The following two A+ objectives maps highlight at a glance the correlation between the A+
the accompanying lab guide. For a more detailed presentation, see Appendix A, "A+ Object

Core Examination

The CompTia organization has established the following objectives for the Core portion of the A+ Certification examination:

A+ Objective	Chapter Coverage	Lab Coverage
1.0 Installation, Configuration, and Upgrading.		
1.1 Identify basic terms, concepts, and functions of system modules including how each module should work during normal operation.	Chapters 1, 2, 3, 4, 6, 8, 9, 11	
1.2 Identify basic procedures for adding and removing field replacable modules.	Chapters 3, 6, 7, 8	Lab Procedures 1, 27, 29
1.3 Identify available IRQs, DMAs, and I/O addresses with procedures for configuring them for device installation.	Chapters 6, 8	
1.4 Identify common peripheral ports, associated cables, and their connectors.	Chapters 6, 7, 8, 10, 11	Lab Procedures 1, 20, 21, 26, 28, 29, 30, 32, 33
1.5 Identify proper procedures for installing and configuring IDE/EIDE devices.	Chapter 8	
1.6 Identify proper procedures for installing and configuring SCSI devices.	Chapter 8	
1.7 Identify proper procedures for installing and configuring peripheral devices.	Chapters 8, 9, 11	
1.8 Identify procedures for upgrading BIOS.	Chapter 4	
1.9 Identify hardware methods of system optimization and when to use them.	Chapters 6, 8	
2.0 Diagnosing and Troubleshooting		
2.1 Identify common symptoms and problems associated with each module and how to troubleshoot and isolate the problems.	Chapters 3, 4, 5 6, 7, 8, 9, 11, 12	Lab Procedures 7, 13, 17, 18, 20, 21, 22, 23, 24, 25, 26, 28
2.2 Identify basic troubleshooting procedures and good practices for eliciting problem symptoms from customers.	Chapters 3, 13	
3.0 Safety and Preventive Maintenance		
3.1 Identify the purpose of various types of preventive maintenance products and procedures, and when to use/perform them.	Chapter 13	
3.2 Identify procedures and devices for protecting against environmental hazards.	Chapter 13	
3.3 Identify the potential hazards and proper safety procedures relating to lasers and high-voltage equipment.	Chapter 13	
3.4 Identify items that require special disposal procedures that comply with environmental guidelines.	Chapter 13	

A+ Objective	Chapter Coverage	Lab Coverage
3.5 Identify ESD (Electrostatic Discharge) precautions and procedures, including the use of ESD protection devices.	Chapter 13	
4.0 Motherboard/Processors/Memory		
4.1 Distinguish between the popular CPU chips in terms of their basic characteristics.	Chapters 2, 6	
4.2 Identify the categories of RAM (Random Access Memory) terminology, their locations, and physical characteristics.	Chapters 2, 6	
4.3 Identify the most popular type of motherboards, their components, and their architecture (e.g., bus structures and power supplies).	Chapters 2, 6, 7	
4.4 Identify the purpose of CMOS (Complementary Metal-Oxide Semiconductor), what it contains, and how to change its basic parameters.	Chapters 4 , 6, 7, 8	
5.0 Printers		
5.1 Identify basic concepts, printer operations, printer components, and field-replaceable units in primary printer types.	Chapter 10	
5.2 Identify care and service techniques and common problems with primary printer types.	Chapters 10, 13	
5.3 Identify the types of printer connections and configurations.	Chapter 10	
6.0 Portable Systems		
6.1 Identify the unique components of portable systems and their unique problems.	Chapters 1, 2, 6, 9	
7.0 Basic Networking		
7.1 Identify basic networking concepts, including how a network works.	Chapter 11	Lab Procedure 33
7.2 Identify procedures for swapping and configuring network interface cards.	Chapter 11	
7.3 Identify ramifications of repairs on the network.	Chapter 11	
8.0 Customer Satisfaction		
8.1 Differentiate effective from ineffective behaviors as these contribute to the maintenance or achievement of customer satisfaction.	Chapter 13	

DOS/Windows Module Examination

In addition to the Core objectives, the following objectives have been established for the DOS/Windows portion of the A+ examination:

A+ Objective	Chapter Coverage	Lab Coverage
1.0 Function, Structure, Operation, and File Management		
1.1 Identify the operating system's functions, structure, and major system files.	Chapters 4, 5	
1.2 Identify ways to navigate the operating system and how to get to needed technical information.	Chapters 4, 5	Lab Procedures 3, 4, 5, 6
1.3 Identify basic concepts and procedures for creating and managing files and directories in DOS/Windows.	Chapter 4	Lab Procedure 2
1.4 Identify the procedures for basic disk management.	Chapter 4, 5, 8, 13	Lab Procedures 27, 28, 36, 37
2.0 Memory Management		
2.1 Differentiate between types of memory.	Chapter 4	
2.2 Identify typical memory-conflict problems and how to optimize memory use.	Chapters 4, 5, 6	Lab Procedure 12
3.0 Installation, Configuration, and Upgrading		
3.1 Identify the procedures for installing DOS, Windows 3.x, and Windows 95 and bringing the software to a basic operational level.	Chapter 8	Lab Procedures 27, 28, and 37
3.2 Identify steps to perform an operating system upgrade.	Chapter 5	Lab Procedure 5
3.3 Identify the basic system boot sequences and alternative ways to boot the system software, including steps to create an emergency boot disk with utilities installed.	Chapters 4, 5	
3.4 Identify procedures for loading/adding device drivers and the necessary software for certain devices.	Chapters 4, 5	

A+ Objective	Chapter Coverage	Lab Coverage
3.5 Identify the procedures for changing options, configuring, and using the Windows printing subsystem.	Chapter 10	Lab Procedure 30
3.6 Identify the procedures for installing and launching typical Windows and non-Windows applications.	Chapter 5	
4.0 Diagnosing and Troubleshooting		
4.1 Recognize and interpret the meaning of common error codes, and startup messages, from the boot sequence and identify steps to correct the problem.	Chapters 4, 5	
4.2 Recognize Windows-specific printing problems and identify the procedures for correcting them.	Chapter 10	
4.3 Recognize common problems and determine how to resolve them.	Chapters 3, 4, 5, 11, 13	Lab Procedures 6, 8, 12, 27, 36
4.4 Identify concepts relating to viruses and virus types—their dangers, their symptoms, sources of viruses, how they infect, how to protect against them and how to identify/remove them.	Chapter 13	
5.0 Networks		
5.1 Identify the networking capabilities of DOS and Windows, including procedures for connecting to the network.	Chapter 11	Lab Procedure 33
5.2 Identify concepts and capabilities relating to the Internet and basic procedures for setting up a system for Internet access.	Chapter 11	

A+
Certification
Concepts & Practice
Second Edition

Charles Brooks

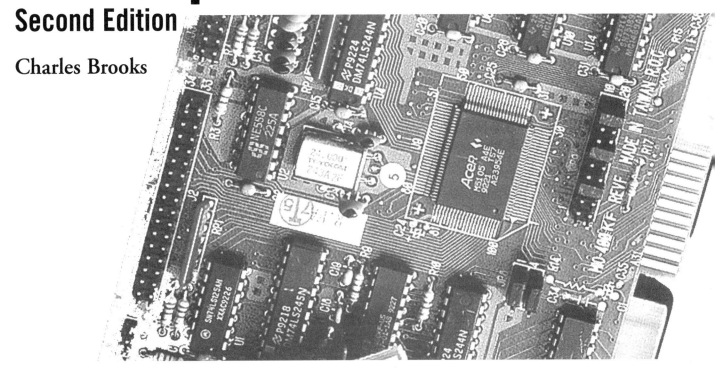

201 West 103rd Street, Indianapolis, Indiana 46290

A+ Certification: Concepts and Practice, Second Edition

Copyright© 1999 by Que® Education and Training

Library of Congress Catalog Number: 98-67621

ISBN: 1-58076-191-7

Trademark Acknowledgments

All terms mentioned in this book that are known to be trademarks or service marks are listed below. Que Education and Training cannot attest to the accuracy of this information. Use of a term in this book should not be regarded as affecting the validity of any trademark or service mark.

IBM®, IBM-PC, PC/XT®, PC-AT, and EGA are registered trademarks of International Business Machines Corporation.

PS/2, Personal System/2, Micro Channel, CGA, and VGA are trademarks of International Business Machines Corporation.

Microsoft®, MS-DOS®, MS-Windows, and Windows 95 are registered trademarks of Microsoft Corporation.

Centronics is a registered trademark of Centronics Corp.

Freon and Mylar are registered trademarks of E.I. du Pont de Nemours and Co., Inc.

AMI is a registered trademark of American Megatrends, Incorporated.

Award is a trademark of the Award Software Company.

Apple, Macintosh, and MAC are trademarks of Apple Computer Company.

Hercules is a registered trademark of Hercules Corp.

Intel, 386, 387, 386SX, 387SX, i486, 486, Pentium, Pentium MMX, and Pentium II are trademarks of Intel Corporation.

Cytrix is a registered trademark of Cyrix Corporation.

NetWare, Novell, and Unix are registered trademarks of Novell, Incorporated.

Tandy is a registered trademark of Tandy Corporation.

Microcom is a registered trademark of Microcom Systems, Incorporated.

SoundBlaster is a registered trademark of Creative Technology, Ltd.

ArcNet is a registered trademark of Datapoint Corporation.

Hayes is a registered trademark of Hayes Microcomputer Products, Incorporated.

Hewlett-Packard and LaserJet are registered trademarks of Hewlett-Packard Company.

Publisher
Robert Linsky

Executive Editor
Jon Phillips

Director of Product Marketing
Susan L. Kindel

Senior Developmental Editor
Lena Buonanno

Senior Editor
Dayna Isley

Copy Editor
Krista Hansing

Book Designer
Louisa Klucznik

Cover Designer
Nathan Clement

Original Graphics
Mike Hall

Proofreader
John Etchison

Page Layout
Eric S. Miller

Indexer
Craig Small

Purpose

The author and Marcraft International Corporation have produced microcomputer architecture and repair courseware since 1988. More than 100,000 students have completed Marcraft's PC repair training course *Microcomputer Systems: Theory & Service* to prepare for successful careers as PC repair technicians. This training course and its accompanying manual have evolved several times to reflect the technician's changing role.

In the 1980s, computer repair was performed by electronic technicians and engineers. Training courses were therefore very hardware-intensive and focused on chip-level isolation and repair techniques. Schematic diagrams and electronic test equipment were key considerations in these courses.

Times have changed, and so has computer repair. The tasks performed by computer repair technicians have changed considerably since that original course was introduced. Computer hardware has become relatively inexpensive, and software has become much more complex. Today's computer technicians spend much more time dealing with software-related problems, configuration problems, and compatibility problems than with hardware problems. As a matter of fact, hardware problems in microcomputers are typically solved at the board level these days. The time and expense of a chip-level repair quickly goes beyond the value of the board, making it unprofitable to do these kinds of repairs. *A+ Certification: Concepts and Practice, Second Edition* and its supporting test file and lab guide are the result of more than 10 years of PC repair training experience.

A+ Certification

A+ Certification: Concepts and Practice, Second Edition provides readers with the knowledge and skills needed to pass the A+ exam required to become a certified computer service technician. A+ certification is recognized nationwide and is a hiring criteria used by companies such as AT&T, IBM, Lotus, Microsoft, and Digital. Therefore, becoming A+ certified will enhance your job opportunities and career advancement potential.

Computing Technology Industry Association (CompTIA) is the organization that establishes certification criteria for service technicians in the computer industry. This organization has created and sponsors the A+ certification exam. A+ certification is a two-step process: You must pass a core exam and either a Microsoft Windows/DOS or a Macintosh specialty exam. The specialty exam must be passed within 90 days of the core exam. For more information on CompTIA and the A+ exam, visit `http://www.comptia.org`.

Audience

A+ Certification: Concepts and Practice, Second Edition and the accompanying lab guide are designed to prepare students to pass the A+ examination. This text and lab guide are not simply to be used to "cram" for the A+ certification exam, however; instead, they are designed to be a complete training package that will help you prepare for the exam and provide you the fundamental knowledge base required to establish a career in this rapidly changing industry.

Key Revisions

A+ Certification: Concepts and Practice, Second Edition has been expanded to include information on all the new A+ objectives established in 1998. The book has maintained the basic coverage of how computer components operate, and it includes several new sections of information concerning advanced computer concepts as well. New information has been added to every chapter to reflect the new A+ standards. In some cases, material has been trimmed to a level more appropriate for a current A+ certification text.

The most notable change to the book occurs in the area of system software. The original chapter on system software has been split into two chapters. The first is Chapter 4, "Operating Systems," which now includes an extensive discussion of the boot-up process, as well as a section covering DOS troubleshooting.

The second software-related chapter is Chapter 5, "Microsoft Windows." This chapter includes coverage of both Windows 3.x and Windows 95. (The A+ exam does not yet cover Windows 98.) The Windows material has been expanded significantly from the previous version. A substantial amount of Windows 95 organizational and troubleshooting information is included. Troubleshooting coverage has been reorganized and integrated in this second edition so that coverage appears in a more intuitive sequence. The Symptoms sections for various microcomputer components have been moved from the chapter, "Troubleshooting the System," and have been integrated with the sections of the chapters in which the component's troubleshooting sequence is discussed.

Special Features

The pedagogical features of this book were carefully developed to provide students with key content information as well as review and testing opportunities. Margin icons are used to clearly signal content directly related to the A+ certification exam.

A+ Core Exam and DOS/Windows Exam Coverage

The A+ core exam objectives are identified with a margin icon that helps students focus on key content that they will be expected to know for the certification exam. The A+ DOS/Windows Exam objectives icon highlights content specific to the DOS/Windows exam.

A+ Test Objectives Appendix

Appendix A, "A+ Objectives Map," is a complete listing of the A+ objectives for both the core exam and the DOS/Windows exam. The items listed in this appendix are directly linked to the margin icons that appear in each chapter.

Boxed Feature

Selected content is boxed in each chapter, helping readers focus on key content.

Evaluation and Test Material

Each chapter closes with 10 multiple-choice questions that test knowledge of the basic concepts presented in the chapter. A set of 15 open-ended review questions are designed to test critical thinking.

Lab Guide Exercises

Applying the concepts of the chapter to hands-on exercises is crucial to preparing for a successful career as a computer technician. Each chapter of this text therefore closes by asking students to complete two or three lab exercises that reinforce the chapter content via hands-on lab work. These exercises are located in the *A+ Certification: Concepts and Practice Lab Guide, Second Edition* that accompanies this text.

TestPrep CD ROM

A+ Certification: Concepts and Practice, Second Edition is accompanied by a comprehensive A+ test bank. This CD-ROM is electronically linked to the 900-question A+ Practice Test Bank. The CD enables students to complete mock tests, determine their weak points, and study more strategically.

The CD provides three styles of testing:

- Flash card-style
- Study card-style
- Full assessment

During the question review, the correct answer is presented on the screen along with the reference heading where the material can be found in the text. A single mouse click takes you quickly to the corresponding section of the electronic text book.

Art Program

Approximately 40 diagrams and screenshots are included in each chapter to provide constant visual reinforcement of the concepts discussed.

Other Pedagogical Features

Each chapter begins with a list of learning objectives that establish a foundation and systematic preview of the chapter. Each chapter concludes with a point-by-point summary of its key content. Key terms are presented in bold throughout the text. A comprehensive glossary of terms appears at the end of the text to provide quick, easy access to key term definitions that appear in each chapter.

Organization

The text is divided into five logical parts. Part I, "Introduction to Computers," is dedicated to computer basics. Chapter 1, "Microcomputer Fundamentals," and Chapter 2, "PC Hardware," introduce basic concepts of microcomputers and describe how these fundamental concepts are actually implemented in working PCs. Chapter 3, "Troubleshooting the System," introduces basic troubleshooting techniques, including FRU troubleshooting techniques.

Part II, "System Software," includes Chapter 4, "Operating Systems," and Chapter 5, "Microsoft Windows." Chapter 4 deals with BIOS and DOS, and Chapter 5 deals with Windows 3.x and Windows 95 issues.

Part III, "The Basic System," concentrates on the components that make up the basic system. This part consists of Chapter 6, "System Boards"; Chapter 7, "Input/Output Devices"; Chapter 8, "Magnetic Storage"; and Chapter 9, "Video Displays."

Part IV, "The Extended System," covers items that extend or customize the function of the basic system. Included in this part are Chapter 10, "Printers"; Chapter 11, "Data Communications"; and Chapter 12, "Multimedia."

Part V, "Skill Enhancement," consists of Chapter 13, "Preventive Maintenance, Safety, and Customer Service," and deals with issues on preventive maintenance, safety considerations, and customer relations.

Coverage

This book is designed to be flexible enough to accommodate a variety of course lengths. In general, it is not necessary to move through this text in the same order that it is presented. Also, it is not necessary to teach any specific portion of the material to its extreme. Instead, the material can be adjusted to fit the length of your course. Alternative syllabi are presented in the Instructor's Resource Manual that is free to qualified adopters of the text.

Chapter 1, "Microcomputer Fundamentals," introduces basic microcomputer architecture by presenting organizational and operational issues associated with a typical microcomputer system. The chapter includes information about the operation of a simple mythical microprocessor to illustrate microprocessor fundamentals.

Chapter 2, "PC Hardware," builds on the fundamental material from Chapter 1 to show how those basic microcomputer structures come together to form an IBM PC-compatible personal computer system. The chapter charts the evolution of the PC from the days when small keyboard units were connected to a television set up to the basis of the most powerful PCs available today.

Chapter 3, "Troubleshooting the System," addresses the fundamentals of troubleshooting microprocessor-based equipment. The chapter covers the use of diagnostic software to isolate system problems, and it describes the Field Replaceable Unit (FRU) method of hardware troubleshooting required for most field and bench repair work.

The software side of the microcomputer system is covered in Chapters 4 and 5. Chapter 4, "Operating Systems," provides a detailed examination of basic operating systems. In particular, this chapter investigates the role of the system's BIOS and the Disk Operating System (DOS) in the operation of the system. The first half of the chapter covers topics associated with the ROM BIOS. This includes system boot-up information, CMOS setup routines, and power-on self-test information.

The second half of Chapter 4 is dedicated to DOS. Topics covered in this section include installing and starting DOS systems, using different types of DOS commands, and using DOS utility programs. The chapter concludes with an extensive section on troubleshooting DOS installation, configuration, and operational problems.

Chapter 5, "Microsoft Windows," is an in-depth study of the Windows 3.x operating environment and the Windows 95 operating system. This chapter looks at installation, startup, structure, and operation of Windows 3.x and Windows 95 system software. Again, an extensive section is included for troubleshooting Windows 3.x and Windows 95 installation, configuration, and operational problems.

Chapter 6, "System Boards," deals with the system boards that make up the heart of every microcomputer system. Microprocessors, microprocessor-support systems, and expansion buses are covered in this chapter. These support systems include timing, DMA, interrupt, common memory structures, and different I/O bus schemes used to connect optional I/O devices to the system. Chapter 6 also covers microprocessors and their operating characteristics, from the 8088 to the Pentium, Pentium MMX, Pentium Pro, and Pentium II. Procedures for troubleshooting system board-related problems and system board upgrading are also presented here. Chapter 7, "Input/Output Devices," begins to examine basic input/output systems. The most common ports found in the PC-compatible world are the parallel and serial I/O ports. However, a host of lesser-known I/O systems are used in PCs. The various I/O systems are examined here. The chapter also investigates the operation of various input devices. In particular, the text covers keyboards, mice, trackballs, joysticks, light pens, touch-sensitive screens, and scanners. Troubleshooting procedures are provided for the various devices.

Chapter 8, "Magnetic Storage," covers mass storage systems commonly used in microcomputers. These include floppy drives, hard drives, RAID systems, and tape drives. Installation and troubleshooting procedures are described for the hard and floppy drive systems, as well as for tape drives.

Chapter 9, "Video Displays," investigates the video display area of I/O devices. Basic CRT construction, operation, and control are featured, and the chapter addresses the various video standards associated with microcomputers, along with troubleshooting procedures for isolating video problems. The end of the chapter deals with troubleshooting the CRT monitor. *Readers should be aware that this section contains information about a potentially dangerous portion of the system and should be practiced only with a trained professional.*

Chapter 10, "Printers," covers printers from the work horse dot-matrix printer to color ink-jet and high-speed laser printers. Theory, operation, and maintenance information is presented for all three types of printers.

Chapter 11, "Data Communications," focuses on one of the hottest areas of microcomputer growth. This chapter covers both local and wide area networks, along with the equipment and software required to operate them. Modems are covered here, along with their application to the Internet. Procedures and precautions for troubleshooting networked systems are provided as well.

Chapter 12, "Multimedia," covers another hot area of microcomputer development. This chapter investigates the components that make up true multimedia systems. These items include CD-ROM drives, sound cards, video capture cards, MIDI sound equipment, and the software required to drive these items. Troubleshooting directions are included for most multimedia systems.

Chapter 13, "Preventive Maintenance, Safety, and Customer Service," investigates topics including cleaning, electrostatic discharges, power line problems, universal power supplies (UPS), and other power-line conditioning devices. Also presented are preventive maintenance procedures for various system components. Important HDD support utilities—such as backup, defragmentation, and anti-virus protection—are highlighted here, and suggested PM schedules are also presented. The chapter closes with safety issues concerning computer systems. Although not an intrinsically unsafe environment, some areas of a computer system can be harmful if approached unaware.

The final section of Chapter 13 completes the A+ certification book by examining customer satisfaction issues. Traditionally, these issues have not been covered in technical books associated with computer maintenance. However, increased demand from computer service providers has finally brought the topic into the spotlight. Many service providers consider the ability to handle customers and their problems effectively as important a skill as having good technical abilities.

Appendix A, "A+ Objectives Map," clearly presents the current objectives for the core and DOS/Window portions of the A+ certification examination, as determined by CompTIA. This map is directly related to the margin icons that appear in each chapter.

Appendix B, "Test Taking Tips," provides basic guidance on successfully preparing for and taking the A+ exam.

The Lab Guide

The *A+ Certification: Concepts and Practice Lab Guide, Second Edition* provides an excellent hands-on component to emphasize the theoretical materials. Three types of procedures are included in the 37 labs:

- Introductory labs that act as introductions to hardware and different types of software.

- Flow-charted troubleshooting labs that enable students to be tested under real problem situations. The instructor can insert software faults, simple hardware faults, or complex hardware faults into the system for the student to track down and isolate.

- Hardware/software installation labs that enable students to install and set up hard drives, CD-ROM drives, modems, network cards, and more.

Instructor's CD-ROM

The Instructor's CD-ROM is available at no cost to qualified adopters of this text. The CD-ROM includes the following components:

- Answers for all the end-of-chapter multiple-choice and review questions, with a reference point in the chapter where that item is covered.

- Sample syllabi that guide instructors on how to use the text and lab manual in a 12-week course and a 1-year course.

- Answers to all lab review questions and fill-in-the-blank steps are provided for an indication of what the expected outcomes should be.

- Descriptions of the numerous Marcraft software faults, hardware faults, and extended hardware faults are presented, along with suggested faults for particular labs, as appropriate.

- 80-100 PowerPoint slides per chapter with key figures and lecture notes.

Acknowledgments

I would like to mention some of the people and groups who have been responsible for the success of this book. First, I would like to thank Greg Michael, formerly of Howard W. Sams, for getting me involved in writing about microcomputer systems back in the early days of the IBM PC.

Several people have given me valuable input for the disk drive chapter. These sources include David Allan (formerly of Tallgrass Technologies, makers of high-speed backup systems), and Michael Arkin, Steve Montero, and Brett McClelland of Silicon Systems, maker of ICs for disk and CD-ROM drive applications.

My staff here at Marcraft makes it easy to turn out a good product. Thanks to Paul Haven, Wanda Dawson, Renia Irvin, and Allen Hoy from the technical services area for trying things out for me. Also, my appreciation goes to Mike Hall, Whitney Freeman, Cathy Boulay, and Yu-Wen Ho from the Marcraft product development department for their excellent work in getting the text ready to go. In addition, I would like to say thanks to Brian Alley and Melissa Ryan of Boston University for their excellent guidance in bringing this version of the book up to speed. I must also say that it has been a pleasure to work with Jon Phillips and Lena Buonanno of Que Education and Training. As always, I want to thank my wife, Robbie, for all her support and help with these projects—and thanks to my son, Robert.

CONTENTS AT A GLANCE

TABLE OF CONTENTS

Part I Introduction to Computers

Chapter 2   PC Hardware   55

Chapter 3   Troubleshooting the System   99

Part III   The Basic System

Chapter 6   System Boards   259

Chapter 7 Input/Output Devices   335

Part VI The Extended System

INTRODUCTION TO COMPUTERS

MICROCOMPUTER FUNDAMENTALS

LEARNING OBJECTIVES

Upon completion of this Chapter and its related Lab Procedures, you should be able to:

1. Define the computer term *word* and describe the three types used in digital computers.

2. State common word sizes used in digital computers and relate the terms *bit*, *byte*, and *nibble* to word size.

3. Define the following terms: *hardware*, *software*, and *firmware*.

4. Explain the functions associated with each of the four fundamental blocks that form a computer.

5. Differentiate between common primary and secondary memory devices or systems and list examples of each.

6. Differentiate between static and dynamic RAM memory devices, and state the conditions that dictate which of the two will be used in a given application.

7. List the three major buses in a computer system and describe the nature of the information each bus carries.

8. Demonstrate the relationship between the size of the computer's address bus and the number of individual memory and I/O locations that it can access.

9. Explain the function of a microprocessor's instruction set.

10. Define the functions of the computer's input/output units.

11. Contrast the four most common methods of initiating an I/O-memory or memory-I/O data transfer (Polling, Interrupts, DMA, and programmed I/O).

12. Explain the function of the system ROM BIOS.

13. Describe the function and purpose of Disk Operating System.

14. Describe the value of a graphical user interface.

15. Describe popular software applications programs.

CHAPTER 1

Introduction

In this chapter, you will examine the fundamental operation and organization of digital computer systems. It lays the foundation for the various in-depth topics covered in subsequent chapters.

The first section of the chapter describes what digital computers actually understand—binary language and logic.

The focus shifts in the second section to cover the basic hardware building blocks that make up a digital computer system. These building blocks include microprocessors, microprocessor support systems, memory units, and buses.

This section is followed by a discussion about how the parts of the computer communicate with the outside world. The four common methods of conducting data transfers are defined, followed by typical input/output hardware conventions and systems.

The final section of the chapter introduces the topic of software. The first portion of the section deals with the system software that controls the operation of the hardware, and the second portion introduces several common application software categories that enable users to create and manipulate different types of data.

Bits, Bytes, and Computer Words

The basic structure of most computers in existence today is composed of digital devices. Digital devices, and therefore digital computers, process electrical signals that can only assume two possible states. These states correspond to a prescribed *high level* of voltage (such as +5.0V dc) and *low level* of voltage (such as +0.5V dc). In digital electronics, these voltage levels are referred to as **high** and **low logic levels**, or as "**1**" and "**0**" **logic states**. Because the computer is an electronic device, these voltage levels are all that it recognizes. However, a number of conventions have been developed to allow humans to more easily relate to the logic understood by digital computers.

> The logic values used in the digital computer correspond directly to the digits of the binary, or Base-2, number system. In this system, each digit can assume only two possible values: 0 and I.

This basic unit of information is referred to as a **bit** (a contraction of ***binary digit***). Very little useful information can be conveyed by a single bit; however, virtually any number, letter, or symbol can be described by organizing a group of related bits into coded bit patterns called **words**.

Within the computer, three types of computer words exist:

- ▶ Pure binary data words
- ▶ Coded data words
- ▶ Instruction words

These classifications describe the type of information that the word is used to convey. These classifications are discussed in the sections that follow, but there is another aspect of computer words that must be covered first—their *length*.

Word Length

Word length is so important to a computer that it is often used to describe the computer because all of its internal hardware devices are constructed to accommodate a given word length. In general, computers that use larger word sizes are more powerful than those with smaller sizes because more information can be conferred at one time. Indeed, the increased number of possible bit patterns provided by larger words allows both a larger range of numeric values and a greater number of characters and symbols that can be specified.

A number of different word sizes are commonly used with digital computers, but the most common is the *8-bit word*, or **byte**. The term byte is so universally accepted in the computer world that even computers with other word sizes, such as 16- or 32-bit, are described in terms of their number of bytes. A computer using 16-bit words is said to have a two-byte word size. The word is divided into a higher- and a lower-order byte. The lower-order byte consists of the eight **least significant bits** (**LSBs**, bits 0–7), and the higher-order byte is made up of the eight **most significant bits** (**MSBs**, bits 8–15). Notice that the least significant bit is always assigned the bit number 0. Figure 1.1 depicts the relationships that exist between nibbles, bytes, decimal, binary, and hexadecimal numbers.

FIGURE 1.1

The relationship of nibbles, bytes, words, and double words.

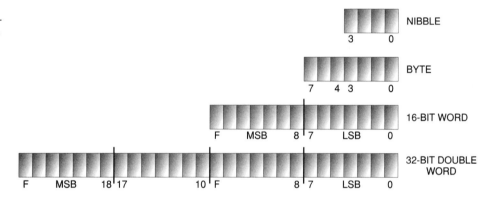

It is also common to divide bytes into two four-bit sub-units called **nibbles**. Therefore, the byte consists of both a higher- and a lower-order nibble. This relationship was contrived largely due to the link between the **binary** (base-2) and **hexadecimal** (base-16) numbering systems. A four-bit binary pattern (nibble) can be easily converted into a single hexadecimal digit, which is much easier to manipulate and communicate than a string of ones and zeros. In this manner, a two-byte computer word can be expressed more simply as a four-digit hexadecimal word. Figure 1.2 depicts the relationship that exists between binary and hexadecimal numbers.

A binary number (10011101) is shown as it would be stored in an eight-bit register. By dividing the byte into its two nibbles, the number can be represented more conveniently in terms of its hex equivalent 9D. When expressing hexadecimal values, it is common to follow the value with a lower case h (that is, 9Dh).

Converting between binary and hexadecimal is a simple matter of grouping the binary word into its respective nibbles and then converting each nibble into its hex equivalent. However, converting between either of these systems and decimal (base-10) is another matter altogether.

In order to convert from either of these systems to decimal, each bit, or digit, must be multiplied by its weighted positional value, as depicted in Figure 1.3.

FIGURE 1.2

The computer-related number systems.

DECIMAL (10)	BINARY (2)	HEXIDECIMAL (16)
0	0000	0
1	0001	1
2	0010	2
3	0011	3
4	0100	4
5	0101	5
6	0110	6
7	0111	7
8	1000	8
9	1001	9
10	1010	A
11	1011	B
12	1100	C
13	1101	D
14	1110	E
15	1111	F
16	10000	10

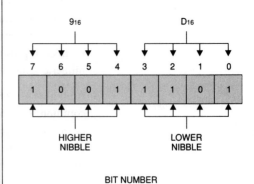

BIT NUMBER

FIGURE 1.3

Converting other number systems to decimal.

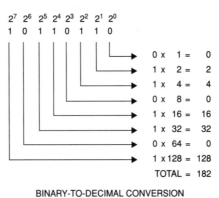

BINARY-TO-DECIMAL CONVERSION

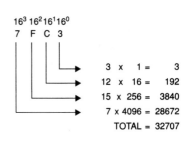

HEX-TO-DECIMAL CONVERSION

Due to the complexity of this operation, computer words are rarely converted into decimal unless done so by the computer's hardware. Whichever number system is being used, it should be remembered that it's only being used for the convenience of humans because all the computer can understand is the high and low logic level voltages used to represent binary numbers.

Numeric Data Words

Now that we've finished our discussion of computer word length and representation, let's return to the topic of the types of words used with computers.

The first type of word we'll discuss is the pure **numeric data word**. As the name implies, these words contain only numeric information and represent a quantity in binary, hexadecimal, or a specialized form of binary called **binary coded decimal** (**BCD**). In the BCD form of binary, the count pattern is limited to binary representations between 0 and 9. After the binary count reaches 9, the next count clears the first BCD digit to 0 and advances the second BCD digit to 1, creating a binary equivalent of the decimal number system.

Like hexadecimal, the BCD system groups binary digits in four-bit digits. But unlike hexadecimal, BCD does not use the binary codes for numbers 10 through 15. These codes are not used in the BCD system and would be considered invalid if they were encountered in a system using BCD. Also, unlike hex, the BCD system can be converted quite easily to decimal because it is not a true weighted number system. Figure 1.4 illustrates the usage of the BCD number system.

FIGURE 1.4

The BCD code.

BASE 10	BCD
0	0000
1	0001
2	0010
3	0011
4	0100
5	0101
6	0110
7	0111
8	1000
9	1001
10	0001 0000

$$9 \quad 4 \quad 3 \quad = 943_{10}$$
$$1001 \quad 0100 \quad 0011 \quad = \text{BCD EQUIVALENT}$$

Another method of representing binary values is the **octal**, or *base-8*, numbering system. Although not as common as hexadecimal, some computers group binary numbers into a three-bit pattern, as depicted in Figure 1.5. The highest binary number that can be represented using this number system is a seven.

FIGURE 1.5

The octal code.

OCTAL (8)	BINARY (2)
0	000
1	001
2	010
3	011
4	100
5	101
6	110
7	111
10	001 000

$$6 \quad 7 \quad 2 \quad 4 \quad = 6724_{8}$$
$$110 \quad 111 \quad 010 \quad 100 \quad = \text{OCTAL EQUIVALENT}$$

Alphanumeric Words

In addition to manipulating numeric values, the computer must also be capable of handling **alphanumeric data** (letters and special characters). Once again, coded binary bit patterns are used to represent these characters and symbols. When you type an alphabetic character on your keyboard, what the key actually does is generate a specific binary bit pattern that the computer recognizes as that particular character. In order to display the character on your monitor, the output device must reconstruct it from the bit pattern stored in the computer.

The alphanumeric code most commonly used in personal computers is the **ASCII** *(American Standard Code for Information Interchange)* code. In ASCII, each character of the alphabet (both upper- and lowercase), decimal numbers 0 to 9, and a variety of special symbols and punctuation marks are assigned a specific seven-bit binary pattern. The seven-bit ASCII code is depicted in Figure 1.6.

Although the basic ASCII code contains only seven bits, it's an 8-bit-oriented world inside the computer. For some applications, a "0" may be added to the MSB of all the ASCII bit patterns, or a "1" may be used to produce an extended (nonstandard) ASCII code of 256 characters. But more often, the extra bit is used as an error-checking bit when ASCII is used for the transmission of alphanumeric data between the computer and its peripherals or another computer.

FIGURE 1.6

ASCII Code.

First group

CTRL	CHARACTER	BINARY BIT 7 TO BIT 0	OCTAL	DECIMAL	HEXADECIMAL
@	NUL	00000000	000	000	00
A	SOW	00000001	001	001	01
8	STX	00000010	002	002	02
C	ETX	00000011	003	003	03
D	EOT	00000100	004	004	04
E	ENQ	00000101	005	005	05
F	ACK	00000110	006	006	06
G	BEL	00000111	007	007	07
H	BS	00001000	010	008	08
I	MT	00001001	011	009	09
J	LF	00001010	012	010	0A
K	VT	00001011	013	011	0B
L	FF	00001100	014	012	0C
M	CR	00001101	015	013	0D
N	SO	00001110	016	014	0E
O	SI	00001111	017	015	0F
P	DLE	00010000	020	016	10
Q	DC1	00010001	021	017	11
R	DC2	00010010	022	018	12
S	DC3	00010011	023	019	13
T	DC4	00010100	024	020	14
U	NAK	00010101	025	021	15
V	SYN	00010110	026	022	16
W	ETB	00010111	027	023	17
X	CAN	00011000	030	024	18
Y	EM	00011001	031	025	19
Z	SUB	00011010	032	026	1A
[	ESC	00011011	033	027	1B
\	FS	00011100	034	028	1C
]	GS	00011101	035	029	1D
^	RS	00011110	036	030	1E
	US	00011111	037	031	1F
_	SP	00100000	040	032	20
	!	00100001	041	033	21
	"	00100010	042	034	22
	#	00100011	043	035	23
	$	00100100	044	036	24
	%	00100101	045	037	25
	&	00100110	046	038	26
	'	00100111	047	039	27
	(	00101000	050	040	28
	)	00101001	051	041	29
	*	00101010	052	042	2A

Second group

CHARACTER	BINARY BIT 7 TO BIT 0	OCTAL	DECIMAL	HEXADECIMAL
+	00101011	053	043	2B
,	00101100	054	044	2C
-	00101101	055	045	2D
.	00101110	056	046	2E
/	00101111	057	047	2F
0	00110000	060	048	30
1	00110001	061	049	31
2	00110010	062	050	32
3	00110011	063	051	33
4	00110100	064	052	34
5	00110101	065	053	35
6	00110110	066	054	36
7	00110111	067	055	37
8	00111000	070	056	38
9	00111001	071	057	39
:	00111010	072	058	3S
;	00111011	073	059	3B
<	00111100	074	060	3C
=	00111101	075	061	3D
>	00111110	076	062	3E
?	00111111	077	063	3F
@	01000000	100	064	40
A	01000001	101	065	41
B	01000010	102	066	42
C	01000011	103	067	43
D	01000100	104	068	44
E	01000101	105	069	45
F	01000110	106	070	46
G	01000111	107	071	47
H	01001000	110	072	48
I	01001001	111	073	49
J	01001010	112	074	4A
K	01001011	113	075	4B
L	01001100	114	076	4C
M	01001101	115	077	4D
N	01001110	116	078	4E
O	01001111	117	079	4F
P	01010000	120	080	50
Q	01010001	121	081	51
R	01010010	122	082	52
S	01010011	123	083	53
T	01010100	124	084	54
U	01010101	125	085	55

Third group

CHARACTER	BINARY BIT 7 TO BIT 0	OCTAL	DECIMAL	HEXADECIMAL
V	01010110	126	086	56
W	01010111	127	087	57
X	01011000	130	088	58
Y	01011001	131	089	59
Z	01011010	132	090	5A
[	01011011	133	091	5B
\	01011100	134	092	5C
]	01011101	135	093	5D
^	01011110	136	094	5E
-	01011111	137	095	5F
'	01100000	140	096	60
a	01100001	141	097	61
b	01100010	142	098	62
c	01100011	143	099	63
d	01100100	144	100	64
e	01100101	145	101	65
f	01100110	146	102	66
g	01100111	147	103	67
h	01101000	150	104	68
i	01101001	151	105	69
j	01101010	152	106	6A
k	01101011	153	107	6B
l	01101100	154	108	6C
m	01101101	155	109	6D
n	01101110	156	110	6E
o	01101111	157	111	6F
p	01110000	160	112	70
q	01110001	161	113	71
r	01110010	162	114	72
s	01110011	163	115	73
t	01110100	164	116	74
u	01110101	165	117	75
v	01110110	166	118	76
w	01110111	167	119	77
x	01111000	170	120	78
y	01111001	171	121	79
z	01111010	172	122	7A
{	01111011	173	123	7B
		01111100	174	124	7C
}	01111101	175	125	7D
~	01111110	176	126	7E
DEL	01111111	177	127	7F

CTRL ABBR. DESCRIPTION table

CTRL	ABBR.	DESCRIPTION	CTRL	ABBR.	DESCRIPTION	CTRL	ABBR.	DESCRIPTION
@	NUL	null, or all zeros	K	VT	vertical tabulation	V	SYN	synchronous idle
A	SOH	start of the heading	L	FF	form feed	W	ETB	end of transmission block
B	STX	start of text	M	CR	carriage return	X	CAN	cancel
C	ETX	end of text	N	SO	shift out	Y	EM	end of medium
D	EOX	end of transmission	O	SI	shift in	Z	SUB	substitute
E	ENQ	enquiry	P	DLE	datalink escape	[	ESC	escape
F	ACK	acknowledge	Q	DC1	device control 1 (X ON)	\	FS	files separator
G	BEL	bell	R	DC2	device control 2	]	GS	group separator
H	BS	backspace	S	DC3	device control 3 (X OFF)	^	RS	record separator
I	HT	horizontal tabulation	T	DC4	device control 4	_	US	unit separator
J	LF	line feed	U	NAK	negative acknowledge		SP	space
							DEL	delete

Under these circumstances, the extra bit, now called a **parity bit**, assumes a certain value dependent upon the number of ones in the character. This bit is used to check the integrity of the transmitted character. Parity checking can be implemented in two forms:

- **odd parity** where the value of the parity bit assumes a value of 1 or 0 so that the total number of "1" bits in the character is odd.

- **even parity** where the parity bit assumes a value of 1 or 0 to make the total number of "1" bits in the character equal to an even number.

When ASCII is being used to transfer information between the computer and one of its peripherals (such as the keyboard, the monitor, or a disk drive) then circuitry in the computer or the peripheral generates the proper type of parity bit as the ASCII characters are transmitted. On the receiving end, the parity bit is regenerated from the received data and compared to the parity bit that was transmitted with the character. If the two bits agree, the communicating devices accept the transmission as a good one and continue. It should be noted that parity checking is the simplest form of error checking used in computer systems to guarantee the integrity of transmitted data. However, parity checking is only capable of detecting single-bit errors. More advanced error checking and correction schemes are widely used to check for and correct data transmission errors.

> Notice in the ASCII code table that some codes are specified as control codes. These characters are special codes that can be used to modify functions associated with other characters. They are also frequently used when working with peripheral devices to specify certain operations or conditions that need to be performed or attended to.

Instruction Words

The last type of computer word to be discussed is the **instruction word**. Unlike binary and coded data words, an instruction word is not used to convey any kind of numeric value or character reference. Instead, this kind of word tells the computer which operation to perform and where to find the data (if any) to perform the operation on. No data is contained in the word, just a complete instruction to the computer. Although the other two types of words are common to most computers, each computer has its own set of operations that it can perform under the direction of a set of instruction words. From computer to computer, the format of instruction words can vary greatly. But generally, instruction words for most computers convey the same types of information.

Figure 1.7 depicts three possible instruction word formats that could be used with an eight-bit computer, depending on the type of operation being specified. In the first example, a **one-byte instruction** containing only coded information about which operation is to be performed (operation code, or **op code**) is presented. This type of instruction is used in operations such as a HALT instruction, where no data is required to carry out the instruction. The second example depicts a **two-byte instruction**. Here, the first byte once again contains the op code, and the second byte contains the **operand** (a piece of data to be worked on) address. The last example illustrates a **three-byte instruction**. The op code is followed by two pieces of data. This format could also be used to indicate a particular operation to be performed, the location of a data word, and a location to store the result of the operation.

These instruction words should not be confused with the instructions given in a higher-order language, such as **BASIC**. The instruction formats described above pertain to the **machine language**—ones and zeros understood by a computer's internal hardware. A single BASIC language instruction can generate several lines of machine language instructions after it has been converted.

Moving Words Around

The most frequent operation performed in a computer is the movement of information from one location to another. This information is moved in the form of *words*. Basically, there are two modes in which the words can be transferred. These modes are **parallel mode**, where an entire word is transferred from location A to location B by a set of parallel conductors at one instant, and **serial mode**, where the bits of the word are transmitted along a single conductor, one bit at a time. Serial transfers require more time to accomplish than parallel transfers because a clock cycle must be used for each bit transferred.

FIGURE 1.7

Instruction word formats.

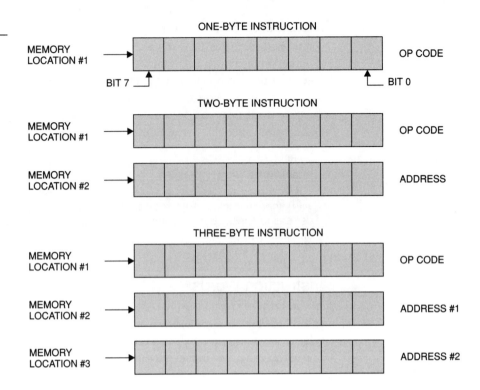

A parallel transfer requires only a single clock pulse. An example of both parallel and serial transfers is depicted in Figure 1.8. Since speed is normally of the utmost importance in computer operations, all data movements within the computer are conducted in parallel, as shown in a. But when information is being transferred between the computer and its peripherals (or another computer), conditions might dictate that the transfer be carried out in serial mode, as shown in b. A good deal more will be said later in this chapter and throughout this text about parallel and serial transmissions, and about the conversions that must take place to convert from one mode to the other.

FIGURE 1.8

Parallel and serial data transfers.

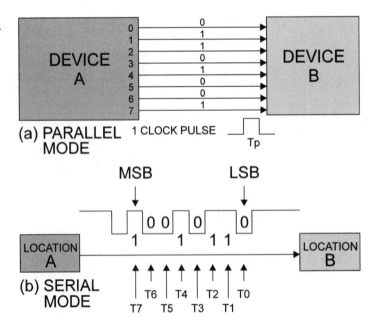

Basic Hardware Structures

Most of the topics discussed so far have dealt with the nonphysical aspects of the computer's organization—its intelligence, if you will.

> The bits, bytes, words, and programs that make the computer function are referred to as **software**. The term software is actually used when referring to any aspect of the computer or its operation that you can't reach out and touch.
>
> The other aspects of the computer system, such as its circuit boards, cables, connectors, magnetic disks, and so forth are referred to as **hardware**. The term hardware is used to indicate any part of the computer system that you can touch with your hand.

The overall performance of any computer system is based on the capabilities of its hardware and software to guide its operation. The most sophisticated computer hardware in the world is useless junk without proper software. And, conversely, the most well-written software is wasted if the hardware doesn't have the capabilities to perform the operations called for in its programs.

Therefore, a digital computer can be defined as a collection of digital devices that can perform logical and mathematical operations under the direction of a program.

Integrated Circuits

The first digital computers were giants that took up entire rooms and required several technicians and engineers to operate. They were constructed with vacuum tubes, and their power was very limited by comparison to modern computers. However, the advent of **integrated circuit** (**IC**) technology in 1964 launched a new era in compact electronic packaging. The much smaller, low-power transistor replaced the vacuum tube, and the size of the computer began to shrink.

Engineers realized very quickly that several transistors could be created simultaneously on the same piece of silicon. Soon, entire electronic circuits were being integrated onto a single silicon chip (that is, an integrated circuit).

The first ICs were relatively small devices that performed simple digital logic. These basic digital devices still exist and occupy a class of ICs referred to as **Small Scale Integration** (**SSI**) devices. SSI devices range up to 100 transistors per chip. As manufacturers improved techniques for creating ICs, the number of transistors on a "**chip**" grew, and complex digital circuits were fabricated together. These devices are categorized as **Medium Scale Integration** (**MSI**) devices. MSI devices range between 100 and 3,000 circuit elements. Eventually, **Large Scale Integration** (**LSI**) and **Very Large Scale Integration** (**VLSI**) devices were produced. LSI devices contain between 3,000 and 100,000 electronic components; VLSI devices exceed 100,000 elements.

> Today's IC technology allows millions of circuit elements to be constructed on a single, small piece of silicon. Some VLSI devices contain complete computer modules.

These devices are commonly referred to as **Application Specific Integrated Circuits**, or **ASICs**. By connecting a few ASIC devices together on a printed circuit board, computers that once inhabited an entire room have shrunk to fit on the top of an ordinary work desk, and, further, into the palm of the hand. Various integrated circuit package types are depicted in Figure 1.9.

FIGURE 1.9

Integrated circuit packages.

Today, there are three general categories of digital computers. In order of their computing power and complexity, these are

▶ Mainframes

▶ Minicomputers

▶ Microcomputers

Mainframes are the largest class of computer, used to service thousands of online users. Mainframes can contain hundreds of megabytes of primary memory and hundreds of gigabytes of secondary memory. **Minicomputers** are medium-sized computers capable of serving hundreds of users. **Microcomputers** are the smallest computers and typically handle a very limited number of users. A **personal computer**, or **PC**, is a type of microcomputer that is intended for use by an individual (that is, personal) either at home or in the work place.

Basic Computer Structure

In their most basic form, all digital computers consist of the four fundamental blocks depicted in Figure 1.10. The computer must have some type of the following:

▶ **Central processing unit (CPU)**

▶ **Memory unit**

▶ **Input unit**

▶ **Output unit**

In many instances, an input unit and an output unit are combined to service some particular device or add-on to the computer. In these cases, the combined unit is referred to as an **input/output (I/O)** unit. Three communications paths called buses normally interconnect the computer's basic units.

Central Processing Unit

A+ CORE 1.1   The CPU section consists of two major sub-sections, an **arithmetic logic unit (ALU)** and a **control unit**. The ALU is the section of the computer where the actual math and logic operations are performed under the direction of the control unit. The control unit receives instructions from the program, decodes them, and then generates signals to inform the ALU as to what operation has been requested. In addition, the control unit orchestrates the operation of all of the other logical blocks by generating the proper timing and control signals necessary to complete the execution of the instruction.

FIGURE 1.10

The fundamental blocks of a digital computer.

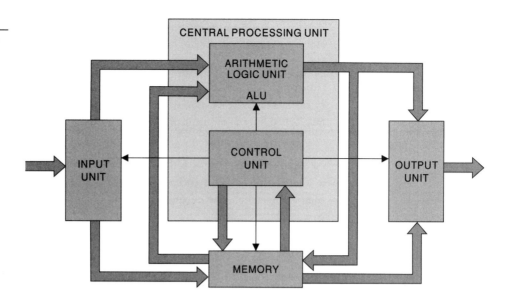

Due to the nature of its hardware structure, the typical microcomputer's operation is limited to performing one instruction at a time, involving a maximum of two quantities. The computer's true value lies in the fact that it can execute a tremendous number of instructions in a short time. A typical personal computer can execute several **million instructions per second** (**mips**).

Microprocessors

People often speak of a microprocessor as the CPU. Others refer to the system's main unit as the CPU. Either terminology is faulty. In the early days of computers, the central processing unit was the area of the computer where logical and mathematical computations were carried out. It was usually composed of discrete circuits or devices.

> One of the earliest VLSI devices brought together a section of special onboard data storage areas, referred to as **registers**, and a CPU in a single IC package. This device is called a **microprocessor** (or **MPU**).

In this manner, a single IC device becomes the brain of the computer.

There are several microprocessor chips in the market, each with its own unique architecture, capabilities, and instruction set (operations that it can execute). The capabilities of the microprocessor used in a particular computer ultimately determine the characteristics and capabilities of the entire computer. Basically, microprocessors are classified by the size of their internal data storage registers. Common microprocessor sizes are 8-bits, 16-bits, and 32-bits.

Basic Microprocessor Operation

The operation of all microprocessors is basically the same. They all execute programs in a cyclic manner. An **instruction cycle** is followed by an **execution cycle**. These two cycles are repeated until the program is terminated or until it reaches its end. During the instruction cycle, the processor retrieves an instruction from memory, decodes it, and prepares to carry out the instruction as directed. The instruction may call for additional data to be retrieved from memory, manipulated in a logical manner, or to be written into a memory location. In any case, the instruction is carried out during the processor's execution cycle.

After completing the operations required by the instruction, the microprocessor moves sequentially to the next instruction. A particular instruction may cause the system to jump to another memory location to receive another instruction. This **instruction jump** can be dictated directly by the instruction, or it can be based on the outcome of some logical operation.

All microprocessors can perform a fixed set of operations. These operations are referred to as a microprocessor's **instruction set**. The size of the instruction set determines how many different operations the microprocessor can perform. This, in turn, determines how quickly data can be processed.

Memory Unit

 A+ CORE 1.1

> The **memory unit** is the section of the computer where instructions and data to be used by the computer are stored.

The memory unit involved directly with the microprocessor consists of high-speed semiconductor devices that are compatible with the microprocessor's speed so as not to slow its operation. In times past, this type of memory was referred to as **internal memory** because it was usually located in the same housing with the microprocessor. Slower, less expensive forms of memory, called **mass storage**, were located in a separate unit. Mass storage systems are used for long-term storage of programs and data, or to hold programs and data too large to be held in the internal memory. In any event, the main emphasis for mass storage devices or systems is the ability to store large amounts of data on a permanent or semi-permanent basis as cheaply as possible.

With the advent of the microcomputer, this method of differentiating memory types blurred. In these computer models, mass storage systems were incorporated into the same housing as the basic system unit. In order to make a clear distinction between the two memory types, the fast semiconductor memories used directly with the microprocessor are referred to as **primary memory,** whereas the slower, less expensive bulk memory systems are designated as **secondary memory**. In this section, our discussion refers only to the primary memory types.

Semiconductor memories can be thought of as a collection of systematically arranged boxes in which computer words are stored. This concept is illustrated in Figure 1.11. Notice that the boxes are arranged so that each has its own unique location, which is specified by a number. This number is referred to as the memory location's **address**. When the microprocessor wants to access a particular box to store or retrieve information, it does so by generating the address of that particular storage space, along with special signals required to perform the operation.

A **read operation**, also referred to as a **fetch operation**, is one where the contents of a specific memory location are sensed by the microprocessor. On the other hand, the act of placing a new word in a specific address is called a **write**, or **store operation**. When the new word is placed in a memory location, it replaces any data that was stored there.

FIGURE 1.11

The logical structure of an IC memory device.

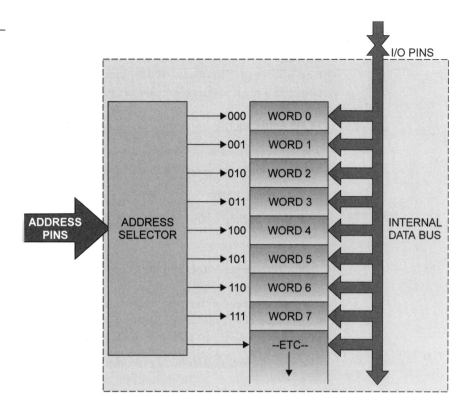

There are actually two major types of semiconductor memories:

- **Read-only memories (ROM)** hold data on a permanent basis.

- **Random access memories (RAM)** are used for temporary storage of data.

ROM Memory

ROM memories generally hold data that was programmed into them at the factory and are not intended to be changed.

The previous description is the classical definition generally applied to ROM, but in reality there are several types of ROM, some of which can be erased and reprogrammed (but not during the normal operation of the computer). These classes include the following:

- Mask-programmed ROM (MROM)—Programmed at the factory.

- Programmable ROM (PROM)—Can be custom programmed by the user (once) using special circuitry

- Erasable-programmable ROM (EPROM)—Can also be programmed and erased by the user using ultraviolet light and special circuitry external to the computer

- Electrically erasable PROM (EEPROM)—Can be erased and reprogrammed by special circuitry within the computer

The one thing all forms of ROM have in common is that they are all **non-volatile**, which means that the data contained in the memory is not lost when the computer is turned off or when electrical power is lost. This allows the computer to begin reading instructions and data from this type of memory as soon as it is powered up.

The term "read-only" truly applies to MROM and PROM memories, which are written once, and cannot be erased or rewritten. The other ROM classes are more appropriately referred to as "read-mostly memories," where the ratio of read operations to write operations is very high. "Read-only" is used with all non-volatile, semiconductor memories that cannot be written to during the normal operation of the computer.

ROM Applications

The different classes of ROM memories are used to perform a wide variety of applications within the computer. Some common ROM applications are listed as follows:

- Firmware storage
- ROM lookup tables
- Code converters
- Character generators for printers and video displays

The most common of these applications includes use as **firmware** storage. In this application, the computer's operating system programs and language interpreters are stored in ROM devices so that the computer can begin operation as soon as it's turned on.

The term "firmware" describes the fact that software is stored in hardware (in this case ICs) on a permanent basis. As an example, the computer's starting address is commonly stored in ROM. This is the address from which the microprocessor takes its first instruction after it has been turned on or reset.

ROM is also used to store tables of data, such as trigonometric functions and code conversion tables, which do not change. Instead of performing a mathematical manipulation each time a function, such as sine, cosine, tangent, or pi, is needed, the microprocessor simply looks up the value associated with the function in a **ROM table**. The CPU does this by decoding an address from the function command, such as sine 37 degrees, and applying it to the ROM table. The output of the table is the numerical value of the function that was stored at that address.

In like manner, ROM tables are often used to convert characters from one code to another within the computer. As an example, Figure 1.12 depicts the ASCII representation of the number 9 being applied to a ROM conversion table as an address, to which the ROM table responds by producing the binary equivalent of 9, for use by the computer.

In addition, ROM memories are frequently used to store dot pattern codes for the character generator sections of alphanumeric output devices, such as video monitors and some printers. Figure 1.13 depicts the dot pattern of the letter *F*, arranged in a 5x7 matrix pattern. The letter is read from ROM by first applying the proper code (such as the ASCII code for the upper case *F*, in this case) as part of the character's address. In order to read the entire dot pattern of the character, a segment of the address is produced by a binary counter whose output is used to step through the dot pattern one horizontal row at a time. In this case, the counter's initial count of 0 would produce the first horizontal row, and its final count of 6 would produce the last, or seventh, row of dots. If a different character must be produced, the ASCII code for that character would simply be used as the upper portion of the address.

FIGURE 1.12

A ROM code conversion generator.

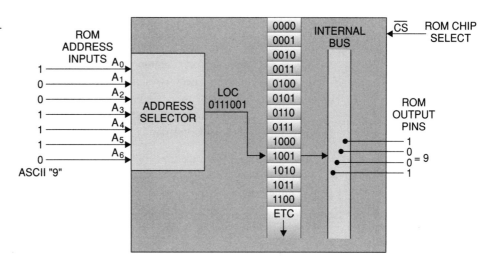

FIGURE 1.13

A ROM character generator.

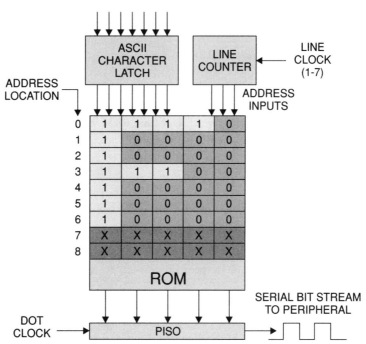

There are several standard ROM look-up tables, code conversion tables, and dot-matrix character generator tables available from IC manufacturers. By storing such information in ROM chips, computer and peripheral manufacturers build a great deal of flexibility into their systems and devices.

Using the examples we have just discussed, it is possible to completely alter the manner in which a computer or peripheral goes about performing its basic function by simply exchanging a handful of IC chips. If an improved operating system is developed for a computer, or a different type style or character font is desired for a printer, the only thing that is required is to change the ROM.

In newer computer systems, special EEPROMs, referred to as **Flash ROMs**, allow the operation of the system to be redefined through software. In these units, it is not necessary to change the ICs to upgrade the system. Simply install the new information from an acceptable source, such as a disk.

RAM Memory

The other type of high-speed semiconductor memory used with computers and peripheral devices is IC **random access memory** or *RAM*. The term "random access" means that any address location in the memory can be accessed as fast as any other location. Since there are other types of RAM memory, IC devices used for primary memory are more appropriately referred to as **read/write (R/W) memories**. In the case of primary memory, the generic term "RAM" always refers to semiconductor R/W memory.

Semiconductor RAM memories are fast enough to work directly with the microprocessor without slowing it down. The computer uses the RAM portion of primary memory to hold programs and data currently being executed by the microprocessor. During the execution of a program, the contents of many RAM address locations are changed as the microprocessor updates the program, by storing intermediate or final results of operations performed.

Like semiconductor ROM, there is more than one type of semiconductor RAM. As a matter of fact, there are two general categories:

▶ Static RAM (SRAM)

▶ Dynamic RAM (DRAM)

Although they both perform the same function, their methods are completely different. **Static RAM** stores binary bits in such a manner that they remain as long as power to the chip is not interrupted. **Dynamic RAM**, on the other hand, requires that data stored in them be **refreshed**, or rewritten, periodically to keep it from fading away. As a matter of fact, each bit in the DRAM must be refreshed at least once every two milliseconds or the data will dissipate. Because it can't be assumed that each bit in the memory will be accessed during the normal operation of the system (within the time frame allotted), the need to constantly refresh the data in the DRAM requires special circuitry to perform this function.

Although the extra circuitry and inconvenience associated with refreshing might initially make DRAM memory seem like a distant second choice behind static RAM, this is not the case. The truth of the matter is that, due to the simplicity of DRAM's internal structure, the bit-storage capacity of a DRAM chip is much greater than that of a similar static RAM chip and offers a much lower rate of power consumption. Both of these factors contribute to making DRAM memory the economical choice in certain RAM memory systems, even in light of the extra circuitry necessary for refreshing.

Generally, static RAM is used in smaller memory systems where the added cost of refresh circuitry would greatly add to the cost per bit of storage. DRAM is used in larger memory systems where the extra cost of refresh circuitry is distributed over a greater number of bits and is offset by the reduced operating cost associated with DRAM chips.

Whether the RAM section of primary memory is made up of static or dynamic RAM chips, all RAM has the disadvantage of being **volatile**, which means that any data stored in RAM will be lost if power to the computer is disrupted. On the other hand, both types of RAM have the advantage of being fast with the ability to be written into and read from with equal ease.

Buses

All of the basic components of the computer are tied together by communications paths called buses. A computer **bus** is simply a parallel collection of conductors that carry data and control signals from one unit to another.

Any computer will have three major system buses identified by the type of information they carry. The three major system buses are

▶ Address bus

▶ Data bus

▶ Control bus

These buses (see Figure 1.14) are actually extensions of the microprocessor's internal communications structure.

FIGURE 1.14

The system buses.

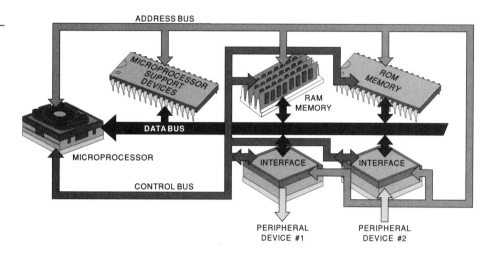

Address Bus

The **address bus** is a **unidirectional** pathway that carries addresses generated by the microprocessor to the memory and I/O elements of the computer. The size of the address bus, determined by the number of conductors in the bus, determines the number of memory locations and/or I/O elements the microprocessor can address. If the address bus is composed of 16 lines (or bits), the microprocessor will be able to generate 2^{16}, or 65,536 distinct address codes. If the address bus size is increased to a 20-bit word size, the microprocessor's capability to address memory and I/O elements is increased to 2^{20}, or 1,048,576 possible addresses.

When discussing addressing capacity, it is common to use the letter **K** (for **kilo**) to represent 1024 (2^{10}) addresses. Using this terminology, the 16-bit bus example above would be capable of addressing up to 64 Kbytes of memory, while the latter example would be capable of directly addressing up to 1,000 Kbytes of memory. This is referred to as a **megabyte** of memory and is denoted by the letter **M** (that is, 1 Mbyte). It is also common to express addresses in hexadecimal form. As a matter of fact, address locations are very rarely specified in a decimal format.

When the microprocessor wants to access a memory location or an input or output element to perform a read or write operation, it does so by placing the appropriate address code on its address pins (A_0-A_N) and generating the proper control signals to perform the operation. Because the memory unit is normally composed of several memory chips (RAM and ROM), special decoding circuitry is required to select the proper IC and then single out the proper memory location and input or output device that the microprocessor is trying to address.

Data Bus

In contrast to the address bus, the **data bus** is **bi-directional** in nature. Data flows along the data bus from the microprocessor to memory during a write operation. Conversely, data moves from memory to the microprocessor during a read operation. The directions for data movement are the same for read and write operations between the microprocessor and input/output devices.

Because all of the computer elements must share the data bus, any device connected to the bus must have the capability to put its outputs in a high-impedance state (floating) when not involved in an operation with the microprocessor. This prevents data from more than one source from being placed on the bus at one time. If two devices attempted to place data on the bus at the same time, confusion and damage to the devices would result. The size of the data bus usually corresponds to the word size of the computer. In general, the larger the data bus, the more powerful the system. Common data bus sizes for microcomputers are 8-bits, 16-bits, and 32-bits.

Control Bus

The **control bus** carries the timing and control signals necessary to coordinate the activities of the entire system. Unlike the other two busses, the control bus signals are not necessarily related to each other. Some are output signals from the microprocessor, whereas others are input signals to the microprocessor from input and output elements. Each different microprocessor type has its own unique set of control signals, which it can generate or respond to. There are many control bus signals common to most microprocessors (or similar to those used by most processors). Therefore, let's discuss the more common control signals in use today:

- System Clock (SYSCLK)
- Read/Write Line (R/W Line)
- Memory Read (MEMR)
- Memory Write (MEMW)
- I/O Read (IOR)
- I/O Write (IOW)

One of the most important control signals in any microprocessor-based system is the **system clock**. This signal provides the timing information around which all of the system's activities take place. Depending on the type of microprocessor being used, the clock signals may be generated on the microprocessor chip or by special IC signal generators. Microprocessors with internal clock generators usually require that an external crystal, or RC network, be connected to its clock input pins.

The control bus also carries the signals that enable selected memory or I/O elements for read and write operations. These signals may range from a simple **Read/Write line (R/W)** to a collection of signals such as **Memory Read (MEMR)**, **Memory Write (MEMW)**, **I/O Read (IOR)** and **I/O Write (IOW)**. These signals are used by the microprocessor in conjunction with addresses on the address bus to perform read and write operations at selected memory or I/O locations.

Microprocessor Operation

To better understand how a microprocessor-based system functions, let's look at a simplified computer system, which we will call the **$1.98 Computer**. This system is based on a mythical 8-bit microprocessor, which has a 4-bit address bus and is capable of performing 16 different operations. The 4-bit address bus means that this processor is only capable of addressing 16 different memory locations, but, for our applications, this should be plenty. Figure 1.15 depicts our mythical microprocessor, its internal block diagram, and a 16x8 (16 address locations and each location stores 8 bits) RAM memory block. The computer's input and output units do not come into play during our discussions of the system's operation. We will simply assume that our programs have been entered into the RAM memory through the input unit and may be displayed through the output unit.

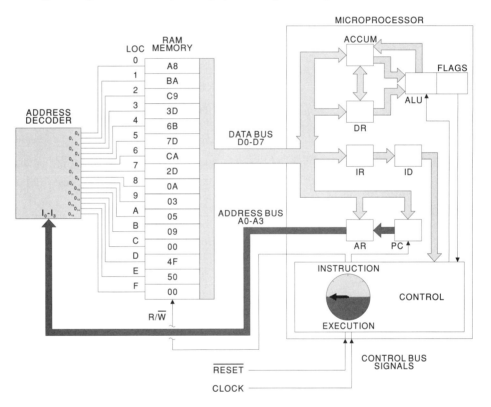

Internal Registers

The microprocessor consists of a group of *Internal Registers*, an *Arithmetic Logic Unit* (ALU), and a *Control Unit*. Different microprocessors will have different numbers and types of internal registers. The ones depicted here are the same as, or similar to, the registers found in almost any microprocessor. They are described as follows:

> **Accumulator (ACCUM).** This type of register is generally used by the microprocessor to store the results of ALU operations. It is also a source of one operand for most ALU operations. Many microprocessors contain more than one accumulator register.

Program Counter (PC). This register/counter keeps track of Instruction Addresses and is always pointing at the address of the next instruction to be fetched from memory. Each time an instruction is fetched from memory, the PC is incremented by one. The control unit may cause the PC to jump to an address out of its normal sequential order. When the control unit receives a branch instruction, such as a JUMP (JMP) or a JUMP-ON-ZERO (JPZ) command, the control unit will cause the PC to be loaded with an address portion of the instruction word. Upon execution of the jump instruction, the PC will continue its normal sequential count, beginning at the new address.

In our example, the PC is automatically reset to a value of 0. This corresponds to the beginning of our program. In real computers, the program counter is reset to some predetermined value, such as a memory location in ROM memory containing the monitor program. This location is referred to as the microprocessor's *vector address* and is determined by the manufacturer of the microprocessor.

Address Register (AR). This register is used to hold the address currently being accessed by the microprocessor. The AR can be loaded from two different places, depending upon which part of the computer cycle is in progress. During an instruction cycle, the contents of the PC are loaded into the AR. Throughout the execution cycle, the AR is used to hold the addresses specified by the operand address portion of the instruction word.

Data Register (DR). This register is used by the microprocessor's accumulator as a temporary storage place for data. Its contents can be applied to the ALU by the accumulator. The number of temporary data registers varies from one microprocessor to the next. Different microprocessors may have several of these registers or none at all.

Instruction Register (IR). This register is loaded with the opcode portion of the instruction word during the instruction cycle and holds it until the completion of the execution cycle.

Instruction Decoder (ID). This device receives the opcode from the IR and decodes it for the control unit.

Arithmetic Logic Unit (ALU). The ALU performs math and logic operations under the direction of the control unit.

Control Unit (CU). The control unit is responsible for generating all of the timing and control signals that are required for the system to execute the instructions contained in the program.

Flag Register. The flag register is not exactly a register in the classical sense. Instead, it is a collection of unrelated bits used to indicate the status of different microprocessor conditions. In our example, the Z-bit of the flag register is set if the last ALU operation produced a result of zero. Likewise, the C-flag is set if the previous operation produced a carry bit beyond the MSB of the accumulator register. Different microprocessors will have different numbers of flags in their flag register. The microprocessor uses these flag bits to allow conditional branching to occur during the execution of the program, with the decision to branch depending on some condition within the microprocessor.

Miscellaneous Registers. Real microprocessors contain a number of specialized registers not covered here. Among these are

- **Index Registers**, used by the programmer to establish and maintain tables and arrays.

- **Stack Pointer Registers**, which are special address registers. These registers are used to create a special area in RAM memory called the **stack**. The stack is normally dedicated to storing the contents of the other microprocessor registers during operations such as interrupt routines.

Instruction Sets

All microprocessors have a specific set of operations that they can perform. These operations are referred to as the microprocessor's **instruction set**. The instruction set defines the operation of the computer very specifically. The instruction set for the $1.98 computer is presented in Table 1.1. Because the $1.98 microprocessor requires only a four-bit opcode and a four-bit address code, the instruction-word format is somewhat different from the more realistic formats described in the previous section. Instead, these instruction words use the four MSBs for the opcode and the four LSBs for the operand address.

Table 1.1 *Instruction Set for $1.98 Computer*

Assembly Language (Mnemonic)	Machine Language Hex Binary	Operation Description
LDA	A 1010	Transfer the contents of the memory location specified by the operand address to the accumulator register.
ADD	B 1011	Add the contents of the memory location specified by the operand address to the contents of the accumulator and store the results in the accumulator register.
SUB	C 1100	Subtract the contents of the memory location specified by the operand address from the contents of the accumulator and store the results in the accumulator register.
JMP	2 0010	Jump unconditionally to the address specified by the operand address. After the jump has been executed, the instructions are taken in order from the new address.
JPZ	3 0011	Jump to the address called for by the operand address, but only if the ZERO flag is set.
STA	4 0100	Store the contents of the accumulator in the memory location specified by the operand address.
STP	5 0101	STOP; halt all operations.
CMP	6 0110	Compare the contents of the memory location specified by the operand address to the contents of the accumulator. If the two are equal, the E-flag is set.
JPE	7 0111	Jump to the address specified by the operand address, if the E-flag was set by the previous operation.

Program Execution

Referring once again to Figure 1.15, examine the hexadecimal program that has been entered into the memory. By referring to the instruction set in Table 1.1, we can interpret the program as described in Table 1.2.

Table 1.2 *Sample Program for $1.98 Computer*

Memory Location	Location Contents	Operation Description
0	A8	LDA with contents of location 8
1	BA	ADD contents of location A to value in ACCUM and store result in the accumulator register
2	C9	SUB contents of location 9 from value in ACCUM and store result in the accumulator register
3	3D	JUMP to location D if ACCUM=0
4	6B	CMP the contents of location B to the value in the ACCUM, set E-flag if equal
5	7D	JUMP to location D if the E-flag if set
6	CA	SUB contents of location A from value in accumulator and store in the accumulator register
7	2D	JUMP to location D unconditionally
8	0A	DATA
9	03	DATA
A	05	DATA
B	09	DATA
C	00	DATA
D	4F	STA the contents of the ACCUM in location F
E	50	STP all operation
F	00	DATA

If you work through the program in sequence and follow the computer's instructions according to their definitions, you will see that this program performs several math functions and makes decisions based on the information available to it. Basically, this is what every computer does. At the end of the program, you should finish with a binary 7 stored in memory location F. If not, go back through the program and follow the instructions in the order that the program dictates, performing the instructions explicitly.

After the program has been loaded into memory, the computer operator must initiate the execution of the program by giving the computer a RUN command or signal. This signal, in turn, applies a RESET input to the microprocessor, which clears its internal registers and sets the program counter to its vector address (0). The RUN signal also causes the computer to enter an **instruction cycle**. During the instruction cycle, the following events occur:

1. The contents of the PC are loaded into the AR and placed on the address bus by the control unit, along with a READ signal on the R/W line of the control bus. Together, these two pieces of information cause the address to be accessed (in our case, location 0) and its contents to be placed on the data bus.

2. The data on the data bus (A8 in this case) is loaded into the microprocessor. The opcode portion (a) of the instruction word is loaded into the IR, and the operand address portion (8) is placed in the AR, replacing the previous address. Both of these operations are performed by the control unit.

3. The IR applies the opcode to the ID, which decodes it for the control unit. The AR places the operand address on the address bus, and the control unit increments the program counter by 1 (to memory location 1).

When the program counter is advanced to the next instruction address, the instruction cycle is ended, and the computer enters an **execution cycle**. During this time, the instruction called for is carried out. At the end of the execution cycle, the computer automatically enters another instruction cycle, where the same sequence of events will be repeated. The computer will continue to perform instruction cycles, followed by execution cycles, until it receives a STOP instruction from the program.

At the beginning of the execution cycle, the control unit issues a READ signal on the R/W line of the control bus, and the data word in the memory location is placed on the data bus. In this instance, the instruction called for the data to be loaded into the microprocessor's accumulator register. During the execution cycle, the control unit develops the signals necessary to latch the data in the accumulator.

There are three other possible courses of action during the execution cycle:

Scenario 1: In the event that the instruction requires an ALU operation, the data word is transferred to the ALU, where it may be placed into the accumulator or the data register. The control unit must generate the control signals required to produce the transfer and also those necessary to carry out the ALU operation.

Scenario 2: If the instruction calls for data to be placed in memory, a *store* operation, the control unit first moves the data to the data register and then places it on the system's data bus. The control unit also generates a WRITE signal on the R/W line, which causes the data to be written into the memory at the address specified by the operand address. Recall that the operand address is still being held in the AR.

Scenario 3: The instruction word calls for some type of jump to occur. If an unconditional jump instruction is received, the control unit simply causes the operand address to be loaded directly into the PC register. If a conditional jump is received and the condition proves false, the execution cycle ends, and the next instruction is taken in order.

Although the $1.98 Computer demonstrates how a typical microprocessor carries out instructions and manipulates data, it does not show the complete scope of microprocessor operations. The $1.98 Computer does not provide any method of entering new instructions or data into the system. It also lacks any provisions for outputting data that has been processed. Without these capabilities, the usefulness of a microprocessor is somewhat limited. In the following section, common methods and equipment for acquiring and outputting data are investigated.

Input/Output (I/O)

In addition to the millions of possible memory locations in a PC, there are typically thousands of addresses set aside for input and output devices in a system.

Referring to the computer system depicted in Figure 1.16, it can be seen that external input and output devices, also called **peripherals**, connect to the computer's bus systems through different interfacing circuits. The interfacing circuits make the peripherals compatible with the system. The system's microprocessor differentiates between memory and I/O addresses through the use of separate read and write signals, as described in the previous section.

FIGURE 1.16

Basic input/output organization.

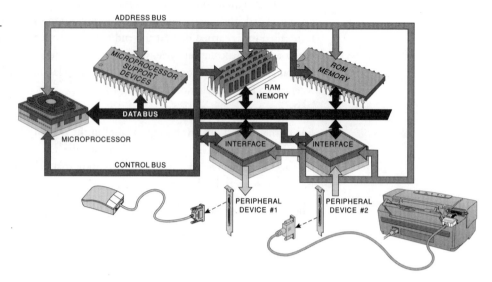

Interface circuits are necessary because the characteristics of most peripherals differ greatly from those of the basic computer.

The microcomputer is a completely solid-state, digital electronic device that uses parallel words of a given length and adheres to basic digital logic levels. However, computer peripherals generally tend to be more mechanical and analogical in nature.

Peripherals may also use parallel or serial transmission modes between themselves and the system board. Although either transmission form may be used with any given type of peripheral, parallel buses are generally used for high-speed devices, such as disk drives and some printers. Conversely, serial transmission is used with remotely located devices or with devices whose operation is more compatible with serial data flow, such as monitors, modems, certain input devices, and some printers.

In addition to these differences, it is not uncommon for a microcomputer system to be composed of a brand-X system unit, a brand-Y printer, and a brand-Z disk drive (not to mention a host of other options from different manufacturers).

This introduces a completely new set of obstacles to the orderly flow of information between the peripherals and the computer. Different manufacturers—or even a single manufacturer from one model to the next—may incorporate a wide variety of signal levels, timing, and formats into their devices that must be matched to those of the host computer. Fortunately, computer and peripheral manufacturers generally adhere to certain conventions—more or less—that allow computers to interface with a variety of different peripheral devices.

More importantly, human beings are **analog** by nature. The computer's input and output units allow it to communicate with the outside world. The input units contain all of the circuitry necessary to accept data and programs from peripheral input devices such as keyboards, light pens, mice, joysticks, and so on, and convert the information into a form that is usable by the microprocessor. The input unit may be used to enter programs and data into the memory unit before execution, or it may be used to enter data directly to the microprocessor during execution. The output units contain all of the circuitry necessary to transform data from the computer's language into a form that is more convenient for the *outside* world. Most often, that is in the form of alphanumeric characters, which are convenient for humans to use. Common output devices include video display monitors, audio speakers, and character printers. Figure 1.17 depicts several common I/O devices associated with personal computers.

FIGURE 1.17

Common I/O devices used with PCs.

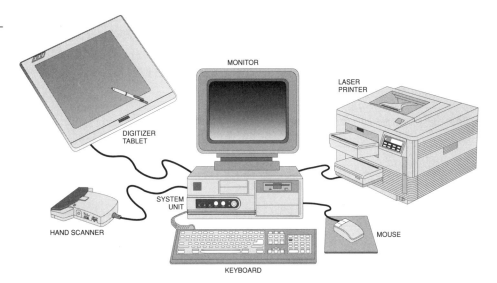

A+ CORE 1.1 Some computer peripherals do double duty as both input and output units. These devices are collectively referred to as **I/O devices** and include secondary storage devices such as hard-disk drives, floppy-disk drives, and magnetic-tape drives, as well as communication devices called **modems** (modulator/demodulators). Modems allow one computer to converse with another over either standard or dedicated telephone lines. In the case of I/O devices, the form data takes is not for the convenience of human beings, but instead, it takes the form most suitable to carry out the function of the device.

Initiating I/O Transfers

During a program's execution, the microprocessor constantly reads from or writes to memory locations. The program may also call on the microprocessor to read from or write to one of the system's I/O devices. Regardless of how the peripheral is connected to the system (serial or parallel), one of four methods may be used to initiate data transfer between the system and the peripheral:

▶ **Polling** is where the microprocessor examines the status of the peripheral under program control.

▶ **Programmed I/O** is where the microprocessor alerts the designated peripheral by applying its address to the system's address bus.

▶ **Interrupt-driven I/O** is where the peripheral alerts the microprocessor that it's ready to transfer data.

▶ **DMA** is where the intelligent peripheral assumes control of the system's buses to conduct direct transfers with primary memory.

Polling & Programmed I/O

Both polling and programmed I/O represent software approaches to data transfer, whereas interrupt-driven and DMA transfers are basically hardware approaches.

In the polling method, the software periodically checks with the system's I/O devices by testing their **READY** lines. When the microprocessor finds a READY line that has been asserted by a peripheral device ready to conduct a data transfer, it begins reading or writing data to the corresponding I/O port. The polling method is advantageous in that it is easy to implement and reconfigure because the program controls the entire sequence of events during the transfer. However, polling is often inconvenient because the microprocessor must be totally involved in the polling routine and cannot perform other functions. A typical polling operation is depicted in Figure 1.18.

FIGURE 1.18

A typical polling operation.

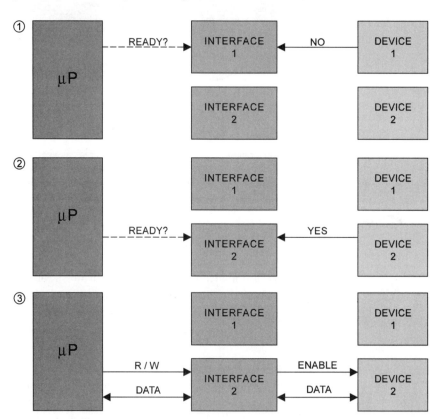

Using the programmed I/O method to conduct data transfers calls for the microprocessor to alert the desired peripheral of an I/O operation by issuing its address to the address bus. The peripheral can delay the transfer by asserting its **BUSY** line. If the microprocessor receives a BUSY signal from the peripheral, it continues to perform other tasks, but periodically checks the device until the BUSY signal is replaced by a READY signal.

In order to establish an orderly flow of data during the transfer, a number of signal exchanges, or **handshakes**, may occur between the peripheral and the system. In a simple handshaking arrangement, the peripheral produces a byte of data at its output register when the microprocessor sends a **Strobe (STB)** signal to the peripheral. The microprocessor reads the word from the data bus. The microprocessor then sends an **Acknowledge (ACK)** signal back to the peripheral, telling it to send the next data word. This method prevents the microprocessor from sending or requesting data at a faster rate than the peripheral can handle. In some systems, the handshaking routine is much more complex. An entire series of handshake signals may be exchanged during the transfer of a single data word. The concept of programmed I/O is illustrated in Figure 1.19.

FIGURE 1.19

A typical programmed I/O operation.

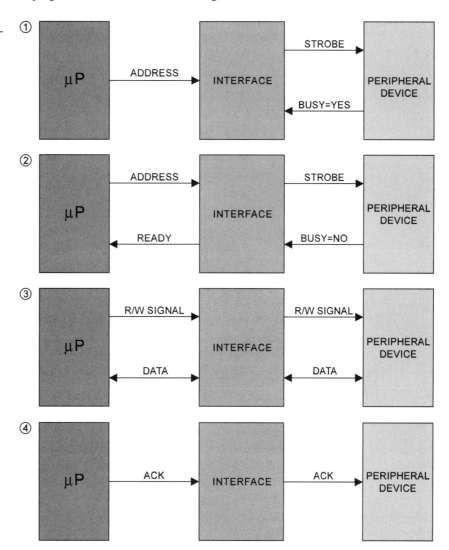

Interrupts

In the course of normal operations, the various I/O devices attached to a PC, such as the keyboard and disk drives, require servicing from the system's microprocessor. Although I/O devices may be treated like memory locations, there is one big difference between the two: I/O devices generally have the capability to interrupt the microprocessor while it is executing a program. The I/O device does this by issuing an **Interrupt (INT)** or **Interrupt Request (INTR or IRQ)** input signal to the microprocessor.

If the microprocessor is responding to INT signals and a peripheral device issues an interrupt request on an IRQ line, the microprocessor will finish executing its current instruction and issue an **Interrupt Acknowledge (INTA)** signal on the control bus. The microprocessor suspends its normal operation and stores the contents of its internal registers in a special storage area referred to as the *stack*.

The interrupting device (or an interrupt controller) responds by sending the starting address of a special program called the **interrupt service routine** to the microprocessor. The microprocessor uses the interrupt service routine to service the interrupting device. After the microprocessor finishes servicing the interrupting device, the contents of the stack are restored to their original locations, and the microprocessor returns to the original program at the point where the interrupt occurred.

Because more than one peripheral device might require the attention of the microprocessor at any given time, all computer systems have methods of handling multiple interrupts in an orderly fashion. The simplest method calls for the microprocessor, or the interrupt controller, to have multiple interrupt inputs that have a fixed priority of service. In this manner, if two interrupt signals occur at the same instant, the interrupt that has the highest priority is serviced first. Actually, there are two varieties of interrupts used in microcomputers:

▶ **Maskable interrupts (MI)**—that the computer can ignore under certain conditions

▶ **Non-maskable interrupts (NMI)**—that it must always respond to

Most microprocessors have an output line called the **Interrupt Enable** (**INTE**) that it uses to inform peripheral devices whether it can be interrupted. The logic level present on this line determines whether the microprocessor will respond to an INT or IRQ input signal. The condition of the INTE line can usually be controlled by software, which means that the program can determine whether the interrupt operation will be activated. Non-maskable interrupt inputs, on the other hand, are signals that cannot be ignored by the microprocessor and, therefore, always cause an interrupt to occur, regardless of the status of the INTE line.

A programmable interrupt controller IC and its relationship to the system's microprocessor are illustrated in Figure 1.20. The interrupt controller chip in the figure accepts prioritized IRQ signals from up to eight peripheral devices on IRQ lines 0 through 7. When one of the peripherals desires to communicate with the microprocessor, it sends an IRQ to the interrupt controller. The controller responds by sending an INT signal to the microprocessor. If two interrupt requests are received at the same instance, the interrupt controller accepts the one that has the higher priority and acts on it first. The priority order is highest for the device connected to the IRQ-0 line and descends in order, with the IRQ-7 input given the lowest priority.

Direct Memory Access (DMA)

Another difference between memory and some intelligent, high-speed I/O devices is that the I/O device may have the capability to perform data transfers (read and write operations) on its own. This type of operation is called **direct memory access** (DMA). DMA generally involves a high-speed I/O device taking over the system's buses to perform Read and Write operations with the primary memory, without the intervention of the system microprocessor.

When the peripheral device has data ready to be transferred, it sends a **DMA request** (**DREQ**) signal to a special IC device called a **DMA controller**, which, in turn, sends a **HOLD** input signal to the microprocessor. The microprocessor finishes executing the instruction it is currently working on and places its address and data pins in a high-impedance state (floating), effectively disconnecting the microprocessor from the buses. At this time, the microprocessor issues a **buses available (BA)** or **hold acknowledge (HLDA)** signal to the DMA controller. The DMA controller then issues a **DMA acknowledge (DACK)** to the peripheral, along with the beginning address of the primary memory block to be used, and the necessary R/W and enable signals for the data transfer to begin. The key to DMA operations is that the DMA controller chip has a speed advantage over the microprocessor in that it can transfer data bytes faster than the microprocessor can.

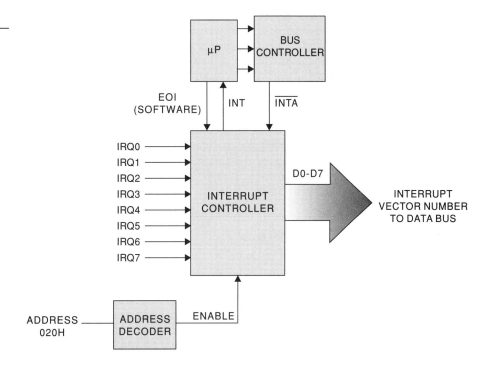

FIGURE 1.20

A programmable interrupt controller operation.

Actually, there are two distinct methods of transferring data using DMA. The crudest and simplest DMA method is referred to as **HALT**, or **Burst Mode DMA**, because the DMA controller takes control of the bus system and transfers a complete block of data to or from memory in a single burst. While the transfer is in progress, the system microprocessor sits idle, performing **No Operation (NOP) instructions** to keep its internal registers refreshed. This is the type of DMA operation performed in most computers.

The second DMA method involves the DMA controller taking control of the bus system for a shorter length of time during periods when the microprocessor is busy with internal operations and does not require access to the buses. In effect, the DMA controller steals clock cycles from the microprocessor when it's not using the bus system. This method of DMA is referred to as **cycle stealing mode**. Cycle-stealing DMA is more complex to implement than HALT DMA because the DMA controller must have the intelligence to sense the periods of time when the system buses are open.

Cycle-stealing DMA can be implemented as **single cycle stealing**, where the microprocessor is halted for a single clock cycle—while the DMA controller transfers a single byte—or as **full cycle stealing**, where the microprocessor is not stopped, and the DMA controller can seize the buses any time the microprocessor is not using them.

Advanced microprocessors offer optimized DMA transfer capabilities because they possess the capability to load several instructions and data internally (called **queuing**) and work for an extended period of time without the need to access the bus system. The microprocessor and DMA controller can have access to the buses for varying lengths of time, as long as the DMA controller does not hold them for too many consecutive clock cycles.

Figure 1.21 depicts a typical DMA controller chip. This controller has provisions for four DMA transfer channels, with each channel consisting of a DREQ line and a corresponding DACK line. This allows the chip to conduct DMA operations for up to four devices. In addition, two of the channels may be used together to perform high-speed memory-to-memory transfers.

FIGURE 1.21

A typical DMA controller.

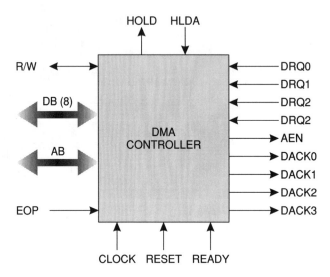

Expansion Slot Connectors

It would be very expensive to design and build a computer that fit every conceivable user application. With this in mind, computer designers include standardized connectors that enable users to configure the system to their particular computing needs.

> Most personal computers use standardized **expansion slot connectors** that allow users to attach various types of peripheral devices to the system. Optional input/output devices, or their interface boards, may be plugged into these slots to connect the devices to the system's address, data, and control buses.

Typical options and interfaces that use these slots include the following:

- Video displays, such as monitors and liquid crystal display (LCD) panels

- Hard and floppy disk drive units for mass storage

- Character/graphics printers to produce hard copy (permanent) output from the system

- Modems to allow the computer to communicate with other computers through commercial telephone lines

- Network adapters that allow computers in a local area to communicate with each other

- Game control units and other pointing devices—such as light pens and mice, and voice generation and recognition systems

⟩ Scanners that convert images from hard copy input into digital information that the computer can process

Adapter Cards

Adapter cards plug into the expansion slots of the computer's main board, as illustrated in Figure 1.22. They typically contain the interfacing and controller circuitry for the peripheral. However, in some cases the entire peripheral may be included on the adapter card. Adapter cards allow peripheral devices to be added to the basic system to modify it for particular applications. For example, adapter cards allow less expensive devices to be used with the system for a beginner and still allow high-end, high-performance peripherals to be used with it for advanced applications. Several companies have developed all types of expansion cards and devices for different types of computer applications. These include I/O controllers, disk drive controllers, video controllers, modems, and proprietary input/output devices, such as scanners.

FIGURE 1.22

Plugging in a typical adapter card.

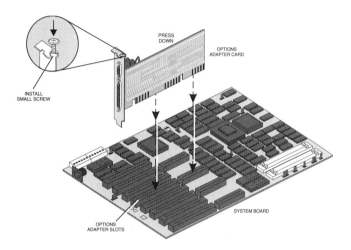

There are three important characteristics associated with any adapter card:

⟩ Function

⟩ Expansion slot connector style

⟩ Size

It is important to realize that any device connected into the system through an adapter card must have a card that is compatible with the expansion slots used in that particular type of computer.

Secondary Memory

 A+ CORE 1.1
Programs and data disappear from the system's RAM when the computer is turned off. In addition, IC RAM devices tend to be too expensive to construct large memories that can hold multiple programs and large amounts of data. Therefore, devices and systems that can be used for long-term data storage are desirable as a second level of memory.

With this in mind, a number of secondary memory technologies have been developed to extend the computer's memory capabilities and store data on a more permanent basis. These systems tend to be too slow to be used directly with the computer's microprocessor.

The secondary memory unit holds the information and transfers it in batches to the computer's faster internal memory when requested.

> From the beginning, most secondary memory systems have involved storing binary information in the form of magnetic charges on moving magnetic surfaces.

This type of storage has remained popular because of three factors:

▶ Low cost per bit of storage

▶ Intrinsically non-volatile in nature

▶ Because it has successfully evolved upward in capacity

The major magnetic storage mediums are floppy disks, hard disks, and tape.

In magnetic disk systems, information is stored in concentric circles around the disk, which are referred to as **tracks**. The tracks on the disk are numbered, beginning with 0, from the outside edge inward. The number of tracks may range from 40 up to 815, depending on the type of disk and drive being used.

Because the tracks at the outer edge of the disk are longer than those at the center, each track is divided into an equal number of equal-sized blocks called **sectors**. The number of sectors on a track may range from 8 to 50, depending on the disk and drive type. A small hole near the center of the disk, called an **index hole**, marks the starting point of the #1 sector on each track. A floppy may have between 40 and 80 tracks per surface, with each track divided into somewhere between 8 and 26 sectors. Each sector holds 512 bytes. The organizational structure of a typical magnetic disk is illustrated in Figure 1.23.

FIGURE 1.23

The organizational structure of a magnetic disk.

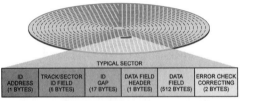

In magnetic tape systems, data is stored in sequential tracks along the length of the tape, as depicted in Figure 1.24. Each track is divided into equal-sized blocks. The blocks are separated by small gaps of unrecorded space. **Multiple tracks** can be recorded across the width of the tape. By using multiple read/write heads, the tracks can be read simultaneously as the tape moves forward. The tracks can also be read in a **serpentine** manner, using a single read/write head.

Although it is possible to directly access any of the sectors on a magnetic disk, the sections on the tape can only be accessed in order. To access the information in block 32 of the tape, the first 31 blocks must pass through the drive.

Most personal computers come from the manufacturer with both a floppy-disk drive unit and a hard-disk drive unit installed. Tape generally represents a cheaper storage option, but its inherent slowness, due to its sequential nature, makes it less desirable than rotating magnetic disks. The disks offer much quicker access to large blocks of data, at a cost that is still affordable to most users.

FIGURE 1.24

*Formats for storing data
on magnetic tape.*

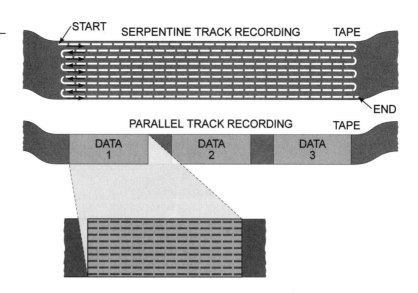

Floppy-Disk Drives

The most widely used data storage systems in personal computers are **Floppy-Disk Drive** (**FDD**) units. These units store information in the form of tiny, magnetized spots on small flexible disks that can be removed from the drive unit. After the information has been *written* on the disk, it remains there until the disk is magnetically erased or written over. The information remains on the disk even if it is removed from the disk drive or if power is removed from the system. Whenever the information is required by the system, it is obtained by inserting the disk back into the drive and causing the software to retrieve (*read*) it from the disk. Information is stored on disks in logical groupings, called **files**. A file is simply a block of related data that is grouped together, given a name, and treated as a single unit.

The disks are relatively inexpensive and are easy to transport and store. In addition, they can easily be removed and replaced if they become full. Popular 3.5-inch and 5.25-inch floppy disk drive units are depicted in Figure 1.25.

FIGURE 1.25

Floppy-disk drives.

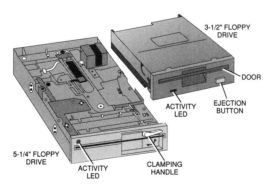

Modern floppy disks come in 5.25- and 3.5-inch diameters, like those depicted in Figure 1.26. Both types are covered with a magnetic coating and encased in protective, semi-rigid envelopes. As the disks are spun inside their envelopes, the drive unit can write data onto them from the computer's RAM memory, or read data from them and store it in RAM. The occurrence of these activities is signaled by a small **disk-drive activity LED** on the front of the unit.

FIGURE 1.26

Floppy disks.

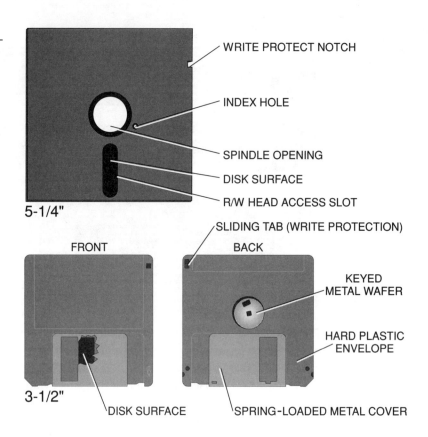

WRITE PROTECT NOTCH

INDEX HOLE

SPINDLE OPENING

DISK SURFACE

R/W HEAD ACCESS SLOT

5-1/4"

SLIDING TAB (WRITE PROTECTION)

FRONT   BACK

KEYED METAL WAFER

HARD PLASTIC ENVELOPE

3-1/2"

DISK SURFACE   SPRING-LOADED METAL COVER

The more popular of the two sizes is the 3.5-inch flexible Mylar disk. The actual disk is housed in a small, hard plastic envelope. The read/write heads access the disk surface from under a spring-loaded metal cover, which the drive unit moves out of the way. The drive spindle does not protrude through the disk. Instead, it drives the disk from a keyed metal wafer attached to the bottom side of the disk. A small, sliding tab in the left-front corner of the envelope performs a **write-protect function** for the disk. Circuitry in the drive checks the condition of this tab to see whether it is allowed to write information on the disk. If the tab covers the opening, the disk may be written to. If the opening is clear, the disk is said to be "**write protected**," and the drive will not write information on the disk.

A typical 5.25-inch floppy disk is also depicted in the figure. There are several openings in the diskette's envelope. In the center of the disk, there is a large circular opening for the drive's spindle. The index hole is the smaller hole just beside the drive-spindle hole. It goes through both sides of the envelope and when the index hole in the disk lines up with the corresponding hole in the envelope, a light shines through the hole and is detected by circuitry on the other side of the disk. This tells the disk-drive controller that the first sector is passing under the drive's **read/write (R/W) heads**.

A semi-elliptical slot on each side of the envelope permits the drive's R/W heads to access the disk's surface. It is through these slots that the R/W heads write and read information to and from the disk. The envelope also has a small square notch along its right edge that provides the write-protect function. If the notch is open, the disk may be written to. The disk cannot be written to if the notch is covered.

Hard-Disk Drives

The system's data storage potential is extended considerably by the high-speed, high-capacity **hard-disk drive** (**HDD**) units like the one shown in Figure 1.27. These units store much more information than floppy disks do. Modern hard drives may have storage capacities ranging up to many gigabytes. Hard drives also differ from floppy-disk units in that they use rigid disks that are permanently sealed in the drive unit (non-removable).

The disks are aluminum platters coated with a nickel-cobalt or Ferro-magnetic material. Two or more platters are usually mounted on a common spindle, with spacers between them, to allow data to be recorded on both sides of each disk. The drive's read/write mechanism is sealed inside a dust-free compartment along with the disks.

Older hard drives used disk platters that ranged in size from 8 to 40 inches in diameter. Modern hard-disk drives come in 5.25-, 3.5-, and 2.5-inch diameters. Of these sizes, the 5.25- and 3.5-inch versions have grown in popularity due to their association with personal and business computers. However, the popularity of the 3.5- and 2.5-inch versions is growing with the rising popularity of smaller laptop and notebook-size computers. Hard drives ranging into the gigabytes are available for these machines.

FIGURE 1.27

Inside a hard-disk drive.

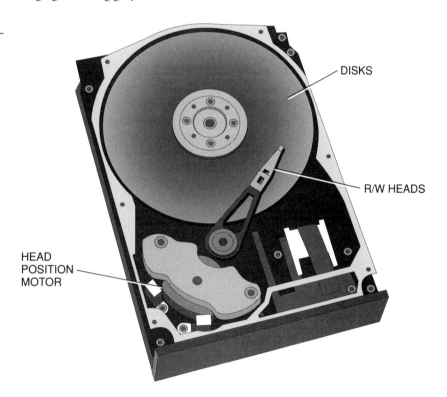

The major differences between floppy- and hard-disk drives are storage capacity, data transfer rates, and cost. Another difference is the fact that hard-disk drives tend to be more delicate than floppy drives. Therefore, they require special handling to prevent both damage to the unit and loss of data. The disks in the HDD are not removable like floppy disks. Therefore, it is possible to fill up a hard-disk drive. When this occurs, it becomes necessary to delete information from the unit to make room for new information.

Conversely, floppy disks are prone to damage due to mishandling, static, temperature, and so on. In addition, they are easy to misplace and provide limited storage of application software. The latter limitation causes the user to "swap" disks in and out of floppy drives when running large programs. But as long as you have a blank disk, you will not run out of storage potential.

Peripherals

> Peripherals are devices and systems added to the basic computer system to extend its capabilities. These devices and systems can be divided into three general categories: **input systems**, **output systems**, and **memory systems**.

Each peripheral device interacts with the basic system through adapter boards that plug into expansion slots inside the system unit. The peripheral systems that are normally included as standard equipment in most microcomputers are the **keyboard**, the **video display monitor**, a **character printer**, and some type of **pointing device**.

A+ CORE 1.1

The most widely used input device for personal computers is the typewriter-like alphanumeric keyboard. Unlike other I/O devices, the keyboard normally requires no interface adapter card. Its interface circuitry is generally built directly into the system's main board.

Pointing devices are small input devices that allow the user to interact with graphical software running in the system. They enable the user to move a cursor or some other screen image around the display screen and choose options from an onscreen menu, instead of typing commands from a keyboard. Most pointing devices are handheld units that enable the user to enter commands and data into the computer easier than is possible with a keyboard. Because they make it easier to interact with the computer than other input devices, they are, therefore, friendlier to the user.

Common input devices are depicted in Figure 1.28. The devices include the keyboard, mouse, joystick, light pen, and trackball.

FIGURE 1.28

Typical input devices.

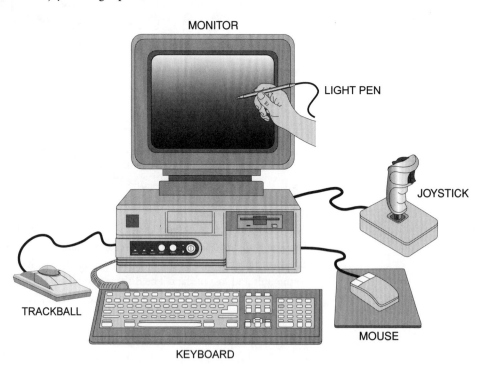

MONITOR

LIGHT PEN

JOYSTICK

TRACKBALL

MOUSE

KEYBOARD

The most widely used pointing device is the **mouse**, which is a handheld device that produces input data by being moved across a surface, such as a (literal) desktop. It may have one, two, or three buttons that can be pressed in different combinations to interact with software running in the system. The mouse enables the user to move a cursor or some other screen image around the display screen. When a position has been selected, clicking one or more of the mouse buttons allows the user to choose options from an onscreen menu, instead of typing commands from a keyboard.

Specialized graphics software enables the user to operate the mouse as a drawing instrument. In this context, the mouse can be used to create elaborate pictures on the screen. The **trackball mouse** detects positional changes through a rolling trackball it rides on.

A+ CORE 1.1 The most widely used output device for personal computers is the **cathode ray tube (CRT)** video display monitor, similar to the one shown in Figure 1.29. Video display monitors often include a tilt/swivel base that enables the user to position it at whatever angle is most comfortable. This offers additional relief from eyestrain by preventing the user from viewing the display at an angle. Viewing the screen at an angle causes the eyes to focus separately, which places strain on the eye muscles.

FIGURE 1.29

Typical output devices.

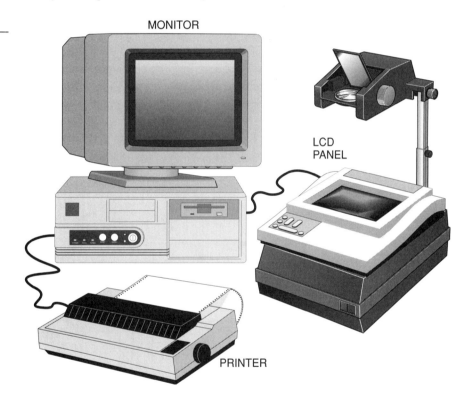

MONITOR

LCD PANEL

PRINTER

Small notebook and laptop computers use non-CRT displays, such as **liquid crystal display (LCD)** and **gas-plasma panels**. These display systems are well-suited to the portability needs of these computers. They are much lighter and more compact than CRT monitors and require less electricity to operate. Both types of display units can operate on batteries.

After the monitor, the next most often added output device is the *character printer*. These peripherals are used to produce hard copy output on paper. They convert text and graphical data from the computer into print on a page.

Software

Once the system's components are connected together and their power connectors have been plugged in, the system is ready for operation. However, there is one thing still missing—the **software**. Without good software to oversee its operation, the most sophisticated computer hardware is worthless.

Three general classes of software need to be discussed:

◗ **System software**

◗ **Applications software**

◗ **Games** and **learning software**

The bulk of the software discussed in this book deals with the system software category, due to the fact that this type tends to require more technical skills to manipulate and, therefore, most often involves the service person.

System Software

The system software category consists of special programs used by the system itself to control the computer's operation. Two classic examples of this type of software are the system's **Basic Input/Output System** (**BIOS**) program and the **Disk Operating System** (**DOS**). These programs, described in Figure 1.30, control the operation of the other classes of software. The BIOS is located in a ROM IC device on the system board. Therefore, it is commonly referred to as **ROM BIOS**. The DOS software is normally located on a magnetic disk.

FIGURE 1.30

System software.

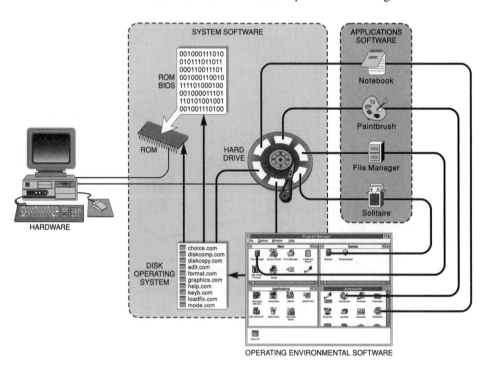

Basic Input/Output Systems

When a PC is turned on, the entire system is reset to a predetermined starting condition. From this state, it begins carrying out software instructions from its BIOS program. This small program is permanently stored in the ROM memory ICs located on the system board. The information stored in these chips is all the inherent intelligence that the system has to begin with.

> A system's BIOS program is one of the keys to its **compatibility**. To be IBM PC-compatible, for example, the computer's BIOS must perform the same basic functions that the IBM PC's BIOS does.

However, because the IBM BIOS software is copyrighted, the compatible's software must accomplish the same results that the original did, but it must do it in some different way.

During the execution of the BIOS firmware routines, three major sets of operations are performed. First, the BIOS performs a series of diagnostic tests (called **POST** or **Power-On Self-Tests**) on the system to verify that it is operating correctly.

If any of the system's components are malfunctioning, the tests will cause an error message code to be displayed on the monitor screen and/or an audio code to be output through the system's speaker.

The BIOS program also places starting values in the system's various programmable devices. These intelligent devices regulate the operation of different portions of the computer's hardware. This process is called **initialization**. As an example, when the system is first started, the BIOS moves the starting address and mode information into the DMA controller. Likewise, the locations of the computer's interrupt handler programs are written into the interrupt controller. This process is repeated for several of the microprocessor's support devices so that they have the information they need to begin operation.

Finally, the BIOS checks the system for a special program that it can use to load other programs into its RAM. This program is called the **Master Boot Record**. The boot record program contains information that allows the system to load a much more powerful control program, called the Disk Operating System, into RAM memory. Once the Operating System has been loaded into the computer's memory, the BIOS gives it control over the system. In this way, the total "intelligence" of the system is greatly increased over what was available with just the ROM BIOS program alone. From this point, the Operating System will oversee the operation of the system.

This operation is referred to as **booting up** the system. If the computer is started from the OFF condition, the process is referred to as a **cold boot**. If the system is restarted from the ON condition, the process is called a **RESET**, or a **warm boot**.

The bootup process may take several seconds, depending on the configuration of the system. If a warm boot is being performed, or if the POST tests have been disabled, the time required to get the system into operation is greatly decreased. The procedure for bootup is shown in Figure 1.31.

FIGURE 1.31A

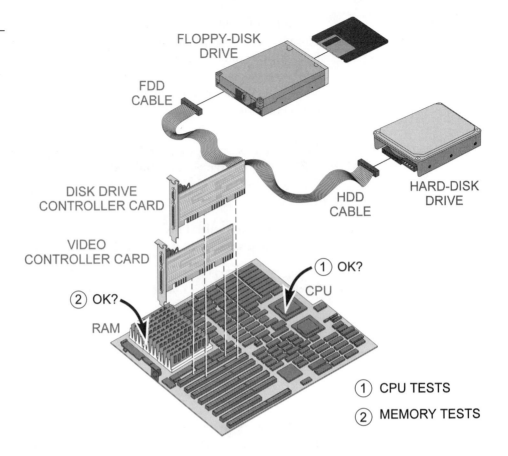

FIGURE 1.31B

① INITIALIZE SYSTEM
   BOARD DEVICES

② INITIALIZE VIDEO
   CONTROLLER

③ INITIALIZE I/O
   CONTROLLER

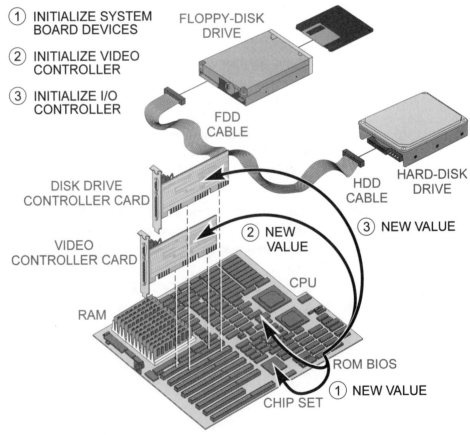

FIGURE 1.31C

The steps of a bootup.

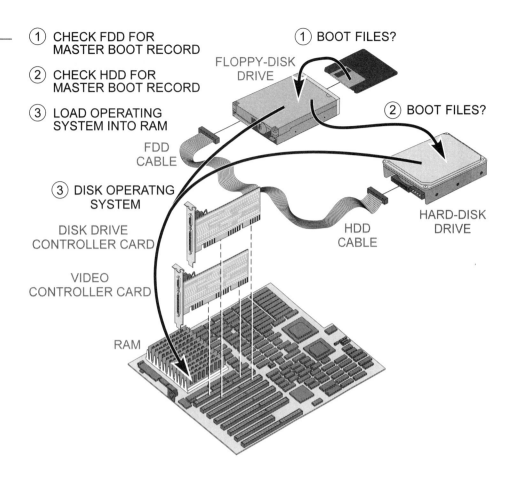

In part a of the operation, the BIOS tests the microprocessor (1) and the system's RAM memory (2). In part b, it furnishes starting information to the system's microprocessor support devices (1), video adapter card (2), and disk drive adapter card (3). Finally, in part c, the BIOS searches through the system in a predetermined sequence looking for a master boot record to which to turn over control of the computer. In this case, it checks the floppy disk drive first (1) and the hard disk drive second (2). If a boot record is found in either location, the BIOS will move it onto the computer's RAM memory and turn over control to it.

Operating Systems

Operating systems are programs designed to control the operation of a computer system. As a group, they are easily some of the most complex programs devised.

> Every portion of the system must be controlled and coordinated so that the millions of operations that occur every second are carried out correctly and on time. In addition, it is the job of the operating system to make the complexity of the personal computer as invisible as possible to the user.

Likewise, the operating system acts as an intermediary between nearly as complex software applications and the hardware they run on. Finally, the operating system accepts commands from the computer user and carries them out to perform some desired operation.

A **Disk Operating System (DOS)** is a collection of programs used to control overall computer operation in a disk-based system. These programs work in the background to enable the user to input characters from the keyboard, to define a file structure for storing records, or to output data to a monitor or printer. The Disk Operating System is responsible for finding and organizing your data, and applications on the disk.

The Disk Operating System can be divided into three distinct sections:

▶ **Boot files**, which take over control of the system from the ROM BIOS during startup

▶ **File management files**, which allow the system to manage information within itself

▶ **Utility files**, which enable the user to manage system resources, troubleshoot the system, and configure the system

The operating system acts as a bridge between the application programs and the computer, as described in Figure 1.32. These applications programs enable the user to create files of data pertaining to certain applications, such as word processing, remote data communications, business processing, and user programming languages.

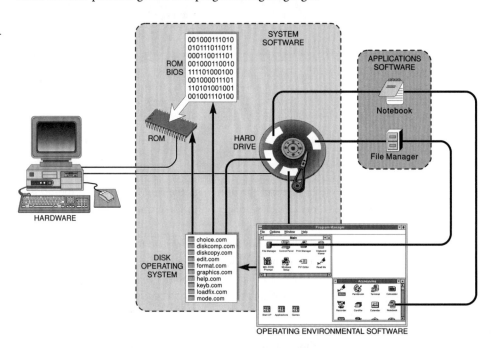

Often, new users are confused because data or programs they have created do not appear from the DOS prompt. The information has been created by an application program that applies its own formatting code to the body of the information. Therefore, the creating program is necessary to properly interpret the created program. As an example, when a text file is created with a given word processing program, formatting codes are added to the document for bold and italic characters, as well as tabs and carriage returns. Although the basic ASCII characters may appear correctly, the codes may be displayed much differently by another word processor. Likewise, there is almost no chance that a BASIC programming package could interpret the control codes so that it could display the text file in any meaningful way.

Operating Environments

Another form of operating environment, referred to as a **graphical user interface** (**GUI**), has gained widespread popularity in recent years. GUIs, like the one depicted in Figure

1.33, use a graphical display to represent procedures and programs that can be executed by the computer. These programs routinely use small pictures, called *icons,* to represent different programs. The advantage of using a GUI is that the user doesn't have to remember complicated commands to execute a program.

FIGURE 1.33

A graphical user interface screen.

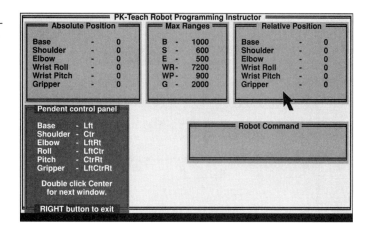

Application Software

The second software category, applications software, is the set of programs that perform specific tasks, such as word processing, accounting, and so forth. This type of software is available in two forms:

▶ Commercially available, user-oriented applications packages, which may be bought and used directly

▶ Programming languages with which you can write your own applications programs

Commercial Application Packages

The openness of the personal computer market has generated a wide variety of different applications programs designed for use with PCs. Even a short discussion of all the software types available for the PC would take up more space than we can afford. However, a small group of these programs makes up the vast majority of the software sold in this category. These programs are

▶ Word processors

▶ Spreadsheets

▶ Data Base Management Systems (DBMS)

▶ Personal productivity tools

▶ Graphic design packages

Word processors are specialized software packages that can be used to create and edit alphanumeric texts, such as letters, memos, contracts, and other documents. These packages convert the computer into a super typewriter. Unlike typewriters, word processors enable the user to edit, check, and correct any errors before the document is committed to paper. Many word processors offer extended functions such as spelling checkers, as well as online dictionary and thesaurus functions that aid the writer in preparing the document. A typical word processor working page is depicted in Figure 1.34.

FIGURE 1.34

A typical word processor.

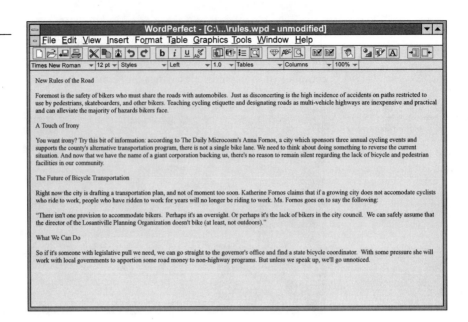

Spreadsheets are specialized financial worksheets that enable the user to prepare and manipulate numerical information in a comparative format. Paper spreadsheets were used by business people for many years before the personal computer came along. Spreadsheets are used to track business information such as budgets, cash flow, and earnings. Because the information in these documents is updated and corrected often, working on paper was always a problem. With electronic spreadsheets, such as the one illustrated in Figure 1.35, this work is much quicker to perform and less fatiguing. This software might be the class most responsible for the growth of personal computers into serious work machines.

FIGURE 1.35

A typical spreadsheet program.

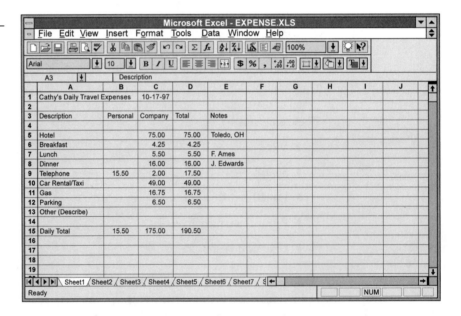

Data Base Management Systems (or simply Databases) are programs that enable the user to store and track vast amounts of related information about different subjects. Databases can be thought of as electronic boxes of note cards. You can keep on these electronic note cards several pieces of information related to a given subject. For example, you might keep information on a note card for each of your relatives. The card might list their phone number, address, and birthday. The database enables you to sort through the information in different ways. With a database program, it would be no problem to sort out all of the relatives who have a birthday in a given month. A typical database working page is shown in Figure 1.36.

FIGURE 1.36

A typical database program.

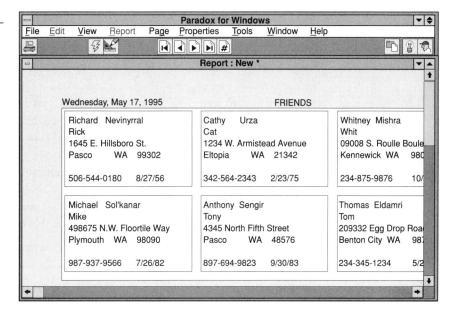

Graphics programs enable the user to create non-alphanumeric output from the computer. Simple graphics programs are used to create charts and graphs that represent data. More complex programs can be used to create artistic output in the form of lines, shapes, and images. Typically, graphic design programs produce graphics in two formats: as **Bitmapped Images** and as **Vector Images**. With bitmapped graphics, every dot (**pixel**) in the image is defined in memory. Vector images are defined as a starting point and a set of mathematical formulas in memory. Because vector images exist only as a set of mathematical models, their size can be scaled up or down easily without major distortions. Vector images can also be rotated easily, allowing three-dimensional work to take place on these images. On the other hand, bitmapped graphics are tightly specified collections of spots across and down the screen. These types of images would be difficult to scale or rotate without distortion. A typical graphics package is depicted in Figure 1.37.

FIGURE 1.37

A typical graphic design program.

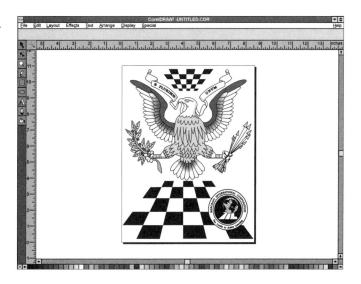

Personal productivity programs, also referred to as **desktop organizers**, encompass a variety of programs that simulate tools found on typical business desks. They normally include items such as telephone directories, calculators, note pads, and calendar programs. Of course, many other types of applications software are available for use with the PC. A meaningful discussion of all these software types are well beyond the scope of this book and certainly goes well beyond the scope of preparing for A+ testing.

Programming Packages

Because the only language that computers understand is their own machine language and most humans don't relate well to machine languages, you'll need a piece of system software to convert whatever language you're programming into the machine's language. These conversion packages exist in two forms: **interpreters** and **compilers**. The distinction between the two is in how and when they convert the user language into machine language. Interpreters convert the program as it is being **run** (executed). Compilers convert the entire user language program into machine code before it is executed. Typically, compiled language programs execute much faster than those written in interpretive languages. In addition, compiled languages typically provide the user with a much higher level of direct control over the computer's operation.

In contrast, interpreted languages are usually slower and less powerful, but their programs tend to be easier to write and use than compiled languages.

BASIC is probably the best-known example of an interpreted *high-level* programming language. The term **BASIC** stands for **Beginners All-purpose Symbolic Instruction Code**, while "high-level" refers to the fact that the language uses commands that are English-like. This all contributes to making BASIC a popular user language, which almost anyone can learn to use (see Figure 1.38 for an example of a **QBASIC** program).

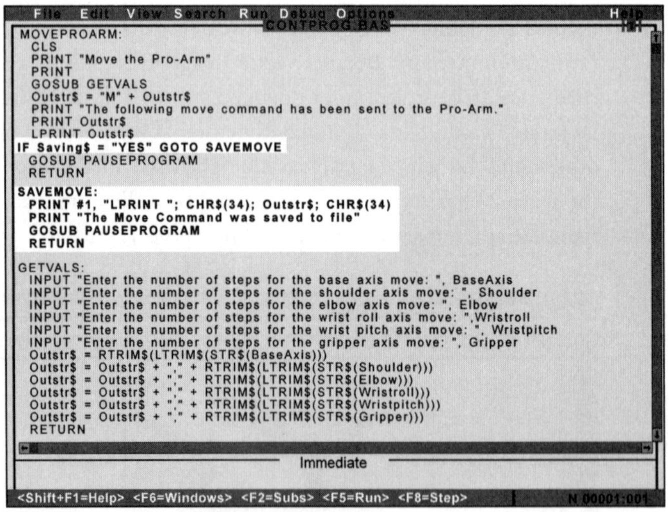

FIGURE 1.38

A QBASIC program.

An example of a compiled language is FORTRAN. FORTRAN is one of the oldest user languages still in use today and is primarily used in engineering and scientific applications. Many of FORTRAN's attributes resemble those you'll find in BASIC. This is due to the fact that most versions of BASIC are modified derivatives of FORTRAN.

There are also commercially available BASIC compiler programs that enable you to take BASIC programs, written with an interpreter, and compile them so that they will run faster. Other compiled language packages that run on almost any PC include COBOL (a business applications language), LISP (an artificial intelligence applications language), and the popular user languages C+, FORTH, and PASCAL.

Another alternative in programming exists for your computer—that is, to write programs in **Assembly Language** (one step away from machine language) and run them through an **Assembler** program. Assembly language is a human-readable form of machine language that uses short, symbolic instruction words, called **mnemonics**, to tell the computer what to do. Each line of an Assembly language program corresponds directly to one line of machine code. Writing programs in Assembly language enables the programmer to precisely control every aspect of the computer's operation during the execution of the program. This makes Assembly language the most powerful programming language you can use. To its detriment, Assembly Language is complex and requires the programmer to be extremely familiar with the internal operation of the system using the program.

A number of steps are required to create an Assembly language program:

1. You must create the program using an alphanumeric text editor.

2. The text file must be run through an **Assembler program** to convert the Assembly language into machine code.

3. Finally, the machine code must be run through a **Linking program**, which puts the assembled machine code into the proper format to work with the operating system. In this final form, the program can be executed from DOS.

For short and simple Assembly language programs, a DOS utility called **DEBUG** can be used to enter and run Machine language and limited Assembly language programs, without going through the various assembly steps. A sample DEBUG program is shown in Figure 1.39.

FIGURE 1.39

The DEBUG Assembly Language program.

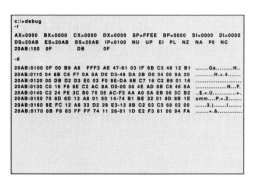

Microsoft introduced a radically different programming environment when it delivered **Visual Basic**. Unlike the previous BASIC language versions, Visual Basic is a graphical programming tool that allows programmers to develop Windows applications in an artistic rather than command-line basis. The programmer draws graphic elements and places them on the screen as desired. This tool is so powerful that it is used to produce large blocks of major applications, as well as finished Windows products. The finished product can be converted into an executable file using a Visual Basic utility. The only major drawback of Visual Basic is that major applications written in it tend to run slowly because it is an interpreted language.

Games and Educational Packages

Games and learning programs are among the leading titles in retail software sales. The games market has exploded as PC speeds have increased and as output graphics have improved. However, on the technical side, there is generally not much call for repair associated with games software. Most games work with well-developed pointing devices, such as trackballs and joysticks, as the primary input devices. Although the housing designs of these products can be quite amazing, they tend to be simple and well-proven devices, requiring relatively little maintenance. Likewise, the software tends to be pretty straightforward from a user's point of view. It simply gets installed and runs.

Computer-Aided Instruction (**CAI**) and **Computer-Based Instruction** (**CBI**) have become accepted means of delivering instructional materials. In CAI operations, the computer assists a human instructor in delivering information and tracking student responses. In CBI operations, the computer becomes the primary delivery vehicle for instructional materials.

As these teaching systems proliferate, more complex input, output, and processing devices are added to the system. A basic teaching system requires a minimum of a sound card, a fast hard drive, a CD-ROM drive, and a high-resolution video card. Beyond this, CAI and CBI systems may employ such wide-ranging peripherals as large LCD display panels, VGA-compatible overhead projectors, intelligent white boards, wireless mice and touch sensitive screens as input devices, full-motion video capture cards, and a host of other multimedia related equipment. Refer to Chapter 12, "Multimedia," for more information on these types of products.

Version Numbers

All types of software are referred to by **version numbers**. When a programmer releases a software program for sale, a version number is assigned to it, such as Windows 3.11 or MS-DOS 6.22. The version number distinguishes the new release from prior releases of that same software. The larger the version number, the more recent the program. When new features or capabilities are added to a program, it is given a new version number. Therefore, referring to a software package by its version number indicates its capabilities and operation. The number to the left of the decimal point is the major revision number, which usually changes when new features are added. The number(s) to the right of the decimal are minor revision numbers, which usually change when corrections are made to the program.

Key Points Review

This chapter has presented a minicourse on the basic organization and operation of the digital computer.

- The logic values used in the digital computer correspond directly to the digits of the binary, or Base-2, number system. In this system, there are only two possible values that each digit can assume, 0 and 1.

- The bits, bytes, words, and programs that make the computer function are referred to as software. The term "software" is used when referring to any aspect of the computer or its operation that you can't reach out and touch.

- The term hardware is used to indicate any part of the computer system that you can touch with your hand.

- IC technology allows millions of circuit elements to be constructed on a single small piece of silicon. Some VLSI devices contain complete computer modules.

- One of the earliest VLSI devices brought together a section of special onboard data storage areas, referred to as registers, and a CPU in a single IC package. This device is called a microprocessor (or MPU).

- The memory unit is the section of the computer where instructions and data to be used by the computer are stored.

- All of the basic components of the computer are tied together by communications paths called buses. A computer bus is simply a parallel collection of conductors that carry data and control signals from one unit to another.

- In addition to the millions of possible memory locations in a PC, there are typically thousands of addresses set aside for input and output devices in a system.

- Interface circuits are necessary because the characteristics of most peripherals differ greatly from those of the basic computer.

- It is not uncommon for a microcomputer system to be composed of a brand-X system unit, a brand-Y printer, and a brand-Z disk drive (not to mention a host of other options from different manufacturers).

- Most personal computers use standardized expansion slot connectors that allow users to attach various types of peripheral devices to the system. Optional input/output devices, or their interface boards, may be plugged into these slots to connect the devices to the system's address, data, and control buses.

- From the beginning, most secondary memory systems have involved storing binary information in the form of magnetic charges on moving magnetic surfaces.

- Peripherals are devices and systems added to the basic computer system to extend its capabilities. These devices and systems can be divided into three general categories: input systems, output systems, and memory systems.

- Without good software to oversee its operation, the most sophisticated computer hardware is worthless.

- A system's BIOS program is one of the keys to its compatibility. For example, to be IBM PC-compatible, the computer's BIOS must perform the same basic functions that the IBM PC's BIOS does.

- Operating Systems are programs designed to control the operation of a computer system. Every portion of the system must be controlled and coordinated so that the millions of operations that occur every second are carried out correctly and on time. The operating system should also make the complexity of the personal computer as invisible as possible to the user.

At this point, review the objectives listed at the beginning of the chapter to be certain that you understand and can perform them. Afterward, answer the review questions that follow to verify your knowledge of the information.

Multiple Choice Questions

1. What does *BCD* stand for?

   a. Binary Counted Decimal

   b. Binary Corrected Decimal

   c. Binary Coded Decimal

   d. Binary Coded Directions

2. Which control bus signal is used to synchronize all microprocessor operations?

   a. The Read/Write signal

   b. The System Clock signal

   c. The Interrupt Request signal

   d. The DMA Request signal

3. What's another name for an eight-bit word?

   a. A bit

   b. A word

   c. A nibble

   d. A byte

4. What determines where a data word will be stored in a memory unit?

   a. Its address

   b. Its size

   c. Its type

   d. Its function

5. What type of operation is being performed when a data word is placed into a memory unit?

    a. A write operation

    b. A read operation

    c. A fetch operation

    d. An interrupt operation

6. What is the major advantage of dynamic RAM over static RAM?

    a. Its speed of operation

    b. Its physical size

    c. Its non-volatility

    d. Its storage capability and low cost of operation

7. What is the major requirement of devices used as internal, or primary, memory?

    a. Storage capacity

    b. Speed

    c. Physical size

    d. Non-volatility

8. What are the major requirements of secondary memory devices or systems?

    a. Low cost and non-volatility

    b. Physical size and speed

    c. Speed and low cost

    d. Non-volatility and speed

9. What components are incorporated to form a microprocessor?

    a. An ALU, an accumulator, and an I/O unit

    b. An input unit, an output unit, and a control unit

    c. An ALU, a control unit, and storage registers

    d. A memory unit, a control unit, and an I/O unit

10. What type of memory device is used to hold data that does not change?

    a. ASIC devices

    b. VLSI devices

    c. ROM devices

    d. RAM devices

Review Questions

The following questions test your knowledge of the material presented in this chapter.

1. What are the differences between an EPROM and EEPROM?

2. Define volatile memory.

3. What is the major disadvantage of dynamic RAM? Primary memory?

4. Name the basic blocks of a typical computer.

5. Where do the contents of the microprocessor's internal registers go during an interrupt operation?

6. What are the three major differences between floppy-disk drives and hard-disk drives?

7. Which bus in the computer is bidirectional and which is unidirectional?

8. Which software category is normally associated with the term "firmware"?

9. Define "files" as they apply to computers.

10. What function do the expansion slots perform in a typical microcomputer?

11. What three functions do the ROM BIOS programs perform?

12. What is the purpose of a GUI?

13. Why is magnetic disk data storage more popular than tape storage?

14. How is magnetic tape storage different from magnetic disk storage?

15. Describe two common formats used to store data on magnetic tape.

Lab Exercises

The lab manual that accompanies this book contains hands-on lab procedures that reinforce and test your knowledge of the theory materials presented in this chapter. Now that you have completed your review of Chapter 1, refer to the lab manual and perform Procedures 14, "QBASIC," and 16, "Advanced QBASIC."

Also, perform the following *paper labs* to become familiar with the basic operation of the computer system:

1. Use the $1.98 Computer's instruction set to write a program that will load a value of 7 from location F into the accumulator. It should then add 2 to the value in the accumulator, compare the result to a value of F, and set the E flag if the two values are equal. Continue to add 2 to the value in the accumulator until the E flag is set. At this point, the program should halt.

2. Use the $1.98 Computer's instruction set to write a program that will multiply 7 by 6 and store the final answer in location F. (Consider the accumulator to be eight bits wide.)

3. Use the $1.98 Computer's instruction set to write a program that will divide the decimal value 105 by 15 and place the answer in location F.

4. Use the $1.98 Computer's instruction set to write a program for it that will count by threes to a value of F and then begin the count again. After counting to F five times, cause the program to halt.

Upon completion of this chapter and its related lab procedures, you should be able to perform the following tasks:

1. Locate the power supply unit, system board, system speaker, disk drive unit, and expansion slots.

2. Discuss differences between different PC case styles and explain strong and weak points associated with each.

3. Recognize the special features associated with portable computers.

4. Describe the function of typical PC power supplies.

5. Locate the system's RAM banks and, by using documentation, determine the amount of RAM installed in the system.

6. Identify different types of RAM modules (DIP, SIPP, SIMM, DIMM).

7. Identify common microprocessor IC package types.

8. Discuss and recognize the different PCMCIA devices currently available.

9. Identify a Video/Graphics/Array (VGA) adapter card.

10. Identify a Multi-I/O (MI/O) card.

11. Recognize different disk drive types associated with PCs.

12. Describe typical external connections associated with PCs.

CHAPTER 2

Introduction

In the previous chapter, basic digital computer concepts were introduced. This chapter illustrates how those basic concepts have been used to develop actual microcomputer systems. The initial portion of the chapter documents the evolution of the personal computer from a variety of small computing systems that started the market, to the Apple and IBM personal computers that brought PCs to prominence, and finally to the clones that currently dominate the market.

The remainder of the chapter deals with the various hardware structures that make up a PC-compatible microcomputer. This section sets the foundation for more in-depth theory and troubleshooting materials in the following chapters.

Personal Computer Evolution

In the early years of microcomputer history, the market was dominated by a group of small companies that produced computers intended mainly for playing video games. Serious computer applications were almost always a secondary concern. Companies such as Commodore, Timex/Sinclair, Atari, and Tandy produced eight-bit machines for the emerging industry based on microprocessors from Intel, Motorola, Zilog, and Commodore.

In 1977 Apple Computers produced the Apple I. This was followed with a series of 8-bit microcomputers: the Apple II, Apple IIc, and Apple IIe. These units were single-board computers with built-in keyboards and a discrete monitor. With the IIe unit, Apple installed seven expansion connectors on its main board. These connectors were included to allow the addition of adapter cards. Apple also produced a set of adapter cards that could be used with the IIe to bring additional capabilities to the basic IIe. These units were very advanced for their time. However, in 1981, Apple introduced their very powerful 16-bit **Macintosh (Mac)** system to the market. The Mac features represented a major shift in computing power. They departed from command line operations by offering a graphical operating method that used a small input device called a mouse to select objects from the output monitor and guide the operation of the system. This method found an eager audience of nontechnical users and public school systems.

Late in 1981, IBM entered the personal computer market with the unveiling of their now famous **IBM PC**. At the time of its introduction, the IBM-PC was a drastic departure from the status quo of the microcomputer world. The PC used an Intel 8088 16/8-bit microprocessor (its registers processed data 16 bits at a time internally, but had an 8-bit external data bus). Relatively speaking, it was fast, powerful, flexible, and priced within the range of most individuals. The general public soon became aware of the tremendous possibilities of the personal computer, and the microcomputer world quickly advanced from one of simple games to one with a seemingly endless range of advanced personal and business applications.

The original Apple Mac and IBM PC are depicted in Figure 2.1.

The success of the PC stemmed largely from IBM's approach to marketing it. IBM actually constructed very little of the PC. Instead, they went to independent manufacturers for most of their system components and software. To do this, IBM made public nearly all of the technical information concerning the PC. This *openness*, in turn, created a rush of small companies developing hardware and software options compatible with the PC.

FIGURE 2.1

In 1983, IBM added a small hard-disk drive to the PC and introduced the **Extended Technology** (**XT**) version of the PC. The success continued when, in 1984, IBM introduced the **Advanced Technology PC** (**PC-AT**). The AT used a true 16-bit microprocessor (it processed 16 bits at a time internally and had a 16-bit external data bus) from Intel, called the 80286. The wider bus increased the speed of the computer's operation because the 80286 was then able to transfer and process twice as much data at a time as the 8088 could.

The IBM PC-AT is depicted in Figure 2.2.

FIGURE 2.2

The IBM PC-AT.

The tremendous popularity of the original IBM PC-XT and PC-AT systems created a set of **Pseudo Standards** for hardware and software compatibility. The AT architecture became so popular that it has become the **Industry Standard Architecture (ISA)**. The majority of microcomputers are both hardware- and software-compatible with the original AT design.

Since the days of the original AT design, Intel has introduced several different microprocessors, such as the 80386, the 80486, the Pentium (80586), the Pentium Pro (80686), and the Pentium II.

In response to microprocessor clone manufacturers using the 80x86 nomenclature, Intel dropped the numbering system and adopted the Pentium name so that they could copyright it. More inclusive information about microprocessor numbering is presented in the Microprocessor section of Chapter 6, "System Boards."

These microprocessors are all upwardly compatible with the 8088 design, which means that programs written specifically for the 8088 can be executed by any of the other microprocessors. However, a program written specifically for an 80386 cannot be executed using an 8088 or 80286. The majority of microcomputers today are based on the AT design but incorporate the newer microprocessors into the system.

With so many PC-compatible software and hardware options on the market, a number of independent companies have developed PC-like computers of their own. These are referred to as **PC look-alikes**, *clones*, or more commonly, **compatibles**. The cloning process was made possible by two events. The government-backed **Electronic Research and Service Organization (ERSO)** in Taiwan successfully produced a noncopyright-infringing version of the XT BIOS firmware, and IBM did not lock up exclusive rights to the Microsoft Disk Operating Software that controls the interaction between the system's hardware and the software applications running on it.

In an attempt to derail the growing market acceptance of clone PCs, IBM introduced a new line of **Personal System/2 (PS/2)** computers, which included a new, patented 32-bit expansion bus standard called **Micro Channel Architecture (MCA)**. The PS/2 desktop is depicted in Figure 2.3.

FIGURE 2.3

Personal System/2 desktop unit.

The Micro Channel Architecture, which was invented, trademarked, and patented by IBM in 1987, provided computing potential that was more closely related to larger mainframe computers than contemporary microcomputers. The advanced design of MCA made provisions that allowed systems using its architecture to work on several tasks at one time and to include several microprocessors working together as a unit.

In developing MCA, IBM disregarded any efforts to remain compatible with the ISA standard architecture. Indeed, the MCA standard stands alone in terms of hardware compatibility. The physical expansion connector is incompatible with the edge connectors on ISA adapter cards. In addition, the interface signals called for in the MCA standard are different in definition, as well as layout. Therefore, the only source for PS/2 peripheral equipment is IBM or one of its approved vendors. Conversely, IBM has maintained software compatibility between its PS/2 line and the older PC, XT, and AT lines.

The majority of the discussion in this text deals with PC-compatible designs because they are the most wide-ranging and because they occupy such a large portion of the personal computer market. You may also notice that most of the discussions tend to lean toward desktop PCs. This information should not be difficult to transfer to other PC styles.

The PC System

A typical personal computer system is modular by design. It is called a system because it includes all of the components required to have a functional computer (see Figure 2.4):

▶ **Input devices**—keyboard and mouse

▶ **Computer**—System Unit

▶ **Output devices**—a CRT monitor and a character printer

FIGURE 2.4

A typical PC system.

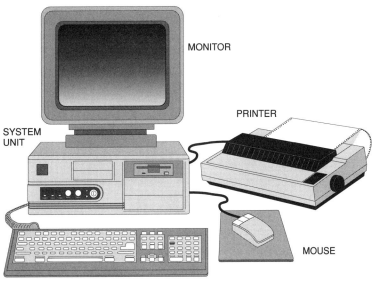

MONITOR

PRINTER

SYSTEM
UNIT

MOUSE

KEYBOARD

The **system unit** is the main portion of the microcomputer system and is the basis of any PC system arrangement.

The components surrounding the system unit vary from system to system, depending on what particular functions the system is supposed to serve.

The components inside the system unit can be divided into four distinct subunits: a switching power supply, the disk drives, the system board, and the options adapter cards, as illustrated in Figure 2.5.

FIGURE 2.5

The components in a system unit.

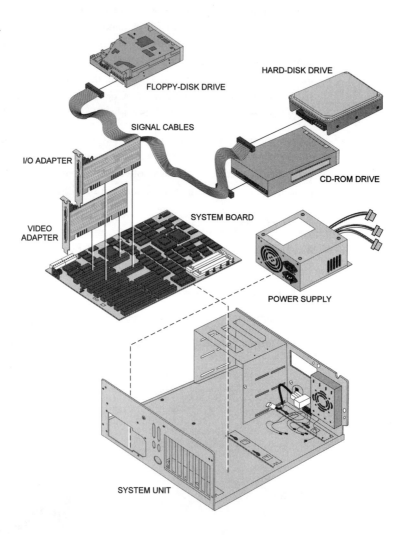

A typical system unit contains a single **power supply unit** that converts commercial power into the various levels required by the different units in the system. The number and types of disk drives in the system varies according to the application the system is designed for. However, a single **floppy-disk drive unit**, a single **hard-disk drive unit**, and a single **CD-ROM drive** are typically installed to handle the system's mass storage requirements.

A+ CORE 1.1

The **system board** is the center of the system. It contains the portions of the system that define its computing power and speed.

System boards are also referred to as **motherboards**, or **planar boards**. Any number of options adapter cards may be installed to handle a wide array of PC peripheral equipment. Typical adapter cards installed in a system include a **Video Adapter Card** and some sort of

Input/Output (I/O) Adapter Card. Peripheral devices such as printers and mice normally connect to options adapter cards through the rear of the system unit. These cards plug into **Expansion Slot Connectors** on the back of the system board. In most desktop cases the keyboard also plugs into the back panel.

Cases

PCs have been built in a number of different case designs. Each design offers characteristics that adapt the system for different environments. These key characteristics for case design include mounting methods for the printed circuit boards, ventilation characteristics, total drive capacity, footprint (the amount of horizontal space they take up), and portability.

Desktops

Some of the most familiar PC case styles are the desktop designs illustrated in Figure 2.6. These units are designed to sit horizontally on a desk top (hence the name). The original IBM PC, XT, and AT designs use this case style. The PC and XT case styles measured 21"wx17"dx5$\frac{1}{2}$"h, whereas the AT case grew to 23"wx17"dx5$\frac{1}{2}$"h.

FIGURE 2.6

Desktop case designs.

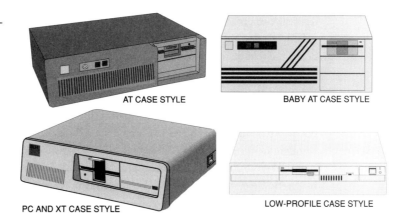

AT CASE STYLE

BABY AT CASE STYLE

PC AND XT CASE STYLE

LOW-PROFILE CASE STYLE

A narrower desktop style, referred to as **baby AT case**, was developed to take up less desk space than the XT and AT. The reduced footprint was accomplished by using a half-height power supply unit and limiting the number of disk drives. The disk-drive cage did not reach down to the floor of the system unit, allowing the system board to slide under the power supply and disk-drive cage. The widths of baby AT cases varied from manufacturer to manufacturer.

A special variety of desktop cases, referred to as **low-profile desktops**, reduce the vertical height of the unit. A short bus-extender card, called a **back plane**, mounts in an expansion slot and allows option adapter cards to be mounted in the unit horizontally. The case is thus enabled to be shorter. The horizontal mounting of the I/O cards in a low-profile case tends to create heat build-up problems. The heat rising from the system board flows around the I/O cards, adding to the heat they are generating. A standard back plane card is depicted in Figure 2.7.

FIGURE 2.7

A back plane card.

Low-profile power supplies and disk drives are also required to achieve the reduced height. Only the very earliest low-profile units tried to incorporate a 5¼" floppy drive into the design. The vast majority of these units allow a single 3½" floppy drive only. IBM's original PS/2 units incorporated these smaller components and shorter microchannel adapter cards to achieve a relatively low profile without mounting the cards horizontally.

In desktop cases, the system board is generally located in the floor of the unit, toward the left-rear corner. The power supply is located in the right-rear corner. Raised reinforcement rails in the floor of the system unit contain threaded holes and slip-in slots that the system board is anchored to. Small plastic feet are inserted into the system board and are set down in the slots. The system board is secured by the sliding of its feet into the narrow portion of the slot.

One or two brass standoffs are inserted into the threaded holes before installing the system board. After the system board has been anchored in place, a small machine screw is inserted through the system board opening and into the brass standoff. This arrangement provides electrical grounding between the system board and the case and helps to reduce **electromagnetic field interference** (**EFI**) emitted from the board.

Every electrical conductor radiates a field of electromagnetic energy when an electrical current passes through it. Computer systems are made of hundreds of conductors. The intensity of these fields increases as the current is turned on and off. Modern computers turn millions of digital switches in their ICs on and off each second, resulting in a substantial amount of energy radiating from the computer. The levels generated by the components of a typical system can easily surpass maximum-allowable radiation levels set by the Federal Communications Commission. The fields generated can potentially interfere with reception of radio, television, and other communications signals under the FCC's jurisdiction. Therefore, computer manufacturers design grounding systems and case structures to limit the amount of EFI that can escape from the case.

Basically, the FCC has established two certification levels for microcomputer systems:

- **Class A** is a level set for computers in business environments.

- **Class B** is a stricter level set for sales directed at general consumers for the home environment.

To be legal, FCC compliance stickers are required on computer units, along with certain information in their documentation.

Looking inside a desktop system unit, as depicted in Figure 2.8, the arrangement of its major components can be seen.

FIGURE 2.8

Inside a desktop unit.

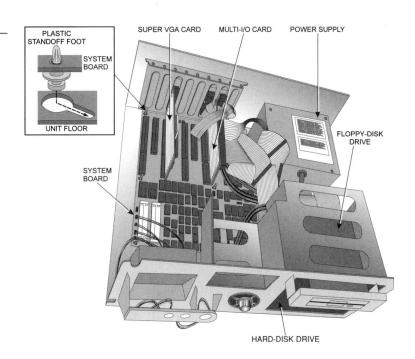

The disk drive units are located in bays at the right-front corner of the system. XT-style units use two side-by-side bays, each capable of handling a **full-height** (3.38"x5.87"x8") 5¹/₄" **drive** unit. Newer desktops are designed to hold between three and five half-height 5¹/₄" drives. Normally, a fixed drive bay capable of holding two or three **half-height drives** is built into the unit. Additional 5¹/₄" or 3¹/₂" removable drive bays may also be included. The removable bays are secured to the system unit with machine screws and provide easier access to the system board when removed. Some cases require that the drive be attached using machine screws, whereas AT-type cases have grooves in the bay that use slide-in mounting rails that are attached to the drive. The drives are held in place by the front panel of the slide-on case. The smaller 3¹/₂" drives require special mounting brackets that adapt them to the 5¹/₄" bays found in many desktop cases.

System **indicator lights** and **control buttons** are built into the front panel. Typical indicator lights include a power light, a hard drive activity light, and a turbo speed indicator light. Control buttons include a power switch, a turbo speed selection switch, and a reset button. Older system units used an on/off flip switch that extended from the power supply at the right-rear edge of the case. Newer units place the on/off switch on the machine's front panel and use an internal power cable between the switch and the power supply unit. The power supply's external connections are made in the rear of the unit. The system's installed options adapter cards are also accessed through the system's back panel. Figure 2.9 shows typical front panel controls and indicators.

The upper portion of the system unit slides (or lifts) off the base, as described in Figure 2.10. The tops of some designs slide forward after screws securing it to the back panel have been removed. In this style of case, the plastic front panel usually slides off with the metal top. In other designs, the top swings up from the rear and slides backward to clear the case. The tops of these units are secured to the base by screws in the rear of the unit and screws or clips along the sides of the case. The plastic front panel is attached directly to the case.

FIGURE 2.9

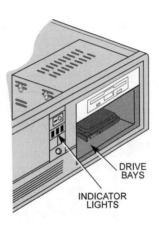

FIGURE 2.10

Removing cases from desktop units.

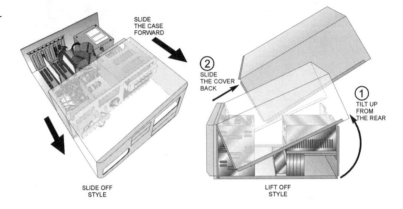

The fit between the top and the case is very important in achieving FCC certification. A tight fit and electrical conductivity between the case and top are necessary to prevent unwanted radio interference from escaping the interior of the case.

The inside face of the plastic front panel is coated with a conductive paint to limit the radio magnetic interference escaping from the case.

A fan in the power supply unit pulls in air through slots in the front of the case. The air flows over the system and options boards, into the power supply unit, and is exhausted through the back of the case. Heat build-up inside the system unit increases as more internal options are added to the system. To compensate for additional heat, it may be necessary to add additional fans to the case. Special **IC cooler fans** are often added to advanced microprocessors. They are designed to be fitted directly onto the IC and plug into one of the power supply's connectors.

Towers

Tower cases are designed to set vertically on the floor beneath a desk. Some AT users resorted to standing the computers on their sides under the desk to provide more usable workspace on the desktop. This prompted computer makers to develop cases that would naturally fit under the desk. IBM validated the tower design when they introduced the PS/2 models 60 and 80. Different tower case styles are depicted in Figure 2.11.

FIGURE 2.11

Tower case designs.

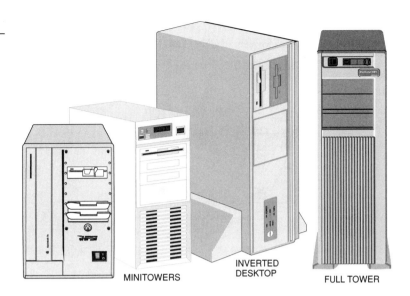

MINITOWERS   INVERTED DESKTOP   FULL TOWER

The system board is mounted to the right side panel of the case. The power supply unit is attached to the back panel. Indicator lights and control buttons are located toward the upper part of the front panel. The drive units are mounted in the disk drive bays located in the upper half of the front panel.

Although there is no real problem mounting hard and floppy drives on their side as they were in the adapted AT cases, older drives could lose tracking accuracy when mounted this way. Tower cases allow the disk drives to be mounted in a horizontal fashion. They also offer extended drive bay capabilities that make them especially useful in file server applications where many disk, CD-ROM, and tape drives are desired.

Many easy-access schemes have been developed to allow quick or convenient access to the inside of the system unit. Some towers use removable trays that the system board and I/O cards are plugged into before being slid into the unit. This allows all of the boards to be assembled outside of the system unit. Other tower cases use hinged doors on the side of the case that allow the system and I/O boards to swing away from the chassis for easy access.

The ventilation characteristics of most tower units tend to be poor. The reason is associated with the fact that the I/O cards are mounted horizontally. This allows the heat produced by lower boards to rise past the upper boards, adding to the cooling problem. To compensate for this deficiency, most tower units include a secondary case fan to help increase the air flow and dissipate the heat.

Minitowers are short towers designed to take up less vertical space. Internally, their design resembles a vertical desktop unit. They are considerably less expensive than the larger towers due to reduced materials needed to produce them. Unlike their taller relatives, minitowers do not provide abundant space for internal add-ons or disk drives. However, they do possess the shortcomings of the full towers. Minitowers exist more as a function of marketing than as an application solution.

Portables

To free the computer user from the desk, an array of **portable PCs** have been developed. The original portables were called **luggables**. Although they were smaller than desktop computers, they were not truly convenient to transport. The first portables included small, built-in CRT displays and detachable keyboards. The battery and CRT equipment made them extremely heavy to carry. Therefore, they never really had a major impact on the PC market. However, they set the stage for the development of future portable computer systems. Examples of different portable computer designs are shown in Figure 2.12.

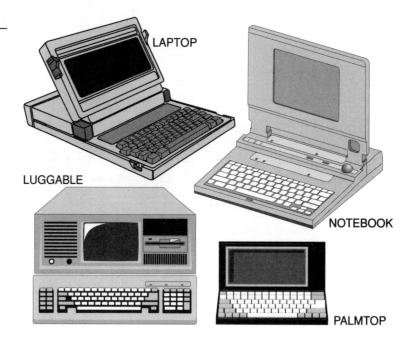

FIGURE 2.12

Portable computers.

LAPTOP

LUGGABLE

NOTEBOOK

PALMTOP

A+ CORE 6.0 With advancements in battery design and the advent of usable, large screen **liquid crystal display (LCD)** panels, the first truly portable PCs, referred to as *laptops*, were introduced. These units featured all-in-one, AT-compatible PC boards. The system board included the I/O and video controller functions. Laptops featured built-in keyboards and hinged LCD display panels that flipped up from the case. They also used an external power supply and a removable, rechargeable battery. The battery life was minimal and the size was still large enough to be inconvenient at times. However, the LCD viewing screen and external power supply/battery arrangement proved to be useful enough to fuel the portable market. The computer user could easily take work from the office to the home or a hotel room while traveling. They could also get work done at traditionally nonproductive times, such as on long automobile or airplane rides. An occasional game of computerized cards or golf was always at hand, as well.

Additional advancements in IC technology allowed the PC's circuitry to be reduced further so that the unit could achieve sizes of 8.75"d$\times$11"w$\times$2.25"h and beyond. Portables in this size range are referred to as **notebook computers**.

Notebook designers work constantly to decrease the size and power consumption of all the computer's components.

Special low-power-consumption ICs and disk drives have been developed to extend battery life. The most widely used notebook keyboard is the 84-key version. The keys are slightly smaller and shorter than those found in full-size keyboards. A number of keys or key functions may be combined or deleted from a notebook keyboard.

The continued minimization of the system comes at a cost. Most notably, the number of I/O ports, memory, and disk drive expansion capabilities are limited. In addition, there is no chance to use common, full-sized options adapter cards that are so inexpensive and easy to find.

To overcome the shortcomings of miniaturization, a wide variety of specialty items aimed at portables has emerged. As mentioned in Chapter 1, small 2¹/₂-inch hard disk drives have been developed expressly for the portable market. Other such items include small internal and external modems, special network adapters that plug into parallel printer ports, docking stations (or ports), special carrying cases and brief cases, detachable key pads, clip-on or built-in trackballs, and touch-sensitive mouse pads.

In addition, a sequence of special credit card-like adapter cards has been designed expressly for portable computers. These adapters are standardized through the **Personal Computer Memory Card International Association** (**PCMCIA**) and are commonly referred to as **PC cards**. The different types of PCMCIA cards are covered in greater detail in the section "Expansion Slots."

A **docking port** is a specialized case in which the entire notebook unit is inserted. In doing so, it allows the notebook to be connected to a collection of desktop I/O devices, such as full-sized keyboards and CRT monitors, as well as modems and other non-notebook devices.

Even smaller **sub-notebook PCs** have been created by moving the disk drives outside the case and reducing the size of the display screen. Very small sub-notebooks, referred to as **palmtop PCs**, were produced for a short time in the pre-Windows days. These units limited everything as far as possible to reach sizes of 7"wx4"dx1"h. Sub-notebooks have decreased in popularity as notebooks have decreased in weight and cost.

The palmtop market has diminished due to the difficulty of running Windows on such small displays. Human ergonomics also came into play when dealing with smaller notebooks. The smaller screens and keyboards become difficult to see and use.

> The drawback of portable computers from a service point of view is that conventions and compatibility disappear. The internal board (or boards) are designed to fit around the nuances of the portable case rather than to match a standard design with standard spacing and connections. Therefore, interchangeability of parts with other machines or makers goes by the wayside.

The only source of most portable parts is the original manufacturer. Even the battery case is proprietary. If the battery dies, you must hope that the original maker has a supply of that particular model. This is true of many of the parts in a portable computer.

Access to the notebook's internal components is usually challenging. Each case design has different methods for assembly and disassembly of the unit. Even the simplest upgrade can be difficult with a notebook computer. Although adding RAM and options to desktop and tower units is a relatively easy and straightforward process, the same tasks in notebook computers can be difficult. In some notebooks, it is necessary to disassemble the two halves of the case and remove the keyboard in order to add RAM modules to the system. In other units, the hinged display unit must be removed to disassemble the unit. Once inside the notebook, you may find several of the components hidden behind other units.

Table 2.1 includes some comparisons between the various computer cases.

Table 2.1 *Case Comparisons*

Types	DD Bays (Inches)	Expansion Slots	PS (Watts)	Dimensions (Inches)
PC/PCXT	5.24 (4)	6-8	56-135	19x17x5.5
AT	5.25e (2) 5.25i (3)	6-8	150-220	21x17x6.5
Baby AT	5.25e (2) (3)	6-8	150-200	19x17x6.5**5.25i
Low Profile	5.25 (1-2*) 3.5 (1-2)	2-4	150-200	16x15x5
Minitowers	5.25e (2-3*) 5.25i (2-3)	6-8	150-250	7.5x18x17-24**
Towers	5.25e (4*) 5.25i (1-4)	8-12	150-400	7.5x18x24-30**

* *The number of internally (i) and externally (e) accessible drive bays varies from manufacturer to manufacturer. Also, some 3.5"-specific bays may be included in case styles.*

** *The dimensions of these case styles vary from manufacturer to manufacturer.*

Power Supplies

A+ CORE 1.1 The system's power supply unit provides electrical power for every component inside the system unit, as well as supplying alternating current (AC) to the video display monitor.

It converts commercial electrical power received from a 120-Vac, 60-Hz (or 220-Vac, 50-Hz outside the U.S.) outlet into other levels required by the components of the system. In desktop and tower PCs, the power supply is the shiny metal box located at the rear of the system unit.

In all, the desktop or tower power supply produces four levels of efficiently regulated direct current (DC) voltage: +5V, –5V, +12V and –12V. It also provides the system's ground. The +5V level is used by the IC devices on the system board and adapter cards. In particular, the P8/P9 connectors provide the system board and the individual expansion slots with up to 1 ampere of current each. All four voltage levels are available for use at the expansion slot connectors.

In the event the power supply detects the presence of inadequate voltage levels and/or damaging **spikes** (**power line transients**), it has the capability to shut down and not supply power to the system. This feature protects the system's circuitry, but the contents of the RAM memory will be lost.

Several bundles of cable emerge from the power supply to provide power to the components of the system unit and to its peripherals. It delivers power to the system board and its expansion slots through two bundles typically marked P8 and P9. The physical construction of these connectors is significantly different than that of the other bundles. They are designed to be plugged into the system board's P1 and P2 power plugs, respectively, as depicted in Figure 2.13.

FIGURE 2.13

The P1/P2—P8/P9 connections.

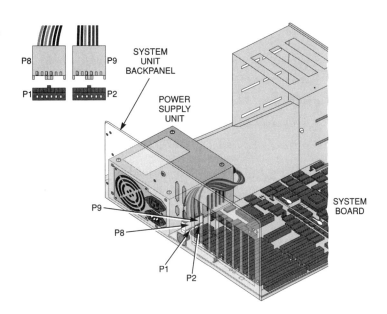

The P8/P9 connectors are normally keyed and numbered. However, their construction and appearance is identical. The voltage levels associated with each plug are different, and *severe damage could result* to the computer by reversing them. The power connector labeled P8 should be plugged into the circuit-board connector nearest the rear of the unit, and connector P9 should be plugged into the connector next to it. A good rule of thumb when attaching these two connectors to the system board is that the black wires in each bundle should be next to each other.

The other power supply bundles are used to supply power to optional systems, such as the disk and CD-ROM drives. These bundles provide a +5 and +12 Vdc supply. The +5V supply provides power for electronic components on the optional devices, and the +12V is used for disk drive motors and other devices that require a higher voltage.

Power is delivered to the monitor through a special plug in the power supply's back plate. The power supply (as well as the rest of the system) is switched on via the power switch. In older units, the power switch is an integral part of the power supply unit and extends from its right side. In most newer units, the on/off switch is located on the front panel of the system unit and is connected to the power supply by a cable. Simply push the button to turn the system on and again to turn it off. Figure 2.14 illustrates the typical power-supply connections found in a desktop or tower unit.

Within the United States, a grounded, three-prong power cord provides the AC input voltage to the power supply. The smaller vertical blade in the connector is considered the *hot* or *phase* side of the connector. A small slide switch on the back of the unit permits the power supply to be switched over to operate on 220-Vac input voltages found outside the United States. When the switch is set to the 220 position, the voltage supplied to the power supply's monitor outlet will also be 220. In this position, it is usually necessary to exchange the power cord for one that has a plug suited to the country the computer is being used in.

Power supply units come in a variety of shapes and power ratings. The shapes are determined by the type of case they are designed to be used in. Figure 2.15 illustrates the various power supply shapes. Typical power ratings include 150, 200, and 250 watt versions.

FIGURE 2.14

Power supply connections.

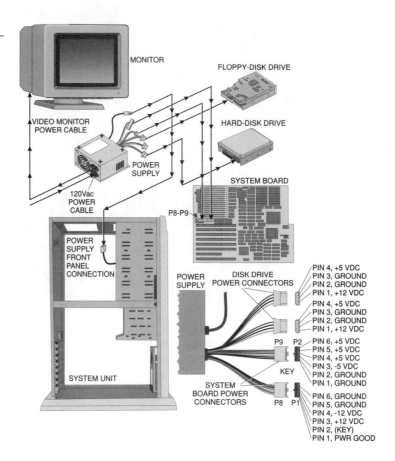

FIGURE 2.15

Desktop/tower power supplies.

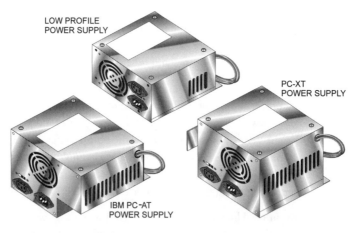

Notebooks and other portables use a detachable, rechargeable battery and an external power supply, as illustrated in Figure 2.16 (battery sizes vary from manufacturer to manufacturer). They also employ power-saving circuits and ICs designed to lengthen the battery's charged time. The battery unit contains a recharging regulator circuit that allows the battery to recharge while it is being used with the external power supply. Like other hardware aspects of notebook computers, there are no standards for the power supply units. They use different connector types and possess different voltage and current delivery capabilities. Therefore, a power supply from one notebook will not necessarily work with another.

FIGURE 2.16

Laptop/notebook power supplies.

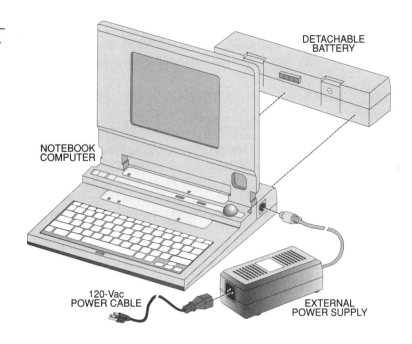

System Boards

The **system board** is the center of the PC-compatible microcomputer system. It contains the circuitry that determines the computing power and speed of the entire system. In particular, it contains the microprocessor and control devices that form the brains of the system. The major components of interest on a PC system board are the microprocessor, the system's primary **read only** (**ROM**), **random access** (**RAM**), and **cache memory** sections, expansion slot connectors, and microprocessor support ICs that coordinate the operation of the system. A typical system board layout is depicted in Figure 2.17.

FIGURE 2.17

The parts of a typical system board.

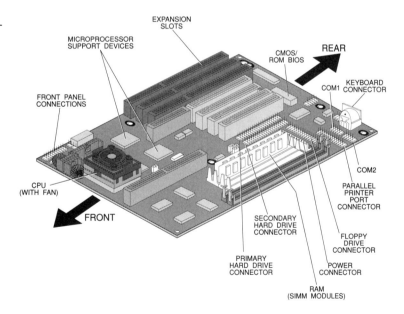

Major Components

For orientation purposes, the end of the board where the keyboard connector, expansion slots, and power connectors are located is generally referred to as the *rear* of the board.

> The system board communicates with various optional **input/output (I/O)** and **memory systems** through adapter boards that plug into its **expansion slots**. These connectors are normally located along the left-rear portion of the system board so that the external devices they serve can access them through openings at the rear of the case.

Several types of expansion slots are in use today. A particular system board may contain only one type of slot, or it may have a few of each type of expansion slot. Be aware that adapter cards are compatible with particular types of slots, so it is important to know which slot is being used. The major expansion slot types are

- 8-bit PC-bus
- 16-bit AT or ISA bus
- 32-bit extended ISA (EISA) and Microchannel Architecture (MCA) buses
- Video Electronics Standards Association (VESA) and Peripheral Component Interconnect (PCI) local buses

These expansion slots are discussed later in this chapter (see the "Expansion Slots" section for more information) and then again in more detail in Chapter 6, "System Boards."

The system board receives power from the power supply unit through a pair of six-pin power supply connectors that are typically labeled P1 and P2. These connectors are always located directly beside each other and are keyed so that the power cable cannot be plugged in backwards. However, the P1 and P2 connectors are identical and can be reversed. This condition will cause *severe* damage to system components if power is applied to the system. The P1/P2 connectors are often located along the right-rear corner of the system board.

Similarly, the keyboard connector is normally located along the back edge of the board. In most PC-compatible systems, the keyboard connector is a round, five-pin DIN connector.

Primary Memory

A+ CORE 1.1

All computers need a place to temporarily store information while other pieces of information are being processed. As discussed in Chapter 1, information storage is normally conducted at two levels in digital computers; **primary memory** (made up of semiconductor RAM and ROM chips) and **mass storage** (usually involving floppy and hard disk drives).

Most of the system's primary memory is located on the system board. Primary memory typically exists in two or three forms on the system board:

- **Read only memory** (ROM)—which contains the computer's permanent startup programs
- **Random access memory** (RAM)—which is quick enough to operate directly with the microprocessor and can be read from and written to as often as desired
- **Cache memory**—which a fast RAM system uses to hold information that the microprocessor is likely to use

ROM devices store information permanently and are used to hold programs and data that do not change. RAM devices only retain the information stored in them as long as electrical power is applied to the IC. Any interruption of power will cause the contents of the memory to vanish. This is referred to as **volatile** memory. ROM, on the other hand, is **non-volatile**.

Every system board contains one or two ROM ICs that hold the system's **basic input/output system** (**BIOS**) program. The BIOS program contains the basic instructions for communications between the microprocessor and the various input and output devices in the system. Until recently, this information was stored permanently inside the ROM chips and could only be changed by replacing the chips. As mentioned in Chapter 1, advancements in EEPRROM technology have produced **flash ROM** devices that allow new BIOS information to be written (**downloaded**) into the ROM to update it. This can be done from an update disk or downloaded from another computer. Unlike RAM ICs, the contents of the flash ROM remain after the power has been removed from the chip. In either case, the upgraded BIOS must be compatible with the system board it is being used in and should be the latest version available.

The information in the BIOS represents all the intelligence the computer has until it can load more information from another source, such as a hard or floppy disk. Taken together, the BIOS software (programming) and hardware (the ROM chip) are referred to as **firmware**. These ICs can be located anywhere on the system board and are usually easy to recognize, due to their size and immediate proximity to each other.

A+ CORE 4.2 In older PC designs—XT and AT—the system's RAM memory was comprised of banks of discrete RAM ICs in **Dual In-line Pin** (**DIP**) sockets. Most of these system boards arranged nine pieces of 1x256 Kbit DRAM chips in the first two banks (0 and 1) and nine pieces of 1x64 Kbit chips in banks two and three. The two banks of 256KB chips provided a total of 512KB of storage (the ninth chip of each bank supplied a parity bit for error checking). The two banks of 64KB chips extended the RAM memory capacity out to the full 640KB. As with the 256KB chips, the ninth bit was for parity.

Some system boards used two 4x256 Kbit chips with a 1x256 Kbit chip to create each of the first two banks. In any event, the system would typically run with one bank installed, two banks installed, or all of the banks installed. Bank 0 had to be filled first, followed by bank 1, and then all four.

Intermediate clone designs placed groups of RAM ICs on small 30-pin daughter boards that plugged into the system board vertically. This mounting method required less horizontal board space. These RAM modules had pins along one side of the board and were referred to as **Single In-line Pin** (**SIP**) modules.

A+ CORE 4.3 Further refinements of the RAM module produced snap in **Single In-line Memory Modules** (**SIMMs**) and **Dual In-line Memory Modules** (**DIMMs**). Like the SIP, the SIMM and DIMM units mount vertically on the system board. However, instead of using a pin and socket arrangement, both use special snap-in sockets that support the module firmly. SIMMs and DIMMs are also keyed, so they cannot be plugged in backwards. SIMMs are available in 30- and 72-pin versions, whereas DIMMs are larger 168-pin boards.

SIMM and DIMM sockets are quite distinctive in that they are normally arranged side by side. However, they can be located anywhere on the system board. SIMMs typically come in 8- or 32-bit data storage configurations. The 8-bit modules must be arranged in **banks** to match the data bus size of the system's microprocessor. In order to work effectively with a 32-bit microprocessor, a bank of four 8-bit SIMMs would need to be used. Conversely, a single 32-bit SIMM could do the same job.

DIMMs, on the other hand, typically come in 32- and 64-bit widths to service more powerful microprocessors. Like the SIMMs, they must be arranged properly to fit the size of the system data bus. In both cases, the modules can be accessed in smaller 8- and 16-bit segments. SIMMs and DIMMs also come in 9-, 36-, and 72-bit versions that include parity checking bits for each byte of storage.

PCs are usually sold with less than their full RAM capacity. This enables users to purchase a less expensive computer to fit their individual needs and yet retain the option to install more RAM if future applications call for it. SIMM and DIMM sizes are typically specified in an a-by-b format. For example, a 2x32 SIMM specification indicates that it is a dual, non-parity, 32-bit (4-byte) device. In this scheme, the capacity is derived by multiplying the two numbers and then dividing by eight (or nine for parity chips). DIP, SIP, SIMM and DIMM modules are depicted in Figure 2.18.

FIGURE 2.18

DIP, SIP, SIMM, and DIMM memory modules.

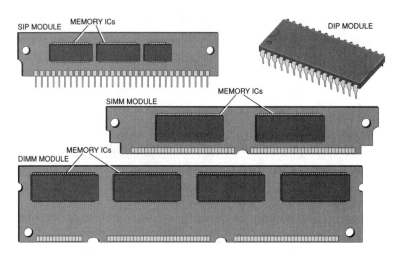

Microprocessors

A+ CORE 1.1

The microprocessor is the major component of any system board. It executes software instructions and carries out arithmetic operations for the system.

These ICs can take on different package styles depending on their vintage and manufacturer. The 8088 processor was housed in a 40-pin DIP package, similar to the one in the previous figure. It was used on the original IBM PC and PC-XT units. It featured a 20-bit address bus, an 8-bit data bus, and a 16-bit internal word size. The 20-bit address bus allowed it to access 1MB of address space. The mismatch between its internal word size and external data bus size required multiplexed, two-transfer operations with external system devices. Another, more expensive version, called the 8086, featured a full 16-bit external data bus. Although some XTs used 8086-based system boards, the vast majority of PCs, XTs, and clones used the 8088.

The 80286 processors used a variety of 68-pin IC types. These processors were used in the IBM PC-AT and its compatibles. It featured a 24-bit address bus, a 16-bit data bus, and a

16-bit internal word size. The 24-bit address bus allowed it to directly access up to 16MB of address space, even though DOS could only handle the 1MB that it had been designed to handle with the 8088 systems. The full 16-bit internal and external word size gave it a 4x speed increase over 8088 systems running at the same clock speed. 80286s were produced in various speed ratings.

The 80386DX followed with a 132-pin **Pin Grid Array (PGA)** IC package, while a more economical 80386SX was produced in a 100-pin surface mount IC package. These microprocessors were mainly used in AT clone systems. The DX version provided a 32-bit address bus, a 32-bit data bus, and a 32-bit internal word size. The 32-bit address bus provided up to 4GB of memory addressing. The SX version featured a reduced 24-bit address bus and 16-bit data bus. Both versions were produced in a variety of operating speeds and included advanced addressing modes.

The 80486 and Pentium microprocessors returned to 168-pin and 273-pin PGA packages. The 80486 featured a 32-bit address bus, a 32-bit external data bus, and a 64-bit internal word size. The Pentium also features a 32-bit address bus. However, both the internal and external word size is 64 bits. Both units include on-board math coprocessors for intense numerical operations and special built-in memory areas, called **cache memory**, for high-speed data access to selected data. Like the 80386, these microprocessors are typically used in advanced AT clone computers. These microprocessor packages are depicted in Figure 2.19.

FIGURE 2.19

Microprocessors.

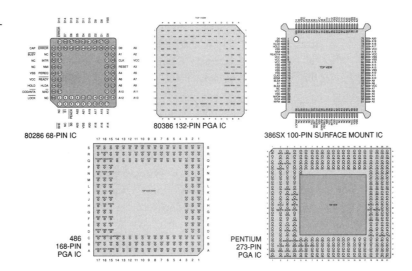

A+ CORE 4.1   PC manufacturers mount microprocessors in **sockets** so that they can be replaced easily. This allows a failed microprocessor to simply be exchanged with a working unit. More often though, the microprocessor is replaced with an improved version to upgrade the speed or performance of the system.

The notches and dots on the various ICs are important keys when replacing a microprocessor. They specify the location of the IC's number 1 pin. This pin must be lined up with the **pin-1 notch** of the socket for proper insertion. In older systems, the microprocessors had to be forcibly removed from the socket using an IC extractor tool. As the typical microprocessor's pin count increased, special **zero insertion force (ZIF)** sockets were implemented that allowed the microprocessor to be set in the socket without force and then clamped in place. An arm-activated clamping mechanism in the socket shifts to the side, locking the pins in place. All of the microprocessors discussed here are covered in greater detail in Chapter 6, along with their significant variations.

For mathematically intensive operations, some programs may shift portions of the work to special *high-speed math coprocessors*, if they are present in the system. These devices are specialized microprocessors that work in parallel with the main microprocessor and extend its instruction set to speed up math and logic operations. They basically add large register sets to the microprocessor, along with additional arithmetic processing instructions. The 8088, 80286, 80386SX/DX, and 80486SX microprocessors used external coprocessors. The 80486DX, and Pentium processors have built-in coprocessors.

Chip Sets

Although the microprocessor is the main IC of the system board, it is certainly not the only IC on the board.

> Microprocessor manufacturers always produce microprocessor-support chip sets that provide auxiliary services for the microprocessor.

The original PC system board used a standard 6-IC 8088 chip set to support the microprocessor. Even so, these early support sets still required a good number of discrete logic ICs to complete the system.

The original AT increased the IC count on the system board by doubling up the DMA and interrupt channel counts. However, when the PC-AT architecture became the acceptable industry standard, several IC manufacturers began developing **Very Large Scale Integration** (**VLSI**) chip sets to perform the standard functions of the AT system board. In the fall of 1985, the company Chips & Technology released a five-chip chip set that replaced the functions of 63 smaller ICs on the PC-AT system board.

For the IC manufacturer, this meant designing chip sets that would use the same basic memory map that was employed in the IBM PC-AT (that is, the chip set's programmable registers, RAM, ROM, and other addresses had to be identical to those of the AT). Therefore, instructions and data in the program would be interpreted, processed, and distributed the same way in both systems. In doing so, the supporting chip set decreased from eight major ICs and dozens of **Small Scale Integration** (**SSI**) devices to two or three VLSI chips and a handful of SSI devices.

In some highly integrated system boards, the only ICs that remain are the microprocessor, one or two ROM BIOS chips, a single chip set IC, and the system's memory modules.

Connectors and Jumpers

A+ CORE 1.3   System boards possess a number of jumpers and connectors of which you must be aware. PC-compatible system boards include micro **switches** and **jumper blocks** (called **BERG connectors**) to select operating options such as speed, video display type (color/mono) being used, memory refreshing Wait-States (special timing periods used by the computer to make certain everything happens on schedule), installed RAM size, and so forth. You might be required to alter these settings if you change a component or install a new module in the system.

Figure 2.20 illustrates the operation of typical configuration jumpers. A metal clip in the cap of the jumper creates an electrical short between the pins that it is installed across. When the cap is removed, the electrical connection is also removed, and an electrically open condition is created.

FIGURE 2.20

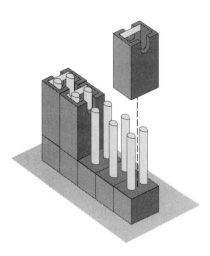

System boards and several types of I/O cards use **micro switches** for configuration purposes. These micro switches are normally integrated into a Dual In-line Pin package, as illustrated in the figure. The switches may use a rocker or slide switch mechanism to create the short or open condition. The switches are typically numbered sequentially and marked for on/off positioning. Because the switches are so small, they may simply be marked with an On or Off, or with a 1 or 0.

It is usually necessary to consult the system board or the adapter's installation guide to locate and properly set configuration jumpers and switches. The installation guide typically provides the locations of all the board's configuration jumpers and switches. It also defines the possible configuration settings, along with corresponding switch or jumper positions.

The system board is connected to the front panel's indicators and controls by BERG connectors. Over time, these connection points have become fairly standard between cases. The normal connections are the **power LED**, **turbo LED**, **turbo switch**, **keylock switch**, **reset switch**, and **system speaker**. A typical front panel connector layout is described in Figure 2.21. It becomes necessary to access these points when the system board is replaced or upgraded. Additional system board connectors that would have to be dealt with include the keyboard and power supply connectors.

FIGURE 2.21

System board connection points.

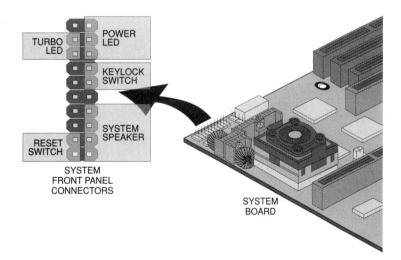

Configuration Settings

Each time the system is turned on or reset, the BIOS program checks the system's **configuration settings** to determine what types of optional devices might be included in the system.

Depending on the model of the computer, the configuration information may be read from hardware jumper or switch settings, from battery-powered RAM, or, in some cases, a combination of jumper and software settings. The PC, PC-XT, and their clones used hardware switches for configuration purposes. When IBM introduced the PC-AT, it featured a battery-powered RAM area that held some of the system's advanced configuration information. This storage area was referred to as CMOS RAM. With that unit, configuration was performed from a floppy disk diagnostic program. Clone BIOS manufacturers quickly added the advanced configuration function to their BIOS chips. Clone system boards also added a rechargeable, Ni-Cad battery to the board to maintain the information when the system was turned off. In newer systems, there is no rechargeable Ni-Cad battery for the CMOS storage. Instead, the CMOS storage area has been integrated with a 10-year, non-replaceable lithium cell in a single IC package.

Because these settings are the system's only way of getting information about what options are installed, they must be set to accurately reflect the actual options being used with the system. If not, an error will occur. You should always suspect configuration problems if a machine fails to operate immediately after a new component has been installed. These CMOS configuration values can be accessed for change by pressing the Control and Delete keys (or some other key combination) simultaneously during the boot-up procedure.

Newer microcomputers possess the capability to automatically reconfigure themselves for new options that are installed. This feature is referred to as **Plug and Play (PnP)** capability.

In 1994, Microsoft and Intel teamed up to produce a set of system specifications that would allow options added to the system to automatically be configured for operation. Under this scenario, the user would not be involved in setting hardware jumpers or CMOS entries. To accomplish this, the system's BIOS, expansion slots, and adapter cards were designed in a manner so that they can be reconfigured automatically by the system software.

During the start up process, the PnP BIOS looks through the system for installed devices. Devices designed for Plug and Play compatibility can tell the BIOS what types of devices they are and how to communicate with them. This information is stored in memory so that the system can work with the device. Plug-and-play information will be scattered throughout the remainder of the text as it applies to the topic being covered.

Expansion Slots

In the back-left corner of most system boards are up to eight expansion slots. These slots allow the system's peripheral devices to be connected to the system board. Optional I/O devices or their PC-compatible interface boards may be plugged into these slots to connect the device to the system unit's address, data, and control buses.

8-Bit Slots

The expansion slots in the original PC, PC-XT, and their compatibles contained an 8-bit, bidirectional data bus and 20 address lines. They also provide six interrupt channels, control signals for memory and I/O read or write operations, clock and timing signals, and three channels of DMA control lines. In addition, the bus offers memory refresh timing signals and an I/O channel check line for peripheral problems, as well as power and ground lines for the adapters that plug into the bus. I/O devices attached to the bus had to be addressed using the system's I/O-mapped address space.

This expansion slot configuration became a **de facto** connection standard in the industry for 8-bit systems. It was dubbed the **PC-Bus** standard. A de facto standard is one that becomes established through popular use rather than through an official certifying organization. Figure 2.22 shows how the PC-Bus's 62 lines are arranged at the expansion slot's connector.

FIGURE 2.22

An eight-bit PC-Bus expansion slot.

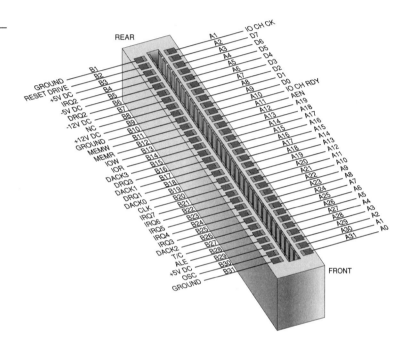

16-Bit Slots

A+ CORE 4.3

The overwhelming popularity of the IBM PC-AT established it as the 16-bit standard to which all other PC-compatible equipment is compared. Its 16-bit expansion bus specification became the industry standard for all 16-bit systems and devices. The 16-bit data bus allowed twice as much data to pass back and forth through the connector in a given amount of time. This made transfers with 16-bit microprocessors smooth. No high/low-byte bus multiplexing was required.

The ISA bus included twice as many interrupt and DMA channels as the PC Bus specification. This made it possible to connect more peripheral devices to these systems. In order to maintain compatibility with older adapter cards, the transfer speed for the ISA bus was limited to the same speed as that of the older PC Bus. Figure 2.23 describes an ISA-compatible expansion slot connector. These expansion slots actually exist in two parts: the slightly altered, 62-pin I/O connector (similar to the standard PC Bus connector) and a 36-pin auxiliary connector.

32-Bit Slots

With the development of fast, 32-bit microprocessors, it was normal for designers to search for a new bus system to take advantage of the 32-bit bus and the higher speed of operation.

IBM introduced a new line, the Personal System/2 (PS/2), that featured a new expansion bus standard that it called **Micro Channel Architecture** (**MCA**). Although similar to the ISA edge connector in appearance, the MCA 16-bit connector is physically much smaller than that of the 16-bit ISA bus connector (the MCA's edge connector is 2.8 inches long, compared to the 5.29-inch length of the ISA bus). The contacts along the edge connector are separated by only 0.05 inches. This is only half the distance allotted between contacts in the ISA connector. The smaller size is also seen in the dimensions of MCA-compatible adapter cards. Both types of edge connectors are depicted in Figure 2.24.

FIGURE 2.23

A 16-bit ISA expansion slot.

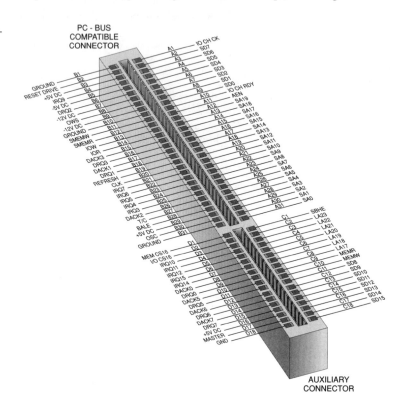

FIGURE 2.24

32-bit MCA and 16-bit ISA edge connectors.

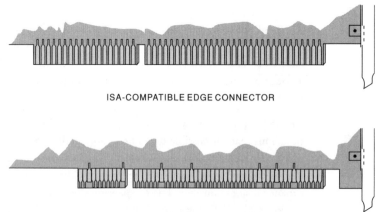

ISA-COMPATIBLE EDGE CONNECTOR

MICRO CHANNEL EDGE CONNECTOR

A+ CORE 4.3 In an attempt to develop an acceptable, 32-bit I/O bus standard that would remain compatible with the large quantities of hardware and software already designed for ISA-compatible computers, a group of computer hardware and software manufacturers (known as **the gang of nine**) banded together and introduced specifications for an extension to the ISA bus. Compaq, AST Research, Epson, Hewlett-Packard, Olivetti, NEC, Tandy, Wyse, and Zenith Data Systems pooled their efforts to extend the ISA world and christened the **EISA bus**.

The key to the EISA bus specification is found in the design of its expansion slot connector. The connector is designed so that it can accept traditional 8- and 16-bit ISA cards, as well as the newer 32-bit EISA cards. This flexibility is achieved by incorporating a two-level approach to the connector, as depicted in Figure 2.25.

FIGURE 2.25

A 32-bit EISA expansion slot.

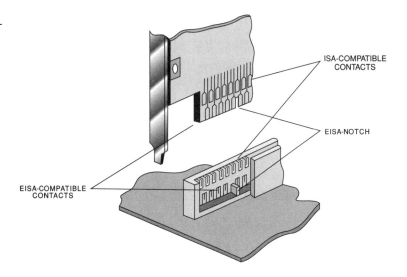

Signals associated with the standard ISA connection are terminated in the upper row of contacts, whereas new EISA signals are interleaved between the ISA signals on the lower row of contacts. In all, the EISA standard adds 55 new signal lines to the bus, along with 35 additional power-supply and ground contacts.

Small raised keys in the bottom of the connector prevent ISA-style cards from being inserted into the full depth of the connector. Therefore, the contacts on the edge connector of the ISA card can only contact the standard ISA signals along the top of the expansion slot connector. However, the edge connectors of EISA cards, which are much deeper than ISA cards (0.52 inches to 0.31 inches), have notches that match the keys in the expansion slot connector and allow the EISA card to be fully inserted. In this way, both rows of contacts make connection when an EISA expansion card is inserted into an EISA expansion slot. It should be apparent that this connection scheme will not work in reverse. An EISA card will not work in a standard ISA slot connector. Although this action should not cause damage, it would render the host computer inoperative until the card is removed.

Both the EISA and MCA architectures were designed with Plug-and-Play capabilities in mind. The EISA bus supports Plug and Play only in a hardware fashion, while MCA supports PnP in both hardware and software manners. All of the adapters used in the MCA architecture possess the capability to automatically identify themselves to the system and be reconfigured by the system for optimum performance. The system is able to obtain information from the adapter cards as to what type they are, where they are located, and what resources they need access to. With this information, the system can check the other adapters and on-board intelligent devices and then reconfigure all of the devices to work together.

Local Bus Slots

In recent years, different manufacturers have implemented proprietary expansion bus designs to improve their system boards. These designs increase the speed and bandwidth between the microprocessor and a few selected peripherals by creating a special bus between them, called a *local bus*.

> The local bus connects special peripherals to the system board (and the microprocessor) through a proprietary expansion slot connector and allows the peripheral to operate at speeds close to the speed of the microprocessor.

When these designs began to appear, the peripherals that could be used in the proprietary slots were only available from the original system board manufacturer. The industry soon realized the benefits of such designs and the need for some "standards." Currently, two local bus designs have gained enough acceptance to have third-party manufacturers design products for them: the VESA and PCI local bus specifications. Most Pentium system boards include a combination of ISA and PCI expansion slots.

A+ CORE 4.3 The VESA local bus was developed by the **Video Electronics Standards Association (VESA)**. This local bus specification, also referred to as the VL-bus, was originally developed to provide a local bus connection to a video adapter. However, its operation has since been defined for use by other adapter types, such as drive controllers, network interfaces, and other hardware. The VESA connector is depicted in Figure 2.26.

FIGURE 2.26

The VESA local bus slot.

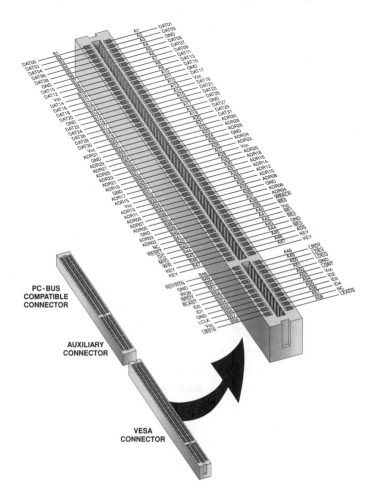

The VL-bus defines a local bus that can operate at up to 66MHz and is designed for use with 386 or 486 microprocessors. However, newer revisions multiplex the address and data buses to provide a 64-bit data bus for use with the Pentium and future microprocessors. This newer revision allows for a 32-bit adapter to operate in a 64-bit slot or visa-versa.

A+ CORE 14.3 The **Peripheral Component Interconnect (PCI)** local bus was developed jointly by IBM, Intel, DEC, NCR, and Compaq. This bus design incorporates three elements: a low-cost, high-performance local bus, an automatic configuration of installed expansion cards, and the capability to expand with the introduction of new microprocessors and peripherals. The data transfer performance of the PCI local bus is 132Mb using a 32-bit bus and 264Mb using a 64-bit bus. This is accomplished even though the bus has a maximum clock frequency of 33MHz

The PCI peripheral device has 256 bytes of on-board memory to hold information about what type of device it is. The peripheral device can be classified as a controller for a mass-storage device, a network interface, a display, or other hardware. The configuration space also contains control, status, and latency timer values. The latency timer register on the device determines the length of time that the device can control the bus for bus mastering operations. Figure 2.27 illustrates the PCI local bus connector.

FIGURE 2.27

The PCI local bus slot.

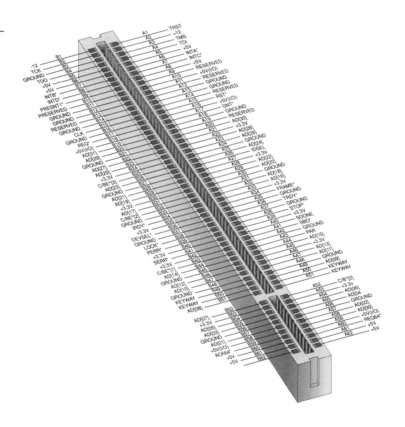

Both local bus specifications include slot addressing capabilities and reserve memory space to allow for reconfiguration of each device installed in the system. Unfortunately, system boards that use these expansion slots also normally have a few ISA-compatible slots. This feature seriously disrupts the Plug-and-Play concept, because no identification of reconfiguration capabilities were designed into the ISA bus specification.

Table 2.2 compares the capabilities of the various bus types commonly found in personal computers. It is quite apparent that the data transfer rates possible with each new version increases dramatically. The reason this is significant is that the expansion bus is a speed-limiting factor for many of the system's operations. Every access of a disk drive, I/O port, video display, and optional system must pass through this bottleneck. When the bus is accessed, the entire computer must slow down to its operating speed.

Table 2.2 *Expansion Bus Specifications*

Bus Type	Transfer Rate	Data Bits	Address Bits	DMA Channels	INT Channels
PC Bus	1MB/s	8	20	4	6
ISA	8MB/s	16	24	8	11
EISA	32MB/s	32	32	8	11
MCA	20-40MB/s	32	32	xx	-11
VESA	150/275MB/s	32/64	32	xx	1
PCI 2	132/264MB/s	32/64	32	xx	3
PCI 2.1	264/528MB/s	32/64	32	xx	3

PCMCIA Buses

> The **PCMCIA** bus was developed to accommodate the space continuous notebook and subnotebook computer market.

Three types of PCMCIA adapters exist. The PCMCIA Type I cards, introduced in 1990, are 3.3mm thick and work as memory expansion units. In 1991, the PCMCIA Type II cards were introduced; they are 5mm thick and support virtually any traditional expansion function, except removable hard drive units. Type II slots are backwardly compatible so that Type I cards will work in them. Currently, Type III PCMCIA cards are being produced; these cards are 10.5mm thick and are intended primarily for use with removable hard drives. Both Type I and Type II cards can be used in a Type III slot.

All three card types adhere to a form factor of 2.12"wx3.37"l and use a 68-pin, slide-in socket arrangement. They can be used with 8- or 16-bit data bus machines and operate on +5V or +3.3V supplies. The design of the cards allows them to be installed in the computer while it is turned on and running. Figure 2.28 shows the three types of PCMCIA cards.

FIGURE 2.28

PCMCIA cards.

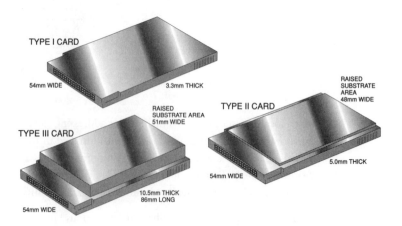

Adapter Cards

The openness of the IBM PC, XT, and AT architectures, coupled with their overwhelming popularity, led companies to develop a wide assortment of expansion devices for them.

The adapter cards in the original IBM PC were 13.2"lx4.2"h. The PC normally came with a disk drive adapter card and a video card. These units were referred to as **Full-Size Adapter Cards** and were so long that plastic guide rails at the front of the system unit were present to keep them from flexing due to system heating or transportation. A smaller (6"lx4.2"h) printer adapter card was also made available for the PC. This size card is referred to as a **Half-Size Card**. When the AT appeared, the I/O cards became more powerful and taller (13.2"lx4.8"h).

The AT cards became the standard against which later I/O cards have been measured. Like system boards, adapter cards have developed into smaller, more powerful units. Most current adapter cards are **2/3-Size Cards**, half-size, or smaller cards. In addition, the height of the cards has been significantly reduced. Many adapters are only half the height, or less, of the original AT cards. Therefore, they are referred to as **Half-Height Cards**.

The only real requirements for adapter cards now are that they fit securely in the expansion slot, cover the slot opening in the rear of the system unit, and provide standard connectors for the types of devices they serve. Various adapter card designs are depicted in Figure 2.29.

FIGURE 2.29

Adapter card designs.

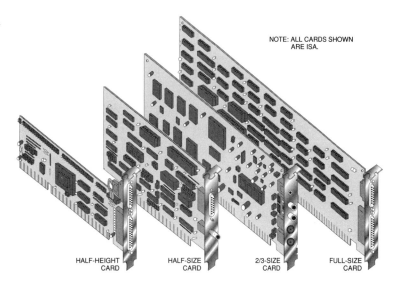

NOTE: ALL CARDS SHOWN ARE ISA.

HALF-HEIGHT CARD   HALF-SIZE CARD   2/3-SIZE CARD   FULL-SIZE CARD

Most of the adapter cards that have been developed use hardware jumpers or configuration switches to allow for configuration for the system they are to be used in. The user sets up the card for operation and solves any interrupt or memory addressing conflicts that occur. These cards are referred to as *legacy* cards.

In newer Plug-and-Play systems, adapter cards should have the capability to identify themselves to the system during the start-up process, along with supplying the system information about what type of device they are, how they are configured, and what resources they need access to. In addition, these cards must be able to be reconfigured by the system software if a conflict is detected between it and another system device.

Prior to the Pentium-based system boards, two types of options adapter cards were traditionally supplied as standard equipment in most desktop and tower PC systems: a video adapter card and a **multi-I/O adapter (MI/O) card**. However, in Pentium units, the MI/O functions have been built into the system board. Similarly, both the video and I/O functions are an integral part of the system board in portable systems.

Video Adapter Cards

> The video adapter card provides the interface between the system board and the display monitor.

The original IBM PCs and XTs offered two types of display adapters, a Monochrome (single color) Display Adapter (MDA) and a Color Graphic Adapter (CGA). Both of these units also included the system's first parallel printer port connector.

These initial units have been followed by a number of improved and enhanced video adapters and monitors. The most common type of video adapter card currently in use is the Video Graphic Adapter (VGA) card, like the one depicted in Figure 2.30. The system uses it to control video output operations.

FIGURE 2.30

A typical VGA card.

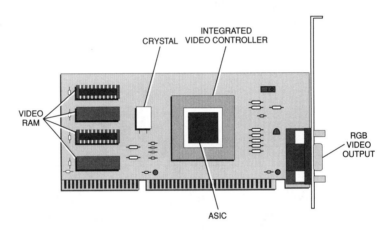

Every aspect of the computer described thus far has dealt with digital signals and circuitry. However, the VGA video standard uses analog signals and circuitry. The main component of most video adapter cards is an Application Specific Integrated Circuit (ASIC) called the **Integrated Video Controller IC**. It is a microprocessor-like chip that oversees the operation of the entire adapter. It is capable of accessing RAM and ROM memory units on the card. The video RAM chips hold the information that is to be displayed on the screen. Its size determines the card's video and color capacities.

The adapter also has a **Video BIOS ROM**, which is similar to the ROM BIOS on the system board. It is used to store firmware routines that are specific only to video functions. The video controller also contains the **Video DAC** (Digital-to-Analog Converter) that converts digital data in the controller into the analog signal used to drive the display. The video output connector is a DB-15 female connector used with analog VGA displays. Unlike earlier video cards, the VGA card does not normally include a parallel printer port.

Multi-I/O Adapter Cards

A multi-I/O (MI/O) adapter card integrates common I/O functions to provide an array of interfaces for the system.

Most MI/O cards combine a **Floppy-Disk Drive Controller (FDC)**, a **Hard-Disk Drive Controller/Interface (HDC)**, a **game port**, a **parallel printer port**, and two **serial ports** all on one board. Before the advent of VLSI technology, the discrete circuitry involved in most of these functions required a separate adapter card for each function. However, the MI/O adapter combines the basic circuitry for all of the these functions into a single ASIC VLSI chip.

Figure 2.31 depicts an MI/O card showing a sample of the IC placement and the location of connectors and configuration jumpers. The disk drives (hard and floppy) are mass storage devices capable of storing large amounts of data and are presented in the following section. The game port is used for input of resistive game devices, such as joysticks. The card also includes a programmable parallel printer port, which allows a wide range of printers to be connected to the system. The last function of the adapter is the RS-232C serial interface port; this port supports serial/asynchronous communications for mice and other serial I/O devices, such as a modems.

FIGURE 2.31

A typical MI/O card.

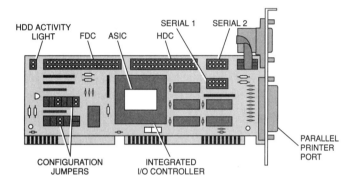

The FDC portion of the adapter is normally capable of controlling two floppy-disk drives (A and B), which connect to the adapter through a 34-conductor flat ribbon cable. Both disk drives can be connected to the cable at once. The system differentiates between the two drives by assigning them **Logical Drive Specifiers** "A:" and "B:", which depend on where they are connected to the cable. The disk drive that is connected to the end of the floppy drive signal cable farthest away from the MI/O card is designated as drive A. When another disk drive is added to the system, it should be plugged into the connector in the middle of the cable, and the system will see it as drive B.

Use caution when connecting the disk drives to the adapter card. Pin 1 of the connector and pin 1 of the adapter must be connected to each other. The connecting signal cable has a stripe on one edge to mark pin 1. Ensure that these markings are lined up together when connecting the cable to the adapter card. This is also true of the signal cable at the disk drive end. The relationship between pin 1 of the disk drive, the controller card, and the signal cable is described in Figure 2.32.

The HDC portion of the adapter is usually capable of controlling two hard-disk drives. The first hard drive is designated as drive C and the second as D. The hard drives are connected to the MI/O through a ribbon cable. The hard drives are connected to the controller in much the same manner as the floppy drives are. The system's first logical hard drive is connected to the end of the cable furthest away from the adapter. Observe the same cable orientation that was used for connecting the floppy-disk drives when connecting the cable to the MI/O adapter for the hard drives.

FIGURE 2.32

Aligning pin 1.

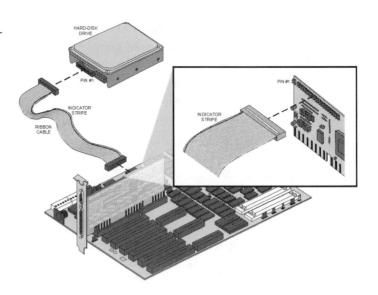

Parallel I/O devices plug into the DB-25 female connector. The MI/O card's serial port connectors might be located on a separate expansion slot cover that is normally located in the slot on either side of the adapter card. At the top of the featured slot cover is a DB-9 male connector where the mouse can be connected. Beneath the 9-pin connector is a DB-25 male connector that serves as the second serial I/O port.

Game port devices connect to the MI/O card through an external 15-pin DB-15 female connector at the rear of the card. The pins of this 15-pin D-Shell are arranged differently than those in the 15-pin VGA connector. In the VGA connector, the pins are arranged in three rows while the pins in the game port are arranged in two rows. Some external connections may be made by using a short ribbon cable to connect an external D-shell connector to a BERG strip connector located on the board. With a Y-cable plugged into the 15-pin connector, the game port will support two joystick-like devices.

Several configuration jumpers are normally found on MI/O adapters. They are used to set the operating characteristics of the different functions on the card. Jumper blocks are also used either to enable or disable the FDC, HDC, game port, and printer port. Other jumpers are used to assign which parallel port the printer will operate from.

Other Adapter Cards

It is safe to say that adapter cards have been designed to add a wide number of different functions to the basic computer system. All of the adapter cards depicted so far have adhered to the PC-Bus and ISA standards for connectors. The various types of adapter cards discussed so far are also available in other expansion slot styles.

Some cards might contain a controller or interface for a single function, such as a simple parallel port. Conversely, the adapter card might hold a complete, complex peripheral system, such as a modem. In any event, by including the correct interface and control circuitry, virtually anything can be connected to the computer system. Some PC board manufacturers have even developed special prototype adapter cards that have no components on them. This allows hobbyists and designers to create specialty adapter cards for their own applications.

Disk Drives

A+ CORE 1.1   The system unit normally comes from the manufacturer with both a floppy-disk drive unit and a hard-disk drive unit installed, as illustrated in Figure 2.33.

FIGURE 2.33

The disk drives of a typical system.

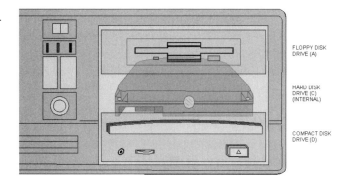

FLOPPY DISK
DRIVE (A)

HARD DISK
DRIVE (C)
(INTERNAL)

COMPACT DISK
DRIVE (D)

However, the system's disk-drive capacity is not usually limited to the standard units installed. In most cases, the system cabinet is designed to hold additional disk-drive units. These units can be either 3.5- or 5.25-inch floppy-disk drives, hard disk drives, or a combination of both. Although three FDD units could physically be installed in most systems, the typical floppy drive controller only supports two floppy-disk drives. Conversely, some systems are smaller and have room for only two disk drives.

One or more hard-disk drive units can be installed in the system unit, along with the floppy drive(s). The system should normally be set up to recognize a single hard-disk unit in the system as *DRIVE C:*. However, a single, physical hard-disk drive can be partitioned into two or more volumes that the system recognizes as *logical drives* C:, D:, and so on.

Floppy-Disk Drives

The standard floppy-disk drive for 8088-based machines was the 5.25-inch, full-height and half-height drive. These drives used disks capable of storing 368,640 (referred to as 360K) bytes of information. The term **Half-Height** was used to describe drive units that were half as tall as the **Full-Height** drive units used with the original IBM PC. Smaller 3.5-inch half-height drives capable of storing 720K (737,280) bytes of information were also used with 8088-based computers.

The PC-AT and its compatibles originally used advanced high-density 5.25-inch drives that could hold over 1,200,000 (1.2M) bytes of information.

In advanced machines, such as PS/2 computers and later AT compatibles, high-density, 3.5-inch floppy drives capable of holding 1.44M (1,474,560) bytes are common.

Floppy Disks

Floppy disks come in 5.25- and 3.5-inch diameters. They are mylar disks that have been coated with a ferro-magnetic material and that are encased in protective, semi-rigid envelopes that contain low-friction liners, which remove dust and contaminants from the disk as it turns within the envelope. Typical floppy drives turn the disk at 300 or 360 revolutions per minute, and the drive's **read/write (R/W) heads** ride directly on the disk surface. Information is **written to** or **read from** the disk as it spins inside the envelope. The small LED on the front of the disk-drive unit lights up whenever either of these operations is in progress.

Current PC systems use a type of floppy disk referred to as **double-sided, high-density (DS-HD)**. This means that the disk can be used on both sides and that advanced magnetic recording techniques may be used to effectively double or triple the storage capacity previously available, using older recording techniques. These disks can hold 1.44MB of information using the **Disk Operating System (DOS)** software.

This type of floppy disk drive can also operate with an older type of floppy disk that is referred to as a **double-sided, double-density (DS-DD)** disk. This notation indicates that the disks are constructed so that they can be used on both sides and that they can support recording techniques that double the storage capacity available with older recording techniques. The older disks were referred to as **single-sided (SS)** and/or **single-density (SD)** disks.

A newer standard for 5.25-inch floppies allows up to three times as much data (1.2MB) to be stored as was possible with the DS-DD disks. These are **double-sided, high-density** (or simply high-density) disks. These disks can usually be distinguished from the other 5.25-inch disk type by the absence of a reinforcing ring around their drive spindle opening.

Hard-Disk Drives

The hard-disk drives normally used with personal computers are referred to as Winchester hard-disk drive units. Both full- and half-height versions are popular in desktop and tower systems. These drives typically contain between one and five disks that are permanently mounted inside a sealed enclosure with the R/W head mechanisms. There is one R/W head for each disk surface. The platters are typically turned at a speed of 5,400 RPM. This high rotational speed creates a thin cushion of air around the disk surface that causes the R/W heads to fly just above the disk.

The **flying R/W heads** glide over the disks at a height of approximately 50 micro inches. This might seem like an unimportant measurement until you consider the size of a common dust particle or a human hair. This relationship is illustrated in Figure 2.34. If the R/W head should strike one of these contaminants as the disk spins at high speed, the head would be lofted into the air and then crash into the disk surface. This action could damage the R/W head and the disk surface and is known as a *head crash*. To avoid this, hard disks are encased in a sealed protective housing. It is important to realize that at no time should the disk housing be opened to the atmosphere. Repairs to hard-disk drives are performed in special repair facilities having **ultra-clean rooms**. In these rooms, even particles the size of those in the figure have been removed from the air.

FIGURE 2.34

Flying R/W heads.

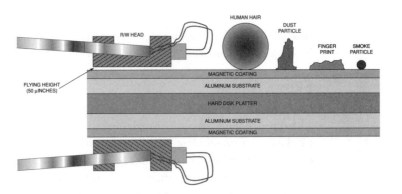

The rigid structure of the hard disk allows its tracks to be placed close together. This makes its storage capacity very high. Typical hard disks may have between 315 and 1,024 sets of tracks (or **Cylinders**) that are divided into between 17 and 50 sectors, depending on the diameter of the disk. Sectors generally contain either 256 or 512 bytes. The high speed at which the hard disk revolves also provides very rapid data transfer rates. On a typical 100MB, 3.5-inch hard disk, there are 1,002 cylinders (tracks per side) divided into 32 sectors.

System Speakers

The system's primary audio output device is a 2.25-inch, 8-ohm, 1/2-watt speaker, similar to the one depicted in Figure 2.35. This unit can be located behind the vertical vents in the front panel or under the power supply unit in a small plastic retainer. The system uses the speaker to prompt the user during certain events and to indicate certain errors in the system, such as video display failures, which can't be displayed on the screen. The speaker can also be controlled by the user through software. Its output frequency range extends through the complete audio range and, with proper programming, can be used to create arcade sounds and music.

FIGURE 2.35

The system speaker.

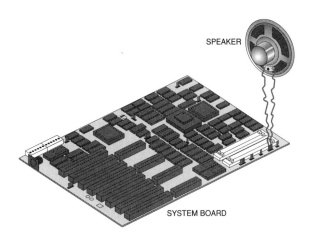

SPEAKER

SYSTEM BOARD

Peripherals

 A+ CORE 1.1

As discussed in Chapter 1, the standard peripherals associated with a personal computer are the keyboard and the CRT monitor. With the rapid growth of GUI-oriented software, the mouse has become a common input peripheral as well. The next most-common peripheral has to be the **character printer**. These peripherals are used to produce hard copy output on paper. Besides these common devices, all types of peripheral equipment are routinely added to the computer. As long as there are open expansion slots or other standard I/O connectors, it is possible to add compatible devices to the system.

The standard input device for PC-compatible computers is the alphanumeric keyboard. Most PCs use a detachable keyboard that is connected to the system by a six-foot coiled cable. This cable plugs into a round five-pin DIN connector located on the rear of the system board. The connector is keyed so that it cannot be misaligned.

The most widely-used display device for current PCs is the **Video Graphics Array (VGA)** color monitor. The monitor's signal cable connects to a 15-pin D-shell connector at the back of the system unit. A power cable supplies 120 Vac power to the monitor from a conventional power outlet or from a special connector on the back of the power supply unit.

The mouse is usually connected to a 9- or 25-pin male D-shell connector on the back panel of the system.

Character printers are normally attached to the system through 25-pin female parallel or 25-pin male serial D-shell connectors at the back of the unit.

External Connections and Devices

The system's peripheral devices typically connect to the back of the system unit. Figure 2.36 shows the external connections for the basic system configuration.

FIGURE 2.36

External connections.

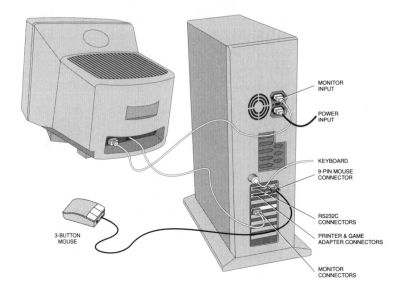

At one side of the system unit is a female power receptacle that may be used to provide power to IBM-PC–compatible monitors. Next to the monitor power receptacle is the power supply's input power connector. Beside the power connector is the power supply's fan vent. In a small opening near the power supply openings is the circular, 5-pin DIN connector for connecting a keyboard to the system. Across the remainder of the back plate are the eight option adapters slot openings. Moving across the panel, we first encounter the system's two RS-232C connectors. The parallel printer and games adapter connectors are in the next opening. In this illustration, the game port connector is located above the parallel port connector. On other systems, the locations of the various connectors may vary. The last connector on the back panel is the VGA adapter's monitor connectors. The 15-pin connector is the VGA-compatible RGB color output port.

Keyboards

The keyboard most widely used with desktop and tower units is a detachable, low-profile 101/102-key model depicted in Figure 2.37. These units are designed to provide the user with a high degree of mobility and functionality. The key tops are slightly concave to provide a comfortable *feel* to the typist. In addition, the key makes a noticeable tap when it bottoms out during a keystroke.

FIGURE 2.37

An alphanumeric keyboard.

The keys are divided into three logical groups according to their function. Along the top of the board are special **function keys** (F1–F12), which assume special functions for different software packages. On the right side of the board is a numeric keypad, which does double duty as cursor control keys, under the control of the numbers-lock (**Num Lock**) key. A separate set of cursor control keys can be found between the normal keyboard keys and the numeric keypad. When power is first applied to the keyboard, the keypad keys function as **cursor control keys**. By pressing the Num Lock key once, the keys function as a numeric keypad. When pressed again, the keys revert to their cursor control functions.

The white keys in the center group normally function as a standard **QWERTY** typewriter keyboard. This is the standard typist's keyboard arrangement. The keyboard's gray keys provide control functions. In addition to the normal typewriter-like control keys (backspace, two shift keys, Return key (also referred to as the **carriage return** or **Enter** key) and a **Tab** key (arrows pointing to both sides), the keyboard has several computer-related control keys. These include two special shift keys (**Ctrl** and **Alt**), three special shift-lock keys (**Caps Lock**, Num Lock, and **Scroll Lock**), and an Esc key. When any of the three shift-lock keys is engaged, its corresponding LED (in the upper-right corner of the board) lights up to show that the function is engaged.

The original PC and XT employed an 84-key version that did not include the separate numeric keypad keys. Laptops, notebooks, and sub-notebooks use a compact 83-key version with many dual-purpose keys. As with the full-size keyboards, these units feature the capability to redefine every key on the board through software. This is an outstanding advantage of the PC keyboard in that it allows the keyboard to assume any function the programmer desires.

Video Displays

A+ CORE 1.1

Desktop and tower units normally use a color **cathode-ray tube** (**CRT**) display monitor, similar to the one shown in Figure 2.38 as standard video output equipment. The PC and PC-XT and PC-AT often used **monochrome** (single color) monitors. They could also use color monitors by simply adding a color video adapter card and monitor. The **color CRT monitor**, shown in Figure 2.38, is sometimes referred to as an **RGB monitor** because the three primary colors that make a color CRT are red, green, and blue.

FIGURE 2.38

The CRT display monitor.

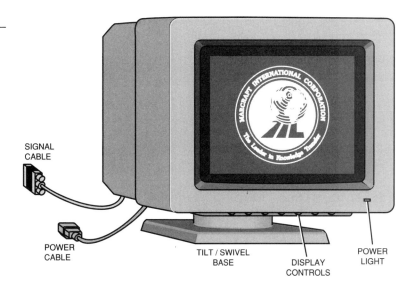

SIGNAL CABLE

POWER CABLE

TILT / SWIVEL BASE

DISPLAY CONTROLS

POWER LIGHT

Modern units normally use high-resolution color monitors for output purposes. The resolution of a monitor refers to the quality of the displayed image. High-resolution monitors produce images with greater detail than lower-resolution monitors. Working with a low-resolution monitor for extended periods can lead to chronic eye, neck, and back strain, and accompanying headaches. Reflected room light has also been shown to increase display-related fatigue.

The monitor can either be plugged into a commercial, three-prong power receptacle or into the special receptacle provided through the power supply at the rear of the unit. This option depends on the type of power cable provided by the manufacturer. A special adapter cable is available to match a standard 120 Vac plug to this power supply receptacle. The **signal cable** (connected to the video adapter card) allows the monitor to be positioned away from the system unit if desired.

The display's normal controls are brightness and contrast. These controls are located in different positions on the monitor depending on the manufacturer. A power on/off switch can be found on the monitor, but its location varies from model to model. If the monitor receives power through the system unit's power supply, the monitor's power switch can be set to on, and the monitor will turn on and off along with the system.

Other Peripherals

A system may employ one or more **pointing devices** as input sources. Most of these devices connect to that system in the rear of the unit. Mice typically plug into a 9-pin or 25-pin male D-shell connector. Joysticks and game paddles are normally connected to the 15-pin female D-shell Game Port connector. Light pens usually require a special connector on the video display card.

Printers are the other most widely-used peripheral. Serial interface versions normally plug into a 9-pin or 25-pin male D-shell connector. Most of the time, it is common to find a serial printer connected to the 25-pin connector that has been set up as the system's second serial port. The first serial port is usually set up with the 9-pin connector and handles the mouse connection. Parallel printers are connected to the 25-pin female connector at the rear of the system. These typical peripheral connections are depicted in Figure 2.39.

FIGURE 2.39

Typical peripheral connectors.

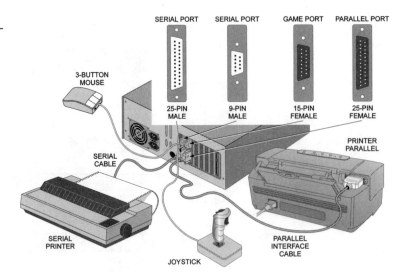

Key Points Review

This chapter has covered the fundamental hardware structures and components associated with PC-compatible personal computer systems.

▶ The tremendous popularity of the original IBM PC-XT and AT systems created a set of pseudo-standards for hardware and software compatibility. The AT architecture became so popular that it has become the Industry Standard Architecture (ISA). The majority of microcomputers are both hardware- and software-compatible with the original AT design.

▶ The system unit is the main portion of the micro-computer system and is the basis of any PC system arrangement.

▶ The system board is the center of the system. It contains the portions of the system that define its computing power and speed.

▶ Notebook computer designers work constantly to decrease the size and power consumption of the computer's components.

▶ The drawback of portable computers from a service point of view is that conventions and compatibility disappear. Therefore, interchangeability of parts with other machines or makers goes by the wayside.

▶ The system's power supply unit provides electrical power for every component inside the system unit, as well as supplying AC power to the video-display monitor.

▶ The system board communicates with various optional input/output (I/O) and memory systems through adapter boards that plug into its expansion slots. These connectors are normally located along the left-rear portion of the system board, so that the external devices they serve can access them through openings at the rear of the case.

▶ The microprocessor is the major component of any system board. It executes software instructions and carries out arithmetic operations for the system.

▶ Microprocessor manufacturers always produce microprocessor-support chip sets that provide auxiliary services for the microprocessor.

▶ Each time the system is turned on, or reset, the BIOS program checks the system's configuration settings to determine what types of optional devices are included in the system.

▶ Newer microcomputers possess the capability to automatically reconfigure themselves for new options that are installed. This feature is referred to as Plug and Play (PnP) capability.

▶ The local bus connects special peripherals to the system board (and the microprocessor) through a proprietary expansion slot connector and allows the peripheral to operate at speeds close to the speed of the microprocessor.

▶ The PCMCIA bus was developed to accommodate the space continuous notebook and sub-notebook computer market.

▶ The video adapter card provides the interface between the system board and the display monitor.

▶ A multi-I/O (MI/O) adapter card integrates common I/O functions to provide an array of interfaces for the system. Most MI/O cards combine a Floppy-Disk Drive Controller (FDC), a Hard-Disk Drive Controller/Interface (HDC), a game port, a parallel printer port, and two serial ports all on one board.

▶ The system unit normally comes from the manufacturer with both a floppy-disk drive unit and a hard-disk drive unit installed.

At this point, review the objectives listed at the beginning of the chapter to be certain that you understand and can perform each item listed there. Afterward, answer the review questions that follow to verify your knowledge of the information.

Multiple Choice Questions

1. What type of IC is the brain of the PC system?

   a. The BIOS

   b. The system board

   c. The ALU

   d. The microprocessor

2. Where would you normally expect to encounter a PCMCIA card?

   a. In an ISA expansion slot

   b. In a serial port

   c. In a notebook computer

   d. In an MCA expansion slot

3. Name one weak feature of tower cases.

   a. Weak framework due to its vertical height

   b. Air flow through tower cases is generally not good

   c. High EFI radiation

   d. Requires excessive desk space in an office environment

4. Where is the system's BIOS program located?

   a. ROM ICs located on the system board

   b. In the CMOS chip

   c. In the keyboard encoder

   d. In the microprocessor's L2 cache

5. How many floppy drives can a typical FDC controller handle? How are these drives identified to the system?

   a. The normal FDC controller can control two floppy disk drives that the system will see as drives A: and B:.

   b. The normal FDC controller can control four floppy disk drives that the system will see as drives A:, B:, C:, and D:.

   c. The normal FDC controller can control one floppy disk drive that the system will see as drive A:.

   d. The normal FDC controller can control two floppy-disk drives that the system will see as drive A: and an assigned drive name.

6. What type of port is indicated by the presence of a nine-pin male connector on the back panel of the computer?

   a. A parallel printer port

   b. A game port

   c. A serial communications port

   d. A VGA port

7. Which 32-bit bus can accept cards from PC and ISA buses?

   a. The ISA bus

   b. The EISA bus

   c. The MCA bus

   d. The PCI bus

8. Where is the MI/O function normally found in a Pentium system?

   a. On the multi-I/O card

   b. On the system board

   c. On the video card

   d. On the SCSI adapter card

9. What two expansion cards were considered as standard equipment in pre-Pentium PCs?

   a. The multi-I/O and video adapter cards

   b. The disk drive and video adapter cards

   c. The system board and video adapter card

   d. The multi-I/O and disk drive adapter cards

10. List the I/O functions associated with a common MI/O adapter.

    a. A Floppy-Disk Drive Controller (FDC) and a Hard-Disk Drive Controller/Interface (HDC)

    b. A game port, a parallel printer port, and two serial ports

    c. Two parallel printer ports and two serial ports

    d. A Floppy-Disk Drive Controller (FDC), a Hard-Disk Drive Controller/Interface (HDC), a game port, a parallel printer port, and two serial ports

Review Questions

1. List four types of ICs commonly found on the system board.

2. List the four subunits typically found inside the system unit.

3. How can you avoid confusion between the DB-15M connectors for VGA and game port connections?

4. List three types of memory typically found on modern system boards.

5. What is the purpose of a back plane? Where is it found?

6. List the devices normally found outside the system unit.

7. Which government agency would be concerned with the characteristics of the computer's case?

8. Describe the major maintenance problem associated with notebook computers.

9. When purchasing a video card to install in a particular unit, what consideration must be taken into account?

10. What type of ASIC device is normally found on a video adapter card, and what are its functions?

11. When connecting a power supply to a system board, what precaution should be taken?

12. What does EFI stand for, and why is it associated with a microcomputer system?

13. What do the terms SIMM and SIPP stand for, and what kind of devices are they?

14. Describe the two input devices that are commonly included in PCs.

15. How is upgrading a system with a flash ROM BIOS different than upgrading a system with a standard ROM BIOS?

Lab Exercises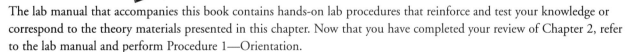

The lab manual that accompanies this book contains hands-on lab procedures that reinforce and test your knowledge or correspond to the theory materials presented in this chapter. Now that you have completed your review of Chapter 2, refer to the lab manual and perform Procedure 1—Orientation.

TROUBLESHOOTING THE SYSTEM

CHAPTER 3

LEARNING OBJECTIVES

Upon completion of this chapter and its related lab procedures, you should be able to perform these tasks:

1. Describe the characteristics of a good work space.

2. Outline steps for using a digital multimeter to perform voltage, resistance, and current checks on a system, as well as identify common DMM tests associated with personal computers.

3. List preliminary steps for diagnosing computer problems.

4. Perform visual inspections of a system.

5. Describe the three general categories of problems into which symptoms can be grouped, and differentiate between them.

6. Differentiate between software- and hardware-based troubleshooting techniques.

7. Use disk-based diagnostic tools to isolate system problems.

8. Describe the function of a POST card.

9. Use DOS batch files to help test selected areas of the system.

10. Describe quick checks that can be used to determine the nature of system hardware problems.

11. Describe FRU-level troubleshooting.

12. Describe steps for isolating power supply problems.

13. Outline checks to isolate problems that produce a dead system.

14. Discuss methods of dealing with symptoms that are not defined well enough to point to a particular component.

Introduction

Effective troubleshooting of electronic equipment is a matter of combining good knowledge of the equipment and its operation with good testing techniques and deductive reasoning skills. In general, the process of troubleshooting microprocessor-based equipment begins at the outside of the system and moves inward. The first step is always to try the system to see what symptoms are produced. Second, you must isolate the problem as either a software- or hardware-related issue. After this, the problem should be isolated to a particular section of the hardware or software. Finally, the problem must be isolated to the specific offending component.

The information in this chapter instructs you on the theory behind successful troubleshooting tools and methods you will need to effectively troubleshoot microprocessor-based equipment.

Tools and Work Space

The first order of business when working on any type of electronic equipment is to prepare a proper work area.

You will need a clear, flat work space on which to rest the device. Make sure that your work space is large enough to accommodate the equipment. Check to make sure that an adequate number of power receptacles is available to handle all the equipment you may need. Try not to locate your work space in a high-traffic area; instead, try to put it somewhere where it won't interfere with other tasks if it's there for a few days.

Good lighting is a prerequisite for the work area because the technician must be able to see small details, such as part numbers, cracked circuit foils, or solder splashes. An adjustable lamp with a shade is preferable, and fluorescent lighting is particularly desirable. In addition, a magnifying glass can prove helpful when you are trying to read small part numbers or when you're looking for cracks in printed circuit board traces.

Organizational Aids

Some troubleshooting problems may require more than one session, so it's a good idea to have some organizational aids on hand before you begin to disassemble any piece of equipment. The following are some of the organizational aids you will need:

1. A parts organizer to keep track of small parts such as screws and connectors you may remove from the device. This organizer need not be extravagant: A handful of paper or Styrofoam cups will do nicely, as will a handful of clear plastic sandwich bags.

2. A roll of athletic or masking tape. The tape can be used to make tags and labels to help identify parts and record where they go and how they are connected in the circuit. The worst thing you can possibly do is attempt to remember everything in your head. Take the time to write notes and stick them on items such as your parts organizers, circuit boards, cables you remove from the system, and so forth.

3. A small note pad or notebook to keep track of your assembly/troubleshooting steps. By the time you begin to disassemble a unit, there should already be quite a few entries logged explaining what preliminary steps led to the decision to remove the outer cover of the device.

Diagnostic and Repair Tools

Obviously, anyone who's going to work on any type of equipment must have the proper tools for the task. Let's discuss the tools and equipment associated with the testing and repair of digital systems.

Using Hand Tools

A+ CORE 1.8 First, you will need some common hand tools. The well-prepared technician's tool kit should contain a wide range of both **flat-blade** and **Phillips-head screwdriver** sizes. At a minimum, it should include a small jeweler's screwdriver, a medium-sized flat-blade screwdriver, and a medium-sized Phillips screwdriver. In addition, you may want to include a small set of miniature nut drivers, a set of **Torx drivers**, and a special nonconductive screwdriver-like device called an **alignment tool**.

You will also need a couple of pairs of needle-nose pliers, which are available in a number of sizes. You will need at least one pair with a sturdy, blunt nose and one with a longer, more delicate nose. You may wish to get a pair that also has a cutting edge built into its jaws, though this same function may be performed by a different type of pliers called diagonals, or cross-cuts. In addition, many technicians carry a pair of surgical forceps to supplement their other pliers.

Another common set of tools associated with computer repair is IC pullers, or **IC extractors**. These tools come in various styles, as illustrated in Figure 3.1, and are used to remove ICs from sockets. On the whole, socket-mounted ICs are not as common on modern PC boards as they were in the past. Potential failures associated with the mechanical connections between sockets and chips—coupled with the industry's reliance on surface-mount soldering techniques—have led to far fewer socket-mounted chips. However, the IC puller still comes in handy on some occasions, such as upgrading a ROM BIOS chip.

FIGURE 3.1

IC pullers.

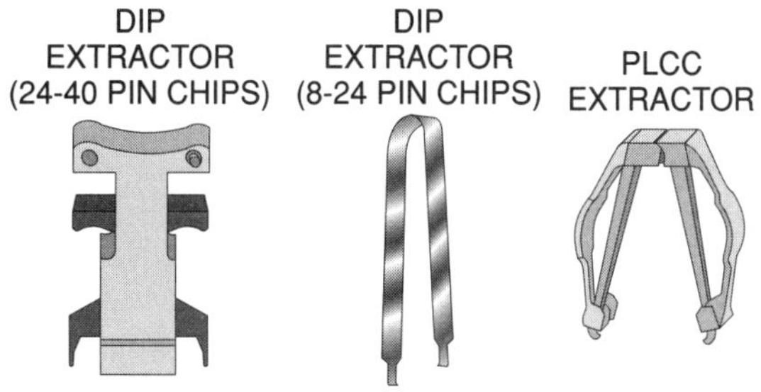

DIP EXTRACTOR (24-40 PIN CHIPS)   DIP EXTRACTOR (8-24 PIN CHIPS)   PLCC EXTRACTOR

A desk-mount vise, a specialized tool to hold the work piece (such as a printed circuit board or similar item) steady during testing and repair, is a valuable asset. Hand tools commonly associated with microcomputer repair are depicted in Figure 3.2.

Using a Multimeter

A+ CORE 1.8 A number of test instruments can be most helpful in isolating problems. One of the most basic pieces of electronic troubleshooting equipment is the **multimeter**. These test instruments are available in both analog and digital read-out form and can be used to directly measure values of **voltage** (V), **current**—either in milliamperes (mA) or amperes (a)—and **resistance**, in Ohms (***). These devices are referred to as **VOMs** (Volt-Ohm-Milliammeters) for analog types, or **DMMs** (Digital MultiMeters) for digital types. Figure 3.3 depicts a Digital Multimeter.

FIGURE 3.2

Hand tools used in micro-computer repair.

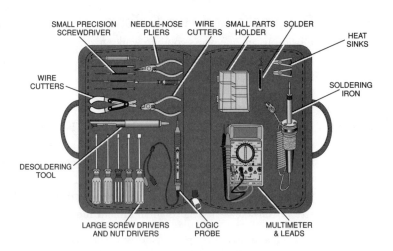

With a little finesse, the multimeter can be used to check diodes, transistors, capacitors, motor windings, relays, and coils. This particular DMM shown in Figure 3.3 contains facilities built into the meter to test transistors and diodes. This capability is in addition to its standard functions of current, voltage, and resistance measurement.

FIGURE 3.3

Digital multimeter.

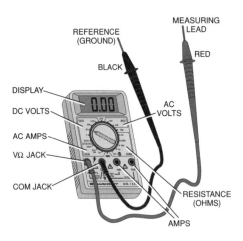

The first step in using the multimeter to perform tests is to select the proper function. For the most part, there is never a need to use the current functions of the multimeter when working with computer systems. However, the voltage and resistance functions can be very valuable tools.

In computer and peripheral troubleshooting, fully 99 percent of the tests made are **dc voltage readings**, measurements that most often involve checking the dc side of the power supply unit. These readings can be made between the ground and one of the expansion slot pins (see Chapter 6, "System Boards," for expansion slot specifications) or at the P8/P9 power supply connectors. It is also common to check the voltage level across a system-board capacitor to verify that the system is receiving power. The voltage across most of the capacitors on the system board is 5-Vdc. The dc voltages that can normally be expected in a PC-compatible system are +12V, +5V, -5V, and -12V. The actual values for these readings may vary by 5 percent in either direction.

The **dc voltage function** is used to take measurements in live dc circuits and should be connected parallel to the device being checked. This could mean connecting the reference lead (black lead) to a ground point and the measuring lead (red lead) to a test point to take a measurement, as illustrated in Figure 3.4.

Normal practice requires first setting the meter to its highest voltage range to make certain that the voltage level being measured does not damage the meter.

As an approximate value is detected, the range setting can be decreased to achieve a more accurate reading. Most meters allow for over-voltage protection, however, it is still a good safety practice to decrease the range of the meter after an initial value has been achieved.

FIGURE 3.4

A dc voltage check.

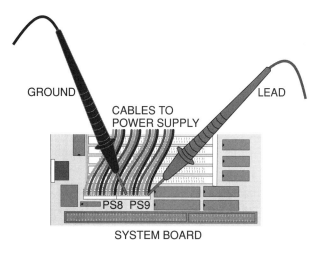

The second most popular test is the **resistance** (or **continuity**) **test**.

Unlike the voltage check, resistance checks are always made after power is removed from the system.

Failure to turn off the power when making resistance checks can cause serious damage to the meter and pose a potential risk to the user. Resistance checks also require that the component being tested be electrically isolated from the system. For most circuit components, this means de-soldering at least one end from the board.

However, the resistance check is very useful in isolating some types of problems in the system. One of the main uses of the resistance function is to test fuses. At least one end of the fuse must be disconnected from the system, and the meter should be set on the 1k-ohm resistance setting. If the fuse is good, the meter should read near zero ohms; if it is bad, the meter will read infinite. The resistance function is also useful in checking for cables and connectors. By removing the cable from the system and connecting a meter lead to each end, the cable's continuity can be checked conductor by conductor to verify its integrity. You can also test the system's speaker with the resistance function. To check the speaker, simply disconnect the speaker from the system and connect a meter lead to each end. If the speaker is good, the meter should read near zero ohms; if the speaker is defective, the resistance reading should be infinite.

Only a couple situations involve using the **ac voltage function** for checking microcomputer systems. The primary use of this function is to check the commercial power being applied to the power supply unit. As with any measurement, it is important to select the correct measurement range. However, the lethal voltage levels associated with the supply power call for additional caution when making such measurements. The second application for the ac voltage function is to measure ripple voltage from the dc output side of the power supply unit. This particular operation is very rarely performed in field service situations.

Initial Troubleshooting Steps

As a general rule, the majority of all equipment problems can be reduced to the simplest things you can think of—the problem is, most people don't think of them. Successful troubleshooting is the result of careful observation, deductive reasoning, and an organized approach to solving problems. These techniques are common to repairing any type of defective equipment. Although we are demonstrating these techniques as they apply to repairing computer systems, it is quite possible to adapt them to other systems as well.

A+ CORE 2.2   The most important thing to do when you approach a malfunctioning device is to be observant. Begin your efforts by talking to the person who reported the problem; many clues to a problem can be determined from this person. You should always try to gather information from the user regarding the environment in which the system is being used, any symptoms or error codes produced by the system, and the situations that existed when the failure occurred. Also be aware that many problems may actually be related to the operator.

> One of the first things to do if you are not personally familiar with the system is to eliminate the user as a possible source of the problem.

List the procedures that led up to the malfunction. This communication can help you narrow a problem down to a particular section of the computer. For example, it does no good to check the video display when the user is having trouble using the disk drive. Next, observe the symptoms of the malfunction to verify the problem for yourself. After you have identified a problem, try to associate the malfunction with a section of the system responsible for that operation.

Performing the Visual Inspection

If you have no prior knowledge of the type of malfunction, you should proceed by performing a careful visual inspection of the system. Check the outside of the system first. Look for loose or disconnected cables. Consult all the external front-panel lights. If no lights are displayed, check the power outlet, the plugs and power cords, and any power switches that may affect the operation of the system. You may also want to check the commercial power-distribution system's fuses or circuit breakers to see whether they are functional.

If part of the system is active, try to localize the problem by systematically removing peripheral devices from the system. Try swapping out suspected devices with known good parts from another computer of the same type. Try to revive the system—or its defective portion—by restarting it several times. As a matter of fact, you should try to restart the system after each correctional step is performed.

> Check all externally accessible switch settings.

For example, check all system jumper settings to see that they are set correctly for the actual configuration of the system. In Pentium-based systems, check the BIOS Advanced CMOS Configuration screen for enabling settings that may not be correct. Also, make certain that any peripheral devices in the system, such as printers or modems, are set up correctly. Consult any additional user or operations manuals liberally. Indeed, many of the computers and peripheral systems on the market, such as printers, have some level of self-diagnostics built into them. Generally, these diagnostics programs produce coded error messages. The key to recognizing and using these error messages is usually found in the device's user's manual. In addition, the user's manual may contain probable causes and suggested remedy information, and/or specialized tests to isolate specific problems.

> Take the time to document the problem, including all the tests you perform and their outcomes. Your memory is never as good as you think it is, especially in stressful situations such as with a down computer. This recorded information can prevent you from making repetitive steps that waste time and may cause confusion. This information will also be very helpful when you move on to more detailed tests or measurements.

Watching the Boot-up Procedure

> Carefully watching the steps of a **boot** procedure can reveal a lot about the nature of problems in a system. Faulty areas can be included or excluded from possible causes of errors during the boot process.

The observable actions of a working system's cold-boot procedure are listed as follows, in their order of occurrence:

1. When power is applied, the power supply fan should work.

2. The keyboard lights should flash as the rest of the system components are being reset.

3. A BIOS message should be visible on the monitor.

4. A memory test should be visible on the monitor.

5. The floppy-disk drive access light should come on briefly.

6. The hard-disk drive access light should come on briefly.

7. An audible beep should be heard.

8. The floppy-disk drive access light should come on briefly before switching to the hard drive.

9. For DOS-based machines, a DOS prompt should be visible on the monitor. For Windows 95/98 machines, the message "Starting Windows" should appear on the screen.

If a section of the computer is defective, some or none of these steps will be observed. By knowing the sections of the computer involved in each of the steps, you can suspect a particular section of causing the problem if the system does not advance past that step. As an example, it would not be logical to replace the floppy-disk drive (5) when a memory test (4) has not been observed on the monitor.

When a failure occurs, components can be eliminated as a possible cause by observing the number of steps that the system completes in the list above; those subsystems associated with steps successfully completed can be eliminated. Efforts should be focused only on those sections responsible for the symptom. When that symptom is cleared, the computer should progress to another step. However, another unrelated symptom still might appear farther down the list. This symptom should be dealt with in the same manner. Always focus on diagnosing the present symptom, and eventually all the symptoms will disappear.

Determining Hardware/Software/Configuration Problems

A+ CORE 2.2 It should be obvious that a functional computer system is comprised of two major parts: the system's hardware and the software that controls it. These two elements are so closely related that it is often difficult to determine which part might be the cause of a given problem. Therefore, one of the earliest steps in troubleshooting a computer problem (or any other programmable system problem) is to determine whether the problem is due to a hardware failure or to faulty programming.

The easiest way to determine whether a problem is hardware- or software-related is to test the hardware with software packages that are known to be good and that have successfully run on the system before. If the system boots up properly and runs these programs correctly, then the problem is very likely to be software-related. If the system will not boot, or if it refuses to run programs that previously ran on it, then the problem is likely to be hardware-related.

> The majority of all problems in computer systems occur in the area of software and configuration settings.

> There's a special category of problems that tend to occur whenever a new hardware option is added to the system, or when the system is used for the very first time. These problems are called **setup problems** and are due to mismatches between the system's programmed configuration and the actual equipment installed in the system.

This mismatch can also occur between the system's configuration settings and the hardware jumper and switch settings.

In three situations it is normally necessary to run the system's CMOS Setup utility:

- The first situation occurs when the system is installed for the first time.

- The second occurrence happens if it becomes necessary to replace the CMOS backup battery on the system board.

- Finally, any time a new option is added to the system it may be necessary to run Setup.

These options normally include the disk drive, the video display, and the installed memory.

Configuration problems occur with some software packages when they are first installed. Certain parameters must be entered into the program by the user to match the capabilities of the software to the actual configuration of the system. These configuration settings are established through the startup software in the ROM BIOS. If these configuration parameters are set incorrectly, the software will be unable to direct the system's hardware properly, and an error will occur.

When you are installing new hardware or software options, be aware of the possibility that this type of error will occur. If configuration, or setup, errors are encountered, refer to the installation instructions found in the new component's user's manual. Table 3.1 lists typical configuration error codes and messages produced when various types of configuration mismatches are incurred.

Table 3.1 *Common Configuration Error Codes*

Configuration Error Message	Meaning
CMOS System Option Not Set	Failures of CMOS battery or CMOS Checksum test
CMOS Display Mismatch	Failure of display type verification
CMOS Memory Size Mismatch	System configuration and setup failure
Strike F1 to Continue	Invalid configuration information

Software Diagnostics

Most PCs have reasonably good built-in self-tests that are run each time the computer is powered up. These tests can prove very beneficial in detecting hardware-oriented problems within the system. Whenever a self-test failure occurs, the system may indicate the error through an audio response (beep codes), a blank screen, or a visual error message on the video display. Some PCs issue a numerically coded error message on the display when an error occurs, and other PCs display a written description of the error.

Basically, software diagnostic routines check the system by running predetermined sets of tests on different areas of the system's hardware. The diagnostic package evaluates the response from each test and attempts to produce a status report for all the system's major components. As with the computer's self-test, these packages produce visual and beep-coded error messages.

The most common software troubleshooting packages test the system's memory, microprocessor, keyboard, display monitor, and the disk drive's speed. If at least the system's CPU, disk drive, and clock circuits are working, you may be able to use one of these special software troubleshooting packages to help localize system failures. These can be especially helpful when trying to track down nonheat-related intermittent problems. However, these test programs normally are only effective down to the board level, not down to a particular chip on a particular board.

If the diagnostic program indicates that multiple items should be replaced, you should replace the units one at a time until the unit starts up. Then replace any units removed prior to the one that caused the system to start. This ensures that there were not multiple bad parts. If all the parts have been replaced and the unit still does not function properly, the diagnostic software is suspect.

Using ROM-Based Diagnostics

In cases where the system is unable to load information from a disk, you can use a ROM-based diagnostic program to check out the partially dead system. In other systems, the diagnostic chips are usually substituted for the system board's ROM BIOS chip.

Several companies offer disk-based and ROM-based diagnostics packages for troubleshooting computer problems. Some are better than others, but as a group, ROM-based diagnostics packages are better than disk-based diagnostic packages simply because they require that much less of the system be operable for use. Disk-based programs require that almost all of the system be functional before they can be used. On the other hand, ROM-based diagnostics require that only a minimal portion of the system be operational for use.

Some versions of the AMI BIOS come with an extensive set of diagnostic routines built into the ROM package. Therefore, the diagnostic routines can be used without removing the system unit's outer cover. These routines can be entered through the BIOS' CMOS Setup menu. To invoke the diagnostic program, turn on the computer, wait for the message "Press DEL if you want to run SETUP or DIAGS," and press the DEL key. After entering the CMOS Setup screen, simply move the screen cursor to the Run Diagnostics position, and press the ENTER key. The BIOS routine responds by placing its diagnostics selection menu (illustrated in Figure 3.5) on the monitor screen. You can select the various sections to test, along with the specific tests to run, using the ARROW keys.

FIGURE 3.5

The CMOS diagnostics menu.

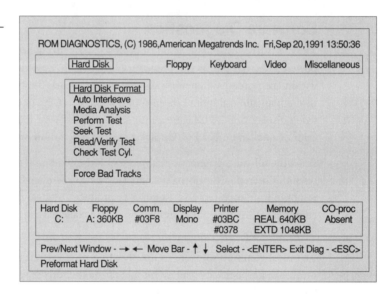

The diagnostic menu screen is divided into three major portions:

- AMI ROM Diagnostics header
- Field for listing available procedures and tests
- List of present devices known to the system

At the top of the screen is the AMI ROM Diagnostics header. This header contains the BIOS version number, the computer's current time and date information, and five headings that can be selected for diagnostic operations. These topics include hard-disk drive procedures and test functions, floppy-disk Drive procedures and test functions, keyboard tests, video display tests, and miscellaneous port tests.

When the highlighted cursor is moved to one of the header topics, a listing of the available procedures and tests appears in the section of the screen underneath the topic. At the bottom of the screen, the program displays a list of the devices that it knows are present in the system. Directions for navigating through the program are also presented at the bottom of the page.

When you select a test listed below one of the diagnostic topics, firmware test routines stored in the ROM BIOS are executed. These diagnostic programs can be used to determine the functionality of the computer's subsystems. The routines are menu-driven and enable you to select a specific test to execute. They also provide information about devices installed in the system.

The printer adapter test checks the signals of the parallel port. During the test, a printer should be connected and the power should be on. This test reports any abnormalities in the printer port status signals, such as if the printer is not loaded with paper. The **Parallel Loopback Plug** is normally used to simulate the presence of a parallel printer.

The communication port test requires that a **Serial Port Loopback Plug** be installed in the port connector. This plug simulates another communication port connection. When the loopback plug is in place, this test transmits data through the port and then verifies that the received data is the same.

Using POST Cards

Most BIOS program chips do not have an extensive set of onboard diagnostics built into them. Therefore, several companies produce **POST cards** and diagnostic software to aid in hardware troubleshooting. A POST card is a diagnostic device that plugs into the system's expansion slot and tests the operation of the system as it boots. These cards can be as simple as Interrupt and DMA channel monitors, or as complex as full-fledged ROM BIOS diagnostic packages that carry out extensive tests on the system.

POST cards are normally used when the system appears to be dead, or when the system cannot read from a floppy or hard drive. The firmware tests on the card replace the normal BIOS functions and send the system into a set of tests. The value of the card lies in the fact that the tests can be carried out without the system resorting to software diagnostics located on the hard disk or in a floppy drive.

The POST tests located in most BIOS chips stop the system if an error is detected. The POST cards note the error and continue through the initialization routine to activate as many additional system resources as possible.

Simple POST cards come with a set of LEDs (Light Emitting Diodes) that produce coded error signals when a problem is encountered. Other cards produce audio beep codes and seven-segment LED read-outs of the error code. A typical XT/AT-compatible POST card is depicted in Figure 3.6.

FIGURE 3.6

A typical POST card.

Using DOS Batch Files

A+ CORE 4.6 Many areas of the PC system can be tested using simple DOS batch files. It is not uncommon for technicians to create short files that test the monitor and floppy drive as well as the serial and parallel ports. These files can be created through the DOS Editor (EDIT.COM),

or by using the DOS COPY CON command. Any DOS command can be used to create a batch file.

FDDTest

A simple FDD test program can be constructed as follows:

```
Copy Con FDDTEST.BAT
DIR A:
FDDTEST.BAT
F6 <Enter>
```

This simple batch program creates a test program named FDDTEST. Typing this filename causes DOS to execute the two lines of the program. These lines cause the system to repeatedly perform directory listings of the floppy drive. The second line causes the program to rerun itself. Pressing the F6 function key stores the program to disk.

VIDTest

The DOS Echo command can be used to set up a short test program for the video system. The program uses the Echo command to display the message "This is a test of the video system" on the monitor screen. The second Echo command, followed by a period, causes the program to create a blank line on the screen. The final line causes the program to automatically rerun and produce the message one line lower on the screen. In this manner, the screen should quickly fill up with this message:

```
Copy Con VIDTEST.BAT
Echo This is a test of the video system
Echo.
VIDTEST
F6 <Enter>
```

PRNTest

Similar test programs can be built to test I/O ports. DOS keeps track of the system's installed ports by assigning them handles (logical device names) such as LPT1, LPT2, and LPT3. DOS also assigns COM port designations to the system's serial ports during boot-up. COM port designations are normally COM1 and COM2 in most systems, but they can be extended to COM4 in some advanced systems:

```
Copy Con PRNTEST.BAT
CD\DOS
PRINT lpt1 This is a printer test
PRINT
PRNTEST
F6 <Enter>
```

The simple printer test batch program causes the system to change directories to the DOS subdirectory, execute a DOS print command to the first logical printer port, and print the message "This is a printer test" to the printer. The next command creates a blank line on the paper.

Batch Commands

These are all simple batch programs for very low-level testing of the system's subsections. By using the logical DOS and batch commands, extensive diagnostic programs can be created. Eight batch commands are particularly helpful in creating test files:

- Call

- If

- Echo

- Pause

- For

- Rem

- Goto

- Shift

Consult the DOS user's manual for more information and suggested usage of these commands.

Using Microsoft Diagnostics (MSD.EXE)

A+ CORE 4.6 Microsoft Windows contains an excellent diagnostic program called Microsoft Diagnostics (MSD.EXE) that can be used to determine what hardware options are installed in the computer without removing the case. This program can also determine whether these options are responding to their correct addresses. MSD provides information about software packages installed during boot-up (such as the operating system's version), the device drivers that are installed, and the **Terminate and Stay Resident** programs **(TSRs)** that are running. MSD is a good tool for eliminating or confirming software conflicts.

This software is particularly useful when adding new options to the system. As the system fills up with options, it becomes increasingly difficult to locate free system resources—such as DMA and interrupt channels—for the new options to use. By running MSD before installing a new option, you can avoid many hardware and software conflicts.

Although MSD is shipped with Windows, it is a DOS-based program. This means that MSD does not have to be executed from within Windows. MSD should be executed from the DOS prompt by simply typing **MSD** at the C:\> prompt. The MSD's menu items can be selected using the mouse or the keyboard. When using the mouse, move the pointer over the desired menu selection and press the left mouse button. When using the keyboard, each menu selection has a highlighted letter that can be pressed to select the menu item.

When the MSD menu appears on the screen, you can choose from 13 options and a separate menu bar with the following options:

- Computer

- Disk Drives

- Memory

- LPT Ports

- Video

- COM Ports

- Network

- IRQ Status

- OS Version
- TSR Programs
- Mouse
- Device Drivers
- Other Adapters

The MSD toolbar includes three options:

- File
- Utilities
- Help

The File pull-down menu enables the user to view system files, such as AUTOEXEC.BAT and CONFIG.SYS, and also shows Windows operating files, such as WIN.INI and SYSTEM.INI. These files are covered in detail in Chapter 5, "Microsoft Windows." Also under this menu is the option called File Find, which enables you to search the disk drive(s) for a specific file. The Print a Report option, located in the File pull-down menu, produces a hard copy of items within each of the options mentioned in the previous paragraphs, as well as any of the system file contents.

The Utilities pull-down menu enables the user to view memory allocation through the Memory Block Display option. Memory contents can also be viewed with the option Memory Browser. The menu includes a Test Printer option as well, which can print an ASCII chart with the symbols and their decimal equivalents if a printer is connected.

The Help pull-down menu shows version and copyright information.

Using CheckIt

The CheckIt diagnostic program can be executed as a single module from the DOS command line to test a specific section of the system. This program can also be run collectively through the GUI depicted in Figure 3.7. The program includes modules to test the following:

- Serial port(s)
- Floppy-disk drive(s)
- Hard-disk drive(s)
- Parallel port(s)
- System board components
- Memory
- Video operation

CheckIt also provides utilities to perform the following tasks: save/restore CMOS settings to/from disk, save device drivers to disk, collect configuration information, calibrate a joystick, and run a virus-detection program. When any of the test applications are executed, they produce a report that lists the results of the test.

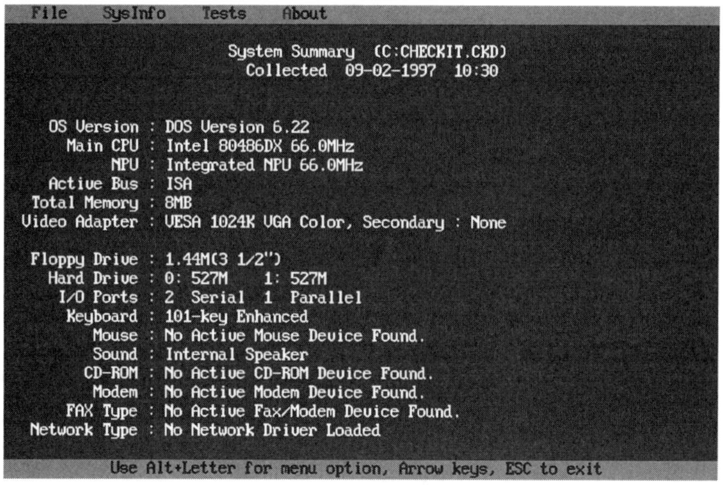

FIGURE 3.7

The CheckIt program screen.

```
 File    SysInfo    Tests    About

                    System Summary  (C:CHECKIT.CKD)
                       Collected   09-02-1997  10:30


     OS Version : DOS Version 6.22
       Main CPU : Intel 80486DX 66.0MHz
            MPU : Integrated MPU 66.0MHz
     Active Bus : ISA
   Total Memory : 8MB
  Video Adapter : VESA 1024K VGA Color, Secondary : None

   Floppy Drive : 1.44M(3 1/2")
     Hard Drive : 0: 527M    1: 527M
      I/O Ports : 2  Serial  1  Parallel
       Keyboard : 101-key Enhanced
          Mouse : No Active Mouse Device Found.
          Sound : Internal Speaker
         CD-ROM : No Active CD-ROM Device Found.
          Modem : No Active Modem Device Found.
       FAX Type : No Active Fax/Modem Device Found.
   Network Type : No Network Driver Loaded

            Use Alt+Letter for menu option, Arrow keys, ESC to exit
```

One of the most interesting features of this program is its capability to customize the test procedure with the use of batch files. The program includes three of these batch files, which script three common test situations. The tests are called Quick test, Certification test, and Burn-in test. The tests vary according to the sections of the system tested and the number of iterations for the testing of each section.

An additional set of programs titled Sysinfo provides a wealth of information concerning the system's setup and performance. This information is particularly valuable when upgrading or installing a new option. The bank of programs enables you to evaluate the performance of the system before and after system changes so that maximum performance standards can be set.

Executing Command-Line Programs

The individual CheckIt programs are executed directly from the DOS command line. The list in Table 3.2 describes the individual program modules included with CheckIt.

Table 3.2 *CheckIt Command Line Programs*

Program	Descriptions
CKCMOS.EXE	Save and restore CMOS settings utility
CKCOM.EXE	COM port test
CKDATA.EXE	Configuration collection utility
CKDRIVER.EXE	Save device driver utility
CKFD.EXE	Floppy drive test
CKHD.EXE	Hard drive test
CKLPT.EXE	LPT port test
CKMEDIA.EXE	Data integrity test
CKMEM.EXE	Memory test
CKRUN.EXE	Batch file execution utility
CKSYS.EXE	System board test
CKVID.EXE	Video test

Executing the GUI Program

If multiple tests are to be executed, it may be easier to use the CheckIt programs collectively. This involves executing the GUI program included with the program. From the graphical interface, you can choose which tests should be run. Most of the parameters are specified before the test is actually executed. When the program starts, it enables you to collect data about that particular computer and then it makes note of the microprocessor type, installed hardware, I/O address map, size and type of drives, and so on. After the data has been collected, it can be saved and loaded into CheckIt the next time the program is executed on that computer.

The GUI main screen operates with pull-down menus, as illustrated in Figure 3.8. On the main screen is a summary of the system's information that was collected when the program started. The pull-down menus are manipulated by the keyboard. Use the ALT key (press and release) to highlight the menu bar, and use the ARROW keys to select a particular menu and a menu option.

FIGURE 3.8

The CheckIt GUI main screen.

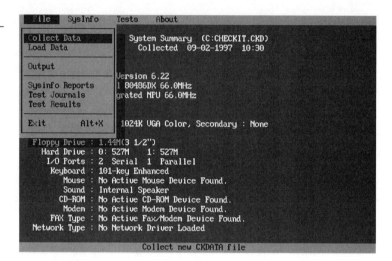

Using PC-Check

Another popular software diagnostic tool is PC-Check, which enables the technician to check system configuration and operation. This tool tests each part of the system and indicates those areas that do not respond correctly. As with other software diagnostic packages, PC-Check requires a working system core, a functional microprocessor, a functional floppy drive, and the display unit.

The types of tests run on the system are somewhat similar to those found in the CheckIt software described in the previous section. PC-Check's Main Menu is depicted in Figure 3.9. The Main Menu is the gateway to information about the system's makeup and configuration, and it serves as the entryway to the PC-Check Advanced Diagnostic Test functions. Utilities for performing low-level formats on older hard drive types and for managing SCSI interface devices are provided through this menu. Additionally, options to print or show test results are available here, as is the exit point from the program.

The first option is the System Information Menu. This option provides access to the system's main functional blocks, as described in Figure 3.10. The menu's IRQ Information, I/O Port Information, and Device Drivers options are valuable aids in locating configuration conflicts.

FIGURE 3.9

The PC-Check main menu.

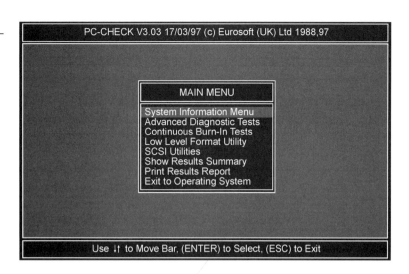

The Advanced Diagnostics Tests selection from the main menu performs extended tests in 13 system areas. These tests, listed in Figure 3.11, contain several lower-level tests that can be selected from submenus. Error notices and diagnostic comments appear on the display in the form of overlay boxes.

FIGURE 3.10

The PC-Check System Information menu.

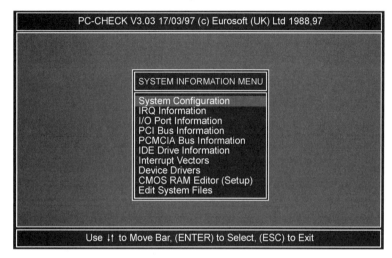

FIGURE 3.11

The Advanced Diagnostics Tests section.

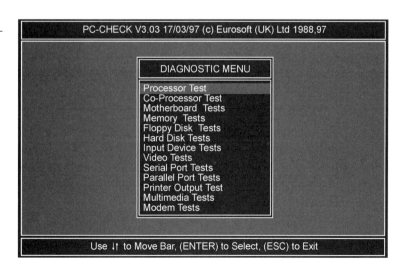

Similar to the other software diagnostic packages, PC-Check performs a number of tests on the floppy drive (5), hard drive (6), input devices (4), display adapter (10), serial ports (1), and parallel ports (1). In addition to these fundamental software tests, PC-Check includes tests for multimedia-related devices such as CD-ROMs to cover both access time and transfer performance, both of which affect the multimedia performance of the system. The multimedia tests also check the system's speaker and sound card capabilities.

For enterprises that repair computers, or for those that build computers from parts, the PC-Check Continuous Burn-In test is a valuable tool. After the system has been built or repaired, this function of the program runs continuous test on the system for an extended (burn-in) period of time without intervention from a technician or operator.

The tests performed are similar to the selections from the main menu. However, these tests are normally used for reliability testing instead of general troubleshooting. Different parts of the system can be selected for the burn-in tests. Because the burn-in tests are meant to be run unattended, the user must be careful to select only tests that apply to hardware that actually exists. PC-Check keeps track of how many times each test has been run and how often it failed during the designated burn-in period. This information is displayed on the monitor, as depicted in Figure 3.12.

FIGURE 3.12

The Burn-In Test report.

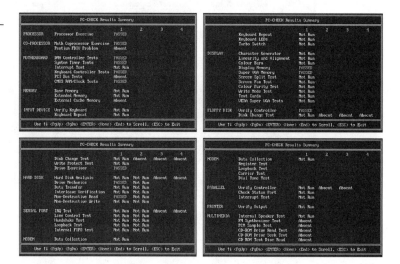

Hardware Troubleshooting

Unfortunately, most software diagnostics packages do not lead to specific components that have failed. Indeed, you may not even be able to use a software package to isolate faults if major components of the system are inoperative. If software and configuration problems have been eliminated, you will need to pull out the test equipment and check the system's internal hardware for proper operation under controlled conditions.

Turn the power off and remove any peripheral devices from the system one at a time. Make sure to restore the power and then retry the system after each peripheral is removed. If all the peripherals have been removed and the problem persists, it will be necessary to troubleshoot the basic components of the system. This usually involves checking the components inside the system unit.

Performing Quick Tests

After you've removed the cover of the system unit, perform a careful visual inspection of its interior.

Look for signs of overheating, such as charred components or wires. When electronic components overheat, they produce a noticeable odor, so you may be able to do some troubleshooting with your nose. If you do find an overheated component, especially a resistor, don't assume that the problem can be cleared up by simply replacing the burnt component. Many times a failed component may cause another component to fail.

A very quick check of the system's integrated circuits can be made by simply touching the tops of the chips with your finger to see if they're hot.

Because the board may contain MOS (Metal Oxide Semiconductor) devices, you'll want to ground yourself before performing this test. This can be done by touching an exposed portion of the unit's chassis, such as the top of the power supply.

If the system has power applied to it, all the ICs should be warm. Some will be warmer than others by nature, but if a chip burns your finger, it probably needs to be replaced. But simply replacing the chip may not clear up your problem. Instead, you may end up with two dead chips: the original and the replacement. The original chip may have been wiped out by some other problem in the system. For this reason, this quick test should be used only to localize problems.

Other items to check include components and internal connections that may have come loose. Check for foreign objects that may have fallen through the device's air vents. Remove any dust build-up that may have accumulated, and then retry the system.

FRU Troubleshooting

Field Replaceable Units (FRUs) are the portions of the system that can be conveniently replaced in the field.

Typical microcomputer FRUs are depicted in Figure 3.13. FRU troubleshooting involves isolating a problem within one section of the system. A section consists of one device, such as a keyboard, video display, video adapter card, I/O adapter card, system board, disk drive, printer, and so on. This is the level of troubleshooting most often performed on PCs. Due to the relatively low cost of computer components, it is normally not practical to troubleshoot failed components to the IC level. The cost of using a technician to diagnose the problem and repair it can quickly exceed the cost of the new replacement unit.

After a hardware error has been indicated, start troubleshooting the problem by exchanging components (cards, drives, and so on) with known good ones.

FIGURE 3.13

The typical FRUs of a microcomputer system.

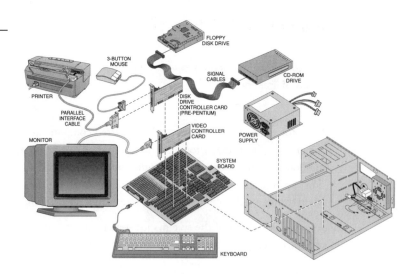

When exchanging system components, be sure to replace the device being removed with another of exactly the same type. Just because two components have the same function does not mean that they can be substituted for each other: For example, an EGA video adapter card cannot be used to replace a monochrome adapter card without making other modifications to the system. Interchanging similar parts is possible in some cases, and not in others. Whether two components can be exchanged depends on the particular modules.

Assume that only a single component has failed. The odds against more than one component failing at the same time are extremely high. At the point where the system's operation is restored, you can assume that the last component removed was defective.

If it is necessary to disconnect cables or connectors from boards, take the time to mark the cables and their connection points so that they will be easy to identify later. The simplest method of marking cables is to place identification marks on tape (masking or athletic) and then attach the tape to the cables and connection points.

Match the markings on the cable with the markings at its connection point. At many connection points, the color of the wire connected to a certain pin may be important. When placing the identifying marks on the tape, you may wish to note the color arrangement of the wires being disconnected so that you can be sure of getting them back in their proper places after the component swap has been performed.

Always check cabling connections after plugging them in. Look for missed connections, bent pins, and other indications of trouble. Also check the routing of cables. Try to establish connections that do not place unnecessary strain on the cable, and route cables away from ICs as much as possible. Some ICs, such as microprocessors, can become quite hot and could eventually damage cables. Avoid routing cables near cooling fans as well.

It is often helpful to simply reseat (remove and reinstall) connections and adapter cards in the expansion slots when a problem occurs. Corrosion may build up on the computer's connection points and cause poor electrical contact. By reseating the connection, the contact problem often disappears.

> Make certain to take the time to document the symptoms associated with the problem, including all the tests you make and any changes that occur during the tests. This information can keep you from making repetitive steps.

> After you have isolated the problem and the computer boots up and runs correctly, work backward through the troubleshooting routines, reinstalling any original boards and other components removed during the troubleshooting process.

These steps should be performed one at a time until all the original parts have been reinstalled except the last one removed. In this way, you will be able to make certain that only one failure occurred in the machine. If the system fails after installing a new card, check the card's default configuration settings against the devices already installed in the system.

Special Troubleshooting Procedures

This section contains three important procedures: isolating power supply problems, troubleshooting dead systems, and isolating undefined problems.

The power supply unit does not need to be developed from a conceptual point. Instead, it is treated as a simple passive FRU. The procedures for a dead system and for undefined problems do not correspond to a single topic that can be expanded as described. Instead, these procedures can involve most of the components in the system.

Isolating Power Supply Problems

A+ CORE 1.2

Typical symptoms associated with power supply failures include the following:

▶ No indicator lights visible, with no disk drive action and no display on the screen. Nothing works; the system is dead.

▶ The ON/OFF indicator lights are visible, but there is no disk drive action and no display on the monitor screen. The system fan may or may not run.

▶ A continuous beep tone is produced by the system.

The power supply unit is one of the few components in the system that is connected to virtually every other component in the system. Therefore, it has the potential to affect all the other components if it fails. Figure 3.14 illustrates the interconnections of the power supply unit with the other components in the system.

When tracking down power supply problems, it's important to remember that in addition to the obvious power connections shown in the diagram, the power supply also delivers power to other components through the system board. These include (1) all the options adapter cards (through the expansion-slot connectors) and (2) the keyboard (through the keyboard connector). Power supply problems can cause symptoms to occur in all these areas, and problems in any areas can affect the operation of the power supply.

Checking a Dead System

Special consideration must be taken when a system is inoperable. A totally inoperable system exhibits no symptoms to give clues where to begin the isolation process. In addition, it is impossible to use troubleshooting software or other system aids to help isolate the problem.

The following discussion describes a standard method of troubleshooting dead microprocessor-based equipment. The first step in troubleshooting any dead system is to visually inspect the system. Check for unseated cards, loose cables, or foreign objects within the system unit.

FIGURE 3.14

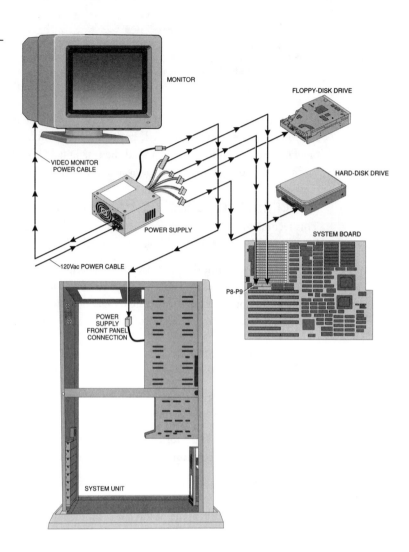

Power supply interconnections.

When the system shows no sign of life—including the absence of lights—the best place to start looking for the problem is at the power supply because the operation of this unit affects virtually every part of the system. Also, the absence of any lights usually indicates that no power is being supplied to the system by the power supply.

Begin by checking the external connections of the power supply. Confirm that the power supply cord is plugged into a functioning outlet. Check the position of the ON/OFF switch. Examine the power cord for good connection at the rear of the unit. Check the setting of the 110/220 switch setting on the outside of the power supply.

If power is reaching the power supply and nothing is happening, the next step in isolating the cause of the problem is to remove the peripheral devices so that only the basic system must be checked. Divide the system into basic and optional sections for testing. Remove all external options from the system, and restart the system. If the system begins to work, troubleshoot the optional portions of the system.

Finally, divide the basic system into optional and basic components. Remove all optional adapter cards from their expansion slots, and restart the system. If the system begins to work, troubleshoot the various options adapters by reinstalling them one at a time until the system fails again.

Before changing any board or connection, always turn the system OFF first.

Isolating Undefined Problems

Normally, symptoms can be divided into three sections. These include configuration problems, boot-up problems, and operational problems.

The system's configuration settings are normally checked first. It is important to observe the system's symptoms to determine the part of the system's operation in which the fault occurs. Error messages typically associated with configuration problems include the following:

- CMOS Display Type Mismatch
- CMOS Memory Size Mismatch
- CMOS Battery State Low
- CMOS Checksum Failure
- CMOS System Options Not Set
- CMOS Time and Date Not Set

These errors occur and are reported before the single beep tone is produced at the end of the POST routines.

After the tone is produced, the system shifts over to the process of booting up. Typical error messages associated with boot-up problems include the following:

- General Failure Error Reading Drive x
- Bad or Missing Command Interpreter
- Non-System Disk or Disk Error
- Bad File Allocation Table

Either type of problem can be caused by a hardware problem. If no configuration settings are incorrect but the symptoms are present, then a hardware problem is indicated. Likewise, boot-up problems are typically associated with the operating system. However, hardware can also produce these symptoms.

Nonclassified Problems

Some problems simply refuse to be classified under any particular symptom. If a multiple failure occurs, or if one failure causes a second failure to occur, the symptoms produced by the computer may not point to any particular cause. Secondary problems may also hide the symptoms of the real failure.

It is best to simply begin with some logical starting point and work through the entire system until the problem is cured.

The system may be made up of the basic computer, monitor, and keyboard, or it may be a highly developed combination of equipment, involving the basic computer and a group of peripherals. For troubleshooting purposes, the system should be divided into logically related subsections.

The first division naturally falls between the components that make up the basic system and other devices. The basic system consists of the system unit, the keyboard, and the video display monitor. Other devices consist of components that are optional as far as the system's operation is concerned. These items can be removed from the system without changing its basic operation. They include such equipment as printers, mice, digitizing tablets, hard-disk drives, tape drives, scanners, and so on.

Optional devices should be the first items removed from the system when a problem occurs. This divides the system in half and determines whether the problem exists in one of the computer's main components or in one of its options.

The second logical division falls between the internal and external options. In cases where you have no idea of what the problem is, all external devices should be tested before removing the outer cover to check internal devices.

Inside the system unit, the next dividing point exists between the system board and all the internal options. The first items to be removed from the system are the options adapters, except for the disk drive and video controller cards. These cards should be checked only if the system still won't work properly with the other options adapters removed.

The next components to exchange are the floppy drives and the power supply unit, in that order. The system board is the last logical and most difficult component to exchange. Therefore, it should be the last component in the system to be exchanged.

Operating Systems Troubleshooting

An interesting troubleshooting point occurs at the single beep in the boot-up process. If the system produces an error message, such as "The system has detected unstable RAM at location XXXX," or a beep-coded error signal before the beep, the problem is hardware-related. In this example, a bad memory device is indicated. Conversely, if the error message or beep code is produced after the beep, the problem is likely to be associated with the operating system.

Troubleshooting an operating system problem involves the same steps as any other logical troubleshooting procedure. The steps are simply adapted to fit the structure of the operating system. Analyze the symptoms displayed, isolate the error conditions, correct the problem, and test the repair.

When dealing with a disk operating system, three tools can be very useful in isolating the cause of operating system problems. These tools are system log files, clean boot disks, and single-step startup procedures. The preliminary steps involved in troubleshooting operating system problems are as follows:

1. Try to reboot the system.

2. Check system log files, if available.

3. Perform a clean boot with minimal configuration settings.

4. Perform a single step boot-up to isolate driver problems.

Key Points Review

This chapter has covered the following fundamental troubleshooting tools and techniques.

- It is normal practice to first set the meter to its highest voltage range to make certain that the voltage level being measured does not damage the meter.

- Unlike the voltage check, resistance checks are always made after power has been removed from the system.

- One of the first things to do if you are not personally familiar with the system is to eliminate the user as a possible source of the problem.

- Check all externally accessible switch settings.

- Carefully watching the steps of a boot-up procedure can reveal a lot about the nature of problems in a system. Faulty areas can be included or excluded from possible causes of errors during the boot-up process.

- A special category exists for problems that tend to occur whenever a new hardware option is added to the system, or when the system is used for the very first time. These problems are called setup problems and are due to mismatches between the system's programmed configuration and the actual equipment installed in the system.

- After you've removed the cover of the system unit, perform a careful visual inspection of its interior.

- Field Replaceable Units (FRUs) are the portions of the system that can be conveniently replaced in the field.

- After a hardware error has been indicated, start troubleshooting the problem by exchanging components (such as cards and drives) with known good ones.

- After you have isolated the problem and the computer boots up and runs correctly, work backward through the troubleshooting routines, reinstalling any original boards and other components removed during the troubleshooting process.

- Special consideration must be taken when a system is inoperable. A totally inoperable system displays no symptoms to give clues where to begin the isolation process. In addition, it is impossible to use troubleshooting software or other system aids to help isolate the problem.

- Some problems simply refuse to be classified under any particular symptom. If a multiple failure occurs, or if one failure causes a second failure to occur, the symptoms produced by the computer may not point to any particular cause. Secondary problems may also hide the symptoms of the real failure.

- An interesting troubleshooting point occurs at the single beep in the boot-up process. If the system produces an error message or beep-code signal before the beep, the problem is hardware-related. Conversely, if the error message or beep-code signal is produced after the beep, the problem is likely to be associated with the operating system.

At this point, review the objectives listed at the beginning of the chapter to be certain that you understand and can perform each item listed there. Afterward, answer the review questions that follow to verify your knowledge of the information.

Multiple Choice Questions

1. If an error occurs before the single beep tone in the boot-up sequence, what type of failure is probable?

   a. The problem is probably associated with the operating system.

   b. The BIOS code has become corrupted.

   c. A setup or configuration problem has occurred.

   d. The problem is hardware related.

2. If an error occurs after the single beep in the boot-up process, what type of problem is likely?

   a. The problem is probably associated with the operating system.

   b. The BIOS code has become corrupted.

   c. A setup or configuration problem has occurred.

   d. The problem is hardware related.

3. If the system refuses to boot after a new component is installed, what type of problem is normally assumed?

    a. The problem is probably associated with the operating system.

    b. The BIOS code has become corrupted.

    c. A setup or configuration problem has occurred.

    d. A hardware-related problem has occurred.

4. What component has the potential to affect the operation of all the other sections of the computer system?

    a. The power supply

    b. The ROM BIOS

    c. The microprocessor

    d. The system board

5. What function and reading would be appropriate for checking a system's speaker?

    a. Infinity

    b. Near zero ohms

    c. 4 ohms

    d. 8 ohms

6. What type of problem is indicated by a continuous beep tone from the system?

    a. A power supply failure

    b. An undefined problem

    c. A configuration problem

    d. A boot-up problem

7. If a system appears to be completely dead, what item should logically be checked first?

    a. The system board

    b. The microprocessor

    c. The hard-disk drive

    d. The power supply

8. The error message "Bad File Allocation Table" indicates _____ problem.

    a. an operating system

    b. a runtime

    c. a configuration

    d. a boot-up

9. If a "CMOS Display Type Mismatch" message appears on the screen, what type of error is indicated?

    a. An operating system problem

    b. A runtime error

    c. A setup or configuration problem

    d. A boot-up failure

10. Which of the following is not normally considered an FRU?

    a. A system board

    b. A floppy-disk drive

    c. A power supply

    d. A video controller IC

Review Questions

1. If the system issues a single beep and the C:\> prompt appears on the screen, what condition is indicated?

2. List the three important tools used to isolate operating system problems.

3. List three situations that would normally require that the CMOS Setup routines be run.

4. What type of problem is indicated by a "Strike F1 to continue" message during booting?

5. What is the recommended method of using a digital multimeter to check voltage in a computer system?

6. If the system functions correctly after all the optional equipment has been removed, what action should be taken next?

7. If you are replacing components one at a time and the system suddenly begins working properly, what can be assumed?

8. List three items commonly tested using the resistance function of a multimeter.

9. What action should be taken first if a software failure is suspected?

10. What resistance reading would normally be expected from a fuse if it is functional?

11. If you are measuring across a capacitor on the system board with a DMM, what voltage reading would you normally expect to see from a DMM?

12. Which noncomputer possibility should be eliminated early in the troubleshooting process?

13. To what range should the voltage function of a DMM be set for an initial measurement?

14. When would a POST card normally be used?

15. Where are loopback plugs used?

Lab Exercises

The lab manual that accompanies this book contains hands-on lab procedures that reinforce and test your knowledge of the theory materials presented in this chapter. Now that you have completed your review of this chapter, refer to the lab manual and perform Procedures 7, "Symptoms"; 8, "MSD"; 10, "PC-Check"; 9, "CheckIt"; 18, "Isolating Power Supply Problems"; 17, "System Inoperable"; 15, "Undefined Problem Isolation"; and 11, "POST Cards."

SYSTEM SOFTWARE

PART II

OPERATING SYSTEMS

LEARNING OBJECTIVES

Upon completion of this chapter and its related lab procedures, you should be able to perform these tasks:

1. Describe the two basic types of operating systems.

2. Define multiuser, multitasking, and multiprocessor operations.

3. Describe the series of events that occurs when power is applied to the system.

4. Configure the system through CMOS Setup procedures.

5. List the events that occur during the boot-up process.

6. Explain the basic organization of a DOS disk.

7. Describe the operation of the DOS command line.

8. Discuss naming conventions as they apply to various types of files.

9. Describe methods of bypassing and correcting inoperable DOS startup sequences.

10. Use the DOS Mode command to test standard I/O ports.

11. Describe different types of DOS memory.

12. Use the AUTOEXEC.BAT and CONFIG.SYS files to optimize system performance.

13. Load driver software for devices added to the system.

14. Describe steps for troubleshooting DOS problems.

15. Edit the AUTOEXEC.BAT and CONFIG.SYS files for troubleshooting purposes.

CHAPTER 4

Introduction

Chapter 1, "Microcomputer Fundamentals," described the general responsibilities of an operating system. This chapter investigates operating systems in greater depth. The first half of the chapter deals with the foundation of the operating system—the BIOS. This topic is discussed in four sections: power-on self-tests and system initialization, the process of booting up to the operating system, system configuration, and BIOS functions.

The second half of the chapter deals with Disk Operating Systems (DOS). In this section, the structure of DOS systems is explored along with typical DOS disk organization. The commands and utilities available through the DOS command line are also presented.

Operating Systems

> Literally thousands of different operating systems are in use with microcomputers. The complexity of each operating system typically depends on the complexity of the application the microcomputer is designed to fill.

The operating system for a fuel mixture controller in an automobile is relatively simple, while an operating system for a multiuser computer system that controls many terminals is relatively complex.

The complete operating system for the fuel controller could be stored in a single small ROM device. It would likely take control of the unit as soon as power is applied, reset the system, and test it. During normal operation, the operating system monitors the sensor inputs for accelerator setting, humidity, and other factors and adjusts the air/fuel mixing valves according to predetermined values stored in ROM. The fuel mixture controller is depicted in Figure 4.1.

FIGURE 4.1

A simple fuel/air mixture controller.

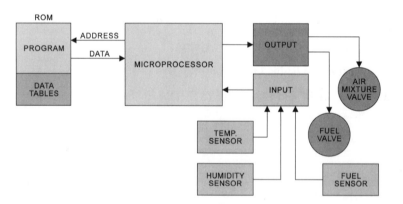

In the large, multiple-user system, the operating system likely is stored on disk and has sections loaded into RAM when needed. As illustrated in Figure 4.2, this type of operating system must control several pieces of hardware, manage files created and used by various users, provide security for each user's information, and manage communications between different stations. The operating system must also be responsible for presenting each station with a user interface that can accept commands and data from the user. This interface can be a command-line interpreter or a Graphical User Interface (GUI).

FIGURE 4.2

A multiuser system.

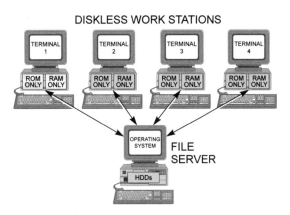

Complex operating systems typically contain several millions of lines of computer instruction. Due to this complexity, large operating systems are typically written in modules that handle the various responsibilities assigned to the system. The operating system for the fuel mixture controller is most likely a single module. However, the operating system for the multiple-user system would likely consist of a core module (called the *kernel*), a task manager, a scheduler, a local file manager, and a host of other manager modules.

Two basic types of operating systems exist:

▶ Single process systems

▶ Multiple process systems

In a single process system, the operating system works with a single task only. These operating systems can operate in **batch mode** or **interactive mode**. In batch mode, the operating system runs one program until it is finished. In interactive mode, the operation of the program can be modified by input from external sources. The simple program presented with the $1.98 computer is an example of a batch mode operating system. If a mechanism were added to the $1.98 so that program jumps could be caused by data from an external entry during the execution of the program, it would then become an interactive system.

In multiple process systems, the operating system is designed so that it can appear to work on several **tasks** simultaneously. A task is a portion of a program under execution. Computer programs are made up of several tasks that may work alone or as a unit. Tasks, in turn, can be made up of several **threads** that can be worked on separately. A thread is a section of programming that can be time-sliced by the operating system to run at the same time that other threads are being executed.

The multiple process system breaks the tasks associated with a process into various threads for execution. Typically, one thread may handle video output, another may handle mouse input, and another may handle output from the printer.

Multiple process operations can be organized in three different ways:

▶ Multiuser

▶ Multitasking

▶ Multiprocessor

These three types of operating systems are described in Figure 4.3.

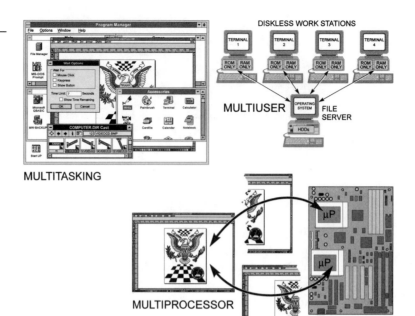

FIGURE 4.3

Multiple process operating systems.

MULTITASKING

MULTIPROCESSOR

> In multiuser and multitasking operations, the appearance of simultaneous operation is accomplished by switching between different tasks in a predetermined order. The multiuser system switches between different users at multiple locations, and multitasking systems switch between different applications at a single location.

In both cases, the information concerning the first task must be stored, and information about the new task must be loaded each time a task switch occurs. The operating system's scheduler module is responsible for overseeing the switching function. In a multiprocessor operating system, tasks are divided among multiple microprocessors. This type of operation is referred to as **parallel processing**.

Simple microcomputers store the entire operating system in ROM, but most microcomputers use a **bootstrapping** process to load the operating system into RAM. Bootstrapping describes an arrangement in which the operating system is loaded into memory by a smaller program called the **bootstrap loader**. The operating system can be loaded from a ROM chip, a floppy disk, a hard-disk drive, or from another computer. The term *bootstrap* refers to the system pulling itself up by its own bootstraps; in loading the more powerful operating system files from the disk, the system has increased its onboard intelligence considerably. In personal computers, the bootstrap operation is one of the functions of the ROM BIOS.

Basic Input/Output Systems

PC system boards use one or two IC chips to hold the system's BIOS firmware. The system's memory map reserves memory locations from E0000h to FFFFFh for the system board BIOS routines. These chips contain the programs that handle system startup, the changeover to disk-based operations, video and printer output functions, and a **Power-On Self-Test** (**POST**).

POST Tests and Initialization

> The POST test is actually a series of tests that is performed each time the system is turned on. The different tests check the operation of the microprocessor, the keyboard, the video display, the floppy- and hard-disk drive units, and the RAM and ROM memory units.

When the system board is reset, or when power is removed from it, the system begins generating clock pulses when power is restored. This action applies a RESET pulse to the microprocessor, causing it to clear most of its registers to 0. However, the system sets the instruction pointer register to 0FFF0h and the CS register to F0000h. The first instruction is taken from location FFFF0h. Notice that this address is located in the ROM BIOS program; this is not coincidental. When the system is started up, the microprocessor must begin taking instructions from this ROM location to initialize the system for operation.

POST Tests and Initialization

The first instruction that the microprocessor executes causes it to jump to the POST tests, where it performs standard tests such as the **ROM BIOS check sum test** (that verifies that the BIOS program is accurate) and the system's various **DRAM tests** (that verify the bits of the memory), as well as testing the system's CMOS RAM (to make certain that its contents have not changed due to a battery failure). During the memory tests, the POST displays a running memory count to show that it is testing and verifying the individual memory locations.

Sequentially, the system's interrupts are disabled, the bits of the microprocessor's flag register are set, and a Read/Write test is performed on each of its internal registers. The test program simply writes a predetermined bit pattern into each register and then reads it back to verify the register's operation. After verifying the operation of the microprocessor's registers, the BIOS program begins testing and initializing the rest of the system. The program moves forward by inspecting the ROM BIOS chip itself; it does this by performing a check sum test of certain locations on the chip and then comparing the answer with a known value stored in another location.

A check sum test involves adding the values stored in the key locations together. The result is a rounded sum of the values. When the check sum test is performed, the sum of the locations is recalculated and compared to the stored value. If they match, no error is assumed to have occurred. If not, an error condition exists and an error message or beep code is produced.

At this point, the program checks to see whether the system is being started from an off condition, or whether it is being reset from some other state. When the system is started from an off condition, a cold boot is being performed. However, simultaneously pressing the CTRL, ALT, and DEL keys while the system is in operation generates a reset signal in the system and causes it to perform a shortened boot-up routine. This operation is referred to as a warm boot and allows the system to be shut down and restarted without turning it off. This function also allows the computer's operation to be switched to another operating system.

If power was applied to the system prior to the occurrence of the RESET signal, some of the POST's memory tests are skipped.

If a cold boot is indicated, the program tests the first 16KB of RAM memory by writing five different bit patterns into the memory and then reading them back to establish the validity of each location. The BIOS start-up steps are illustrated in Figure 4.4.

FIGURE 4.4

The Startup sequence.

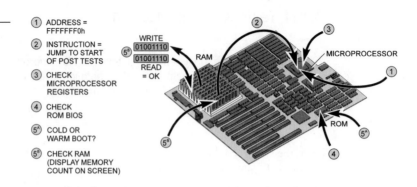

① ADDRESS = FFFFFFF0h

② INSTRUCTION = JUMP TO START OF POST TESTS

③ CHECK MICROPROCESSOR REGISTERS

④ CHECK ROM BIOS

⑤ᴬ COLD OR WARM BOOT?

⑤ᴮ CHECK RAM (DISPLAY MEMORY COUNT ON SCREEN)

System Initialization

> If the first 16KB of RAM successfully pass all five of the bit-pattern tests, the BIOS routine initializes the system's intelligent devices. During this part of the program, start-up values stored in the ROM chip are moved into the system's programmable devices to make them functional.

The BIOS loads starting information into all the system's standard AT-compatible components, such as the interrupt, DMA, keyboard, and video controllers, as well as its timer/counter circuits. The program checks the DMA controller by performing an R/W test on each of its internal registers and then initializes them with start-up values.

The program continues by setting up the system's interrupt controller. This includes moving the system's interrupt vectors into address locations 00000h through 003FFh. In addition, an R/W test is performed on each of the interrupt controller's internal registers. The routine then causes the controller to mask (disable) all its interrupt inputs and then test each one to assure that no interrupts occur.

The programming of the interrupt controller is significant because most of the events in a PC-compatible system are interrupt-driven. The operation of the interrupt controller affects the operation of the computer in every phase from this point forward. Every peripheral or software routine that needs special services from the system makes use of the interrupt controller.

Following the initialization of the interrupt controller, the program checks the output of the system's timer/counter channels. It does this by counting pulses from the counters for a given period of time to verify that the proper frequencies are being produced.

If the timer/counter frequencies are correct, the routine initializes and starts the video controller. The program obtains information about the type of display (monochrome, color, or both) being used with the system by reading configuration information from registers in the system's CMOS RAM. After this has been established, the program conducts R/W tests on the video adapter's RAM memory. If the video adapter passes all these tests, the program causes a cursor symbol to be displayed on the monitor. The steps of the initialization process are described in Figure 4.5.

Additional POST Checks

After the display adapter has been checked, the BIOS routine resumes testing the system's onboard memory. First, R/W testing is performed on all the additional RAM on the system board (beyond the first 16KB). In addition, the BIOS executes the system's built-in setup program to configure its day/time setting, its hard- and floppy-disk drive types, and the amount of memory actually available to the system.

FIGURE 4.5

System initialization.

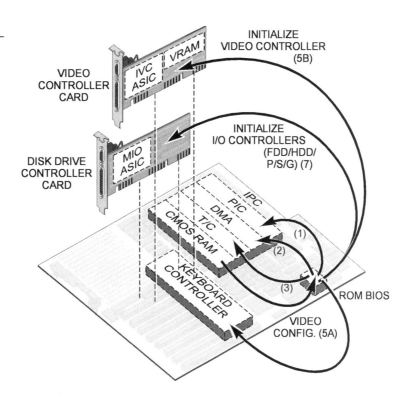

Following the final memory test, the remaining I/O devices and adapters are tested. The program begins by enabling the keyboard circuitry and checking for a scan code from the keyboard. The absence of a scan code indicates that no key has been depressed. The program then proceeds to test the system's parallel printer and RS-232C serial ports. In each case, the test consists of performing R/W tests on each of the port's registers, storing the addresses of functional ports (some ports may not be installed or in use), and storing time limitations for each port's operation. The steps of the POST process are described in Figure 4.6.

FIGURE 4.6

Completion of the POST test.

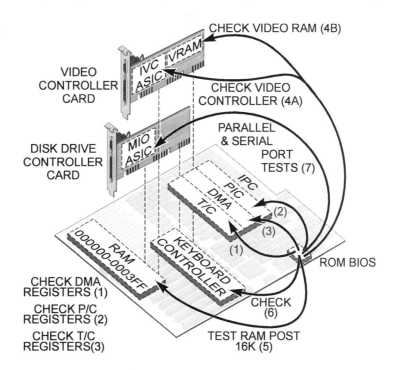

BIOS Extensions

After the initialization and POST tests are completed, the BIOS checks the area of memory between C0000h and DFFFFh for BIOS extension programs.

IBM system designers created this memory area so that new or nonstandard BIOS routines could be added to the basic BIOS structure. These extended firmware routines match software commands from the system to the hardware they support. Therefore, the software running on the system does not have to be directly compatible with the hardware.

BIOS extensions are created in 512-byte blocks that must begin at a 2KB marker (such as C8000h, C8200h, C8400h, C8800h, and so on), as illustrated in Figure 4.7. A single extension can occupy multiple blocks, but it can start only at one of the markers. When the main BIOS encounters the special 2-byte extension code at one of the 2KB markers, it tests the block of code and then turns control over to the extension. Upon completion of the extension code, control is passed back to the main BIOS, which then checks for an extension marker at the next 2KB marker.

Although the extension addresses are memory addresses, the extension code may be located anywhere in the system. In particular, BIOS extensions are often located on expansion cards. The system simply accesses them through the expansion bus.

FIGURE 4.7

BIOS extension blocks.

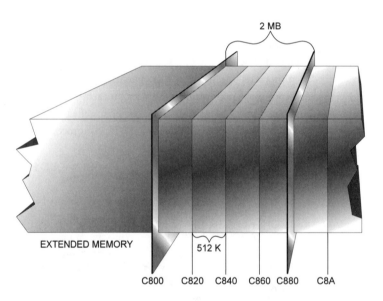

Advanced video cards contain video BIOS code, either in a ROM IC or built directly into the video controller ASIC. The IBM EGA and VGA standards allow for onboard ROM that uses addresses between C0000h and C7FFFh.

Likewise, different types of HDD controller cards contain a BIOS extension IC. The HDD controllers in XT units had BIOS extensions that used the address space between C8000h and C9FFFh. Some current HDD controllers, such as ESDI and SCSI adapters (described in Chapter 8, "Magnetic Storage") reserve memory blocks between C8000h and CBFFFh.

Another type of device that commonly uses the C000h–D000h blocks are network adapter cards. With these cards, the computer can be connected to other computers in the local area. The BIOS extension code on a network card may contain an **Initial Program Load** (**IPL**) routine that causes the local computer to load up and operate from the operating system of a remote computer. Refer to the boot-up section of this chapter and the networking information in Chapter 11, "Data Communications," for more information about these BIOS extensions.

The system can accommodate as many extensions as will mathematically fit within the allotted memory area. However, two extension programs cannot be located in the same range of addresses. With this in mind, peripheral manufacturers typically include some method of switching the starting addresses of their BIOS extensions so that they can be set to various markers.

CMOS Setup Routines

Just prior to completing the boot-up process, PCs and PC-XTs checked a set of configuration switches on the system board to determine what types of options were being used with the system. On newer systems, the configuration information is stored on the system board in a battery-powered storage area called the CMOS RAM. Newer BIOS enable the user to have access to this configuration information through the Setup utility.

While performing its normal tests and boot-up functions, the BIOS program displays a header on the screen and shows the RAM memory count as it is being tested. Immediately following the RAM test count, the BIOS program places a prompt on the monitor screen to tell the user that the CMOS setup program can be accessed by pressing a special key, or a key combination. Typical keys and combinations include the DEL key, the ESC key, the F2 function key, the CTRL and ESC keys, and the CTRL+ALT+ESC key combination.

Arguably, the most popular BIOS in the world are those from American Megatrends Inc. (AMI). These programs uses the DEL key, but other BIOS programs may use different keys or key combinations for accessing their setup menus. If the DEL key is not depressed within a predetermined amount of time, the BIOS program continues with the boot-up process. However, if the DEL key is pressed during this time, the boot-up routine is put on hold and the program displays a CMOS Setup Selection screen similar to the one depicted in Figure 4.8.

FIGURE 4.8

A CMOS Setup Selection screen.

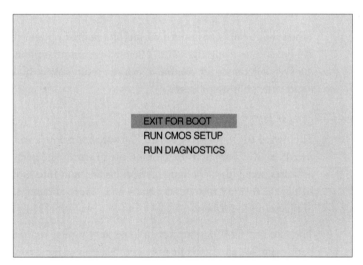

Every chipset variation has a specific BIOS designed for it. Therefore, some functions are specific to the design of system boards using that chipset. Referring to the example in the figure, three options can be selected from the screen: return to the boot-up process and continue normal operation, select the Run CMOS Setup routine, or run a built-in diagnostics program. This particular example is relatively simple. BIOS screens from other manufacturers, or for other chip sets, may have several options to consider. The example is also unusual in that it possesses a set of onboard diagnostics routines. These can be quite helpful when portions of the system are not functional, but they are not common in the industry.

If you are setting up the computer for the first time or adding new options to the system, it will be necessary to run the CMOS Configuration Setup program. The values input through the setup utility are stored in the system's CMOS Setup registers. These registers are examined each time the system is booted to tell the computer what types of devices are installed.

The AMI Configuration Setup screen is shown in Figure 4.9. Through this screen, the user enters the desired configuration values into the CMOS registers. The cursor on the screen can be moved from item to item using the keyboard's cursor control keys.

FIGURE 4.9

The CMOS Configuration Setup screen.

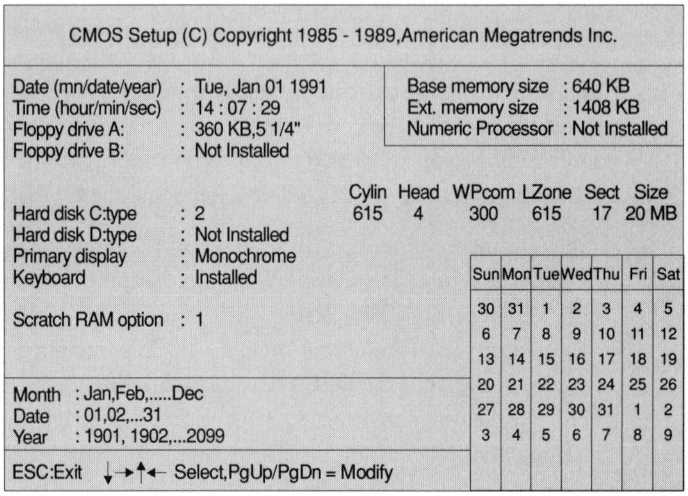

When the cursor is positioned on top of a desired option, the PgUp and PgDn cursor keys can be used to change its value. When all the proper options have been configured, pressing the ESC key causes the routine to exit the setup screen, update any changes made, and resume the boot-up process.

Other BIOS Manufacturers

The Award BIOS from the Award Software company is another widely used BIOS. An Award BIOS Configuration selection menu screen is depicted in Figure 4.10. As the menu indicates, many user-configurable options are built into modern BIOS. Unlike the AMI BIOS, the Award firmware uses the + and – keys to manipulate the settings of menu items displayed on the screen.

The standard CMOS setup screen looks very similar to the AMI screen in Figure 4.9. In both examples, the BIOS first presents a screen of basic configuration information. As both figures show, this screen typically includes information about the time and date, microprocessor, system memory organization, floppy-disk drives, hard-disk drives, and video configurations.

FIGURE 4.10

The Award BIOS Configuration
Setup screen.

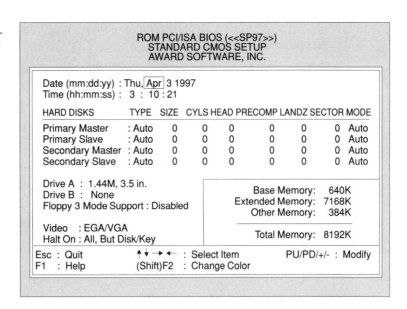

A third major BIOS is produced by Phoenix Technologies, Ltd. Its main features are identical to the AMI and Award BIOS. The main screen covers time and date, hard- and floppy-disk drives, and system memory. The Phoenix BIOS uses the F2 function key to enter the Setup function's main menu, depicted in Figure 4.11. Notice that the select keys for manipulating the Setup program are identified at the bottom of the display.

FIGURE 4.11

The Phoenix BIOS
Configuration Setup screen.

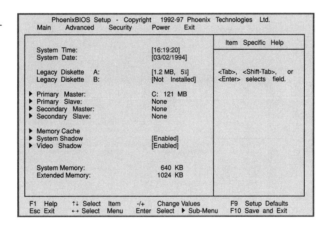

In most CMOS displays, the total memory does not equal the summation of the base and extended memory. This is due to the fact that the BIOS reserves 384KB for shadowing purposes.

The other area in this screen that typically requires some effort to set up is the HDD parameters section. All BIOS come with a list of hard drive types that they can support directly. However, they also provide a position for user-definable drive settings. Historically, this has been referred to as the Type 47 entry, but this entry may be located at any number in the list.

Advanced CMOS Setup

A second CMOS Configuration screen, referred to as the BIOS Features Setup screen or the Advanced CMOS Setup screen, provides extended user control over the configuration of the system. A relatively simple Award Features screen is illustrated in Figure 4.12. In this example, several boot-up options can be enabled in CMOS, such as the boot drive sequence and password enabling.

The boot-up sequence enables the system to boot up without checking all the drives in order. This setting may need to be adjusted to include the A: floppy drive if it becomes impossible to boot to the hard drive.

The password setting prevents users without the password from accessing the system. If the system has an unknown password, it will be necessary to clear the CMOS. Most system boards have a jumper block that can be shorted to reset the CMOS to its default settings. If this option is used, it will be necessary to re-enter the original configuration information.

On Pentium-based system boards, the configuration jumpers and switches for enabling functions have been replaced by BIOS enabling settings. These settings usually include the disk drives, keyboard, and video options, as well as onboard serial and parallel ports.

In addition, the user can turn certain sections of the system's RAM on or off for shadowing purposes, as well as establish parity or nonparity memory operation.

All of these enabling settings must be taken into account when troubleshooting the system's hardware. Incorrectly setting BIOS enabling parameters causes the corresponding hardware to fail. Therefore, be sure to check the enabling functions of the Advanced CMOS settings as a part of every hardware-configuration troubleshooting procedure.

FIGURE 4.12

The Award BIOS Features Setup screen.

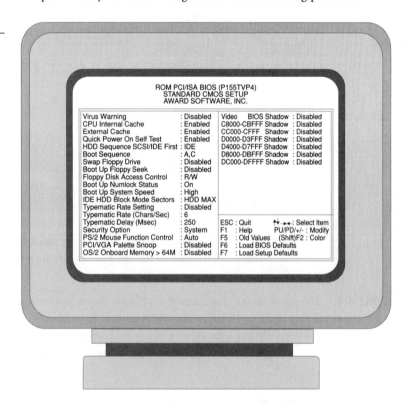

The complexity of modern system boards has created a huge number of configuration options for their BIOS. This is reflected in the complexity of their Advanced CMOS Configuration screens. Working in these screens, it is very easy to place the system in a condition in which it is unable to respond. Because the problem lies at the BIOS level, it is often difficult to get back into the CMOS to correct the problem. Therefore, system designers have included a couple of options to safeguard the system from this condition. In some BIOS, holding down the DEL key throughout startup erases the CMOS contents and starts from scratch. Jumpers also may be placed on the system board and can be set to start the contents from a bare-essentials setting. In either case, it will be necessary to rebuild any advanced features in the CMOS configuration afterward.

BIOS Entry and Exit

Even the option selection pages for newer BIOS can be complex. A typical Options page is depicted in Figure 4.13. This screen serves as the main menu for entering and exiting the CMOS Setup, as well as for moving between its configuration pages.

BIOS designers have built two options into newer BIOS to help users avoid the complexity of the advanced CMOS configuration settings. These options are Auto Configuration and Default Settings.

FIGURE 4.13

A complex entry menu.

All newer system boards have an auto-configuration mode that takes over most of the setup decisions. This option works well in the majority of applications because its settings produce an efficient, basic level of operation for standard devices in the system. However, they will not optimize the performance of the system. To do that, it is necessary to turn off the auto-configuration feature and insert desired parameters into the configuration table. Two options typically exist for the auto-configuration function: Auto Configure with Power-On Defaults, and Auto Configure with BIOS Defaults.

Using power-on defaults for auto-configuration loads the most conservative options possible into the system from the BIOS. This is the most effective method of detecting BIOS-related system problems. These settings replace any user-entered configuration information in the CMOS Setup registers. Any turbo speed mode is disabled, all memory caching is turned off, and all wait states are set to maximum. This enables the most basic part of the system to start up. If these default values fail to get the system to boot, it is an indication of hardware problems, such as incorrect jumper settings or bad hardware components.

Using auto-configuration with BIOS defaults provide a little more flexibility than the power-on option. If you have entered an improper configuration setting and cannot determine which setting is causing the problem, this option is suggested. As with the power-on option, this selection replaces the entered configuration settings with a new set of parameters from the BIOS. Choosing this option likely gets you back into the CMOS Setup screen so that you can track down the problem. This is also the recommended starting point for optimizing the system's operation.

The many configuration options available in a modern BIOS require the user to have a good deal of knowledge about the particular function being configured. Therefore, an extended discussion of the advanced CMOS setup options cannot be conducted at this point. However, such information is covered along with the system component to which it relates as the book moves through various system components.

With older Award BIOS, the CMOS Setup screen was accessed during boot-up by pressing the ESC key. However, newer versions have adopted the same DEL-key strategy used with the AMI units. The exit routine is also different in that you can either scroll through several exit options or press the F10 key to save any changes and then exit the CMOS Setup. Older units require you to press the F5 key to confirm the exit selection. The newer units require a yes or no answer to exit.

Some BIOS may also offer a wide array of exit options. Typically, though, the options all involve writing the information away in CMOS and exiting, or not writing the information to CMOS and exiting. One common mistake in working with CMOS configuration settings is not saving the new settings before exiting. When this happens, the new settings are not stored and the old settings are still in place when the system boots up.

BIOS Error Codes

A+ CORE 2.1

> If an error or setup mismatch is encountered, the BIOS issues an error code, either in message form on the display screen or in beep-coded form through the system's speaker.

Figure 4.14 defines the AMI BIOS error messages and beep codes. Likewise, the Award BIOS produces display and beep-coded error messages when a boot-up or configuration problem is encountered during the boot process.

A+ CORE 3.4

In the case of **Plug-and-Play (PnP)** systems, the BIOS must also communicate with the adapter cards located in the expansion slots to determine their characteristics. When the system is turned on, the PnP devices involved in the boot-up process become active in their default configurations. Other logical devices not required for boot-up start up in an inactive mode.

Before starting the boot-up sequence, the PnP BIOS checks the devices installed in the expansion slots to see what types they are, how they are configured, and which slots they are in. It then assigns each adapter a software handle (name) and stores their names and configuration information in a RAM table. Next, the BIOS checks the adapter information against the system's basic configuration for resource conflicts. If no conflicts are detected, all the devices required for boot-up are activated.

FIGURE 4.14

Error messages and beep codes.

```
                    BEEP CODE MESSAGES

  1 beep - DRAM refresh failure
  2 beeps - RAM failure (bare 640kB)
  3 beeps - System Timer failure
  5 beeps - Microprocessor failure
  6 beeps - Keyboard Controller failure
  7 beeps - Virtual Mode Exception failure
  9 beeps - ROM BIOS checksum failure
  1 long, 3 short beeps - Conventional and Extended test failure
  1 long, 8 short beeps - Display test failure
```

```
                 VISUAL DISPLAY ERROR MESSAGES

                     SYSTEM HALTED ERRORS
  (a) CMOS INOPERATIONAL - Indicated failure of CMOS shutdown register test.
  (b) 8042 GATE A20 ERROR - Error getting into protected mode.
  (c) INVALID SWITCH MEMORY FAILURE
  (d) DMA ERROR - DMA controller failed page register test.
  (e) DMA #1 ERROR - DMA device #1 failure.
  (f) DMA #2 ERROR - DMA device #2 failure.

              NON FATAL ERRORS - WITH SETUP OPTION
  (a) CMOS BATTERY LOW - Indicates failure of CMOS battery or CMOS checksum
         test.
  (b) CMOS SYSTEM OPTION NOT SET - Indicates failure of CMOS battery or CMOS
         checksum test.
  (c) CMOS CHECKSUM FAILURE - Indicates CMS battery low or CMOS checksum test
         failure.
  (d) CMOS DISPLAY MISMATCH - Failure of display type verification.
  (e) CMOS MEMORY SIZE MISMATCH - System Configuration and Setup failure.
  (f) CMOS TIMER AND DATE NOT SET - System Configuration and Setup failure in timer
         circuitry.

              NON FATAL ERRORS - WITHOUT SETUP OPTION
  (a) CH-X TIMER ERROR - Channel X (2, 1, or 0) TIMER failure.
  (b) KEYBOARD ERROR - Keyboard test failure.
  (c) KB INTERFACE ERROR - Keyboard test failure.
  (d) DISPLAY SWITCH SETTING NOT PROPER - Failure to verify display type.
  (e) KEYBOARD IS LOCKED - Unlock it.
  (f) FDD CONTROLLER ERROR - Failure to verify floppy-disk setup by System
         Configuration file.
  (g) HDD CONTROLLER FAILURE - Failure to verify hard-disk setup by System
         Configuration file.
  (h) C:DRIVE ERROR - Hard-disk setup failure.
  (i) D:DRIVE ERROR - Hard-disk setup failure.
```

The devices not required for boot-up may be configured and activated by the BIOS, or they may simply be configured and left in an inactive state. In either event, the operating system is left with the task of activating the remaining intelligent devices and resolving any resource conflicts that the BIOS detected and could not resolve. If the PnP option is not working for a particular device, or if the operating system cannot resolve the remaining resource conflicts, then it is necessary to use the manufacturer's setup instructions to perform manual configurations.

The Boot-Up Process

If the option to enter the Setup routine is bypassed, or if the routine has been exited, the BIOS begins the process of booting up to the operating system. A simple single-operating system, single-disk boot-up process is described in Figure 4.15. As you can see, it is a multiple-access operation that uses two different bootstrap routines to locate and load two different boot records.

The boot-up process starts when the BIOS begins looking through the system for a master boot record. This record can reside on drive A: or C:, or at any other location.

FIGURE 4.15

The bootstrap operation.

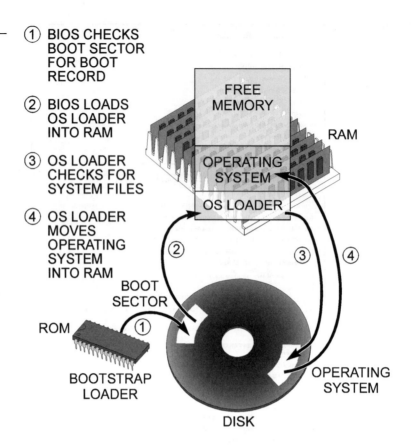

① BIOS CHECKS BOOT SECTOR FOR BOOT RECORD

② BIOS LOADS OS LOADER INTO RAM

③ OS LOADER CHECKS FOR SYSTEM FILES

④ OS LOADER MOVES OPERATING SYSTEM INTO RAM

The very first section on any logical DOS disk is called the **boot sector.** This section contains information about how the disk is organized, and it may also contain the small, optional master boot record that can access a larger, more powerful bootstrap loader program located elsewhere on the disk (normally in an area known as the root directory). In most systems, the master boot record is found at sector-0, head-0, and track-0 of the first logical hard drive. If the disk possesses a master boot record, it can boot up the hardware system to the operating system. The disk is then referred to as a bootable disk, or a system disk. If not, the disk is simply a data disk that can be used for storing information.

Traditionally, BIOS programs search for the master boot record in floppy-disk drive A: first. If a bootable disk exists in the floppy-disk drive, the BIOS executes the primary bootstrap loader routine to move the master boot record into RAM and then begin the process of loading the operating system. In the original IBM PC, the BIOS searches in the floppy-disk drive for the boot record. If it is not located there, the BIOS routine turns over control to a BASIC program located in the PC's ROM BIOS IC.

In the PC-XT, the BIOS looks first in the floppy drive(s) and then in the hard-disk drive. If neither location contains the boot record, the system loads up the ROM BASIC program. In clone systems, no ROM BIOS is present to which the system can default when no boot record is found. If the BIOS does not locate the boot record in the floppy or hard drive, it simply displays a "Non-System Disk or Disk Error" or "ROM BASIC Interpreter Not Found" message on the screen.

In newer systems, the order in which the BIOS searches drives for the boot record is governed by information stored in the system's CMOS configuration RAM. The order can be set to check the floppy drive first and then the hard drive, or to check the hard drive first, or to check the hard drive only.

In a networked system, a bootstrap loader routine can also be located in the ROM extension of a network card, as described earlier. When the system checks the BIOS extensions, the bootstrap routine redirects the boot-up process to look for a boot record on the disk drive of another computer. Any boot record on the local drive is bypassed. Networking is covered in Chapter 11.

To accomplish the boot-up, the BIOS enables the system's nonmaskable interrupts and causes a single, short tone to be produced by the speaker circuitry. The single beep indicates that the POST portion of the boot-up has been successfully completed.

The next BIOS instruction executes an Interrupt19 Disk Drive service routine. This interrupt routine carries out the primary bootstrap loader program, which looks for the master boot record in the first section of the floppy and hard disks. When located, it moves the master boot record into system RAM to be executed.

The master boot record contains the secondary bootstrap loader, also called the operating system loader. This routine looks for an operating system boot record, typically located on the disk. When found, it loads the bigger boot record into RAM and begins executing it. This boot record brings special operating system files into memory so that they can control the operation of the system (such as the operating system).

The operating system loader looks for a command processor file. The command processor can belong to any operating system, such as Microsoft MS-DOS, UNIX, IBM PC DOS, or Novell Netware. The default command processor for DOS is a system file called COMMAND.COM, which interprets the input entered at the DOS prompt. When the bootstrap program finds the command processor, it moves it into system RAM along with the operating system support files.

In the case of Microsoft DOS, the special files in the OS boot record are the IO.SYS and MSDOS.SYS files. The BIOS recognizes these files by special extensions added to their names (.SYS and .COM).

In the original PC-DOS from IBM, the files were titled IBMBIO.COM, IBMDOS.COM, and COMMAND.COM. This step marks the end of the BIOS routine. The three system files must be found in the root directory (the starting point for any disk-based operations) to successfully boot DOS. The total boot-up process is described in Figure 4.16.

FIGURE 4.16

The boot-up process.

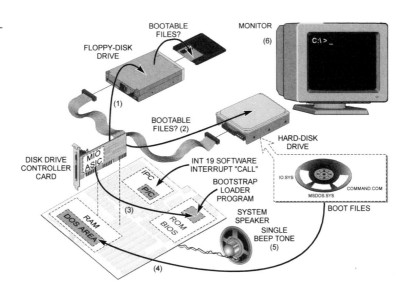

If the system has performed a standard DOS boot-up without any modifications, it should print date and time prompts on the monitor screen, followed by the DOS command-line prompt (A:\>> or C:\>>). The prompt indicates that DOS is operational and that the currently active drive is the A: floppy drive or the C:\ hard drive. Now the DOS software controls the movement of data and overall operation of the system. DOS enables the basic boot-up to be modified through two special utility files, called CONFIG.SYS and AUTOEXEC.BAT, both of which are discussed later in this chapter.

The operation of the system is now in the control of the operator and whatever software is being used with the system. The system waits for the user to do something, such as enter commands and instructions, or run programs from the other two software categories. The user hasn't had anything to do with the operation of the system yet. This is why this type of software is referred to as system software.

BIOS Services

While the system is operating, the BIOS continues to perform several important functions. It contains routines on which the operating system calls to carry out basic services. These services include providing BIOS interrupt CALLs (software interrupt routines) for such operations as printer, video, and disk-drive accesses.

The ROM BIOS services are organized into groups identified by interrupt numbers. Each interrupt may cover several different services. When the microprocessor jumps to a particular interrupt, the software calling the interrupt must have already loaded the service number into the microprocessor to tell it which section of the interrupt handler to access.

The most notable BIOS interrupt calls include the following:

- 10h—Video services (16)
- 13h—Hard and floppy drive services (17 and 11)
- 14h—Serial port services (6)
- 16h—Keyboard services (7)
- 17h—Parallel printer port services (3)
- 18h—ROM BASIC (old systems)/network card services (newer systems)
- 19h—Primary bootstrap loader
- 1Ah—Realtime clock services

The numbers in parenthesis refer to the number of different services available through the interrupt—10h—Video services (16) indicates that there are 16 different services available through interrupt call 10.

This list represents just a few of the more notable BIOS interrupts. The most important thing for a technician to remember about BIOS interrupt CALLs is that they form the backbone of the system's operation. The BIOS and DOS are constantly handing control of the system back and forth as normal system functions are carried out. This relationship is illustrated in Figure 4.17. These BIOS interrupt CALLs are also responsible for most of the drawbacks of the PC system; that is why so much effort is exerted in software to work around them. Advanced operating systems implement newer methods of handling system functions just to avoid handing control over to the BIOS interrupts.

FIGURE 4.17

The DOS/BIOS relationship.

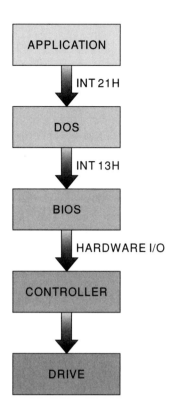

Some older PCs have trouble supporting newer hardware because the BIOS does not support the new item. To correct this situation, it is usually necessary to load a software driver program to support the device. Another possibility is to replace the BIOS with an improved version. This operation is not performed often because an upgraded BIOS must be compatible with the older chip set. Figure 4.18 shows a sample boot-up screen featuring the BIOS revision number.

FIGURE 4.18

BIOS version information.

MS-DOS

A+ DOS/WINDOWS 4.4

MS-DOS is a disk operating system for IBM PC-compatible computers. It is easily the most popular operating system in the world. As with any other operating system, its function is to oversee operation of the system by providing support for executing programs, controlling I/O devices, handling errors, and providing the user interface. MS-DOS is a disk-based, single-user, single-task operating system.

The main portions of MS-DOS are the IO.SYS, MSDOS.SYS, and COMMAND.COM files mentioned earlier. The IO.SYS and MSDOS.SYS files are special hidden system files that do not show up in a normal directory listing. The IO.SYS file implements the MS-DOS default control programs (referred to as **device drivers**) for various hardware components. These include the following:

▶ Boot disk drive

▶ Console display and keyboard

▶ System's time-of-day clock

▶ Parallel and serial communications port

Conversely, the MSDOS.SYS file provides default support features for software applications. These features include the following:

▶ Memory management

▶ Character input and output

▶ Realtime clock access

▶ File and record management

▶ Execution of other programs

The COMMAND.COM command interpreter contains the operating system's most frequently used commands. When a DOS command is entered at the DOS prompt, the COMMAND.COM program examines it to see whether it is an internal DOS command or an external DOS command. Internal commands are understood directly by COMMAND.COM, and external commands are stored in a directory called DOS. If the command is one of the internal commands, the COMMAND.COM file can execute it immediately. If not, COMMAND.COM looks in the \DOS directory for the command program.

Likewise, when DOS runs an application, COMMAND.COM finds the program, loads it into memory, and then gives it control of the system. When the program is shut down, it passes control back to the command interpreter.

The remainder of the operating system is comprised of utility programs to carry out DOS operations such as formatting disks (Format), printing files (Print), and copying files (XCOPY).

MS-DOS Structure

A+ DOS/WINDOWS 1.2 It is important to consider that MS-DOS is a *disk* operating system. Therefore, you must understand how DOS organizes disks. The DOS organizational structure is typically described as being like a common office file cabinet, similar to the one depicted in Figure 4.19. Think of DOS as the filing cabinet structure. Our example has four drawers that can be opened. Think of these as **disk drives** labeled A, B, and C-D. Inside each drawer are hanging folders that can hold different types of items. Think of these as **directories**. The hanging folders may contain different types of items or other individual folders. Think of these individual folders as **subdirectories**. For organizational purposes, each hanging folder and each individual folder must have a unique label on it.

Inside of each hanging folder or individual folder are the items being stored. In a real filing cabinet, these items in the folders are usually documents of different types. However, pictures, tapes, and other items related to the folder can also be stored in them.

Think of the items inside the folders as **files**. Disk-based systems manage data blocks by giving them filenames. Recall that a file is simply a block of logically related data given a single name and treated as a single unit. As with the contents of the folders, files can be programs, documents, drawings or other illustrations, sound files, and so on.

FIGURE 4.19

DOS organization.

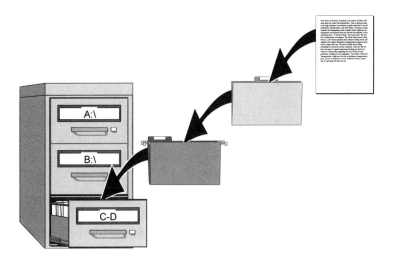

To find an item in the cabinet, you simply need to know the drawer, hanging folder, and folder in which it is located. This concept can be translated directly to the computer system: To locate a particular file, you simply need to know the drive, directory, and subdirectory in which it is located. In MS-DOS, the path to any file in the system can be written as a direction to the computer so that it knows where to find the file you're seeking. This format for specifying a path is as follows:

```
C:\directory name\subdirectory name\file name
```

In this example, the *C:* specifies the C disk drive. The directory, subdirectory, and filenames would naturally be replaced by their real names. The back slashes (\) after each item indicate the presence of a directory or subdirectory. The first slash indicates a special directory, called the root directory, that is present on all DOS disks.

If the direction points to a file, the **filename** is always placed at the end of the path. MS-DOS can accommodate a basic filename of up to eight characters, with an extension of up to three characters. The extension is separated from the main portion of the filename by a period and is normally used to identify the type of file—for example, the filename file1.*ltr* could be used to identify a letter created by a word processor.

Filename extensions are not actually required for most files. However, they become helpful in sorting files in a congested system. You should be aware that the operating system reserves some three-letter combinations, such as .COM and .SYS, for its own use. More information about filenames and extensions is presented in the subsequent section concerning file-level DOS commands.

DOS Disk Structure

It is also important to understand how DOS views disks. In the earlier section on booting up, we mentioned that the first area on each DOS disk is the boot sector. Though all DOS disks have this sector, they do not all have the optional master boot record located in the sector. Only those disks created to be bootable disks have this record.

File Allocation Tables

The second section of a DOS disk is an area referred to as the **File Allocation Table (FAT)**, a table of information about how the disk is organized. Basically, the system logs the use of the space on the disk in this table.

In older versions of DOS, the amount of space dedicated to tracking the sectors on the disk was 16 bits. Therefore, only 65,536 sectors could be accounted for. This parameter limited the size of a DOS partition to 32MB (33,554,432 bytes). To more effectively manage the space on the disk, newer versions of DOS divide the disk into groups of logically related sectors, called **allocation units**, or **clusters**.

As described in Chapter 1, the sectors on a DOS disk hold 512 bytes each. On the other hand, files can be any length. Therefore, a single file may occupy several sectors on the disk. The DOS disk routine breaks the file into sector-sized chunks and stores it in a cluster of sectors. In this manner, DOS uses the cluster to track files instead of sectors. Because the file allocation table must handle information only for a cluster instead of for each sector, the number of files that can be tracked in a given length table is greatly increased.

The organization of a typical FAT is described in Table 4.1. The first two entries are reserved for DOS information. Each sector after that holds a value. Each value may represent one of three conditions. A value of 0 indicates that the cluster is empty and can be used for storage. Any number besides 0 or FFFh indicates that the cluster contains data, and the number provides the location of the next cluster in a chain of clusters. Finally, a value of FFFh (or FFFFh in a 16-bit entry) indicates the end of a cluster chain.

Table 4.1 *File Allocation Table Structure*

Cluster Number	Contents
Cluster 0	Reserved for DOS
Cluster 1	Reserved for DOS
Cluster 2	3 (contains data go to Cluster 3)
Cluster 3	4 (contains data go to Cluster 4)
Cluster 4	7 (contains data go to Cluster 7)
Cluster 5	0 (free space)
Cluster 6	0 (free space)

Cluster Number	Contents
Cluster 7	8 (contains data go to Cluster 8)
Cluster 8	FFFh (end cluster chain)
Cluster 9	0 (free space)
Cluster x	0 (free space)
Cluster y	0 (free space)
Cluster z	0 (free space)

On floppy disks, common cluster sizes are one or two sectors long. With hard disks, the cluster size may vary from 1 to 16 sectors in length. The FAT keeps track of which clusters are used and which ones are free. It contains a 12- or 16-byte entry for each cluster on the disk. The 12 byte entries are used with floppy disks and hard disks that are smaller than 17MB. The 16-byte entries are employed with hard disk drives larger than 17MB. Obviously, the larger entries enable the FAT to manage more clusters.

In version-b of Windows 95 (also referred to as OSR2) Microsoft supplied a 32-bit file allocation table system called FAT32 to make efficient use of large hard drives (larger than 2GB). Under the previous FAT structure, large drives used large partitions, which, in turn, required large cluster sizes and wasted a lot of disk space.

The FAT32 format in OSR2 supports hard drives up to 2TB in size. FAT 32 uses 4KB cluster sizes for partitions up to 8GB in size.

In free clusters, a value of zero is recorded. In used clusters, the cluster number is stored. In cases where the file requires multiple clusters, the FAT entry for the first cluster holds the cluster number for the next cluster used to store the file. Each subsequent cluster entry contains the number of the next cluster used by the file. The final cluster entry contains an end-of-file marker code that tells the system that the end of the file has been reached.

These cluster links enable DOS to store and retrieve virtually any size file that will fit on the disk. However, the loss of any link makes it impossible to retrieve the file and use it. If the FAT becomes corrupted, chained files can become cross-linked with each other, making them useless. For this reason, two complete copies of the FAT are stored consecutively on the disk under the DOS disk structure. The first copy is the normal working copy, and the second FAT is used as a backup measure in case the contents of the first FAT become corrupted.

The Root Directory

A+ DOS/WINDOWS 1.2

The next section following the FAT tables is the disk's **root directory**, a special directory present on every DOS disk. The root directory is the main directory of every logical disk and serves as the starting point for organizing information on the disk.

The location of every directory, subdirectory, and file on the disk is recorded in this table.

Each directory and subdirectory (including the root directory) can hold up to 512 32-byte entries that describe each of the files in them. The first 8 bytes contain the file's name, followed by 3 bytes for its filename extension.

The next 11 bytes define the file's attributes. Attributes for DOS files include the following:

- Read-only
- System file
- Volume label
- Subdirectory entry
- Archive (backup) status

Two bytes are used to record the time the file was created or last modified. This is followed by 2 additional bytes that record the date the file was created or last modified.

The final 4 bytes are divided equally between the value for the starting cluster number and a byte count number for the file. Unlike the previous information in the directory, the information associated with the last 4 bytes is not displayed when a directory listing is displayed on the screen.

Because each root directory entry is 32 bytes long, each disk sector can hold 16 entries. Consequently, the number of files or directories that can be listed in the root directory is dependent on how many disk sectors are allocated to it. On a hard-disk drive, there are normally 32 sectors set aside for the root directory. Therefore, the root directory for such a disk can accommodate up to 512 entries. A typical 3¹/₂-inch, 1.44MB floppy has 16 sectors reserved for the root directory and can hold up to 224 entries.

Figure 4.20 describes the organization of a DOS disk and illustrates the position of the boot sector, FATs, and the root directory. The remainder of the disk is dedicated to data storage. On a floppy disk the logical structure normally has a group of files located under the root directory. Directory structures can be created on a floppy, but this is not normally done due to their relatively small capacity. However, a hard drive is another matter. With hard drives, it is normal to organize the disk into directories and subdirectories, as described earlier in this chapter.

FIGURE 4.20

DOS disk organization.

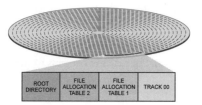

Technically, every directory on a disk is a subdirectory of the root directory. All additional directories branch out from the root directory in a tree-like fashion. Therefore, a graphical representation of the disk drive's directory organization is called a **directory tree**. Figure 4.21 depicts the directory organization of a typical hard drive.

Under DOS, hard disk drives can be divided into multiple logical drives. This operation is referred to as **partitioning** the drive. With earlier versions of DOS this became necessary as the capacity of hard drives exceeded the FAT's capability of tracking all the possible sectors.

By creating a second logical drive on the hard disk, another boot sector, FAT, and root directory are created. DOS sees this new structure on the hard drive as a completely new disk. Therefore it must have its own drive letter assigned to it.

FIGURE 4.21

The DOS directory tree structure.

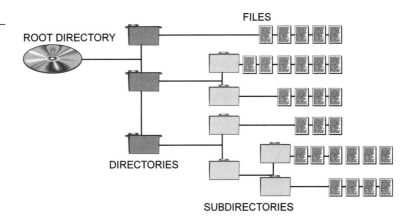

In some applications, partitioning is popular because the system can be booted up to different operating systems. Because each partition contains its own boot sector, FAT, and root directory, each partition can be set up to hold and boot up a different operating system.

DOS Command Line

> The operating system is responsible for providing the user interface. The main user interface for DOS is the command line. The command line is the space immediately following the DOS prompt on the screen.

The MS-DOS prompt for using the C: hard disk drive as the active directory is displayed in Figure 4.22.

FIGURE 4.22

The DOS prompt.

```
Mouse Version 8.00
1988 - 1993

Driver Installed : Mouse Systems Mode
Dynamic Resolution OFF
Mouse setup on COM1:

C:\MOUSE>
```

From the DOS prompt, all DOS functions can be entered and executed; many programs can be started from this prompt as well. These files can be discerned by their filename extensions. Files with .COM, .EXE, or .BAT extensions can be started directly from the prompt. The .COM and .EXE file extensions are reserved by DOS and can be generated only by programs that can correctly configure them. BAT files are simply ASCII text files that have been generated using DOS functions. Because they contain DOS commands mixed with .COM and .EXE files, DOS can execute .BAT files from the command line.

Programs with other types of extensions must be associated with one of these three file types to be operated. The user can operate application software packages such as graphical user interfaces, word processors, business packages, data communications packages, and user programming languages (such as QBASIC and DEBUG). As an example, the core component of a word processor could be a file called WORDPRO.EXE. Document files produced by word processors are normally given filename extensions of .DOC (for document) or .TXT (for text file). To view one of the documents electronically, you first need to run the executable file and then use its features to load up, format, and display the document. Likewise, a BASIC file normally has an extension of .BAS assigned to it. To execute a file with this extension, it is necessary to run a BASIC interpreter (such as QBASIC.EXE) to load the .BAS file and then run the file.

The user can also type DOS commands on the command line to perform DOS functions. These commands can be grouped into drive-level commands, directory-level commands, and file-level commands. The format for using DOS commands is as follows:

```
COMMAND (space) SOURCE location (space) DESTINATION location
COMMAND (space) location
COMMAND
```

The first example illustrates how the process by which DOS operations involving a source and a final destination (such as moving a file from one place to another) are entered. The second example illustrates how single location DOS operations (such as formatting a disk in a particular disk drive) are specified. The final example applies to DOS commands that occur in a default location, such as obtaining a listing of the files on the current disk drive.

Many DOS commands can be modified by placing one or more software switches at the end of the basic command. A switch is added to the command by adding a space, a foreslash (/), and a single letter:

```
COMMAND (space) option /switch
```

Common DOS command switches include /P for page, /W for wide format, and /S for system. Different switches are used to modify different DOS commands. In each case, the DOS user's guide should be consulted for switch definitions available with each command.

Drives and Disks

It is important to note that each disk drive in the system is identified by DOS with a single-letter name (such as A:), and this name must be specified when giving the system commands so that they are carried out using the proper drive. The format for specifying the drive to perform a DOS operation calls for the presence of the drive's identifier letter in the command, followed by a colon (for example, A: or C:).

Figure 4.23 shows how the various disk drives are seen by a typical standalone system. DOS assigns the letters A: and B: to the first and second floppy drives. Multiple hard-disk drive units can be installed in the system unit along with the floppy drive(s). DOS recognizes a single hard-disk unit in the system as DRIVE C:. As described previously, DOS utilities can be used to partition a single, physical hard-disk drive into two or more volumes that the system recognizes as logical drives (for example, C: or D:).

Figure 4.23 shows a CD-ROM drive as drive D: because this is becoming the most common PC configuration. In the case of networked systems, logical drive letters may be extended to define up to Z drives. These drives are actually the hard drives located in remote computers. The operating system in the local machine treats them as additional logical drives (such as F, G, and so on).

FIGURE 4.23

The system's disk drives.

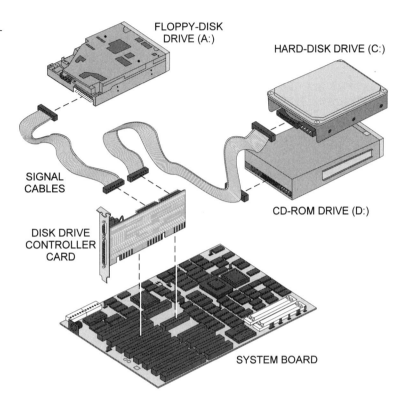

Conversely, a second hard-disk drive can be added to the system and set up as logical drive D:. This second drive may also be partitioned into smaller logical drives that the system recognizes as drives E:, F:, and so on. Logical drives and disk partitioning are covered in Chapter 8.

Some DOS operations are simplified by allowing the system to choose the location for the command to be carried out through the use of **default settings** (special predetermined settings that are automatically used by the system when no specific directions are given to change the setting). These settings are remembered in DOS and used by the system when the operator does not specify a particular location for events to happen. The default setting in your system is the A: drive. In systems with two or more drives, it is imperative that the user specify exactly where the action is to occur.

The following DOS commands pertain to drive-level operations that must be typed at the DOS prompt. These commands carry out the instruction along with any drive modifiers given.

▶ **DISKCOPY**: This command is used to make a duplicate of a disk. The DISKCOPY operation is normally used to make backup disks and is usually followed by a DISKCOMP operation, as shown in this code:

```
C:\>DISKCOPY A: B:
```

▶ **DISKCOMP**: This command is used to compare the contents of two disks, not only to see whether they are alike, but also to see that the data is located in the same place on both disks. The DISKCOMP operation is normally used to check backup disks and usually follows a DISKCOPY operation, as shown in this code:

```
C:\>DISKCOMP A: B:
```

▶ **FORMAT**: This command is used to prepare a new disk for use. Actual data locations are marked on the disk for the tracks and sectors, and bad sectors are marked. In addition, the directory is established on the disk. New disks must be formatted before they can be used.

`C:\>FORMAT B:` is used even in a single-drive system. The system issues prompts to insert the proper disks at the correct times. A self-booting diskette can be created by using a /S modifier (for system files) at the end of the normal FORMAT command.

`C:\>FORMAT B:/S` causes three system files (boot files) to be copied onto the disk after it has been formatted. The new disk then boots up without a DOS disk.

`C:\>FORMAT A:/Q` causes the system to perform a quick format operation on the disk. This amounts to removing the FAT and root directory from the disk.

Directories

As mentioned earlier, in hard drive-based systems it is common to organize related programs and data into areas called directories. This makes the programs and data easier to find and work with because modern hard drives are capable of holding large amounts of information. As described earlier, most directories can hold up to 512 directory or filename entries.

It would be difficult to work with directories if you could not know the one in which you were working. The DOS prompt can be set up to display the directory being used. This particular directory is referred to as the current, or working, directory. As an example, C:\DOS\forms would indicate that you were working with programs located in a subdirectory of the DOS directory named Forms. The first backslash represents the root directory on the C: hard drive. The presence of two dots (..) near the top of a directory listing identifies it as a subdirectory. These dots indicate the presence of a parent directory above the currently active subdirectory.

The following DOS commands are used for directory-based operations. The format for using them is identical to disk-related commands discussed earlier.

▶ **DIR**: The Directory command gives a listing of the files on the disk located in the drive indicated by the drive specifier.

`C:\>DIR` or `DIR B:` may be used with modifiers to alter the way in which the directory is displayed. If DIR is used without any drive specifier, the contents of the drive indicated by the prompt will be displayed.

`C:\>DIR/W` displays the entire directory at one time across the width of the display.

`C:\>DIR/P` displays the contents of the directory one page at a time. You must press a key to advance to the next display page.

▶ **MKDIR (MD)**: This command creates a new directory in an indicated spot in the directory tree structure.

`C:\>MD C:\DOS\XXX` creates a new subdirectory named XXX in the path that includes the ROOT directory (C:\) and the DOS directory.

- **CHDIR (CD)**: This command changes the location of the active directory to a position specified with the command.

  `C:\>CD C:\DOS` changes the working directory from the C: root directory to the C:\DOS directory.

- **RMDIR (RD):** The Remove Directory command erases the directory specified in the command. You cannot remove a directory until it is empty, and you cannot remove the directory if it is currently active.

  `C:\>RD C:\DOS\forms` would remove the DOS sub-directory "forms," provided it was empty.

- **PROMPT:** The Prompt command changes the appearance of the DOS prompt

  `C:\>PROMPT $P$G` causes the form of the prompt to change from simply C: to C:\> and causes the complete path from the main directory to the current directory to be displayed at the DOS prompt (for example, C:\DOS>).

- **TREE:** This command lists all the directory and subdirectory names on a specified disk.

  `C:\>TREE C:` displays a graphical representation of the organization of the C: hard drive.

- **DELTREE:** This command removes a selected directory and all the files and sub-directories below it.

  `C:\>DELTREE C:\DOS\DRIVER\MOUSE` deletes the subdirectory Mouse and any sub-directories it may have.

Files and Filenames

A+ DOS/WINDOWS 1.3 Disk-based systems store and handle related pieces of information in groups called files. The system recognizes and keeps track of the different files in the system by their filenames. Therefore, each file in the system is required to have a filename that is different from that of any other file in the directory. If two files with the same name were present in the system at the same time, the computer would become confused and fail to operate properly because it could not tell which file was supposed to be changed. Each time you create a new file of information, you must give it a unique filename by which DOS can identify it.

With DOS, you must remember a few rules when creating new filenames. As described earlier in this chapter, the filename consists of two parts: a name and an extension. The filename is a combination of alphanumeric characters and is between one and eight characters in length. The extension is an optional addition to the name that begins with a period and is followed by between one and three characters. Extensions are not required on filenames, but they often prove useful in describing the contents of a file or in identifying different versions of the same file. If a filename that already exists is used to store another file, the computer writes the information in the new file over that of the old file, assuming that they are both the same. Therefore, only the new file still exists, and the information in the old file is lost.

Many software packages automatically generate filename extensions for files they create. The software does this so that other parts of the program, which may work with the same file, can identify where the file came from or what form it is in.

In any event, you should remember these seven items when assigning and using filenames:

1. All files must have a filename.

2. All filenames must be different than any other filename in the system or on the disk presently in use.

3. Filenames can be up to eight characters long with an optional three-character extension (separated from the basic filename by a period).

4. When using a filename in a command, you must also use its extension, if one exists.

5. Some special characters are not allowed in filenames. These are: [,], :, ;, +, =, \, /, and ,.

6. When telling DOS where to carry out a command, you must tell it on which disk drive the operation is to be performed. The drive must be specified by its letter name followed by a colon (such as A:, B:, C:, and so on).

7. The complete and proper way to specify a file involves calling for the drive specifier, the filename, and the filename extension, in that order (for example, B:filename.ext).

The following DOS commands are used to carry out file-level operations. The format for using them is identical to the disk- and directory-related commands discussed earlier. However, the command must include the filename and its extension at the end of the directory path. Depending on the operation, the complete path may be required, or a default to the currently active drive will be assumed.

- **COPY**: The File Copy command copies a specified file from one place (disk or directory) to another, as in the following code:

```
C:\>COPY A:filename.ext B:filename.ext
```

```
C:\>COPY A:filename.ext B:
```
is used if the file is to have the same name in its new location; the second filename specifier can be omitted.

In a single-drive system, it is necessary to switch disks in the middle of the operation. (Notice that the drive B specifier is used even though only drive A: is present.) Fortunately, the DOS produces a prompt message to tell you when to put the target disk in the drive. This is not required in a two-drive system, and no prompt is given. The transfer can be specified in any direction desired:

```
C:\>COPY B:filename.ext A:
```

The only thing to keep in mind in this situation is to place the source disk in drive B and the target disk in drive A: before entering the command.

- **XCOPY:** This command copies all the files in a directory, along with any subdirectories and their files. This command is particularly useful in copying files and directories between disks with different formats (such as from a 1.2Mb disk to a 1.44Mb disk:

```
C:\>XCOPY A: B: /s
```

This command would copy all the files and directories from the disk in drive A: (except hidden and system files) to the disk in drive B:. The /s switch instructs the XCOPY command to copy directories and subdirectories.

▶ **DEL or ERASE**: This command enables the user to remove unwanted files from the disk when typed at the DOS prompt:

```
C:\>DEL filename.ext
```

```
C:\>ERASE B:filename.ext
```

A great deal of care should be taken when using this command. If a file is erased accidentally, it may not be retrievable.

▶ **REN**: This command enables the user to change the name or extension of a filename:

```
C:\>REN A:filename.ext newname.ext
```

Using this command does not change the contents of the file; it changes only its name. The original filename (but not the file) is deleted. If you wish to retain the original file and filename, a copy command (using different filenames) can be used:

```
C:\>COPY A:filename.ext B:newname.ext
```

▶ **TYPE**: This command shows the contents of a designated file on the monitor screen.

```
C:\>TYPE AUTOEXEC.BAT
```
displays the contents of the AUTOEXEC.BAT file.

▶ **FC:** This command compares two files to see whether they are the same. This operation is normally performed after a file copy has been performed to ensure that the file was duplicated and located correctly:

```
C:\>FC A:filename.ext B:
```

If the filename was changed during the copy operation, the command would have to be typed as follows:

```
C:\>FC A:filename.ext B:newname.ext
```

A+ DOS/WINDOWS 4.6

▶ **ATTRIB:** This command changes file attributes such as read-only (+R or –R), archive (+A or –A), system (+S or –S), and hidden (+H or –H). The + and – signs are used to add or subtract the attribute from the file.

```
C:\>ATTRIB +R C:\DOS\memos.doc
```
sets the file memos.doc as a read-only file.

Read-only attributes protect the file from accidentally being overwritten. Similarly, one of the main reasons for giving a file a hidden attribute is to prevent it from accidentally being erased. The system attribute is reserved for use by the operating system and marks the file as a system file.

▶ **SETVER:** This command sets the DOS version number that the system reports to an application. Programs designed for previous DOS versions may not operate correctly under newer versions unless the version has been set correctly:

```
C:\>SETVER C:
```

This entry causes all the files on the C: drive to be listed in the DOS version table. If the current DOS version is not known, typing **VER** at the DOS prompt displays it on the screen. These commands are particularly useful in networking operations in which multiple computers are connected to share information. In these applications, several versions of DOS may exist on different machines attached to the network.

DOS Shortcuts

DOS provides some **command-line shortcuts** through the keyboard's function keys. Some of the most notable are the F1 and F3 function keys. The F1 key brings the previous command back from the command-line buffer, one character at a time. Likewise, the F3 key brings back the entire previous command, through a single keystroke.

When using filenames in DOS command-line operations, the filename appears at the end of the directory path in the source and destination locations. The * notation is called a **wildcard** and permits operations to be performed with only partial source or destination information. Using the notation as *.* tells the software to perform the designated command on any file found on the disk using any filename and extension.

A question mark (?) can be used as a wild card to represent a single character in a DOS name or extension. Multiple question marks can be used to represent multiple characters in a filename or extension.

Data from a DOS command can be modified to fit a prescribed output format, through the use of **filter commands**. The main filter commands are More, Find, and Sort. The filter command is preceded by a pipe symbol (|) on the command line when output from another DOS command is to be modified. For example, to view the contents of a batch file that is longer than the screen display can present at one time, type `C:\xxx.bat¦more`. If the information to be modified is derived from another file, the less than (<<) symbol is used.

The Find command searches through files and commands for specified characters. Likewise, the Sort command presents files in alphabetical order.

DOS I/O Commands

> The DOS mode command is used to configure the system's I/O devices. These devices include the parallel and serial ports, as well as the monitor display and the keyboard.

DOS keeps track of its different parallel and serial ports by assigning them logical designations during the initialization phase of the system boot-up. A parallel port is designated as an LPT port and can be assigned to the system as LPT1, LPT2, or LPT3. Likewise, serial ports are designated as COM, or communications ports. Any of the system's serial ports can be configured as COM1, COM2, COM3, or COM4. However, the serial ports cannot share the same COM port designation.

The format for using the Mode command to configure the parallel printer port is as follows:

```
mode LPT1:n,m,P
```

In this code, n is the number of characters per line across the page, m is the number of lines of print down the page, and the value of P sets up continuous retry on **time-out errors** (errors that occur when actions do not occur during a prescribed amount of time). The value of n can be set to 80 or 132 characters. Common values for m are 6 or 8 lines.

The Mode command is also used to set up the serial ports.

The format for the serial port is as follows:

```
mode COMn:baud,parity,databits,stopbits,P
```

In this code, *n* represents one of the four serial ports in the system. **Baud** is the transmission rate by which the port sends and receives data. Common values for this variable are 110, 150, 300, 600, 1,200, 2,400, 4,800, 9,600 and 19,200. Only the first two digits of the speed rating are placed in the command (for example, 9,600 = 96).

Parity describes the type of error checking used by the port (the topics of error checking and parity are discussed later in Chapter 7, "Input/Output Devices," and Chapter 11). Parity can be set to E for *even*, O for *odd*, or N for *none*.

The data bit entry tells the receiver how many data bits to expect. The usual setting for data bits is 7, but an 8-bit data word can also be selected. Likewise, different numbers of special **stop bits** can be used in serial communications to mark the end of a character or message. Typical stop bit values can be 1 or 2. The P value is used to indicate whether the port is being used with a serial printer or some other serial device. If a value is included for P, the system assumes that it is connected to a serial printer and performs continuous retries on time-out errors.

In addition to setting up the operation of the system's I/O ports, the Mode command can be used to alter the output format of the video display. The format for using the Mode command to alter the output on the video display is as follows:

```
mode n,m,T
```

In this code, *n* is the number of columns and color selection for the display. Typical values for this variable are 40, 80, BW40, BW80, CO40, CO80, and mono. The 40 and 80 values indicate the numbers of characters on a text line. The BW40 and BW80 options also indicate the number of characters per line but include a reference to the color graphics adapter with color turned off. Conversely, the CO40 and CO80 values indicate the color graphics adapter with color enabled. Mono indicates a monochrome display adapter.

The *m* variable can be set to *r* (for right-shift) or *l* (for left-shift). If the *T* value is present in the command, a test pattern is presented on the screen so that it can be aligned properly.

To use the Mode command to set the display mode, a device statement must be included in the CONFIG.SYS file for the ANSI.SYS device driver.

Finally, the Mode command can be used to shift data from one output port to another. As an example, it is possible to shift data intended for a serial port to the parallel port. This is a quick and useful troubleshooting tool when working with ports. If data intended for a suspect port can be successfully redirected to another port, then a hardware problem with the first port is indicated. An example of redirecting data from one port to another follows:

```
mode LPT1:=COM2
```

This example would redirect data intended for the first parallel port to the second parallel port.

The Mode command can be used inside the AUTOEXEC.BAT file to automatically reconfigure the system at startup.

DOS Utilities

A subclass of system software, called **utilities**, can be used to perform some basic system operations. These programs enable the system to be optimized for operations in particular functions or with different options.

In the DOS operating system, two of these utilities—called the CONFIG.SYS and AUTOEXEC.BAT files—can be included in the DOS boot-up process. As the system moves through the boot-up procedure, the BIOS checks in the root directory of the boot disk for the presence of a file named CONFIG.SYS. Afterward, it searches for the COMMAND.COM interpreter and finally looks in the root directory for the AUTOEXEC.BAT file. In particular, the CONFIG.SYS and AUTOEXEC.BAT files play key roles in optimizing the system's memory and disk drive usage. This operation can be summarized as follows:

1. BIOS performs INT19 to search drives for the master boot record.

2. The primary bootstrap loader moves the master boot record into memory.

3. The system executes the secondary bootstrap loader from the master boot record.

4. The secondary bootstrap loader moves IO.SYS and MSDOS.SYS into memory.

5. DOS checks for the CONFIG.SYS file in the root directory.

6. If CONFIG.SYS is found, DOS reconfigures the system.

7. DOS loads COMMAND.COM.

8. COMMAND.COM checks for the AUTOEXEC.BAT file in the root directory.

9. If the AUTOEXEC.BAT file is found, COMMAND.COM carries out the commands found in the file.

10. If no AUTOEXEC.BAT file is found, COMMAND.COM displays the DOS time and date prompt, as described earlier.

DOS Memory

A+ DOS/WINDOWS 2.1

To understand how the CONFIG.SYS and AUTOEXEC.BAT files improve the performance of the system, you must understand how DOS views memory.

The original DOS version was constructed in two sections. The first 640KB of memory were reserved for use by DOS and its programs. The remaining section was reserved for use by the BIOS and the system's peripherals (such as the video card, the hard drive controller card, and so on). This arrangement utilized the entire 1MB addressing range of the 8088 microprocessor.

As more powerful microprocessors entered the market (80286 microprocessors can access up to 16MB of memory, and the 80386 and 80486 can handle up to 4GB of memory), DOS retained the limitations imposed on it by the original version to remain compatible with older machines and software.

Special add-on programs called **memory managers** have been created to allow DOS to access and use the additional memory available to more powerful microprocessors.

Basic Memory Organization

Every computer has a memory organization plan called a **memory map**. A simplified memory map showing RAM, ROM, and I/O address allocations is shown in Figure 4.24.

When the original PC was designed, the programmers decided to divide the 8088's 1MB of memory address space, giving the Intel microprocessors a separate memory map for I/O addresses. These decisions were implemented by the original DOS program and, by necessity, carried over into the address allocations of all DOS-based PC-compatible systems, as described in Figure 4.25.

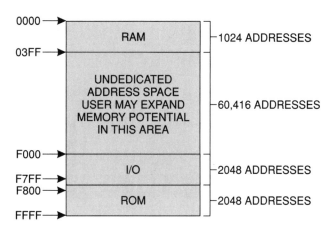

FIGURE 4.24

A computer memory map.

0000 → | RAM — 1024 ADDRESSES
03FF →

UNDEDICATED ADDRESS SPACE USER MAY EXPAND MEMORY POTENTIAL IN THIS AREA — 60,416 ADDRESSES

F000 → | I/O — 2048 ADDRESSES
F7FF →
F800 → | ROM — 2048 ADDRESSES
FFFF →

FIGURE 4.25

PC memory allocations.

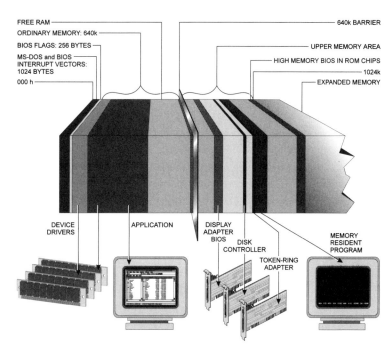

FREE RAM
ORDINARY MEMORY: 640k
BIOS FLAGS: 256 BYTES
MS-DOS and BIOS INTERRUPT VECTORS: 1024 BYTES
000 h

640k BARRIER
UPPER MEMORY AREA
HIGH MEMORY BIOS IN ROM CHIPS
1024k
EXPANDED MEMORY

DEVICE DRIVERS

APPLICATION

DISPLAY ADAPTER BIOS
DISK CONTROLLER
TOKEN-RING ADAPTER

MEMORY RESIDENT PROGRAM

Basically, DOS can recognize the following classifications of memory: conventional memory, upper memory blocks, high memory area, expanded memory, extended memory, and virtual memory.

Conventional Memory

The **conventional memory** area is divided into two sections referred to as **base memory** and the **upper memory area** (**UMA**). These sections are illustrated in Figure 4.26. Base memory occupies the first 640KB of addresses, and the remaining 384KB is referred to as **upper memory**.

Base memory (locations 00000h through 9FFFFh) is the standard memory area for all PC-compatible systems. This section traditionally holds DOS, interrupt vector tables, and relocated ROM BIOS tables. The remaining space in the base memory area is referred to as DOS program memory. Programs written to operate under PC or MS-DOS use this area for program storage and execution.

FIGURE 4.26

Conventional memory.

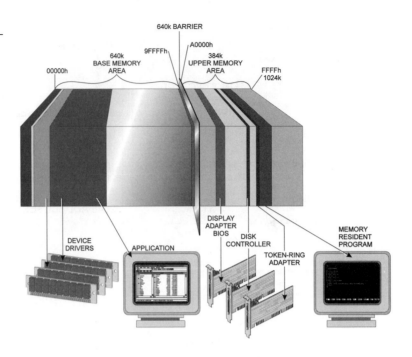

The upper memory area occupies the 384KB portion of the PC's address space, from A0000h to FFFFFh. This space is segmented into 64KB **upper memory block** regions, as illustrated in Figure 4.27. Although the addresses are allocated, no actual memory exists here. The upper memory area was originally dedicated to different forms of video display memory and ROM-based functions. However, many advanced systems reserve space in this area to incorporate a memory-usage scheme called Shadow RAM to improve the overall performance of the computer.

FIGURE 4.27

Upper memory blocks of the UMA.

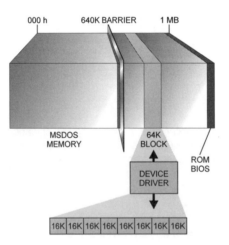

With this feature, the contents of the ROM BIOS and/or Video BIOS are rewritten (shadowed) into the upper memory area. Under this scheme, the system operates faster when application software makes use of any BIOS CALL routines. Instead of accessing an IC ROM device—which takes up to four wait states to complete—BIOS calls are redirected by the shadow feature to the same information located in fast DRAM devices with no wait states. Some benchmark tests have shown performance increases between 300% and 40% in systems where the shadow feature is used.

Extended Memory

With the advent of the 80286 microprocessor and its protected operating mode, it became possible to access physical memory locations beyond the 1MB limit of the 8088. Memory above this address is generally referred to as **extended memory**. With the 286 microprocessor, this could add up to an additional 15MB of RAM, for a total of 16MB (24-bit address). Extended memory is illustrated in Figure 4.28.

FIGURE 4.28

Extended memory.

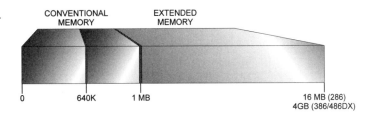

Even though the 80286 could physically access this type of memory using its special addressing mode, it was impossible for application programs to access it at the time. This was due to the 640KB DOS limit imposed by earlier architectures. Extended memory could range up to 4GB in 80386- and 80486-based computers (32-bit address). It was not that software couldn't access memory at these addresses; it was simply that DOS didn't have the capability to do so.

Applications programs can be written to specifically take advantage of these memory locations, but few are. Operating systems such as Microsoft DOS versions beyond 4.0 and Windows versions beyond 3.0 (as well as IBM's OS/2 operating system) can take full advantage of extended memory through the protected addressing modes of the more advanced microprocessors. This capability of managing higher memory enables the system to free up more of the base memory area for use by application programs.

The DOS versions above 4.0 contain a memory-management program called HIMEM.SYS that manages extended memory above the 1024KB level. This utility operates under the Microsoft **Extended Memory Specification** (**XMS**). When the utility is loaded into memory, it shifts most of the operating system functions into an area known as the **high memory area** (**HMA**) of extended memory. The HMA takes up the first 64KB of addresses above the 1MB boundary and is a result of a quirk in the design of advanced Intel microprocessors.

The HIMEM function is activated by adding a line of instruction to the system's CONFIG.SYS file so that it is executed when the computer boots. When the HIMEM utility is encountered, the program assumes control of the system's **A20 interrupt handler** routine. This function is part of the BIOS program and takes control of the system's A20 address line when activated.

The A20 interrupt handler is located at BIOS interrupt INT15 and is used to transfer data blocks of up to 64KB in length between the system and extended memory. The INT15 function also supplies entries for the various microprocessor tables that are required for protected virtual addressing mode.

Expanded Memory (EMS)

Some publications may refer to memory above the 1MB limit as expanded memory. However, the term **expanded memory** is generally reserved to describe another special memory option. In 1985, three companies (Lotus, Intel, and Microsoft) joined together to define a method of expanding the 8088's memory-usage capabilities by switching banks of memory from outside the DOS memory area into the usable address ranges of the 8088. This method became known as the **LIM EMS** (for *Lotus, Intel,* and *Microsoft Expanded Memory Specification*) standard.

This idea of **bank switching** was not exactly new; it had been used with older computer systems before the advent of the IBM line. The LIM EMS standard simply defined how this technique should be applied to IBM PCs and their compatibles. The original standard defined specifications for both hardware and software elements of the EMS system. Figure 4.29 illustrates the basic principle behind the EMS standard.

FIGURE 4.29

Expanded memory (EMS) operations.

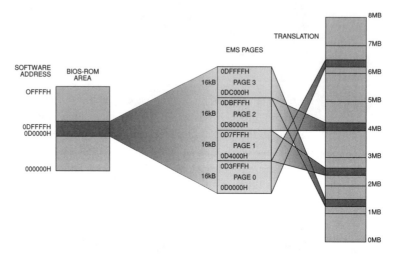

The specification provides for four 16KB areas of memory between C0000h and EFFFFh, referred to as **pages**, to be used as windows to predefined RAM locations above the 1MB address limit. Originally, these RAM addresses were located on special EMS RAM cards that plugged into one of the system board's expansion slot connectors. Newer system boards based on the 80486 and Pentium microprocessors can use their advanced virtual memory paging capabilities to handle the EMS function directly on the board.

Figure 4.29 depicts hex locations D0000h through DFFFFh as windows through which the expanded memory addresses are translated. In reality, the four 16KB windows can be selected from anywhere within the LIM EMS-defined address range and can be relocated to anywhere within the 32MB physical address range.

The EMS software specifications consist of predetermined programs called **Expanded Memory Manager** (**EMM**) drivers that work with application software to control the bank-switching operations. These drivers contain special function calls that application programs can use to manipulate the expanded memory. Note, however, that the application software must be written to take advantage of the EMS function calls. EMS versions before 4.0 made provision for the expanded memory to be used only as data storage areas. Programs could not actually be executed in these areas. Versions 4.0 and later support much larger bank-switching operations, as well as program execution and multitasking.

Virtual Memory

The term **virtual memory** is used to describe memory that isn't what it appears to be. Virtual memory is actually disk drive space that is manipulated to seem like RAM. Software creates virtual memory by swapping files between RAM and the disk drive, as illustrated in

Figure 4.30. Because there is a major transfer of information that involves the hard disk drive, an overall reduction in speed is encountered with virtual memory operations.

FIGURE 4.30

Virtual memory operations.

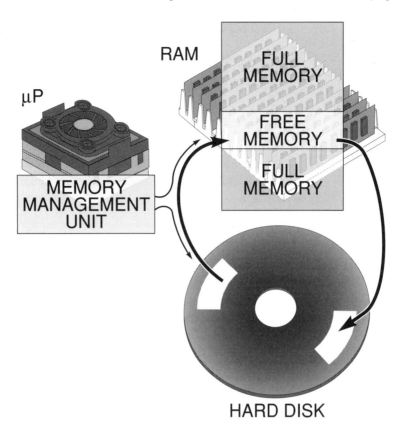

CONFIG.SYS

A+ DOS/WINDOWS 1.1

During installation, DOS versions from 5.0 forward create a system file called CONFIG.SYS. This particular filename is reserved by DOS for use with a special file that contains setup (configuration) instructions for the system. When DOS is loaded into the system, a portion of the boot-up program automatically searches in the default drive for a file named CONFIG.SYS. The commands in this file configure the DOS program for use with options devices and application programs in the system.

> The CONFIG.SYS program is responsible for: (1) setting up any memory managers being used, (2) configuring the DOS program for use with options devices and application programs, (3) loading **device-driver software** and installing **memory-resident programs**.

These activities are illustrated by the sample CONFIG.SYS file:

1 Device=C:\DOS\HIMEM.SYS
  Device=C:\DOS\EMM386.EXE 1024 RAM

2 FILES=30
  BUFFERS=15
  STACKS=64,500

```
3  DEVICE=C:\DOS\SMARTDRV.SYS 1024
   DOS=HIGH, UMB
   DEVICEHIGH=C:\MOUSE\MOUSE.SYS
   DEVICEHIGH=C:\DOS\RAMDRIVE.SYS 4096/a

4  DOSKEY
   INSTALL=C:/DOS/SHARE.EXE
```

Memory Managers

In the first section, the system's memory-manager programs are loaded. In this case, the HIMEM.SYS command loads the DOS **extended memory driver**. This driver manages the use of extended memory installed in the system. This memory manager should normally be listed in the CONFIG.SYS file before any other memory managers or devices drivers.

The EMM386.EXE program provides the system's microprocessor with access to the upper memory area. Operating together with the HIMEM.SYS program, this enables the system to conserve conventional memory by moving device drivers and memory resident programs into the UMA. This concept is described in Figure 4.31.

HIMEM.SYS also creates a 64KB area of memory just above the 1MB address space called the high memory area. With this, the DOS=HIGH statement is used to shift portions of DOS from conventional memory into the HMA.

Similarly, the EMM386.EXE command could load the DOS expanded memory simulator driver. A file called LIM EMS 4.0 is another commonly used expanded memory manager that you could encounter in a CONFIG.SYS file set up for expanded memory operations.

FIGURE 4.31

Loading memory managers.

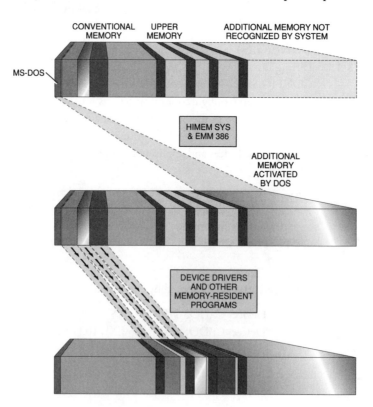

Files, Buffers, and Stacks

In the second section of the file are the commands that define DOS for operation with optional devices and applications. The **FILES command** causes the DOS program to establish 30 as the number of files that DOS can handle at any one time. This just happens to be the minimum number required to load Windows for operation. The **BUFFERS command** sets aside 15 blocks of RAM memory space for storing data being transferred to and from disks. Similarly, the **STACKS command** establishes the number and length of some special RAM memory storage operations at 64 memory stacks, with each being 500 bytes long.

Device Drivers

Device drivers are loaded in the third part of the file. Device drivers are programs that tell DOS how to control specific devices. DEVICEHIGH=C:\MOUSE\MOUSE.SYS is a command that loads a third-party device driver supporting the particular mouse being used with the system.

Some device manufacturers include software **installation utilities** that automatically install its device drivers into the CONFIG.SYS (or AUTOEXEC.BAT) files during the installation process. With other devices, the device drivers must be installed by manually updating the CONFIG.SYS and AUTOEXEC.BAT files. The device's installation instructions identify which method must be used to install its drivers.

The order in which device drivers appear in the CONFIG.SYS file is important. The recommended order for listing device drivers is: (1) HIMEM.SYS, (2) the expanded memory manager, if installed, (3) the EMM386.EXE command, and (4) then any other device drivers being used.

The SMARTDRV.SYS driver establishes a disk cache in an area of extended memory as a storage space for information read from the hard-disk drive. A **cache** is a special area of memory reserved to hold data and instructions recently accessed from another location. A **disk cache** holds information recently accessed from the hard disk drive. Information stored in RAM can be accessed much more quickly than information on the hard drive. When a program or DOS operation requests more data, the SMARTDRV program redirects the request to check the cache memory area to see whether the requested data is located there. If SMARTDRV finds the information in the cache, it operates on it from there. If the requested information does not exist in the cache, the system accesses the hard drive for it.

Using this technique, the overall operating speed of the system is improved. When the system is shut down, SMARTDRV copies the most current information onto the hard drive. Therefore, no data is lost simply because it is stored in RAM. The idea behind SMARTDRV operations is described by Figure 4.32.

The 1024 modifier establishes a memory cache size of 1MB (1024KB of memory) in extended memory. This is a typical cache size for SMARTDRV, but 2MB (2048KB) is probably the most efficient size for the cache. This is because the larger the cache size, the greater the chance the requested information will be in the cache—there is no need to go to the hard drive for the information. If the command is modified further by an /a extension, the cache is established under an expanded memory operation instead of extended memory. Extended memory is the default for SMARTDRV operations.

The RAMDRIVE.SYS driver simulates the organization of a hard-disk drive in RAM memory. This type of drive is called a **virtual disk**. In this case, the DEVICEHIGH= command loads the RAMDRV into the upper memory area instead of the base memory area, where a simple DEVICE= command would run it. Likewise, the DOS=HIGH,UMB command shifts the operation of DOS into the high memory area, and gives the application access to the upper memory area.

FIGURE 4.32

How SMARTDRV works.

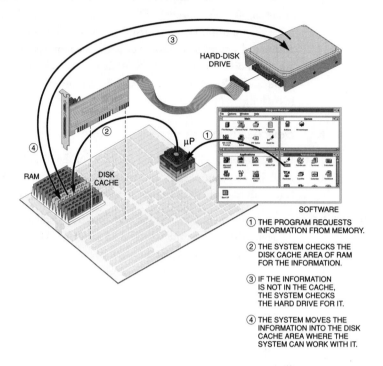

SOFTWARE

① THE PROGRAM REQUESTS INFORMATION FROM MEMORY.

② THE SYSTEM CHECKS THE DISK CACHE AREA OF RAM FOR THE INFORMATION.

③ IF THE INFORMATION IS NOT IN THE CACHE, THE SYSTEM CHECKS THE HARD DRIVE FOR IT.

④ THE SYSTEM MOVES THE INFORMATION INTO THE DISK CACHE AREA WHERE THE SYSTEM CAN WORK WITH IT.

The operation of both the SMARTDRV.SYS and RAMDRIVE.SYS device drivers is governed by the HIMEM.SYS memory manager. This is only normal because both programs involve the use of memory beyond the 1MB conventional memory level. Likewise, the DEVICEHIGH= and DOS=HIGH commands that move programs into the upper memory area perform under the guidance of the HIMEM.SYS manager.

The fourth portion of the file sets up the system to use special keyboard shortcuts available in the DOSKEY program. DOSKEY is a type of program referred to as a **memory-resident program**. Memory-resident programs are programs that run in the background of other programs.

The DOS INSTALL command is placed in the CONFIG.SYS file to load memory-resident files into memory when DOS starts. These files remain in memory as long as the system is on. A common install command is as follows: **INSTALL=C:\DOS\SHARE.EXE**. The SHARE program provides the capability of sharing files in a networked, or multitasking, environment.

Other common CONFIG.SYS commands include these:

- ❯ BREAK
- ❯ COUNTRY
- ❯ DRIVPARM
- ❯ LASTDRIVE
- ❯ NUMLOCK
- ❯ REM

- ▶ SET

- ▶ SHELL

- ▶ INCLUDE

- ▶ MENUCOLOR

- ▶ MENUDEFAULT

- ▶ SUBMENU

The definitions and usage of these commands are covered in detail in the MS-DOS user's guide. The DOS installable device drivers are also defined in that publication.

Altering CONFIG.SYS Steps

A+ DOS/WINDOWS 1.1
The operation of the CONFIG.SYS file can be altered or bypassed by pressing selected keyboard keys during the boot-up process. Holding the SHIFT key, or pressing the F5 key while the MS-DOS message "Starting DOS..." is on the screen, causes the boot-up process to skip all the commands in the CONFIG.SYS file. This action also bypasses all the steps of the AUTOEXEC.BAT file (discussed in the next section).

When this option is used, the system boots with a complete set of default settings. No installable device drivers are installed, the current directory is set to C:\DOS, and you may receive a "Bad or missing command interpreter" message. If this message is received, the system asks you to manually enter the path to the COMMAND.COM file.

Similarly, pressing the F8 function key while the DOS message is on the screen causes the system to stop between each CONFIG.SYS command and ask for verification before proceeding. This can be very helpful in troubleshooting configuration and boot-up problems. This action also causes the system to ask the user if the AUTOEXEC.BAT file should be run or skipped. Placing a question mark after a CONFIG.SYS command (before the = sign) causes the system to automatically seek verification whenever the system is booted.

DOS comes with several other standard device driver programs. These include the following:

- ▶ KEYBOARD.SYS

- ▶ DISPLAY.SYS

- ▶ ANSI.SYS

- ▶ DRIVER.SYS

- ▶ PRINTER.SYS

KEYBOARD.SYS is the DOS default keyboard definition file. The DISPLAY.SYS driver supports code-page switching for the monitor type in use by the system. A **code page** is the set of 256 characters that DOS can handle at one time when displaying, printing, and manipulating text. ANSI.SYS supports ANSI escape-code sequences used to modify the function of the system's display and keyboard. This file is also required to display colors on the monitor in DOS. DRIVER.SYS creates the logical drive assignments for the system (such as A: and C:). Finally, the PRINTER.SYS driver supports code-page switching for parallel ports. All these drivers are normally found in the DOS directory.

POWER.EXE

A special power-saving program called POWER.EXE is designed for use in notebook computers. When it is loaded in the last line of the CONFIG.SYS file, and when the system hardware meets the **Advanced Power Management (APM)** specification, the power savings can be as high as 25%. This is an important savings when discussing the operation of a battery before it needs to be recharged. The POWER.EXE file must be available in the C:\DOS directory.

AUTOEXEC.BAT

After completing the CONFIG.SYS operation, DOS searches for the presence of a file called the AUTOEXEC.BAT file. This file contains a **batch** of DOS commands that are automatically carried out when DOS is loaded into the system.

This file can also be re-executed from the DOS prompt by simply typing the command **AUTOEXEC**. This is not true of the CONFIG.SYS file, however. The system must be restarted to perform the commands in this file.

Refer to the following sample AUTOEXEC.BAT file:

```
DATE
TIME
PROMPT=$P$G
SET TEMP=C:\TEMP
PATH=C:\;C:\DOS;C:\MOUSE
DOSKEYSMARTDRV.EXE 2048 1024
CD\
DIR
```

The first two commands cause DOS to prompt you for the date and time (DOS does not automatically do this when an AUTOEXEC.BAT file is present). The PROMPT=PG command causes the active drive and directory path to be displayed on the command line. The SET TEMP= line sets up an area for holding data temporarily in a directory named TEMP.

The PATH command creates a specific set of paths that DOS uses to search for program files. In this case, DOS searches for executable files first in the root directory, followed by the DOS directory, and finally through the MOUSE directory. This statement effectively enables the Mouse program to be executed from anywhere in the system. Upon receiving the command, the operating system looks through all the directories in the path until it finds the specified filename.

The syntax (punctuation and organization) of the PATH command is very important. Each entry must be complete from the root directory and must be separated from the previous entry by a semicolon. No spaces should be present in the PATH command.

The DOSKEY command loads the DOSKEY program into memory. Following this, the SMARTDRV.EXE 2048 1024 command configures the system for a 2MB disk cache in DOS and a 1MB cache for Windows. After the cache has been established, the CD\ command causes the DOS default directory to change to the root directory. The last line causes a DOS DIR command to be performed automatically at the end of the operation.

The execution of the AUTOEXEC.BAT file can be interrupted by pressing the Pause key on the keyboard; the program can be restarted by pressing any key. With DOS version 6.2, the F8 interactive bypass procedure (described for use with the CONFIG.SYS file) was extended to include the AUTOEXEC.BAT file.

You can use the DOS batch file commands to construct elaborate start-up procedures. Other programs designed to test ports and peripherals can be constructed using these commands as well. These test files can be named using the DOS filename conventions. They must be stored with a .BAT extension to be executed from the DOS prompt, but the extension does not need to be entered to run the program.

Neither of these two special files are required for normal operation of the computer with DOS. However, they can prove to be very useful in tailoring the operation of the system to your personal use, or to the requirements of different software applications packages. To determine whether either of these files already exist on your DOS disk, simply type the DIR command at the DOS prompt (with the disk in the default drive).

Refer to the MS-DOS® user's guide manual for more information about the creation and use of the CONFIG.SYS and AUTOEXEC.BAT files. Other DOS utilities for disk management are covered in the disk drive and preventive maintenance chapters (Chapter 8 and Chapter 13, "Preventive Maintenance, Safety, and Customer Service").

DOS Editor

A+ DOS/WINDOWS 4.6

Later versions of DOS contain a small text editor program (EDIT.COM) that enables users to easily modify text files. This package is started by typing **EDIT** and the filename at the DOS prompt. The DOS editor's working screen is depicted in Figure 4.33. The editor is an unformatted text-file editor that is particularly useful in modifying the CONFIG.SYS and AUTOEXEC.BAT files. It does not introduce formatting codes, such as underlining and italics, into the text in the manner that more powerful word processors do. This is an important consideration when dealing with DOS utility files. Formatting codes can introduce errors in these files because DOS cannot recognize them.

FIGURE 4.33

The DOS Editor screen.

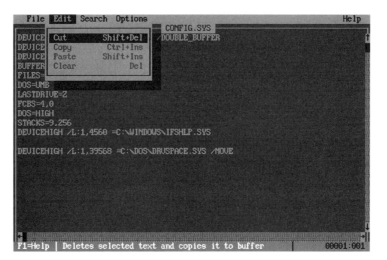

DOS Versions

Although DOS has remained compatible with its original design, this does not mean that it has not changed significantly since its original version.

In July 1981, Microsoft purchased the rights to a personal computer DOS from the Seattle Computer Products and promptly named it MS-DOS. A month later IBM began shipping a private labeled version of the Microsoft package that it named PC-DOS 1.0.

In May 1982, Microsoft released MS-DOS version 1.1 to IBM for its units and then released its own brand-name DOS product, MS-DOS 1.25, for PC-compatible computers. This version added support for 360KB double-sided floppy disk drives.

In March 1983, MS-DOS 2.0 was announced. This version added support for 10MB hard drives, a directory tree structure, and 360KB floppy drive support to the operating system. A minor revision, entitled MS-DOS 2.11, added foreign language and date features to the operating system in March 1984.

Version 3.0 of MS-DOS, released in August 1984 along with IBM's AT model, added support for 1.2MB floppy disk drives and larger hard-disk drives. In November of the same year, version 3.1 added support for Microsoft networks. By January 1986, version 3.2 had entered the market and brought support for 3-1/2-inch, 720KB floppy-disk drives to the operating system.

In August 1987, version 3.3 delivered a 1.44MB floppy-disk drive and multiple 32MB partitions for hard drives.

Version 4.0 of MS-DOS was released in June 1988. This new version introduced a graphical shell for DOS, a mouse interface, and expanded memory drivers. By November, version 4.01 was being shipped to clean up problems with the 4.0 version.

The next version of MS-DOS didn't appear until June 1991. Version 5.0 brought a full screen editor, task-swapping capabilities, Undelete and Unformat commands, and QBASIC to the operating system. In addition, it included support for upper memory blocks, larger hard disk partition sizes (up to 2GB), support for 2.88MB floppies, and the capability of loading DOS into the HMA and loading device drivers into the UMBs.

Microsoft began shipping the 6.0 version of MS-DOS in March 1993. This new version included a DoubleSpace disk compression utility that enabled users to double the storage capacity of their hard-disk drives. More than 1 million copies of this version sold within the first month and a half. An enhanced version, MS-DOS 6.2, was released in November of the same year. By February 1994, legal problems over the compression utility caused Microsoft to release version 6.21 with the utility removed. However, by June, version 6.22 appeared with the compression software back in the operating system under the name DriveSpace.

In April 1994, IBM released a new version of PC-DOS: version 6.3. In January 1995, the company followed with PC-DOS 7, which included data compression for hard-disk doubling. This marked the last release of a major command line-based DOS operating system. Table 4.2 summarizes the development of DOS products.

Table 4.2 *DOS Development Timeline*

Year	Version	Features
1981	V1.0	First operating system for IBM-PC.
	V1.25	Double-sided disk support and bug fixes added; widely distributed by OEMs.
1983	V2.0	Hierarchical file support and hard-disk support.
	V2.01	International support added.
	V2.11	V2.01 with bug fixes.
1984	V3.0	Introduced with AT model. Support for 1.2MB floppy and larger hard-disk sizes.
	V3.1	Support for Microsoft Networks added.
1986	V3.2	Enhanced support for new media types added.

1987	V3.3	Support for 1.44MB floppy, support for four serial ports, hard-disk partitions greater than 32MB, improved national language support.
	V4.0	DOSSHELL, support for TSRs, expanded memory drivers, an install program (Select), and the MEM command.
	V4.01	V4.0 with bug fixes.
1992	V5.0	Support for upper memory blocks, larger partition sizes (greater than 2GB), loading device drivers in UMB, improved DOSSHELL and online help, support for 2.88MB drives, Qbasic, improved system editor (Edit).
1994	V6.0	DoubleSpace disk compression introduced.
	V6.22	DriveSpace disk compression, replaces DoubleSpace.

Installing DOS

A+ DOS/WINDOWS 3.3

In the earliest versions of DOS, the operating system was contained on two disks, the **system disk** and the **supplemental disk**. Because the early PCs operated from floppy-disk drives, they booted directly to the system disk. The most used DOS utility functions were loaded into RAM. For advanced DOS functions, the supplemental disk was inserted in the drive when requested by the system.

When the PCs moved to hard-drive operations, the main DOS files were placed on the hard disk as part of its formatting process. The other DOS files were typically copied into a C:\DOS directory when the unit was set up.

The installation of newer DOS versions (after 5.0) is a relatively easy process controlled by the file SETUP.EXE. The only response required by this program is to tell it whether DOS should be installed on the hard-disk drive. The installation process is so automated in newer versions that it runs the SETUP.EXE program automatically on new systems. This is accomplished simply by starting the system with the first DOS disk (one of three) in the floppy drive.

The setup program's installation screen default to the C:\DOS subdirectory to install the DOS files. The files on the installation floppies are compressed so that they cannot simply be copied onto the hard drive. As the DOS files are installed, the setup program automatically determines the amount of memory, the number of drives, and other configuration information about your computer.

With versions of MS-DOS from 5.0 forward, the setup program also creates the files AUTOEXEC.BAT and CONFIG.SYS. After setup has determined the configuration, the findings are presented for the user to check. If the setup program incorrectly determines the configuration, it can be changed during the setup.

DOS Shell

Versions of DOS from 4.0 forward offer an option to install the **DOS shell**, a multiple-window user interface that simplifies performing DOS operations. The DOS shell interface is depicted in Figure 4.34.

As illustrated in the figure, the DOS shell divides the screen into four basic areas:

- Title bar
- Directory tree window
- File list window
- Program list window

FIGURE 4.34

The DOS shell.

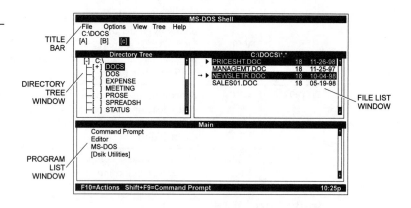

The **drive icons** under the **title bar** are used to select the disk drive to carry out any DOS functions. The drive icon is selected by highlighting it with the cursor and then pressing the Enter key. When the drive is selected, its directory structure appears in the directory tree window.

The **directory tree window** shows the organization of the selected disk's directory structure. As with drive selection, a particular directory or subdirectory can be selected using the cursor. When this is done, the contents of the directory appear in the file list window.

The program list window shows programs that can be run directly from the shell, such as QBASIC and DOS Editor.

Versions beginning with version 4.0 MS-DOS enabled task swapping. By enabling the Task Swapper utility in the title bar's Options menu, multiple programs could be run simultaneously. The execution of the programs was not simultaneous, but there was no need to exit from one program to start another. All the active programs appear in the Active Task window; switching among them involves a simple operation of getting to the shell and then clicking on the desired program in the window.

The shell made it easy to locate and start files on the disk. Any program could be located by scrolling through the different windows. When the desired file is located, it can be run by simply highlighting it with the cursor and pressing the Enter key, or by clicking a mouse button. No cryptic commands must be remembered, and no long paths must be typed.

Troubleshooting DOS

A+ DOS/WINDOWS 4.1

MS-DOS problems can be divided into two basic categories: **startup problems** and **operating problems**. DOS does not produce a log file, so it is necessary to perform a minimal boot if the system does not respond to a normal reboot.

DOS Startup Problems

Typical DOS startup error messages include the following:

▶ Unrecognized command in CONFIG.SYS

▶ Bad or Missing Command interpreter

A+ DOS/WINDOWS 4.2 These and other error messages during the boot-up process indicate that a problem exists that must be sorted out before the system can boot up and operate correctly. If the DOS system will not boot up correctly, it is necessary to use the F5 function key startup method to bypass the CONFIG.SYS and AUTOEXEC.BAT commands. This boots the system to a minimum configuration and establishes a point to begin troubleshooting the problem. The same function can be performed by running a clean boot disk to start the system. A guide for creating a **clean boot disk** is presented in the next section.

If the system boots up from the minimal condition, restart the system and press the F8 function key while the "Starting MS-DOS" message is on the screen to move through the CONFIG.SYS and AUTOEXEC.BAT files individually. The **single step method** can be used to isolate the problem command. If the system crashes while trying to execute a particular command, restart the boot-up process and skip the offending command. Repeat the process until the system reaches a successful boot. Track all offending commands so that they can be corrected individually.

Another common setup problem occurs when the system displays a "There is not enough free space on drive C to install MS-DOS" message. When this occurs, run the CHKDSK C:(check disk) command from the floppy drive. This provides a description of the free space available on the hard drive. Remove files from the disk until enough room has been cleared to perform the installation. It is recommended that the files be backed up to some other medium before erasing them from the drive.

DOS Operating Problems

A+ DOS/WINDOWS 4.1

A+ DOS/WINDOWS 4.6

The most common DOS operating problems involve memory-management issues. One of the most common errors occurs when a DOS program displays an "Out of memory" message. When this happens, it becomes necessary to free up additional memory. The first step in this process is to use the DOS MEM command to determine how much memory is actually in the system and how it is organized.

The real objective in memory management is to free up additional conventional memory. This can be accomplished by running the DOS Memmaker command from the DOS prompt. Memmaker moves device drivers and other memory resident programs into the system's upper memory area by modifying entries in the CONFIG.SYS and AUTOEXEC.BAT files. In particular, Memmaker changes switches associated with the EMM386.EXE entry. It also changes some of the device= lines to devicehigh= statements, and it may add loadhigh commands to some of the AUTOEXEC.BAT lines.

Use the steps outlined in the "Optimizing DOS" section that follows to free up as much memory as possible.

Another typical DOS operating error message is "Incorrect DOS version." This message is produced when a DOS utility such as DISKCOPY, FDISK, or MEM does not find the version of the operating system with which it is designed to work. This condition exists whenever a system has been booted from a different version of DOS than the one that resides on the hard drive, or when the system files of the hard disk have been repaired with a SYS command using a different version of DOS. In these cases, the correct version of DOS required to run the utility must be used. Use the VER command to determine which DOS version is in use.

Self-Booting DOS Disk

It is always good to have a clean boot disk to start the system. This tool provides a well-defined point to begin troubleshooting operating system problems.

To create a self-booting DOS disk, place a new disk in the floppy drive and enter the following lines at the DOS prompt:

```
Format A:/s
MD C:\DOS
CD \DOS
```

To make the disk truly useful, the following files should be copied to the boot disk under the DOS directory:

```
FDISK
FORMAT
SYS
EDIT
CHKDSK
MSD
```

New minimum configuration CONFIG.SYS and AUTOEXEC.BAT files should be created for the startup disk. The files should include the following entries:

```
CONFIG.SYS
FILES=40
BUFFERS=40
SHELL=COMMAND.COM C:\DOS /p /e:256

AUTOEXEC.BAT
PATH=c:\;C:DOS
PROMPT $P$G
SET COMSPEC=C:\DOS
```

Optimizing DOS

A+ DOS/WINDOWS 2.2

The following steps can be used to optimize the operation of the system at the DOS level:

1. Use a dos=high or dos=high,umb command in the CONFIG.SYS file to load DOS into the HMA.

2. Check the CONFIG.SYS and AUTOEXEC.BAT files for lines that load the HIMEM.SYS, EMM386.EXE, SMARTDRV.EXE, and RAMDRIVE.SYS drivers. In each case, make certain that the latest version of the driver is located in the specified directory.

3. Check the order of commands in the CONFIG.SYS file to make certain that the HIMEM.SYS driver is loaded before any other extended memory application or driver. If not, move the command closer to the beginning of the file.

4. Set the memory cache size for the SMARTDRV.EXE command in the AUTOEXEC.BAT file to the largest size possible.

5. Optimize the CONFIG.SYS lines for buffers and files. Set files equal to 30, unless a currently installed application requires more handles. This step should also be used if DOS or Windows 3.x operations return a "Too Many Files are Open" message. The number of buffers should be set to 10 if SMARTDRV is being used, and to 20 if not. Using more than 10 buffers with SMARTDRV decreases efficiency; using more than 20 buffers without SMARTDRV uses more of the system's conventional memory area.

6. Set up the RAMDRIVE to use the TEMP environment. This improves printing performance and the operation of other applications that use .TMP files.

7. Load EMM386.EXE to allocate upper memory blocks for TSRs and device drivers.

Even using the setup steps listed above, the system's performance will deteriorate over time. Most of this deterioration is due to unnecessary file clutter and segmentation of the system's hard disk drive. The following steps can be used to periodically tune up the performance of the system. These steps are explained in greater detail in Chapter 13.

1. Periodically remove unnecessary .TMP and .BAK files from the system.

2. Check for and remove lost file chains and clusters using the DOS CHKDSK and CHKDSK /f commands.

3. Use the DOS DEFRAG utility to realign files on the drive that may have become fragmented after being moved back and forth between the drive and the system.

Key Point Review

This chapter has examined basic operating systems in depth. In particular, it has concentrated on the ROM BIOS and MS-DOS disk operating systems.

▶ Literally thousands of different operating systems are in use with microcomputers. The complexity of each operating system typically depends on the complexity of the application the microcomputer is designed to fill.

▶ In multiuser and multitasking operations, the appearance of simultaneous operation is accomplished by switching between different tasks in a predetermined order. The multiuser system switches between different users at multiple locations, and multitasking systems switch between different applications at a single location.

▶ The POST test is actually a series of tests that are performed each time the system is turned on. The different tests check the operation of the microprocessor, the keyboard, the video display, the floppy- and hard-disk drive units, and both the RAM and ROM memory units.

▶ If the first 16KB of RAM successfully passes all five bit-pattern tests, the BIOS routine initializes the system's intelligent devices. During this part of the program, startup values stored in the ROM chip are moved into the system's programmable devices to make them functional.

▶ After the initialization and POST tests are completed, the BIOS checks the area of memory between C0000h and DFFFFh for BIOS extension programs.

▶ On Pentium-based system boards, the configuration jumpers and switches for enabling functions have been replaced by BIOS enabling settings. These settings usually include the disk drives, keyboard, and video options, as well as on-board serial and parallel ports.

▶ If an error or setup mismatch is encountered, BIOS issues an error code, either in message form on the display screen or in beep-coded form through the system's speaker.

▶ The boot-up process starts when BIOS begins looking through the system for a master boot record. This record can reside on drive A: or C:, or at any other location.

▶ While the system is operating, the BIOS continues to perform several important functions. In particular, BIOS contains routines that the operating system calls on to carry out basic services; these include providing BIOS interrupt CALLs (software-interrupt routines) for such operations as printer, video, and disk-drive accesses.

▶ MS-DOS is a disk operating system for IBM PC-compatible computers. As with any other operating system, its function is to oversee operation of the system by providing support for executing programs, controlling I/O devices, handling errors, and providing the user interface. MS-DOS is a disk-based, single-user, single-task operating system.

- The second section of a DOS disk is an area referred to as the File Allocation Table (FAT). This area is a table of information about how the disk is organized. Basically, the system logs the use of the space on the disk in this table.

- The next section following the FAT tables is the disk's root directory, a special directory that is present on every DOS disk. The root directory is the main directory of every logical disk, and it serves as the starting point for organizing information on the disk.

- The operating system is responsible for providing the user interface. The main user interface for DOS is the command line, which is the space immediately following the DOS prompt on the screen.

- The DOS Mode command is used to configure the system's I/O devices. These devices include the parallel and serial ports, as well as the monitor display and the keyboard.

- Basically, DOS can recognize the following classifications of memory: conventional memory, upper memory blocks, high memory area, expanded memory, extended memory, and virtual memory.

- The CONFIG.SYS program is responsible for: (1) setting up any memory managers being used, (2) configuring the DOS program for use with options devices and application programs, (3) loading device-driver software, and installing memory-resident programs.

- After completing the CONFIG.SYS operation, DOS searches for the presence of a file called the AUTOEXEC.BAT file. This file contains a batch of DOS commands that will be carried out automatically when DOS is loaded into the system.

- MS-DOS problems can be divided into two basic categories: startup problems and operating problems. DOS does not produce a log file, so it is necessary to perform a minimal boot-up if the system does not respond to a normal reboot.

- It is always good to have a clean boot disk to start the system. This tool provides a well-defined point to begin troubleshooting operating system problems.

At this point, review the objectives listed at the beginning of the chapter to be certain that you understand and can perform each item listed there. Afterward, answer the review questions that follow to verify your knowledge of the information.

Multiple Choice Questions

1. Which DOS command prepares a disk to function as a self-booting disk?

    a. Boot /s

    b. FDISK /s

    c. Format /s

    d. MEM /s

2. Choose the DOS prompt for a default directory of mouse on the D: drive.

    a. C:\dos\mouse

    b. C:\mouse.exe

    c. D:\mouse.exe

    d. D:\dos\mouse

3. In terms of managing processes, what type of operating system is DOS?

    a. A single-process, batch-mode operating system

    b. A multiple-process, interactive-mode operating system

    c. A multiple-process, batch-mode operating system

    d. A single-process, interactive-mode operating system

4. For which file is the operating system loader looking during the boot-up process?

    a. An OS loader

    b. A primary bootstrap loader

    c. A master boot record

    d. The root directory

5. What is the purpose of placing a SMARTDRV.EXE command in the CONFIG.SYS file?

   a. To establish a disk cache in conventional memory

   b. To establish a disk cache in extended memory

   c. To establish a disk cache in base memory

   d. To establish a RAM disk in extended memory

6. Where would you find the system's memory managers listed?

   a. In the CONFIG.SYS file

   b. In the boot record

   c. In the AUTOEXEC.BAT file

   d. In the COMMAND.COM file

7. List the three files that must be located in the root directory to successfully boot MS-DOS.

   a. MSDOS.SYS, IO.SYS, and COMMAND.COM

   b. CONFIG.SYS, COMMAND.COM, and AUTOEXEC.BAT

   c. FILES, STACKS, and BUFFERS

   d. HIMEM.SYS, EMM386.EXE, and COMMAND.COM

8. Which filename extensions enable programs to be started directly from the DOS prompt?

   a. .TXT, .BAT, and .DOC

   b. .EXE, .COM, and .BAT

   c. .EXE, .DOC, and .BAT

   d. .BAT, .EXE, and .BAS

9. What does HIMEM.SYS do?

   a. It governs the use of shadow RAM.

   b. It governs the use of conventional memory.

   c. It governs the use of extended memory.

   d. It governs the use of base memory.

10. Write a DOS command that can be used to make a duplicate of another disk.

   a. COPY A:

   b. DISKDUP A:

   c. DUPCOPY A:

   d. DISKCOPY A:

Review Questions

1. What function does the POWER.EXE file perform, and where is it commonly found?

2. Under what conditions is it normally necessary to run the CMOS Configuration Setup program?

3. What type of operating system breaks the tasks associated with a process into its various threads for execution?

4. What advantage does the DOS shell offer to the system?

5. What is the first event that occurs when the system is turned on or reset?

6. Which memory manager should always be listed before any other memory managers or device drivers?

7. If the system locks up while the message "Starting DOS" is on the screen, what two actions should be performed?

8. Pressing the F8 key while the "Starting DOS" message is on the screen will have what effect on the system?

9. From the system start-up point of view, how do a cold and a warm boot differ?

10. What does the "*" character stand for when used in a DOS filename?

11. How does the XCOPY command differ from the COPY or DISKCOPY command?

12. How are multitasking and multiuser systems different?

13. Write a DOS command that can be inserted in the AUTOEXEC.BAT file to cause the active path and directory to be shown on the DOS command line.

14. What condition is indicated by the presence of an A:\> prompt on the monitor screen?

15. What does the BUFFERS= command in the CONFIG.SYS file do?

Lab Exercises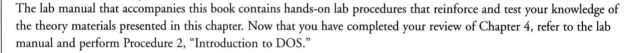

The lab manual that accompanies this book contains hands-on lab procedures that reinforce and test your knowledge of the theory materials presented in this chapter. Now that you have completed your review of Chapter 4, refer to the lab manual and perform Procedure 2, "Introduction to DOS."

MICROSOFT WINDOWS

Upon completion of this chapter and its related lab procedures, you should be able to perform these tasks:

1. Use the various Windows 3.x Setup modes to install Windows into a system.

2. List the core files in the Windows 3.x and Windows 95 structures.

3. Alter typical Windows 3.x Control Panel values.

4. List the standard .INI files in Windows 3.x and describe their functions.

5. Describe multitasking operations in Windows 3.x and Windows 95.

6. State reasons for implementing security measures in multiuser or networked systems.

7. Create a clean boot disk for troubleshooting Windows 3.x problems.

8. State major differences between Windows 3.x and Windows 95.

9. Describe the boot-up sequence employed by Windows 95.

10. Manipulate the Windows 95 Registry structure.

11. Use the Policy Editor to change Windows policy settings.

12. Use various Safe Mode startup scenarios.

13. Bypass and correct inoperable Windows startup sequences.

14. Create an emergency start disk for troubleshooting Windows 95 startup problems.

15. Use log files to determine the location of Windows 95 operating system problems.

CHAPTER 5

Introduction

The previous chapter explored operating systems in some detail. Most of the information covered BIOS operations and DOS command-line structure, and the chapter concluded with a discussion of a graphical user interface for MS-DOS—the DOS shell. It may be easy to think that the Windows programs evolved out of the DOS program, but this is not the case. Microsoft Windows was first introduced in 1984; 10 years before Microsoft introduced its final version of MS-DOS. The pressure for a GUI operating system for PCs actually came from the Apple operating systems.

This chapter continues with operating system software by examining Microsoft's Windows programs. The first half of the chapter deals with the 3.x versions of Windows. In these versions, Windows operates as an **operating environment**. This can most easily be thought of as a three-layer operating system—the BIOS, DOS, and Windows.

The final sections of the chapter deal with Windows 95. Unlike its predecessors, Windows 95 is a true operating system: No DOS foundation is required.

Windows Evolution

In April 1983 Microsoft demonstrated a **graphical interface manager** that would later become Windows. This system gave the appearance of overlapping window panes, with various programs running in each window. In November of the same year, Microsoft formally announced Windows and set a release date of April 1984. Interestingly, IBM passed on the opportunity to market Windows with its units three different times—the company was busy developing a GUI called TopView for its systems.

Microsoft announced Windows 1.0 in June 1985 and began shipping it in November. The product found a PC market that was steeped in command-line operations. Many industry analysts predicted it would come and go and that "real computer users" would hold on to their DOS disks.

Version 2.0 was announced in April 1987 and actually hit the market in October, along with a version called Windows/386. By December of that year, Microsoft had shipped more than 1 million copies of Windows. Two versions of Windows 2.1 shipped in June 1988 under the titles Windows/286 and Windows/386.

Windows 3.0 did not make it to the market until May 1990. However, it opened with a $3 million first-day advertising campaign. In March 1992, Microsoft produced its first television advertising campaign for the upcoming Windows 3.1 version. The new version began shipping in April and reached a level of 1 million copies shipped by June. The 3.1 version migrated into Windows for Workgroups (WfW) in November 1992. This version integrated peer-to-peer networking directly into the operating environment. It was quick and easy to install. It also set up a workgroup network to share information and resources between different computers, concepts that were not usually associated with the process of networking computers. By April 1993, the number of licensed units sold had risen to 25 million copies of Windows. By October, Microsoft had begun shipping 3.11, the final 3.x version of Windows.

In September 1994, Microsoft announced the next version of Windows: Windows 95. The first version was released in August 1995, and 1 million copies were sold during the first week on the market. Within a month, the sales of Windows 95 climbed to more than 7 million copies and by March 1996 had topped 30 million copies.

From this historical outline, it is easy to see why this chapter focuses on Windows 3.x and Windows 95. Due to the huge installed base of these products, any technician must be familiar with these operating systems for the immediate future. Table 5.1 summarizes the versions and their features.

Table 5.1 *Windows Development Time Line*

Year	Version	Features
1983		Graphics Interface Manager demonstrated
1985	V1.0	First official Windows release
1987	V2.0 Windows/286 Windows/386	Task switching of applications Use of all the extended memory for applications Cooperative multitasking of applications
1990	V3.0	Pre-emptive multitasking of applications, enhanced memory support, use of icons, Program Manager interface
1992	V3.1	(Windows for Workgroups) Integrated peer-to-peer networking directly into the operating environment
1993	V3.11	Upgraded 32-bit software and disk capabilities; BIOS calls removed from file accesses
1995	Windows 95	Improved multimedia support, plug-and-play hardware support, 32-bit advanced multitasking function, improved email and fax capabilities, WAN usage
1998	Windows 98	Upgraded Windows 95 and integrated Internet Explorer into the Windows 98 interface.

Microsoft Windows 3.x

A+ DOS/WINDOWS 1.1

Windows is a **graphical working environment** that makes it easier for people to use computers. Under Windows, each application runs in a window on the screen that can open or close. It is possible to run multiple applications at the same time, each in its own window, and to switch easily between them.

Windows can be installed on any computer using a 286 or higher microprocessor.

Windows works most effectively with the pointing device known as a **mouse**. The mouse is used to select graphical program options from the screen to be executed. It works with Windows software by moving a screen symbol, called a **cursor**, across the screen as the mouse is rolled across a desktop.

When the cursor points to an **icon** (a graphical symbol) on the screen, the program represented by the icon can be selected by simply pressing (clicking) the left button on the mouse. Likewise, the program can be run by double-clicking the mouse button on the icon. Remember that a single click selects and a double click executes. The icon images are usually created by the software manufacturer and are different for each application. However, the same icon can be used to represent different programs within the system or within a single window.

Moving the mouse in a given direction produces corresponding movement of the cursor on the screen. To select an object on the screen, simply move the cursor over the item, as illustrated in Figure 5.1, and click one of the mouse buttons.

FIGURE 5.1

Selecting an item from the screen.

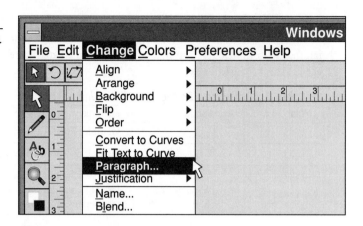

Installing Windows 3.x

Windows 3.x is relatively simple to install. A standard setup involves placing the setup disk 1 in the A: drive and then typing **SETUP** at the A:\>> prompt. The SETUP program examines the system to determine what hardware is being used, installs the Windows files on the hard disk, configures its initialization files with default information, searches for existing application programs on the hard disk, creates **Program Information Files** (**PIF**s) about any DOS-based files it finds, and modifies the existing CONFIG.SYS and AUTOEXEC.BAT files.

When installing Windows 3.x on a system, it is important to examine the requirements of any TSR programs that may be on the drive. These programs remain on the drive after the installation and could create conflicts with Windows components.

The command SETUP/A can be used to install a shared copy of Windows on a network drive. Likewise, the command SETUP/I sets up Windows to start, without regard to any automatic hardware detection.

Windows 3.1 requires a minimum of a 286 system with 2MB of RAM to start in Standard mode. This includes 256KB of free conventional memory and 192KB of free extended memory. A memory manager such as HIMEM.SYS must also be loaded before starting Windows. Windows 3.11 requires a 386 system with a total of 4MB of RAM to start in Standard mode.

To start Windows in 386 Enhanced mode, a minimum of an 80386SX microprocessor, 256KB of free conventional memory, and an extended memory of 1024KB are required. A memory manager must also be loaded before Windows.

Windows checks the system memory before selecting the mode in which it will start. If Windows finds less than 1MB of extended memory present, it automatically defaults to Standard mode. If the system possesses an 80386 microprocessor and 2MB of RAM, it can run efficiently in 386 Enhanced mode. This mode makes use of the virtual memory capabilities of 80386 and newer microprocessors.

Running Windows

A+ DOS/WINDOWS 1.1

The Windows program can be loaded into the system by typing **WIN** at the C:\>> prompt. This command executes the WIN.COM program in the Windows directory. The WIN.COM file checks the system type, memory arrangements, and device drivers to determine the mode in which to start. Typing **WIN/S** forces the system to start Windows in

Standard mode. Conversely, the command **WIN/3** forces the system to run in Enhanced 386 mode, if possible. WIN.COM uses the file DOSX.EXE to start in Standard mode, and it uses WIN386.EXE to start in Enhanced mode. An extended memory manager (XMS)—such as HIMEM.SYS, QEMM, or 386-MAX—is required before either mode can be used.

Win/s could be considered 80286 mode. The 80286 microprocessor had no capability of running separate applications simultaneously and keeping them from interfering with each other. Although it was possible to task-switch in Standard mode, multitasking was not possible.

The Windows 386 Enhanced mode was designed to take advantage of the 80386 micro-processor's **virtual protected mode**. In this mode, the 80386 can act like multiple 8086 microprocessors operating simultaneously. This is also known as **virtual 86 mode**. Each virtual 86 environment established is known as a **virtual machine** and operates like a completely independent 8086 machine.

This mode is extremely useful for running DOS applications from the Windows environment. This condition is discussed in greater detail later in the section "DOS and Windows."

In any event, WIN.COM brings together the Windows core files, driver files, fonts, support files for non-Windows applications, and DOS mode-specific programs.

The core files are as follows:

▶ KRNL386.EXE (Windows kernel)

▶ USER.EXE

▶ GDI.EXE

The kernel is the file that controls the usage of the systems memory and I/O resources, as well as loading and executing Windows applications. The USER.EXE file creates and controls the various windows on the screen, and it is responsible for handling requests to create, move, size, or delete windows on the screen. In addition, the USER.EXE file controls user input and output through the mouse, keyboard, and communications ports. The GDI file controls the Windows GUI functions. These files are located in the \Windows\System directory created when Windows was installed.

The driver files provide the hardware-specific interface between the Windows software and the physical devices in the system. What appears on the screen next is the **Program Manager**, depicted in Figure 5.2. The Program Manager is the application coordinator that is used to associate related software applications and data into groups. The Program Manager uses icons to quickly locate and run applications that you use. On the same screen as the Program Manager are the different groups of applications. Each group has its own icon to represent that group of applications. The default groups included when Windows is installed are Main, Startup, Accessories, Games, and Applications.

The Main group includes system applications that control files and printing, set up peripherals, customize the appearance of Windows (called the **desktop**), and manage files and disks. The Startup group includes optional applications that Windows activates immediately upon startup. The Accessories group includes desktop accessories such as a simple word processor, a calculator, a calendar, a card file, a note pad, and a painting program. The Games group includes two games: Solitaire and Minesweeper. The Applications group includes programs that Windows found when it was installed, such as Backup, and anti-virus programs that run under both DOS and Windows.

FIGURE 5.2

Windows Program Manager.

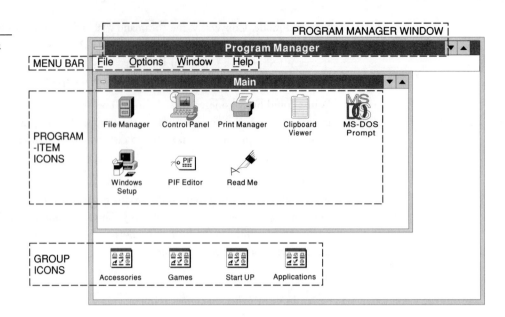

The Windows program can be operated from the keyboard, but it was designed to be used with a mouse. When the mouse is used, a pointer is produced on the screen. By first moving the mouse, which moves the pointer over a selection, and then pressing the left mouse button twice in rapid succession (called double-clicking), the selection is chosen. That item can be dragged across the screen by moving the pointer over it, holding down the mouse button, and then moving the mouse. Afterward, release the mouse button to drop the item. Windows uses only the left button of the mouse.

Main Window

The Main group, depicted in Figure 5.3, contains the File Manager, Control Panel, Print Manager, Clipboard Viewer, MS-DOS Prompt, and Windows Setup icons.

FIGURE 5.3

The Main window.

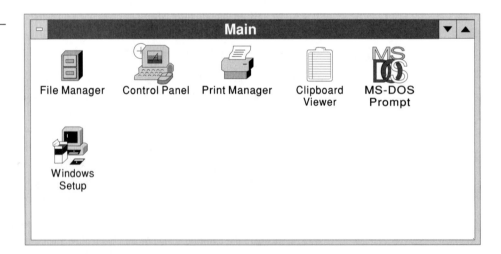

File Manager

The **File Manager** is an application that is used to manage files and disks. This application enables the user to copy, move, and delete files on any of the system's drives. Its icon resembles a file cabinet. The File Manager's screen is divided into three parts. The bar at the top of the screen with File, Disk, Tree, View, Options, Window, and Help options is called the

menu bar. The left side shows a directory tree, with one directory or subdirectory highlighted to show that it is selected. The right side of the screen shows the files contained in the selected directory or subdirectory. At the bottom of the screen is the **status bar**, which shows the number of files and bytes the selected directory consumes. This is illustrated in Figure 5.4.

FIGURE 5.4

The File Manager screen.

MENU
BAR

STATUS
BAR

Multiple directories can be displayed on the same screen, making it easier to perform file operations. Files can be moved or copied from one directory to another. In a move operation, selected files are picked up from one directory or disk and deposited into another directory or disk. In a copy operation, the file is deposited into the new directory and remains in the original directory.

Multiple files can be selected for Move or Copy operations. To select sequential files from the list, click on the first file. Then press SHIFT and click on the last file. All the files between and including the first and last file will be selected. To select nonsequential files for file operations, press the CTRL key and click on each filename. When the desired files have been selected, a move, copy, or delete operation can be performed on all the highlighted files.

The File Manager can perform other DOS-like file-management functions. These functions include disk formatting, as well as directory and file organization and management. Under the Disk entry on the menu bar, options to format, label, and copy disks are available. Self-booting system disks can also be created from this menu.

Under the File option, you will find the capability to open or run selected files. It is also possible to create new directories, search selected directories for a given file, and sort files by their attributes from this menu.

The correct procedure for installing a program or running it from the File Manager window is as follows: Click on the drop-down File option on the menu bar, click on the Run entry, and enter the filename of the program to be installed or run. The same steps can be used to start programs from the menu bars of other windows.

Programs can also be set up to automatically start along with Windows. This operation can be accomplished by placing the program's icon in the Startup window, or by placing a **RUN=programname** or **LOAD=programname** line in the WIN.INI file.

The View menu option enables the user to control how files and directories appear in the File Manager window. Files can be sorted by name, type, size, and date of creation through this menu. Other options in this menu control how the directory tree is displayed on the screen.

Control Panel

The **Control Panel**, which is depicted in Figure 5.5, enables users to modify the system's date and time and to determine how Windows responds to the mouse and keyboard. Its options can be accessed by double-clicking on its icon in the Main window. The Control Panel also facilitates the installation of the system printer(s) and customization of the desktop, as well as featuring Color, Desktop, Fonts, International, and Sound options that can be used to customize Windows to the user's preference.

FIGURE 5.5

The Windows Control Panel.

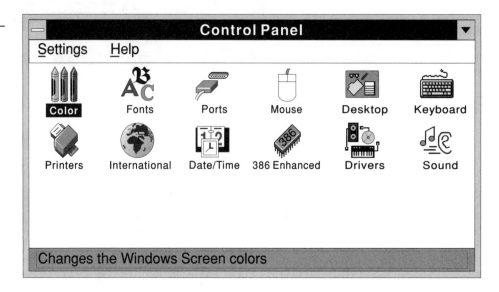

Customizing the Window's desktop from the Control Panel involves setting screen colors and features, such as the Window's wallpaper. Wallpaper is the picture that is displayed behind the Program Manager window.

Still other options, such as Ports and Drivers, are used to further configure the operation of Windows. The **Ports** option is used to set up the serial ports of the computer, and the **Drivers** option is used to install software drivers for other purposes, such as sound boards, mice, and CD-ROM drives.

Windows 3.1 introduced 32-bit access to the Windows package. This feature can be found in the Control Panel window under the Virtual Memory option of the 386 Enhanced icon. Contrary to the sound of its name, 32-bit access has nothing to do with moving data in 32-bit blocks. Instead, 32-bit access is a method of reducing the need to move back and forth between real and protected memory modes when an access request is made.

Before version 3.1 came out, a simple request for a hard-disk access while running in protected mode would result in Windows, DOS, and the BIOS handing the request back and forth a number of times (for example, application to Windows to DOS to Windows to BIOS to Windows to DOS to Windows to application). This operation is illustrated in Figure 5.6.

FIGURE 5.6

The Windows/DOS/BIOS relationship.

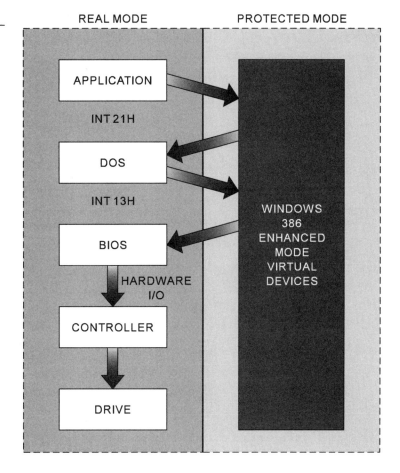

In Windows 3.11, the work associated with this type of operation was reduced by removing the BIOS completely from the loop. A protected-mode device driver called **FastDisk** emulates the BIOS routines in Windows. The upgraded 32-bit software capabilities in 3.11 sped up the operation of the system by eliminating the changes between real and protected modes that occurred each time Windows had to hand over control to the DOS or BIOS. Additional speed was obtained due to the reduced information processing required by cutting the BIOS portion out of the loop. The advanced 32-bit access process using FastDisk is depicted in Figure 5.7.

Windows 3.11 adds 32-bit access capabilities to file accesses as well as disk accesses. This further increases the system's overall operating speed by removing BIOS calls from file accesses.

Windows establishes a swap file on the hard disk to free up memory and speed up operation in 386 Enhanced mode. This file reserves space on the hard drive to allow data to be swapped back and forth between the drive and system memory.

A temporary swap file named WIN386.SWP is created when Windows starts, and it disappears when Windows is shut down. If possible, Windows creates a permanent swap file through its Setup program. This file is governed by two files located on the HDD: SPART.PAR and 386SPART.PAR. The organization and operation of the swap file is controlled through the Virtual Memory option, under the Control Panel's 386 Enhanced icon.

FIGURE 5.7

The 32-bit access with FastDisk.

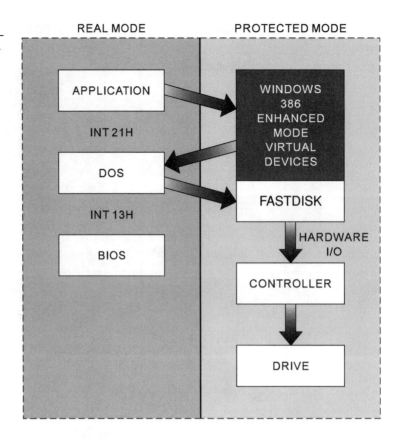

The swap file's size determines how many applications can use the swap file. The best virtual memory performance is achieved by establishing a permanent swap file on the drive. However, for drives that are heavily segmented, or for redirected network drives, a temporary swap file is highly recommended.

The FastDisk function also sets up a **disk cache** area in extended memory to hold data that has already been read from the hard disk. The next time the system tries to read that information, it reads from RAM instead of accessing the hard drive. Data to be written to the disk can be temporarily stored in the cache as well. The default size of the cache is normally 512KB. If the system has sufficient RAM (above 4MB), the size of the cache may be extended to 1MB.

Windows Setup

Windows Setup enables the user to add new applications after Windows has been installed. The Windows Setup icon is available through the Main group window. Double-clicking on its icon brings up the Windows Setup dialog box, depicted in Figure 5.8. The window shows the current driver settings for the video, keyboard, mouse, and network functions. These settings represent the hardware that Windows detected at the time of installation.

To change any of these settings, select the Options entry on the menu bar and choose the Change System Settings command. Select the system setting to be changed by clicking on the down arrow button by its entry. This action brings up a list of options available for that setting.

The Set Up Applications option is used to install new Windows applications. This option either searches the drive for an existing application or asks the user to specify an application to be added to Windows.

FIGURE 5.8

The Windows Setup screen.

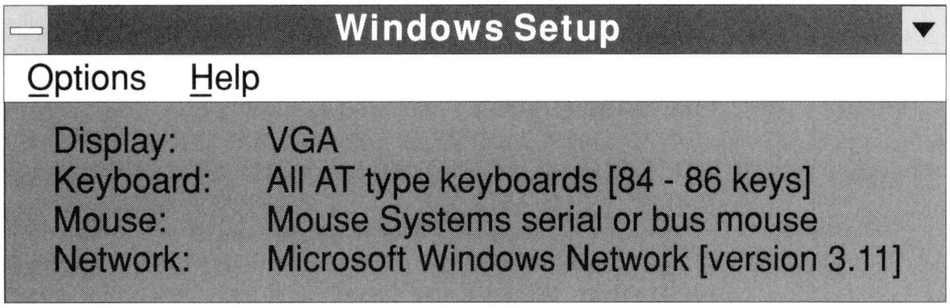

Windows Setup

Options   Help

Display: VGA
Keyboard: All AT type keyboards [84 - 86 keys]
Mouse: Mouse Systems serial or bus mouse
Network: Microsoft Windows Network [version 3.11]

The Add/Remove Windows Components option enables the user to add or remove items that are not essential to Windows operation. If the hard-disk drive becomes full, these items can be removed to free up about 2MB of memory.

Some manufacturers include a proprietary setup program for their Windows applications. In these cases, installation is as easy as selecting File from the Program Manager's menu bar, and then selecting the Run option. These actions present a dialog box in which the user can enter the path of the setup program to be installed. Whenever a new device driver is installed or a device driver is changed, Windows must be restarted for the changes to take effect.

Other icons commonly found in the Main window include the Clipboard Viewer, the Print Manager, and the MS-DOS Prompt. The Clipboard Viewer function enables the user to cut and paste text from different Windows applications. The Print Manager controls printing for all Windows applications. The MS-DOS icon enables the user to exit from the Windows environment and execute DOS commands and programs.

Initialization (INI) Files

A+ DOS/WINDOWS 1.1

When Windows 3.x is installed, several **initialization files** are copied into the Windows directory. All of these files have an extension of .INI. Within these files are the default or current startup settings for various Windows components. These files are updated when changes are made, and the Save Changes Upon Exit option is set in the Program Manager's Options pull-down menu. You can also use a shortcut to update these settings by selecting the File menu from the Program Manager. From this point, press and hold the SHIFT key and then select Exit Windows from the File menu. This updates these files with current settings, such as open groups or minimized programs.

The major initialization files are listed here:

▶ WIN.INI

▶ CONTROL.INI

▶ WINFILE.INI

▶ PROGMAN.INI

▶ SYSTEM.INI

Several other .INI files also exist in the Windows directory. In fact, when a new Windows application is installed, it usually installs its own .INI file at that time as well. These files can be modified to customize or optimize the program's execution.

Some of the parameters in these files are modified through normal Windows menus or dialog boxes. Others can be changed only by modifying the .INI file directly. The files are broken into sections that contain the individual parameters that can be altered.

Normal system functions that alter INI settings include changing Control Panel, Program Manager, or File Manager entries. Changing system settings through the Windows Setup program also modifies the contents of the INI files.

A+ DOS/WINDOWS 4.6

Windows provides a System Editor utility called **SysEdit** that can be used to modify the SYSTEM.INI, WIN.INI, CONFIG.SYS, and AUTOEXEC.BAT files. This utility can be accessed by simply typing **SysEdit** in the Windows File/Run dialog box.

The files can be modified directly using the DOS/Windows text editor or some other word processing/text-editing program. Windows has two word processing packages that can be used to modify text and .INI files. These are the Notepad and Write editors, under the Accessories window. Notepad is a small ASCII editor, and Write is a simple word processor package that supports document formatting, incorporation of graphics files, and **Object Linking and Embedding (OLE)**.

The format of all the INI files is consistent. Each INI file is divided into logical sections. Each section consists of a list of entries in the format of keyname=value. Each section has a name that is enclosed in brackets. The keyname is simply a name that describes the function of the entry; it is normally followed by an equals sign. The keyname can be any combination of characters and numbers, and the value entry can be any integer or string. Typical enabling entries include On, True, Yes, and 1. Conversely, disabling entries are Off, False, No, and 0.

```
[Section name]
keyword=value
```

WIN.INI

The WIN.INI file contains parameters that can be altered to change the Windows environment to suit the user's preferences. This is one of the largest INI files installed by Windows. The major sections of the WIN.INI file are Windows, Desktop, Extensions, and Colors.

The [Windows] Section

The [Windows] section can be used to alter several attributes of the environment, such as the mouse settings. Other items controlled by this section include warning beeps, printing operations, border width of windows, keyboard speed, and applications that automatically start when Windows is started.

```
[windows]
spooler=yes
run=c:\mcafee\viruscan\vshldwin.exe
Beep=yes
NullPort=None
BorderWidth=3
CursorBlinkRate=530
DoubleClickSpeed=452
Programs=com exe bat pif
Documents=
DeviceNotSelectedTimeout=15
TransmissionRetryTimeout=45
KeyboardDelay=2
```

```
KeyboardSpeed=31
ScreenSaveActive=1
ScreenSaveTimeOut=1200
MouseThreshold1=0
MouseThreshold2=0
MouseSpeed=0
CoolSwitch=1
DosPrint=no
SwapMouseButtons=0
device=Panasonic KX-P4420,HPPCL,LPT1:
```

The [Desktop] Section

The [Desktop] section sets the appearance of the desktop and groups. It controls the appearance of the background on the screen and the position of the windows and icons.

```
[Desktop]
Pattern=0 0 84 124 124 56 146 124
Wallpaper=arcade.bmp
GridGranularity=0
IconSpacing=75
TileWallPaper=1
```

The [Extensions] Section

The [Extensions] section sets association of file types to an application. This enables icons to be used to automatically start an application when one of its documents is selected.

```
[Extensions]
cal=calendar.exe ^.cal
crd=cardfile.exe ^.crd
trm=terminal.exe ^.trm
txt=notepad.exe ^.txt
ini=notepad.exe ^.ini
pcx=pbrush.exe ^.pcx
bmp=pbrush.exe ^.bmp
wri=write.exe ^.wri
rec=recorder.exe ^.rec
hlp=winhelp.exe ^.hlp
```

The International Section

The international [intl] section defines how different information is formatted on the screen. It controls how dates, times, and currencies are displayed.

```
[intl]
sLanguage=enu
sCountry=United States
iCountry=1
iDate=0
iTime=0
iTLZero=0
iCurrency=0
iCurrDigits=2
iNegCurr=0
iLzero=1
```

```
iDigits=2
iMeasure=1
s1159=AM
s2359=PM
sCurrency=$
sThousand=,
sDecimal=.
sDate=/
sTime=:
sList=,
sShortDate=M/d/yy
sLongDate=dddd, MMMM dd, yyyy
```

Windows Ports

The [ports] section is the Windows equivalent of the DOS Mode command. In this section, it is possible to establish and configure up to 10 **logical ports**.

```
[ports]
; A line with [filename].PRN followed by an equal sign causes
; [filename] to appear in the Control Panel's Printer Configuration
dialog
; box. A printer connected to [filename] directs its output into this
file.
LPT1:=
LPT2:=
LPT3:=
COM1:=9600,n,8,1,x
COM2:=9600,n,8,1,x
COM3:=9600,n,8,1,x
COM4:=9600,n,8,1,x
EPT:=
FILE:=
LPT1.DOS=
LPT2.DOS=
```

The entries at the top of this example are notes about how the system handles filenames with a .PRN extension. Windows recognizes up to three parallel ports and assigns them LPTx designations. The COMx assignments apply to the system's serial communications ports (COM1–COM4). The values to the right of the equal sign establish the speed and character parameters the port uses to conduct communications with remote devices.

Alphanumeric characters can be created in a number of different type styles. A certain set of characters may be curved in appearance, and another set might be quite square and blocky. A given set of characters designed in a common style is called a **font**. The [fonts] section describes the **screen fonts** that are loaded at startup. New font sets can be added to the list (from a third-party disk, for example), but they must be installed through the Fonts icon in the Control Panel. (More information about fonts is provided in Chapter 10, "Printers.") Be sure to remember also that the topic of fonts relates equally to other output devices, such as display monitors, as well as printers.

Windows Fonts

```
[fonts]
Arial (TrueType)=ARIAL.FOT
```

```
Arial Bold (TrueType)=ARIALBD.FOT
Arial Bold Italic (TrueType)=ARIALBI.FOT
Arial Italic (TrueType)=ARIALI.FOT
Courier New (TrueType)=COUR.FOT
Courier New Bold (TrueType)=COURBD.FOT
Courier New Italic (TrueType)=COURI.FOT
Times New Roman (TrueType)=TIMES.FOT
Times New Roman Bold (TrueType)=TIMESBD.FOT
Times New Roman Bold Italic (TrueType)=TIMESBI.FOT
Times New Roman Italic (TrueType)=TIMESI.FOT
```

The [FontSubstitutes] section sets fonts (types of characters) recognized by Windows equal to another type of font. This relationship enables character sets used with other software programs to be recognized and substituted for an appropriate Windows font. As an example, Helvetica is a widely used character font. The Arial font in Windows is very similar to it. According to the equation in the example, if Windows encounters a document with Helvetica type, it substitutes the Arial font for the Helvetica characters.

```
[FontSubstitutes]
Helv=MS Sans Serif
Tms Rmn=MS Serif
Times=Times New Roman
Helvetica=Arial
```

The [TrueType] section defines how Windows applications treat a special type of fonts known as TrueType fonts. In this example, the system is enabled to handle TrueType fonts if they are available in the system.

```
[TrueType]
TTEnable=1
TTOnly=0
```

Media File Control

The [mci extensions] section defines how various media files interact with the Windows Media Control Interface. (This interface is discussed in greater detail in Chapter 12, "Multimedia.") In this case, a file with a .WAV extension is routed to the Waveaudio driver.

```
[mci extensions]
wav=waveaudio
mid=sequencer
rmi=sequencer
```

Embedding

The [embedding] section lists types of objects that can be embedded in Windows applications. The format of the entry is as follows:

```
object=description, description, program file, format
[embedding]
SoundRec=Sound,Sound,SoundRec.exe,picture
PBrush=Paintbrush Picture,Paintbrush Picture,pbrush.exe,picture
ScreenCamMoviev2=Lotus ScreenCam Movie 2.0,Lotus ScreenCam Movie
2.0,A:\SCPLAYER.EXE,picture
MPlayer=Media Clip,Media Clip,mplayer.exe,picture
```

Windows Color Control

The [Colors] section defines colors to use for the different Windows components. The format for defining colors is red value, green value, blue value. The range of possible values runs from 0 to 255, where 0 is minimum intensity and 255 is maximum intensity. The parts of a typical Windows window are described in Figure 5.9.

```
[colors]
Background=0 64 64
AppWorkspace=192 192 192
Window=255 255 255
WindowText=0 0 0
Menu=192 192 192
MenuText=0 0 0
ActiveTitle=0 128 64
InactiveTitle=64 128 128
TitleText=255 255 255
ActiveBorder=0 128 64
InactiveBorder=64 128 128
WindowFrame=0 0 0
Scrollbar=192 192 192
ButtonFace=192 192 192
ButtonShadow=128 128 128
ButtonText=0 0 0
GrayText=128 128 128
Hilight=0 128 0
HilightText=255 255 255
InactiveTitleText=0 0 0
ButtonHilight=255 255 255
```

FIGURE 5.9

The parts of a Windows screen.

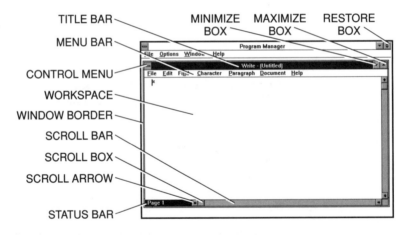

The [Windows Help] Section

The [Windows Help] section defines the placement and appearance of the Windows Help window when it is on the screen. Entries for the window occur in this format:

▶ Starting x position of the window's upper-left corner

▶ Starting y position of the window's upper-left corner

▶ Default width of the window

- Default height of the window

- Window maximized (1) or minimized (0)

```
[Windows Help]
H_WindowPosition=[213,160,213,160,0]
```

Windows Sounds

The [sound] section identifies the events that produce sound in the system, along with the particular sound generated and its description.

```
[sounds]
SystemAsterisk=chord.wav,Asterisk
SystemHand=chord.wav,Critical Stop
SystemDefault=ding.wav,Default Beep
SystemExclamation=chord.wav,Exclamation
SystemQuestion=chord.wav,Question
SystemExit=chimes.wav,Windows Exit
SystemStart=tada.wav,Windows Start
```

Windows I/O Ports

The [Printer Ports] section lists the printers, both active and inactive, that have Windows drivers installed. The entry for each printer also lists its time-out values. **Time-outs** are used to determine whether the printer has taken too long to respond (indicating that a problem has been encountered) and how long to wait before trying to communicate again. Both values are specified in seconds.

```
[PrinterPorts]
HP LaserJet Series II=HPPCL,LPT1:,600,1000
Panasonic KX-P4420=HPPCL,LPT1:,15,45
[devices]
HP LaserJet Series II=HPPCL,LPT1:
Panasonic KX-P4420=HPPCL,LPT1:
```

Other sections may be added to the WIN.INI file by software programs when they are installed. In the following sections, entries have been added to define the operation of the Windows Terminal communications package and Paintbrush graphics package. In the final entry, a software package has added a User Identification section to the file.

```
[Terminal]
Port=COM2
[Paintbrush]
width=640
height=480
clear=COLOR
OmitPictureFormat=0
[MS User Info]
DefName=Charles Brooks
DefCompany=Marcraft
```

SYSTEM.INI

The SYSTEM.INI file contains information on hardware settings for the drivers and modules that Windows uses to configure itself when started. The key sections of the SYSTEM.INI file are the [boot], [keyboard], [drivers], and [386enh] sections. Setup assigns values to the entries under each of these headings, and they must exist in the SYSTEM.INI file for Windows to operate properly. As a matter of fact, the SYSTEM.INI file is the only INI file that actually needs to be present to load Windows 3.x.

Windows Boot-up Settings

The [boot] section lists devices that can be changed by running the Windows Setup function. These items are used by Windows to configure itself during boot-up. Values are assigned to each entry according to the selections made in the Windows Setup menu.

```
[boot]
mouse.drv=MSCMOUSE.DRV
shell=progman.exe
network.drv=
language.dll=
sound.drv=mmsound.drv
comm.drv=comm.drv
keyboard.drv=keyboard.drv
system.drv=system.drv
386grabber=vga.3gr
oemfonts.fon=vgaoem.fon
286grabber=vgacolor.2gr
fixedfon.fon=vgafix.fon
fonts.fon=vgasys.fon
display.drv=vga.drv
drivers=mmsystem.dll WTNIPM
SCRNSAVE.EXE=C:\WINDOWS\SSMYST.SCR
```

The [keyboard] section provides the startup codes for the operation of the keyboard. The keyboard files shipped with Windows are **dynamic link library** (**DLL**) files. These are executable modules whose code can be loaded on demand, linked at run-time, and unloaded when finished.

```
[keyboard]
subtype=
type=4
keyboard.dll=
oemansi.bin=
```

The [boot.description] section lists the devices that can be changed through the Setup menu. There is no reason for the user to change these values directly; doing so disables Setup's capability of updating drivers.

```
[boot.description]
mouse.drv=Mouse Systems serial or bus mouse
keyboard.typ=Enhanced 101 or 102 key US and Non US keyboards
network.drv=No Network Installed
language.dll=English (American)
system.drv=MS-DOS System
codepage=437
woafont.fon=English (437)
aspect=100,96,96
display.drv=VGA
```

Windows Mode Settings

The [386enh] section contains information specifically related to running Windows in Enhanced mode, such as virtual memory and page swapping.

Entries in this section can appear as a filename of a virtual driver and its path, or as an asterisk (*) followed by a device name.

```
[386Enh]
keyboard=*vkd
mouse=MSCVMD.386
32BitDiskAccess=OFF
device=*int13
device=*wdctrl
network=*dosnet,*vnetbios
ebios=*ebios
woafont=dosapp.fon
display=*vddvga
EGA80WOA.FON=EGA80WOA.FON
EGA40WOA.FON=EGA40WOA.FON
CGA80WOA.FON=CGA80WOA.FON
CGA40WOA.FON=CGA40WOA.FON
device=vtdapi.386
device=*vpicd
device=*vtd
device=*reboot
device=*vdmad
device=*vsd
device=*v86mmgr
device=*pageswap
device=*dosmgr
device=*vmpoll
device=*wshell
device=*BLOCKDEV
device=*PAGEFILE
device=*vfd
device=*parity
device=*biosxlat
device=*vcd
device=*vmcpd
device=*combuff
device=*cdpscsi
local=CON
FileSysChange=off
PagingFile=C:\WINDOWS\WIN386.SWP
MaxPagingFileSize=20480
COM1Irq=4
COM1Base=03F8
device=c:\dos\vfintd.386
device=vsertd.386
device=vshare.386
MinTimeslice=20
WinTimeslice=100,50
WinExclusive=0
Com1AutoAssign=2
```

The [standard] section contains information that Windows uses to run in Standard mode. In this example, no values are installed.

```
[standard]
```

The [NonWindowsApp] section is used to hold information required by non-Windows applications. These values affect the performance of the system when non-Windows applications are running.

```
[NonWindowsApp]
localtsrs=dosedit,ced
```

Windows Drivers

The [mci] section lists the drivers that use Windows Media Control Interface (MCI). The MCI and devices that use it are described in greater detail in Chapter 12.

```
[mci]
WaveAudio=mciwave.drv
Sequencer=mciseq.drv
CDAudio=mcicda.drv
```

The [drivers] section contains names assigned to the installable driver programs. These files control and communicate with the system's hardware options.

```
[drivers]
timer=timer.drv
midimapper=midimap.drv
WTNIPM=wtnipm.drv
```

CONTROL.INI

The CONTROL.INI file contains settings for the Control Panel. This file is relatively small and mostly contains current color settings and screen saver settings. The major sections of the CONTROL.INI file are Current, Color Schemes, and Custom Colors.

Windows Colors and Patterns

The [Current] heading parameter defines the current color scheme name.

```
[current]
color schemes=Emerald City
```

The [Color Schemes] parameters define color values for each Windows component. Each scheme is identified with a name and carries a set of default color values for the various screen components. The following example shows two sample schemes: Arizona and Emerald City. However, even the minimum installation has several default schemes and any optional schemes that have been defined:

```
[color schemes]
Arizona=804000,FFFFFF,FFFFFF,0,FFFFFF,0,808040,C0C0C0,FFFFFF,4080FF,C0C
0C0,0,C0C0C0,C0C0C0,808080,0,808080,808000,FFFFFF,0,FFFFFF
Emerald
City=404000,C0C0C0,FFFFFF,0,C0C0C0,0,408000,808040,FFFFFF,408000,808040
,0,C0C0C0,C0C0C0,808080,0,808080,8000,FFFFFF,0,FFFFFF
```

The [Custom Colors] parameters specify colors that have been added to the basic color palette. This example shows that a single custom color has been defined (B–D and beyond are default values). These values are adjusted through the Control Panel's Color icon.

```
[Custom Colors]
ColorA=968AFF
ColorB=FFFFFF
ColorC=FFFFFF
ColorD=FFFFFFcx
```

The patterns for different bitmapped colors are specified in the [Patterns] section. These values are set through the Desktop icon.

```
[Patterns]
(None)=(None)
Boxes=127 65 65 65 65 65 127 0
Paisley=2 7 7 2 32 80 80 32
Weave=136 84 34 69 136 21 34 81
Waffle=0 0 0 0 128 128 128 240
Tulip=0 0 84 124 124 56 146 124
```

The [installed] Section

The currently installed version of Windows and its installed printers are listed in the [installed] section.

```
[installed]
3.1=yes
PSCRIPT.DRV=yes
HPIII522.WPD=yes
PSCRIPT.HLP=yes
TESTPS.TXT=yes
HPPCL.DRV=yes
UNIDRV.DLL=yes
FINSTALL.DLL=yes
FINSTALL.HLP=yes
UNIDRV.HLP=yes
```

Multimedia Settings

Values associated with items under the Control Panel's Multimedia icon are specified in the [MMCPL] section.

```
[MMCPL]
NumApps=13
X=0
Y=0
W=430
H=240
ODBC=C:\WINDOWS\SYSTEM\ODBCINST.DLL
```

Screen Savers

The [Screen Saver.*] section defines how the selected screen saver is to be displayed, including speed and density of the objects moving on the screen. The Screen Saver feature is provided to prevent static displays from remaining on the system's monitor for too long. Over time, the display would become permanently etched in the display's screen and ruin it.

```
[Screen Saver.Stars]
Density=25
```

```
WarpSpeed=4
PWProtected=0
```

The [drivers.desc] Section

The information in the [drivers.desc] section describes the functions of the Windows Midimapper and Timer.

```
[drivers.desc]
mciwave.drv=[MCI] Sound
mciseq.drv=[MCI] MIDI Sequencer
timer.drv=Timer
midimap.drv=MIDI Mapper
```

WINFILE.INI

The WINFILE.INI contains settings and defaults for the File Manager. This file essentially contains only one section: [Settings]. Its parameters specify default settings that are used during File Manager operations.

These default settings deal with confirmations that when enabled, are required before the requested operation is performed. When Windows is installed, all these confirmations are enabled. Another parameter indicates whether the filenames are displayed in uppercase or lowercase. Windows defaults to lowercase.

```
[Settings]
Window=0,0,640,480, , ,1
dir1=0,0,500,279,-1,-1,1,30,201,1814,250,C:\IC100\CHAP3\*.*
```

In this example, the Windows= setting describes the size of the window on the screen that is maximized when opened. The dir1= line indicates the current directory settings.

PROGMAN.INI

The PROGMAN.INI file contains settings for the Program Manager. It can have three sections: Settings, Groups, and Restrictions.

The [Settings] Section

The [Settings] section holds general configuration information. This example depicts typical entries in this section. The first line indicates the position of the window on the screen, with the final number indicating whether the window is maximized.

```
[Settings]
Window=-4 61 641 467 1
display.drv=vga.drv
Order= 2 3 1 7 22 4 5 15 19 8
AutoArrange=0
SaveSettings=1
```

The [Groups] Section

The [Groups] section defines the valid group names, sizes, and locations for the group icons. A **group file** (.grp) contains information about the objects included in the program group. This section also indicates the order in which the group icons are presented on the screen.

```
[Groups]
Group1=C:\WINDOWS\MAIN.GRP
```

```
Group2=C:\WINDOWS\ACCESSOR.GRP
Group3=C:\WINDOWS\GAMES.GRP
Group4=C:\WINDOWS\STARTUP.GRP
Group5=C:\WINDOWS\APPLICAT.GRP
Group7=C:\WINDOWS\WPW51US.GRP
Group8=C:\WINDOWS\CORELVEN.GRP
Group15=C:\WINDOWS\MCAFEE.GRP
Group19=C:\WINDOWS\MCAFEEVI.GRP
Group22=C:\WINDOWS\MARCRAFT.GRP
```

The [Restrictions] Section

The [Restrictions] section is optional and may not be included in all PROGMAN.INI files. However, this section can be added to prevent access to certain Program Manager functions and menus. The parameters in this section override any other configuration settings.

```
[Restrictions]
NoRun=1
NoClose=1
NoSaveSettings=1
NoFileMenu=1
EditLevel=4
```

The NoRun=1 and NoClose=1 lines disable the Run and Close commands in the File menu. Only icons can be used to run programs. Similarly, the NoFileMenu=1 command disables the File menu altogether.

The NoSaveSettings=1 command disables the Save Settings entry in the Options menu. The EditLevel= command provides five editing-level settings that restrict user access to the Program Manager. The 0 level grants the user free access to all options. The level 4 restriction prevents users from changing any program item information.

DOS and Windows

In many instances, it is desirable to run a DOS application from the Windows environment. From the earlier discussion about how Windows, DOS, and the BIOS interact, it should be apparent that running a DOS program from this position can be difficult. DOS applications can be run from inside a Windows window or in **full-screen mode**. However, these applications can be operated only within a window while in 386 Enhanced mode. The About Program Manager option, selected from the Program Manager's Help menu, can be consulted to determine the mode in which Windows is currently operating.

> When a non-Windows application runs in 386 Enhanced mode, Windows establishes a virtual 86 environment for it that simulates 8086 Real mode operation. Within the virtual 86 machine, Windows establishes a DOS environment with the drivers that were in operation when the system left DOS and entered Windows. Windows keeps a picture of the original DOS environment stored in memory. Under this organizational structure, the Windows kernel and Windows applications run in Protected mode and remain active while each non-Windows application runs in a virtual 86 time slice. This requires Windows to shift between Protected mode for Windows applications and Virtual 86 mode for DOS applications.

Under Windows 3.x, the operating system gives control to the Windows application when it is running. When the application completes its task, it returns control of the system back to the operating system. The operating system then gives control to the next scheduled application. This transfer of control from the operating system to the application during multitasking operations is called **cooperative multitasking**. The various tasks cooperate with each other, more or less, in sharing control of the system.

In the case of DOS applications running in Windows, the operating system does not give total control of the system to the application. Instead, Windows runs the application in a time slice and then moves on to the next application at the end of the designated time period. This type of multitasking in which the operating system retains control is referred to as **pre-emptive multitasking**. Even though the system runs the DOS session in a pre-emptive mode, the Windows applications running on the system operate in a cooperative mode.

Running DOS programs from inside a window is more resource-intensive than running them from a full screen. The application can be switched to a full-screen operation by pressing the ALT and ENTER keys together. Windows can be configured to run multitasking operations in the foreground while DOS programs are operating in the background. Due to the interactions between DOS and Windows, programs that directly access the hard drive and bypass Windows safeguards should be avoided in Windows-based operations.

Windows for Workgroups 3.11

The 3.11 version of Windows for Workgroups adds networking capabilities to the Windows environment. The updated File and Print Managers enable resources such as printers and directories. When directories are enabled for sharing, other terminals on the network can have access to your files. This is particularly useful when you are working in a group setting, where various members of your team or workgroup need access to items on which you are working.

Security

When a computer is networked to another computer, a certain amount of security is lost. Because a physical path has been established into the computer, data stored in the system is now potentially available to anyone on the network. Therefore, all networking software includes some type of data security system. In Windows 3.11, the data on a particular computer is protected by a logon **password**. When Windows is started, a **logon box**, such as the one in Figure 5.10, pops up asking for a password to enter the system. This password can be up to 14 characters in length. As with any security system, the password should be easy to remember and should be changed periodically.

After the second user has logged on, both users may connect to shared directories and resources around the network. Some resources may require an additional password to be accessed. In Windows, it is possible to create a password list under a **logon name** that enables the user to connect to these resources without entering the password. That is, after you have access to a resource you can always have access to it as long as its password is not changed. The logon process also enables the system to create a custom environment for each user that might work at any given station. Information specific to a particular user can be stored in the system and recalled when that person logs on.

FIGURE 5.10

The Windows 3.11 logon
dialog box.

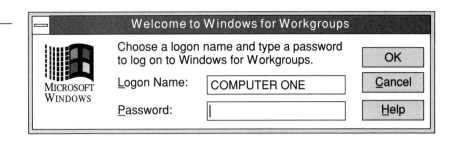

File Manager

The 3.11 File Manager window contains four new icons dedicated to network management. These icons are located on a tool bar near the top of the screen. The new icons, illustrated in Figure 5.11, are Connect Network Drive, Disconnect Network Drive, Share As, and Stop Sharing. Only shared directories and resources can be accessed across the network. The Share As icon notifies other potential users that this resource or directory can be accessed. To access a shared resource, the Connect Network Drive icon must be activated. When engaged, this icon creates a new logical drive on the local machine to handle the shared directory. The File Manager assigns the directory to the next logical drive available in the local system.

The path to the shared directory must contain a little more information than the path to a local directory. The remote path must include the remote computer's name and shared directory name. The format of a shared path is \\computer name\directory name. The Disconnect Network Drive icon is used to terminate the connection to a shared resource. Likewise, the Stop Sharing icon is used to discontinue access to a locally shared resource or directory.

FIGURE 5.11

The Windows for Workgroups
File Manager window.

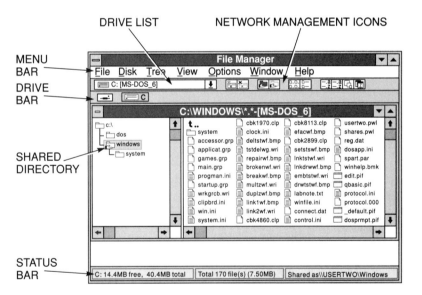

Print Manager

As with the 3.11 File Manager, the Print Manager window has been modified to accommodate networking. In particular, two new icons have been added to the Print Manager Tool Bar. These are the Share Printer As and Stop Sharing Printer icons, depicted in Figure 5.12. Clicking on the printer sharing icons enables the local system to share its printer with other stations on the network and grant the local system access to other printers and printer types around the network. For example, the local printer may be a small ink-jet or personal laser printer, but the more powerful network printers used for special projects or heavy output may be available at remote locations.

FIGURE 5.12

The Windows for Workgroups Print Manager window.

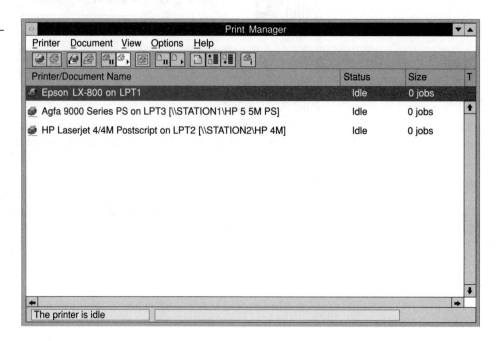

Clicking the Share Printer As icon grants remote units access to the local printer. You can also click this icon to update the password for using the printer. The local printer is connected to a serial or parallel port in the back of the local computer and is identified by the proper DOS handle (such as COM1 or LPT1). The remote printers are connected to other units around the network and are logically linked to a **port name** in the local computer. When the port name is active in Print Manager, no local printer hardware is required. The network redirects the printer operation to the remote printer's port. As with the File Manager paths, network printer ports require a network path in the format of `\\Computer Name\Share Name`.

Control Panel

Two new icons have been added to the Control Panel window, as illustrated in Figure 5.13. These icons are the Network and Fax options.

FIGURE 5.13

The Windows 3.11 Control Panel.

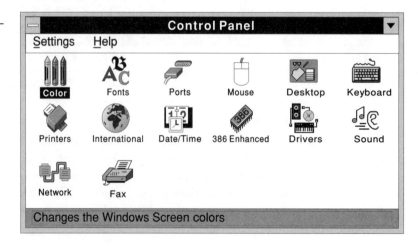

The Network option is used to establish and change the local computer's network name, logon password, and workgroup in which the local system is operating. This option also enables you to specify how the local CPU's time is allocated between local duties and resource-sharing operations. Figure 5.14 shows the WfW Network Settings dialog box.

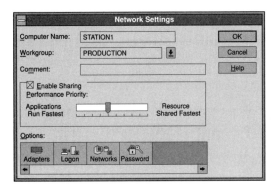

Double-clicking on the Fax icon opens the Fax Modems window, illustrated in Figure 5.15. This window enables the user to configure the system so that it can be used to send and receive faxes. The icon can be used to set up a local fax/modem or a shared fax/modem located remotely on the network. To share a fax modem on the network, a special directory must be established to store outgoing faxes. The directory must be shared and have full access privileges to be used with the remote fax/modem.

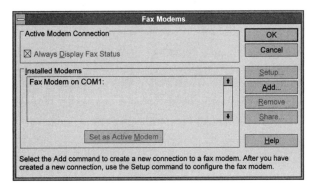

Troubleshooting Windows 3.x

Until Windows 95, the Windows operating environment had a DOS layer running under it. Therefore, it was necessary to isolate DOS problems from Windows problems. Typical DOS problems were described in the previous chapter. Typical Windows 3.x problems include the following:

- Windows setup problems

- Windows hardware problems

- Windows printing problems

- Windows operating problems

- Windows multimedia problems

This section examines only Windows 3.x problems associated with setup and general Windows operation. Hardware, printing, and multimedia-related Windows problems are discussed in the chapters related to these topics.

Creating a Clean Boot Disk

A+ DOS/WINDOWS 4.6

One of the best tools to have when troubleshooting Windows problems is a clean boot disk. When the Windows program becomes nonfunctional, it often becomes necessary to use the boot disk to restore the system to proper operation. The steps involved in creating the boot disk are listed here:

1. Create a self-booting troubleshooting disk.

   a. Place a blank disk in Drive A.

   b. At the DOS prompt, type **FORMAT A:/s** and press Enter.

2. Create a new CONFIG.SYS file on the boot disk.

   a. At the C:\> DOS prompt, type **COPY CON A:config.sys** and press ENTER.

   b. Enter the following lines of text, pressing the ENTER key at the end of each line:

   ```
   buffers=20
   files=40
   stacks=9256
   device=c:\windows\himem.sys
   device=c:\windows\vga.sys
   shell=c:\dos\command.com c:\dos /p /e:256
   ```

3. Save the new CONFIG.SYS file to the floppy disk.

   a. Hold down the CONTROL key and press the Z key.

4. Create a new AUTOEXEC.BAT file on the boot disk.

   a. At the DOS prompt, type **EDIT A:autoexec.bat**.

   b. Enter the following lines of text, pressing the ENTER key at the end of each line:

   ```
   path=c:\dos;c:\windows
   set temp=c:\windows\temp
   prompt $p$g
   ```

5. Save the new AUTOEXEC.BAT file to the floppy disk.

   a. Hold down the ALT key and press the F key.

   b. Use the DOWN Arrow key to highlight the Save option, and press ENTER.

6. Copy the system's .INI files to the floppy disk.

   a. Copy \windows\win.ini a:.

   b. Copy \windows\system.ini a:.

   c. Copy \windows\progman.ini a:.

   d. Copy \windows\control.ini a:.

The Clean Boot disk should be stored in a convenient space and labeled so that it is easy to find. Without it, getting the system up and running after a crash becomes a much more difficult undertaking.

Windows 3.x Setup Problems

A+ DOS/WINDOWS 4.1

> Two typical problems can occur when setting up Windows 3.x software. First, Windows can **hang up** (stop) the system during installation; second, the setup process can fail and return an error message to the screen.

Typical Windows 3.x Setup error messages include the following:

- HIMEM.SYS not loaded
- Unable to initialize display adapter
- Swapfile corrupt
- Device referenced in WIN.INI could not be found

As with the DOS messages described in the previous chapter, these and other Windows 3.x Startup error messages indicate that an error has occurred that must be remedied before the system can boot and run properly. If the system hangs up while trying to run Setup, record any error messages displayed on the screen and troubleshoot that portion of the system. If no error message is returned, reboot the machine using the clean startup disk. Try to run Setup again.

Setup actually carries out two routines when it is executed. It first performs an MS-DOS setup routine to install Windows critical system files. This is followed by running a Windows Setup routine. The second routine sets up the Program Manager groups and Windows applications.

A+ DOS/WINDOWS 4.5

Three common failure points exist in the Setup process. These occur primarily during the detection of TSRs, memory manager programs, and device drivers in the system. However, they can also occur during the auto-detection phase of the MS-DOS mode setup, as well as while Windows is being loaded into the system. In each case, it is possible that the system may do any of the three following:

1. Lock up completely
2. Give an error message
3. Simply return to the command line

If the system will not run the standard Setup routine after booting from the clean disk, attempt to run a modified setup using the /t switch (that is, Setup /t). This switch setting checks the system for conflicting memory resident programs.

It is a good idea to check any TSR programs running in the system against the list of known problem TSRs located in the SETUP.TXT file on the first Windows disk. Use the Windows SysEdit function to disable any TSRs in the system by REMing their statements in the AUTOEXEC.BAT and CONFIG.SYS files. This should make it possible to successfully install Windows after rebooting the system. The disabled TSRs can be added back to the system one at a time after Windows has been installed. When offending programs are found, try replacing them with standard Windows options available on the installation disks. If standard drivers will not work with the system, contact the manufacturer for Windows 3.x compatible products.

The DOS Editor utility, or another word processor, can be used to examine the SETUP.INF (setup information) file in the System subdirectory for listings of problem TSRs. These files are listed under the [incompTSR1] and [incompTSR2] sections of the file.

A common symptom of Windows loading problems involves the Windows startup screen (also called a **splash screen**), which appears on the screen and stops the system from moving forward. When this occurs, the boot-up sequence is looking for the operating system. This usually indicates a "Bad or missing COMMAND.COM" condition.

Windows 3.x Operating Problems

In general, two classes of Windows 3.x operation problems exist: general protection faults and operating problems. Operating problems can be divided into Standard mode operating problems and 386 Enhanced mode operating problems.

General Protection (GP) Faults

A **general protection** (**GP**) **fault** occurs when Windows or one of its applications attempts to access an unallocated memory location. When this memory conflict occurs, the data in the violated memory location is corrupted and may crash the system. In Windows 3.0, a GP fault usually requires that the user exits Windows and reboots the system. Version 3.1 provides improved control of GP faults. In this version, the error notice includes information about where the error occurred and which application caused the error. In addition, Windows 3.1 remains stable enough after a GP fault to enable the user to save the work in progress before exiting the program. Some GP faults are not fatal and provide an option to ignore the fault and continue working, or to simply close the application. Although the application may continue to operate, it is generally not stable enough to continue working on an extended basis. It is recommended that the application be used only long enough to save any existing work.

Using Dr. Watson

Windows 3.1 also includes a diagnostic tool, called **Dr. Watson**, which can be used to monitor the operation of the system and log its key events. The log provides a detailed listing of the events that led up to the failure. The information is automatically stored in a file named DRWATSON.LOG.

If Dr. Watson is not running, it should be activated so that it can serve as a reference for further troubleshooting steps. This can be accomplished by running the DRWATSON.EXE file from the Windows directory, or by installing its icon in the Startup window. This action causes Dr. Watson to run in the background each time Windows is started. Complete the following steps:

1. Check the DOS version to see that it is correct.

2. Check the HIMEM.SYS version to see that it is 3.01 or higher.

3. Check the device drivers in the CONFIG.SYS file.

4. Perform a CHKDSK /F operation from the DOS prompt to check for cross-linked files.

5. If the fault occurs in 386 Enhanced mode, start Windows using the WIN /D:XSV switch.

   If the GP fault continues, you must reinstall Windows from scratch.

   If the GP fault disappears, reduce the switch to WIN /D:XS.

   If the fault returns with the shortened switch, insert the line **VirtualHDIRQ=OFF** in the [386Enh] section of the SYSTEM.INI file.

   If the GP fault does not return, reduce the switch to WIN /D:X.

   If the fault returns, insert the line **SystemPointBreakpoint=False** in the [386Enh] section of the SYSTEM.INI file.

   If the GP fault does not return, search for an EMMExclude= line in the [386Enh] section of the SYSTEM.INI file. If the line is not present, create it and set it to a value of A000-EFFF. If it is present, decrease the size of the address range.

Standard Mode Problems

If Windows has successfully been installed, changes in the system must occur to prevent Windows from running in Standard mode. These changes include the following:

- Low conventional memory
- Altered "PATH=" command
- Corrupted or missing files in the Windows directory
- Incorrect or missing HIMEM.SYS file
- Incorrect A20 handler routine loaded
- Conflicting third-party device drivers
- Hardware devices installed after Windows was installed

If Windows will not start with the WIN /s switch, check to see that the machine has an 80286 or newer microprocessor, with at least 256KB of conventional memory free. Also check to make certain that HIMEM.SYS, or some other extended memory manager, is installed with at least 192KB of extended memory free.

Attempt to boot the system using the clean boot disk, and attempt to start Windows in Standard mode. If the system runs Windows from the clean boot, then use the single-step boot-up method to locate the offending configuration step so that it can be corrected.

Normally, if the system does not start in Standard mode, then some program or device is taking up too much memory. If the system has enough physical memory to run Windows, you must free up additional extended memory for use.

Items to check include the following:

1. Check the CONFIG.SYS and AUTOEXEC.BAT files for commands that load unnecessary programs into extended memory. Remove these commands and retry the system.

2. Check the CONFIG.SYS file for memory managers and device drivers that use too much memory. Replace the driver with an updated driver or a standard Windows driver, if possible.

3. Check for a RAMDrive installation that is using too much extended memory. Decrease the size of the RAM drive.

4. The XMS driver could be defective. The A20 handler routine of the HIMEM.SYS file may be incorrect. Check the HIMEM.SYS version to make sure that it is version 3.01 or higher. Replace the HIMEM.SYS file with the version in the current Windows installation disks.

386 Enhanced Mode Problems

If Windows runs in Standard mode but will not run in 386 Enhanced mode, a conflict may exist in the allocation of the upper memory blocks (UMBs). Windows may not detect the presence of an adapter card and may try to use memory areas the card has taken if any of the following exist:

▶ An incorrect or missing HIMEM.SYS file

▶ An incorrect A20 handler routine loaded

▶ Conflicting third-party device drivers

To detect this type of memory conflict, start Windows using a Win /d:x switch. This avoids the complete upper memory portion of the startup process. If Windows starts successfully using this switch, then a UMB conflict exists and must be corrected.

If conflicting device drivers are suspected, the DOS MEM /p command or the MSD.EXE diagnostic should be run to examine the drivers using the UMBs and their addresses. When a conflicting device driver has been located, add an **emmexclude=** line to the [386enh] section of the SYSTEM.INI file. The statement must include the address range of the device. The emmexclude statement prevents Windows from trying to use the space to establish buffers.

Shadow ROM and RAM should also be checked to see whether either is enabled in the E0000h area. If so, turn shadowing off for this memory section.

If the system crashes while running in Enhanced mode, add the line **emmexclude=A000-EFFF** to the [386enh] section of the SYSTEM.INI file, and restart Windows so that the change takes effect. This line prevents Windows from accessing the range of addresses between A000h and EFFFh.

If the system runs Windows Enhanced mode after the SYSTEM.INI file has been modified, begin limiting the address range of the emmexclude command to find the location of the problem. It may also be necessary to turn off Shadow RAM features in these memory areas.

If the system produces a Stack Overflow Error message in Windows enhanced mode, check the **STACKS=** line in the CONFIG.SYS file. The stacks setting should be set to 9,256.

Reinstalling Windows 3.x

Many times it will be necessary to reinstall Windows 3.x to return a corrupted system to service. Usually, though, the technician will want to maintain the system's old settings, if possible. To do this, you must install Windows in a new directory and try to run it from that location.

If the new installation will not run, use the DOS MEM command to check the system for low conventional memory. Also check for defective hardware and corrupted Windows files. If no apparent cause is present, completely erase the original Windows installation and reinstall Windows using standard Setup procedure.

If the new installation runs correctly, rename its .GRP and .INI files with .GRN and .INN (N = new) extensions. Copy all the files from the new installation into the old installation directories, and try to run Windows. If the system still will not run, one of the old .INI file entries is probably corrupt. Rename the original .INI files and replace them with the .INN versions copied from the new installation. As an alternative, reinstall all applications so that their drivers will be updated throughout the system.

Optimizing Windows 3.x

A+ DOS/WINDOWS 2.2

The performance of a Windows 3.x system can be optimized by setting up the system using the following steps:

1. Use the 386 Enhanced icon in the Control Panel to establish a permanent swap file on the hard drive (select the fastest drive in multiple hard-drive systems). Also select the options in the Virtual Memory dialog box.

2. Select the lowest video resolution that is practical for the system. This option is selected through the Windows Setup icon or command. In most cases, this comes down to selecting the standard VGA driver from the option list.

3. Implement the DOS optimization steps given earlier in this chapter. Load DOS into the HMA, as illustrated in the following CONFIG.SYS lines:

    Device=path\HIMEM.SYS

    Device=path\EMM386.EXE noems

    DOS=HIGH,UMB

The **noems switch** in the EMM386 line establishes the upper memory blocks. A similar **RAM switch** option provides UMBs but imposes a 64KB EMS page frame. The noems switch does not produce a page frame and provides an additional 64KB in the UMB area. An **x= switch** can also be added to the noems line to exclude unused UMB addresses. This option enables Windows to move translation buffer memory that it establishes for non-Windows applications into the UMB to free up some additional conventional memory space. UMBs that can be excluded may be detected by using the MEM /p command at the DOS prompt.

Some optimization steps depend on the system's makeup and purpose. Generally, optimization considerations are divided between operating speed and disk space. The previous steps all lead to optimizing the system for maximum speed. Additional steps that produce speed include the following:

1. Remove any unnecessary TSRs and device drivers (such as non-Windows mouse drivers) from the AUTOEXEC.BAT and CONFIG.SYS files.

2. Install SMARTDRV for caching.

3. Create a permanent swap file for 386 Enhanced mode.

4. Establish the TEMP variable to the fastest hard disk in the system, and establish the SwapDisk function to the drive with the most space available. This function is set up through the [NonWindowsApp] section of the SYSTEM.INI file.

Conversely, to optimize a system for maximum hard disk space, perform the following steps:

1. Establish a RAMDRIVE using the TEMP environment.

2. Use a temporary swap file, or eliminate swapping altogether. This can be accomplished by entering **none** in the New Settings Type box of the Control Panel's Virtual Memory dialog box.

3. Use the minimum Windows installation possible.

Windows 95

A+ DOS/WINDOWS 1.1

In 1995, Microsoft released a radically different Windows environment called **Windows 95**. This Windows featured many new and improved features over previous versions. Win 95 offered improved multimedia support for video and sound-file applications, Plug-and-Play hardware support, 32-bit advanced multitasking functions, improved email and fax capabilities through Microsoft Exchange, and the Microsoft Network for easy **wide area network (WAN)** usage.

Even though Windows 95 is optimized for running 32-bit applications, it is still fully compatible with 16-bit Windows 3.x and DOS applications. The only real concern when installing Windows 95 over either of these operating systems is that the system has the hardware resources needed to run Windows 95.

Windows 95 offers full built-in Plug-and-Play (PnP) capability. When Win 95 is combined with a hardware system that implements PnP BIOS, expansion slots and adapter support, and is supported with PnP adapter drivers, fully automated configuration and reconfiguration can take place.

Win 95 also does away with the 8+3 character filename system implemented under DOS. In Windows 95, long filenames of up to 255 characters can be used so that the user can be more descriptive when naming files. When these filenames are displayed in non-Windows 95 systems, they are truncated (shortened) and identified by a tilde character (~). This mark shows that the filename is being displayed in a shortened manner. Customers with older operating systems may overlook files because they are saved in this manner. Windows 95 also uses the right mouse button (referred to as right-clicking, or as alternate-clicking for right-handers) to display a pop-up menu of functions, such as arranging icons, creating short cuts, and changing display properties.

Installing Windows 95

A+ DOS/WINDOWS 3.2

Windows 95 must be installed over an existing operating system, such as MS-DOS or Windows 3.x. In particular, the Windows 95 installation program must find a recognizable MS-DOS FAT-16 partition on the drive. This prevents it from being installed over some other operating system. The system must be at least an 80386DX or higher machine, operating with at least 4MB of RAM (8MB is recommended).

The system should also possess a mouse and a VGA or better monitor. The system's hard drive should have at least 20MB of free space available to install Windows 95 successfully.

With the Windows 95 Setup disk or CD-ROM in the drive, the Windows 95 Setup routine can be executed from the DOS command line, from the Windows 3.x Program Manager's Run box, or from the File Manager window. The preferred method is to run the Setup program from Windows 3.x.

To run the Setup program from Windows 3.x, follow these steps:

1. Boot the computer and start Windows.

2. Insert the Windows 95 Start Disk (Disk 1) in the A: drive, or place the Windows 95 CD in the CD-ROM drive.

3. Open the File Manager and select the proper drive.

4. Double-click on the SETUP.EXE file entry.

5. Follow the directions from the screen, and enter the information requested by the program for the type of installation being performed.

To run the Setup program from DOS, follow these steps:

1. Boot the computer.

2. Insert the Windows 95 Start Disk (Disk 1) in the A: drive, or place the Windows 95 CD in the CD-ROM drive.

3. Move to the drive that contains the Windows 95 Installation files.

4. At the DOS prompt, type **Setup** and press Enter.

5. Follow the directions from the screen, and enter the information requested by the program for the type of installation being performed.

The Setup program provides options for performing **Typical** (default), **Portable, Compact,** and **Custom** installations. Figure 5.16 depicts the Windows 95 Setup Wizard's Setup Options screen. The Typical process installs most of the Windows 95 files without intervention from the user. The Portable option installs those options most closely associated with portable computer systems. The Compact option is a minimal installation for those units with limited disk space available. The Custom option enables the user to make customized selections for most device configurations.

One custom installation feature includes retaining the Windows 3.x Program Manager for those who are comfortable with the look and fields of the 3.x environment. This is accomplished by selecting the Custom setup option, moving into the Computer Settings dialog box, and clicking on the User Interface option. At this point, click on Change and select Windows 3.1. The Program Manager can be run by setting up a shortcut to the PROGMAN.EXE file. However, Windows 95 folders and some other desktop-related functions will not work with Program Manager. In addition, you must Shut Down Windows 95 after leaving the Program Manager.

If Setup detects the presence of a Windows 3.x operating system, it asks whether it should install its files in the same directory. If the prompt is answered with "Yes," then Windows 95 acts as an upgrade over the existing Windows structure. It obtains existing configuration information from the SYSTEM.INI, WIN.INI, and PROTOCOL.INI files and moves it into a new configuration known as the **Registry**. This enables these settings to work automatically when Windows 95 is first started. Windows 95 also moves the contents of the existing Windows 3.x Group (.GRP) files into the Registry during installation. Because Windows 95 rummages around in these files, both the .INI and .GRP files from the original Windows 3.x setup should be backed up before installing Windows 95.

FIGURE 5.16

The Windows 95 Setup Options Screen.

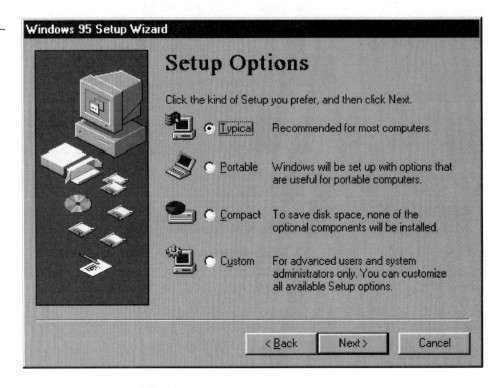

Windows 95 draws from the existing DOS or Windows 3.x structure when it is being installed, so an interruption or crash during the installation process may leave the system with no workable operating system in place. If this occurs, you must boot the system from a bootable floppy disk and reinstall Windows 95 from that point. If the MS-DOS version that Setup detects on the hard drive is older than 3.1, the system displays an "Incorrect MS-DOS version" message on the screen. If this happens, the hard drive must be reformatted with a more current version of DOS.

If the answer to the installation directory question is "No," you will be asked where the Windows 95 files should be installed. By installing Win 95 in a new directory, it is possible to preserve the old DOS or Windows environment. To boot to both operating systems, you must configure the system with dual boot options.

Dual-Boot Configuration

A+ DOS/WINDOWS 3.3

By establishing a **dual-boot configuration**, it is possible to install Windows 95 on an existing system and still retain the original operating system.

As stated previously, the first step in establishing a dual boot system is to install the copy of Windows 95 into a new directory.

To dual-boot with DOS, the system must be running a copy of DOS 5.0 or higher. In addition, the setting for the Windows 95 MSDOS.SYS file's BootMulti= entry must be set to a value of 1. This can be done by bringing the file into a text editor, such as Notepad, and then changing the setting to the desired value. After rebooting the system, it is possible to boot into the old DOS/Windows 3.x environment by pressing the F4 function key when the Starting Windows message appears during boot-up.

If Windows 95 is already installed in the system, you must copy the IO.SYS and MSDOS.SYS files to a floppy, rename them IO.DOS and MSDOS.DOS, and then copy them back into the root directory. These files also must be handled as any other hidden, read-only, system files (use the Attribute command to read and copy them). You must perform the same copy/rename/copy operations on the existing COMMAND.COM file. Finally, create new CONFIG.DOS and AUTOEXEC.DOS files that are appropriate for the version of DOS you are using in the system. Simply restart the system to run DOS or Windows 95. The reasons for changing the filenames will become more apparent as the chapter explains the organizational structure that Windows 95 takes.

WIN 95 Startup

Unlike previous versions of Windows, Win 95 does not overlay a DOS structure. Instead, Win 95 takes over the DOS boot-up functions as a normal part of its operation. This seamless boot-up may be convenient, but it can offer some interesting problems when the system will not boot up—there's no DOS level to fall back to for troubleshooting purposes.

Basically, the Win 95 portion of the boot-up sequence occurs in five phases:

- ▶ Phase 1: Bootstrap with the BIOS

- ▶ Phase 2: Loading DOS drivers and TSR files

- ▶ Phase 3: Real Mode initialization of static **Virtual Device Drivers (VxDs)**

- ▶ Phase 4: Protected Mode switch-over

- ▶ Phase 5: Loading of any remaining VxDs

VxDs are protected mode drivers that enable multiple applications to access a system hardware or software resource. The x in the acronym represents a particular type of driver—for example, VDD is a display driver, VPD is a printer driver, and so forth.

Two types of VxDs exist: those that must be **statically loaded** and those that may be **dynamically loaded**. Static VxDs are loaded into memory and stay there while the system is operating. All virtual device drivers are loaded this way in Windows 3.x. The problem is that these types of drivers use a lot of memory. Win 95 dynamically loads some drivers into memory as they are needed. Win 95 VxDs files have an extension of .VXD, but Win 3.x drivers retain the .386 extension.

Phase 1: The Bootstrap Process

During the bootstrap process, the BIOS is in control of the system and functions as described in the previous chapter. However, most newer BIOS contain Plug-and-Play features designed to work with the Windows 95 architecture. In particular, the BIOS passes configuration information about the system to the Win 95 Configuration Manager. At startup, the PnP BIOS checks the CMOS RAM to determine which PnP devices should be activated and where their PnP should be stored, as well as what their DMA, INT, and I/O addressing assignments should be. Upon completion of the configuration check operation, the BIOS configures the PnP cards and the intelligent system board devices. The BIOS then performs the POST and Initialization functions for the system.

Phase 2: Loading DOS Drivers and TSR Files

After the disk boot, Win 95 checks the system's hardware profile to determine its actual configuration. This profile is a function of the BIOS' detection process during the initialization phase. At this point, the CONFIG.SYS and AUTOEXEC.BAT files are executed. These files are present to maintain compatibility with applications written for earlier operating systems and environments. In the Windows 95 environment, the CONFIG.SYS file contains a name listing for each hardware profile used.

In the next phase, Win 95 loads the WIN.COM file to control the loading and testing of the Win 95 core components.

Phase 3: Initializing Static VxDs

The previous phase is followed by loading first the **VMM32.VXD virtual machine manager** and, finally, the SYSTEM.INI file so that its information can be used to maintain compatibility with nondynamic VxDs.

The VMM32.VXD file creates the virtual environment and loads the VxD files. This file contains a list of all the VxD files the system requires. These files are stored in a branch of the Windows 95 Registry, a centralized, improved replacement for the old 3.x INI files. If the value in the listing is represented by a StaticVxD= statement, the VMM32.VXD file loads and initializes it in Real mode. This file also statically loads any VxDs that have a device=xxxVxD entry; the dynamic VxD files are not loaded by the VMM32.VXD file.

Phase 4: Protected Mode Change-Over

After loading all the static VxDs, the VMM32.VXD file shifts the microprocessor into Protected mode operation and begins loading the Protected mode components of the system.

The Configuration Manager is loaded and initialized with configuration information from the PnP BIOS. If no PnP information is available, the Configuration Manager develops a PnP tree by loading dynamically loadable drivers. When the tree is in place, the Configuration Manager reconciles the configuration information for each device, resolves any conflicts, and then reconfigures any devices necessary.

Phase 5: Loading Remaining Components

A+ DOS/WINDOWS 1.1

Following the initialization process, the final Win 95 components are loaded into the system. These components include the following:

▶ The KERNEL32.DLL and KERNEL386.EXE files

▶ The GDI.EXE and GDI32.EXE files

▶ The USER.EXE and USER32.EXE files

▶ All fonts and other associated resources

▶ The WINI.INI file

▶ The Win 95 shell and desktop files

A+ DOS/WINDOWS 2.2

The KERNEL32.DLL and KERNEL386.EXE files contain the Win 95 core and load its device drivers. The GDI files provide the base of the graphical device interface, and the USER files provide the user interface. The GDI files graphically represent and manage the system hardware devices.

The WIN.INI, SYSTEM.INI, and WINFILE.INI files are included in the Windows directory to maintain compatibility functions with older software. These files are retained for use with older 16-bit applications and are not necessary used for the operation of Windows 95 applications. However, these files must be checked if the Windows 95 system has conflicts with any 16-bit applications.

When the shell and desktop components are loaded, the system displays a prompt on the screen for the user to log on, as depicted in Figure 5.17. Similar to the logon process associated with networked systems, the Win 95 logon enables the operating system to configure itself for specific users. Normal logon involves entering a username and password. If no logon information is entered, then default values are loaded into the system. The logon screen appears only if the system is in use with a network, or when there are settings for the user to customize.

FIGURE 5.17

The Windows 95 logon dialog box.

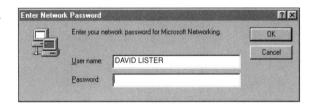

Windows 95 possesses system startup files that replace the DOS files described in the previous chapter. The Win 95 version of IO.SYS is a Real mode operating system that replaces the DOS version. It also takes over many of the functions associated with the CONFIG.SYS file. An MSDOS.SYS file is created to retain compatibility, but the VMM32 and VxDs take control of the system from the IO.SYS file during the startup process.

Even though the CONFIG.SYS and AUTOEXEC.BAT files are not required to start Windows 95, they are retained from the previous operating system to maintain compatibility with older applications. However, entries in the CONFIG.SYS file override the values in the Win 95 IO.SYS file. The IO.SYS file also handles some of the AUTOEXEC.BAT commands. In both cases, the system uses REM statements to deactivate those CONFIG.SYS and AUTOEXEC.BAT functions that are implemented in the IO.SYS file. Similarly, the functions of the SYSTEM.INI and WIN.INI files have been moved to the Windows 95 Registry.

The Windows 95 Setup routine stores existing MS-DOS files under .DOS extensions when it is installed as an upgrade over a previous operating system. In particular, the AUTOEXEC.BAT, COMMAND.COM, CONFIG.SYS, I/O.SYS, and MSDOS.SYS files are stored with this extension. If the system is started with the other operating system (see the Dual-Boot Configuration section earlier in this chapter), the Windows 95 versions of these files are stored under .W40 extensions and the original DOS files are returned to their normal extensions.

As with Windows 3.x, the SYSTEM.INI, WIN.INI, PROTOCOL.INI, CONFIG.SYS, and AUTOEXEC.BAT files can be modified through the **System Editor** in Windows 95. The **Sysedit** utility can be accessed by selecting the SysEdit option in the Start/Run dialog box.

The Windows 95 startup sequence can be summarized as follows:

1. Post tests occur.

2. Plug-and-Play BIOS starts.

3. OS Bootup looks for MBR.

4. System loads IO.SYS.

5. IO.SYS loads and executes CONFIG.SYS.

6. IO.SYS loads MSDOS.SYS.

7. System loads and executes COMMAND.COM.

8. Windows 95 Core files load.

9. Windows 95 checks the Startup folder.

Windows 95 enables programs to be started automatically whenever Windows starts by adding them to the system's Startup folder. This is accomplished by accessing the Start Menu Programs tab and selecting Add. Browse until the desired program is found, and then double-click on it. Finish the addition by clicking Next and then double-clicking on the Startup folder. These programs can be bypassed for troubleshooting purposes by pressing the Spacebar during startup.

Win 95 Desktop

When Win 95 is started, it produces the basic desktop screen depicted in Figure 5.18. The new user interface features four basic icons: My Computer, Network Neighborhood, Recycle Bin, and the Start button.

FIGURE 5.18

The Windows 95 Desktop screen.

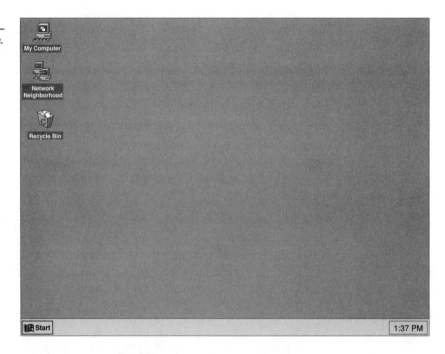

The My Computer icon enables the user to see the local system's contents and manage its files. The Network Neighborhood icon provides information about the world around the system, when used in a networked environment. The Recycle Bin is a storage area for deleted files that enables you to retrieve such files if they are deleted by mistake. This icon should always be present on the desktop; it can be removed only through the Registry. If the Recycle Bin icon is missing, you have two alternatives to restoring it: establish a short-cut to the Recycle Bin using a new icon, or simply reinstall Windows 95. This second action always places the Recycle Bin on the desktop. The Start button is used to accomplish several different tasks, depending on the context of the operation. For example, the Start button is used to start programs, alter system settings, and open documents.

A+ DOS/WINDOWS 1.2 All operations begin from the Start button. When you click on the button, a pop-up menu of options appears, as illustrated in Figure 5.19. This menu normally contains the options Programs, Documents, Settings, Find, Help, Run, and Shut Down.

FIGURE 5.19

The Start Button menu.

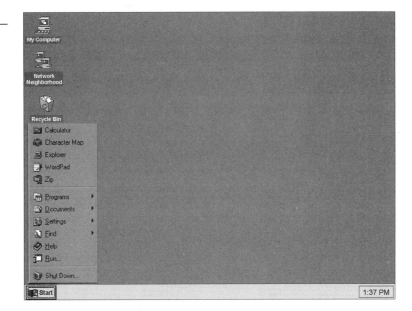

Placing the cursor over designated menu items causes any submenus associated with that option to pop up on the screen. An arrow to the right of the option indicates a submenu is available. To open the selected item, simply left-click on it, and its window appears on the screen.

Just to the right of the Start button is an area called the taskbar. This area is used to display all the applications currently open. Each time a program is started or a window is opened, a corresponding button appears on the taskbar. To switch between applications, simply click on the desired program button to make it the active window.

The Programs submenu, depicted in Figure 5.20, has several options that include Accessories, Online Services, Start Up, Windows 95 Training, MS-DOS Prompt, and Windows Explorer.

Several functions from Windows 3.x are combined under the Programs option. The Windows groups appear when this option is selected. The File Manager function from 3.1x is performed by the Windows Explorer option. By clicking on this option, the system's directory structure appears, as shown in Figure 5.21.

A+ DOS/WINDOWS 1.2 As with the Windows 3.x file manager, the Windows Explorer enables the user to copy, move, and erase files on any of the system's drives. Its screen is divided into two parts. The left side displays the directory tree showing all the directories and subdirectories of the system's available drives. In Windows 95, directories and subdirectories are referred to and depicted as folders (and subfolders). Any drive or directory can be selected by clicking the cursor on its icon or folder. The contents of the folder can be expanded by clicking on the (+) sign beside the folder. Conversely, the same folder can be contracted by clicking on the (-) sign in the same box.

FIGURE 5.20

The Programs submenu.

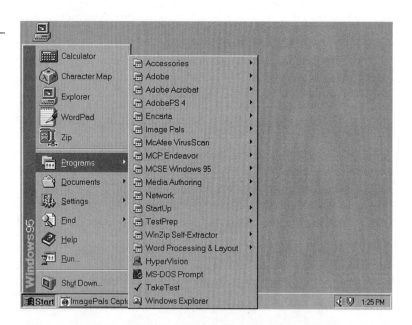

FIGURE 5.21

The system's directory structure.

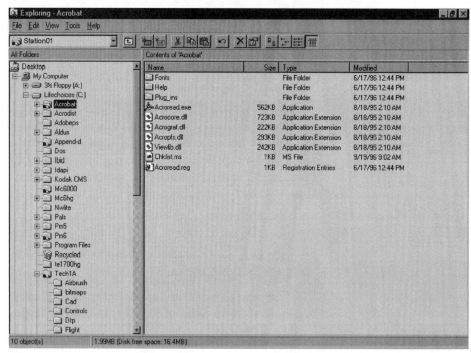

The right side of the Windows Explorer screen displays the files of the selected directory. The Status bar at the bottom of the screen provides information about the number and size of the files in the selected directory.

It is possible to display multiple directories on the Explorer screen. This feature makes it easy to perform file operations by simply opening another window. As with Windows 3.x, Win 95 provides drag-and-drop file copies and moves for single and multiple files. The Windows Explorer is also used to perform other DOS-like functions, such as formatting and copying disks.

The MS-DOS prompt also can be accessed through the Programs option.

The Start menu's Documents entry displays a list of documents previously opened.

The Settings option, accessed from the Start button menu, displays values for the system's configurable components and combines previous Windows functions. The Control Panel and Print Manager functions can be found here, and you can access the Win 95 taskbar. The Win 95 taskbar uses new button icons for the Minimize, Maximize, and Close functions, as illustrated in Figure 5.22. Each time a program is started, a button representing that program is displayed on the lower line of the taskbar. Changing from one program to another is as simple as clicking on the button of the program you want. The button disappears from the taskbar if the program is closed.

FIGURE 5.22

Windows 95 Minimize, Maximize, and Close functions.

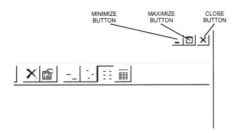

The **Find** utility is used to locate folders, files, mail messages, and shared computers. The Find function can be accessed directly from the Start menu on the taskbar, or it can be reached by right-clicking on the My Computer icon. The selection from the Start menu enables you to search for files, folders, and computers. The My Computer option searches only for files and folders. To locate a file, simply type its name in the Named window, tell the system the drive in which to look, and click Find. Standard DOS wildcards can be included in the search name.

The **Help** file system provides information about many Win 95 functions and operations. It also supplies an exhaustive list of guided troubleshooting routines for typical system components and peripherals.

The **Run** option is used to start programs or open folders from a command line.

The Start button is also used to correctly shut down Windows 95. The **Shut Down** option from the Start menu shuts down the system, restarts the computer, or logs off the user. This option must be used to avoid damaging files and to ensure that your work is properly saved. When you use the Shut Down option, the Shut Down Windows dialog box depicted in Figure 5.23 appears. After selecting an option from the dialog box, the unit tells you to wait until you receive a screen message that it is OK to turn off the system.

FIGURE 5.23

The Shut Down dialog box.

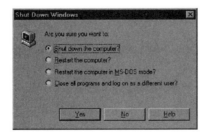

Win 95 Control Panel

A+ DOS/WINDOWS 4.6

The Control Panel in Windows 95 is located under the My Computer icon. The Control Panel window, depicted in Figure 5.24, contains icons for every device attached to the system. Each icon accesses the configuration information for the system's installed devices specific to its type. The icons are visually different from those used in the Win3.x Control Panel.

FIGURE 5.24

The Windows 95 Control Panel.

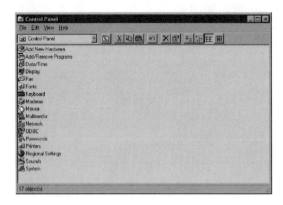

One of the main functions of the Control Panel is to enable users to customize the Win 95 Desktop. This customization includes setting screen colors, changing the Windows **wallpaper**, and selecting **screen savers**. Wallpaper is the pattern that appears behind the various application windows. Screen savers are screen displays that remain in motion while the system is idle. This utility prevents a single display from remaining on the screen for a prolonged time. This keeps the image from being "burned into" the screen. When this happens, the image becomes a permanent ghost on the screen and the monitor is ruined.

The Control Panel is also used to assign ports for printers and mice, as well as specifying how various peripheral devices respond. The Add New Hardware and Add/Remove Programs icons are used to set up interrupt and port assignments for new hardware devices, as well as to install device driver programs to support the hardware.

Installing Hardware and Software

A+ DOS/WINDOWS 3.7

Windows 95 is designed to assist the user in setting up any new hardware components that may be added to the system. An icon named Add New Hardware can be found under the Control Panel option of the Settings menu.

Double-clicking on this icon activates the Win 95 Wizard, depicted in Figure 5.25. The Wizard program is designed to guide you through hardware setup steps. The new card or device should already be installed in the system before running this procedure.

A+ DOS/WINDOWS 3.2

As with the Hardware Wizard, Win 95 offers the user assistance in installing new programs. The **Add/Remove New Programs** icon under the Control Panel option is used to install new programs automatically.

Setup

The Windows Setup function is located under the Control Panel's Add/Remove Programs icon. Configuration changes can be made through its dialog boxes. Some component manufacturers include a proprietary setup program for their Windows 95 applications. The Apply option searches the available drives for applications and installs them in the system.

FIGURE 5.25

The Win 95 Wizard.

DOS and Windows 95

A+ DOS/WINDOWS 4.7

DOS-based applications are installed in Windows 95 by simply running their executable file from the Run dialog box or Windows 95 Explorer. If the file has never been run under Windows 95, the operating system creates a default entry in its APPS.INF file for that program. A copy of the new entry is also used to create a .PIF file for the application.

After the APPS.INF entry has been created, it can be accessed and modified through the Properties window for that application. These Properties windows replace the PIF editor used in previous versions of Windows. The Properties window contains six tabs that enable the operation of the application to be modified. These tabs are as follows:

- ▶ General
- ▶ Program
- ▶ Font
- ▶ Memory
- ▶ Screen
- ▶ Misc

The **Program** tab enables the user to define where the DOS program is located, what it is called, and how it should be displayed. The tab's Run entry is used to establish the initial window size setting for the application. Options for this setting include normal window, maximized window, and minimized window.

A+ DOS/WINDOWS 3.3

Nearly every DOS-based program should run successfully in Windows 95. Even DOS programs that require access to all the system's resources can run successfully in the Windows 95 **MS-DOS mode**. In this mode, basically all but a small portion of Windows exits from memory. When the application is terminated, Windows restarts and returns to the desktop screen.

MS-DOS mode is established for the application by configuring its properties in the Advanced dialog box under My Computer/Properties/Program. Simply right-click on the application's executable filename in the My Computer window, and select the MS-DOS Mode setting in the Advanced screen.

It is also possible to adjust the memory allocated to the program through My Computer/ Properties/Memory. This function is accessed by right-clicking its executable filename, moving to the Memory window, and increasing or decreasing the memory available.

The **Memory** tab enables the user to establish memory allocation properties for the application. Values can be selected for Conventional, Extended, and Expanded memory usage, as well as for configuring HMA and UMB operations. These settings are still dependent on the information that may exist in the CONFIG.SYS file. In particular, check the

CONFIG.SYS file for noems parameters in the EMM386 statement. If present, replace them with an appropriate ram or x=mmmm-nnnn parameter.

The **Screen** tab provides several options for how the application is presented onscreen. It is possible to set the window size in which the application will run. These options include Full Screen, a user-definable window size, and a default window size based on the size determined by the graphic mode the application is using.

This tab also enables the Windows 95 toolbar to be displayed on the bottom of the screen. This feature can be valuable if the application becomes unstable or has trouble running in Windows.

Finally, the Screen tab enables the application to use the Windows 95 Fast ROM emulation and **dynamic memory allocation** features. These functions are selected to speed up video output operations.

Win 95 Structure

When fully installed, the Win 95 structure appears as depicted in Figure 5.26. The new Registry, Configuration Manager, and Virtual Machine Manager have already been introduced. However, they are joined by an **Installable File System (IFS) Manager** to function between the Win 95 core and the device drivers that service the system's hardware. On the other side of the Win 95 core, applications running on the system are accessed through the new 32-bit shell and user interface tools.

FIGURE 5.26

The Windows 95 organizational structure.

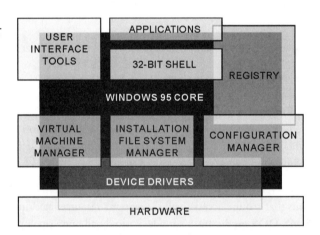

The Win 95 Core consists of three components: the **kernel**, the **GDI**, and the **USER** files. The kernel is the foundation of the system and includes basic memory and I/O management, task scheduling, error (exception) handling, and program execution functions. The USER files manage input from hardware devices and output to the user interface components, such as the icons and screen structures. The GDI components control what appears on the display. The GDI includes two main subsystems: the Graphics subsystem and the Printing subsystem. More is mentioned about these components as the text continues.

The Registry

A+ DOS/WINDOWS 1.1 Many of Windows 3.1's SYSTEM.INI, CONTROL.INI, PROGMAN.INI, and WIN.INI management functions have been relocated to an area known as the **Registry**. The system's configuration information—including local hardware configuration information, the network environment information, file associations, and user configurations—is held in the Win 95 Registry. When applications were removed from the system in earlier Windows versions, the configuration information distributed between the various .INI files remained unless the user or a special Windows Uninstall program looked them up and removed them individually. With Windows 95, headings and the associated configuration information are all removed from the registry, unlike the old .INI method of tracking this information.

The Registry files are located in the Windows\System directory. Each time Windows 95 boots up successfully, these files are backed up with a .DA0 extension. The contents of the registry can be viewed and altered through the **Registry Edit** utility, as depicted in Figure 5.27.

The Registry uses English-language descriptions and a hierarchical organization strategy. The hierarchy is divided into headkeys, keys, subkeys, and values. Keys are descriptive section headers that appear at the left side of the RegEdit window. Values, on the other hand, are definitions of topics organized under the keys. This organization can be thought of in the same terms as the organization of any book; the head keys are similar to chapter titles, the keys and subkeys are equivalent to the major and minor headings of the chapters, and values are equal to the sentences that convey information.

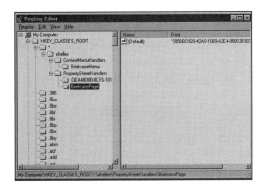

Values can contain a wide variety of information types. They can contain interrupt and port address information for a peripheral system, or simply information about an installed application program. The information can be encoded into binary, DWORDS, or strings. Values are always located at the right side of the RegEdit window.

If you examine the My Computer heading using the RegEdit option, you will find six categories listed. The head keys all start with an HKEY_ notation. Under My Computer, the categories are HKEY_CLASSES_ROOT, HKEY_CURRENT_USER, HKEY_LOCAL_MACHINE, HKEY_USERS, HKEY_CURRENT_CONFIG, and HKEY_DYN_DATA.

Most of the HKEY titles should appropriately describe their contents. The Classes_Root key divides the system's files into two groups by file extension type and by association. This key also holds data about icons associated with the file.

The Current_User key holds the data about the user specific configuration settings of the system, including color, keyboard, desktop, and start settings. The values in the Current_User key reflect those established by the user currently logged onto the system. If a different user logs on, then the contents of the HKEY_USERS section are moved into the Current-User key.

The Local_Machine key contains information about the system's hardware. All the hardware drivers and configuration information is contained in this key. The system cannot use peripheral devices that are not properly documented in the Local_Machine key.

Finally, the Users key contains the information about the various users who have been defined to log onto the system. The information from the Current_User key is copied into this section whenever a user logs off the system, or when the system is shut down.

Windows 95 System Policies

Because Windows 95 provides multiuser operations, operational policies are necessary to govern the rights and privileges of different users. Windows 95 System Policies establish guidelines to restrict user access to the options in the Control Panel and desktop. They also enable an administrator to customize the desktop and configure network settings.

The system policies that govern these functions are established and modified using an editor similar to the Registry Editor, called the **System Policy Editor**.

The Policy Editor is another tool that can be used to access the information in the Registry. Unlike the RegEdit utility, the Policy Editor can access only subsets of keys. The Registry Editor can access the entire Registry.

The Policy Editor utility is located on the Windows 95 CD, under the Admin folder, so only the keeper of the CD can adjust the system's policies. The path to access the Policy Editor on the CD is ADMIN\APPTOOLS\POLYEDIT. After the utility is located, it can be executed by entering **poledit** in the Run box. This should bring the Policy Editor screen, depicted in Figure 5.28, to the display.

FIGURE 5.28

The Windows 95 Policy Editor.

A+ DOS/WINDOWS 1.1 With any multiuser system, it may be necessary to establish various working environments for different users. Some users are entrusted with access to more of the system than other users. As described earlier, this is the purpose of logon procedures. The Win 95 policy file tracks policies for different users in a file named CONFIG.POL. The contents of this file are moved into the USER.DAT and SYSTEM.DAT files when a user logs on.

The Policy Editor enables system administrators to configure the Windows Desktop differently for different users. For some users, it may not be necessary to grant access to certain system options, such as printers or Registry Editor tools. Through the Policy Editor, access to these options can be removed from the desktop for a given user.

The window in Figure 5.29 contains an icon for a default user and a default computer. When the user logs onto the system, Windows searches for a user profile that matches the user logging on. If none is found, the default policies are copied into the new user's profile and are used until modified by a system administrator. The editing screen used to modify the Default User's policies is depicted in Figure 5.29.

As with the Registry Editor, the branches of the Policy Editor can be expanded or contracted by clicking on the plus and minus signs in the nodes of the tree. Three options can be selected for each setting: checked, cleared, or grayed. When a policy is checked, it is being implemented. If it is cleared (open), then the policy is not implemented. When the policy is grayed out, then the policy has not been changed since the last time the user logged on. As an example of the effects of these settings, let's use the system's wallpaper setting from the Control Panel. If the setting is checked, the designated wallpaper is displayed. If the setting is cleared, no wallpaper is displayed. Finally, if the setting is grayed out, the user can select a different wallpaper pattern through the Control Panel.

FIGURE 5.29

Inside the Policy Editor.

Configuration Manager

The **Configuration Manager** oversees the complete configuration process. Its primary purpose is to ensure that each device in the system can access an interrupt request channel without conflict and that each device has a unique I/O Port address. The I/O Port address is located where the system communicates with an intelligent programmable device. This address constantly tracks the number and location of devices in the system and reconfigures them when required.

The Configuration Manager charts a hardware tree for the system similar to the one illustrated in Figure 5.30. The tree represents all the buses and intelligent devices in the system. Information about the buses and devices is collected by the Configuration Manager's **Bus Enumerators**. The information can be obtained from the BIOS interrupt services used by the devices, device drivers installed for the devices, and the hardware itself.

The Configuration Manager assigns the system's resources to the devices, using **resource arbitrator** routines to provide interrupts, DMA channels, I/O addressing, and memory allocations for all the system's devices. The arbitrators resolve any conflicts between the devices and then inform each device driver about its particular resource allocations.

Virtual Machine Manager

Windows brought multitasking to the personal computer with version 3.0. This system worked its way around all the open applications, enabling them to run for a period of time before resetting and moving to the next application. One of the simplest forms of multitasking is **task switching**. In a task-switching operation, several applications can run at the same time. When you have multiple applications open in Windows, the window that is currently being accessed is called the active window and appears in the foreground (over top of the other windows). The activity of the other open windows is suspended, as denoted by their gray color, and they run in the background.

Special key combinations enable the user to move between tasks easily. By pressing the ALT and TAB keys together, you can move quickly through the open applications. The ALT+ESC combination also enables the user to cycle through open application windows.

In a Windows 3.x cooperative multitasking system, some applications gained control of the system and used the resources until they were finished. Some Win 3.x applications took up more than their share of the system's resources.

FIGURE 5.30

The Configuration Manager's tree structure.

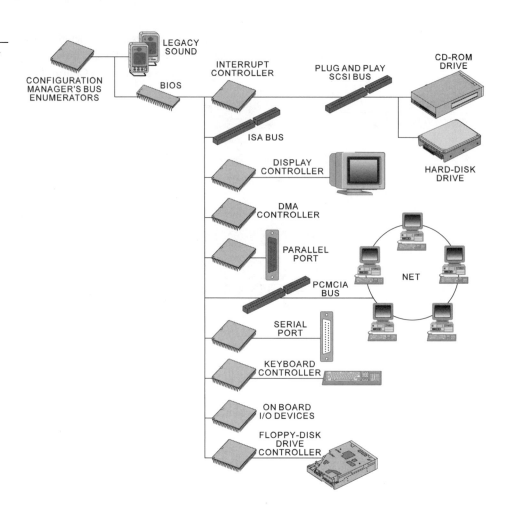

When Microsoft designers created Windows 95, they designed it for pre-emptive multitasking operation so that the operating system allowed applications to run for only a predetermined amount of time, based on how critical the task was in the overall scheme of the system. More time was allotted to high-priority tasks than to low-priority tasks. However, the operating system remained the controlling force. When the application's time was up, the operating system simply cut it off.

Under cooperative multitasking, the system is tied up with a single application whenever Windows displays an hourglass on the screen. With pre-emptive multitasking, a new task can be opened while the hourglass is being displayed on the screen. Work can be performed under that task window while the system is working on the other task. More importantly, if the system locks up while working on a specific task in Windows 95, you can simply end the task instead of restarting the machine.

32-Bit Access with Windows 95

A+ DOS/WINDOWS 1.6

Windows 95 streamlines the 32-bit file and disk access operations by removing both the DOS and the BIOS from the access equation, as illustrated in Figure 5.31. This enables Win 95 to always run in Protected memory mode so that no mode switching need occur.

Microsoft refers to this portion of the system as the Protected Mode FAT File System, or VFAT. As its full name implies, the VFAT provides a protected mode method of interacting with the file system on the disk drive. VFAT operates in 32-bit mode, but the actual FAT structure of the disk remains as 12- or 16-bit allocations. Because the system does not normally have to exit and re-enter Protected mode, performance is increased considerably. The logical blocks of the VFAT are illustrated in Figure 5.32.

FIGURE 5.31

32-bit access in Windows 95.

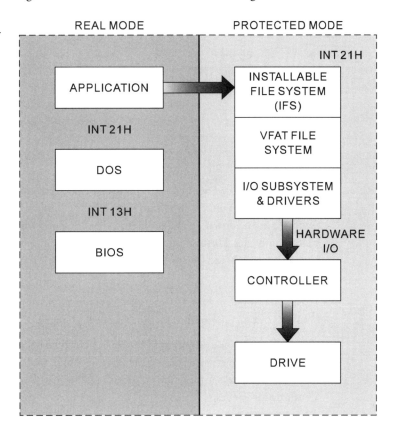

The VFAT system replaces the SMARTDRV disk caching utility with a Protected mode driver named **VCACHE**. Under VCACHE, the size of the cache data pool is based on the amount of free memory in the system instead of a fixed amount. The program automatically allocates blocks of free memory to caching operations as needed. Under Windows 95, the VCACHE driver controls the cache for the system's CD-ROM drive, in addition to the hard disk and file operations.

When a file or disk access request is received by Win 95, a subsection of the interface known as the **Installable File System** (**IFS**) processes the request by passing it to the proper **file system driver** (**FSD**). The FSDs communicate with the IFS manager and the drivers that work directly with the hardware device controllers. These device-specific drivers work within the **I/O subsystem layer** (**IOS**). The IOS layer handles I/O systems that transmit and receive data in multiple-byte transfers. Devices in this category include hard-disk drives, CD-ROM drives, tape drives, and network controllers.

Safe Mode Startup

A+ DOS/WINDOWS 3.3

Because no DOS level is present in the Windows 95 startup routine, special precautions and procedures must be used to protect the system in case of startup problems. Two very good tools to use in these situations are an emergency startup disk and the Startup menu.

FIGURE 5.32

The Win 95 VFAT interface.

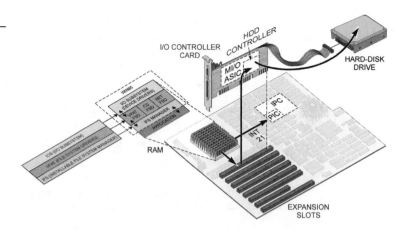

During the Windows Setup operation, the software provides an option for creating an emergency startup disk. This option should be used for every Windows 95 installation. Setup copies the operating system files to the disk along with utilities for troubleshooting startup problems. The disk can then be used to boot up the system in **Safe Mode** and display a DOS command-line prompt.

A startup disk can also be created through the Control Panel's Add/Remove Programs icon. This option is normally used to create a new startup disk after new hardware has been installed or configuration information has been changed.

The 95 Startup Menu, depicted in Figure 5.33, can be obtained on a nonstarting system by holding the F8 function key when the Starting Windows 95 display is on the screen. The menu offers several startup options, including: Normal, Logged, Safe, and Step-by-Step Confirmation modes.

FIGURE 5.33

The Startup menu.

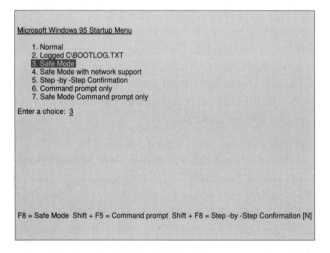

In **Normal mode**, the system simply tries to restart as it normally would, loading all its normal Startup and Registry files. The Logged mode option also attempts to start the system in Normal mode but keeps an error log file that contains the steps performed and the outcome. This text file (BOOTLOG.TXT) can be read with any text editor or can be printed out on a working system.

A+ DOS/WINDOWS 4.1

If Win 95 determines that a problem has occurred that prevented the system from starting, it attempts to restart the system in Safe mode. This mode bypasses several startup files to provide access to the system's configuration files. In particular, the CONFIG.SYS and AUTOEXEC.BAT files are bypassed, along with the Win 95 Registry and the SYSTEM.INI's [Boot] and [386enh] sections. In this mode, the keyboard, mouse, and standard mode VGA drivers are active. Unless modified, the Safe mode screen appears as depicted in Figure 5.34. Active functions appear on the screen along with the Safe mode notice in each corner.

FIGURE 5.34

The Safe mode startup screen.

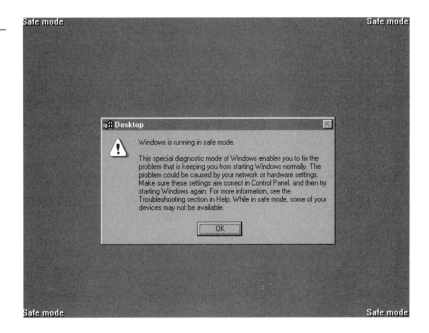

Safe mode can also be accessed by typing **Win /d:m** at the DOS prompt, or by pressing the F5 function key during startup.

The **Step-by-Step Confirmation mode** displays each startup command line by line and waits for a confirmation from the keyboard before moving ahead. This isolates and avoids an offending startup command so that it can be replaced or removed. This option is obtained by pressing the F8 function key at the Startup menu.

Other startup options may also be available from the menu, depending on the configuration of the system. Some options start the system and bring it to a DOS command-line prompt. Depending on which option is selected, the system may boot up to the command line, using the Startup files and the Registry, or start in Safe mode with a command-line prompt only.

Windows can be started from the command line using a number of different switches. These switches can be used to check for startup conflicts. The Win /d:m example given earlier starts Windows in Safe mode. The /d:x switch is used to check for an upper memory conflict. The /d:f switch can be used to check for 32-bit disk access conflicts. Finally, the /d:v switch is used to check for hard disk I/O conflicts.

Windows 95 maintains a number of log files that track system performance and can be used to assess system failures. These log files are SETUPLOG.TXT, DETLOG.TXT, and BOOTUPLOG.TXT and are stored in the drive's root directory. All three are text files that can be viewed with a text editor package.

These filenames are indicative of the types of information they log. As described earlier, the BOOTUPLOG.TXT file tracks the events of the startup procedure. Likewise,

SETUPLOG.TXT tracks the events of the Setup process. The DETLOG.TXT file monitors the presence of detected hardware devices and identifies the parameters for them.

Windows 95(b)–OSR2

A+ DOS/WINDOWS 1.6

Windows 95 **OSR2**, also known as Win **95(b)**, is an upgrade of the original Windows 95 package that includes patches and fixes for version 1, along with Microsoft Internet Explorer 3.0 and Personal Web Server. This upgrade also includes an enhanced File Allocation Table system, referred to as **FAT32**.

Previous versions of DOS and Windows supported what is now termed **FAT16** (or **FAT 12**). As described in Chapter 3, "Troubleshooting the System," the size of the operating system's FAT determines the size of the clusters for a given-size disk partition. Of course, smaller cluster sizes are better because even a single byte stored in a cluster removes the entire cluster from the available storage space on the drive. This can add up to a lot of wasted storage space on larger drives. Table 5.2 describes the relationships between clusters and maximum partitions for various FAT entry sizes.

Table 5.2   FAT Relationships

FAT Type	Partition Size	Cluster Size (In bytes)
FAT12	16MB	4096
FAT16	32MB	2048
FAT16	128MB	2048
FAT16	256MB	4096
FAT16	512MB	8192
FAT16	1GB	16384
FAT16	2GB	32768
FAT32	<260MB	512
FAT32	8GB	4096
FAT32	16GB	8192
FAT32	32GB	16384
FAT32	>32GB	32768

To use the FAT32 system, the hard drive must be formatted using the FDISK/FORMAT functions in OSR2. This makes FAT32 incompatible with older versions of Windows (even Windows 95(a)and Windows NT) and with disk utilities and troubleshooting packages designed for FAT12/16 systems.

To use the FAT32 FDISK function in OSR2, you must enable the Large Disk Support option. After completing the FDISK function and exiting, you must manually reboot the system. After this, it is usually a simple matter of performing a FORMAT operation using the OSR2 CD or start disk to install the FAT32 drive. Failure to reboot between the FDISK and FORMAT operations produces an error.

To verify that the hard drive is formatted with FAT32, select the My Computer option from the desktop and right-click on the C: drive icon. This produces the [C:] properties window displayed in Figure 5.35. The Type entry should read Local Disk [FAT 32]. The hard disk usage pie chart will not work correctly with drives larger than 2GB; it will show the drive as empty until at least 2GB of space is used.

FIGURE 5.35

*Showing FAT32 in the HDD
Properties window.*

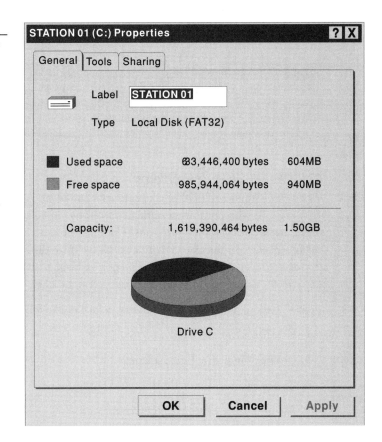

OSR2 does not require that FAT32 be used; it operates just as well, if not better, using the FAT16 format. Depending on the application of the system, OSR2 may run slower with FAT32. Remember that FAT32 is designed to optimize storage space, not performance. The simple fact that FAT32 offers more potential for more clusters makes it slower than a drive with fewer clusters. With this in mind, the decision to use FAT32 or FAT16, or to use different cluster sizes in FAT32, usually depends on the balance the user establishes between performance and storage. The default cluster size set by Microsoft for FAT32 is 4KB.

In addition to the FAT32 system, OSR2 offers improved **power management (APM)** functions, **bus mastering** support, **MMX** multimedia support, and enhanced PCMCIA functions over version a (which is referred to as OSR1, or Service Pack 1).

Also new in OSR2 is HDD/CD-ROM DMA access support. This feature is located in the Control Panel/System/Device Manager/Disk Drives window. At this point, choose the desired drive, select Properties, and click the Settings tab. Check the DMA box and reboot the system. The same procedure should be performed for the CD-ROM drive as well. This box appears for only IDE drives, and only when using properly installed and configured OSR2 bus mastering drivers for the drive.

Interestingly, OSR2 is not sold in the retail market; it is available legally only through OEMs selling system board and HDD hardware, or with new systems. Version b can be identified by 0796 Part No. 000-45234 nomenclature on the CD, or by a B in the part number under the System Properties tab. Version b may also be denoted by a 4.00.950.1111 version number when a VER operation is performed.

Troubleshooting Windows 95

Windows 95 offers many improved features over previous operating systems. However, it can suffer many of the same problems as any other operating system. To overcome some of the typical system problems, Windows 95 includes several built-in troubleshooting tools. These tools include several Safe mode startup options, a trio of system log files, and an extensive interactive troubleshooting help file system.

Windows 95 Startup Problems

A+ DOS/WINDOWS 3.3

Windows 95 requires 420KB of conventional memory and at least 3MB of extended memory to start. As with previous operating systems, two important tools can be used with a system that is having startup problems. These are the clean boot disk and the step-by-step startup sequence. In the case of Windows 95, the clean disk is referred to as an **emergency start disk**. Pressing the Shift and F8 function keys simultaneously when the Starting Windows 95 message appears onscreen can access the single-step startup process.

A+ DOS/WINDOWS 4.1

Typical Windows 95 Startup Error messages include the following:

- HIMEM.SYS not loaded
- Unable to initialize display adapter
- Device referenced in WIN.INI could not be found
- Bad or missing COMMAND.COM
- Swapfile Corrupt
- Damaged or Missing Core files
- Device referenced in SYSTEM.INI could not be found

These and other Windows 95-related startup messages indicate the presence of problems that must be corrected before the system can boot up and run correctly. As with DOS and Windows 3.x startup problems, the logical procedure for isolating and correcting these problems in Windows 95 involve booting the system from the emergency start disk or starting the system in Safe mode, and then single-stepping through the startup sequence until the offending steps have been isolated.

In the case of the HIMEM.SYS error, use the DOS editor to check the syntax and correctness of the entry in the CONFIG.SYS file. Also check the HIMEM.SYS file to make sure it is the correct version and in the correct location. You should also be able to bypass the display adapter problem by starting the system in Safe mode and then sorting out the display driver/hardware problem as directed in the Video Troubleshooting section of Chapter 9, "Video Displays." To correct the missing core file problem, run the WIN 95 Setup in Safe Recovery mode, using the Verify option to replace the files. The missing files referenced from the .INI files should be correctly reloaded from the emergency startup disk to correct the offending references.

Creating an Emergency Start Disk

A+ DOS/WINDOWS 4.3

Windows 95 does not start up through DOS, so it is very difficult to gain access to the system if Windows becomes disabled. Therefore, it is helpful to have a clean startup disk to troubleshoot Windows 95-related problems. In the event that the Windows program becomes nonfunctional, you must use the Start disk to restore the system to proper operation.

In addition to creating a startup floppy, Windows 95 transfers a number of diagnostic files to the disk. These utilities are particularly helpful in getting a Windows 95 machine operational again. Because no path to DOS exists except through Windows, this disk provides one of the few tools for the technician to service a down machine with this operating system. The steps involved in creating the boot disk are as follows:

1. Create the emergency startup disk.

   a. Click the Start button.

   b. Move to the Settings option in the Start menu.

   c. Select the Control Panel from the list.

   d. Double-click the Add/Remove Programs icon.

   e. Select the Startup Disk tab.

   f. Click the Create Disk button.

   g. Place the WIN 95 CD in the CD-ROM drive, when prompted.

   h. Follow the menu items as directed.

   i. Place a blank disk in Drive A, when prompted.

   j. Remove the WIN 95 CD from the drive when the operation is complete.

2. Examine the Startup disk.

   a. Close the Control Panel window.

   b. Select the Windows Explorer option from the Start/Programs menu.

   c. Click on the 3.5-inch Floppy A: option from the list in the All Folders window.

   d. Label the disk as an Emergency Startup Disk.

3. Examine the new CONFIG.SYS file on the boot disk.

   a. Select the Notepad utility in the Start/Programs/Accessories menu.

   b. Click the File and Open options in the Notepad window.

   c. Select the 3.5-inch Floppy (A:) option in the Look in window.

   d. Select the All File (*.*) option from the Files of Type window.

   e. Double-click the CONFIG.SYS entry in the window.

4. Add helpful files to the Start disk.

   a. Close the Notepad utility.

   b. Select the Windows Explorer option from the Start/Programs menu.

   c. Click the File and Open options in the Notepad window.

   d. Select the 3.5-inch Floppy (A:) option in the Look in window.

   e. Select the Folder option from the File/New menu.

   f. Type your three initials in the box for the new subdirectory.

   g. Select the (C:) option in the Look in window.

     h. Locate the AUTOEXEC.BAT file in the "Contents of C:\" window.

     i. Click, hold, and drag the file to the 3.5-inch Floppy (A:) option on the Look in window, and release.

     j. Repeat Step 5-i for the SYSTEM.DAT, CONFIG.SYS, WIN.INI, and SYSTEM.INI files.

     k. Exit Windows Explorer.

5. Examine the new AUTOEXEC.BAT file on the boot disk.

     a. Select the Notepad utility in the Start/Programs/Accessories menu.

     b. Click on the File and Open options in the Notepad window.

     c. Select the 3-1/2-inch Floppy (A:) option in the Look in window.

     d. Select the All File (*.*) option from the Files of Type window.

     e. Double-click the AUTOEXEC.BAT entry in the window.

As with the DOS and Windows 3.x boot disks, the Windows 95 emergency start disk should be stored in a convenient place and clearly labeled so that it is easy to find when you need it.

WIN Switches

When Windows 95 refuses to start up, a number of options are available for starting it from the command line. Starting Window using a /d switch is often helpful in this situation (that is, using the WIN /d command). The /d switch can be modified to start Windows in a number of different configurations.

Using an :f modifier disables 32-bit disk access. The :m and :n modifiers start Windows in Safe mode, or Safe with Networking mode. An :s modifier inhibits Windows from using address space between F0000h and FFFFFh. The :v modifier prevents Windows from controlling disk transfers. Instead, HDD interrupt requests are handled by the BIOS. Using the :x modifier prevents Windows from using the A000h-FFFFh area of memory.

Windows 95 Log Files

> Windows 95 maintains four log files named BOOTLOG.TXT, SETUPLOG.TXT, DETLOG.TXT, and DETCRASH.LOG. These files maintain a log of different system operations and can be used to see what events occurred leading up to a failure.

The .TXT files can be read with Notepad, DOS Editor, or any other text editor.

BOOTLOG.TXT

The BOOTLOG.TXT file contains the sequence of events conducted during the Startup of the system. A bootlog can be created by pressing the F8 key during startup, or by starting Windows 95 with a WIN /b switch. The log information is recorded in five basic sections.

1. Loading Real Mode Drivers

This section records a two-part loading report during the boot-up process. In the example section that follows, the system successfully loads the HIMEM.SYS and EMM386.EXE memory managers. Afterward, a list of other Real mode drivers are loaded. In the case of an unsuccessful load operation, the report returns a LoadFailed= entry.

```
[000E3FDC] Loading Device = C:\WINDOWS\HIMEM.SYS
[000E3FE0] LoadSuccess   = C:\WINDOWS\HIMEM.SYS
[000E3FE0] Loading Device = C:\WINDOWS\EMM386.EXE
[000E3FEC] LoadSuccess   = C:\WINDOWS\EMM386.EXE
[000E3FEC] Loading Device = C:\WINDOWS\SETVER.EXE
[000E3FEF] LoadSuccess   = C:\WINDOWS\SETVER.EXE
[000E3FEF] Loading Device = C:\PWRSCSI!\MCAM950.SYS
[000E406B] LoadSuccess   = C:\PWRSCSI!\MCAM950.SYS
[000E406B] Loading Device = C:\PWRSCSI!\FDCD.SYS
[000E40BD] LoadSuccess   = C:\PWRSCSI!\FDCD.SYS
[000E40BD] Loading Device = C:\WINDOWS\IFSHLP.SYS
[000E40C0] LoadSuccess   = C:\WINDOWS\IFSHLP.SYS
```

2. Loading VxDs

In the second section, the system loads the VxD drivers. The following list includes a sample of various VxDs that have been loaded. The asterisks in the sample listing are included to indicate sections of omitted lines. This is done to shorten the length of the file for illustration purposes.

```
[000E4198] Loading Vxd = VMM
[000E419B] LoadSuccess = VMM
*
[000E41AA] Loading Vxd = CONFIGMG
[000E41AB] LoadSuccess = CONFIGMG
*
[000E41AC] Loading Vxd = VWIN32
[000E41AC] LoadSuccess = VWIN32
[000E41AC] Loading Vxd = VFBACKUP
[000E41AC] LoadSuccess = VFBACKUP
[000E41AC] Loading Vxd = VCOMM
[000E41AD] LoadSuccess = VCOMM
[000E41AD] Loading Vxd = COMBUFF
[000E41AD] LoadSuccess = COMBUFF
*
[000E41B1] Loading Vxd = VFAT
[000E41B2] LoadSuccess = VFAT
[000E41B2] Loading Vxd = VCACHE
[000E41B2] LoadSuccess = VCACHE
*
[000E41B5] Loading Vxd = V86MMGR
[000E41B6] LoadSuccess = V86MMGR
[000E41B6] Loading Vxd = PAGESWAP
[000E41B6] LoadSuccess = PAGESWAP
*
[000E41F3] Loading Vxd = int13
[000E41F3] LoadSuccess = int13
[000E41F3] Loading Vxd = vmouse
[000E41F4] LoadSuccess = vmouse
[000E41F6] Loading Vxd = msmouse.vxd
[000E41F9] LoadSuccess = msmouse.vxd
```

```
[000E41F9] Loading Vxd = vshare
[000E41F9] LoadFailed  = vshare
*
[000E4208] Loading Vxd = EBIOS
[000E4208] LoadFailed  = EBIOS
```

3. Initialization of Critical VxDs

Check this section to verify that system-critical VxDs have been initialized.

```
[000E420A] SYSCRITINIT    = VMM
[000E420A] SYSCRITINITSUCCESS  = VMM
[000E420A] SYSCRITINIT    = VCACHE
[000E420A] SYSCRITINITSUCCESS  = VCACHE
[000E420A] SYSCRITINIT    = PERF
[000E420A] SYSCRITINITSUCCESS  = PERF
[000E420A] SYSCRITINIT    = VPICD
[000E420A] SYSCRITINITSUCCESS  = VPICD
[000E420A] SYSCRITINIT    = VTD
[000E420A] SYSCRITINITSUCCESS  = VTD
*
*
```

4. Device Initialization of VxDs

This section of the log shows the VxDs that have been successfully initialized. In each cycle, the system attempts to initialize a VxD and then reports its success or failure.

```
[000E420D] DEVICEINIT    = VMM
[000E420D] DEVICEINITSUCCESS  = VMM
[000E420D] DEVICEINIT    = VCACHE
[000E420D] DEVICEINITSUCCESS  = VCACHE
[000E420E] DEVICEINIT    = PERF
[000E420E] DEVICEINITSUCCESS  = PERF
*
[000E421F] Dynamic load device  isapnp.vxd
[000E4225] Dynamic init device   ISAPNP
[000E4226] Dynamic init success ISAPNP
[000E4226] Dynamic load success isapnp.vxd
*
*
```

The bold information in the listing points out the dynamic loading and initialization of the ISA bus PnP driver.

5. Successful Initialization of VxDs

The entries in this section verify the successful completion of the initialization of the system's VxDs. A partial listing of these activities follows:

```
[000E4430] INITCOMPLETE = VMM
[000E4430] INITCOMPLETESUCCESS = VMM
[000E4430] INITCOMPLETE = VCACHE
[000E4430] INITCOMPLETESUCCESS = VCACHE
[000E4430] INITCOMPLETE = PERF
[000E4430] INITCOMPLETESUCCESS = PERF
*
*
```

SETUPLOG.TXT

The SETUPLOG.TXT file holds setup information that was established during the installation process. The file is stored on the system's root directory and is used in safe recovery situations. The log file exists in seven basic sections, as described in the following sample sections. Entries are added to the file as they occur in the setup process. Therefore, the file can be read to determine what action was being taken when a setup failure occurred.

```
[OptionalComponents]
"Accessories"=1
"Communications"=1
"Disk Tools"=1
"Multimedia"=1
"Screen Savers"=0
"Disk compression tools"=1
"Paint"=1
"HyperTerminal"=1
"Defrag"=1
"Calculator"=1
"Backup"=0
"Phone Dialer"=1
"Flying Windows"=1
"Desktop Wallpaper"=0
*

*

[System]
"Display"="S3"
"Keyboard"="Standard 101/102-Key or Microsoft Natural Keyboard"
"SelectedKeyboard"="KEYBOARD_00000409"
"MultiLanguage"="ENGLISH"
"Machine"="MS_CHICAGO"
"Monitor"="(Unknown Monitor)"
"Mouse"="Standard Serial Mouse"
"Power"="No_APM"
"Locale"="L0409"
"UI_Choice"="Win95UI"
*

*

[Setup]
InstallType=1
Customise=0
Express=0
ChangeDir=1
Network=1
OptionalComponents=1
System=1
MBR=1
Reboot=1
*
CleanBoot=0
Win31FileSystem=-8531
CopyFiles=1
Verify=-8531
*
```

```
CHKDSK=0
UNINSTALL=1
DevicePath=0
InstallDir=C:\WINDOWS,0,400
[Started]
version=262144,950
OldLogFile
SourcePath=C:\WININST0.400
CmdLine=/T:C:\WININST0.400 /SrcDir=D:\WIN95 /IZ /IS /IQ /IT /II /C
/U:xxxxxxxxxxxxxxxx
WinVer=Mini
ExePath=C:\WININST0.400
FilePath=D:\WIN95\
RunVer=3.1
Init:Setup initialization sucessful.
Started=Passed

[Detection]
Detection=Passed
Detection Passed
loading 'C:\WININST0.400\suexpand.dll' returned c4f0ea6
VcpClose:About to close
VcpClose:About to End
VcpClose:About to Terminate
CacheFile() C:\WINDOWS\system.ini returns=0
*
Display_InitDevice:Checking display driver. No PNP registry found.
Mouse_InitDevice:Checking mouse driver. No PNP registry found.
```

The bold text in the sample section shows the system's response to not finding a PnP registry entry for different devices.

```
[FileQueue]
CacheFile() C:\WINDOWS\win.ini returns=0
CacheFile() C:\WINDOWS\exchng32.ini returns=0
CacheFile() C:\WINDOWS\control.ini returns=0
CacheFile() C:\WINDOWS\qtw.ini returns=0
CacheFile() C:\WINDOWS\system.cb returns=0
SrcLdid:(11)skyeagle.cpl
CacheFile() C:\WINDOWS\msoffice.ini returns=0
SrcLdid:(25)reg.dat
Winver (0400) specific Section:win4.0, reRet=0.
Calling Netdi to install
CacheFile() C:\WINDOWS\protocol.ini returns=0
*
*
[FileCopy]
VcpClose:About to close
VcpClose:Delete 1514
VcpClose:Rename 4
VcpClose:Copy 827
CAB-No volume name for LDID 2, local copy - path C:\WININST0.400
adapter.inf=17,,7915,20032
appletpp.inf=17,,7915,20032
applets.inf=17,,7915,20032
```

```
awfax.inf=17,,7915,20032
awupd.inf=17,,7915,20032
bkupagnt.inf=17,,7915,20032
cemmf.inf=17,,7915,20032
cheyenne.inf=17,,7915,20032
command.com=30,command.new,7915,20032
decpsmw4.inf=17,,7915,20032
diskdrv.inf=17,,7915,20032
drvspace.bin=13,,7915,20032
drvspace.sys=13,,7915,20032
dskmaint.dll=11,,9063,24692
enable.inf=17,,7915,20032
extract.exe=13,,9063,24685
fonts.inf=17,,7915,20032
*
*
[Restart]
loading 'C:\WININST0.400\suexpand.dll' returned c4f0ea6
SrcLdid:(30)SYSTEM.NEW
SrcLdid:(30)COMMAND.NEW
SrcLdid:(30)WINBOOT.NEW
SrcLdid:(26)SETVER.WIN
SrcLdid:(30)SULOGO.SYS
SrcLdid:(30)USER.NEW
Ver:C:\DRVSPACE.BIN=:262144:256:
Ver:C:\WININST0.400\DRVSPACE.BIN=:262144:256:
SrcLdid:(2)DRVSPACE.BIN
Ver:C:\DBLSPACE.BIN=:262144:256:
Ver:C:\WININST0.400\DRVSPACE.BIN=:262144:256:
SrcLdid:(2)DRVSPACE.BIN
VcpClose:About to close
VcpClose:Delete 101
VcpClose:Copy 10
CAB-No volume name for LDID 2, local copy - path C:\WININST0.400
Resolve Conflict:C:\DBLSPACE.BIN ConflictType: 240
drvspace.bin=31,DBLSPACE.BIN,7915,20032
Resolve Conflict:C:\drvspace.bin ConflictType: 240
drvspace.bin=31,,7915,20032
drvspace.sys=13,dblspace.sys,7915,20032
LDID is ffff failed CtlGetLdd
CAB-No volume name for LDID ffff, local copy - path Absolute
COMMAND.NEW=30,command.com,7915,20032
COMMAND.NEW=26,command.com,7915,20032
*
*
```

The bold lines in the example demonstrate the capability of the PnP system to resolve conflicts between programs and devices. In this case, a conflict occurs between a driver named DBLSPACE and another named DRVSPACE.

DETCRASH.LOG

This **Detect Crash** log file is created when the system crashes during the hardware detection portion of the startup procedure. The file contains information about the detection module that was running when the crash occurred. This file is a binary file and cannot be read directly. However, a text version of the file, named DETLOG.TXT, is available under the Root directory of the drive.

DETLOG.TXT

The **DETLOG.TXT** file holds the text equivalent of the information in the DETCRASH.LOG file. This file can be read with a text editor to determine which hardware components have been detected by the system and what its parameters are. The following section of a sample DETLOG.TXT file demonstrates the type of information logged in this file.

```
[System Detection: 11/07/97 - 12:05:11]
Parameters "", InfParams "", Flags=01004233
SDMVer=0400.950, WinVer=0700030a, Build=00.00.0, WinFlags=00000419
LogCrash: crash log not found or invalid
SetVar: CDROM_Any=
Checking for: Programmable Interrupt Controller
QueryIOMem: Caller=DETECTPIC, rcQuery=0
        IO=20-21,a0-a1
Detected: *PNP0000\0000 = [1] Programmable interrupt controller
        IO=20-21,a0-a1
        IRQ=2
Checking for: Direct Memory Access Controller
QueryIOMem: Caller=DETECTDMA, rcQuery=0
        IO=0-f,81-83,87-87,89-8b,8f-8f,c0-df
Detected: *PNP0200\0000 = [2] Direct memory access controller
        IO=0-f,81-83,87-87,89-8b,8f-8f,c0-df
        DMA=4
Checking for: System CMOS/Real Time Clock
QueryIOMem: Caller=DETECTCMOS, rcQuery=0
        IO=70-71
Detected: *PNP0B00\0000 = [3] System CMOS/real time clock
        IO=70-71
        IRQ=8
Checking for: System Timer
QueryIOMem: Caller=DETECTTIMER, rcQuery=0
        IO=40-43
Detected: *PNP0100\0000 = [4] System timer
        IO=40-43
        IRQ=0
Checking for: System Speaker
QueryIOMem: Caller=DETECTSPEAKER, rcQuery=0
        IO=61-61
Detected: *PNP0800\0000 = [5] System speaker
        IO=61-61
Checking for: Numeric Data Processor
QueryIOMem: Caller=DETECTNDP, rcQuery=0
        IO=f0-ff
Detected: *PNP0C04\0000 = [6] Numeric data processor
        IO=f0-ff
        IRQ=13
Checking for: System Board
```

```
Detected: *PNP0C01\0000 = [7] System board
Checking for: Keyboard
QueryIOMem: Caller=DETECTKBD, rcQuery=0
     IO=60-60,64-64
GetKbdType: Keyboard ID=faab41
Detected: *PNP0303\0000 = [8] Standard 101/102-Key or Microsoft
  Natural Keyboard
     IO=60-60,64-64
     IRQ=1
Checking for: System Bus
CheckInt86xCrash: int 1a,AX=b101,rc=0
Detected: *PNP0A00\0000 = [9] ISA Plug and Play bus
Checking for: S3 801/805/928/864/964 Display Adapter
QueryIOMem: Caller=DETECTS3801, rcQuery=0
     Mem=c0000-c07ff
QueryIOMem: Caller=DETECTS3801, rcQuery=0
     Mem=c0000-c7fff
VerifyHWReg: failed verification of *PNP0913\0000
Checking for: Future Domain TMC-950 SIC-based SCSI Host Adapter
QueryIOMem: Caller=DETECTFD8XX, rcQuery=0
     Mem=cbc00-cbfff
Detected: *FDC0950\0000 = [10] Future Domain TMC-850/M/MER/MEX SCSI
  Host Adapter
     Mem=ca000-cbfff
     IRQ=5
Checking for: Standard Floppy Controller
QueryIOMem: Caller=DETECTFLOPPY, rcQuery=0
     IO=3f2-3f5
QueryIOMem: Caller=DETECTFLOPPY, rcQuery=0
     IO=372-375
Detected: *PNP0700\0000 = [11] Standard Floppy Disk Controller
     IO=3f2-3f5
     IRQ=6
     DMA=2
Checking for: Serial Communication Port
QueryIOMem: Caller=DETECTCOM, rcQuery=0
     IO=3f8-3ff
GetCOMIRQ: IIR=1
Detected: *PNP0500\0000 = [12] Communications Port
     IO=3f8-3ff
     IRQ=4
SetVar: COMIRQ3f8=4,0
Checking for: Serial Communication Port
QueryIOMem: Caller=DETECTCOM, rcQuery=0
     IO=2f8-2ff
GetCOMIRQ: IIR=1
Detected: *PNP0500\0001 = [13] Communications Port
     IO=2f8-2ff
     IRQ=3
SetVar: COMIRQ2f8=3,0
Checking for: Serial Mouse
QueryIOMem: Caller=DETECTSERIALMOUSE, rcQuery=2
     IO=3f8-3ff
```

```
Serial mouse ID: M (004d)
Detected: *PNP0F0C\0000 = [14] Standard Serial Mouse
SetVar: COMIRQ3f8=4,0
Checking for: Standard IDE/ESDI Hard Disk Controller
QueryIOMem: Caller=DETECTESDI, rcQuery=0
      IO=1f0-1f7
QueryIOMem: Caller=DETECTESDI, rcQuery=0
      IO=3f6-3f6
Detected: *PNP0600\0000 = [15] Standard IDE/ESDI Hard Disk Controller
      IO=1f0-1f7,3f6-3f6
      IRQ=14
Checking for: Parallel Printer Port
QueryIOMem: Caller=DETECTLPT, rcQuery=0
      IO=378-37a
Detected: *PNP0400\0000 = [16] Printer Port
      IO=378-37a
Checking for: Sound Blaster Compatible
SetVar: SkipGUSResources=
QueryIOMem: Caller=DETECTSB, rcQuery=0
      IO=220-22f
QueryIOMem: Caller=DETECTSB, rcQuery=0
      IO=388-38b
Detected: *ESS4881\0000 = [17] ESS ES488 AudioDrive
      IO=220-22f,388-389
      IRQ=7
      DMA=1
Checking for: Sound Blaster Compatible
QueryIOMem: Caller=DETECTSB, rcQuery=0
      IO=201-201
Detected: *PNPB02F\0000 = [18] Gameport Joystick
      IO=201-201
VerifyHW: manual device UNIMODEM535147EF\COM2: 14.4 Data FAX Modem
```

Referring to the information in the sample file, it should be easy to see the type of information that is logged about the system. The detection routine cycles through a three-part process. First it identifies the activity it is about to perform (for example, Checking for: Serial Mouse), then it queries the system at addresses normally allocated to that type of device (IO=3f8-eff), and finally it verifies whether this device was detected. Some entries also include a listing of the IRQ and DMA resources allocated to the device. The sample list includes information about many of the system and I/O devices already mentioned in Chapters 1, "Microcomputer Fundamentals," and 2, "PC Hardware."

In each case, the PnP system inquires about particular system devices and logs the parameters of the device it detects. The sample also shows that, at least in this case, no crash log has been created. To use the file for crash detection purposes, simply check the last entry created in the log. To determine exactly where a problem has occurred, it may be necessary to compare this information to the listing in a file named DETLOG.OLD. This file is the old version of the DETLOG file that was renamed before the latest detection phase began.

Windows 95 Operating Problems

The Windows 95 structure provides a much improved multitasking environment over Windows 3.x. However, applications can still attempt to access unallocated memory locations or attempt to use another application's space. When these memory conflicts occur, the system can either return an error message or simply stop processing.

Windows 95 typically indicates that such a problem has occurred by placing a "This program has committed an Illegal Operation and is about to be shut down" message on the screen. When this happens, Windows may take care of the error and enable you to continue operating by simply pressing a key.

If the system locks up, it is possible to gain access to the Windows task list by pressing the CTRL+ALT+DEL key combination. When the task list is on the screen, it is possible to close down the offending application and continue operating the system without rebooting.

If the system locks up and will not start, the swap file may have become corrupted, or the Virtual Memory setting may have been changed to "disabled." In this case, it will be necessary to reinstall Windows.

If a DOS-based program is running and the system locks up, it will be necessary to restore Windows 95. To accomplish this, try to restart the system from a cold boot. If the system comes up in Windows 95, check the properties of the DOS application under the Advanced button of the My Computer/Filename/Properties/Program path. If the application is not already set for MS-DOS mode operation, click the box to select it. Also select the Prevent MS-DOS-based programs from detecting Windows option. Return to the failing application to see whether it will run correctly in this environment.

If the DOS program causes the system to stall during Windows 95 boot-up, shut down the system and then boot up the computer. When the Starting Windows 95 message appears on the screen, press the F8 key. This brings up the Startup menu. Select the Restart in MS-DOS mode? option from the list. From this point, it will be necessary to edit the AUTOEXEC.BAT and CONFIG.SYS files to remove selected lines. In the AUTOEXEC.BAT file, rem the following lines:

- \Windows\command
- \call c:\windows\command***
- \windows\win.com/wx
- rem the "dos=single" line in the CONFIG.SYS file

Windows 95 stores its files in a compressed Cabinet(.CAB) format on the distribution CD. If corrupted Windows 95 files are found in the system, it is not possible to simply copy new ones into the system from the CD. Instead, it will be necessary to run Setup using the distribution CD and the Validate/Restore option. The EXTRACT.EXE command can also be run from the Windows COMMAND directory to extract selected compressed files from the CD. The preferable method is the Setup option.

Windows 95 Help Files

Windows 95 comes with a built-in Troubleshooting Help file system. This feature includes troubleshooting assistance for a number of different Windows 95 problems.

The Troubleshooting Help system can be accessed from the Start button or from the Help menu entry on the taskbar. In either case, the Help Topic Window appears as illustrated in Figure 5.36.

FIGURE 5.36

The Windows 95 Help Topics Window.

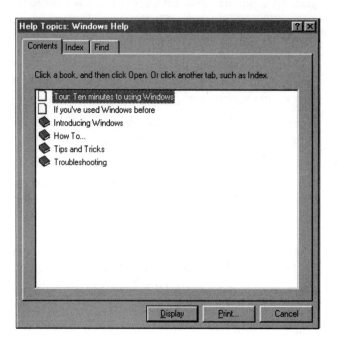

Double-clicking the Troubleshooting entry accesses the Troubleshooting Help section. This section contains a list of several entries with information about common Windows problems and situations. Clicking a topic produces a Help window with information about the troubleshooting process associated with that particular problem (such as Hardware Conflict Troubleshooting). This window is depicted in Figure 5.37. The interactive text contains a step-by-step procedure for isolating the problem listed.

FIGURE 5.37

Hardware Conflict troubleshooting window.

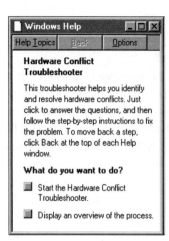

Using Device Manager

A+ DOS/WINDOWS 4.6

Hardware and configuration conflicts can also be isolated manually using the Windows 95 Device Manager from the Control Panel's System icon. The Device Manager can be used to identify installed ports, update device drivers, and change I/O settings. From this window, the problem device can be examined to see where the conflict is occurring. The Device Manager displays an exclamation point (!) inside a yellow circle whenever a device is experiencing a direct hardware conflict with another device. Similarly, when a red "X" appears at the device's icon, the device has been disabled due to a user selection conflict. When a conflict is suspected, simply click the offending device in the listing, make sure that the selected device is the current device, and then click the Resources tab to examine the Conflicting devices list. Make sure that the device has not been installed twice.

The System Tools

Windows 95 includes several helpful utilities that can be accessed through the Start/ Programs/Accessories/System Tools path. Among these utilities are the **System Monitor** and **System Resource Meter** programs. The System Monitor can be used to track the performance of key system resources for both evaluation and troubleshooting purposes. If system performance is suspect but there is no clear indication of what might be slowing it down, the System Monitor can be used to determine which resource is operating at capacity, thereby limiting the performance of the system.

Typical resources that the System Monitor is capable of tracking include those associated with processor usage and memory management. Results can be displayed in real-time using Statistical mode, Line Chart mode, or Bar Chart mode. Figure 5.38 illustrates the monitor operating in Line Chart mode. The System Monitor can be set up to run on top of other applications so that it can be used to see what effect they are having on the system.

FIGURE 5.38

Using the System Monitor.

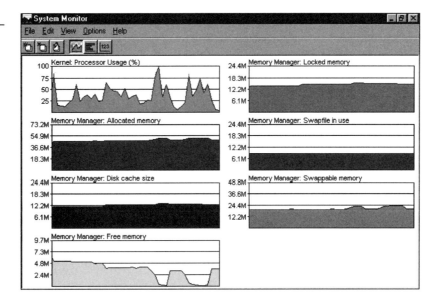

The Resource Meter is a simple bar chart display that shows the percent usage of the system resources, user resources, and GDI resources. When activated, the meter normally resides as an icon on the extreme right side of the Start button bar at the bottom of the desktop. Double-clicking the icon brings the bar chart display to the desktop. As with the System Monitor, the Resource Meter can be used to evaluate hardware and software performance.

Key Points Review

This chapter has presented an extensive exploration of the Windows 3.x operating environment and the Windows 95 operating system.

▶ Windows is a graphical working environment that makes it easier for people to use computers. Under Windows, each application runs in a window on the screen that can open or close. It is possible to run multiple applications at the same time, each in its own window, and to switch easily between applications.

▶ Before Windows 3.1 came out, a simple request for a hard-disk access while running in Protected mode would result in Windows, DOS, and the BIOS handing the request back and forth a number of times.

▶ When a non-Windows application runs in 386 Enhanced mode, Windows establishes a virtual 86 environment for it that simulates 8086 Real mode operation. Within the virtual 86 machine, Windows establishes a DOS environment with the drivers that were in operation when the system left DOS and entered Windows.

▶ When a computer is networked to another computer, a certain amount of security is lost. Because a physical path has been established into the computer, data stored in the system is now potentially available to anyone on the network. Therefore, all networking software includes some type of data security system.

▶ One of the best tools to have when troubleshooting Windows problems is a clean boot disk. When the Windows program becomes nonfunctional, it often becomes necessary to use the boot disk to restore the system to proper operation.

▶ Two typical problems can occur when setting up Windows 3.x software. First, Windows can hang up (stop) the system during installation; second, the setup process can fail and return an error message to the screen.

▶ In general, two classes of Windows 3.x operation problems exist: general protection faults and operating problems. Operating problems can be divided into Standard mode operating problems and 386 Enhanced mode operating problems.

▶ Normally, if the system will not start in Standard mode, then some program or device is taking up too much memory. If the system has enough physical memory to run Windows, it will be necessary to free up additional extended memory for use.

▶ Windows 95 must be installed over an existing operating system, such as MS-DOS or Windows 3.x. The system must be at least an 80386DX or higher machine, operating with at least 4MB of RAM (8MB is recommended).

▶ By establishing a dual-boot configuration, it is possible to install Windows 95 on an existing system and still retain the original operating system.

▶ Windows 95 is designed to assist the user in setting up any new hardware components that may be added to the system. An icon named Add New Hardware can be found under the Control Panel option of the Settings menu.

▶ Because no DOS level is present in the Windows 95 startup routine, special precautions and procedures must be used to protect the system in case of startup problems. Two very good tools to use in these situations are an emergency startup disk and the Startup menu.

▶ Windows 95 offers many improved features over previous operating systems. However, it can suffer many of the same problems as any other operating system. To overcome some of the typical system problems, Windows 95 includes several built-in troubleshooting tools. These tools include several Safe mode startup options, a trio of system log files, and an extensive interactive troubleshooting help file system.

▶ Windows 95 maintains four log files named BOOTLOG.TXT, SETUPLOG.TXT, DETLOG.TXT, and DETCRASH.LOG. These files maintain a log of different system operations and can be used to see what events occurred leading up to a failure.

- The Windows 95 structure provides a much improved multitasking environment over Windows 3.x. However, applications can still attempt to access unallocated memory locations or attempt to use another application's space. When these memory conflicts occur, the system can either return an error message or simply stop processing.

- Windows 95 comes with a built-in Troubleshooting Help file system. This feature includes troubleshooting assistance for a number of different Windows 95 problems.

At this point, review the objectives listed at the beginning of the chapter to be certain that you understand and can perform each item listed there. Afterward, answer the review questions that follow to verify your knowledge of the information.

Multiple Choice Questions

1. What are the maximum and minimum color value settings for Windows screen components?

   a. 0 to 100

   b. 0 to 255

   c. 0 to 1024

   d. 0 to 5

2. How many parallel ports does Windows recognize?

   a. 1

   b. 2

   c. 3

   d. 4

3. What type of multitasking is performed in Windows 3.x Standard mode operation?

   a. Pre-emptive

   b. None

   c. Cooperative

   d. Bank switching

4. The minimum amount of extended memory required to start Windows 3.1 in Enhanced mode is _____.

   a. 512KB

   b. 1MB

   c. 2MB

   d. 4MB

5. What function does the BOOTUPLOG.TXT file serve?

   a. It tracks the events of the Startup procedure.

   b. It carries out the steps of the Startup procedure.

   c. It tracks the events of the Shut Down procedure.

   d. It tracks the events of the POST sequence.

6. How are the branches of a Win 95 Registry or policy tree expanded and contracted?

   a. Clicking on the Expand and Contract buttons.

   b. Clicking on the right mouse button.

   c. Clicking on the plus and minus signs.

   d. Clicking on the left mouse button.

7. The file that loads the Windows 3.x environment is _____.

   a. WIN.COM

   b. COMMAND.COM

   c. VxDs

   d. IO.SYS

8. What is the major input device for a Windows-based system?

   a. The keyboard

   b. The scanner

   c. The mouse

   d. The touch screen

9. What are the requirements to start Windows in 386 Enhanced mode?

   a. An 80286 microprocessor, 512KB of free conventional memory, and 512KB of extended memory

   b. An 80486 microprocessor, 256KB of free conventional memory, and 512KB of extended memory

   c. A Pentium microprocessor, 1024KB of free conventional memory, and 1024KB of extended memory

   d. An 80386SX microprocessor, 256KB of free conventional memory, and 1024KB of extended memory

10. Where is the Windows 95 Policy Editor located?

    a. Under the Polyedit folder on the Windows 95 CD

    b. Under the Admin folder on the Windows 95 CD

    c. Under the Regedit folder on the Windows 95 CD

    d. Under the Sysedit folder on the Windows 95 CD

Review Questions

1. What type of multitasking is performed in Windows 3.x 386 Enhanced mode operation?

2. What is a .PIF file, and what does it do?

3. Which Windows utility is used to edit ASCII files, such as COMMAND.COM and the .INI files?

4. Describe the basic responsibilities of the .INI files in Windows 3.x.

5. Why are logon procedures used, and where are they used?

6. Name two important tools for solving startup problems in Windows 95.

7. What practical function does 32-bit access serve in the Windows 95 system?

8. What is the significance of placing items in the Windows Startup window?

9. What type of multitasking is performed in Windows 95 386 Enhanced mode operation? Why is it different than the 3.x-multitasking operation?

10. Using the System Policy Editor, what effect does a grayed-out setting have on an option?

11. List two methods of performing a Safe mode startup in Windows 95.

12. What .INI functions does the Windows 95 Registry file take over from Windows 3.x, and why?

13. Why would a step-by-step Confirmation mode startup be performed?

14. How are the Setup, Setup/A, and Setup/I commands different?

15. How are the Win, Win/s, and Win/3 commands different?

Lab Exercises

The lab manual that accompanies this book contains hands-on lab procedures that reinforce and test your knowledge of the theory materials presented in this chapter. Now that you have completed your review of Chapter 5, refer to the lab manual and perform Procedures 3, "Windows"; 4, "Advanced Windows"; 5, "Windows 95"; and 6, "Advanced Windows 95."

THE BASIC SYSTEM

PART III

SYSTEM BOARDS

LEARNING OBJECTIVES

Upon completion of this chapter and its related lab procedures, you should be able to perform these tasks:

1. Define AT-compatible interrupt and DMA addresses.

2. List advantages of chip-set-based circuit design.

3. Identify various microprocessors from their package type.

4. Define Real, Protected, and Virtual addressing modes.

5. Discuss the major attributes of popular microprocessors.

6. Describe the internal structure of a typical Integrated Peripheral Controller (IPC) IC.

7. Describe operation of the real-time clock circuitry.

8. Name the use of the Timer/Counters output signals in the typical PC-compatible system.

9. List the sequence of events that occurs during a typical interrupt operation.

10. Identify conditions that will cause an NMI interrupt to occur.

11. Describe the events of a typical DMA operation and differentiate between the different modes of DMA transfers.

12. Differentiate between static and dynamic RAM memory devices, and state the conditions that dictate which of the two will be used in a given application.

13. Describe how the microprocessor works with a first- or second-level cache memory.

14. Describe steps to troubleshoot various system board problems.

15. List symptoms and error messages associated with system board problems.

CHAPTER 6

Introduction

The system board contains the components that form the basis of the computer system. Even though the system board's physical structure has changed over time, its logical structure has remained relatively constant. Since the original PC, the system board has contained the microprocessor, its support devices, the system's primary memory units, and the expansion slot connectors. A typical system board layout is depicted in Figure 6.1.

FIGURE 6.1

A typical system board layout.

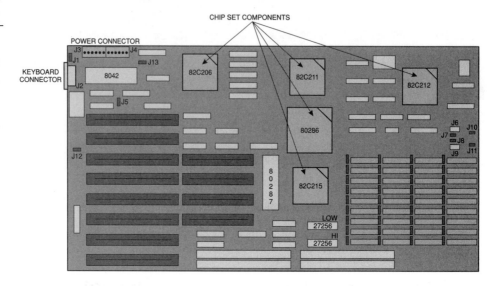

System Board Evolution

 A+ CORE 1.1

> System boards fundamentally change for three reasons: new microprocessors, new expansion-slot types, and reduced chip counts. Reduced chip counts are typically the result of improved microprocessor support chip sets. Chip sets combine PC- and AT-compatible structures into larger Integrated Circuits (ICs).

Several IC manufacturers produce single ICs that contain the AT's interrupt, DMA, timer/counter, and real-time clock circuitry. These ICs also contain the address decoding and timing circuitry to support those functions.

The original IBM PC used a six-chip set to support the 8088 microprocessor. These devices included the following intelligent support devices:

- ▶ An 8284 Clock Generator

- ▶ An 8288 Bus Controller

- ▶ An 8255 Parallel Peripheral Interface (PPI)

- ▶ An 8259 Programmable Interrupt Controller (PIC)

- ▶ An 8237 DMA Controller

- ▶ An 8253 Programmable Interval Timer (PIT)

- ▶ An 8042 Intelligent Keyboard Controller

The clock generator and bus controller ICs assisted the microprocessor with system clock and control bus functions. The PPI chip handled system configuration and onboard addressing functions for the system's intelligent devices.

The interrupt controller provided the system with eight channels of programmable interrupt capabilities. The 8237 DMA Controller provided four channels of high-speed DMA data transfer service for the system. The 8253 was used to produce three programmable timer channel outputs to drive the system's time-of-day clock, DRAM refresh signal, and system speaker output signal. The PC/XT interrupt and DMA controller functions are described in Figure 6.2.

FIGURE 6.2

PC/XT Interrupt and DMA Controller functions.

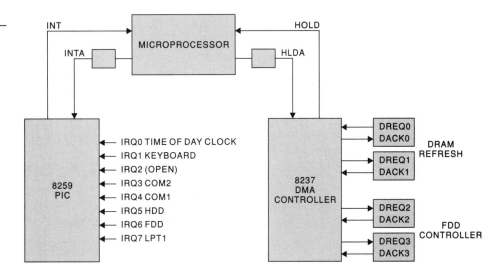

When the IBM PC-AT came to the market, it brought an upgraded chip set that expanded the capabilities of the system. IBM improved the basic 8284 and 8288 devices by upgrading them to 82284 and 82288 versions. Likewise, the keyboard controller and the three-channel timer/counter were updated in the AT. The AT's interrupt and DMA channel capabilities were both doubled—to 15 and 7, respectively—by cascading two of each device together. In each case, one IC is the master device and the other is the slave device. The PC-AT interrupt and DMA controller functions are described in Figure 6.3.

Chip Sets

> Because chip set-based system boards require much fewer SSI, MSI, and LSI devices to produce, manufacturers of printed circuit boards have been able to design much smaller boards.

The original **PC-AT system board** measured 30.5 cm x 33 cm. Initially, manufacturers of printed circuit boards reduced the size of their chip set-based system boards to match that of the original PC and PC-XT system boards (22 cm x 33 cm). This allowed the new 286 boards to be installed in the smaller XT-style cases. This particular size of system board is described as a **Baby AT system board.**

FIGURE 6.3

*PC-AT interrupt DMA
Controller functions.*

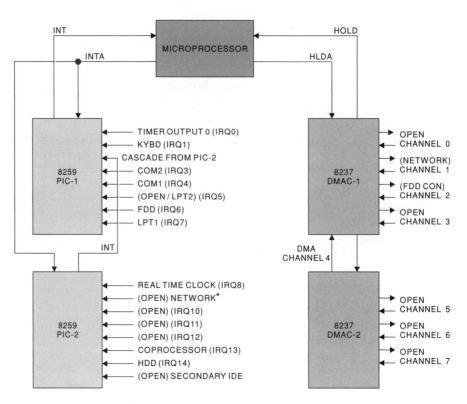

A+ CORE 4.3   As VLSI technology improves, IC manufacturers continue to integrate higher levels of circuitry into their chips. All the functions of the four-chip chip set system board of Figure 6.1 is duplicated using the two-chip chip set depicted in Figure 6.4. The high level of circuit concentration in this chip set allows the size of the system board to be reduced even further: It is approximately half the length of a standard Baby AT system board; therefore, this size system board is referred to as a **half-size system board**.

FIGURE 6.4

A half-size system board.

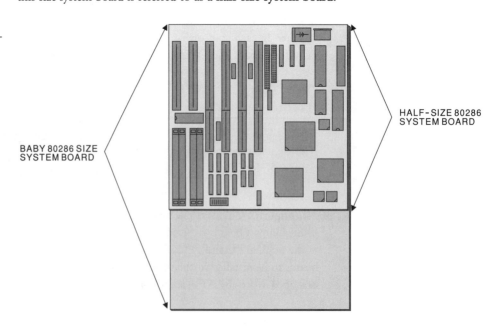

The first chip set-based system boards came with special configuration software that had to be loaded from disk. However, it is now normal to consider the ROM BIOS as an integral part of the chip set because it is designed to support the register structure of the chip set. Therefore, replacing a ROM BIOS chip on a system board is not as simple as placing another ROM BIOS in the socket. The replacement BIOS must be correct for the chip set used.

By combining larger blocks of circuitry into fewer ICs, a price reduction spiral is created. Fewer ICs on the board leads to reduced manufacturing costs to produce the board. The material cost of the board is decreased due to its smaller physical size. The component cost is decreased because it is cheaper to buy a few VLSI chips than several SSI or MSI devices. Finally, the assembly cost is less because only a few items must be mounted on the board.

Reduced board costs create lower computer prices, which in turn creates greater consumer demand for the computers. Increased demand for the computers—and therefore the chip sets—acts to further push down the prices of all the computer components.

A+ CORE 4.3 Chip set-based system boards and I/O cards tend to change often, as IC manufacturers continue to integrate higher levels of circuitry into their devices.

The newest system board designation is the **ATX form factor** developed by Intel for Pentium-based systems. This specification is an evolution of the Baby AT form factor that moves the standard I/O functions to the system board. The ATX specification basically rotates the Baby AT form factor by 90 degrees, relocates the power supply connection, and moves the microprocessor and memory modules away from the expansion slots.

The power supply orientation enables a single fan to be used to cool the system. This provides reduced cost, reduced system noise, and improved reliability. The relocated microprocessor and memory modules permit full-length cards to be used in the expansion slots, while providing easy upgrading of the microprocessor, RAM, and I/O cards.

Figure 6.5 depicts a Pentium-based **ATX system board** that directly supports the FDD, HDD, serial, and parallel ports. The board is 12 inches (305 mm) wide and 9.6 inches (244 mm) long. A revised, mini-ATX specification allows for 11.2-inch-by-8.2-inch system boards. The hole patterns for the ATX and Mini-ATX system boards require a case that can accommodate the new boards. Although ATX shares most of its mounting hole pattern with the Baby AT specification, it does not match exactly.

The fully implemented ATX format also contains specifications for the power supply and I/O connector placements. In particular, the ATX specification for the power supply connection calls for a single 20-pin power cable between the system board and the power supply unit, instead of the typical P8/P9 cabling. The new cable adds a +3.3 Vdc supply to the traditional +/- 12 Vdc and +/- 5 Vdc supplies. A software-activated power switch can also be implemented through the ATX power connector specification. The PS-ON and 5VSB (5-volt standby) signals can be controlled by the operating system to perform automatic system shutdowns.

FIGURE 6.5

An ATX Pentium system board.

System boards designed for use in notebooks typically include the video circuitry as an integral part of the board. These units must also provide the physical connections for the unit's parallel and serial I/O ports, as well as onboard connectors for auxiliary disk drive, monitor, and keyboard units.

Microprocessors

A+ CORE 1.1

A+ CORE 4.0

The microprocessors used in the vast majority of all PC-compatible microcomputers include the 8088/86, the 80286, the 80386, the 80486, and the Pentium (80586 and 80686) microprocessors.

The 8088 material that follows provides the background for the microprocessors that have been used to advance the PC-compatible line of microcomputers to the computational levels they now possess. The popularity of the original PCs (and the software developed for them) has caused limitations to be built into the microprocessors that followed the 8088 to maintain compatibility with it.

The 8088 Microprocessor

At the heart of PC- and PC-XT-compatible systems is the 40-pin **8088 microprocessor**. The 8088 is a high-performance HMOS microprocessor that has attributes of both 8- and 16-bit processors. Its internal structure supports 16-bit words, but it uses only an 8-bit data bus. In this manner, its internal data registers can be used as single 16-bit registers, divided into higher- and lower-order bytes, or used as independent 8-bit register pairs.

The 8088 supports a 20-bit address bus that enables it to directly access 1MB of memory and I/O addresses. The 8088-2 version can run at either of two standard clock rates: a 4.77MHz normal clock frequency and a high-speed (turbo) 8MHz clock frequency.

8088 Pin Assignments

The pin assignments and definitions of the 8088 microprocessor are detailed in Figure 6.6. To hold the number of pins on the IC down to a reasonable level, the 8088's designers **multiplexed** many of its pins to perform different functions, depending upon the part of the machine cycle in which the microprocessor is located.

FIGURE 6.6

8088 pin assignments.

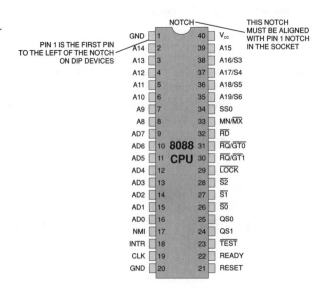

The most notable of the multiplexed pins are the **address/data lines** (AD0–AD7) and the **address/status pins** (A16/S3–A19/S6). Pins AD0 through AD7 are time-multiplexed to act as address lines during the first clock pulse of the machine cycle, and they then turn into bi-directional data lines throughout the remainder of the machine cycle. Likewise, the address/status pins are multiplexed to act as address lines during the first clock pulse and then change to processor status lines for the remainder of the machine cycle.

Collectively, the AD0–AD7, A8–A15, and A16/S3–A19/S6 lines are combined to form the system's address bus. The 8088 uses the entire 20 bits when addressing memory locations, but it uses only lines A0 through A15 when addressing Input/Output devices. This provides a total of 1,048,576 (1MB) of memory addresses and 65,535 (64KB) of I/O addresses.

After the address has been latched, the AD0–AD7 lines are available for bi-directional data transfers. The computer system uses a bi-directional line buffer to assist the 8088 in driving the system's data bus. A pair of signals from the bus controller handles the transfer of data through the line buffer. The bus controller issues a **data enable signal** (**DEN**) to activate the buffer, along with a **data transmit/receive direction signal** (**DT/R**), which properly configures the buffer so that the microprocessor can read (receive) or write (transmit) through them. Figure 6.7 illustrates how the 8088's address/data/status pins are multiplexed to form the address and data buses.

FIGURE 6.7

8088 bus multiplexing.

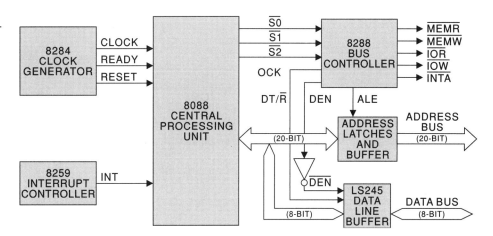

8088 Register Set

Figure 6.8 illustrates the basic architecture of the 8088 in block diagram form. One of the most noticeable features of the 8088's internal structure is its large and very flexible register set. The register set consists of 14 16-bit registers that can be divided into four functional groups, as follows: the data group the index and pointer registers, the segment registers, and the instruction pointer and flag registers.

The most interesting of these registers is the data group (AX, BX, CX, and DX). These highly flexible registers are unique in that each can be treated as a single 16-bit register, or they may be used as two independent 8-bit registers (AH and AL, BH and BL, CH and CL, and DH and DL). The "H" and "L" designators refer to the higher- and lower-order bytes of the basic 16-bit register. All of these registers correspond roughly to the accumulator register described in Chapter 1, "Microcomputer Fundamentals." Arithmetic and logic operations can be performed, and results can be stored in each of the data registers. (These operations can also be performed in the two index and pointer registers.)

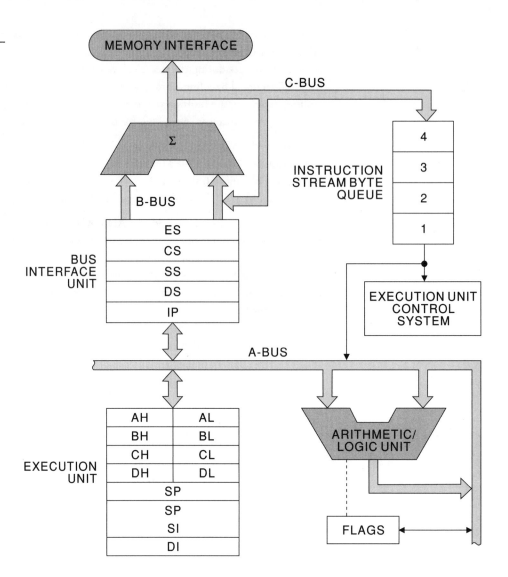

FIGURE 6.8

Inside the 8088.

8088 Addressing

You may wonder how the 8088 can support a 20-bit address bus if its internal registers are only 16 bits wide. Actually, the 20-bit address is constructed inside the 8088 by combining the contents of two registers. The 8088's memory addresses are divided into 64KB blocks called **segments**. These segments can be assigned to the segment registers in the 8088. Within each 64KB segment, individual addresses can be accessed using only a 16-bit address, called the **offset address**. To obtain the entire 20-bit address, the 16-bit offset address is added to a 16-bit segment address, which has been shifted left four binary places. This concept is illustrated in Figure 6.9.

During instruction cycles, the 8088's address is the sum of the **Instruction Pointer** (**IP**) and **Code Segment** (**CS**) registers. During execution cycles, the address produced is the sum of the operand address portion of the instruction word and the contents of one of the segment registers (DS, SS, or ES).

In special addressing operations involving the **stack**, the contents of the **Stack Segment** (**SS**) register are added to the contents of either the **Base Pointer** (**BP**) or the **Stack Pointer** (**SP**) registers to obtain the address. The **Data Segment** (**DS**) register is used whenever data is moved to or from the memory.

FIGURE 6.9

8088 addressing.

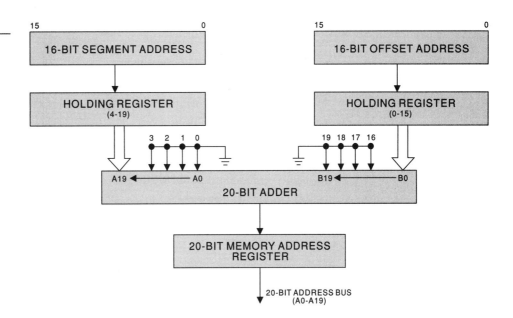

Normally, these registers and their use are more important to a programmer than to a technician. The reason for mentioning the 8088's addressing here is to illustrate how the address is generated. In many publications and diagnostic software packages, addressing is presented in an XXXX:YYYY format (that is, FFFF:0000). The reason for this is found in the segmented nature of how the 8088 viewed addressing. The first set of numbers represent the segment value, and the number to the right of the colon is the offset value.

The 80286 Microprocessor

One of the key elements of the IBM-PC AT system board is the 80286 16-bit **microprocessor** chip, depicted in Figure 6.10. The 80286 is backward-compatible with the 8088 microprocessor found on the original PC and XT system boards. This means that the 80286 can run the same software that the 8088 does, but it runs it much faster. However, the 80286 is much more than a fast 8088 microprocessor.

Unlike the 8088 (or its full 16-bit equivalent—the 8086), the 80286 microprocessor is designed to support **multiuser** and **multitasking** operations. In these types of operations, the 80286-based machine appears to work on several tasks, or to serve several users simultaneously. Of course, the microprocessor can't actually work on more than one item at a time; the appearance of simultaneous operations is created by storing the parameters of one task, leaving the task, loading up the state of another task, and beginning operation on it.

Figure 6.11 shows the 80286 microprocessor in block diagram form. The special memory management and memory protection circuitry in the **Address Unit (AU)** of the 286 handles task separation, program and data integrity between tasks, and isolation of the operating system from the **task-switching** operation. When two or more programs are running together in Protected mode, this circuitry keeps track of the different tasks on which the 286 is working and keeps them from interfering with each other's data or program space.

As its name implies, the **Bus Interface Unit (BU)** controls the action between the 286's internal structures and the system's local buses. In addition, the BU sets priorities between the **Code Prefetch Unit (CU)** and the **Execution Unit (EU)**. Execution Unit operations (where instructions are actually processed) are given the highest priority by the BU.

However, the BU allows the code Prefetch Unit to sequentially fetch instructions from memory during spare clock cycles. The Prefetch Unit stores the instructions in a 6-byte queue, and await decoding and execution.

The **Instruction Decoding Unit (IU)** decodes instruction words and stores them in a three-instruction, first-in/first-out (FIFO) queue. In this way, the execution unit does not have to wait for a new instruction to be fetched from memory because the instruction is already waiting in the decoded instruction queue.

The 80286's internal register set is shown in Figure 6.12. As you can see, it is identical to the register set found in the 8088. However, the 286 possesses an extended 8088/86 instruction superset that enables it to operate in two distinctly different addressing modes: **Real mode** and **Virtual Protected mode**.

FIGURE 6.10

The 80286 microprocessor.

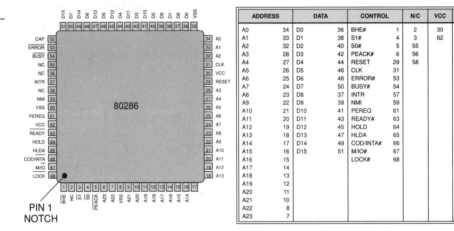

ADDRESS		DATA		CONTROL		N/C		VCC		VSS
A0	34	D0	36	BHE#	1	2		30		9
A1	33	D1	38	S1#	4	3		62		35
A2	32	D2	40	S0#	5	55				60
A3	28	D3	42	PEACK#	6	56				
A4	27	D4	44	RESET	29	58				
A5	26	D5	46	CLK	31					
A6	25	D6	48	ERROR#	53					
A7	24	D7	50	BUSY#	54					
A8	23	D8	37	INTR	57					
A9	22	D9	39	NMI	59					
A10	21	D10	41	PEREQ	61					
A11	20	D11	43	READY#	63					
A12	19	D12	45	HOLD	64					
A13	18	D13	47	HLDA	65					
A14	17	D14	49	COD/INTA#	66					
A15	16	D15	51	M/IO#	67					
A16	15			LOCK#	68					
A17	14									
A18	13									
A19	12									
A20	11									
A21	10									
A22	8									
A23	7									

FIGURE 6.11

Inside the 80286.

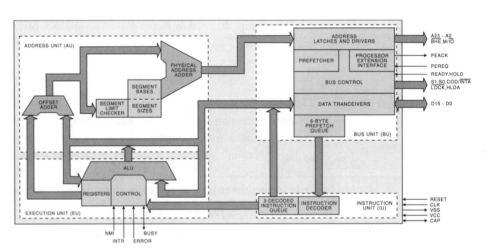

FIGURE 6.12

The 80286 register set.

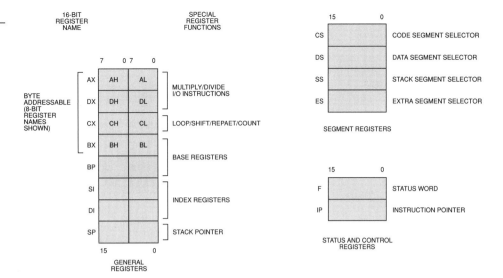

In Real mode, the 286 operates like an 8088/86 microprocessor and can directly access 1MB of RAM addresses in segments of 64KB. It also uses real addresses up to 1MB and can work on only one task at a time. In this mode, addresses are specified by the bits present on the 80286's A0–A19 pins. If software increments the 80286's addresses past FFFFFh in this mode, the address simply rolls over to 00000h, and address bits A20–A23 are not activated.

In Protected mode, address bits A20–A23 are enabled, and the 286 can access up to 16MB of physical memory addresses. This mode can also be used to perform **virtual memory operations**. In these operations, the system treats an area of disk space as an extension of RAM memory. It can shift data from RAM memory to disk (and vice-versa) to simulate large areas of RAM (up to 1024MB, or 1GB).

However, the 286 requires external support circuitry and special software to conduct virtual memory operations. Using Protected mode addressing, the 80286 maps up to 1GB (2^{30}) of memory into an actual address space of 16MB (2^{24}).

The 80286 is available in 68-pin **Ceramic Leadless Chip Carrier** (**CLCC**), 68-pin **Plastic Leaded Chip Carrier** (**PLCC**), and 68-pin **Pin Grid Array** (**PGA**) packages, as depicted in Figure 6.13. These microprocessors are also available with different clock/speed ratings. For example, a microprocessor marked 80286-12 is rated for stable operation with internal clock signals up to 12MHz. (The 286 divides the external clock input by a factor of 2 to arrive at this value. Therefore, the maximum external clock frequency for the 286-12 is 24MHz.)

The 80386 Microprocessor

 A+ CORE 4.1

The **80386DX** (or simply 80386) **microprocessor** is the 32-bit successor of the 80286. This microprocessor improves on previous 80x86 architectures by offering 32-bit registers as well as 32-bit address and data buses. The 80386 is produced in the 132-pin PGA package shown in Figure 6.14.

FIGURE 6.13

The 80286 microprocessor packages.

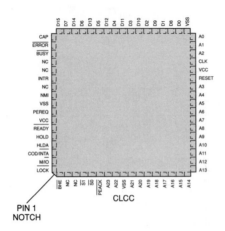

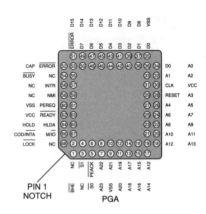

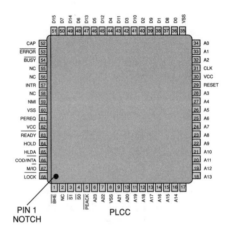

FIGURE 6.14

The 80386DX microprocessor.

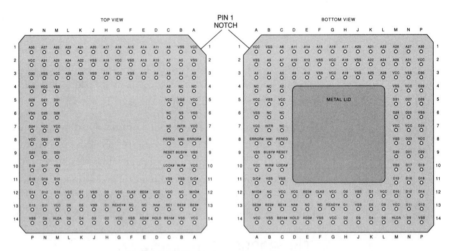

SIGNAL/PIN		SIGNAL/PIN		SIGNAL/PIN		SIGNAL/PIN		SIGNAL/PIN		SIGNAL/PIN	
A2	C4	A24	L2	D6	L14	D28	M6	VCC	C12	VSS	F2
A3	A3	A25	K3	D7	K12	D29	P4		D12		F3
A4	B3	A26	M1	D8	L13	D30	P3		G2		F14
A5	B2	A27	N1	D9	N14	D31	M5		G3		J2
A6	C3	A28	L3	D10	M12	D/C#	A11		G12		J3
A7	C2	A29	M2	D11	N12	ERROR#	A8		G14		J12
A8	C1	A30	P1	D12	N13	HLDA	M14		L12		J13
A9	D3	A31	N2	D13	P13	HOLD	D14		M3		M4
A10	D2	ADS#	E14	D14	P12	INTR	B7		M7		M8
A11	D1	BE0#	E12	D15	M11	LOCK#	C10		M13		M10
A12	E3	BE1#	C13	D16	N11	M/IO#	A12		N4		N3
A13	E2	BE2#	B13	D17	N10	NA#	D13		N7		P6
A14	E1	BE3#	A13	D18	P11	NMI	B8		P2		P14
A15	F1	BS16#	C14	D19	P10	PEREQ	C8		P8	W/R#	B10
A16	G1	BUSY#	B9	D20	M9	READY#	G13	VSS	A2	N.C.	A4
A17	H1	CLK2	F12	D21	N9	RESET	C9		A6		B4
A18	H2	D0	H12	D22	P9	VCC	A1		A9		B6
A19	H3	D1	H13	D23	N8		A5		B1		B12
A20	J1	D2	H14	D24	P7		A7		B5		C6
A21	K1	D3	J14	D25	N6		A10		B11		C7
A22	K2	D4	K14	D26	P5		A14		B14		E13
A23	L1	D5	K13	D27	N5		C5		C11		F13

Ironically, most 80386 microprocessors were used in systems with AT-compatible architectures. Therefore, its data bus had to support a 16-bit I/O channel. However, operations that were confined to the system board, such as memory reads and writes, could be carried out as full 32-bit transfers. The 80386 microprocessor can actually conduct data transfers in three distinct ways: It can transfer data in 8-bit bytes, in 16-bit words, or in **32-bit dwords** (double words).

In addition to handling data in one of these three basic definitions, the 80386 possesses two methods of manipulating memory units in very large blocks. These memory units are called **pages** and **segments**. The 80386 has the capability to divide memory into one or more variable-length segments that can be swapped to and from disk, or shared between different programs.

The 80386 has built-in circuitry that can be used to organize RAM memory into one or more 4KB sections referred to as pages. This memory-management scheme effectively divides programs into multiple uniform-sized modules that can be manipulated as individual blocks, and it is particularly useful in virtual memory multitasking operations.

> The advanced memory-mapping capabilities of the 80386 enable it to implement **ROM shadowing**. This speeds up system operation by enabling BIOS-related functions to be conducted from fast 32-bit RAM locations instead of slower 8-bit ROM locations.

Figure 6.15 depicts the 80386's internal structure in block diagram form. It illustrates the 80386's six functional units: the Bus Interface Unit (BU), the Code Prefetch Unit (CU), the Instruction Decoding Unit (IU), the Execution Unit (EU), the Segmentation Unit (SU), and the Paging Unit (PU). By comparing these blocks to those of the 80286 microprocessor, you can see that several of them are carryovers from the 286.

FIGURE 6.15

Inside the 80386DX.

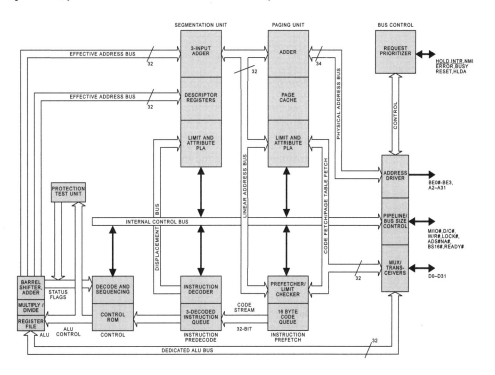

In addition to offering the 80286 version of Protected mode addressing, the 80386 offers an improved Protected-addressing mode, referred to as **Virtual 86 mode**. This mode enables the 80386 to simulate several 8086 microprocessors running at the same time. Each 8086 environment is referred to as a **virtual 86 machine**.

Subsequently, the 80386 is capable of running several applications at the same time. This type of machine uses paging to re-map memory and brings each virtual machine to the microprocessor as the program running in it requires attention.

The 80386DX possesses an internal divide-by-2 clock system. Therefore, the maximum clock frequency applied to the chip is twice its rated operational frequency (for example, the maximum external clock frequency of an 80386DX-25 is 50MHz).

The 80386SX Microprocessor

The **80386SX microprocessor**, depicted in Figure 6.16, is a 16/32-bit hybrid version of the 80386DX. It was developed to achieve a compromise between the power of the 80386DX and the lower cost of the 80286 microprocessors. The 80386SX is constructed using high-speed CHMOS III technology and is packaged in a surface-mount, 100-pin, plastic, **Plastic Quad Flatpack** package.

FIGURE 6.16

The 80386SX microprocessor.

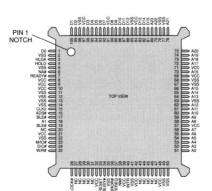

ADDRESS		DATA		CONTROL		N/C	VCC	VSS
A1	18	D0	1	ADS#	16	20	8	2
A2	51	D1	100	BHE#	19	27	9	5
A3	52	D2	99	BLE#	17	28	10	11
A4	53	D3	96	BUSY#	34	29	21	12
A5	54	D4	95	CLK2	15	30	32	13
A6	55	D5	94	D/C#	24	31	39	14
A7	56	D6	93	ERROR#	36	43	42	22
A8	58	D7	92	HLDA	3	44	48	35
A9	59	D8	90	HOLD	4	45	57	41
A10	60	D9	89	INTR	40	46	69	49
A11	61	D10	88	LOCK#	26	47	71	50
A12	62	D11	87	M/IO	23		84	63
A13	64	D12	86	NA#	6		91	67
A14	65	D13	83	NMI	38		97	68
A15	66	D14	82	PEREQ	37			77
A16	70	D15	81	READY#	7			78
A17	72			RESET	33			85
A18	73			W/R#	25			98
A19	74							
A20	75							
A21	76							
A22	79							
A23	80							

On the inside, the 80386SX is, for all practical purposes, identical to the 80386DX chip. Compare the 80386SX's block diagram, shown in Figure 6.17, with that of the 80386DX in Figure 6.15. As you can see, they appear identical. The major difference between these microprocessors is found in their external address and data buses. Although the 80386SX's internal registers are 32 bits wide (like the 80386DX), this system does not support a 32-bit external data bus. Instead, it supports a 16-bit external data bus.

This makes the 80386SX readily adaptable to the 16-bit architectures originally designed for 80286 microprocessors. Because of the register/bus-size mismatch created by this arrangement, the 80386SX must handle data in a high-byte/low-byte register format for reading or writing data. This is similar to the 16-bit register/data bus format found in the 8088 microprocessor.

Likewise, the 80386SX's address bus is also smaller than that of the 80386DX. The 80386SX supports a 24-bit address bus. Both processors use the same **logical address space**, but the 80386SX is limited to only 16MB of **physical address space**, as opposed to the 4GB available to the 80386DX.

FIGURE 6.17

Inside the 80386SX microprocessor.

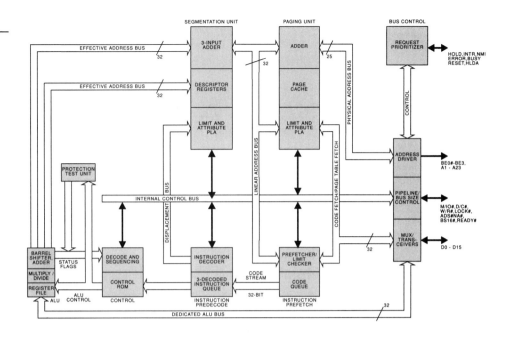

By incorporating these few differences into its makeup, the 80386SX can offer all the performance benefits associated with 32-bit programming, while providing the cost savings associated with 16-bit computer systems. The 80386SX is 100% software-compatible with the 80386DX, 286, and 8088/86 microprocessors. Therefore, systems based on it can access and run software already developed for these popular systems.

Other 80386 Microprocessors

Due to the 80386 microprocessor's popularity, other manufacturers have produced similar microprocessors based on the 80386 architecture without infringing on the Intel design. The following are some of the other 80386 variations that you may encounter.

The **80386SL** microprocessor is used in laptop or notebook computers because this chip uses less power compared to Intel's other 80386s. This microprocessor is a mixture of the 80386DX and 80386SX microprocessors; its processor retains the 32-bit address bus, like the 80386DX, but has an external 16-bit data bus. The 80386SL still has an internal 32-bit data path, like either the 80386DX or the 80386SX. The 80386SL also keeps the virtual memory capability of the 80386DX or 80386SX.

The **AM80386DX** was the first **clone microprocessor**. Manufactured by **Advanced Micro Devices (AMD)**, it was released in early 1991. The AM80386DX exactly mimics the operation of Intel's 80386DX. This includes the 32-bit address and data buses and addressable virtual memory. The **AM80386SX** is AMD's release to compete with Intel's 80386SX. This processor is actually more like Intel's 80386SL microprocessor in architecture. This chip also has the 32-bit address bus and a 16-bit external data bus. The AM80386SX does have one advantage of consuming less power than Intel's 80386SX.

The **IBM 80386SLC** microprocessor is the result of a joint venture between Intel and IBM, for exclusive use in IBM products. This chip is actually similar to Intel's 80386SX, which has a 24-bit address bus and a 16-bit external data bus. The enhancements implemented in this design include an 8KB cache and an increased instruction set.

The 80486 Microprocessor

A+ CORE 4.1

The **80486 (486) microprocessor** is the successor to the 80386DX. The block diagram of the 80486 is presented in Figure 6.18.

> Basically, the 80486 brings an improved 80386DX microprocessor, a high-performance 80387 coprocessor, and an 82385 cache memory controller together in a single package.

Both of these additions greatly improve the speed at which the microprocessor can manipulate numbers. The 80486 also incorporates an onboard 8KB-memory cache, as well as internal parity generation and checking circuitry.

All this circuitry is combined into a single 168-pin, Ceramic Pin Grid Array package. Even though most of the overall package is used for heat dissipation purposes, the 80486 still generates so much heat that additional fans are often required. A number of companies have developed snap-on and stick-on fan units for 80486 processors. These units typically derive power from one of the system power supply's auxiliary power connectors.

FIGURE 6.18

Inside the 80486 microprocessor.

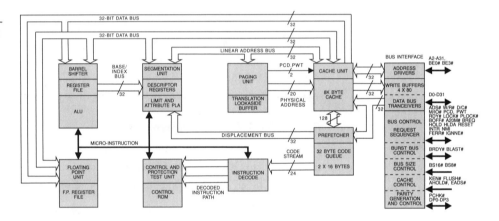

Naturally, the 80486 offers the three addressing modes (Real, Protected, and Virtual 86) that the 80386 does. It can access 4GB (2^{32}) of physical addresses and 64TB (2^{46}) of virtual address space. The 80486's paging mechanism allows the 20-bit linear address produced by the Virtual mode program to be divided into up to 256 pages. Each page can be located anywhere within the 4GB of the 80486 physical addressing space. An additional I/O protection feature enables the operating system to set aside a selected set of I/O ports for device protection.

The 80486 microprocessor offers vastly improved memory access and instruction execution speed over the 80386DX. It also greatly increases floating-point calculation speed due to the presence of the onboard coprocessor unit. Transfers between the 80486's ALU and coprocessor unit are carried out in the form of 64-bit words.

When the 80486 performs memory read operations that require more than a single bus cycle to complete, it can shift into a special high-speed **Burst mode**. Recall from the discussion of 80386 bus cycles that a normal bus cycle is made up of at least two bus states. In Burst mode, the normal two-state bus cycle is reduced to one clock cycle after the initial two-state read cycle.

Burst mode is most useful when the 80486 is filling its internal cache memory from the system memory. The cache is updated each time the microprocessor performs a memory read (I/O read operations are not recorded in the cache). When the 80486 performs a memory read operation, it first checks the cache to see whether the requested data is there. If the data is in the cache, no memory is read (and, therefore, no external bus access is required). This makes for a very fast read operation. However, if the data is not in the cache, the 80486 reads the actual memory location and then places the data in the cache.

Conversely, all 80486 memory-write operations are performed at the system memory, even if the data is already in the cache. If the bus is busy when the 80486 needs to write data to memory, it can store the data in one of its four onboard **write registers**. This enables the microprocessor to continue processing internally and wait for a convenient time to write the data into memory. IO write operations may also be stored temporarily inside the 80486, but unlike memory-write buffering, multiple IO writes must be written to memory before other internal processing can continue.

The 80486's **internal cache controller** monitors the system's address bus when other processors or bus masters gain control of the bus system. The reason for this is to keep track of addresses where new data may be written into memory, but not into the cache. By keeping track of these address locations, the cache controller can update the cache as soon as the 80486 regains control of the buses. Many manufacturers of 80486-based systems opt to include additional external cache memories on their system boards.

In these systems, the 80486's internal cache memory is referred to as the **first-level cache**, and the external cache is called the **second-level cache,** or **L2 cache**. Secondary caches are normally 128KB or 256KB.

When the 80486 writes data into memory, it generates a parity bit for each byte. As in other systems, the parity bit is stored in system RAM along with the data. When the data is read from memory, the parity bit is also read. If an error condition is detected by the 80486, the microprocessor activates its PCHK output line to notify the system. It is the responsibility of the system's decision circuitry to handle the error condition. The 80486's parity check circuitry checks only information retrieved from RAM, not internally generated data.

Excluding its floating-point coprocessor's registers, the 80486's general register structure (detailed in Figure 6.19), is very similar to that of the 80286 and 80386 processors. These registers can be divided into three distinct groups: the **Base Architecture Registers**, the **System Level Registers**, and the **Floating-Point Registers**. The 80486's basic register set is identical with those in the 80386 processor. Registers are 32-bits wide but can be accessed in 8- or 16-bit formats.

Likewise, the floating-point registers are identical to those of the 80387 coprocessor. The instruction and data pointer registers perform the same functions as their 387 counterparts in determining the cause of coprocessor exceptions.

The 80486's pin groupings are displayed in Figure 6.20. Most of these lines should be familiar to you from previous microprocessor discussions. Naturally, the coprocessor interface lines used with previous microprocessors have been discarded on the 80486. However, new lines have been added for cache and Burst mode control, as well as to provide parity generation and checking functions.

FIGURE 6.19

The 80486 register structure.

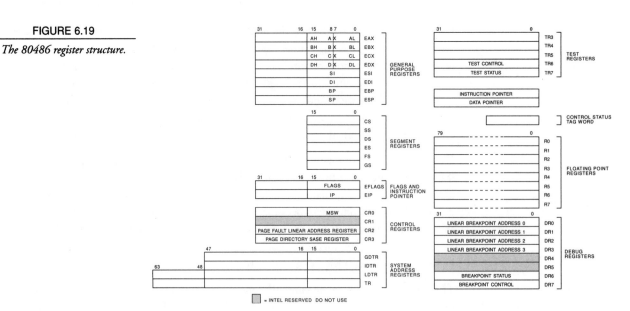

= INTEL RESERVED DO NOT USE

FIGURE 6.20

The 80486 pins.

(TOP SIDE VIEW)

ADDRESS		DATA		CONTROL		N/C	VCC	VSS
A2	Q14	D0	P1	A20M#	D15	A3	B7	A7
A3	R15	D1	N2	ADS#	S17	A10	B9	A9
A4	S16	D2	N1	AHOLD	A17	A12	B11	A11
A5	Q12	D3	H2	BE0#	K15	A13	C4	B3
A6	S15	D4	M3	BE1#	J16	A14	C5	B4
A7	Q13	D5	J2	BE2#	J15	B10	E2	B5
A8	R13	D6	L2	BE3#	F17	B12	E16	E1
A9	Q11	D7	L3	BLAST#	R16	B14	G2	E17
A10	R12	D8	F2	BOFF#	D17	B16	G16	G1
A11	S13	D9	D1	BRDY#	H15	C10	H16	G17
A12	S7	D10	E3	BREQ#	Q15	C11	J1	H1
A13	Q10	D11	C1	BS8#	D16	C12	K2	H17
A14	S5	D12	G3	BS16#	C17	C13	K16	K1
A15	R7	D13	D2	CLK	C3	G15	L16	K17
A16	Q9	D14	K3	D/C#	M15	R17	M2	L1
A17	Q3	D15	F3	DP0	N3	S4	M16	L17
A18	R5	D16	J3	DP1	F1		P16	M1
A19	Q4	D17	D3	DP2	H3		R3	M17
A20	Q8	D18	C2	DP3	A5		R6	P17
A21	Q5	D19	B1	EADS#	B17		R8	Q2
A22	Q7	D20	A1	FERR#	C14		R9	R4
A23	S3	D21	B2	FLUSH#	C15		R10	S6
A24	Q6	D22	A2	HLDA	P15		R11	S8
A25	R2	D23	A4	HOLD	E15		R14	S9
A26	S2	D24	A6	IGNNE#	A15			S10
A27	S1	D25	B6	INTR	A16			S11
A28	R1	D26	C7	KEN#	F15			S12
A29	P2	D27	C6	LOCK#	N15			S14
A30	P3	D28	C8	M/IO#	N16			
A31	Q1	D29	A8	NMI	B15			
		D30	C9	PCD	J17			
		D31	B8	PCHK#	Q17			
				PWT	L15			
				PLOCK#	Q16			
				RDY#	F16			
				RESET	C16			
				W/R#	N17			

The rated clock input to the 80486 is different than that of the previous 80x86 micro-processors in that there is no internal division factor to arrive at the chip's speed rating. In other words, an 80486-25 microprocessor must operate from a 25MHz clock input signal. Conversely, a 16MHz 80386SX requires a clock signal of 32MHz to operate properly. In addition, no provision exists for slowing the 80486 microprocessor down during operation to accommodate expansion bus usage (normal/turbo operations). This may adversely affect software that relies on clock-dependent timing loops to accomplish tasks.

Other 80486 Microprocessors

The **80486SX** microprocessor, produced by Intel, is an 80486DX version that does not have a built-in math coprocessor. This translates into a lower cost for the computer system. Most of the systems that use the 80486SX have the capability of adding a separate math coprocessor, if desired. The math coprocessor for the 80486SX is identified as an 80487SX. The 80486SX maintains the same bus sizes as the 80486DX.

The **80486DX2** is identical to the 80486DX in operation and bus size. However, the 80486DX2 adds a feature called **clock doubling**. This technology, introduced by Intel, gives the appearance of doubling the frequency of the clock internally to decrease execution time. The external bus operation, though, is still at the speed determined by the input clock frequency. This feature is actually achieved by increasing the internal efficiency of the chip design. For example, an 80486DX2 with an input clock frequency of 33MHz has the appearance of the same chip operated at 66MHz.

The **80486DX4** microprocessor, also produced by Intel, takes the clock-doubling technology to the next level to produce a **clock-tripling** design. This, again, is achieved by increasing the internal efficiency of the architecture.

The **Cyrix CX486SLC** is technically more like an 80386SX microprocessor in architecture. It has a 24-bit address bus and a 16-bit external data bus. The math coprocessor is also not included in this design. The Cyrix **CX486DLC** microprocessor is Cyrix's version of Intel's 80486DX. Like the 80486DX, this chip includes the 32-bit address and data buses and math coprocessor. The **CX486DRU2**, Cyrix's answer to Intel's 80486DX2, offers the same architecture and features as the 80486DX2.

The design of the **80486SLC2** is IBM's version of the 80486DX2 and the 80386SX. This chip has the bus size of the 80386SX and the clock-doubling technology of the 80486DX2 integrated in one package. This design does not include a math coprocessor, but it does use the 80486 instruction set.

The Pentium Processor

A+ CORE 4.1 The **Pentium processor** succeeds the 80486 microprocessor and maintains compatibility with other 80X86 microprocessors. The Pentium is a 32/64-bit microprocessor contained in a 273-pin PGA package. As in the 80486 package, the Pentium generates so much heat during normal operation that an additional **CPU cooling fan** is required.

All registers for the microprocessor and floating-point sections of the Pentium are identical to those of the 80486. The Pentium has a 64-bit data bus that enables it to handle **quad word** (or **Qword**) data transfers. The Pentium also contains two separate 8KB caches, compared to only one in the 80486. One of the caches is used for instructions or code, and the other is used for data. The internal architecture of the Pentium resembles an 80486 in expanded form. The floating-point section operates up to five times faster than that of the 80486.

The internal architecture of the Pentium is shown in Figure 6.21. It is called a **superscalar** microprocessor because its architecture enables multiple instructions to be executed simultaneously. A pipelining process achieves this. Pipelining is a technique that uses multiple stages to speed up instruction execution. Each stage in the pipeline performs a part of the overall instruction execution, with all operations being completed at one stage before moving on to another stage.

This technique enables streamlined circuitry to perform a specific function at each stage of the pipeline, thereby improving execution time. When an instruction moves from one stage to the next, a new instruction moves into the vacated stage. The Pentium contains two separate pipelines that can operate simultaneously. The first is called the **U-pipe**, and the second is the **V-pipe**. Most instructions execute in both pipelines in a single clock cycle.

A few pins on the Pentium differ from the 80486. A pinout for the Pentium is shown in Figure 6.22 and defined in Figure 6.23. The Pentium has been produced in a variety of clock-frequency versions: 75/90/100/120/133/150/166/200MHz. The external frequency applied to its clock input is the same frequency the Pentium uses internally. The address bus connections are labeled A3–A31. These lines are bi-directional, as was the case with the 80486, and are used as inputs for cache inquiries. D0–D63 are the 64-bit bi-directional data bus pins.

FIGURE 6.21

Inside the Pentium microprocessor.

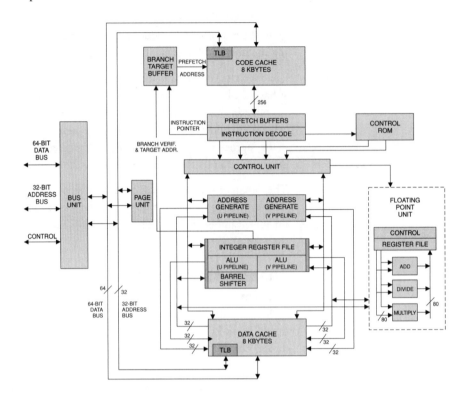

FIGURE 6.22

Pinout for the Pentium.

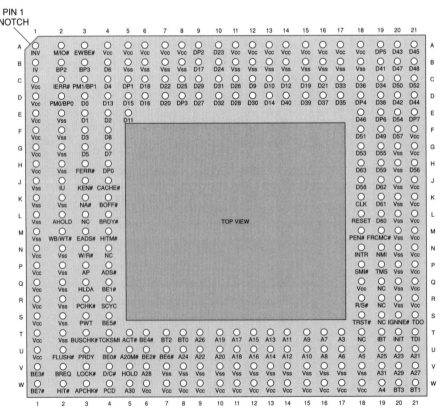

FIGURE 6.23

The pins of the Pentium microprocessor.

ADDRESS									
A3	AL35	A9	AK30	A15	AK26	A21	AF34	A27	AG33
A4	AM34	A10	AN31	A16	AL25	A22	AH36	A28	AK36
A5	AK32	A11	AL31	A17	AK24	A23	AE33	A29	AK34
A6	AN33	A12	AL29	A18	AL23	A24	AG35	A30	AM36
A7	AL33	A13	AK28	A19	AK22	A25	AJ35	A31	AJ33
A8	AM32	A14	AL27	A20	AL21	A26	AH34		

DATA									
D0	K34	D13	B34	D26	D24	D39	D10	D52	E03
D1	G35	D14	C33	D27	C21	D40	D08	D53	G05
D2	J35	D15	A35	D28	D22	D41	A05	D54	E01
D3	G33	D16	B32	D29	C19	D42	E09	D55	G03
D4	F36	D17	C31	D30	D20	D43	B04	D56	H04
D5	F34	D18	A33	D31	C17	D44	D06	D57	J03
D6	E35	D19	D28	D32	C15	D45	C05	D58	J05
D7	E33	D20	B30	D33	D16	D46	E07	D59	K04
D8	D34	D21	C29	D34	C13	D47	C03	D60	L05
D9	C37	D22	A31	D35	D14	D48	D04	D61	L03
D10	C35	D23	D26	D36	C11	D49	E05	D62	M04
D11	B36	D24	C27	D37	D12	D50	D02	D63	N03
D12	D32	D25	C23	D38	C09	D51	F04		

CONTROL								
A20M#	AK08	BREQ	AJ01	HIT#	AK06	PRDY	AC05
ADS#	AJ05	BUSCHK#	AL07	HITM#	AL05	PWT	AL03
ADSC#	AM02	CACHE#	U03	HLDA	AJ03	R/S#	AC35
AHOLD	A04	CPUTYP	Q35	HOLD	AB04	RESET	AK20
AP	AK02	D/C#	AK04	IERR#	P04	SCYC	AL17
APCHK#	AE05	D/P#	AE35	IGNNE#	AA35	SMI#	AB34
BE0#	AL09	DP0	D36	INIT	AA33	SMIACT#	AG03
BE1#	AK10	DP1	D30	INTR/LINT0	AD34	TCK	M34
BE2#	AL11	DP2	C25	INV	U05	TDI	N35
BE3#	AK12	DP3	D18	KEN#	W05	TDO	N33
BE4#	AL13	DP4	C07	LOCK#	AH04	TMS	P34
BE5#	AK14	DP5	F06	M/IO#	T04	TRST#	Q33
BE6#	AL15	DP6	F02	NA#	Y05	VCC2DET#	AL01
BE7#	AK16	DP7	N05	NMI/LINT1	AC33	W/R#	AM06
BOFF#	Z04	EADS#	AM04	PCD	AG05	WB/WT#	AA05
BP2	S03	EWBE#	W03	PCHK#	AF04		
BP3	S05	FERR#	Q05	PEN#	Z34		
BRDY#	X04	FLUSH#	AN07	PM0/BP0	Q03		
BRDYC#	Y03	FRCMC#¹	Y35	PM1/BP1	R04		

¹ The FRCMC# pin is not defined for the Pentium ® processor with MMXTM technology. This pin should be left as a "NC" or tied to VCC3 via an external pullup resistor on the Pentium processor with MMX technology.

Advanced Pentium Architectures

Intel has advanced its Pentium line of microprocessors by introducing three new specifications: the **Pentium MMX, Pentium Pro**, and **Pentium II** processors.

Pentium MMX

 A+ CORE 4.1

> In the **Pentium MMX** processor, the multimedia and communications-processing capabilities of the Pentium device are extended by the addition of 57 multimedia-specific instruction to the instruction set.

Intel also increased the L1 onboard cache size to 32KB. The cache has been divided into two separate 16KB caches: the instruction cache and the data cache. The external L2 cache used with the MMX is typically 256KB or 512KB.

The MMX adds an additional multimedia-specific stage to the integer pipeline. This integrated stage handles MMX and integer instructions quickly. Improved branching prediction circuitry has also been implemented to offer higher prediction accuracy and thereby provide higher processing speeds. The MMX's four prefetch buffers can hold up to four successive streams of code. The four write buffers are shared between the two pipelines to improve the MMX's memory write performance. The block diagram of the Pentium MMX is presented in Figure 6.24.

FIGURE 6.24

Inside the Pentium MMX.

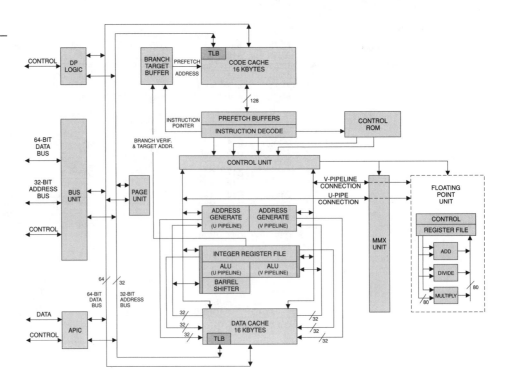

The Pentium MMX processor is available in 166MHz and 200MHz versions and is pin-for-pin compatible with previous Pentium processors (273-pin PGA format). However, it requires two separate operating voltages. One source is used to drive the Pentium processor core, and the other is used to power the processor's I/O pins. The pinout of the Pentium MMX is identical to that of the basic Pentium illustrated in Figure 6.22 and 6.23.

Pentium Pro

A+ CORE 4.1

Intel departed from simply increasing the speed of its Pentium processor line by introducing the **Pentium Pro** processor. Though compatible with all the previous software written for the Intel processor line, the Pentium Pro is optimized to run 32-bit software.

However, the Pentium Pro did not remain pin-compatible with the previous Pentium processors. Instead, Intel adopted a 2.46-inch-by-2.66-inch, 387-pin PGA configuration to house a Pentium Pro **processor core** and an onboard 512KB or 256KB L2 cache. The L2 cache complements the 16KB L1 cache in the Pentium core. This arrangement is illustrated in Figure 6.25. Notice that though they exist on the same PGA device, the two components are not integrated into the same IC. A gold-plated, copper/tungsten heat spreader covers the unit.

The Pentium Pro uses dynamic execution techniques to manipulate the data flow through it instead of simply processing it. The Pentium Pro performs three types of special data manipulation:

▶ Multiple branch prediction

▶ Data-flow analysis

▶ Speculative execution

FIGURE 6.25

The Pentium Pro microprocessor.

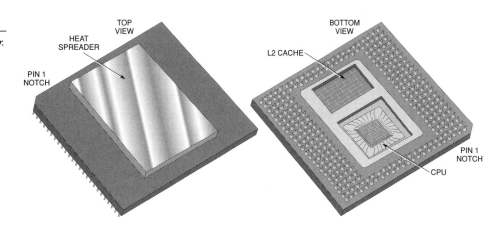

A multiple branch prediction algorithm enables the Pentium Pro to anticipate branching in the instruction sequence. It predicts where the next instruction address will be located in memory by looking ahead in the **instruction queue**. As the processor decodes instructions, its data flow analysis circuitry determines whether the instruction can be executed right away or whether it is dependent on the outcome of other instructions. This technique enables the processor to execute the instruction flow in the most efficient manner. In addition, the Pentium Pro processor uses the **look-ahead function** to process up to five instructions in the pipeline on a speculative basis. When the final state of the instruction sequence is available, the instructions are returned to their proper order and the final results can be output.

The level-2 (L2) onboard cache stores the most frequently used data not found in the processor's internal L1 cache, as close to the processor core as it can be without being integrated directly into the IC. A high-bandwidth cache bus connects the processor and cache unit. The bus (0.5 inches in length) enables the processor and external cache to communicate at a rate of 1.2GB per second.

The Pentium Pro is designed so that it can be used in typical single-microprocessor applications or in multiple processor environments, such as with high-speed, high-volume file servers and work stations. Several dual-processor system boards have been designed for twin Pentium Pro processors. These boards, such as the one shown in Figure 6.26, are created with two Pentium Pro sockets so that they can operate with either a single processor or with dual processors. When dual processors are installed, logic circuitry in the Pentium Pro's core manages the requests for access to the system's memory and 64-bit buses.

FIGURE 6.26

A dual-processor system board.

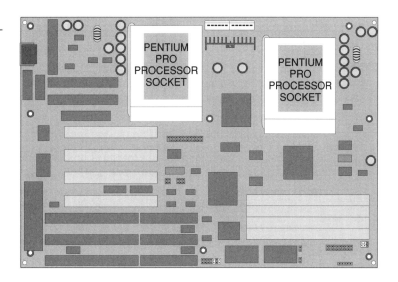

Pentium II

A+ CORE 4.1 Intel radically changed the form factor of the Pentium processors by housing the **Pentium II** processor in a new **single-edge contact** (SEC) cartridge, depicted in Figure 6.27. This cartridge uses a special **retention mechanism** built into the system board to hold the device in place. The new proprietary socket design is referred to as the Slot 1 specification and is designed to enable the microprocessor to eventually operate at bus speeds in excess of 300MHz—this is the upper operating frequency limit for pin grid sockets.

The cartridge also requires a special **fan heatsink** (FHS) module and fan. As with the SEC cartridge, the FHS module requires special support mechanisms to hold it in place. The fan draws power from a special power connector on the system board, or from one of the system's options power connectors.

Figure 6.27 depicts the Pentium II's cartridge contents. Inside the cartridge is a substrate material on which the processor and related components are mounted. The components consist of the Pentium II processor core, a **TAG RAM**, and an L2 Burst SRAM.

> The Pentium II includes all the multimedia enhancements from the MMX processor, and it retains the power of the Pentium Pro's dynamic execution and 512KB L2 cache features. The L1 cache is increased to 32KB, and the L2 cache operates with a half-speed bus.

FIGURE 6.27

The Pentium II cartridge.

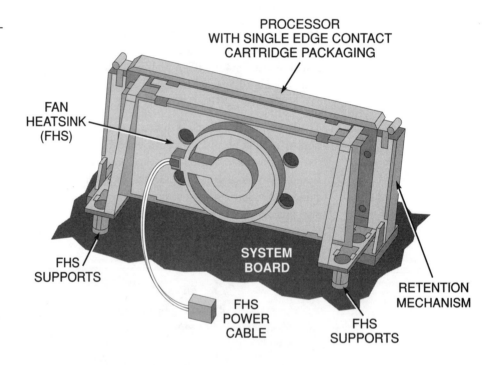

Figure 6.28 depicts the Pentium II's cartridge contents.

The operation of Pentium Pro and Pentium II processors can be modified by uploading processor update information into BIOS that have **application programming interfaces (API)** capabilities built into them. The microprocessor manufacturer places update information on its Web site that can be downloaded onto a floppy disk by customers. The user transfers the update information from the update disk to the system's BIOS via the API. If the updated data is relevant (as indicated by checking its processor stepping code), the API writes the updated microcode into the BIOS. This information, in turn, is loaded into the processor each time the system is booted. Table 6.1 summarizes the characteristics of the Intel microprocessors covered in this chapter.

FIGURE 6.28

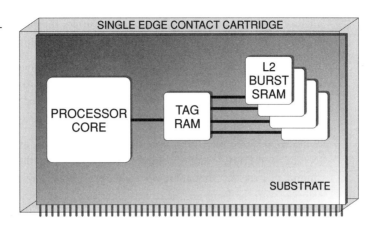

Inside the Pentium II cartridge.

Table 6.1 *Characteristics of Intel Microprocessors*

Type	Address Bus Width	Space	Internal Clock Speed (MHz)	Data Bus Width	Math Coprocessor	Main Use
8088	20	1MB	4.77 (Normal) 8 (Turbo)	8 (supports 16)	8087	XT
80286	20 24 24	1MB (Real mode) 16MB (Protected mode) 16MB (Protected mode, addressing & GB of virtual memory)	12	16	80287	AT
80386 (DX)	32	4GB	25	32	80387	AT-compat
80386SX	24	16MB (Physical)	16	16-external 32-internal	80387SX	AT-compat
80386SL	32	4GB	20	16-external 32-internal	80387SL	Notebooks
AM386DX	32	4GB	25	32	AM387DX	AT-compat
AM386SX	32	4GB	25	16	AM387SX	AT-compat
IBM386SLC	24	16MB	20	16		PS/2
80486	32	4GB	25	32-external 64-internal	NA	AT-compat
80486SX	32	4GB	20	32	80487SX	AT-compat Notebooks
80486DX2	32	4GB	50	32	NA	AT-compat
80486DX4	32	4GB	100	32	NA	AT-compat
CX486SLC	24	16MB	20	13	CX487SLC	Notebooks
CX486DLC	32	4GB	25	32-internal	NA	AT-compat
CX486- DRU	32	4GB	50	32	NA	AT-compat
IBM-486SLC2	24	16MB	50	16		PS/2
Pentium	32	4GB	60, 66	64	Onboard	AT-compat
Pentium MMX	32	4GB	133, 150, 166	64	Onboard	AT-compat
Pentium Pro	36	4GBX4	150, 166, 180, 200	64	Onboard	AT-compat
Pentium	36	64GB	233, 266	64	Onboard II	AT-compat

Pentium Clones

A+ CORE 4.1 As mentioned in Chapter 2, "PC Hardware," Intel abandoned the 80x86 nomenclature in favor of names that could be copyrighted in an effort to distance themselves from the clone microprocessor manufacturers. When this occurred, the other manufacturers largely followed the 80x86 path but moved toward alternate numbering schemes as well.

Table 6.2 shows the relationship between the various numbering systems. In addition to the 8x86 numbering system, Intel used a Px identification up to the Pentium II. The Pentium II is identified as the Klamath processor. Subsequent improved versions have been dubbed Deschutes, Covington, Mendocino, Katmai, Willamette, Flagstaff (P7), Merced, and Tahoe.

NexGen produced three processors capable of performing at the same level as the **P5** (Nx586) and **P54C** (Nx686) Pentium devices. However, these devices use proprietary pinouts that are not compatible with other processors. Although the performance levels compete with the Pentium, the devices offer compatibility only with 80386/87 operation.

Cyrix uses an Mx numbering system in addition to the 5x/6x86 numbers. The **M5/M6/M7** devices are compatible with their Intel counterparts in performance, compatibility, and pinout. The 5x86 device is compatible with the 80486DX4 in performance, compatibility, and pinout. The M1 (6x86) and **M2** (6x86MX) processors are compatible with the Intel P54C and P55C units in performance and pinout. The M1 unit is operationally compatible with the 80486DX4, and the M2 processor is compatible with the Pentium MMX and Pro processors.

AMD offers five clone microprocessors: the 5x86 (**X5**), the 5x86 (**K5**), the **K6**, the **K6PLUS-3D**, and **K7** microprocessors. The X5 offers operational and pinout compatibility with the DX4, and its performance is equal to the Pentium and MMX processors. The K5 processor is compatible with the Pentium, and the K6 is compatible with the MMX. The K6PLUS-3D is compatible operationally and in performance with the Pentium Pro, and the K7 is compatible operationally and in performance with the Pentium II. However, neither of these units have a pinout compatibility with another processor.

Table 6.2 Clone Processors

Intel	Cyrix	-AMD	NextGen	Centaur
80386SX (P9)				
80486DX (P4)	M6			
80846SX (P4S/P23)	M5			
80486DX2 (P24)	M7			
80486DX4 (P24C)	M1SE (5X86)	-X5 (5X86)		
Pentium (P5/P54C)	M1 (6X86)	-K5 (5X86)	NX586/686	C6
Pentium MMX (P55C)	M2 (6X86MX)	-K6		C6PLUS
Pentium Pro (P6)	MXi	-K6PLUS-3D		
Pentium II	M3	-K7		

A+ CORE 4.3 In addition to the previously described clones, Intel has developed a line of upgrade microprocessors for their original units. These are referred to as **OverDrive processors**. The OverDrive unit may simply be the same type of microprocessor running at a higher clock speed, or it may be an advanced architecture microprocessor designed to operate from the same socket/pin configuration as the original. To accommodate this option, Intel has created specifications for eight socket designs, designated Socket-1 through Socket-8.

The specifications for **Socket-1** through **Socket-3** were developed for 80486SX, DX, and OverDrive versions that use different pin numbers and power supply requirements. Likewise, **Socket-4** through **Socket-6** deal with various Pentium and OverDrive units that use different speeds and power supply requirements. The **Socket-7** design works with the fastest Pentium units and includes provision for a **Voltage Regulator Module** (**VRM**) to enable various power settings to be implemented through the socket. Finally, the **Socket-8** specification is specific to the Pentium Pro processor.

Power Supply Requirements

A+ CORE 4.1 You must consider three compatibility issues when dealing with clone processors: performance, operation, and pinout compatibility. In addition to these three issues, it is important to be aware of the power supply requirements for the various types of microprocessors. In the quest for higher operating speeds, one method of improving microprocessor performance is to use a lower voltage level. This in effect moves the high and low logic levels closer together, requiring less time to switch back and forth between them.

Beginning with the Pentium MMX, Intel adopted dual-voltage supply levels for the overall IC and for its core. Common Intel voltage supplies are +5/+5 for older units, and +3.3/+3.3, +3.3/+2.8, +3.3/+1.8 for newer units. Clone processors may use compatible voltages (especially if they are pinout-compatible) or may use completely different voltage levels. Common voltages for clone microprocessors include +5, +3.3, +2.5, and +2.2. Special regulator circuits on the system board typically generate the additional voltage levels. In each case, the system board's user's guide should be consulted any time the microprocessor is being replaced or upgraded.

Microprocessor Support Systems

> As powerful as modern microprocessors are, they still require a certain amount of **support circuitry** to be considered a system. Over time, these support systems have been reduced to just a few ASIC devices.

The system boards displayed in Figures 6.1 and 6.4, as well as most other AT-compatible system boards, employ a single ASIC to perform most of the system's AT-compatible functions. This IC is referred to as an **Integrated Peripheral Controller** (**IPC**) chip.

Integrated Peripheral Controllers (IPC)

The functional blocks of a typical IPC are shown in Figure 6.29. This IC contains the equivalent of the AT's two 8237 four-channel DMA Controllers, two 8259 eight-line Interrupt Controllers, an 8253 three-channel Timer/Counter IC, and a 74LS612 Memory Mapper. In addition, the IPC incorporates the system's real-time clock circuit, non-volatile RAM configuration registers, and all the AT system's discrete support circuitry for these devices.

Timing Systems

The main clock signal on any system board is the processor clock signal. This signal serves as the reference for all system operations and is specified in megahertz (MHz). Normally, all the system board's auxiliary clock signals are derived from this signal.

FIGURE 6.29

*An Integrated Peripheral
Controller.*

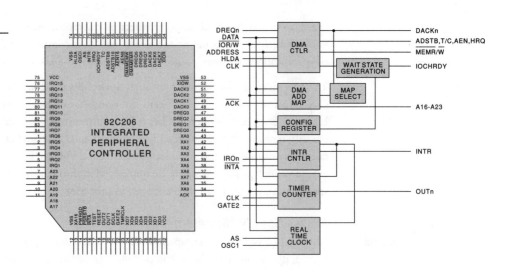

Typical auxiliary system board frequencies include a 14.318MHz signal that is applied to the PC-Bus, ISA, and EISA expansion slots to form their **oscillator (OSC) line**. A 1.19318MHz signal is also generated to provide the system's **peripheral clock (PCLK)** signal that drives the system's timer/counter channels.

Most system boards support a **software speed switch** that can be activated directly from the keyboard to speed up or slow down the operation of the unit. To place the system in **turbo speed**, press down and hold the CTRL and ALT keys. While holding these keys, press the + (plus) key on the keyboard's numeric keypad. This operation is written as CTRL/ALT/+. The system is now running in high-speed turbo mode.

To return the system to **normal speed** operation, press the CTRL/ALT/- (minus) key combination. In addition to setting turbo speed operation from the keyboard, the user can select the system's operating speed through a push-button turbo switch located on the front panel of the system unit. To return to hardware speed selection, press the CTRL+ALT+* key combination.

Real-Time Clock

The **real-time clock (RTC)** module is included for maintaining the system's time and date. In a PC-compatible system, this time and date information is attached to files when they are written to a disk. This operation is a function of the operating system's file handling routines. This subsystem contains 114 bytes of RAM information. The IPC's internal clock circuitry uses 14 bytes, and the remainder is used to hold the system's configuration information. An external, rechargeable battery backs up this information so that it is retained when the computer is turned off. Table 6.3 shows the addresses and descriptions of the IPC's internal RAM memory locations.

Table 6.3   *IPC's Internal RAM Configuration Locations*

Address	Description	Address	Description
00	Seconds	10	FDD A: and B: type byte
01	Second alarm	12	HDD type byte
02	Minutes	14	Equipment byte
03	Minutes alarm	15	Low base memory
04	Hours	16	High base memory

Address	Description	Address	Description
05	Hour alarm	17	Low expansion memory
06	Day of week	18	High expansion memory
07	Date of month	19	High expansion memory
08	Month	1A	Disk C: Extended byte
09	Year	1B	Disk D: Extended byte
0A	Status Register A	1C	CMOS checksum (2 bytes)
0B	Status Register B	1E-2F	Low expansion memory byte
0C	Status Register C	30	High expansion memory byte
0D	Status Register D	31	Data century byte
0E	Diagnostic status byte	32	Information flags
0F	Status byte	34-7E	User RAM

The first 10 bytes of the RTC hold the time, calendar, and alarm data for the system's software. The DOS date and time commands obtain their values from this table. These bytes are updated once every second. Information is stored in these locations as BCD data.

The alarm bytes can be programmed to generate interrupts at specific times or on a periodic basis. Simply entering the desired time into the alarm byte registers can generate specifically timed alarm interrupts. Conversely, periodic alarms are generated by programming logic 1s into the two most significant bits of any of the three alarm registers.

The 114 bytes of general-purpose user RAM, located between hex addresses 0E and 7F, are not affected by the RTC update circuitry. These registers hold the system's CMOS Setup configuration information and can be accessed by the system at any time. Due to its nonvolatile nature (battery backup), this memory area is often used to hold these configuration and calibration parameters that must be preserved when the computer is turned off. In Pentium systems, this includes enabling settings for the system board's integrated I/O devices.

Timer/Counter Channels

The operation of any PC-compatible timer/counter subsystem is identical to the three-channel 8253 Timer/Counter IC used in PCs and XTs. All three counters are driven from the system's 14.318MHz OSC signal. Counter 0 is connected to the interrupt controller and is used as a general-purpose timer for the system, providing a constant time base for implementing the system's time of day clock. Counter 1 may be programmed to produce pulses that initiate dynamic RAM refresh operations. Counter 2 is used to support tone generation for the system's speaker. Table 6.4 lists the system's timer/counter channel definitions.

Table 6.4 *System Timer/Counter Channel Definitions*

Timer	Function
Channel 0	System timer
GATE0	Tied on (internally)
CLOCK	1.19318MHz TMRCLK
OUT0	Drives IRQ0 (internally) with 15 μSEC Pulse
Channel 1	Refresh request generator
GATE1	Tied on (internally)
CLOCK	1.19318MHz TMRCLK
OUT1	Request refresh cycle

continues

Table 6.4 *continued*

Timer	Function
Channel 2	Tone generator for speaker
GATE2	PORT-B bits 0 and 1 (HEX address 61)
CLOCK	1.19318MHz TMRCLK
OUT2	Drives speaker

The internal timer/counter circuitry is depicted in Figure 6.30. Each counter can be programmed individually by writing control words into the IPC's control register at hex address locations 040h–043h. The control logic circuitry decodes the control information and provides the internal signals necessary to load, configure, and control each counter.

FIGURE 6.30

The timer/counter circuits.

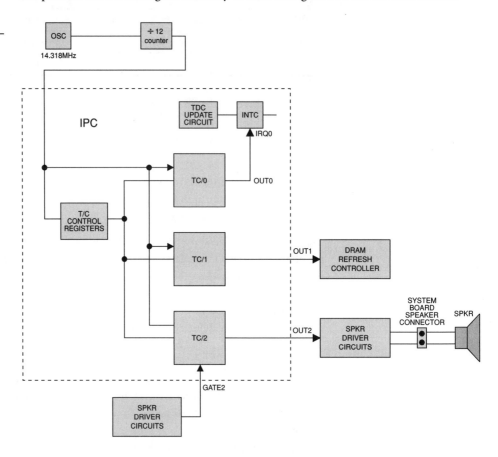

Each of the timer/counter's channels consists of a 16-bit down-counter that can accept an input clock signal ranging from 0MHz to 2MHz. The three channels operate independently of each other, and each can be programmed to produce an output frequency that is equal to its input frequency divided by any whole number between 1 and 65,535.

All three counters receive clocking through the IPC's **Timer-Clock** (**TMRCLK**) input signal. This signal originates from an external clock source and is, therefore, independent from all other IPC clock signals. The 14.318MHz OSC clock signal is applied to a divide-by-12 counter. The counter outputs the 1.19318MHz (TMRCLK) clock signal.

The timer's **OUT0** output is connected directly to the master interrupt controller's IRQ0 input and is used by the system for time-keeping and task-switching functions. The internal interrupt controller uses this signal to drive the system's time-of-day clock update circuitry.

Counter 1 is used to generate pulses that act as a time-base for the system's memory refresh operations. The **OUT1** signal is used to provide the 15-microsecond clock pulses that set up the system's dynamic RAM refresh operations.

The output of Counter 2 is used to drive the system's speaker circuitry. This is the only timer/counter channel that has an external inhibit line (**GATE2**). To activate the speaker, the speaker circuit must enable Counter 2 and the speaker. The entire range of audio frequencies can be produced by the system's speaker circuitry.

Interrupt Controllers

An AT-compatible interrupt controller device provides two eight-line interrupt controllers (**INTC1** and **INTC2**), each of which is equivalent to the 8259 PIC used in the original PCs, XTs, and ATs. These interrupt controllers are internally cascaded together to provide the 16 interrupt channels necessary for AT compatibility. Like those discrete 8259's used in the original AT, the IPC's controllers must be programmed to operate in cascade mode. INTC1 is located at hex addresses 020 and 021, and INTC2 is located at 0A0 and 0A1.

A+ CORE 1.3

Of the 16 interrupt channels (IRQ0 through IRQ15) available, three are generally used inside the IPC. Therefore, they do not have external IRQ pins. The other 13 IRQ inputs are available to the system for user-definable interrupt functions. As with the PC and XT, each IRQ input is assigned a priority level. IRQ0 is the highest, and IRQ15 is the lowest. The three internally connected channels are as follows:

Channel 0 (IRQ0) Timer/Counter interrupt is OK

Channel 2 (IRQ2) Cascaded to INTC2

Channel 8 (IRQ8) Real-time clock interrupt

Table 6.5 shows the designations for the various interrupt levels in the system.

Table 6.5 *System Interrupt Levels*

Interrupt	Description	Interrupt	Description
NMI	Parity check error or I/O channel check error		
	INTC1		*INTC2*
IRQ0	Minute alarm	IRQ8	Real-time clock
IRQ1	Keyboard buffer full	IRQ9	Cascade to INTC1
IRQ2	Cascade from INTC2	IRQ10	Spare
IRQ3	Serial port 2	IRQ11	Spare
IRQ4	Serial port 1	IRQ12	Spare
IRQ5	Parallel port 2	IRQ13	Coprocessor
IRQ6	FDD controller	IRQ14	Primary IDE CTRL
IRQ7	Parallel port 1	IRQ15	Second IDE CTRL

A typical PC's interrupt circuitry is illustrated in Figure 6.31. Its operation is as follows:

1. When one or more of the interrupt controller's IRQ inputs becomes active, the interrupt controller checks its internal registers for priority levels.

2. The priority resolver evaluates the priority of the IRQ(s) received and asserts an INTR signal to the microprocessor.

FIGURE 6.31

The interrupt circuitry.

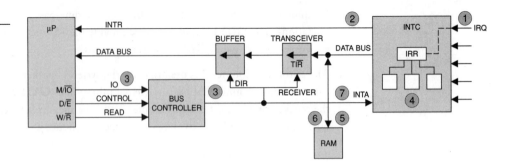

3. When the microprocessor accepts the interruption, it enters into INTA cycles. These cycles produce the necessary signals (M/IO, D/E, and W/R = 0) to cause the bus controller to issue an INTA signal to the interrupt controller. These conditions also create the proper XDIR and T/R conditions for data movement from the IPC to the microprocessor.

4. Each I/O system must have a special program called an **Interrupt Service Routine**. This program is specific to that system's function and operational needs. After the controller informs the microprocessor that an interrupt has occurred, it must produce an address to point the microprocessor to the starting address of the service routine that corresponds to the level of interrupt being serviced. This pointing address (**vector address**) is located in a portion of RAM memory called the vector table. These addresses are physically located in the lowest 1KB (0–3FF) of RAM memory in the system and contain the starting addresses of the various service routines.

5. The interrupt controller places an 8-bit interrupt vector address (nn) on the XD0–XD7 data pins. The *nn* value corresponds to the priority of the interrupt being serviced. The microprocessor pushes the contents of its internal registers on a stack and latches the vector address bits during this time.

6. The microprocessor jumps to the address specified by the vector byte and loads a 4-byte address. This address represents the beginning address of the service routine for the interrupting device. The microprocessor services the interrupting device until an **End Of Interrupt** (**EOI**) instruction is encountered in the routine.

7. The EOI command from the CPU causes the interrupt controller's ISR bit to be cleared at the end of the second INTA cycle. This marks the end of the service routine. The microprocessor retrieves the contents of its internal registers from the stack and resumes its normal operation at the point where it left off when the interrupt was accepted.

Table 6.6 lists the interrupt vectors and functions used in PC-compatible computer systems. These vectors can also be used by software designers to execute software interrupts in the system. By doing so, they can take over direct control of the system's I/O devices.

Table 6.6 *Interrupt Vectors*

Interrupt	Function
0	Divide by zero
1	Single step
2	Non-maskable interrupt (NMI)
3	Break point instruction
4	Overflow
5	Print screen

Interrupt	Function
6, 7	Reserved
8	Time-or-day hardware interrupt (18.2/sec.)
9	Keyboard hardware interrupt
A	Reserved
B, C	Serial communications hardware interrupt
D	Fixed-disk hardware interrupt
E	Disk hardware interrupt
F	Printer hardware interrupt
10	Video I/O call
11	Equipment check call
12	Memory check call
13	Disk I/O call
14	RS232 I/O call
15	(Not used)
16	Keyboard I/O call
17	Printer I/O call
18	ROM basic entry code
19	Bootstrap loader
1A	Time of day call
1B	Get control on keyboard break
1C	Get control on timer interrupt
1D	Pointer to video initialization table
1E	Pointer to disk parameter table
1F	Pointer to graphics character generator
20	DOS program terminate
21	DOS function call
22	DOS terminate address
23	DOS CTRL-BRK exit address
24	DOS fatal error vector
25	DOS absolute disk read
26	DOS absolute disk write
27	DOS terminate, fix in storage
28–3F	Reserved for DOS
40–5F	Reserved
60–67	Reserved for user software interrupts
68–7F	(Not used)
80–85	Reserved by BASIC
86–F0	Used by BASIC interpreter while running
F1–FF	(Not used)

Non-Maskable Interrupts (NMI)

Two system board-based conditions cause a **Non-Maskable Interrupt** (**NMI**) signal to be sent to the microprocessor. The first condition occurs when an active **IO Channel Check** (**IOCHCK**) input is received from an options adapter card located in one of the board's expansion slots. The system's BIOS program enables this signal during initialization. The other event that causes an NMI signal to be generated is the occurrence of a **Parity Check** (**PCK**) **Error** in the DRAM memory. The BIOS program also enables the parity check signal during the system's initialization.

DMA Controllers

Before a DMA data transfer begins, the starting address and number of bytes to be transferred are sent to the DMA controller on the data bus, along with information specifying the type and direction of transfer to be performed (I/O-memory, memory-I/O, or memory-to-memory). This information is stored in the DMA controller's internal registers.

During the transfer, the address that the controller applies to the memory unit is decremented by 1 each time a byte is transferred. An internal count register, which was originally loaded with the number of bytes to be transferred, is also decremented by 1. After it has been activated, the data transfer continues until the count register has been decremented to 0 or until the I/O device activates the **End Operation** (**EOP**) line to terminate DMA operations.

The IPC's DMA subsystem provides an AT-compatible PC with four channels for 8-bit DMA transfers (DMA1) and three channels (DMA2) for 16-bit DMA transfers. The DMA1 channels are used to carry out DMA transfers between 8-bit options adapters and 8- or 16-bit memory locations. These 8-bit transfers are conducted in 64KB blocks and can be performed throughout the system's entire 16MB-address space. The DMA2 channels (channels 5, 6, and 7) are used only with 16-bit devices and can transfer words only in 128KB blocks. The first 16-bit DMA channel (DMA channel 4) is used internally to cascade the two DMA controllers together. Table 6.7 describes the system's DMA channel designations.

Table 6.7 *System's DMA Channel Designations*

Channel	Function	Controller	Page Register Address
CH0	Spare	1	0087
CH1	SDLC (network)	1	0083
CH2	FDD controller	1	0082
CH3	Spare	1	0081
CH4	Cascade to CNTR 1	2	
CH5	Spare	2	008B
CH6	Spare	2	0089
CH7	Spare	2	008A

DMA Controller Modes

The typical DMA subsystem operates in three distinctly different modes:

- Idle mode
- Program mode
- Active mode

When no DMA requests are pending, the DMA subsystem operates in Idle mode. In this mode, the DMA controller performs single-state (S1) operations. This is the DMA controller's default mode and the mode in which it operates unless a DMA request is presented to the controller, or until one of its internal registers is accessed by the system for programming.

When the system places a valid address on the address bus that corresponds to one of the IPC's DMA registers (along with an IOR or IOW signal), the DMA subsystem enters Program mode. In this mode, all programmable aspects of the DMA channel can be written to (or read from) the DMA controller.

When the DMA subsystem is presented with a DMA request on one of its DRQ lines, it enters into its Active mode. A normal active DMA cycle consists of three states (S2, S3, and S4) that require four DMA clock cycles to complete. State S3 is normally executed twice to create a wait-state condition in the DMA timing sequence. However, the DMA channel can be programmed to produce higher data throughput by excluding the second S3 state and terminating the DMA cycle in S4. This would, of course, produce a zero wait-state condition.

A Typical DMA Operation

Figure 6.32 depicts a typical DMA transfer from floppy disk to memory. In this case, the IPC's DMAMEMW, XIOR, and DACK2 output lines are used to move bytes of data from the disk drive controller through the expansion-slot connector and I/O buses and into RAM memory. The DMAMEMW line works in conjunction with the address that the DMA controller places on the address bus to select the location in RAM memory where the byte of information from the disk drive controller will be stored.

FIGURE 6.32

A typical DMA operation.

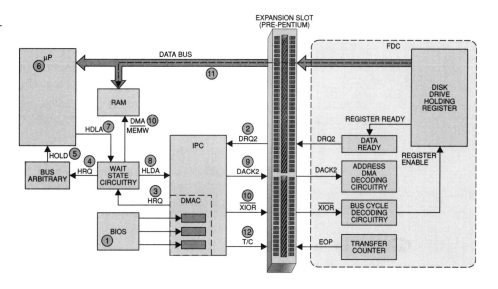

The XIOR line works with the DACK2 line to access and read the disk drive controller's output register. Because the address bus is being used at this time to access the RAM memory location, the DACK line is needed to act as the chip select signal that addresses the output latch on the controller board. Therefore, the DACK line performs the same task as a decoded I/O address would on the controller card. Note that during **I/O-to-memory** or **memory-to-I/O transfers**, the DMA controller does not handle any of the data being transferred internally; it simply manipulates the I/O device and the memory structure to carry out the data transfer.

The floppy-disk drive DMA transfer operation can be summarized as follows:

1. The IPC's internal registers are loaded with information such as this:

    a. The address in RAM memory where the data from the FDD will be stored

    b. The number of bytes to be transferred

    c. The size of the block (sector) to be transferred

    d. The mode of transfer (block or byte-by-byte)

2. The FDD controller signals the IPC by activating the system's **DMA Request-2 (DRQ2)** line.

3. The DMA controller responds by sending a **Hold Request (HRQ)** signal to the system's wait-state logic.

4. The wait-state circuitry applies the HRQ signal to the bus arbitrator circuitry.

5. The bus arbitrator issues a HOLD signal to the microprocessor.

6. The microprocessor finishes its current instruction and places its address, data, and control bus lines in a high impedance state.

7. The microprocessor generates the **Hold Acknowledge (HLDA)** signal.

8. The HLDA is applied to the IPC. The HLDA signal is also converted into the **Acknowledge (ACK)** signal that is applied to the IPC.

9. The IPC activates the **DMA Acknowledge-2 (DACK2)**, signal which is applied to the expansion slot and to the peripheral device (FDD unit) to enable it.

10. The IPC directs the data transfer from the FDC to RAM memory (data does not flow through the controller).

11. As the last byte is transferred, the **Terminal Count (T/C)** and EOP signals should be generated simultaneously if the transfer has been carried out successfully.

Memory Systems

> Normally three types of semiconductor memory are found on a typical system board. These include the system's ROM BIOS ICs, the system's RAM memory, and the second-level cache memory unit.

A+ CORE 4.3   A typical PC system board uses one or two 256KB/128KB x 8 ROM chips to hold the system's BIOS firmware. The system's memory map reserves memory locations from F0000h to FFFFFh. These chips contain the firmware routines to handle startup of the system, the changeover to disk-based operations, video and printer output functions, and the Power-On Self-Test.

A+ CORE 4.2   Basically two types of semiconductor RAM exist: **static RAM (SRAM)** and **dynamic RAM (DRAM)** used on system boards. Although they both perform the same types of functions, the methods they use are completely different. Static RAM stores bits in such a manner that they remain as long as power to the chip is not interrupted. Dynamic RAM requires periodic refreshing to maintain data, even if electrical power is applied to the chip.

Dynamic RAM stores data bits on rows and columns of IC capacitors. Capacitors lose their charge over time, and this is why dynamic RAM devices require data-refreshing operations. Static RAM uses IC transistors to store data and maintain it as long as power is supplied to the chip. Its transistor structure makes SRAM memory much faster than DRAM. However, static RAM can store only about 25% as much data in a given size as a DRAM device. Therefore, it tends to be more expensive to create large memories with SRAM.

Whether the RAM is made up of static or dynamic RAM devices, all RAM systems have the disadvantage of being volatile. This means that any data stored in RAM will be lost if power to the computer is disrupted for any reason. On the other hand, both types of RAM have the advantage of being fast and can be written to and read from with equal ease.

Generally, static RAM is used in smaller memory systems, such as cache and video memories, where the added cost of refresh circuitry would increase the cost-per-bit of storage. Cache memory is a special memory structure that works directly with the microprocessor; video memory is a specialized area that holds information to be displayed onscreen. On the other hand, DRAM is used in larger memory systems, such as the system's main memory, where the extra cost of refresh circuitry is distributed over a greater number of bits and is offset by the reduced operating cost associated with DRAM chips.

Memory Overhead

It has already been mentioned that the DRAM devices commonly used for the system's RAM require periodic refreshing of their data. Regular reading and writing of the system's memory performs some refreshing simply. However, additional circuitry must be used to ensure that every bit in the memory is refreshed within the allotted time frame. In addition to the circuitry, the reading and writing times used for refreshing must be taken into account when designing the system.

Another design factor associated with RAM is data **error detection**. A single incorrect bit can shut down the entire system instantly. With bits constantly moving in and out of RAM, it is crucial that all the bits be transferred correctly. The most popular form of error detection in PC-compatibles is **parity checking**. In this method, an extra bit is added to each word in RAM and is checked each time that it is used. As with refreshing, parity checking requires additional circuitry and memory overhead to operate.

DRAM Refresh

Dynamic RAM devices require that data stored in them be **refreshed**, or rewritten, periodically to keep it from fading away. As a matter of fact, each bit in the DRAM must be refreshed at least once every 2 milliseconds, or the data will dissipate. Because it can't be assumed that each bit in the memory will be accessed during the normal operation of the system (within the time frame allotted); the need to constantly refresh the data in the DRAM requires special circuitry to perform this function.

The extra circuitry and inconvenience associated with refreshing may initially make DRAM memory seem like a distant second choice behind static RAM. However, due to the simplicity of DRAM's internal structure, the bit-storage capacity of a DRAM chip is much greater than that of a similar static RAM chip; furthermore, DRAM offers a much lower rate of power consumption. Both of these factors contribute to making DRAM memory the economical choice in certain RAM memory systems—even in light of the extra circuitry necessary for refreshing.

Parity Checking

A+ CORE 4.2

Parity is a simple self-test used to detect RAM read-back errors. When a data byte is being stored in memory, the occurrences of logic "1s" in the byte are added by the parity generator/checker chip. This chip produces a parity bit that is added to and stored with the data byte. Therefore, the data byte becomes a 9-bit word. Whenever the data word is read back from the memory, the parity bit is reapplied to the parity generator and is recalculated. The recalculated parity value is then compared to the original parity value stored in memory. If the values do not match, a parity-error condition occurs and an error message is generated. Traditionally, two approaches to generating parity bits exist: The parity bit may be generated so that the total number of 1-bits equals either an even number (**even parity**) or an odd number (**odd parity**).

A+ CORE 4.4

To enable parity checking, an additional ninth bit is added to each byte stored in DRAM. On older systems, an extra memory chip was included with each bank of DRAM. In newer units, the extra storage is built into the SIMM and DIMM modules. Whether a particular system employs parity checking or not depends on its chip set. Many newer chip sets have moved away from using parity checking altogether. In these cases, SIMMs and DIMMs with parity capability can be used, but the parity function will not perform. In Pentium systems, the system board's user's guide or the BIOS' Extended CMOS Setup screen should be consulted to determine whether parity is supported. If so, the parity function can be enabled through this screen.

The system's parity generator/checker circuitry consisted of discrete 74LS280 ICs in the original PC, PC-XT, PC-AT, and 80386-based compatibles. Figure 6.33 illustrates how the system's RAM and parity-checking circuit work together.

FIGURE 6.33

How parity checking works.

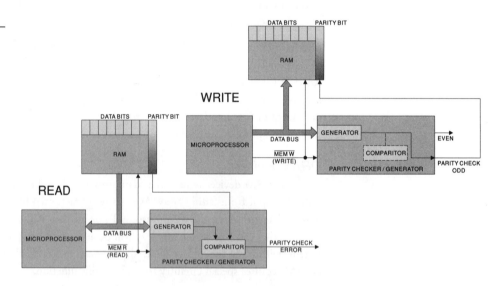

With the advent of the 80486 processor, the parity-checking function is built directly into the microprocessor. However, some 486 and Pentium system boards retain the discrete parity generator/checkers for DMA data.

When a parity error occurs, an NMI signal is co-generated in the system, causing the BIOS to execute its NMI handler routine. This routine normally places a parity error message on the screen, along with an option to shut down the system or continue.

Advanced Memory Structures

As the operating speeds of microcomputers have continued to increase, it has become increasingly necessary to develop new memory strategies to keep pace with the other parts of the system. Some of these methods, such as developing faster DRAM chips or including wait states in the memory-access cycles, are very fundamental in nature. However, these methods do not enable the entire system to operate at its full potential. Other more elaborate memory management schemes have been employed on faster computers to maximize their overall performance.

Cache Memory

One method of increasing the memory-access speed of a computer is called **caching**. This memory-management method assumes that most memory accesses are made within a limited block of addresses. Therefore, if the contents of these addresses are relocated into a special section of high-speed SRAM, then the microprocessor could access these locations without requiring any wait states.

Cache memory is normally small, to keep the cost of the system as low as possible. However, it is also very fast, even in comparison to fast DRAM devices.

Cache memory operations require a great deal of intelligent circuitry to operate and monitor the cache effectively. The cache controller circuitry must monitor the microprocessor's memory-access instructions to determine whether the specified data is stored in the cache. If the information is in the cache, the control circuitry can present it to the microprocessor without incurring any wait states. This is referred to as a **hit**. If the information is not located in the cache, the access is passed on to the system's RAM and is declared a **miss**.

The primary objective of the cache memory's control system is to maximize the ratio of hits to total accesses (hit rate) so that the majority of memory accesses are performed without wait states. One way to do this is to make the cache memory area as large as possible (thus raising the possibility of the desired information in the cache). However, the relative cost, energy consumption, and physical size of SRAM devices work against this technique. Practical sizes for cache memories run between 16KB and 256KB.

Two basic methods exist for writing updated information into the cache. The first is to write data into the cache and the main memory at the same time. This is referred to as **write thru cache**. This method tends to be slow because the microprocessor must wait for the slow DRAM access to be completed. The second method is known as **write back cache**. A write back cache holds the data in the cache until the system has a quiet time and then writes it into the main memory.

A+ CORE 4.3

The 80486 and Pentium microprocessors have a built-in first-level cache that can be used for both instructions and data. The internal cache is divided into four 2KB blocks containing 128 sets of 16-byte lines each. Control of the internal cache is handled directly by the microprocessor. The first-level cache is also known as an L1 cache. However, many system boards extend the caching capability of the microprocessor by adding an external second-level 128/256KB-memory cache. As with the L1 cache, the second-level cache may also be referred to as an L2 cache. An external L2 cache memory system is depicted in Figure 6.34.

Both types of RAM are brought together to create an improved DRAM, referred to as **enhanced DRAM (EDRAM)**. By integrating an SRAM component into a DRAM device, a performance improvement of 40% can be gained. An independent write path enables the system to input new data without affecting the operation of the rest of the chip. These devices are used primarily in L2 cache memories.

SRAM is available in a number of different types:

▶ **Asynchronous SRAM** is standard SRAM that delivers data from the memory to the microprocessor and returns it to the cache in one clock cycle.

▶ **Synchronous SRAM** uses special buffer storage to deliver data to the CPU in one clock cycle after the first cycle. The first address is stored and retrieves the data as the next address is on its way to the cache.

▶ **Pipeline SRAM** uses three clock cycles to fetch the first data and then accesses addresses within the selected page on each clock cycle.

▶ **Burst mode SRAM** loads a number of consecutive data locations from the cache over several clock cycles, based on a single address from the microprocessor.

FIGURE 6.34

An external cache.

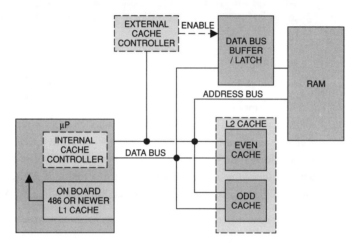

Memory Paging and Interleaving

Other commonly used methods of organizing RAM memory exist so that this memory can be accessed more efficiently. Typically, memory accesses occur in two fashions: instruction fetches (which are generally sequential) and operand accesses (which tend to be random). **Paging** and **interleaving** memory schemes are designed to take advantage of the sequential nature of instruction fetches from memory.

The basic idea of paged-mode DRAM operations is illustrated in Figure 6.35. Special memory devices called **Page-Mode** (or **Static-Column**) **RAM** are required for memory paging structures. In these memory devices, data is organized into groups of rows and columns, called **pages**. When a ROW access is made in the device, it is possible to access other column addresses within the same row without pre-charging its **Row Address Strobe** (**RAS**) line. This feature produces access times that are half that of normal DRAM memories. **Fast Page Mode RAM** is a quicker version of page-mode RAM, with improved **Column Address Strobe** (**CAS**) access speed.

FIGURE 6.35

Page-mode DRAM operation.

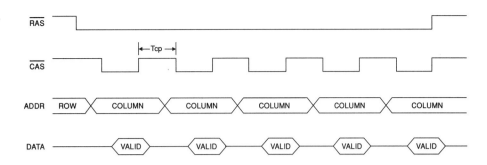

A+ CORE 4.2 The operating principal behind memory interleaving is depicted in Figure 6.36. Typical interleaving schemes divide the memory into two **banks** of RAM, with one bank storing even addresses and the other storing odd addresses. The RAS signals of the two banks overlap so that the time required to pre-charge one bank's RAS line is used for the active RAS time of the other bank. Therefore, there should never be a pre-charge time for either bank as long as the accesses continue to be sequential. If a nonsequential access occurs, a miss is encountered and a wait state must be inserted into the timing. If the memory is organized into two banks, the operation is referred to as two-way interleaving. It is also common to organize the memory into four equal-sized banks. This organization effectively doubles the average 0 wait-state hit space in the memory.

FIGURE 6.36

Memory interleaving.

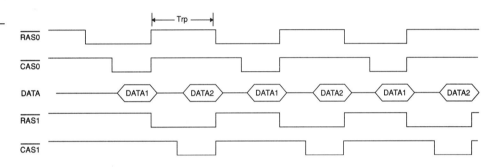

Other RAM Types

A+ CORE 4.2 Another modified DRAM, referred to as **Synchronous DRAM (SDRAM)**, uses special internal registers and clocks to organize data requests from memory. This enables the microprocessor to perform other tasks while the data is being organized.

Extended data out (EDO) memory increases the speed at which RAM operations are conducted by cutting out the 10 nanosecond wait time normally required between issuing memory addresses. This is accomplished by not disabling the data bus pins between bus cycles. EDO is an advanced type of fast page-mode RAM also referred to as **hyper page mode RAM**. The advantage of EDO RAM is encountered when multiple sequential memory accesses are performed. By not turning off the data pin, each successive access after the first access is accomplished in two clock cycles instead of three.

Special memory devices have also been designed to optimize video-memory–related activities. Among these are **video RAM (VRAM)** and **Windows RAM (WRAM)**. In typical DRAM devices, access to the data stored inside is shared between the system microprocessor and the video controller. The microprocessor accesses the RAM to update the data in it and to keep it refreshed. The video controller moves data out of the memory to make it screen information. Normally, both devices must access the data through the same data bus. VRAM employs a special **dual-port access** system to speed up video operations.

WRAM is a special version of VRAM optimized to transfer blocks of data at a time. This enables it to operate at speeds of up to 150% of typical VRAM—and costs up to 20% less.

On-Board I/O

When dealing with a PC-compatible, you must contend with two forms of I/O. These include the system board's **on-board I/O** and peripheral devices that interact with the system through its expansion slots.

In a PC-compatible system, some system I/O addresses are associated with intelligent devices on the system board, such as the interrupt and DMA controllers, timer counter channels, and the keyboard controller. Other system I/O ports and their interfaces are located on optional plug-in cards. These easily installed options give the system a high degree of flexibility in adapting to a wide variety of peripheral devices.

Most of the I/O functions associated with PC-compatible systems have become so standardized that IC manufacturers produce them in single-chip ASIC formats. Figure 6.37 illustrates an IPC ASIC for standard AT-compatible system board functions.

FIGURE 6.37

On-board I/O.

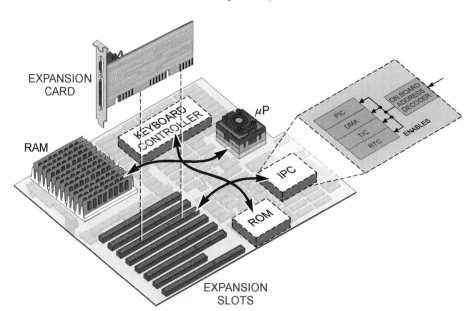

Certain I/O connections have become standards associated with PC-compatibles. These include the system's parallel printer ports, RS-232 serial ports, and the game port. Figure 6.38 depicts an M/IO ASIC for standard peripheral control.

In both cases, the I/O controllers integrated into the ASIC are responsible for matching signal levels and protocols between the system and the I/O device.

I/O Addressing

Each I/O device must have its own specific address. Computers can use two common methods to handle I/O addressing. In some computers, the microprocessor addresses I/O in the same manner as it does memory locations. This is because the I/O devices are granted a portion of the available address codes, and the same control signals are used to read and write both I/O and memory locations. This method of I/O addressing is referred to as **memory-mapped I/O**.

FIGURE 6.38

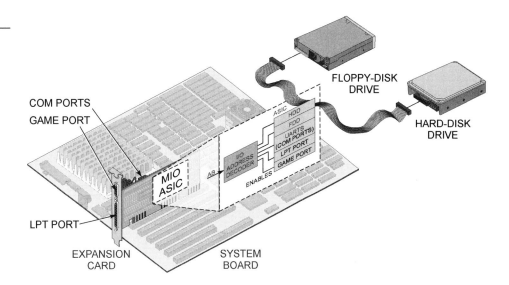

In the second method, separate microprocessor control signals and address decoders are used for I/O addressing. Microprocessors in these systems use separate outputs such as **memory request (MREQ)** and **I/O request (IORQ)** to distinguish between memory and I/O operations. This practice of distinguishing between memory and I/O addressing is the more accepted method of handling I/O and is referred to as **direct I/O** or **isolated I/O**.

Advantages and disadvantages exist for both addressing methods. In the memory-mapped method, the same instructions used to reference memory can also be used to move data to or from an I/O device. However, the I/O devices use up a portion of the available address codes, limiting the actual amount of storage available in the memory. In direct I/O systems, none of the memory allocations are used up by I/O devices, but extra control lines are required.

Address Decoding

As the microprocessor's address bus runs through the system and connects the various components, the binary information on the bus is decoded into a single signal. This decoded signal is used to access the one location in the system where a data read or write is to be performed.

In IBM-compatible systems, the microprocessor differentiates between memory and I/O accesses because these activities are specified by different instructions in the instruction set. Data transfers between the microprocessor and memory locations, or between the microprocessor's internal registers, are called for by program code that takes the form of an assembly language **move instruction** (MOV), as described here:

> **MOV** (destination memory location; source memory location). Input and Output operations are carried out between the microprocessor and an I/O port when an IN or OUT assembly language instruction is encountered.
>
> **IN** (microprocessor register location; I/O port location).
>
> **OUT** (I/O port location; microprocessor register). The microprocessor responds to these different types of instructions by applying an appropriate logic level to its M/IO pin. The microprocessor holds the M/IO pin active for the MOV instruction and deactivates it when an IN or an OUT instruction is executed.

The system treats its onboard intelligent devices as I/O addresses. The onboard address decoder, like the one displayed in Figure 6.39, converts address bits from the address bus into chip-select enabling bits for the system's intelligent devices. These addresses are included in the overall I/O addressing map of the system.

FIGURE 6.39

Address decoding.

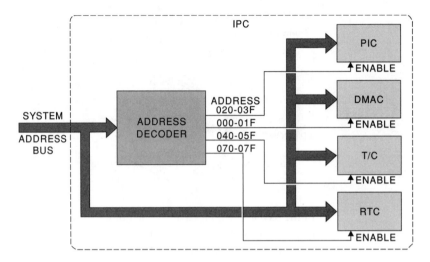

The various I/O port addresses listed in Table 6.8 are used by standard I/O adapters in the PC-compatible system. Notice that these addresses are redundant with those stated for the system's interrupt vectors given in Table 6.9. This method of addressing is referred to as **redundant addressing**. Figure 6.40 illustrates how a system address is routed through the system to an I/O port location.

Table 6.8   *I/O Port Addresses*

Hex Address	Device	Usage
000–01F	DMA controller (IPC)	System
020–03F	Interrupt controller (IPC)	System
040–05F	Timer/counter (IPC)	System
060–06F	Keyboard controller	System
070–07F	Real-time clock, NMI mask (IPC)	System
080–09F	DMA page register (IPC)	System
0A0–0BF	Interrupt controller (IPC)	System
0F0	Clear math coprocessor busy	System
0F1	Reset math coprocessor	System
0F8–0FF	Math coprocessor	System
1F0–1F8	Hard-disk controller	I/O
200–207	Game port	I/O
278–27F	Parallel printer port #2	I/O
2F8–2FF	Serial port #2	I/O
378–37F	Parallel printer port #1	I/O
3B0–3BF	MGA/First printer port	I/O
3D0–3DF	CGA	I/O
3F0–3F7	FDD controller	I/O
3F8–3FF	Serial port #1	I/O

Table 6.9 *System Memory Map*

Address	Function
0–3FF	Interrupt vectors
400–47F	ROM-BIOS RAM
480–5FF	BASIC and special system function RAM
600–9FFFF	Program memory
0A0000–0AFFFF	VGA/EGA display memory
0B0000–0B0FFF	Monochrome display adapter memory
0B8000–0BFFFF	Color graphics adapter memory
0C0000–0CFFFF	Hard-disk ROM
0D0000–0D7FFF	Spare ROM
0D8000–0DFFFF	Spare ROM
0E0000–0E7FFF	Spare ROM
0E8000–0EFFFF	Spare ROM
0F0000–0F3FFF	Spare ROM
0F4000–0F7FFF	Spare ROM
0F8000–0FBFFF	Spare ROM
0FC000–0FDFFF	ROM BIOS
0FE000–0FFFFF	ROM BIOS

FIGURE 6.40

Address routing to an I/O port.

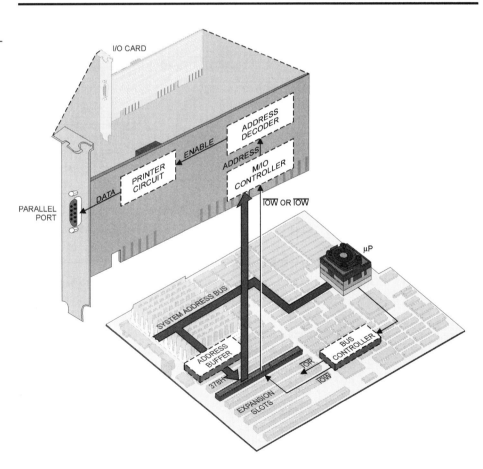

Expansion Slots

> The system's expansion slots provide the connecting point for most of its I/O devices. Interface cards communicate with the system through the extended microprocessor buses in these slots.

As mentioned in Chapter 1, expansion slots basically come in three formats: 8-bit, 16-bit, and 32-bit data buses. The **PC-bus** slot is the most famous example of an 8-bit expansion slot, and the ISA slot is the consummate 16-bit expansion bus. The 32-bit expansion buses include the MCA bus, the EISA bus, the VESA bus, and the PCI bus.

PC-Bus Expansion Slot

This expansion bus provided the I/O channel in the original PC, PC-XT, and their compatibles. It became the de facto connection standard in the industry for 8-bit systems. Figure 6.41 shows how the PC-bus's 62 lines are arranged at the expansion slot's connector.

FIGURE 6.41

Standard PC-bus expansion slot.

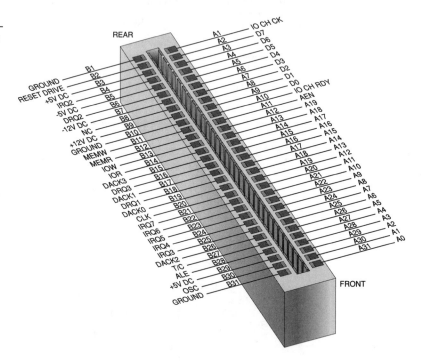

ISA Expansion Slots

 A+ CORE 4.3

The 16-bit **Industry Standard Architecture (ISA)** slot is the most common expansion slot used with microcomputers. This bus specification originally appeared on the 16-bit, 80286-based PC-AT system board. At that time it was called the **AT bus**. However, its widespread acceptance earned it the ISA title it now carries. Even in units that have newer, faster 32-bit expansion slots, it is not uncommon to find one or more ISA slots. Figure 6.42 presents the signal lines of the ISA-compatible expansion slot connector.

Notice that although the physical aspects are identical, some of the pins of the 62-pin expansion slot have been redefined from the PC-bus. In particular, pins SLB4 and SLB19 have been changed from IRQ2 and DACK0 to IRQ9 and REFRESH, respectively. The definition of SLB8 has changed from Reserved to 0WS, a line used with memory devices to enable 0 wait-state operations. Finally, many of the address, data, and control lines have had an "S" (for system) identifier added to their definitions.

FIGURE 6.42

The ISA expansion slot.

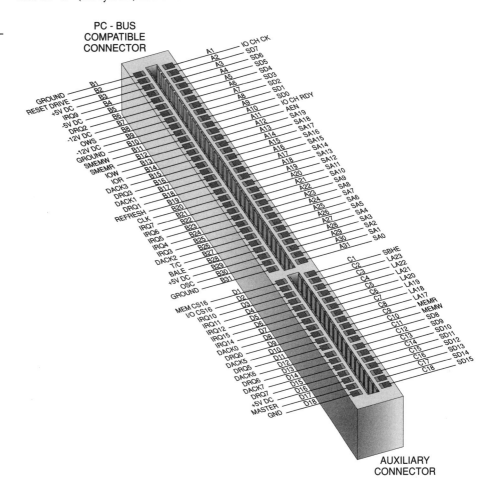

One of the most interesting features of the 36-pin auxiliary slot is the presence of a second pair of read/write enable lines: MEMR and MEMW. These lines serve memory locations associated with the highest four address bits (LA20–LA23). Addresses in the lowest megabyte of memory are served by the SMEMR and SMEMW lines in the 62-pin slot.

On many AT-compatible system boards, it is common to find that the designer has retained two or three of the 62-pin, 8-bit PC-bus expansion slots. Only options adapter cards with a PC-bus-compatible, 8-bit edge connector can be used in these slots. However, this does not mean that these 8-bit cards must be installed in one of the 8-bit slots; they function just as well if they are placed in the 62-pin portion of an ISA-compatible 16-bit slot.

Advanced 32-Bit Architectures

As 32-bit microprocessors have gained popularity, the shortcomings and restrictions of the 16-bit ISA bus have become more noticeable. As we have already noted, the ISA bus cannot support the full 32-bit capabilities of microprocessors such as the 80386DX and i486. In addition, the physical organization of the signal lines in the ISA bus produce unacceptable levels of **radio frequency interference** (**RFI**) as the bus speed increases.

When the 80386DX first appeared, some manufacturers began producing computers that reserved one special 32-bit expansion slot for proprietary I/O cards. The 32-bit slot is usually constructed by adding a second 62-pin connector to the standard 8-bit PC-bus connector. The signals in the first portion of the connector are normally identical to those of the normal PC-bus slots. The manufacturer adds all the new address, data, and control signals for the 32-bit function to the second 62-pin connector. All other expansion slots remain ISA-compatible.

Most of the I/O boards produced for these slots are large memory cards that enable the system's microprocessor and memory to operate together (at very high speeds), separately from the system board's I/O functions. The slot effectively provides a 32-bit memory bus structure that works in parallel with the system's main bus. This technique of separating the buses is called **bifurcation**.

The main problem with this approach to achieving a 32-bit expansion bus is the lack of compatibility that results. Because the memory boards are proprietary, it is not usually possible to use one manufacturer's memory card in another manufacturer's system board. In addition, a large part of what personal computers do involves accessing disks, video output systems, and other I/O devices. Therefore, the system will still be prevented from performing at its maximum potential much of the time.

Two legitimate 32-bit bus standards have been developed to take advantage of the full power of the 32-bit microprocessors. These are the **Expanded Industry Standard Architecture** (**EISA**) bus (which, as its name implies, is an extension of the existing ISA standard bus) and a new IBM-sponsored bus standard called **Micro Channel Architecture** (**MCA**).

EISA Systems

A+ CORE 4.3
The EISA bus specification, illustrated in Figure 6.43, naturally adds 16 more data lines and 16 additional address lines to the ISA bus. In the EISA design, all 32 address lines on the bus are latched so that they can hold the address information throughout the complete address cycle. Several of the control lines associated with more powerful microprocessors (such as the 80386DX and 80486) are extended directly to the EISA bus. These lines enable the system to transfer 8-, 16-, or 32-bit words.

Conversely, the standard also includes lines to enable I/O cards to specify the type of transfer they can perform. These are the EX16 and EX32 lines. If neither line is activated during a data transfer, the EISA system assumes that an 8-bit transfer is being performed. The EISA standard calls for systems to incorporate bus controller circuitry that automatically dissects larger data words into sizes manageable by the I/O card.

To retain compatibility with the older ISA options adapters, the clock speed of the bus must be restricted to between 6MHz and 10MHz in EISA systems. To overcome the relative slowness of the bus, the EISA standard provides two high-speed data-transfer options.

First, the EISA standard makes provisions to enable full burst-mode DMA transfers to occur. In typical PC architectures, DMA transfers are carried out one word at a time. However, the EISA structure enables the DMA controller to seize the bus and conduct continuous transfers.

The second high-speed data-transfer method allowed in the EISA specification is called **compressed transfer**. Using the compressed method causes the data to move twice as quickly across the bus as it normally would be.

Bus Mastering

The point where the EISA standard departs from previous microcomputer architecture occurs in its bus-sharing capabilities. The microcomputer systems you have studied thus far were designed on the premise that a single microprocessor (and maybe a math coprocessor) would be working on a single task. However, more powerful architectures, such as those of mainframe and minicomputers, enable multiple **bus masters** (microprocessors and intelligent controller devices) to access the bus and perform multitasking and parallel-processing applications. In these applications, it is possible for different processors within the system to divide the workload and attack different parts of a task simultaneously.

FIGURE 6.43

EISA bus specifications.

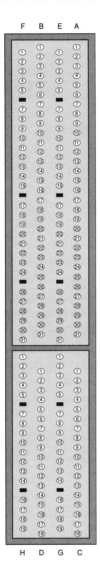

In these systems, options are divided into two categories: bus masters (those devices that can take control of the system's buses) and **slaves** (those devices that must be controlled by some other intelligent device). The EISA standard provides for up to seven bus masters (the system's microprocessor and six bus masters) to operate within the system at any given time.

Bus-mastering systems require special circuitry to act as a referee between all the potential bus masters within the system. This circuitry arbitrates between different devices that request access to the system buses at the same time, and decides which device should be given access. Under the EISA standard, arbitration levels are assigned to devices in a fixed three-tiered arrangement, as illustrated in Figure 6.44.

FIGURE 6.44

EISA bus mastering.

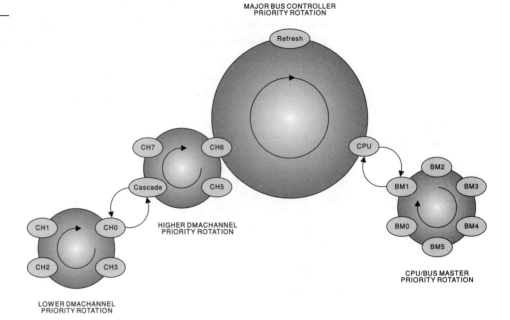

The highest level of access is given to the DRAM refresh circuitry, the second level of access is assigned to DMA operations, and the third level is shared between the system microprocessor and the other six possible bus masters. Different levels of priority are assigned to the different members of tiers two and three. For example, if several channels are requesting service when control is passed to the DMA phase of the cycle, then only the DMA channel with the highest priority assignment will be granted access to the buses at that time. Within the DMA channels, priority levels are assigned on a rotating basis. As the priority level is shifted around the upper tier of DMA channels, the cascade position is eventually reached. When this occurs, the DMA channel with the highest priority in the lower tier is granted access to the buses. After the DMA operation is completed, control shifts to the microprocessor/bus-master tier. As in the DMA tier, control in this tier passes back and forth between the microprocessor and bus-master positions. When control passes to the bus-master position, the bus master with the highest priority level is granted access to the buses.

The **bus-master arbitration** function is designed into a special VLSI bus controller device that contains the EISA-compatible bus control functions. Because hardware, not software, is used to control bus access, this action is referred to as **hardware-mediated bus arbitration**. Recall that it is possible to perform multitasking operations using a 286-based PC. However, in a typical ISA architecture, software is responsible for deciding when and how the system performs tasks. Therefore, multitasking in these computers is referred to as **software-mediated bus arbitration**.

When an expansion board containing a bus master desires to gain control of the system, it activates the slot's **Master Request (MREQx) line**. Each EISA slot has its own MREQ line. The "x" corresponds to the physical location of the slot on the board. The EISA standard enables each adapter card to be addressed independently. The EISA standard makes provisions for up to 15 slots to exist in a system.

Micro Channel (PS/2) Systems

The Micro Channel Architecture—which was invented, trademarked, and patented by IBM—provides computing potential that is more closely related to mainframe computers. This design has provisions that accommodate multitasking, as well as true parallel processing.

The MCA standard has built-in bus-sharing provisions that enable up to eight microprocessors and eight other bus masters to operate within the system.

In developing the Micro Channel Architecture, IBM disregarded any efforts to remain compatible with the ISA standard architecture. Indeed, the MCA standard stands alone in terms of hardware compatibility. The physical expansion connector is incompatible with the edge connectors on ISA adapter cards. In addition, the interface signals called for in the MCA standard are different in definition as well as layout. Therefore, the only source for PS/2 peripheral equipment is IBM, or one of its approved vendors. Conversely, IBM has maintained software compatibility among its PS/2 line and the older PC, XT, and AT lines.

The total Micro Channel signal layout is depicted in Figure 6.45. In the MCA standard, the organization of the signal lines can be broken down into three primary sections. First is a section of basic 8-bit signals (A/B01–A/B45), located at the rear of the card. A notch in the edge connector that is two contacts wide follows this section. The second section of signal lines is the 16-bit extension that runs between contact positions A/B48 and A/B58. The final section of standard signals is the 32-bit extension that runs from positions A/B59 to A/B89.

FIGURE 6.45

The MCA expansion slot signals.

Pin	FOIL (A) SIDE CONTACTS	FOIL (B) SIDE CONTACTS
	BASIC 8-BIT SECTION	BASIC 8-BIT SECTION
1	CARD SETUP	AUDIOGND
2	MADE 24	AUDIODAT
3	GND	GND
4	A11	OSC
5	A10	GND
6	A9	A23
7	+5V	A22
8	A8	A21
9	A7	GND
10	A6	A20
11	+5V	A19
12	A5	A18
13	A4	GND
14	A3	A17
15	+5V	A16
16	A2	A15
17	A1	GND
18	A0	A14
19	+12V	A13
20	ADL	A12
21	PREEMPT	GND
22	BURST	INT9
23	-12V	INT3
24	ARB0	INT4
25	ARB1	GND
26	ARB2	INT5
27	-12V	INT6
28	ARB3	INT7
29	ARBGRNT	GND
30	T/C	RESERVED
31	+5V	RESERVED
32	STATUS0	CHCK
33	STATUS1	GND
34	M/IO	COMMAND
35	+12V	CHRDY RETURN
36	CARDRDY	CARDSLCTFB
37	D0	GND
38	D2	D1
39	+5V	D3
40	D5	D4
41	D6	GND
42	D7	CHRESET
43	GND	RESERVED
44	DS16 RETURN	RESERVED
45	REFRESH	GND
46	NOTCH	NOTCH
	16-BIT SECTION	16-BIT SECTION
47	NOTCH	NOTCH
48	+5V	D8
49	D10	D9
50	D11	GND
51	D13	D12
52	+12V	D14
53	RESERVED	D15
54	SBHE	GND
55	DS16	INT10
56	+5V	INT11
57	INT14	INT12
58	INT15	GND
	32-BIT SECTION	32-BIT SECTION
59	RESERVED	RESERVED
60	RESERVED	RESERVED
61	GND	RESERVED
62	RESERVED	RESERVED
63	RESERVED	GND
64	RESERVED	D16
65	+12V	D17
66	D19	D18
67	D20	GND
68	D21	D22
69	+5V	D23
70	D24	RESERVED
71	D25	GND
72	D26	D27
73	+5V	D28
74	D30	D29
75	D31	GND
76	RESERVED	BE0
77	+12V	BE1
78	BE3	BE2
79	DS32 RETURN	GND
80	DS32	TRANSLATE32
81	+12V	A24
82	A26	A25
83	A27	GND
84	A28	A29
85	+5V	A30
86	RESERVED	A31
87	RESERVED	GND
88	RESERVED	RESERVED
89	GND	RESERVED

AUXILLIARY VIDEO EXTENSION

Pin	FOIL (A)	FOIL (B)
V0	NOTCH	NOTCH
V1	VIDEO	GND
V2	VIDDAT7	VIDDAT0
V3	GND	VIDDAT1
V4	DOTCLK	VIDDAT2
V5	EDCLK	GND
V6	VIDDAT6	VIDDAT3
V7	GND	VIDDAT4
V8	BLANKING	VIDDAT5
V9	HORZ SYNC	GND
V10	VERT SYNC	ESYNC

MATCHED MEMORY EXTENSION

Pin	FOIL (A)	FOIL (B)
M1	MATCHED MEM CYC	RESERVED
M2	GND	MATCHED MEM CYC RQST
M3	MATCHED MEM CYC COMMAND	RESERVED
M4	RESERVED	GND

The MCA bus standard also provides signal and connector specifications for a pair of auxiliary interface connections. These are the **auxiliary video extension** and the 32-bit **matched memory extension**. The video extension to the bus is a small auxiliary connector (usually included with only one of the expansion slots) that grants access to the system's built-in VGA circuitry.

The 32-bit matched memory extension enables I/O cards with higher-speed capabilities to signal the microprocessor that they can operate faster. This, in turn, causes the system to transfer the information 25% faster.

Many of these signals are similar to those already discussed in association with the PC-bus, the ISA bus, and the EISA bus. Of course, the most notable features of the interface are that the address and data buses have been expanded to the desired 32-bits.

The MCA design includes a single-channel analog audio line that provides audio output, with a frequency range of nearly 10KHz, that approaches the quality of an FM radio signal.

The video extension connector is normally added to one of the slots in the MCA system. This extension grants video enhancement cards access to the VGA-compatible circuitry that is built into MCA system boards. The extension's signals must be applied to D/A converters before it can be used to drive a VGA monitor.

Another important aspect of the interface layout is that it incorporates a high number of ground lines placed adjacent to high-speed signal lines. This design technique enables the MCA bus to operate at much higher speeds than possible before, while generating much less RFI. The MCA bus is capable of operating at frequencies as high as 80MHz without generating unacceptable levels of RFI.

MCA Bus Operations

Many of the new signal lines in the MCA bus are dedicated to coordinating bus activities between the different microprocessors and bus masters that can be combined in the Micro Channel-based system. These lines arbitrate between the different devices wanting to gain access to the bus to keep them from interfering with each other.

During the configuration process, the system creates a set of disk files, called the **adapter description files**, in which it stores each expansion card's assigned priority level, along with other information related to the card. The individual expansion cards supply this information when their slot's **CARDSETUP line** is activated. Likewise, the expansion card confirms that it is at its correct address by activating its **Card Selected Feedback line** during configuration and diagnostic situations.

When the system boots up, the software routine compares the contents of the disk files with information stored in the system's CMOS setup memory to verify that the hardware's configuration has not changed. The boot-up software also reads a section of firmware from each expansion card to obtain their ID numbers. Their manufacturers assign these numbers to the cards when they are made. The startup software compares the information found on the cards with the CMOS and disk-file configuration information to ensure that the current setup is correct. The card's firmware also contains information concerning its installation and use within the system.

During normal operation of the system, MCA-compatible cards routinely exchange information with system devices concerning their bus sizes. The intelligent devices that control the system signify the size of the information they are placing on the data bus by activating either the **Card Data Size 16** or **Card Data Size 32** line. The cards respond by activating either the **Data Size 16 Return** or **Data Size 32 Return** line. Similarly, the system's intelligent devices can specify whether they are using 24-bit, 80286-compatible or extended 32-bit, 80386-compatible addresses by activating (or not activating) the **Memory Address Enable 24** line.

Proprietary Bus Designs

Even though other advanced bus specifications added more data lines to their expansion slot, they continued to operate at about 8MHz to 10 MHz. These low bus speeds were required to ensure that compatibility with older I/O cards was maintained. **Local buses** are designed to improve system performance by enabling the devices attached to the bus to operate directly with the system's microprocessor. These devices operate at speeds nearly equal to that of the microprocessor's clock speed. The most famous local buses are the PCI and VESA buses.

PCI Local Bus

A+ CORE 4.3 Figure 6.46 illustrates the structure of the **Peripheral Component Interconnect (PCI)** local bus components.

> The main component in the PCI bus is the PCI bus controller, called the **host bridge**. This device monitors the microprocessor's address bus to determine whether addresses are intended for devices in a PCI slot or for one of the system board's other types of expansion slots. Each PCI adapter can perform up to eight different functions and support multiple bus-mastering cards on the bus.

In PC-compatible systems, the PCI bus normally co-exists with the ISA bus. The PCI portion of the bus structure functions as a **mezzanine bus** removed from the system's main bus system. Figure 6.46 depicts a PCI-to-ISA bridge that enables ISA adapters to be used in the PCI system. Other bridge devices can also be used to accommodate either EISA or MCA adapters.

FIGURE 6.46

PCI bus structure.

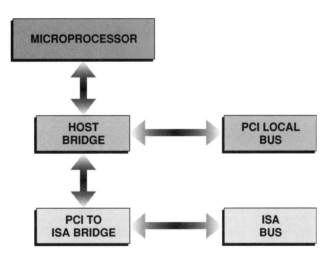

The host bridge routes 32-bit PCI data directly to the expansion slots through the local bus. These transfers occur at speeds compatible with the microprocessor. The host bridge routes non-PCI data to the ISA bridge, which converts it into a format compatible with the expansion slot. In the case of ISA slots, the data is converted from 32-bits to the 16-bit ISA format. These transfers occur at typical ISA bus speeds. In EISA and MCA machines, the data is simply rerouted in 32-bit format.

The PCI bus specification also uses the host bridge to buffer its bus lines, and it supports data buffering for **burst write operations**. A burst write operation is performed when the processor supplies a beginning address and then outputs only data to be written to consecutive address locations. The PCI bus even supports burst writes for systems that include a microprocessor, such as an 80386, that doesn't have burst write capability. Unlike other designs that have a fixed length for a burst write, PCI burst writes can be of indefinite length.

Figure 6.47 shows the pinout of a PCI connector. The PCI local bus specification uses multiplexed address and data lines to conserve the pins of the basic 62-pin PCI connector. Within this connector are signals for control, interrupt, cache support, error reporting, and arbitration.

FIGURE 6.47

PCI slot pinout.

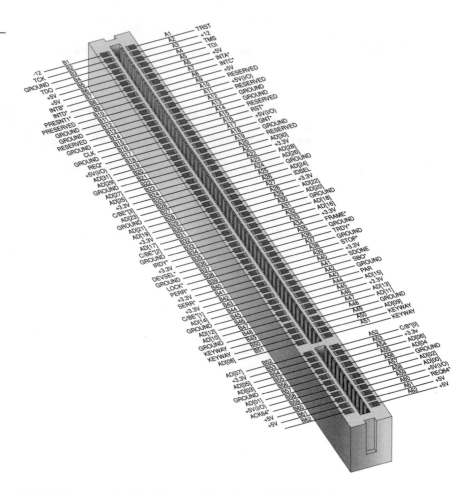

The PCI bus uses 32-bit address and data buses (AD0–AD31).

However, its specification also defines 64-bit multiplexed address and data buses for use with 64-bit processors such as the Pentium. The CLK line was originally defined for a maximum clock frequency of 33MHz and a 132MBps-transfer rate, but it can be used with microprocessors operating at higher clock frequencies (66MHz under the PCI 2.1 specification).

The **Request (REQ)** and **Grant (GNT)** lines provide arbitration conventions for bus-mastering operations. The arbitration logic is contained in the host bridge. To provide for faster access, a bus master can request use of the bus while the current bus cycle is in progress. When the current bus cycle ends, the master can immediately begin to transfer data, assuming the request has been granted.

The bus master uses bus commands to specify the type of transaction to be performed. These commands are encoded on the **Command/Byte Enable lines (C/BE0–C/BE3)**. These four lines are driven with command information during the first portion of the bus cycle, called the address phase. The lines then switch to byte-enable lines for the remaining portion of the bus cycle. The byte-enable pins duplicate the operation of the byte enables on the 80386DX,

80486, and Pentium microprocessors. The commands issued by the bus master include interrupt acknowledge (INTA), I/O read (IOR), I/O write (IOW), memory read (MEMR), memory write (MEMW), configuration read (CR), and configuration write (CW).

PCI Configuration

The PCI standard is part of the Plug-and-Play hardware standard. As such, the system's BIOS and system software must support the PCI standard. Although the PCI function is self-configuring, many of its settings can be viewed and altered through the CMOS setup utility. Figure 6.48 depicts the PCI PnP configuration information from a typical BIOS.

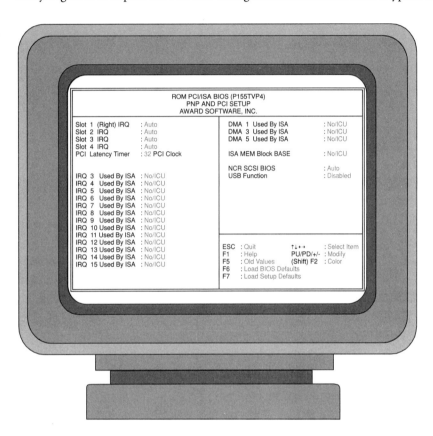

During boot-up, the PCI PnP-compatible BIOS checks the system for devices installed in the expansion slots to see what types they are, how they are configured, and which slots they are in. For PnP-compatible PCI cards, this information is held in a ROM device on the adapter card. As described in the Boot-up section of Chapter 3, "Troubleshooting the System," the BIOS reads the information from all the cards and then assigns each adapter a logical name (**handle**) in the PnP registry. It then stores the configuration information for the various adapters in the registry as well. This process is described in Figure 6.49. Next, the BIOS checks the adapter information against the system's basic configuration for resource conflicts. After evaluating the requirements of the cards and the system's resources, the PnP routine assigns system resources to the cards as required.

Depending on the CMOS settings available with a particular PCI chip set, the startup procedure may be set up to configure and activate all the PnP devices at startup. With other PCI chip sets, it may also be possible to check all cards but only enable those actually needed for startup. Some CMOS routines may contain several user-definable PCI configuration settings. Typically, these settings should be left in default positions. The rare occasion for changing a PCI setting occurs when directed to do so by a product's installation guide.

FIGURE 6.49

PCI information acquisition.

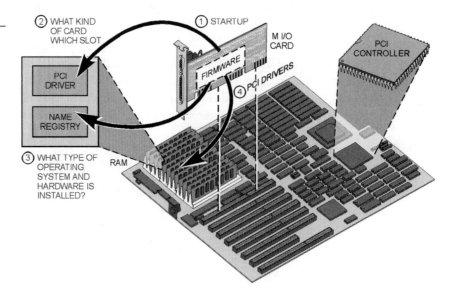

Systems may theoretically contain an unlimited number of PCI slots. However, a maximum of four slots is normally used on a system board due to signal loading considerations. The PCI bus includes four internal interrupt lines (INTa–INTd, or INT1–INT4) that enable each PCI slot to activate up to four different interrupts. PCI interrupts should not be confused with the system's IRQ channels, although they can be associated with them if required by a particular device. In these cases, IRQ9 and IRQ10 are typically used.

The **latency timer** value in the figure refers to the length of time a PCI device can maintain control of the bus after another device has requested it. This feature is necessary because the PCI bus runs much faster than the ISA bus. The latency timer setting defines how long the PCI bus will wait for the ISA bus. Values assigned to the timer range from 0 to 255, with the lower number representing quicker access to the bus.

In the example CMOS configuration screen, a block of memory in the UMA can be set aside as an **ISA memory block base area**. This feature enables the system to temporarily write data to a buffer memory so that the microprocessor is not disturbed. Data from the buffer can be handled as system priorities allow.

VESA Local Bus

A+ CORE 4.3   Figure 6.50 illustrates the flow of information through the **VL-bus**-based computer. It also indicates data-transfer priority levels.

> As with the PCI bus, the VL-bus controller monitors the microprocessor's control signals and addresses on the local bus to determine what type of operation is being performed and where the address is located in the system.

The highest level of activity occurs between the microprocessor and the system's cache memory unit. The second level of priority exists between the microprocessor and the system's DRAM memory unit. The third priority level is between the microprocessor and the

VL-bus controller. The final priority level exists between the VL-bus controller and the non-VESA bus controller.

VL-bus data is passed to the VESA slots on the local bus in 32-bit format at VL-bus speeds. The VL-bus controller passes non-VESA data to the ISA bus controller to be applied to the ISA expansion slots. These transfers are carried out in 16-bit ISA format at ISA-compatible speeds.

FIGURE 6.50

VL-bus block diagram.

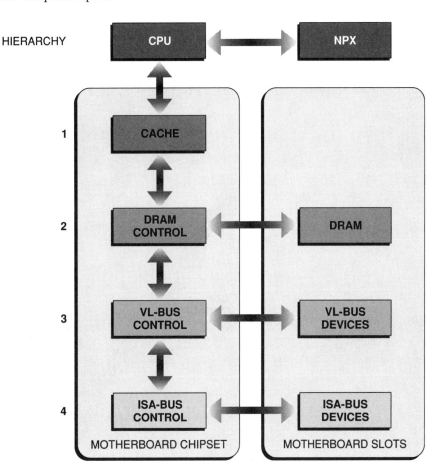

The VL-bus also defines the operation of devices connected to the bus and classifies them as **local bus controller**, **local bus master**, or **local bus target**. The local bus controller arbitrates requests for use of the bus between the microprocessor and local bus masters. A local bus master is any device, such as a SCSI controller, that is capable of initiating data transfers on the VL-bus. A local bus target is any device capable of only answering requests for a data transfer. The data transfer can be either a read or a write operation. The VL-bus also supports burst writes for faster transfers and increased efficiency.

The VL-bus connection pinout is shown in Figure 6.51.

The VL local bus clock can operate at speeds up to 66MHz. However, if the VL-bus devices are installed into an expansion slot, the maximum frequency allowed is 50MHz. The 66MHz-clock rate can be used only if the VL-bus device is built directly on the system board.

The PCI bus is more widely used on Pentium system boards, but the VL-bus offers higher performance and lower costs than similar boards with PCI buses. In addition, the VL bus is typically implemented in such a way that 16-bit ISA cards can use the traditional part of the expansion slot.

FIGURE 6.51

VL-bus pinout.

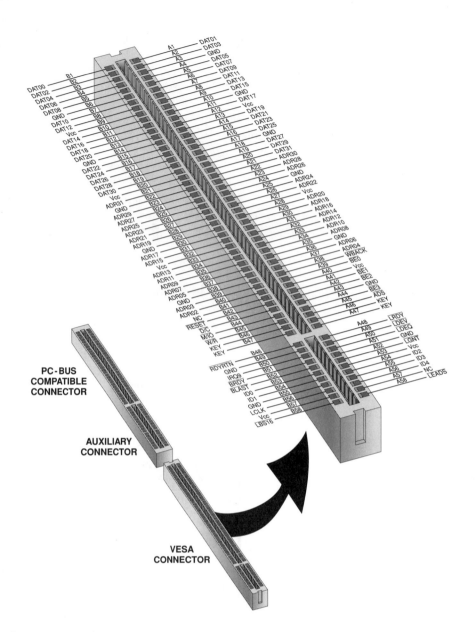

PCMCIA Slots

A+ CORE 4.3   As more desktop users began to use laptop and notebook computers, they demanded that additional peripheral systems be included. With the limited space associated with these units, it became clear that a new method for installing options would need to be developed. At first, laptop and notebook manufacturers included proprietary expansion connections for adding such devices as fax/modems, additional memory, and additional storage devices.

A+ CORE 6.1   In 1989, the PCMCIA bus was introduced with the **68-pin JEIDA connector standard**, depicted in Figure 6.52. A small form-factor expansion-card format was also adopted for use. This format was derived from earlier laptop/notebook memory card designs. The definitions of the connector's 68 pins, listed in Table 6.10, enable the interface to be used for a wide variety of peripheral devices.

FIGURE 6.52

PCMCIA connector standard.

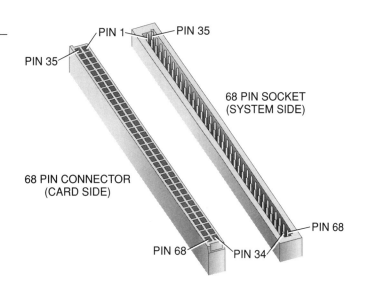

Table 6.10 *68-Pin Connector Definitions*

Pin	Name	Description	Pin	Name	Description
1	GND	Ground	35	GND	Ground
2	D3	Data bit 3	36	CD1	Card detect 1
3	D4	Data bit 4	37	D11	Data bit 11
4	D5	Data bit 5	38	D12	Data bit 12
5	D6	Data bit 6	39	D13	Data bit 13
6	D7	Data bit 7	40	D14	Data bit 14
7	CE1	Card enable 1	41	D15	Data bit 15
8	A10	Address bit 10	42	CE2	Card enable 2
9	OE	Output enable	43	RFSH	Refresh input
10	A11	Address bit 11	44	IORD	I/O Read strobe
11	A9	Address bit 9	45	IOWR	I/O Write strobe
12	A8	Address bit 8	46	A17	Address bit 17
13	A13	Address bit 13	47	A18	Address bit 18
14	A14	Address bit 14	48	A19	Address bit 19
15	WE/-PGM	Write enable	49	A20	Address bit 20
16	IREQ	Interrupt request	50	A21	Address bit 21
17	VCC	Card power	51	VCC	Card power
18	VPP1	Programming supply voltage 1	52	VPP2	Programming supply voltage 2
19	A16	Address bit 16	53	A22	Address bit 22
20	A15	Address bit 15	54	A23	Address bit 23
21	A12	Address bit 12	55	A24	Address bit 24
22	A7	Address bit 7	56	A25	Address bit 25
23	A6	Address bit 6	57	RFU	Reserved

continues

Table 6.10 *continued*

Pin	Name	Description	Pin	Name	Description
24	A5	Address bit 5	58	RESET	Card reset
25	A4	Address bit 4	59	WAIT	Extend bus cycle
26	A3	Address bit 3	60	INPACK	Input port acknowledge
27	A2	Address bit 2	61	REG	Register and IO select enable
28	A1	Address bit 1	62	SPKR	Digital audio waveform
29	A0	Address bit 0	63	STSGNG	Card status changed
30	D0	Data bit 0	64	D8	Data bit 8
31	D1	Data bit 1	65	D9	Data bit 9
32	D2	Data bit 2	66	10	Data bit 10
33	IOIS16	IO port is 16 bits	67	CD2	Card detect 2
34	GND	Ground	68	GND	Ground

The interface is designed so that it can be inserted into the unit while it is turned on (**hot insertion**). Although the PCMCIA connection scheme was never intended to be used with a full-sized unit, its design is compatible with all the other bus types. As a matter of fact, PC-card adapters are available for use in desktop and tower units. These slots are often designed so that they can be mounted in a standard disk drive bay of the desktop's case.

The standard defines a methodology for software programmers to write standard drivers for PC-card devices. The standard is referred to as **Socket Services** and provides for a software head to identify the type of card being used, its capabilities, and its requirements. Its software can be executed directly on the card (instead of moving it into RAM for execution). This is referred to as **Execute In Place mode**. In addition, the cards for this standard can use the same file allocation system used by floppy- and hard-disk drives. This also increases the ease with which programmers can write code for PCMCIA devices.

System Board Upgrading

A+ CORE 1.10

Typically five serviceable components exist on the system board:

▶ The microprocessor

▶ The RAM modules

▶ The CMOS backup battery

▶ The ROM BIOS IC(s)

▶ The cache memory

Of the five items listed, three—the microprocessor, the RAM modules, and the cache memory—can be exchanged to increase the performance of the system. These devices are normally mounted in sockets to make replacing or upgrading them an easy task.

Great care should be taken when exchanging these parts to avoid damage to the ICs from **electrostatic discharge (ESD)**. ESD prevention is covered in detail in Chapter 13, "Preventive Maintenance, Safety, and Customer Service." In addition, care should be taken during the extraction and replacement of the ICs to avoid misalignment and bent pins. Make sure to correctly align the IC's pin #1 with the socket's pin #1 position. In the case of microprocessors that plug into standard socket types (also referred to as **low insertion force,** or **LIF**, sockets), the force required to insert them might overstress the system board if not properly supported.

As stated earlier in this chapter, microprocessor manufacturers have devised upgrade versions for virtually every type of microprocessor in the market. It is also common for clone microprocessors to be pin-compatible with older Intel socket designs. This strategy means that the end user not only realizes a speed increase by upgrading, but also sees a processing power increase as well.

Upgrading the processor is a fairly easy operation after gaining access to the system board. Simply remove the microprocessor from its socket and replace it with the upgrade. The physical upgrade should also be accompanied by a logical upgrade. When the microprocessor is upgraded, the BIOS should also be flashed with the latest compatibility firmware. If the BIOS does not possess the flash option and does not support the new microprocessor, the entire system board typically must be upgraded. Two items must be observed when changing the microprocessor:

▶ Make sure the replacement is pin-out-compatible with the original.

▶ Make sure to properly orient the new processor in the socket so that its pin #1 matches the socket's pin #1.

Upgrading system board memory is also a fairly simple process. Having more RAM on board enables the system to access more data from extended or expanded memory without having to access the disk drive. This, of course, speeds up system operation considerably. Normally, upgrading memory simply amounts to installing new memory modules in vacant SIMM or DIMM slots. If the slots are already populated, you must remove them to install faster or higher-capacity modules.

The system board user's guide should be consulted to determine the speed for which the memory devices must be rated. You should be aware that RAM and other memory devices are rated in access time instead of clock speed. Therefore, a -70 nanosecond (ns) RAM device is faster than an -80ns device. The guide should also be checked for any memory configuration settings that must be made to accept the new memory capacity.

If the system has socketed cache memory, some additional performance can be gained by optimizing the cache. Upgrading the cache on these system boards normally requires only that additional cache ICs be installed in vacant sockets. If the sockets are full but the system's cache size is less than maximum, it is necessary to remove the existing cache chips and replace them with faster, higher-capacity devices. Make sure to observe the pin #1 alignment as well as check the system board's user's guide for any configuration jumper changes.

Before upgrading the system board's FRU units, it is always advisable to check the cost of the proposed component upgrade against the cost of upgrading the system board itself. In many cases, the RAM from the original board can be used on a newer, faster model that should include a more advanced microprocessor. Before finalizing the choice to install a new system board, however, make sure that the current adapters, software, and peripherals can operate with the updated board. If not, the cost of upgrading may be unexpectedly higher than simply replacing an FRU component.

System Board Troubleshooting

Troubleshooting problems related to the system board can be difficult to solve due to the board's relative complexity. So many system functions at least partially rely on the system board that certain symptoms can be masked by other symptoms.

As with any troubleshooting procedure, begin by observing the symptoms produced by boot-up and operation. Observe the steps that led to the failure, and determine under what conditions the system failed. Were there any unusual operations in progress? Note any error messages or beep codes.

Try any obvious steps, such as adjusting brightness controls on a dim monitor or checking for loose connections on peripheral equipment. Check power switch settings on every system component. Retry the system several times to observe the symptoms clearly. Take the time to document the problem—write it down.

Refer to the system board and peripheral units' user's guides to look for configuration problems. Check the CMOS Setup for configuration problems. Diagnose the problem to a section of the system (in this case, the system board). In Pentium systems, check the Advanced CMOS Setup parameters to make certain that all the appropriate system board enabling settings have been made.

If possible, run a software diagnostics package to narrow the possible problem causes. Remember that the microprocessor, RAM modules, ROM BIOS, CMOS battery, and possibly cache ICs are typically **Field Replaceable Units** (**FRU**s) on the system board. If enough of the system is running to perform tests on these units, they can be replaced. If symptoms suggest that one or more of these devices may be defective, they can be exchanged with a known good unit of the same type.

If the diagnostics program indicates a number of possible bad components, replace them one at a time until the bad unit has been isolated. Then insert any possible good units back into the system and check them. The possibility of bad software should also be considered when multiple FRU problems are indicated.

If possible, back up the contents of the hard drive before removing the system board. Record the CMOS configuration settings, along with the settings of all jumpers and switches, before exchanging the system board.

System Board Symptoms

So much of the system's operation is based on the system board that it can have several different types of symptoms. Typical symptoms associated with system board hardware failures include the following:

- The ON/OFF indicator lights are visible, the display is visible on the monitor screen, but there is no disk drive action and no boot-up.

- The ON/OFF indicator lights are visible, the hard drive spins up, but the system appears dead and there is no boot-up.

- System locks up during normal operation.

- A beep code with 1, 2, 3, 5, 7, or 9 beeps is produced by the system.

- A beep code of 1 long and 3 short beeps is produced by the system.

- System will not hold date and time.

- An "8042 Gate A20 Error" message occurs when getting into Protected mode.

- An "Invalid Switch Memory Failure" message appears.

- A "DMA Error" message occurs; the DMA controller failed page register test.

- A "CMOS Battery Low" message indicates failure of CMOS battery or CMOS checksum test.

- A "CMOS System Option Not Set" message indicates failure of CMOS battery or CMOS checksum test.

- A "CMOS Checksum Failure" message indicates CMOS battery low or CMOS checksum test failure.

- A 201-error code is displayed on the screen to indicate a RAM failure.

- A Parity Check error message on the screen indicates a RAM error.

Typical symptoms associated with system board setup failures include the following:

- A "CMOS Inoperational" message indicates failure of CMOS shutdown register.

- A "Display Switch Setting Not Proper" message indicates failure to verify display type.

- A "CMOS Display Mismatch" message indicates failure of display type verification.

- A "CMOS Memory Size Mismatch" message indicates system configuration and setup failure.

- A "CMOS Time & Date Not Set" message indicates system configuration and setup failure.

- An IBM-compatible error code displayed on the screen indicates that a configuration problem has occurred.

Typical symptoms associated with system board I/O failures include the following:

- The speaker doesn't work.

- The keyboard does not function after being replaced with a known good unit.

Most of the hardware problems that occur with computers, outside of those already described, involve the system board. Because the system board is the center of virtually all the computer's operations, it's only natural that it will need to be checked at some point in most troubleshooting efforts. The system board normally marks the end of any of the various troubleshooting schemes given for different system components. It occupies this position for two reasons. The first reason is that the system board supports most of the other system components, either directly or indirectly. Second, it is the system component that requires the most effort to replace and test.

Other System Board Problems

A+ CORE 2.1   In addition to containing the circuitry that directs all the system's operations, the system board contains a number of other circuits on which the rest of the system's components depend. These include the system's DRAM memory (which all software programs use) and the system's data, address, and signal buses. The parts of the buses you are most familiar with are the expansion slots.

Problems with key system board components produce symptoms similar to those described for a bad power supply. As a matter of fact, part of the Power Supply Problem Isolation procedure (Procedure 18 in the Hands-on Lab Procedures) refers to checking the system board. Both the microprocessor and the ROM BIOS can be sources of these problems. Both should be checked by substitution when dead system symptoms are encountered but the power supply is good.

In the case of the microprocessor, the system may issue a slow, single beep, with no display or other I/O operation. This indicates that an internal error has disabled a portion of the processor's internal circuitry (usually the internal cache). Internal problems may also allow the microprocessor to begin processing but ultimately fail as it attempts operations. Such a problem results in the system continuously counting RAM during the boot-up. The system may also lock up while counting RAM. In either case, the only method of repair is to replace the microprocessor.

If the system continually locks up after being on for a period of time, this is a good indication that the microprocessor's fan is not running, or that some other heat buildup problem is occurring. The microprocessor should also be checked if its fan has not been running but the power is on. This may indicate that the microprocessor has been without adequate ventilation and is overheated. When this happens, you must replace the fan unit and the microprocessor. Check to make certain that the new fan works correctly, or a second microprocessor will be damaged.

As with the microprocessor, a bad or damaged ROM BIOS typically stops the system dead. When a dead system board is encountered, examine the BIOS chip (or chips) for physical damage. If these devices overheat, it is typical for them to crack or blow a large piece out of the top of the IC package. Another symptom of a damaged BIOS is indicated by the boot-up moving into the CMOS configuration but never returning to the boot-up sequence. In any case, the defective BIOS must be replaced with a version that matches the chip set used by the system.

The system board's memory is a very serviceable part of the system. Many of the symptoms listed in the preceding paragraphs pertain to the system's RAM. A class of memory errors, called **soft memory errors**, is caused by infrequent and random glitches in the operation of applications and the system. Simply restarting the system can clear these events. However, the other errors listed normally relate to **hard memory errors** and require either that memory units be checked by substitution or that a configuration jumper be reset.

All of the system's options adapters connect to the buses through the expansion slots, so failure of any component attached to one of the slots can prevent information movement between other components along the bus. In this case, you must remove the offending component from the bus before any operation can proceed.

A number of other optional devices may be added to the system simply by installing an appropriate options adapter card in one of the system board's expansion slots and then connecting the option to it. Figure 6.53 illustrates the flow of information between the system board and a typical connection port (a parallel printer port) located on an options adapter card.

FIGURE 6.53

*Moving information to an
I/O port.*

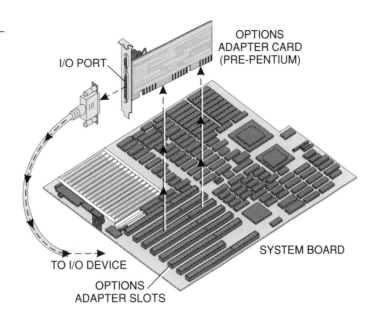

An often-overlooked output device is the system's speaker. Unlike other I/O devices, all the circuitry that controls the speaker is contained on the system board. Therefore, there are only a few reasons that the speaker should fail: The speaker itself is defective, the speaker circuitry on the system board is defective, the speaker is unplugged from the system board, or the software is failing to drive the speaker circuits. The speaker-related components are depicted in Figure 6.54.

FIGURE 6.54

Speaker-related components.

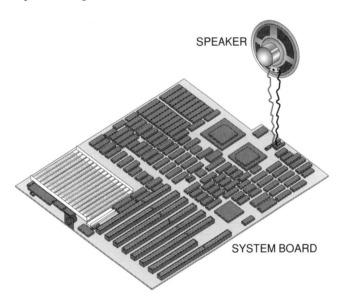

The keyboard is another I/O device supported directly from the system board. When examining keyboard problems, there are only three items to check: the keyboard, the system board, and the keyboard driver software.

Configuration Checks

Observe the boot-up RAM count to see that it is correct for the amount of physical RAM actually installed in the system. If not, swap RAM devices to see if the count changes. Use logical movement of the RAM devices to locate the defective part.

Normally, the only time a configuration problem occurs is when the system is being set up for the first time, or when a new option is installed. The other condition that causes a configuration problem involves the system board's CMOS backup battery. If the battery fails or has been changed, then the contents of the CMOS setup will be lost. After replacing the battery, it is always necessary to run the CMOS Setup utility to reconfigure the system.

The values stored in this memory must accurately reflect the configuration of the system, or an error will occur. These values can be accessed for change by pressing the CTRL and DEL keys (or some other key combination) simultaneously during the boot-up procedure.

Typically, if the boot-up process reaches the point where the system's CMOS configuration information is displayed on the screen, it can be assumed that no hardware configuration conflicts exist in the system's basic components. After this point in the boot-up process, the system begins loading drivers for optional devices and additional memory. If the error occurs after the CMOS screen is displayed and before the boot-up tone sounds, it is necessary to clean-boot the system and single-step through the remainder of the boot-up sequence.

Software Checks

Boot up the system and start the selected diagnostic program, if possible. Try to use a diagnostic program that deals with the system board components. This should include memory, microprocessor, interrupt, and DMA tests.

Run the program's **System Board Tests** function, and perform the equivalent of the ALL tests function. These types of tests are particularly good for detecting memory errors, as well as interrupt and DMA conflicts. Note all the errors indicated by the tests. If a single type of error is indicated, it may be possible to take some corrective actions, such as replacing a memory module or reconfiguring interrupt/DMA settings, without replacing the system board. However, if more complex system board problems are indicated, exit the diagnostic program and use the following Hardware Checks and Installation/Removal procedure to troubleshoot and replace the system board.

The DOS **MEM command** ;can be used to view the system's memory utilization scheme. It displays both the programs currently loaded into memory and the system's free memory areas. The /C switch can be used with the MEM command as a valuable tool to sort out TSR conflicts in upper memory.

The **MEMMAKER utility** modifies the CONFIG.SYS and AUTOEXEC.BAT files on your system so that device drivers and memory resident programs take up less conventional memory space. This is accomplished by loading these types of programs into the upper memory area. This utility requires a microprocessor capable of running in Virtual memory mode. MemMaker is often used to resolve memory conflicts in the lower 64KB of memory.

Hardware Removal and Installation

After a problem has been isolated to the system board hardware, it is necessary to remove and replace it. The removal procedure can be defined in five steps:

1. Remove all external I/O systems.

2. Remove the system unit's outer cover.

3. Remove the option adapter cards.

4. Remove the cables from the system board.

5. Remove the system board.

During this operation, you must disconnect several connectors from the old system board and reconnect them to the new system board. The easiest method of handling this is to use tape (preferably masking tape) to mark the wires and their connection points (on the new system board) before removing any wires from the old system board.

Removing All External I/O Systems

Unplug all power cords from the commercial outlet. Remove all peripherals from the system unit. Disconnect the mouse, keyboard, and monitor signal cable from the rear of the unit. Finally, disconnect the monitor power cable from the system unit (or the outlet). Figure 6.55 illustrates the system unit's back-panel connections.

FIGURE 6.55

System unit back panel connections.

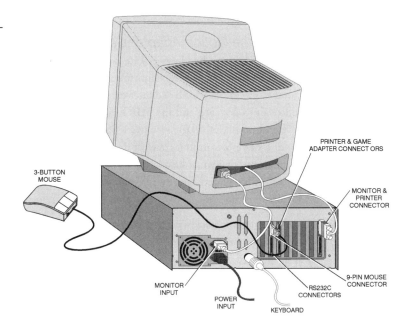

Removing the System Unit's Outer Cover

Unplug the 120-Vac power cord from the system unit. Determine the type of case on which you are working. If the case is a desktop model, does the cover slide off the chassis in a forward direction, bringing the front panel with it, or does it raise off the chassis from the rear? If the back lip of the outer cover folds over the edge of the unit's back panel, then the lid raises up from the back after the retaining screws are removed. If the retaining screws go through the back panel without passing through the lip, then the outer cover slides forward after the retaining screws have been removed.

Check to see how many screws hold the outer cover to the chassis. Do not confuse the power supply retaining screws with those holding the back panel. The power supply unit requires four screws. Check for screws along the lower edges of the outer cover that would hold it to the sides of the chassis. Remove the screws that hold the cover to the chassis. Store the screws properly.

Remove the system unit's outer cover, as illustrated in Figure 6.56, and set it aside. Slide the case forward. Tilt the case upward from the front, and remove it from the unit. You can also lift the back edge of the outer cover to approximately 45 degrees and then slide it toward the rear of the chassis.

FIGURE 6.56

Removing the case.

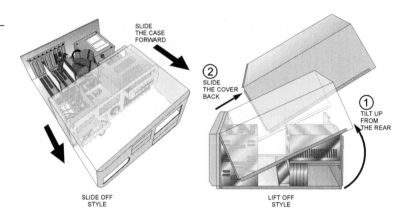

Removing the Option Adapter Cards

A wide variety of peripheral devices are used with PC-compatible systems. These devices communicate with the main system through options adapter cards that fit into slot connectors on the system board. The adapter cards that come in most pre-Pentium PC systems are the video controller card and the MI/O card. The MI/O card contains the disk drive controller circuitry, as well as the system's serial and parallel port connections. The hard- and floppy-disk drives communicate with this card through ribbon cables. These cables have indicator stripes that must be aligned properly on both ends. In Pentium systems, the MI/O card is integrated directly into the system board. It is a good practice to place adapter cards back into the same slots from which they were removed, if possible.

Remove the retaining screws that secure the options adapter cards to the system unit's back panel. Remove the video adapter card from the expansion slot. Store the screws properly. Refer to Figure 6.57 to perform this procedure.

If the system uses an MI/O card, disconnect the floppy-drive signal cable (the smaller signal cable) and the hard-drive signal cable (the larger signal cable) from the MI/O card. Also disconnect any I/O port connections from the MI/O card. Remove the MI/O adapter card from the expansion slot.

FIGURE 6.57

Removing adapter cards.

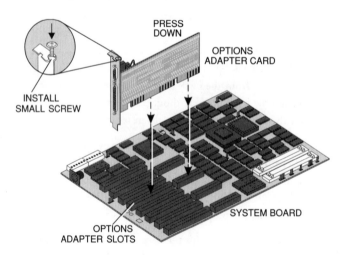

Removing the Cables from the System Board

The system board provides an operator interface through a set of front-panel indicator lights and switches. These indicators and switches connect to the system board by BERG connectors, as depicted in Figure 6.58.

FIGURE 6.58

Front-panel connections.

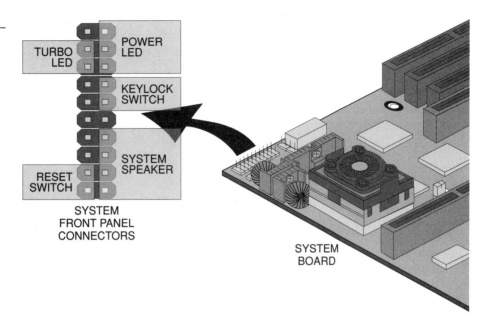

The **front-panel connectors** must be removed to exchange the system board for a new one. It is quite easy to get these connections reversed, so make sure that you mark them for identification purposes before removing them from their connection points. Record the color and function of each connection. Trace each wire back to its front panel connection to determine its purpose. This will ensure that they are reinstalled correctly after the exchange is completed.

Disconnect the P8 and P9 power supply connections from the system board as well.

Removing the System Board

Check the positions of all jumper and switch settings on the old system board. Record these settings and verify their meanings before removing the board from the system. This may require the use of the system board's user's manual, if available. Remove the retaining screw (or screws) that secure the system board to the floor of the chassis. Store the screw(s) properly.

In a desktop unit, slide the system board toward the left side of the system unit (as you face the front of the unit) to free its plastic feet from the slots in the floor of the system unit. Tilt the left edge of the board up, and then lift it straight up and out of the system unit, as illustrated in Figure 6.59.

In a tower unit, slide the system board toward the bottom of the system unit to free its plastic feet from the slots in the side panel. Tilt the bottom edge of the board away from the unit, and pull it straight out of the chassis, as shown in Figure 6.60.

FIGURE 6.59

Removing the system board from a desktop case.

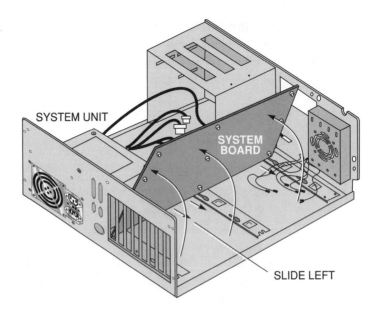

SYSTEM UNIT

SYSTEM BOARD

SLIDE LEFT

FIGURE 6.60

Removing the system board from a tower case.

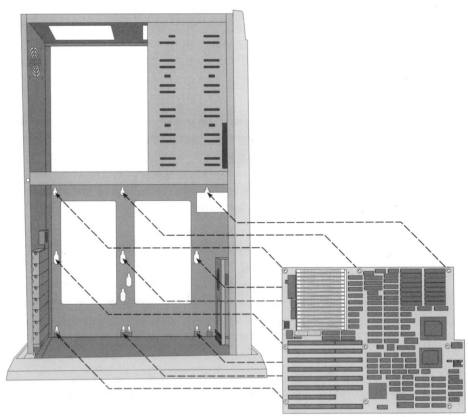

Reassembling the System

The system board installation procedure is basically the removal procedure in reverse. However, the CMOS setup and hardware configuration must be reset after the new system board has been installed. Also, try to replace the options adapter cards in the same expansion slots from which you removed them.

Hardware Checks

If the system's CMOS configuration setup appears to be correct and a system board hardware problem is suspected, the first task is to remove all the externally connected devices from the rear of the system, except for the monitor and keyboard. Try to boot the system with just the basic I/O options installed.

If the system operates correctly with the external options removed, it is safe to assume that one of them is the cause of the problem. To verify which external device is causing the problem, reconnect the devices one at a time until the problem reappears. The last device reinstalled before the problem reappeared is defective. Replace this item and continue reinstalling options one at a time until all the options have been reinstalled. If another failure occurs while reinstalling options, replace that option as well. Repair or replace the defective option, and return the system to full service.

If none of the external options seem to be causing the problem, the next easiest item to test is the operation and configuration of the hard disk drive. This is accomplished by trying to boot the system to a clean, self-booting disk in the A: floppy drive. This test can be accomplished without removing the outer cover of the system unit.

Check the CMOS setup, if possible, to make sure that the system checks the A: drive as part of the boot sequence. Place a bootable disk (or a clean boot disk) in floppy drive A: and turn on the system. If the system boots to the floppy, a failure has occurred in the hard drive or controller. Refer to Procedures 27 and 28 in the lab guide to service the HDD section of the system.

The process for isolating system board problems is reinforced and expanded in the accompanying hands-on lab book in Procedure 13.

Checking Inside the System Unit

Remove the system unit's outer cover, and then remove all the internal options adapter cards except for the video and disk-drive controller cards from the system board's expansion slots. Try to reboot the system. If the system works correctly with the additional adapter cards removed, it is reasonable to assume that one of them was causing the problem. To verify which option is causing the problem, reinstall them one at a time until the problem reappears. The last adapter reinstalled before the problem reappeared is defective. Replace this adapter with a working unit and continue reinstalling adapters one at a time until all the cards have been reinstalled. If another failure occurs while reinstalling adapters, replace that unit as well.

If the system boots up with the internal options removed, it is reasonable to assume that one of them is the cause of the problem. Therefore, you should reinstall the internal options one at a time until the problem reappears. As always, the last option reinstalled before the problem returned is defective. Replace the defective device or card with a new one, reinstall any options removed from the system, and return the system to full service.

Checking Basic Components

If the system still refuses to boot up, the basic adapter cards should be checked next. It doesn't really matter which card is checked first unless some symptom points to a particular card. In older units, try the MI/O card first because it contains a variety of system functions. Turn off the system, and remove the disk-drive controller card from the system board's expansion slot. If the system produces an HDD or FDD error message on the screen, exchange the disk-drive controller (in pre-Pentium systems) with a known good one. Make certain to mark the cable and its connection point to ensure proper reconnection after the exchange. Try to reboot the system with the new disk-drive controller installed.

If problems continue, remove the video controller card from the system board's expansion slots and turn on the system. Does the FDD activity light come on? If so, exchange the video controller card with a known good one of the same type.

Check for +5 and +12 Vdc on the system board, as illustrated in Figure 6.61. If these voltages are missing, turn off the system, disconnect power to all disk drives, and swap the power supply unit with a known good one.

FIGURE 6.61

The system board voltage check location.

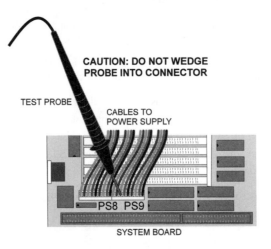

Exchanging the System Board

If the system still won't boot up, remove the video and disk-drive controller cards from the system board's expansion slots. Disconnect the system board from the power supply unit (P8–P9) and the system board/front-panel connections. Take care to mark any connection removed from the system board and its connection point, to ensure proper reconnection. Exchange the system board with a known good one. Reconnect all the power-supply and front-panel connections to the system board. Reinstall the video and disk-drive controller cards in the expansion slots, and try to reboot the system.

Reconfigure the system board to operate with the installed peripherals. Reseat the video and disk-drive controller cards in the system unit. Reset the CMOS Setup to match the installed peripherals, and turn on the system.

When the system boots up, reinstall any options removed from the system and replace the system unit's outer cover. Return the system to full service and service the defective system board. If the system still does not boot up, retest all the system components one at a time until a cause is found. Check the small things, such as cable connections and key switches, carefully.

A few serviceable items exist on the system board. These include the RAM modules, the microprocessor (and its cooling fan), the ROM BIOS chip(s), and the system battery.

The RAM modules can be swapped out one at a time to isolate defective modules. These modules are also swapped out when a system upgrade is being performed. The burn-in tests in most diagnostic packages can be helpful in locating borderline RAM modules.

The microprocessor can be exchanged easily on most system boards. Only the 80386SX is soldered-in, so it would be much more difficult to exchange and would not likely be worth the expense involved. However, the fact that most microprocessors, as well as the BIOS chips, are mounted in sockets brings up another point. These items should be pulled and reseated in their sockets if they seem to be a possible cause of problems. Sockets are convenient for repair and upgrade purposes, but they can also attract corrosion between the pins of the device and those of the socket. After some time, the electrical connection may be too poor for the device to operate properly.

Corrosion can also affect the system clock over time. If a system refuses to maintain time and date information after the backup battery has been replaced, check the contacts of the holder for corrosion. Two types of batteries are commonly used for CMOS backup: These are nickel-cadmium (Ni-Cad) and lithium batteries. Of the two, Ni-Cads have historically been the most favored. Conversely, lithium batteries are gaining respect due to their long life capabilities when installed in systems designed to recharge lithium batteries. However, lithium battery life is noticeably short when it is installed in systems designed for the higher-current-draining Ni-Cads. Therefore, the correct type of battery should always be used to replace a system board battery.

Key Points Review

The system board is the main component of any personal computer system. This chapter has examined the major components that make up typical PC-compatible system boards. These items include microprocessors, memory types, microprocessor support systems, and expansion buses.

- System boards fundamentally change for three reasons: new microprocessors, new expansion-slot types, and reduced chip counts. Reduced chip counts are typically the result of improved microprocessor support chip sets. Chip sets combine PC- and AT-compatible structures into larger ICs.

- Because chip set-based system boards require much fewer SSI, MSI, and LSI devices to produce, manufacturers of printed circuit boards have been able to design much smaller boards.

- Chip set-based system boards and I/O cards tend to change often as IC manufacturers continue to integrate higher levels of circuitry into their devices.

- The microprocessors used in the vast majority of all PC-compatible microcomputers include the 8088/86, the 80286, the 80386, the 80486, and the Pentium (80586 and 80686) microprocessors.

- In Protected mode, address bits A20 and above are enabled, and the microprocessor can access physical memory addresses above the 1MB limit. The microprocessor can also be used to perform virtual memory operations. In these operations, the system treats an area of disk space as an extension of RAM memory.

- The advanced memory-mapping capabilities of the 80386 enable it to implement ROM shadowing. This speeds up system operation by enabling BIOS-related functions to be conducted from fast 32-bit RAM locations instead of slower 8-bit ROM locations.

- The 80386 offers an improved Protected-addressing mode, referred to as Virtual 86 mode. This mode enables the 80386 to simulate several 8086 microprocessors running at the same time.

- Basically, the 80486 brings an improved 80386DX microprocessor, a high-performance 80387 coprocessor, and an 82385 cache memory controller together in a single package.

- The Pentium is called a superscalar microprocessor because its architecture enables multiple instructions to be executed simultaneously. A pipelining process that uses multiple stages to speed up instruction execution achieves this.

- In the Pentium MMX processor, the multimedia and communications-processing capabilities of the Pentium device are extended by the addition of 57 multimedia-specific instructions to the instruction set.

- Intel departed from simply increasing the speed of its Pentium processor line by introducing the Pentium Pro processor.

- The Pentium II includes all the multimedia enhancements from the MMX processor and retains the power of the Pentium Pro's dynamic execution and L2 cache features.

- As powerful as modern microprocessors are, they still require a certain amount of support circuitry to be considered a system. Over time, these support systems have been reduced to just a few ASIC devices.

- Normally three types of semiconductor memory are found on a typical system board: the system's ROM BIOS ICs, the system's RAM memory, and the second-level cache memory unit.

- Caching is a memory-management method that assumes that most memory accesses are made within a limited block of addresses. Therefore, if the contents of these addresses are relocated into a special section of high-speed SRAM, the microprocessor could access these locations without requiring any wait states.

- Paging and interleaving memory schemes are designed to take advantage of the sequential nature of instruction fetches from memory.

- When dealing with a PC-compatible, you must contend with two forms of I/O: the system board's onboard I/O, and peripheral devices that interact with the system through its expansion slots.

- The system's expansion slots provide the connecting point for most of its I/O devices. Interface cards communicate with the system through the extended microprocessor buses in these slots.

- The main component in the PCI bus is the PCI bus controller, called the host bridge. This device monitors the microprocessor's address bus to determine whether addresses are intended for devices in a PCI slot or one of the system board's other types of expansion slots.

- As with the PCI bus, the VL-bus controller monitors the microprocessor's control signals and addresses to determine what type of operation is being performed and where it is located in the system.

- The microprocessor, the RAM modules, and the cache memory can be exchanged to increase the performance of the system. These devices are normally mounted in sockets to make replacing or upgrading them an easy task.

- Typically, if the boot-up process reaches the point where the system's CMOS configuration information is displayed on the screen, it can be assumed that no hardware configuration conflicts exist in the system's basic components. If an error occurs after this point and before the boot-up tone, you must clean-boot the system and single-step through the remainder of the boot-up sequence.

Multiple Choice Questions

1. Where is the CMOS setup stored in the system?

   a. In the registers of the RTC

   b. In the BIOS chip

   c. In the registers of the microprocessor

   d. In the intelligent keyboard controller chip

2. How many hardware interrupt channels are there in a PC- or XT-compatible system?

   a. 16

   b. 2

   c. 4

   d. 8

3. What maximum clock frequency should be applied to an 80286-12 microprocessor?

    a. 12MHz

    b. 24MHz

    c. 48Mhz

    d. 16Mhz

4. Where can interrupt request #1 be found in a PC-compatible system?

    a. At the keyboard's encoder chip

    b. At the system board's keyboard controller chip

    c. At the system's DRAM refresh controller chip

    d. At the system's FDD controller chip

5. How many total addresses can the 8088 microprocessor select when executing memory operations?

    a. 640KB

    b. 384KB

    c. 1MB

    d. 512KB

6. What function does IRQ-0 play in a PC-compatible system?

    a. It drives the system's DRAM refresh signal.

    b. It drives the system's time-of-day clock.

    c. It drives the system's FDD interrupt.

    d. It drives the system's keyboard interrupt.

7. How many DMA channels are included in a PC- or XT-compatible system?

    a. 8

    b. 16

    c. 1

    d. 4

8. What function does DMA channel 2 serve in a PC-compatible system?

    a. It provides the system's HDD DMA channel.

    b. It provides the system's keyboard DMA channel.

    c. It provides the system's FDD DMA channel.

    d. It provides the system's video DMA channel.

9. What items can cause an NMI to occur?

    a. Power good and **** errors

    b. Power supply and disk-drive errors

    c. System board and power supply errors

    d. I/O channel check and parity check errors

10. What is the maximum allowable clock frequency that should be used to drive an 80486-33 microprocessor?

    a. 66MHz

    b. 16MHz

    c. 15.5MHZ

    d. 33MHz

Review Questions

1. What categories of devices are checked before actually checking the system board? Why is this?

2. Describe three different types of symptoms associated with system board failures.

3. Why should you try to boot the system from a clean, self-booting disk before removing the system unit's cover?

4. From the troubleshooting information in this chapter, what is indicated if the boot-up reaches the CMOS setup screen before failing? What does this information have to do with troubleshooting system board problems?

5. In the hardware troubleshooting checks, is there any reason that the MI/O card was tested before the video card?

6. How many hardware interrupt channels are available in an AT-compatible system?

7. Describe the operation of the system when it receives a DMA request.

8. What function does IRQ 2 serve in an AT-compatible system?

9. Which IRQ channel services the FDD in PC-compatible systems?

10. Name two events that can mark the end of a DMA transfer.

11. List the functions of the system's timer/counter outputs.

12. Name three advantages of the 80286 microprocessor over the 8088.

13. List at least four microprocessor support circuits common to all PC-compatibles.

14. List the three major sections of the 80486 microprocessor.

15. Name two advantages of using chip sets to design circuit boards.

Lab Exercises

The lab manual that accompanies this book contains hands-on lab procedures that reinforce and test your knowledge of the theory materials presented in this chapter. Now that you have completed your review of Chapter 6, refer to the lab manual and perform Procedures 12, "Memory Optimization"; 13, "System Board Problem Isolation"; and 19, "Speed Indicators."

INPUT / OUTPUT DEVICES

LEARNING OBJECTIVES

Upon completion of this chapter and its related lab procedures, you should be able to perform the following tasks:

1. Identify the various port connectors used in PC-compatible systems.

2. List typical parallel port applications.

3. Explain the operation of a Centronics-type parallel interface port.

4. Describe the need for parallel/serial conversions.

5. Describe the differences between synchronous and asynchronous transmissions, stating advantages and disadvantages for both.

6. Explain the operation of an RS-232C serial interface port and define its signal lines.

7. Describe the operation of the Universal Serial Bus (USB).

8. State the three tasks that must be performed by a keyboard to present meaningful data to the computer.

9. List the events that occur when a key is depressed on the keyboard.

10. Describe steps to troubleshoot keyboard problems.

11. Explain the operation of a mouse and a trackball.

12. Describe the operation of a game port used with joysticks and game paddles.

13. Describe the operation of a light pen.

14. Describe the operation of handheld and flat-bed scanners.

15. Describe steps to troubleshoot scanner problems.

CHAPTER 7

Introduction

Although the circuitry on the system board forms the nucleus of the personal computer system, it cannot stand alone. The computer must be capable of acquiring data from the outside world. In most applications, it must also be capable of delivering results of operations it performs to the outside world in a useful format. Many different systems have been developed for both inputting and outputting data.

A PC-compatible system contains more than 65,000 input and output addresses. Part of the previous chapter described how the system treats its onboard intelligent devices as I/O devices. This chapter examines peripheral I/O in detail. The first portion covers the standard I/O port assignments and configurations in PC systems. The second half of the chapter deals with typical input devices associated with PC systems.

Standard I/O Ports

 A+ CORE 1.4

Although many different methods have been developed to connect devices to the PC-compatible system, three ports have been standard since the original PCs were introduced:

- ▶ The IBM versions of the Centronics parallel port
- ▶ The RS-232C serial port
- ▶ The game port

Typical connectors found on the PC's back panel are described in Figure 7.1.

FIGURE 7.1

Typical I/O ports.

    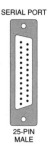  

VGA	MGA & CGA	PARALLEL PORT	SERIAL PORT	SERIAL PORT	GAME PORT
15-PIN FEMALE	9-PIN FEMALE	25-PIN FEMALE	25-PIN MALE	9-PIN MALE	15-PIN FEMALE

Parallel Ports

> Parallel ports have been a staple of the PC system since the original PCs were introduced. They are most widely used to connect printers to the computer.

In many instances, parallel ports are referred to as **parallel printer ports**. Due to the parallel port's capability of quickly transferring bytes of data in a parallel mode, this type of port has been adopted to interface a number of other peripheral devices to the computer. These devices include X-Y plotters; fast computer-to-computer transfer systems; high-speed, high volume, removable disk backup systems; and optical scanners. The parallel port's simplicity makes it a natural for hobbyists and designers to use for specialized interface projects.

Parallel Port Operations

A simplified parallel port operation is illustrated in Figure 7.2. The system applies a decoded port address and an I/O write signal to the port. It then moves data to the port in parallel format from the system's data bus. If the device attached to the port is ready to receive data, it moves through the port still in parallel format.

FIGURE 7.2

Parallel port transfers.

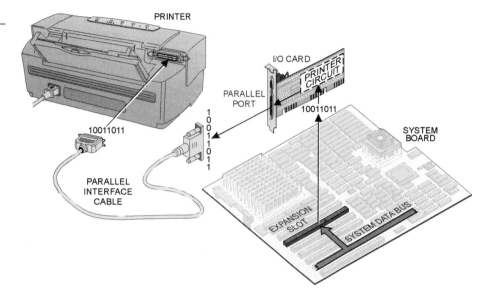

The port's address decoder compares each address placed on the address bus with its preset address. This address may be designated by a set of jumper wires, a bank of DIP switches, or firmware/Plug-and-Play settings. All of these methods enable the peripheral device's address to be changed, by rearranging the jumpers, reconfiguring the positions of the switches, or allowing it to be detected by the BIOS's PnP firmware. Other address-decoding tactics include using SSI and MSI logic circuit arrangements or PROM devices to decode the bits of the address bus.

When the address on the bus matches the port address, the decoder produces an enabling output (EN) that is used to enable the peripheral's sending and receiving circuits.

When a **data-out** (microprocessor-to-peripheral) operation is performed, the microprocessor places a data word on the data bus and sends an I/O write signal to the port. The port applies a **data available strobe** signal to the peripheral, indicating the presence of valid data on the bus. The strobe signal causes the data word to be transferred to the peripheral in parallel format. At the input to the peripheral, the data is latched (held) in its inbound register for processing.

When a **data-in** (peripheral-to-microprocessor) operation is performed, one of the four transmission methods previously discussed occurs to initiate the transfer of data. When the attention of the microprocessor has been gained, the peripheral's outbound register dumps its contents onto the system's data bus, where it is read by the microprocessor.

The Centronics Standard

A+ CORE 1.4

Figure 7.3 shows a typical parallel printer connection, using the IBM version of the **Centronics standard**. This interface enables the computer to pass information to the printer, 8 bits at a time, across the eight data lines. The other lines in the connection carry control signals (handshaking signals) back and forth between the computer and the printer.

The original Centronics interface used a 36-pin D-shell connector at the adapter, and the IBM version reduced the pin count to 25. Table 7.1 defines the signals of the IBM parallel printer port connection standard.

FIGURE 7.3

Parallel port signals.

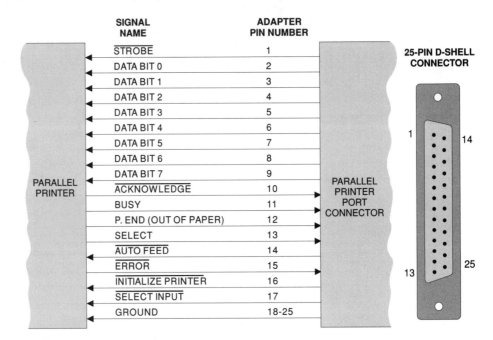

Table 7.1 Pin Assignments

Pin No.	Signal	Direction*	Description
1	STROBE	In	STROBE pulse to read data in. Pulse width must be more than 0.5μs at the printer. The signal level is normally "high"; read-in of data is performed at the "low" level.
2	DATA1	In	
3	DATA2	In	
4	DATA3	In	
5	DATA4	In	
6	DATA5	In	
7	DATA6	In	
8	DATA7	In	
9	DATA8	In	These signals represent information of the 1st to 8th bits of parallel data, respectively. Each signal is at "high" level when data is logical "1" and "low" when logical "0."

Pin No.	Signal	Direction*	Description
10	ACK	Out	Approximately 5µs pulse; "low" indicates that data has been received and the printer is ready to accept other data.
11	BUSY	Out	A "high" signal indicates that the printer cannot receive data. The signal becomes "high" in the following cases: ▶ During data entry ▶ During printing operation ▶ In "Off line" state ▶ During printer error status
12	PE	Out	A "high" signal indicates that the printer is out of paper.
13	SLCT	Out	The signal indicates that the printer is in the selected state.
14	AUTO-FEED	In	With this signal being at "low" level, the paper is automatically fed one line after printing.
15	ERROR	Out	The level of this signal becomes "low" when the printer is in "Paper End" state, "Off line" state, and "Error" state.
16	INIT	In	When the level of this signal becomes "low," the printer controller is reset to its initial state and the print buffer is cleared. This signal is normally at "high" level, and its pulse width must be more than 50µs at the printer.
17	SLCT IN	In	Data entry to the printer is possible only when the level of this signal is "low."
18–25	GND		These pins provide the interface's ground reference points.

*As viewed from the printer

The **Data Strobe (STROBE)** line is used by the computer to signal the printer that a character is available on the Data lines. The printer reads the character from the Data lines into its buffer, to be printed at the printer's convenience. If, for some reason, the printer cannot accept the character from the Data lines (for example, if the printer is out of paper or if its buffer is full), the printer sends a "busy" signal to the computer on the **Busy** line, telling the computer not to send any more data.

After the peripheral device has read the data word from the Data lines, it pulses the **Acknowledge (ACK)** line to tell the computer it is ready to accept another data word, as long as the Busy line is not asserted. The printer also uses the **Select (SLCT)** line to let the computer know that data can be sent to it. In the event that the SLCT signal is not present, the computer can't send the printer any data.

In addition to the lines discussed above, the Centronics standard calls for additional printer-related control lines, which include **Paper End (PE)**, **Auto Feed (AUTO-FD)**, **Error**, **Initialize Printer (INIT)**, and **Select Input (SLCT-IN)**. Not all printers use the complete standard and all its control lines. In many instances, only a few of the lines are used and nonstandard pin numbers and connector types may be used.

Parallel Printer Interface

A PC-compatible parallel port interface typically offers 8-bit parallel data words and nine I/O control lines at a 25-pin, female D-shell connector at the rear of the system unit. In early PCs, the parallel port was located on the back of the video adapter card, on a dedicated parallel printer card or on a multi I/O card. The primary port was always located on the video adapter card. With the VGA card, the primary printer port was normally located on an MI/O card in one of the slots.

> In earlier MI/O cards, discrete circuit devices controlled all the I/O functions. On newer MI/O cards, the various standard I/O functions were increasingly integrated into more complex ICs. Finally, IC manufacturers combined the standard MI/O functions (HDD/FDD/1P/2S/1G ports) into ASIC devices. When the Pentium system boards were developed, the ASIC chip containing the parallel port circuitry moved to the system board.

The printer port connector may be located directly on the back plate of an I/O card, or the port's circuitry may be connected via a ribbon cable to the 25-pin D-shell connector on the unit's back panel.

Figure 7.4 depicts a block diagram of a typical parallel printer port. The interface includes a port address decoder, data-latching register, data bus buffer, control-line latching register, status-line buffer, and control-line drivers. In operation, the adapter performs five I/O instructions, which correspond to three different port addresses and the condition of the system's IOR line. The adapter supports the two-way handshaking scheme using the Strobe, Acknowledge, and Busy lines described earlier.

FIGURE 7.4

Block diagram of printer interface.

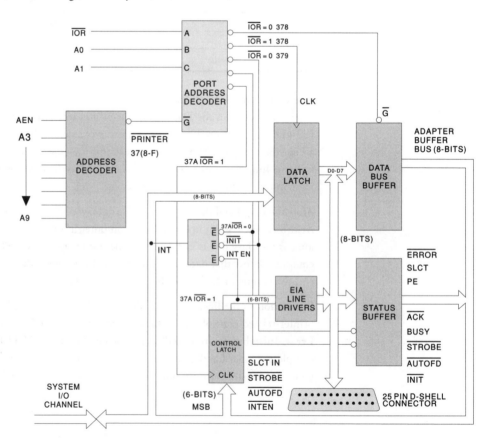

Writing to the Printer Port

The printer adapter is enabled by port addresses 378h–37Fh. When the system wishes to send a byte of data to the printer, it must place the data byte on the data bus, set its IOR line to an inactive state (this is equivalent of IOW being active to the adapter), and apply an address of 378h to the adapter. This action causes the adapter's **data latch** to accept the data from the data bus and latch it.

Next, the computer must read the adapter's **status buffer** to check the condition of the printer's Busy line. To read the printer's status bits, the computer must make its IOR line active and apply an address of 379h to the adapter. This places the ERROR, SLCT, PE, INIT, and BUSY status bits on the adapter's data bus.

If the Busy line is active, indicating that the printer can accept data, the system unit pulses the Strobe line to tell the printer that a valid data byte is present on the Data lines from the port. Actually, the system unit writes a complete 6-bit control word into the control latch by placing the control word on the adapter's data bus, making the IOR line inactive, and applying an address of 37Ah to the adapter. This places the control word in the latch, which, in turn, applies the individual bits to the line driver amplifiers and then to the printer's input control lines.

Reading from the Printer Port

Two other instructions enable the system to read the contents of the two latches. To read the current contents of the data-latching register, the microprocessor must make the IOR line active and apply an address of 378h to the adapter. This action enables the data bus buffer and places the outputs of the data latch register on the adapter's data bus.

When the system unit reads the status of the printer, it activates the IOR line and applies an address of 37Ah to the adapter. This enables the system to read the printer's SLCT-IN, ACK, Strobe, and AUTO-FD status lines as well as the port's IRQ line. If the printer is not driving these pins, the system reads the last control word written into the control latch register. In the event that the printer is driving these pins, the status bits from the printer is logically ORed with the bits of the control latch and is placed on the adapter's data bus.

In addition to the primary handshaking lines (Strobe, ACK, Busy), the parallel printer interface provides secondary control lines for PE, SLCT, and ERROR input signals from the printer, and AUTO-FD, INIT, and SLCT-IN outputs to the printer.

The interrupt level of the printer port section may be set at a number of different levels by changing its configuration jumpers or CMOS enabling setting. The interrupt from the printer is actually obtained through the INIT line. This signal is gated to the adapter's interrupt line by the **interrupt enable (INT EN)** bit of the control word stored in the control latch. The status of this bit determines whether the printer adapter can interrupt the system unit. In this manner, the printer can use the printer port's INIT input to cause an interrupt to occur, provided the system unit has not masked the interrupt through the interrupt enable bit of the control word. Normal interrupt settings for printer ports in a PC-compatible system are IRQ5 or IRQ7.

All the signals discussed earlier are transmitted between the adapter card and the printer at standard **Transistor-Transistor Logic (TTL)** levels. This means that the signals can deteriorate quickly with long lengths of cable. The cable length used for the parallel printer should be kept to less than 10 feet. If longer lengths are needed, the cable should have a low capacity value. The cable should also be shielded so as to minimize interference.

LPT Handles

If a printer port is found at 3BCh, then DOS assigns it the title of LPT1. If, however, no printer port is found at 3BCh but one exists at 378h, then DOS assigns LPT1 to the latter address. Likewise, a system that has printer ports at physical addresses 378h and 278h would have LPT1 assigned at 378h, and LPT2 at location 278h.

Parallel printer ports located on video display cards are normally set for 3BCh operation. Therefore, this is the parallel port that the system normally defines as LPT1. This is also true of system boards that come equipped with built-in parallel ports. Problems arise in any system with different parallel ports that share the same physical address. If this occurs, you must disable or readdress one of the ports before either of them will work. This is usually accomplished through jumpers located on the I/O cards.

The address of the printer port can normally be changed to respond as LPT1, LPT2, or LPT3, depending on the setting of address selection jumpers. The printer port can also be disabled completely through these jumper settings. IRQ7 is normally assigned to the LPT1 printer port, and IRQ5 typically serves the LPT2 port, if installed.

A+ CORE 4.4 Although the data pins of the parallel printer port are defined as output pins, the figure illustrates that they are actually bidirectional. Many PC-compatible parallel ports are bi-directional, but some cheaper ports may not have the electronics built into them to handle the input function. This is not important for printer operations, so most users won't notice.

Serial Ports

In this manner, the number of conductors connecting the computer and the peripheral is reduced from eight or more data lines from and any number of control lines to one (or two) communications lines, a ground line, and maybe a few control lines. Therefore, the cost of connecting equipment is reduced by using serial communication techniques when a peripheral device must be located at some distance from the computer.

The simplest method of converting a parallel computer word into a serial bit stream is depicted in Figure 7.5 using a **parallel-in, serial-out (PISO)** shift register. In this arrangement, a parallel word is loaded into the register with a single clock pulse. After the word has been loaded into the register, the logic level on its mode control pin is reversed and the bits are shifted out of the register's serial output by eight consecutive clock pulses.

FIGURE 7.5

A PISO register.

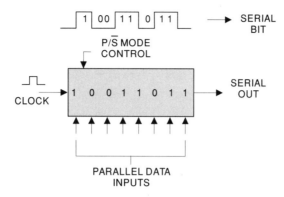

Conversely, serial data sent from a remote computer or a peripheral must be converted back into parallel form to be compatible with the computer's internal bus structure. The simplest method of implementing this operation is shown in Figure 7.6, using a **serial-in, parallel-out** (**SIPO**) shift register. Here, the serial bit stream is shifted into the register by eight clock pulses.

FIGURE 7.6

A discrete SIPO register.

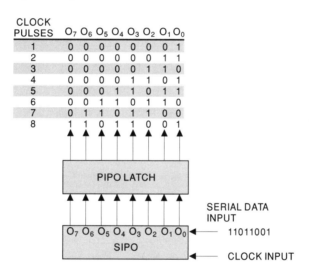

Serial Transmission Modes

The biggest problem encountered when sending data serially is keeping the transmitted data-bit timing synchronized between the two devices.

> Two methods are used to provide the proper timing for serial transfers: the data bits may be sent **synchronously** (in conjunction with a synchronizing clock pulse) or **asynchronously** (without an accompanying clock pulse).

When data is transmitted synchronously, the bits of a word, or character, are synchronized by a common clock signal, which is applied to both the transmitting and receiving shift registers. The two registers are initialized before data transmission begins, when the transmitting circuitry sends a predefined bit pattern that the receiver recognizes as the initialization command. After this, the receiving circuitry processes the incoming bit stream by counting clock pulses and dividing the bit stream into words of a predetermined length. If the receiver misses a bit for any reason, all the words that follow will be processed erroneously. Figure 7.7 depicts a simplified synchronous transmission scheme.

FIGURE 7.7

Synchronous transmission.

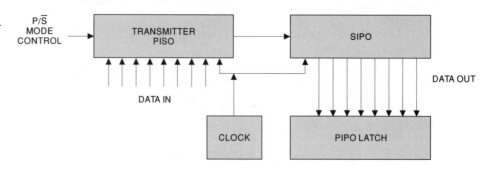

When data is transferred asynchronously, the receiving system is not synchronized with the sending system. In asynchronous communications, the transmission is dependent on the capability of two separate clocks, running at the same frequency, to remain synchronized for a short period of time. The transmitted material is sent character by character (usually ASCII), with the beginning and end of each character framed by character start and stop bits. Between these marks, the bits of the character are sent at a constant rate, but the time interval between characters may be irregular. Figure 7.8 depicts a typical format for transmitting an 8-bit ASCII character asynchronously.

FIGURE 7.8

Asynchronous character format.

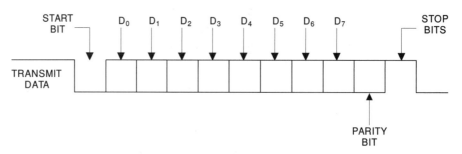

When no bits are being transmitted, the Data line is held in a high logic state, also referred to as a **mark**. At the beginning of a character, the transmitter sends a **start bit**, which is always a low logic pulse (**space**). After the start bit, the data bits are transmitted, beginning with the least significant bit. A number of bits may be transmitted after the data bits. In this case, a **parity bit** has been added for error-detection and correction purposes, and one **stop bit** has been added to identify the end of the character.

Although this format is fairly common, on different systems the number of data bits range between five and nine. There may be one, one-and-a-half, or two stop bits included. The use of an error-checking bit is optional.

Over a given period of time, synchronous communications are much faster than asynchronous methods. This is due to the extra number of bits required to send each character asynchronously. PC serial ports and analog modems use asynchronous communications methods, and digital modems and local area network adapters use synchronous methods.

Serial Interface ICs

Computer systems do not normally rely on the discrete PISO and SIPO shift registers described in the previous sections. As with the single-chip parallel ports, IC manufacturers have developed a number of single-chip devices that perform all the functions necessary for serial transfers to occur. These serial port IC's are referred to as **Asynchronous Communication Interface Adapters (ACIAs)** or as **Universal Asynchronous Receiver/Transmitters (UARTs)**. Synchronous devices are usually called **Universal Synchronous/Asynchronous Receiver/Transmitters (USARTs)**. Not only do these devices provide the parallel-to-serial and serial-to-parallel conversions required for serial communications, they also handle both the parallel interface required with the computer's bus and all the control functions associated with the transmission.

UARTs

A functional block diagram of a UART is illustrated in Figure 7.9. A UART consists of two major sections: the transmit section and the receive section. The transmit section is primarily made up of two registers: the **Transmit Output Shift Register** and a **Transmit Holding Register**. The transmit holding register holds the next data word to be transmitted until the shift register has completed the serialization of the previous data word.

FIGURE 7.9

Blocks of a UART.

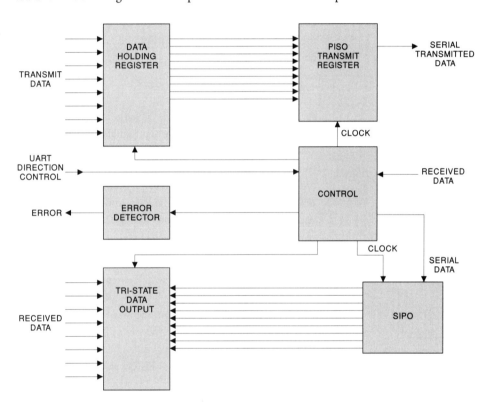

The UART's receiver section is basically the reverse of the transmit section. Serial data is shifted into the **Serial Receive Shift Register** until the predetermined number of bits has been accumulated. At this point, the bits are loaded (in parallel form) into the **Receive Holding Register**. Both the transmit and receive functions are under the direction of the UART's control section. Many of the device's parameters, such as the number of start and stop bits and the type of parity (if any) to be used during transmission, may be programmed by the user through the control section.

In pre-Pentium units, the system's MI/O card provided a pair of fully programmable, asynchronous communication channels through two serial port connections. On earlier I/O cards, a pair of **8250 UART**s were used as the basic port circuitry. In newer MI/O cards, a single VLSI device, called an integrated I/O controller, provides the interfacing and UART functions. In most Pentium systems, the serial port adapter function is incorporated into the system board's integrated I/O controller IC.

The original serial adapters featured programmable baud rates from 50 baud to 9600 baud, a fully programmable interrupt system, and variable character lengths (5-, 6-, 7-, or 8-bit characters). In addition, the adapter added and removed start, stop, and parity bits, had false start-bit detection, had line-break detection and generation, and possessed built-in diagnostics capabilities. As modems became faster, upgraded UARTs were included, or integrated, to keep up.

Notable advanced UART versions include the **16450** and **16550**. The 16450 was the 16-bit improvement of the 8250, and the 16550 was a high-performance UART with an onboard 16-byte buffer. The buffer enables the UART to store or transmit a string of data without interrupting the system's microprocessor to handle them. This provides the 16550 with an impressive speed advantage over previous UARTs. These advanced UARTs enable serial ports to reach data transmission rates of up to 115Kbps. Though some features have changed between these UARTs, and though they are sometimes integrated directly into an integrated I/O chip, the units must still adhere to the basic 8250 structure to remain PC-compatible.

USARTs

As their name implies, USARTs have the capability to perform asynchronous communications as the UART does, but when higher-performance data transfers are required, the USART is used in synchronous mode. A few words of clarification about why synchronous transmission would offer higher performance (speed) than asynchronous transmission are in order at this point. Recall that, for asynchronous communications, a start bit is required to mark the beginning of each character, and at least one stop bit is required to identify the end of the character. This means that at least 10 bits (and therefore 10 bit times) are required to send an 8-bit data character.

On the other hand, synchronous transmissions require no nondata bits after the transmitter and receiver have been initialized. Therefore, 8 bits of data are transmitted in 8 bit times. The only drawback is that any break in the data stream causes the transmitter and receiver to become desynchronized. To minimize this problem, the USART incorporates extra internal circuitry to generate "dummy" or "null" characters for transmission. This keeps the data flow rate in sync when no actual data is being sent. In addition, the USART also incorporates a set of **first-in, first-out** (**FIFO**) registers. These registers can be filled in advance (this is called **queuing**) so that a constant flow of data—and, therefore, constant synchronization—can be maintained between the transmitter and receiver.

Serial Interface Connections

Because of the popularity of asynchronous serial data transmissions and the number of devices that use them (including printers and modems), standardized bit-serial signals and connection schemes have been developed to simplify the process of connecting serial devices to computers. The most popular of these serial interface standards is the **Electronic Industry Association** (**EIA**) RS-232C interface standard.

The RS-232C Standard

A+ CORE 1.4

Basically, the IBM version of the **RS-232C** standard calls for a 25-pin, male D-type connector, as depicted in Figure 7.10. This standard also designates certain pins for data transmission and receiving, along with a number of control lines. These pin designations are expressed in Table 7.2. The standard was developed to cover a wide variety of peripheral devices, so not all the lines are used in any given application. Different device manufacturers may use different combinations of RS-232C lines, even between peripherals of the same type.

FIGURE 7.10

RS-232C connector.

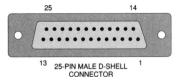

25   14

13   25-PIN MALE D-SHELL   1
      CONNECTOR

Table 7.2 *RS-232C Signal Lines*

Pin No.	Common Name	RS-232C Name	Description
1		AA	Protective ground
2	TxD	BA	Transmitted data
3	RxD	BB	Received data
4	RTS	CA	Request to send
5	CTS	CB	Clear to send
6	DSR	CC	Data set ready
7	GND	AB	Signal ground (common return)
8	CD	CF	Received line signal detector (RLSD)
9			Reserved for data set testing
10			Reserved for data set testing
11			Unassigned
12	SI	SCF	Secondary RLSD
13		SCB	Secondary clear to send
14		SBA	Secondary transmitted data
15		DB	Transmission signal element timing (DCE source)
16		SBB	Secondary received data
17		DD	Received signal element timing (DCE source)
18			Unassigned
19		SCA	Secondary request to send
20	DTR	CD	Data terminal ready
21		CG	Signal quality detector
22	RI	CE	Ring indicator
23		CH/CI	Data signal rate selector (DTE/DCE source)
24		DA	Transmit signal element timing (DTE source)
25			Unassigned

In addition to defining the type of connector to be used and the use of its individual pins, the RS-232 standard also establishes acceptable voltage levels for the signals on the pins. A logic "1" is represented by a voltage between −3 and −20V dc. Conversely, a logic "0" is signified by a voltage between +3 and +20V dc. These levels are generally converted to and from

TTL-compatible signals by CMOS driver and receiver chips. Under these conditions, a maximum baud rate of 20,000 baud can be achieved for distances of less than 50 feet.

Advanced Serial Standards

Since the adoption of the RS-232C standard, the EIA has also adopted two more improved serial standards: the **RS-422** and **RS-423**, which are enhancements of the RS-232C standard. The RS-422 uses twisted-pair transmission lines and differential line signals to provide a high degree of noise immunity for transmitted data. The RS-423 standard uses coaxial cable to provide extended transmission distances and higher data-transfer rates.

A+ CORE 1.4 With the advent of the mouse as a common input device, a 9-pin, male D-shell version of the RS-232 serial port became common. This version is commonly used as the COM1 serial port for the mouse in Windows-based systems. Figure 7.11 depicts the 9-pin version of the interface being used to connect a serial printer through a common connection scheme referred to as a "null modem."

FIGURE 7.11

RS-232C 9-pin serial printer connection.

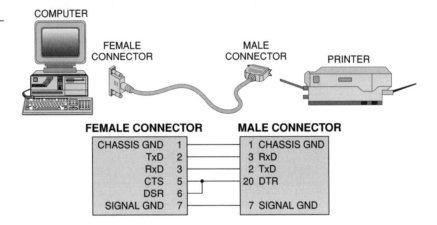

The exchanging of pins 2 and 3 between the two devices forms the basis of the **null modem**. Because the device in Figure 7.11 is a serial printer, pins 5 and 6 of the DTE equipment are tied to the DTR pin of the DCE equipment. In a true null modem, pins 4 and 5 of the interface would need to be cross-connected to facilitate two-way communications.

The character bit stream is transmitted to the printer on the line designated as the **Transmit Data (TXD)** line at the computer connector, and the **Receive Data (RXD)** line at the printer connector. A reciprocal line (TXD at the printer connector and RXD at the computer connector) is also used in the printer interface. Because data does not flow from the printer to the computer, this line basically informs the computer that a printer is connected to the interface, is turned on, and is ready to receive data (much like the Select line in the Centronics interface standard).

The flow of data to the printer is moderated by a line referred to as the **Data Set Ready (DSR)** line at the computer connector, and the **Data Terminal Ready (DTR)** line at the printer connector. The printer uses this line in much the same manner as the Busy line of the Centronics interface. When the buffer is full, the printer signals on this line to tell the computer not to send any more data. More complex serial interfacing may include a line called the **Clear to Send (CTS)** line at the computer connector and the **Ready to Send (RTS)** line at the printer connector, and its reciprocal line, where the identifications are reversed.

At the printer's end of the cable, another UART receives the serial bit stream, removes the start and stop bits, checks the parity bit for transmission errors, and reassembles the character data into parallel form.

Because the movement of data is asynchronous using the UART, an agreement must be established between the computer's UART and the printer's UART concerning the speed at which characters will be sent. The transmission rate, or **baud** rate, of the computer's UART is generally set by software. On the other hand, the printer's baud rate is usually designated by a set of DIP switches in the printer. Common baud rates used with serial printers are 300, 1200, 2400, and 9600 **bits per second** (**bps**). One of the most common problems associated with getting a serial interface to work is mismatched baud rate.

Character Framing

In the Centronics type parallel port, the data is specifically sent in individual 8-bit packages. However, in serial communications there is more flexibility in how the data is transmitted. Typical RS-232 transmission formats enables 7- or 8-bit characters to be sent as a package inside a **character frame**. Each frame also contains various numbers of nondata bits for marking the starting and stopping points of the frame. An additional bit is often added to the frame for error-checking purposes. The composition of the character frame must be the same at both the sending and receiving ends of the transmission. It shouldn't be too difficult to understand what problems would arise if a device is set to receive a 7-bit character with two start bits, one stop bit, and an error-checking bit, but receives an 8-bit character with two start bits, two stop bits, and no error-checking bit.

Using the serial printer as an example, it should be easy to envision simple communications taking place. However, most serial port applications involve two-way communications. In these types of applications, control of the communication port becomes more complicated. In addition to matching baud rates and character framing between the two devices, a mechanism for controlling the flow of information between the two ports must be established. This method of controlling the flow of information between the two devices is called a **protocol** and must be agreed to by both devices for the transfer to be successful. Both hardware and software flow-control protocols have been devised for use with serial ports. More information about character framing and protocols is presented in Chapter 11, "Data Communications."

DOS Serial Port Names

As with parallel ports, DOS assigns COM port designations to the system's serial ports during boot-up. COM port designations are normally **COM1** and **COM2** in most systems, but they can be extended to **COM3** and **COM4** in advanced systems.

Either RS-232 port may be designated as COM1, COM2, COM3, or COM4, as long as both ports are not assigned to the same COM port number. In most PCs, COM1 is assigned as port address hex 3F8h and uses IRQ4. The COM2 port is typically assigned port address hex 2F8h and IRQ3. Likewise, COM3 uses IRQ4 and is assigned an I/O address of 3E8h, and COM4 usually resides at 2E8 and uses IRQ4.

Game Port

The **Game Control Adapter** enables up to four **game paddles** or two **joysticks** to be used with the system. The adapter converts resistive input values into relative paddle or joystick positions in much the same manner described in the previous section. This adapter can also function as a general-purpose I/O converter, featuring four analog and four digital input points. Figure 7.12 depicts a block diagram of the Game Control Adapter.

FIGURE 7.12

The Game Control Adapter.

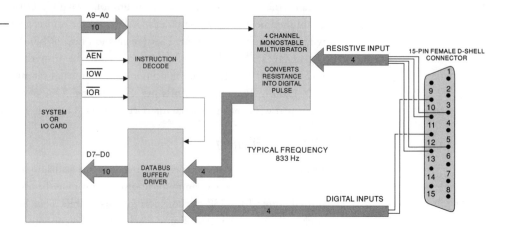

The input to the game port is generally a set of resistive joysticks or game paddles. Joysticks are defined as having two variable resistances, and game paddles are defined as consisting of one variable resistance. Each resistance should be variable between 0k ohms and 100k ohms. Joysticks may have one or two **fire buttons** normally open. Game paddles have only one button. Under this definition, the Game Control Adapter will support two game paddles (A and B), four game paddles (A, B, C, and D), or two joysticks (A and B). The order of fire buttons should correspond with that of the resistive elements (A and B or A, B, C, and D).

This interface is simple and straightforward, combining elementary hardware and software techniques. When the software issues the adapter's address (201h) and an IOW signal, the timers are triggered into their active state. The individual timer outputs remain active for a length of time, dictated by the setting of each resistive input and timing capacitor at each timer's input. As each timer times out according to its own resistive/capacitive (RC) time constant, its output returns to an inactive state.

The software periodically polls the adapter's latching register data to determine whether each output has timed out. A software counter keeps track of the number of times the port has been read before the timers time out. The number of read cycles (0 to 255) before a logic low is encountered is directly proportional to the resistive setting of the joystick or game paddle. The wiring structure for the 15-pin, D-shell female connector is shown in Figure 7.13.

FIGURE 7.13

Game port connections.

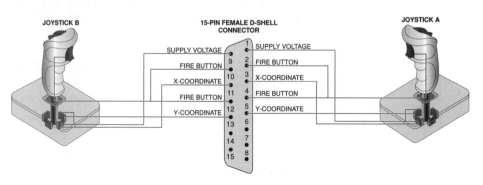

Troubleshooting Port Problems

Basically three levels of testing apply to troubleshooting port problems. These are the **DOS level**, the **Windows level**, and the **hardware level**.

Before concentrating on any of these levels, troubleshooting should begin by observing the symptoms produced by operation of the port. Observe the steps that led to the failure. Determine under what conditions the port failed. Was a new peripheral device installed in the system? Were any unusual operations in progress? Note any error messages or beep codes. Use the troubleshooting hints that follow to isolate the parallel, serial, or game-port circuitry as the source of the problem. Retry the system several times to observe the symptoms clearly. Take the time to document the problem.

Figure 7.14 illustrates the components involved in the operation of the serial, parallel, and game ports. Failures in these devices tend to end with poor or no operation of the peripheral. Generally, only four possible causes exist for a problem with a device connected to an I/O port:

▶ The port is defective.

▶ The software is not configured properly for the port.

▶ The connecting signal cable is bad.

▶ The attached device is not functional.

FIGURE 7.14

Components associated with I/O ports.

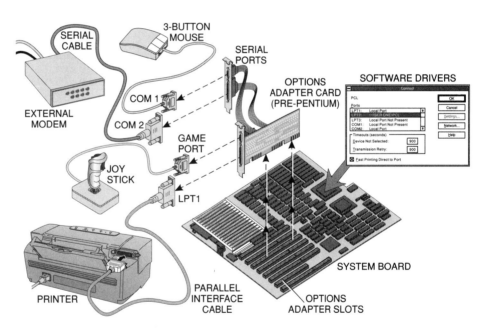

Port Problem Symptoms

A+ CORE 2.1

Typical symptoms associated with serial, parallel, or game port failures include the following:

▶ A 199, 432, or 90x IBM-compatible error code is displayed on the monitor (printer port).

▶ Online light is on, but the printer prints no characters.

▶ A 110x IBM-compatible error code is displayed on the monitor (serial port).

- "Device not found" error message, or unreliable connection.

- Input device will not work on the game port.

As you can see from the symptom list, I/O ports do not tend to generate many error messages on the screen.

Port Hardware Checks

A+ CORE 4.3
In the area of hardware, only a few items pertain to the system's ports: the port connector, signal cabling between the port circuitry and the connector in some units, the port circuitry itself, and the system board. As mentioned earlier, the port circuitry can be found on video cards in some older units, on specialized I/O cards in other units, and on the system board in newer units. In any of these situations, some configuration settings must be correct.

Check the board containing the I/O port circuitry, and its user's guide for configuration information. This normally involves LPT, COM, and IRQ settings. Occasionally, you will be required to set up hexadecimal addressing for the port addresses, but this is becoming rare.

> With newer Pentium systems, you must check the Advanced CMOS Setup to determine whether the port in question has been enabled and, if so, if it has been enabled correctly.

For example, a modern parallel port must be enabled and set to the proper protocol type to operate advanced peripherals. For typical printer operations, the setting can normally be set to **Standard Printer Port (SPP)** mode. However, devices that use the port in a bidirectional manner must be set to EPP or ECP mode for proper operation. In both cases, the protocol must be set properly for both the port and the device to carry out communications.

Figure 7.15 illustrates the movement of data to the parallel port mounted on an I/O adapter card.

FIGURE 7.15

Moving information through a port.

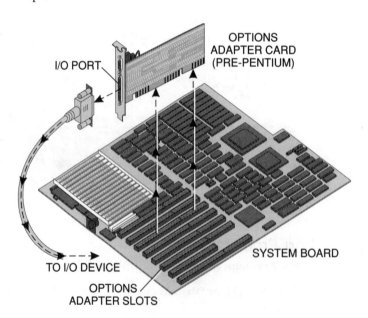

I/O PORT

OPTIONS ADAPTER CARD (PRE-PENTIUM)

SYSTEM BOARD

TO I/O DEVICE

OPTIONS ADAPTER SLOTS

A+ CORE 4.4
It is helpful to single-step through the boot-up to read the port assignments in the boot-up window. If serial or parallel port problems are occurring, the CMOS configuration window

is the first place to look. If the system does not detect the presence of the port hardware at this stage, then none of the more advanced levels will find it either. If values for any of the physical ports installed in the system do not appear in this window, check for improper port configuration jumpers or switches.

Because the unit has not loaded DOS at the time the configuration widow appears, DOS and Windows cannot be sources of port problems at this time. If all jumpers and configuration settings for the ports appear correct, assume that a hardware problem exists. Diagnose the hardware port problem to a section of the system (in this case, the board containing the port).

DOS Checks

If possible, run a software diagnostics package to narrow the possible problem causes. This is not normally a problem because port failures do not generally affect the main components of the system. Try to use a diagnostic program that deals with the system board components. This should include parallel and serial port tests, as well as a game port test if possible.

Run the program's **Port Tests function** and perform the equivalent of the ALL tests function. Note all the errors indicated by the tests. If a hardware error is indicated, such as those already mentioned, it may be possible to take some corrective actions (such as resetting or reconfiguring LPT, COM, or IRQ settings) without replacing the unit containing the port hardware. However, if more complex port problems are indicated, exit the diagnostic program and replace the port hardware.

DOS Parallel Ports

Software diagnostic packages normally ask you to place a **loop-back test plug** in the parallel port connector to run tests on the port. The loop-back plugs simulate a printer device by redirecting output signals from the port into port input pins. Figure 7.16 describes the signal rerouting scheme used in a parallel port loop-back plug.

FIGURE 7.16

Parallel port loop-back connections.

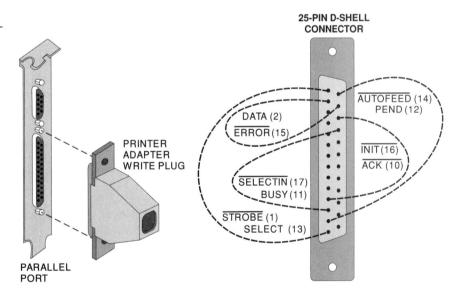

A live printer can be used with the port for testing purposes, but this action elevates the possibility that the printer can inject problems into the troubleshooting process.

If the software diagnostic program does not provide enough information to solve the problem, attempt to print to the first parallel port from the DOS level. To do this, type **COPY AUTOEXEC.BAT LPT1:** at the DOS prompt, and press the ENTER key.

If the file is not successfully printed, at the C:\>> DOS prompt, type **EDIT AUTOEXEC.BAT**. Check the file for a SET TEMP = command. If the command is not present, add a SET TEMP statement to the AUTOEXEC.BAT file. At the C:\>> DOS prompt, type **EDIT AUTOEXEC.BAT**. Create a blank line in the file, and type **SET TEMP=C:\WINDOWS\TEMP** into it. Save the updated file to disk, and reboot the system. Make sure to check the SET TEMP= line for blank spaces at the end of the line.

Is there a printer switch box between the computer and the printer? If so, remove the print-sharing equipment, connect the computer directly to the printer, and try to print from the DOS level, as previously described.

Check the free space on the HDD. Remove any unnecessary files to clear space on the HDD, and defragment the drive, as described in Chapter 13, "Preventive Maintenance, Safety, and Customer Service."

DOS Serial Ports

As with parallel ports, diagnostic packages typically ask you to place a loop-back test plug in the serial port connector to run tests on the port. Use the diagnostic program to determine whether are any IRQ or addressing conflicts exist between the serial port and other installed options. The serial loop-back plug is connected different physically than a parallel loop-back plug so that it can simulate the operation of a serial device. Figure 7.17 describes the signal rerouting scheme used in a serial port loop-back plug.

FIGURE 7.17

Serial port loop-back connections.

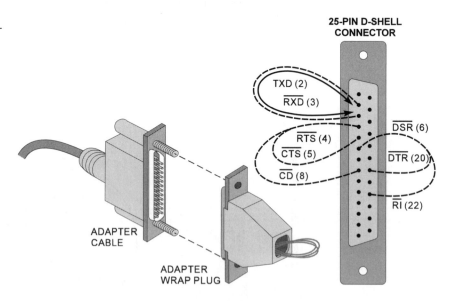

A live serial device can be used with the port for testing purposes, but as with the printer, this elevates the possibility that nonport problems can be injected into the troubleshooting process.

If the software diagnostic program does not provide enough information to solve the problem, attempt to print to the serial port from the DOS level. To do this, type **DIR. COMx** at the DOS prompt. The value of *x* is equal to the COM port to which you're printing.

Windows 3.x Checks

Windows adds another level of complexity to isolating port problems. Windows was designed to perform the printer and communication functions for the system. If DOS-level port operation is working but Windows is not, check under the Control Panel icon in the Main window. There is no Game Port setting in Windows, so this port can be tested only from the DOS level.

The [Ports] entry of the WIN.INI file is used to define parallel printer and serial ports. Up to 10 ports may be defined in this section: four serial ports, three parallel ports, two logical ports, and a file port. The SYSTEM.INI device-driver files control and communicate with the port hardware.

Windows 3.x Parallel Ports

Try to print from a non-Windows environment. Return to the DOS prompt and open a non-Windows application that has a print function. Attempt to print from the application.

If the system will print from DOS but not from Windows, determine whether the Print option from the application's File menu is unavailable (gray). If so, check the Windows Control Panel/Printers window for correct parallel port settings. Make certain that the correct printer driver is selected for the printer being used. If no printer is selected, or if the wrong printer type is selected, simply set the desired printer as the default printer. To add the desired printer as the default printer, enter the Main window, double-click the Control Panel icon, double-click the Printer icon, and set the desired printer as the default printer.

Click the Setup button to examine the selected printer's settings. If these settings are correct, click the Connect button to ensure that the printer information is being routed to the correct port. This sequence is depicted in Figure 7.18.

FIGURE 7.18

Printer and connect windows.

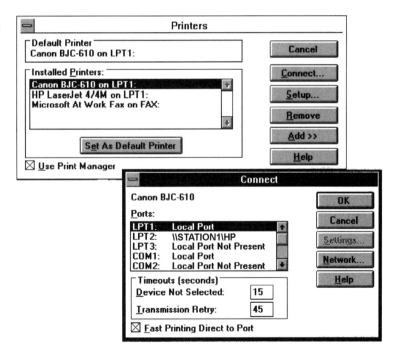

The final place to check for Windows printer-port problems is in the Print Manager. This area of Windows is reached through the Main window by double-clicking on the Print Manager icon. Check the Print Manager for errors that have occurred that may be holding up the print jobs that follow. If an error is hanging up the print function, highlight the offending job and remove it from the print spool by clicking the Delete Document entry of the Document menu (see Figure 7.19).

FIGURE 7.19

Print Manager window.

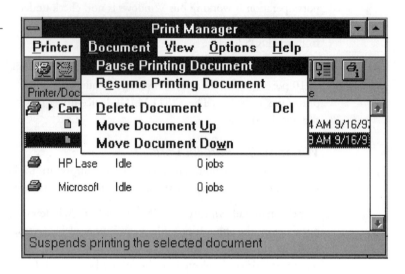

Windows 3.x Serial Ports

Check the Windows Control Panel/Ports window for correct serial port settings. This is accomplished by double-clicking the main tile. Double-click the Control Panel icon to access it, click the Ports option, and click the Settings button. Most serial printers use settings of 9600 baud, No Parity, 8 bits, 1 stop bit, and Hardware Handshaking. Click on the Advanced button to determine the IRQ setup for the port. These steps are illustrated in Figure 7.20. Check the user's manual to document the correct settings for the device using the port in question.

FIGURE 7.20

*Main/Control Panel/
Port/Settings path for COM1.*

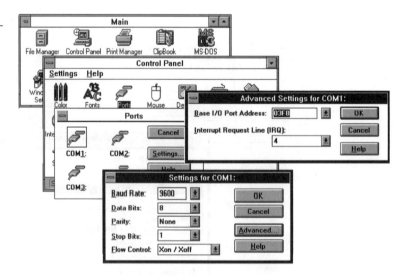

It is possible to check the internal setup of the Windows serial ports. From the DOS editor, check the SYSTEM.INI file for COM port configuration information. At the DOS prompt, type **Edit C:\WINDOWS\SYSTEM.INI**. Scroll down to the [386enh] section, and check the COM Port values. In Windows, mice are normally installed on COM1 or COM2. IRQ4 is normally assigned to COM1 and COM3, and IRQ3 is usually designated for COM2 and COM4.

Windows 95 Checks

The I/O port functions in Windows 95 can be reached through two avenues. Port information can be accessed through the desktop's Start/Settings buttons. This information can also be reached through the My Computer icon on the desktop. Printer port information can be viewed through the Printers icon, and serial port information is accessed through the System/Device Manager entries under the Control Panel icon.

Windows 95 Parallel Ports

Isolate the problem to the Windows 95 program by attempting to print from a non-Windows environment. Restart the computer in MS-DOS mode, and attempt to print a batch file from the DOS prompt.

If the system will print from DOS but not from Windows 95, check to see whether the Print option from the application's File menu is unavailable (gray). If so, check the My Computer/Printers window for correct parallel port settings. Make certain that the correct printer driver is selected for the printer being used. If no printer is selected, or if the wrong printer type is selected, use the **Add Printer Wizard** to install and set up the desired printer.

The system's printer configuration information is also available through the Device Manager tab under the System icon in the Control Panel. Check this location for printer port setting information. Also, check the definition of the printer under the Control Panel's Printer icon.

A+ DOS/WINDOWS 4.4

Windows 95 comes with an online tool, called **Print Troubleshooter**, to help solve printing problems. To use the Print Troubleshooter, click the Troubleshooting entry in the Windows 95 Help system, as illustrated in Figure 7.21. Press F1 to enter the Help system. The Troubleshooter will ask a series of questions about the printing setup. After all its questions have been answered, the Troubleshooter returns a list of recommendations for fixing the problem.

FIGURE 7.21

Accessing Windows 95 Troubleshooting Help.

If the conclusions of the troubleshooter do not clear up the problem, try printing a document to a file. This enables you to separate the printing software from the port hardware. If the document successfully prints to a file, use the DOS COPY command to copy the file to the printer port. The format for doing this is `COPY /B FILENAME.PRN LPT1:`. If the document prints to the file but will not print on the printer, then the hardware setup and circuitry are causing the problem.

Continue troubleshooting the port by checking the printer driver to ensure that it is the correct driver and version number. Click the Printer icon and select the Properties entry from the menu. Click the Details tab to view the driver's name. Click the About entry under the Device Options tab to verify the driver's version number.

Click the printer port in question (under the Printer icon) to open the Print Manager screen. Check the Print Manager for errors that have occurred that may be holding up the print jobs that follow it. If an error is hanging up the print function, highlight the offending job and remove it from the print spool by clicking the Delete Document entry of the Document menu.

Windows 95 Serial Ports

Information on the system's serial ports is contained in three areas under the **Device Manager**. These are the **Resources** entry, the **Driver** entry, and the **Port Settings** entry. The Resources entry displays port-address ranges and IRQ assignments. The Driver entry displays the names of the installed device drivers and their locations. The Port Settings entry, depicted in Figure 7.22, contains speed and character frame information for the serial ports. The Advanced entry under Port Settings enables the transmit and receive buffer speeds to be adjusted for better operation.

FIGURE 7.22

Port Settings entry.

Check under the Windows 95 Control Panel/System/Device Manager window for correct serial port settings. Click the Port Settings option to view the setup for the ports. Most serial printers use settings of 9600 Baud, No Parity, 8 bits, 1 stop bit, and Hardware Handshaking (**Xon-Xoff**). Click on the Resources button to determine the IRQ setup for the port. Check the user's manual to document the correct settings for the device using the port in question.

Universal Serial Bus (USB)

> A new serial interface scheme, called the **Universal Serial Bus (USB)**, has been developed to provide a fast, flexible method of attaching up to 127 peripheral devices to the computer. The USB provides a connection format designed to replace the system's traditional serial and parallel port connections.

USB peripherals can be daisy-chained or networked together using connection hubs that enable the bus to branch out through additional port connections. The resulting connection architecture is a tiered-star configuration, such as the one depicted in Figure 7.23.

The USB system is composed of a **USB host** and **USB devices**. The devices category consists of **hubs** and **nodes**. In any system, one USB host exists. This unit contains the interface that provides the USB **host controller**. The controller is actually a combination of USB hardware, firmware, and software.

FIGURE 7.23

Universal Serial Bus architecture.

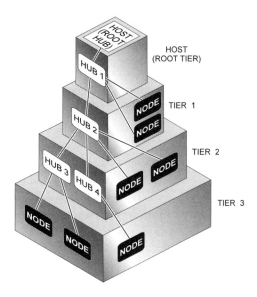

Hubs are devices that provide additional connection points for other USB devices. A special hub, called the **root hub**, is an integral part of the host system and provides one or more attachment points for USB devices.

Although the tiered architecture depicted in Figure 7.23 approaches the complexity and capabilities of the local area networks covered in Chapter 11, "Data Communications," a more practical desktop connection scheme is presented in Figure 7.24. It is evident that some of the components of the system (including the keyboard and the monitor) serve as both a function and as a hub. In these devices, the package holds the components of the function and provides an embedded hub to which other functions can be connected. These devices are referred to as **compound devices**.

FIGURE 7.24

USB desktop connection scheme.

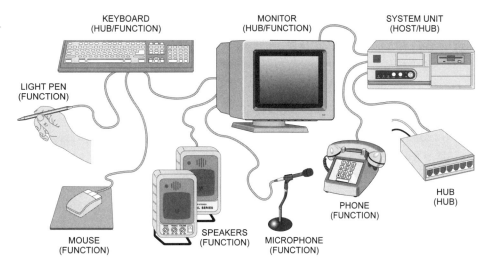

USB Cabling and Connectors

USB transfers are conducted over a four-wire cable, as illustrated in Figure 7.25. The signal travels over a pair of twisted wires (D+ and D–) in a 90 ohm cable. The differential signal and twisted-pair wiring provide minimum signal deterioration over distances and high noise immunity.

FIGURE 7.25

The USB cable.

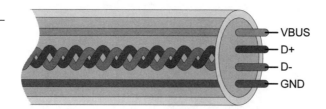

VBUS
D+
D-
GND

A Vbus and ground wire are also present. The Vbus is the +5 Vdc power cable. The interface provides power to the peripheral attached to it. The root hub provides power directly from the host system to those devices directly connected to it. Hubs also supply power to the devices connected to them. Even though the interface supplies power to the devices, they are allowed to have their own power sources, if necessary. In these instances, the device must be designed specifically to avoid interference with the bus's power distribution scheme. The USB host's power-management software can apply power to devices when needed and suspend power to it when not required.

The USB specification defines two types of plugs: Series-A and Series-B. **Series-A connectors** are used for devices in which the USB cable connection is permanently attached to devices at one end. Examples of these devices include keyboards, mice, and hubs. Conversely, the **Series-B plugs and jacks** are designed for devices (such as printers, scanners, and modems) that require detachable cabling. Both are four-contact plugs and sockets embedded in plastic connectors, as shown in Figure 7.26. The sockets can be implemented in vertical, right-angle, and panel-mount variations. The icon used to represent a USB connector is also depicted in the figure.

FIGURE 7.26

USB connectors.

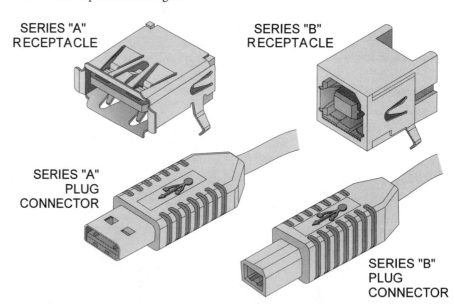

SERIES "A"
RECEPTACLE

SERIES "B"
RECEPTACLE

SERIES "A"
PLUG
CONNECTOR

SERIES "B"
PLUG
CONNECTOR

The connectors for both series are keyed so that they cannot be plugged in backward. All hubs and functions possess a single, permanently attached cable with a series B connector at its end. The connectors are designed so that the A and B series connections cannot be interchanged.

USB Data Transfers

Unlike traditional serial interfaces that transmit framed characters one at a time, data moves across the USB in the form of **data packets**. Packet sizes vary with the type of transmission being carried out. However, they are typically 8, 16, 32, or 64 bytes in length. All transmissions require that two or three packets of information be exchanged among the host, the source location, and the destination location.

All data transfers are conducted between the host and an **endpoint device**. The flow of data can occur in either direction. USB transactions begin when the host controller sends a **token packet** that contains information about the type of transaction to take place, the direction of the transmission, the address of the designated USB device, and an **endpoint number**. If the device is the source of the transaction, it either places a data packet on the bus or informs the host that it has no data to send. If the host is the source, it simply places the data packet on the bus. In either case, the destination returns a **handshake packet** if the transfer was successful. If an error is detected in the transfer, a **not acknowledge (NACK)** packet is generated. Figure 7.27 demonstrates the USB's four packet formats: the **token packet**, the **start-of-frame (SOF) packet**, the **data packet**, and the **handshake packet**.

Each type of packet begins with an 8-bit **packet ID (PID)** section. The SOF packet adds an 11-bit frame number section and a 5-bit **cyclic redundancy check (CRC)** error-checking code section. In the data packet, a variable-length data section replaces the frame number section, and the CRC frame is enlarged to 16 bits. The data section can range up to 1023 bytes in length. The handshake packet simply consists of a PID byte.

FIGURE 7.27

USB packet formats.

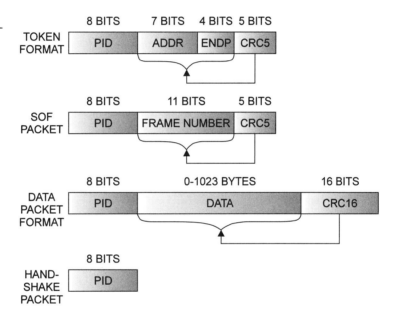

The USB management software dynamically tracks what devices are attached to the bus and where they are. This process of identifying and numbering bus devices is known as **bus enumerating**. The USB specification enables **hot-swap** peripheral connection, which does not require the system to be shut down. The system automatically detects peripherals and configures the proper driver. Instead of simply detecting and charting devices at startup in a PnP style, the USB continuously monitors the bus and updates the list whenever a device is added to or removed from it.

The USB specification provides for four types of transfers to be conducted:

▶ **Control transfers** are used by the system to configure devices at startup or time of connection. Other software can use control transfers to perform other device-specific operations.

- **Bulk data transfers** are used to service devices, such as scanners and printers that can handle large batches of data. Bulk transfers are typically made up of large bursts of sequential data. The system arranges for bulk transfers to be conducted when the bus has plenty of capacity to carry out the transfer.

- **Interrupt transfers** are small, spontaneous transfers from a device that are used to announce events, provide input, coordinate information, or transfer characters.

- **Isochronous transfers** involve large streams of data. This format is used to move continuous real-time data streams such as voice or video. Data delivery rates are pre-determined and correspond to the sampling rate of the device.

Input Devices

Input devices convert physical quantities into electronic signals that can be manipulated by interface units. The input devices typically used with microcomputers convert human physical activity into electronic impulses that can be processed by the computer. The chief devices of this type are keyboards, joysticks, mice, and light pens and touch panel screens.

These devices are illustrated in Figure 7.28. Other types of input devices convert physical quantities (such as temperature, pressure, and motion) into signals that can be processed. These devices are normally found in industrial control applications.

FIGURE 7.28

Input devices.

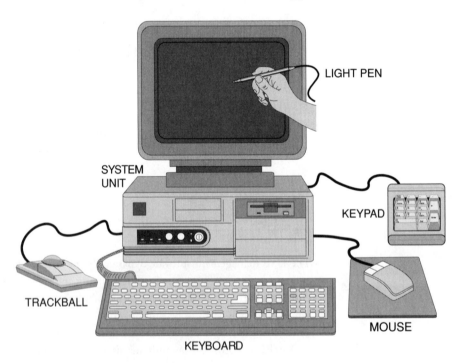

LIGHT PEN

SYSTEM UNIT

KEYPAD

TRACKBALL

MOUSE

KEYBOARD

Keyboards and Keypads

The **alphanumeric keyboard** is the most widely used input device for microcomputers. It provides a simple, finger-operated method of entering numbers, letters, symbols, and special control characters into the computer.

362   PART III   THE BASIC SYSTEM

Modern computer keyboards are actually adaptations of earlier typewriter-like keyboards used with teletypewriters. These devices served as both input and output systems for the earliest generation of computers. In addition to the alphabetic and numeric keys found on conventional typewriters, the computer keyboard may also contain any number of special function and command keys to extend its basic operation and provide special-purpose entry functions.

In smaller microcomputers, such as those programmed in hexadecimal code, numeric-only **keypads** may be used as the sole means of entering programs and data. In some computer keyboards, numeric keypads resembling calculator keypads are included with the alphanumeric keys. When large amounts of numeric data must be entered into the computer, the keypad usually proves more efficient than the numeric keys associated with the alphanumeric portion of most keyboards.

Keyboard Designs

The pattern in which keyboards are arranged and constructed has traditionally sparked some debate among users. Everyone seems to have a favorite key pattern in a keyboard. Obviously, an individual who is trained to touch-type on a standard QWERTY typewriter keyboard would prefer that the computer keyboard be laid out in the same manner. The contour of the key top, the amount of pressure, and the length of the stroke that must be applied to the key to actuate it are also important **ergonomic considerations** in keyboard design. Some keyboards offer a defined click at the bottom of the keystroke to identify a complete entry. Others offer shorter key strokes with a soft bottom and no feedback click.

Keyboard design is part form and part function. Although the **QWERTY keyboard** remains the standard for key arrangement, a second key pattern, known as the **DVORAK keyboard**, has gained some notoriety. This keyboard layout, depicted in Figure 7.29, attempts to arrange the keyboard characters in a more logical pattern that should lead to faster operation. Its basic premise is that the new key placement should lead to alternate hand usage.

Although the layout is quite old, (devised in 1936) and does offer some speed advantages, the DVORAK keyboard has gained only minimal acceptance by users. However, the programmability of PC-compatible keyboards make DVORAK conversion easy if desired. The only physical action required to implement a DVORAK layout involves repositioning the keyboard's keycaps.

FIGURE 7.29

A DVORAK keyboard.

Still other designs have been adapted to make using the keyboard more comfortable for the user. Some units include a special cushion along the front edge to provide support for the wrists. Another innovative design divides the keyboard in half and angles each side back slightly, as illustrated in Figure 7.30. This design is supposed to offer a more natural angle for the human hands than straight-across designs.

FIGURE 7.30

An ergonomic keyboard design.

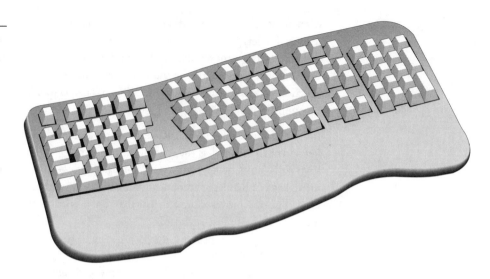

Keyboard Encoding

Inside, a keyboard is basically an **X–Y matrix** arrangement of switch elements, as shown in Figure 7.31. To produce meaningful data from a key depression, the keyboard must be capable of detecting and identifying the depressed key, debounce it, and encode the key closure into a form the computer can use.

FIGURE 7.31

A typical keyboard matrix.

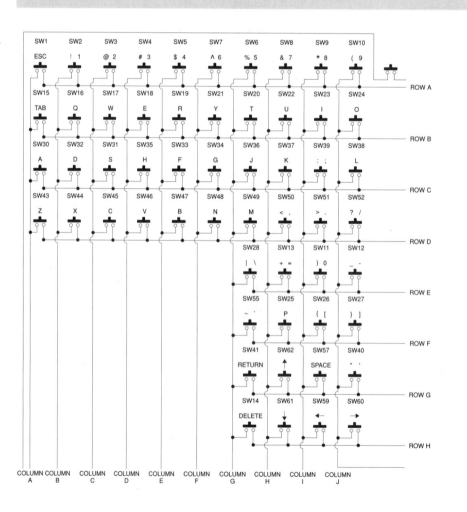

Depressing one of the keys shorts a row to a column. The closure is detected by applying an active logic level to the rows, either one at a time or collectively, and scanning the columns for an active level. When an active logic level is detected on a column, the row/column intersection represents the key closure.

After the detection and identification process has been completed, a short delay is imposed and the key is rechecked. A **time delay** is one method of eliminating a characteristic associated with all types of keyboard switches, known as **key bounce**. Key bounce occurs just prior to the switch closure and just after its release, while the switch contacts are in close proximity to each other. During these periods (5–20 milliseconds), contact-arcing can produce pulses that may be erroneously interpreted as additional digital signals.

To transform the coordinates of the key closure into a more conventional code (such as hex, EBCDIC, or ASCII), the row and column information is applied as an address to a ROM lookup table. This table holds the corresponding character codes. The same function can also be performed by a software routine.

As a matter of fact, all the functions discussed so far can be performed with software routines. Software interfacing has the advantages of lower cost and less board space than would be required to perform the same tasks with hardware. The disadvantage of software interfacing is the fact that the system microprocessor must expend a great deal of time involved in keyboard operations.

On the other hand, advancements in LSI chip technology have produced single-device **keyboard encoders** that contain all the circuitry necessary to interface the computer to an electronic keyboard. By enabling hardware to handle the keyboard functions, the system's microprocessor is freed to perform other more important functions. The system's microprocessor needs to be involved with the keyboard only long enough to transfer the character from the keyboard after it has been notified that a valid key closure has occurred. Figure 7.32 depicts a block diagram of a typical hardware keyboard encoder.

FIGURE 7.32

A keyboard encoding scheme.

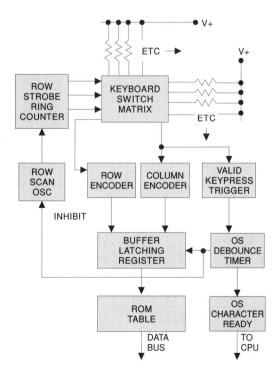

A **row-scan oscillator** is used to clock a **row strobe ring counter**. The counter circulates an active output level sequentially to the rows of the matrix. When a key is depressed and the row strobe places the active level on that row, an active level is produced at the corresponding column. The high-to-low transition on any of the column lines triggers the one-shot debounce timer. The row and column logic patterns are combined through two encoders to form an address for the ROM lookup table.

The debounce timer performs three functions. When a key closure is detected, the timer output inhibits the scan oscillator to prevent further scanning until the closure encoding is completed. Secondly, the debounce timer clocks the **scan-code latch** to enable the combined row/column address code to be applied to the ROM table. Finally, the debounce timer triggers a second one-shot, which produces a **character-ready** signal to inform the system that a valid character has been entered.

A more advanced hardware-encoding method uses a dedicated microprocessor, called a **microcontroller,** to monitor the keyboard matrix, as depicted in Figure 7.33. The microcontroller scans the matrix and generates an interrupt request signal when a key closure occurs. The microcontroller performs all the functions previously discussed and offers greater flexibility in operation. This includes the capability to evaluate multiple, simultaneous key closures for legitimate entries; simplified multiple-key entries (such as control characters, lowercase letters, and so on); faster scan rates; and the capability of redefining the function of various keys.

FIGURE 7.33

Keyboard encoding with a controller.

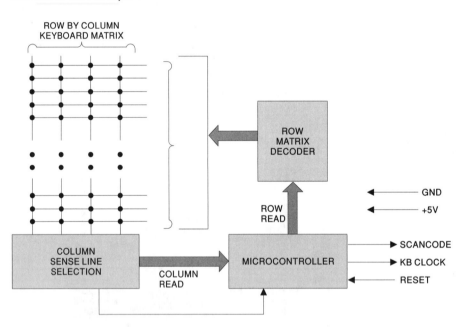

Switching Techniques

Several methods of switching are used to perform the keying function in computer keyboards. The oldest of these is the simple **mechanical switch**, depicted in Figure 7.34. The mechanical switch functions in much the same manner as a common light switch. Though mechanical switches have been the mainstays of switching technology for some time, techniques using electronic parameters (such as capacitance and inductance) have gained widespread acceptance.

FIGURE 7.34

A hard-contact switch.

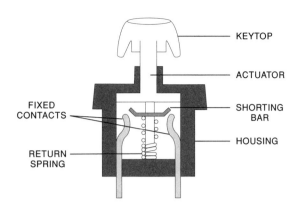

Mechanical Switches

The term *mechanical switch*, as it applies to computer keyboards, actually covers a fairly wide range of mechanical devices. Mechanical keyboards can be separated into two basic groups:

- The hard-contact keyboard, in which individual switches provide the keys
- Key panels, constructed as integrated units

The switch in Figure 7.34 depicts a typical **hard-contact key switch**. These switches are widely used in keyboards because they are relatively inexpensive. They do, however, tend to suffer from excessive key bounce and a relatively short life span.

A somewhat newer mechanical-switching technique is the **snap-action dome switch**, shown in Figure 7.35. A small stainless-steel dome is connected to a conductor on a PC board. A second conductor passes beneath the dome. When pressure is applied to the top of the dome by a key plunger or by touching a plastic overlay, contact occurs between the dome and the center conductor.

FIGURE 7.35

A snap-action dome switch.

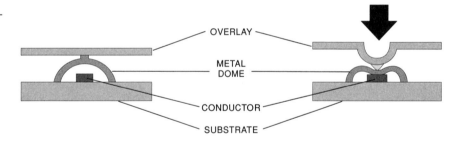

When pressure is released, the dome snaps back to its original shape, and contact between the dome and the conductor is removed.

The snap-action dome switch may be used with key caps, where the individual switches are set in a **keyboard arrangement**. The switches may also be used in a dome switch field, covered by a common overlay. This is referred to as a **key panel arrangement**. Another key panel technology is the simple **membrane key panel**, depicted in Figure 7.36.

The membrane key panel is a flexible, three-layer lamination whose upper and lower layers are etched with adjacent metallic contact points. The separating layer holds the contact points apart under normal circumstances. However, this layer has openings between the contact points to enable contact to occur under pressure. The membrane is normally attached to a rigid substrate to prevent unintentional flexing of the laminations, causing the contact points to meet erroneously. The entire assembly is covered by a plastic overlay containing graphic images that identify and mark the location of the contact points.

FIGURE 7.36

A membrane key panel.

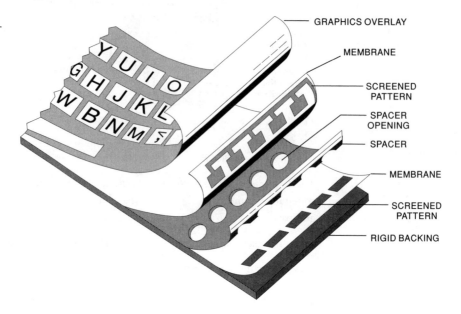

Solid State Switches

New types of noncontact electronic switching techniques have gained wide acceptance in computer keyboards. This is due to their low cost, high performance, and longevity of operation. Two of these methods are the **capacitive switching** and the **magnetic-core switching** techniques, depicted in Figures 7.37 and 7.38.

FIGURE 7.37

A capacitive switch.

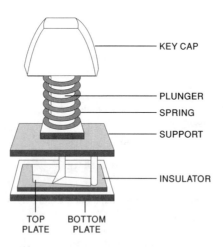

Capacitive switches work by using the varying capacitance between two switch contacts to change the frequency of an oscillator. The change in oscillator frequency is detected by the keyboard encoder and converted to a key closure signal.

The switch works on the most basic principle of a capacitor: A capacitor is simply two conductive plates separated by a dielectric (an insulator such as air). The capacitance of a switch is directly proportional to the area of its plates and is inversely proportional to the distance between them. In the switch, a movable plate approaches a fixed plate when the key is depressed. The capacitance of the switch increases as the plates approach each other, and the oscillator's output frequency decreases. The capacitive switch is easily the most popular technology used in keyboards today.

Magnetic-core switches use a ferro-magnetic keystroke plunger to alter the magnetic coupling between the two coils of a small transformer, as illustrated in Figure 7.38. When the plunger is in its nondepressed state, the magnetic core is out of the transformer, and its windings are loosely coupled. Depression of the key moves the core into the transformer, increasing its coupling. This enables pulses applied to the primary coil to be induced into the secondary coil with enough amplitude to be recognized as a valid output signal.

FIGURE 7.38

A magnetic-core switch.

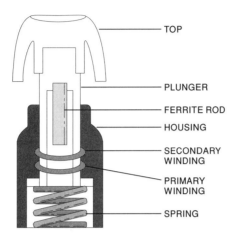

- TOP
- PLUNGER
- FERRITE ROD
- HOUSING
- SECONDARY WINDING
- PRIMARY WINDING
- SPRING

Interfacing and Connection

Most early microcomputers included the keyboard as an integral part of the system unit. However, most manufacturers now produce **detachable keyboards** that connect to the computer by a flexible cable. This grants the user greater movement potential and, therefore, increased comfort.

Extending the detachable keyboard concept one step further, the IBM PCjr offered completely cordless operation by transferring keyboard entries to the system over an infrared link.

A+ CORE 1.4 Most detachable keyboards use a round, 0.5-inch; 5-pin DIN connector to plug into the PC's system board. The connection is most often made through a round opening in the rear of the system unit's case. In some case designs, a front-mounted 5-pin plugin is included. The front-mounted connector is routed to the system board through an extension cable.

With the IBM PS/2 line, a smaller (0.25-inch), 6-pin mini-DIN connector was adopted. Other PC-compatibles use a modular 6-pin AMP connector to interface the keyboard to the system. Figure 7.39 shows the various connection schemes used with detachable keyboards.

PC-Compatible Keyboards

Figure 7.40 is a diagram of a typical 101-key keyboard that comes with most PC systems. It contains an onboard microprocessor, which provides fast scan rates, and has the capability to evaluate multiple key closures. As mentioned earlier in this section, the keyboard encoder is actually an 8-bit microprocessor specifically adapted for intelligent keyboard operations. The keyboard encoder has both internal RAM (128 x 8) and ROM (2k x 8), along with specialized electronics to handle keyboard control functions. The keyboard manufacturer programs the encoder to handle the particular keyboard being manufactured.

FIGURE 7.39

Connection schemes for detachable keyboards.

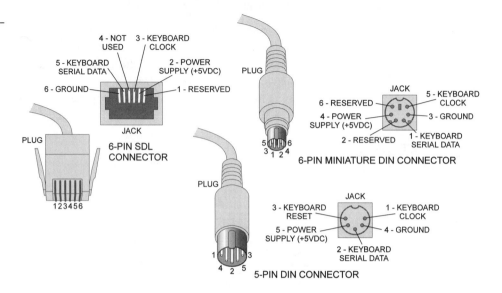

The system's keyboard-handling routines provide a **keyboard buffer** area in memory, which enables the user to type up to 10 characters ahead of the present operation. It also enables the user to redefine the keys in any manner desired, via software routines. Transfers of data from the keyboard to the system unit are performed serially.

FIGURE 7.40

A 101-key keyboard.

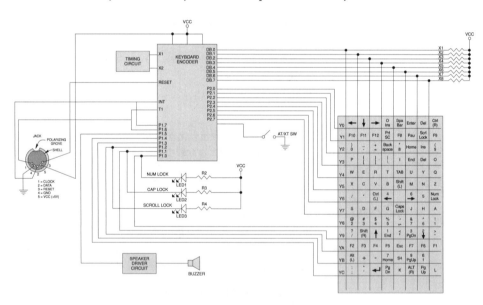

The keys of this PC's keyboard are arranged in a matrix of 13 active low Strobe lines and 8 normally high Sense lines. The keyboard encoder scans the lines of the matrix by sequentially dropping each of its scan lines to a low logic level. This causes each row of the matrix to be active for a short duration. The keyboard encoder sets the row-scan rate much faster than it is humanly possible to close one of the key switches and release it. The encoder scans the entire keyboard within 3 to 5 milliseconds.

When a switch closure shorts a particular row to a particular column, an active logic level appears at one of the keyboard encoder's sense inputs. When the active logic level is detected, the keyboard encoder pauses for a few milliseconds to enable the switch closure to **settle out**. In this manner, the keyboard encoder provides its own switch-debouncing, without using any additional hardware. After this short delay, the keyboard encoder stores the closure in its buffer and continues scanning until all the rows have been scanned.

At the end of the scan, the status of the entire keyboard has been stored in the encoder's internal buffer. This enables it to evaluate the keyboard for **phantom switch closures** and legitimate **multiple key closures** (such as CTRL+ALT+DEL). When the encoder detects two or more switches closed in the same row, it concludes that a phantom closure has occurred and generally ignores the condition completely.

Each time the keyboard encoder receives a valid key closure from the matrix, it generates two serially coded characters. The first is a distinct 8-bit code (referred to as a **scan code**) that corresponds to the key closure. The second is a **break code** that is generated when the key closure is broken. The break code is the same as the scan code, with the exception that the most significant bit of the break code is high.

The keyboard encoder's scan codes are listed in Figure 7.41. These codes are transmitted to the PC's system unit on the **Scan Code Data** (**KBDATA**) line. When no code is being sent, the keyboard encoder holds this line high. If a key (or a set of keys other than the Shift key) is held for more than half a second, the keyboard encoder begins regenerating the same scan code, at a rate of 10 times per second, until key-break is detected.

FIGURE 7.41

Keyboard scan codes.

Key	Make/Break Code	Key	Make/Break Code	Key	Make/Break Code	Key	Make/Break Code
Esc	01 / 81	J	24 / A4	' / ~	29 / A9	7 / Home	47 / C7
1 / !	02 / 82	K	25 / A5	Lft Shift	2A / AA	8	48 / C8
2 / @	03 / 83	L	26 / A6	\ /		2B / AB	9 / PgUp	49 / C9
3 / #	04 / 84	M	32 / B2	, /	33 / B3	-	4A / CA
4 / $	05 / 85	N	31 / B1	. /	34 / B4	4	4B / CB
5 / %	06 / 86	O	18 / 98	/ / ?	35 / B5	5	4C / CC
6 / ^	07 / 87	P	19 / 99	Rt Shift	36 / B6	6	4D / CD
7 / &	08 / 88	Q	10 / 90	*	37 / B7	+	4E / CE
8 / *	09 / 89	R	13 / 93	Lft Alt	38 / B8	1 / End	4F / CF
9 / (	0A / 8A	S	1F / 9F	Rt Alt	E0 38 / E0 B8	2	50 / E0
0 /)	0B / 8B	T	14 / 94	Space	39 / B9	3 / PgDn	51 / E1
- / _	0C / 8C	U	16 / 96	Caps Lock	3A / BA	0 / Ins	52 / E2
= / +	0D / 8D	V	2F / AF	F1	3B / BB	. / Del	53 / E3
Backspace	0E / 8E	W	11 / 91	F2	3C / BC	F11	57 / D7
Tab	0F / 8F	X	2D / AD	F3	3D / BD	F12	58 / D8
A	1E / 9E	Y	15 / 95	F4	3E / BE	Up Arrow	E0 48 / E0 C8
B	30 / B0	Z	2C / AC	F5	3F / BF	Dn Arrow	E0 50 / E0 D0
C	2E / AE	[/ {	1A / 9A	F6	40 / C0	Lft Arrow	E0 4B / E0 CB
D	20 / A0	] / }	1B / 9B	F7	41 / C1	Rt Arrow	E0 4D / E0 CD
E	12 / 92	Enter	1C / 9C	F8	42 / C2	Home	E0 47 / E0 C7
F	21 / A1	Lft Ctrl	1D / 9D	F9	43 / C3	End	E0 4F / E0 CF
G	22 / A2	Rt Ctrl	E0 1D / E0 9D	F10	44 / C4	Ins	E0 52 / E0 D2
H	23 / A3	; / :	27 / A7	Num Lock	45 / C5	Del	E0 53 / E0 D3
I	17 / 97	' / "	28 / A8	Scroll Lock	46 / C6	PgUp	E0 49 / E0 C9
						PgDn	E0 51 / E0 D1

The encoder notifies the system unit that it is ready to transmit a scan code by dropping the serial data line to an active logic level for 0.2 milliseconds. This forms a start-bit. The encoder then begins transmitting the code, with the least significant bit first, with each bit-time defined as 0.1 milliseconds in length. To coordinate the serial bit stream with the receiving circuitry, the keyboard encoder sends a **keyboard clock** (**KBCLK**) signal to the system unit.

Keyboard Interfacing

On PC and XT system boards, the keyboard interfacing function was handled by discrete logic circuits. The interfacing was based on a 74LS322 SIPO shift register. The incoming data bits from the keyboard were shifted into the register serially. A special two-pulse delay circuit in the Data line caused the register to ignore the two start bits at the beginning of the incoming data stream. When the 8 bits of the register became full, the shift register IC produced the system's IRQ1 signal and placed its bits on the system's data bus.

Intelligent Keyboard Controllers

On many AT-compatible system boards, a single-chip microcontroller performs the keyboard-interfacing functions. This specialized microcontroller is called an **intelligent keyboard controller**. It contains built-in control software, stored in an internal ROM area that enables its operation to be customized for keyboard control.

When the keyboard controller receives serial data from the keyboard, it checks the parity of the data, converts it into a scan code (which it stores in its output buffer), and generates an interrupt (IRQ1) to the system.

Figure 7.42 depicts the internal block diagram of an 8042/8742 intelligent keyboard controller. This type of device has been widely used in AT-compatible systems. From its internal structure, it should be easy to see that this is indeed a microprocessor, with an ALU, onboard control circuitry and a wealth of internal registers. This structure gives hardware and software designers a great deal of flexibility in the design and use of the computer's keyboard interface. However, for most purposes, the greatest points of interest in the keyboard controller are input and output data bus buffers (DBBIN and DBBOUT), its Input Port Register (P1.0–P1.7), its Output Port Register (P2.0–P2.7), and its Test lines (T0–T1).

FIGURE 7.42

A typical keyboard controller IC.

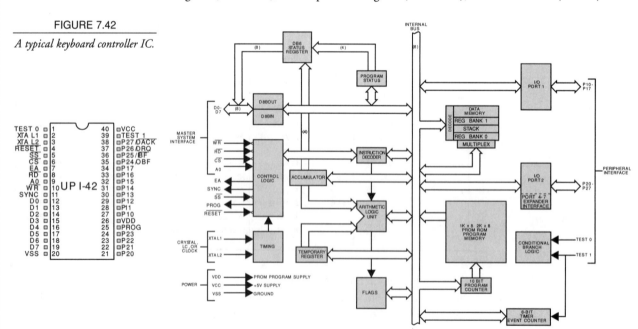

The keyboard interface enables data to be sent serially to the keyboard. This is accomplished by writing the data into the controller's input buffer. The data byte written into this location can be transmitted to the keyboard (with an odd parity bit added for error-detection purposes). Afterward, the controller waits for an acknowledge signal from the keyboard before allowing another byte to be written to the keyboard.

Figure 7.43 depicts a typical system board's keyboard controller circuitry. The interface circuitry supports a round, 5-pin DIN socket compatible with the keyboard plug found on nearly all keyboards manufactured for use with compatibles. Keyboard data passes through pin 2 of the connector (KBDATA), and clocking signals move through pin 1 (KBCLK). A keyboard reset, which can be connected to the system's RESET line, is included at pin 3. Ground and +5 Vdc connections are applied to the keyboard through pins 4 and 5, respectively.

FIGURE 7.43

The keyboard receiver circuitry.

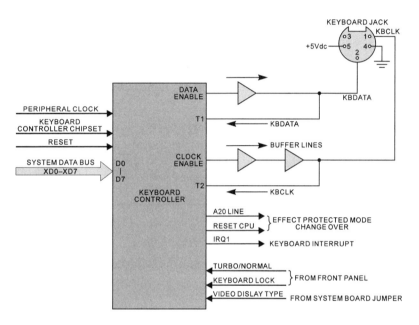

The front panel connections of most PCs have a BERG connector that enables an external **keylock switch** to be used to control access to the computer. If this switch is set to the lock position when the system performs its initialization routine, the boot-up program halts without reaching the DOS prompt or desktop.

The Input Buffer

The microcontroller's 8-bit input buffer serves two functions, depending upon how it is addressed. At hex address 60h, data written into the buffer is interpreted as data to be transmitted to the keyboard. However, data written to this buffer using address 64h is handled as a command to the controller.

The system's software writes to this buffer to manipulate the keyboard controller's Output Port Register. Through this register, software can enable or disable the Keyboard Data Clock lines. These functions are performed through the **Keyboard Data Enable (KBEN)** and **Keyboard Clock Enable (KBCLKEN)** bits. Other bits of this register cause the system to move back and forth between Real and Protected addressing modes and change the system's operating speed between Normal and Turbo modes. The interface is constructed in such a way that, when the system sends commands to the keyboard, it uses the KBEN and

KBCLKEN lines as its data and clock outputs to the keyboard. Table 7.3 defines the bits of the keyboard controller's output port (P2.0–P2.7).

Table 7.3 *The Keyboard Controller's Input- and Output-Port Bit Definitions*

Input Port		Output Port	
Bit	**Definition**	**Bit**	**Definition**
0	Reserved	0	CPU reset 0=CPU reset 1=CPU not reset
1	Reserved	1	Gate address but A20 0=A20 inhibited 1=A20 line not inhibited
2	Reserved	2	Reserved
3	Software turbo	3	Software turbo switch
4	Switch	4	Output buffer full (IRQ1) 0=Buffer not full 1=Buffer full (IRQ1)
5	Reserved	5	Reserved
6	Reserved	6	Keyboard clock (out) KBCLKEN 0=KB clock enabled 1=KB clock disabled
7	Keyboard inhibit 0=Keyboard inhibited 1=Keyboard unlocked	7	Keyboard data (out) KBEN

Real/Protected Mode Switching

The **A20** bit of the address bus is used when the system changes over from Real to Protected Addressing mode and back. To switch into Protected mode, the system software must do the following:

▶ Enable the system's A20 address line

▶ Clear all interrupts

▶ Store the address to which the processor should return when it re-enters Real mode

▶ Load the microprocessor's Protected mode tracking registers

▶ Unmask the interrupt handler routines

▶ Set the microprocessor's Protected-Mode Enable (PE) bit

When the microprocessor is first powered up, it starts in Real mode, and address lines from A20 up are disabled. A block of circuitry called the CPU reset circuitry produces a signal that indicates that the microprocessor will execute instructions only in the lower 1MB of physical memory. In this condition, shadow RAM can be moved into the top of the physical memory space.

The system's A20 line is enabled by writing a logic "1" into the Bit-1 position of the keyboard controller's output port. This signal is used to enable the microprocessor's **A20 Enable** pin (**AM20**). In this condition, the full range of the microprocessor's addressing capability becomes available when the microprocessor is reset. At this point, the system performs a special reset operation that affects only the microprocessor. This is accomplished as the software writes a logic 0 into Bit-0 of the keyboard controller's output port. This action resets the microprocessor through the system's **Reset CPU (RC)** line. The microprocessor basically goes to sleep in Real mode and wakes up in Protected mode.

To switch back from Protected mode to Real mode, the system must produce an appropriate logic level at the AM20 pin and activate the RC line. This action should not be confused with the system RESET signal, which resets all the devices in the system.

During boot-up and initialization, the keyboard controller reads and stores information gathered at its input port. The system's software issues commands to the controller that causes this information to be moved into the output buffer. From this register, the system can check the contents of this buffer for its hardware configuration information. The table also describes the functions of the keyboard controller's input port bits (P1.0–P1.7).

The Output Buffer

The controller also contains an 8-bit **output buffer** that duplicates the activities of the SIPO keyboard receiver register, found on PC- and XT-compatible system boards. The output buffer receives serial data bits from the keyboard through its T_1 input. These bits are clocked into the keyboard controller's buffer in conjunction with the KBCLK signal at the keyboard controller's T_0 input. Under the direction of its internal programming, the keyboard controller shifts the data bits from the keyboard into its output buffer. When the buffer becomes full, the keyboard controller generates the system's keyboard interrupt request (IRQ1), and the BIOS's keyboard interrupt handler routine examines the contents of this register to determine which key has been pressed.

On the system board, the KBCLK signal is shifted into the controller's T_0 input. Inside the controller, the signal is delayed by two clock periods and is then applied to the output buffer as its clock input. This action synchronizes the data bits to the clock signal to ensure that the data bits are read in the middle of the bit time. The scan code from the keyboard is applied serially to the controller's T_1 input. The two-pulse time delay prevents the scan code's start bits from being shifted into the register. When the eighth bit of the scan code has been shifted into the register, and when the keyboard controller receives another clock signal on the KBCLK line, the system generates and latches the IRQ1 to the system's interrupt controller.

The interrupt controller responds by placing an INT9 code on the data bus, which causes the microprocessor to call up the INT9 keyboard routine from the ROM BIOS program.

The system's BIOS routines convert the scan code into its ASCII-coded equivalent and stores both codes in a 16 x 16 FIFO character buffer. This action clears the interrupt request and enables other interrupts occurring in the system to be serviced. The keyboard buffer is actually organized in the 8-bit address locations of the system's RAM memory. The buffer permits up to 16 characters to be entered before they must be retrieved by the system. The unit beeps when the buffer is full. This arrangement enables the user to enter characters from the keyboard while the system is busy executing a previous command.

The scan codes from the keyboard are stored in the most significant byte of each buffer location, and the ASCII-coded character is stored in the corresponding lower byte of each location. Special keys, such as the numeric keypad and function keys (F1 through F12), store a 00 in their lower byte. This differentiates them from the ASCII-coded characters of the keyboard.

To cause the system to read the keyboard entries out of the buffer, the user, or the software package, an **INT16** signal must be generated. This interrupt causes the ROM BIOS routine to retrieve the character codes (both scan and ASCII) from the buffer and place them in the microprocessor's AX register. The scan code is placed in the AH portion of the register, and the ASCII code is stored in the AL byte. The scan code in AH enables the system to differentiate between keys that may return the same ASCII codes. The BIOS routine also checks the status of the codes to see whether any special keys were pressed (CTRL, ALT, DEL, SHIFT, and so on) If no character has been entered when the interrupt is encountered, and if AH=0, then the INT16 waits for a character to be entered.

Finally, the routine sends the ASCII character code to the program that called for it. The program delivers the code to the activated output device (monitor, modem, or printer). Sending a character to a display device through the CPU is called an **echo** and may be suppressed by programming so that the character is not displayed.

Troubleshooting Keyboard Problems

> Most of the circuitry associated with the computer's keyboard is contained in the keyboard itself. However, some keyboard interface circuitry is located on the system board. Therefore, the steps required to isolate keyboard problems are usually confined to the keyboard, its connecting cable, and the system board.

This makes isolating keyboard problems relatively easy: Simply check the keyboard and the system board.

> Some of the same symptoms given for keyboard problems are also described in Chapter 9, "Video Displays," under the section for video display problems. This is because most software packages (including DOS) echo keyboard entries through the system board's RAM memory to the monitor for display.

Keyboard Symptoms

A+ CORE 2.1

Typical symptoms associated with keyboard failures include the following:

▶ No characters appear onscreen when entered from the keyboard.

▶ Some keys work, while others don't.

▶ A "Keyboard Is Locked—Unlock it" error is displayed on the screen.

▶ A "Keyboard Error—Keyboard test failure" error is displayed on the screen.

▶ A "KB/Interface Error—Keyboard test failure" error is displayed on the screen.

▶ An error code of six short beeps is produced during boot-up.

▶ Wrong characters are displayed on the screen.

▶ An IBM-compatible 301-error code is displayed on the screen.

Configuration Checks

Keyboard information is stored in the CMOS setup memory and must accurately reflect the configuration of the system, or an error will occur. In most CMOS screens, the setup information includes keyboard enabling, Num Lock key condition at startup, **typematic**

rate, and **typematic delay**. The typematic information applies to the keyboard's capability to repeat characters when the key is held down. The typematic rate determines how quickly characters will be repeated, and the delay time defines the amount of time the key can be held before typematic action occurs. A typical typematic rate setting is 6 characters per second, and the delay is normally set at 250 milliseconds.

As with other components, the only time a configuration problem is likely to occur is when the system is being set up for the first time or when a new option is installed. The other condition that will cause a configuration problem involves the system board's CMOS backup battery. If the battery fails or has been changed, then the contents of the CMOS setup will be lost. After replacing the battery, it is always necessary to run the Setup utility to reconfigure the system.

Software Checks

Turn on the system and observe the BIOS screens as the system boots up. Note the **keyboard type** listed in the BIOS summary table. If possible, run a selected diagnostic program to test the keyboard. Run the program's **Keyboard Tests** function, and perform the equivalent of the ALL tests function, if available. These tests are normally very good at testing the keyboard for general operation and sticking keys.

If a stuck key or keys is detected, the individual key switches can be desoldered and replaced with a good key from a manufacturer or a similar keyboard. However, the amount of time that may be spent repairing a keyboard will quickly drive the cost of the repair beyond the cost of a new unit.

If the keyboard functions properly in DOS but not in Windows, check the Windows Keyboard settings. In Windows 3.x, start Windows and double-click the Main tile. Double-click the Setup icon, and note the keyboard listed in the Setup window. If the keyboard is not installed or is incorrect, install the correct keyboard type.

Keyboard Hardware Checks

If a hardware problem is suspected, the first task is to isolate the keyboard as the definite source of the problem. This is a fairly easy task. Because the keyboard is external to the system unit, is detachable, and is inexpensive, begin by exchanging the keyboard with a known good keyboard. Turn on the system and type characters from the keyboard. If the characters appear correctly on the screen using the new keyboard, check the bottom and backsides of the original keyboard for an **88/286/386 selector switch**. If the switch is present, make sure it is set to the correct position for the type of computer being used.

If the selector switch is not there, or if it is in the correct position, return the system to full service and then service the defective keyboard appropriately. Remove the back cover from the keyboard and check for the presence of a fuse in the +5 Vdc supply (refer to the connector pinout in Figure 7.43) as well as for continuity. Disconnecting or plugging in a keyboard with this type of fuse while power is on can cause it to fail. If the fuse is present, simply replace it with a fuse of the same type and rating.

If the system still won't boot up, recheck the CMOS Setup to make sure that the keyboard is enabled. Check the keyboard cabling for continuity. Finally, check the video display system (monitor and adapter card) to make sure that it is functional.

If replacing the keyboard does not correct the problem, and if no configuration or software reason is apparent, then the next step is to troubleshoot the keyboard receiver section of the system board. In most cases, this involves removing the system unit's outer cover and replacing the system board. After the cover is off, examine the keyboard connector on the system board. Also, look for auxiliary BERG connectors for the keyboard. Make certain that no item is shorting the pins of this connector together. Check for enable/disable jumpers for the keyboard on the system board.

Remove all the options adapter cards from the system board's expansion slots. Disconnect the system board from the power supply unit (P8–P9) and the system board/front panel connections. Take care to mark any connection removed from the system board and its connection point to ensure proper reconnection. Exchange the system board for a known good one. Reconnect all the power supply and front panel connections to the system board. Reinstall the video and disk-drive controller cards in the expansion slots, and try to reboot the system.

If the system boots up, turn it off, reinstall any options cards removed from the system, replace the system unit's outer cover, and return the unit to full service.

Mouse/Trackballs

A+ CORE 1.1

A mouse is a handheld pointing device that produces input data by being moved across a surface. Basically, the mouse is an X-Y positioning device that enables the user to move a cursor or some other screen image around the display screen.

The mouse also enables users to choose options from an onscreen menu instead of typing in commands from the keyboard or to use specialized software to create elaborate pictures on the screen. Currently, two methods exist by which a mouse can produce positional input data.

The first type of mouse is the **optical mouse**. The optical mouse requires a special pad, which is divided into a number of X and Y coordinates by horizontal and vertical lines on the surface of the pad. The mouse detects motion by emitting an infrared light stream, which is disturbed when the mouse crosses one of the lines on the pad.

The second mouse type is the **trackball mouse**, depicted in Figure 7.44. This type of mouse detects positional changes through a freewheeling trackball upon which it rides.

FIGURE 7.44

A typical trackball mouse.

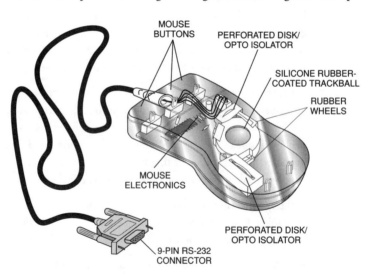

Both types of mice have similar appearances, although they may differ in the number of buttons on the top.

In the trackball mouse, movement of the mouse causes the trackball to roll. Inside the mouse, the trackball drives two small wheels that are attached to the rotors of two potentiometers (one X-pot and one Y-pot). As the trackball rolls, the wheels turn and the resistance of the pots' wipers varies proportionally. The varying resistance is converted to a varying analog output voltage. The output voltage undergoes A/D conversion, where it is changed into a digital input that represents movement of the mouse.

Some trackball mice use **opto-coupling** techniques to generate a string of digital pulses when the ball is moved. These devices are referred to as **opto-mechanical mice**. The mouse trackball moves two perforated wheels by friction. Light from LEDs shines through holes in the wheels (which are not attached to potentiometers) as the mouse moves. The light pulses are detected by a photoconductive device that converts them into digital voltage pulses. The pulses are applied to counters that tabulate the distance (both X and Y) that the mouse moves.

A+ CORE 1.2

In some applications, such as notebook computers, it is desirable to have a pointing device that does not require a surface to be moved across. The trackball can be thought of as an inverted mouse that enables the user to directly manipulate it. Trackballs, such as the one depicted in Figure 7.45, may be separate units that sit on a desk or clip to the side of the computer and connect to one of the system's serial ports. In many laptop and notebook computers, trackballs are frequently built directly into the system housing and are connected directly to its I/O circuitry. As with mice, trackballs may come with one to three buttons.

FIGURE 7.45

A trackball unit.

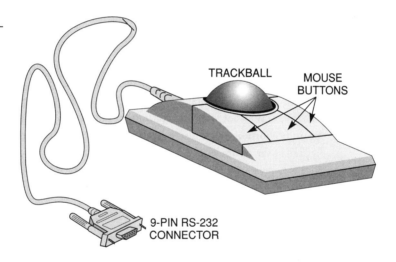

Mouse Communications

> Mice may also be classified by the method they use to communicate with the host computer. The most common type of mouse sends data to the computer serially. However, other mice, called **bus mice**, use dedicated cards to connect directly to the system's buses and communicate in parallel with the computer.

The serial mouse connects to the system through a DB-9M connector and uses the RS-232C interface. In older systems, a 25-pin-to-9-pin adapter may be required to physically connect the mouse to the unit.

A+ CORE 1.4   Bus mice use a 9-pin mini-DIN connector. This prevents them from being erroneously plugged into a serial bus connection. In addition, the bus mouse uses a completely different driver than the typical serial mouse to control its operation.

The circuitry of a typical serial mouse is shown in Figure 7.46. Notice that the typical serial mouse uses only four of the RS-232 serial connection lines. The power for the mouse is obtained from the interface's TXD line and signal ground (GND) line. The TXD line is normally at –12V, and the GND line is at signal ground.

FIGURE 7.46

Mouse circuitry.

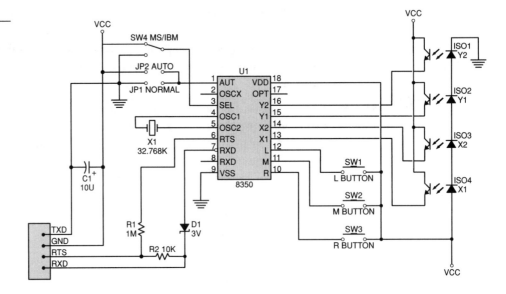

The mouse detects movement through the pulses of light created by the turning perforated wheels. These wheels rotate between the LED and photo-transistor sections of the opto-isolators (ISO1–ISO4). The intermittent pulses of light cause the transistors to turn off and on in proportion to the distance the trackball rolls. The transistors pulse the X and Y inputs of the mouse encoder IC, which determines the speed and direction of movement and generates a pulse train that corresponds to the movement. This information is applied to the serial port through the RXD line.

A+ CORE 1.7   The same type of action occurs when the mouse encoder detects that one of the mouse buttons has been depressed. The encoder generates and transmits a different series of pulses to the interface for each of the various actions of the mouse.

> Most mice require special **driver software** programs to control their operation. The driver software decodes the pulses sent by the mouse to determine what action the mouse is performing.

The driver software also supplies the instructions that interface software applications to the mouse. The driver tracks the position of the mouse based on information from the mouse and your software application. As it receives data from the mouse, the software displays a text cursor or graphics pointer on the screen.

A+ DOS/WINDOWS 3.5   Mouse manufacturers normally supply their device driver programs with the mouse. In DOS operations, the driver must be installed in the system before using the mouse. If the driver file is included in the AUTOEXEC.BAT file, it will be loaded into memory each time the computer is booted. Conversely, some mouse drivers are loaded in CONFIG.SYS as device drivers. As mentioned in Chapter 3, "Troubleshooting the System," the installation of the driver software may be performed automatically by the installation software, or the technician/user may have to do this manually. This depends on the nature of the device manufacturer's installation program.

Typically, a MOUSE.COM file is called for in the AUTOEXEC.BAT file, and a MOUSE.SYS file is referenced in the CONFIG.SYS file. Driver software for several common mice are included in the Windows software package. These drivers can be installed and set up at the time Windows is installed. The driver setup can also be changed anytime a new mouse is installed by accessing the Setup window.

Windows Mouse/Trackball Operation

The Windows software provides drivers for a number of different mice. The action of the mouse can be changed through the Mouse option of the Control Panel. To do this, select the Control Panel icon from the Main window. Double-click on the Mouse option, and move into the Mouse dialog box, depicted in Figure 7.47.

FIGURE 7.47

The Windows 3.x Mouse dialog box.

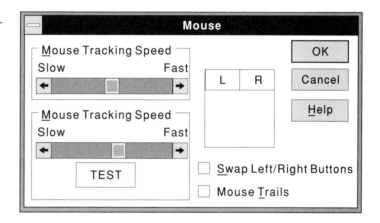

The mouse **tracking speed** and **double-click speed** can be modified from this dialog box. The tracking speed determines how fast the mouse pointer moves on the screen when you move the mouse. This option can be varied between the extremes of slow and fast. The tracking speed is changed by clicking the mouse on the arrow beside each extreme, to move the scrollbar in that direction.

The double-click speed is changed in the same manner. Often, the speed at which the user double-clicks the mouse button increases with more use of Windows. This can lead to frustration when you try to activate an icon and double-click too fast. After a new setting is implemented, you can sample the double-click speed through a test box under the option. The test box is highlighted when a valid double-click is recognized, according to the current setting of the double-click speed option.

The Mouse dialog box also enables the user to change the function of the mouse buttons for those who are left-handed. In the bottom right corner of the dialog box is a Swap Left/Right Buttons check box. By clicking on this check box, an X is placed in the box to indicate that the buttons are now reversed. Under this check box is another check box labeled Mouse Trails. When activated, this box causes mouse movement to leave a trail of mouse pointers on the screen.

Troubleshooting Mouse Problems

A+ CORE 2.1

> The levels of mouse troubleshooting move from configuration problems to software problems (including DOS, Windows, and applications) to hardware problems.

Maintenance of the mouse is fairly simple. Most of the problems with mice are related to the trackball. As the mouse moves across the tabletop, the trackball picks up dirt or lint, which can hinder its movement. This is typically evident by the cursor periodically freezing and jumping on the screen. On most mice, the trackball can be removed by a latching mechanism on its bottom. Twisting the latch counter-clockwise permits the removal of the trackball. Dirt can then be cleaned out of the mouse.

Mouse Configuration Checks

A common problem encountered when a new mouse is being installed is the setting of its 2/3-button switch. This switch, depicted in Figure 7.48, is located on the bottom of the mouse and may be marked with a 2/3 designation, or as PC/MS. The PC designation stands for three-button operation; the MS (Microsoft) setting specifies two-button operation. This switch setting must correspond to the software driver configuration.

FIGURE 7.48

The 2/3 button selection switch.

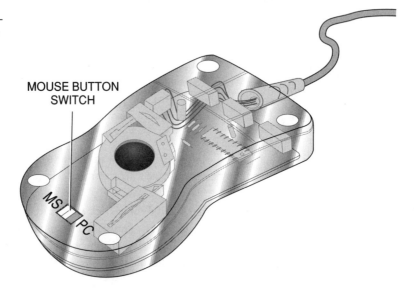

MOUSE BUTTON
SWITCH

MS   PC

Mouse Software Checks

Test the operation of the mouse in DOS first. Most mouse drivers come with a built-in test for DOS operation. If so, run the test program from the Mouse directory. If no self-test software is included, check the mouse in a non-Windows application.

If the mouse will not operate in DOS, check the BIOS Setup screen during boot-up for the presence of the serial port to which the mouse is connected. Check the directory structure of the system for a Mouse directory. Examine the AUTOEXEC.BAT and CONFIG.SYS files to see where the system looks for the mouse drivers. Two common driver files that may be present are the MOUSE.COM file called for in the AUTOEXEC.BAT file and the MOUSE.SYS file referenced in the CONFIG.SYS file.

If the driver software is not present in the directory indicated by the AUTOEXEC.BAT file, you must install it. At the C:\>> DOS prompt, type **MD\MOUSE**. Then type **CD\MOUSE** to move into the new subdirectory. Locate the manufacturer's driver disk, and insert it into drive A. Copy the mouse driver software into the Mouse subdirectory on drive C.

A+ CORE 2.1 If the mouse functions properly in DOS but not in Windows 3.x, then the Windows mouse driver and mouse settings must be checked. Begin by checking the Windows mouse driver in the Setup window. Move into the Main window by clicking its tile, and then click the Setup icon. Click the Options entry from the tool bar, and choose the Change System Settings option from the menu. Use the scroll arrow at the right of the window to move through the available driver options. Select the correct driver from the list, if available.

If the correct driver is not available in the Windows list, place the manufacturer's driver disk in the floppy drive, and load it using the Other Mouse (Requires Disk from OEM) option. If the OEM driver fails to operate the mouse in Windows, contact the mouse manufacturer for an updated Windows driver. Windows normally supports mice only on COM1 and COM2. Therefore, check the COM settings under the Control Panel's Ports icon. If several serial devices are being used in the system, it may be necessary to establish alternate IRQ settings for COM3 and COM4.

Check the IRQ and Base Address settings for Windows. Compare these settings to the actual configuration settings of the hardware. If they are different, change the IRQ or base address setting in Windows to match those of the installed hardware. Check the AUTOEXEC.BAT and CONFIG.SYS files for conflicting device drivers. In particular, look for a DEVICE = command associated with the mouse. Also check in the CONFIG.SYS file for device statements that apply to the mouse.

In Windows 95, click the Mouse icon in the Control Panel window to check the configuration and settings for the mouse. Follow this by checking the port configuration in Windows 95's Control Panel. Consult the Device Managers entry under the Control Panel's System icon. Select the Ports option, click the COM x Properties option in the menu, and click Resources. Make certain that the selected IRQ and address range match that of the port.

Mouse Hardware Checks

If the 2/3-button switch and driver setup is correct, then you must divide the port circuitry in half. For most systems, this involves isolating the mouse from the serial port. Simply replace the mouse to test its electronics.

If the replacement mouse works, then the original mouse is probably defective. If the electronics are not working properly, few options are available for servicing the mouse. The mouse may need cleaning or a new track ball. However, the low cost of a typical mouse generally makes it a throwaway item if simple cleaning will not fix it.

If the new mouse does not work, either, then the chances are very high that the mouse's electronics are working properly. In this case, the driver software or port hardware must be the cause of the problem.

Joysticks and Game Paddles

Joysticks are very popular peripheral devices for use with computer video games. However, these devices also provide a convenient computer/human interface for a number of other applications. Nearly every computer in the personal/business category includes ports for joysticks.

Most joysticks are X-Y positioning devices with a handle (gimbal) that can be moved forward, backward, left, right, or at any angular combination between these four basic directions. The joystick converts the movement of the handle, along either axis, into a digital signal that can be used to move a cursor on a display or that can be processed as a data input.

Two major types of joysticks exist: **analog** and **digital**. The analog version illustrated in Figure 7.49 employs two resistive potentiometer elements, one for **X-direction** and one for **Y-direction**. Both potentiometers are mechanically connected to the movable gimbal. A dc voltage applied across the resistance elements produces variable levels of output voltage when the gimbal is moved along the X-axis, Y-axis, or at some angle between them (this varies both the X and Y voltages). These analog voltages are applied to A/D converter circuits, which produce digital X-Y coordinate information for input to the computer. When this type of joystick is used to position a screen image, the position of the image on the screen corresponds to the X-Y position of the gimbal.

FIGURE 7.49

An analog joystick.

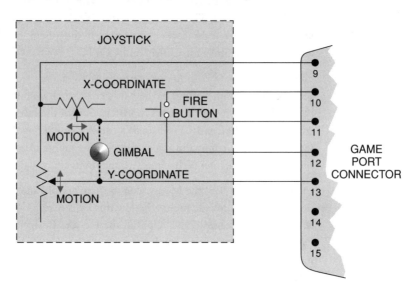

Figure 7.50 shows a simplified version of the A/D conversion process used with joysticks. The portion of the joystick's resistance picked off by the position of the gimbal becomes part of an RC proportional time constant that controls the timing factor of a one-shot timer. The duration of the one-shot's output pulse (Tp) is determined by the value of the RC time constant. More resistance produces a longer pulse duration, and less resistance causes the timing pulse to be shorter.

FIGURE 7.50

A/D conversion.

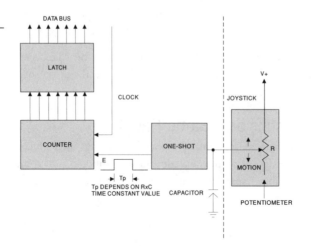

The output of the timer is used to clear and enable a digital pulse counter. This counts pulses produced by an oscillator with a predetermined output frequency. If the counter is enabled for a relatively long duration, the binary count will be higher than if the counter were enabled for a shorter time period. At the end of the enabling pulse, the output of the counter is latched into a PIPO register, where the system can read it. The counter is then cleared and, after a short reset delay, the one-shot is retriggered for another count sequence.

A somewhat simpler design is used in the construction of digital joysticks. The gimbal is used to mechanically open and close different combinations of an internal four-switch arrangement, as depicted in Figure 7.51. The joystick produces a single-byte output, which encodes the gimbal's movement in any of eight possible directions. Unlike analog joysticks, the position of the controlled image on the screen does not correspond to the X-Y position of the gimbal. Instead, the gimbal position produces only the direction of movement for the screen image. When the gimbal is returned to its neutral position, the screen image simply stops where it is.

FIGURE 7.51

A digital joystick.

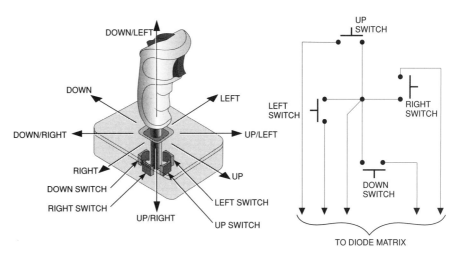

Game Port

A+ CORE 1.2 The **game port** enables game paddles or joysticks to be used with the system. The port's interface circuitry converts resistive input values into relative paddle or joystick positions in much the same manner described in the previous section. This port can also function as a general-purpose I/O converter featuring four analog and four digital input points. Figure 7.52 depicts a block function diagram of the game port.

The input to the game port is a set of **resistive joysticks** or **game paddles**. Joysticks are defined as having two variable resistances, and game paddles are defined as consisting of one variable resistance. Each resistance should be variable between 0 k ohms and 100 k ohms. Joysticks may have one or two normally open (fire) buttons. Game paddles have only one button. Under this definition, the Games Adapter supports two game paddles (A and B), four game paddles (A, B, C, and D), or two joysticks (A and B). The order of fire buttons should correspond with that of the resistive elements (A and B, or A, B, C, and D).

This interface is simple and straightforward, combining elementary hardware and software techniques. When the software issues the adapter's address (201_h) and an IOW active I/O write signal, the timers are triggered into their active state, and their outputs go to a high logic level. The individual timer outputs remain high for a length of time, dictated by the setting of each resistive input and timing capacitor at each timer's input. As each timer times out according to its own RC time constant, its output returns to a low logic state.

FIGURE 7.52

The Game Control Adapter

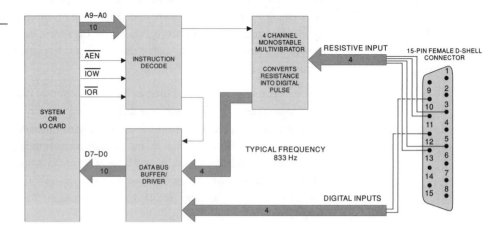

A+ CORE 1.4   Figure 7.53 shows a connection scheme for attaching joysticks to the 15-pin, D-Type connector at the rear of the system. Unlike the 3-row, 15-pin, D-shell connector used for VGA video, the game port connector has only two rows of pins. When attaching game paddles to the adapter, four separate +5 Vdc supplies are furnished (pins 1, 8, 9, and 15), one for each paddle. The adapter also provides separate grounds for paddles A and B (pins 4 and 12). Paddles C and D may also use these grounds, or they may share a ground connection at pin 5. The wipers of the resistance elements are connected to pins 3, 6, 11, and 13 (A, B, C, and D). The order of the fire buttons should correspond with that of the resistive elements. Therefore, connect the A, B, C, and D buttons to pins 2, 7, 10, and 14, respectively. The buttons should be of the normally open variety.

FIGURE 7.53

Joystick connection.

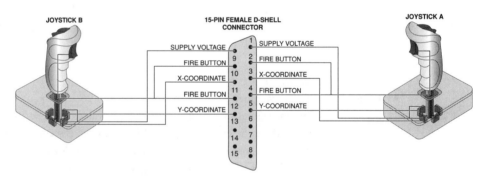

Game Software

The game software periodically polls the adapter's data bus buffer/driver latch to determine whether each output has timed out. A software counter keeps track of the number of times the port has been read before each timer times out. The number of read cycles (0–255) before a logic low is encountered is directly proportional to the resistive setting of the joystick or game paddle.

The software reads the fire buttons in the same manner as the resistive inputs. In the button's inactive (open) state, the digital inputs are at a high logic state. When a button is depressed, its input is pulled to a low logic level. When the software reads the output latch, it detects a low at the bit position reserved for that button and interprets it as a closure.

Troubleshooting Joystick Problems

As with other input devices, three levels of possible problems can occur with a joystick: configuration, software, and hardware problems.

Attempt to run the joystick with a DOS-based program. If the joystick will not work at the DOS level, check the game port's hardware configuration settings. Compare the hardware settings to that of any software using the game port. Try to swap the suspect joystick for a known good one.

Windows 3.x makes no provision for a joystick device. However, Windows 95 contains a joystick icon in the Start/Settings/Control Panel window. Figure 7.54 shows the contents of the Windows 95 Joystick Properties dialog box. The joystick icon is not loaded into the Control Panel window if the system does not detect a game port during installation. If the port is detected during boot-up but no joystick device is found, the window will say that the joystick is not connected correctly.

FIGURE 7.54

The Joystick Properties dialog box.

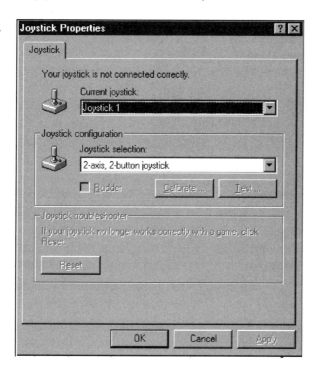

The Joystick Properties dialog box is used to select different numbers of joysticks (1–16) that can be used. This dialog box shows the currently selected joystick type and enables other devices to be selected. The default joystick setting is a 2-axis, 2-button device. You can also select None or Custom joystick types. Other selections include 2-axis, 4-button joysticks, and 2-button game pads, as well as specialized flight yoke and flight stick assemblies.

The Joystick Properties dialog box also contains a button to calibrate the joystick's position. This button enables you to set the zero-position of the stick for the center of the screen. The Test button enables you to check the movement of the stick and its button operation, as directed by the test program. Windows 95 also enables you to add a rudder device to the system. The Joystick Troubleshooter section contains a reset button to reinitialize the game port. This function is normally used if the stick stops responding to the program.

Light Pens

Light pens, as depicted in Figure 7.55, are handheld light-sensing devices that work in conjunction with the scanning electron beam of a CRT display.

As the electron beam sweeps the screen of the CRT, it "paints a picture" on the face of the screen by selectively striking **phosphor** spots located on its face. When the electron beam strikes a phosphor, the phosphor glows, leaving a spot of light that remains for a predetermined length of time. The length of time depends on the type of phosphor and the intensity of the electron beam when the phosphor was struck. The location of each phosphor spot has a specific X- and Y-coordinate on the face of the screen. The light pen uses the scanning electron beam to produce X/Y-coordinate information about the position of images on the screen for input into the CRT controller.

FIGURE 7.55

A typical light pen.

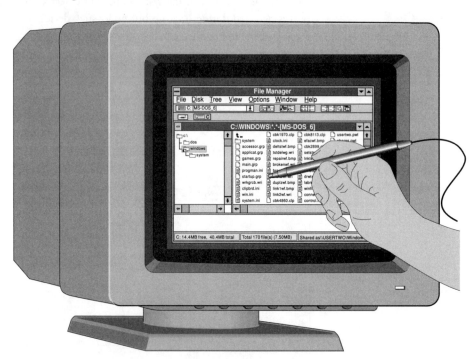

Light Pen Operation

The light pen contains a light-sensitive device (see Figure 7.56), such as a phototransistor or photodiode that produces a pulse when struck by the passing CRT electron beam. The monitor's CRT controller can determine the exact position of the light pen against the face of the screen by checking the horizontal and vertical position of the scanning electron beam at the time it receives the pulse from the light pen.

The CRT controller obtains the Y-coordinate (number of raster scans down the screen) and the X-coordinate (number of dot clock pulses since the last horizontal synchronization [HSYNC] signal) from the horizontal and vertical counters used to access the CRT's screen memory. These values are combined and loaded into the CRTC's **Light Pen Address Register** when enabled by the pulse from the light pen. At the same instant, the CRTC sends an interrupt input signal to the computer.

FIGURE 7.56

The Light Pen Register.

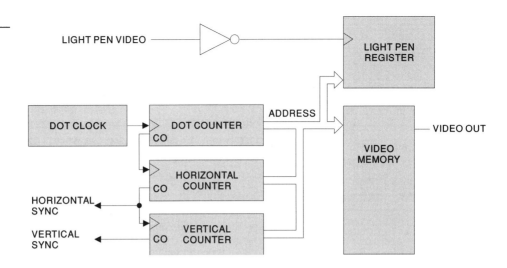

The light pen may seem like a very simple device, and electronically it is. Some simple light pen designs are available through hobby magazine articles. But a truly useful and accurate light pen must overcome some very troublesome design problems (see Figure 7.57). In addition to the fact that the space allotted for electronics in the light pen is somewhat limited, the light pen must be capable of resolving the electron beam's position accurately (**resolution**) and must reject noise and nonintended light from being interpreted as input (**ambient light rejection**).

FIGURE 7.57

Inside the light pen.

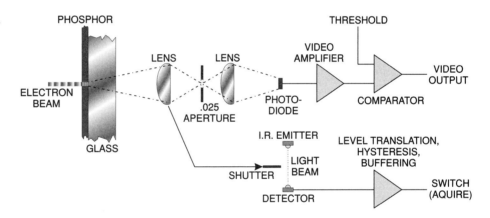

The pen uses a mechanical aperture, which is opened when the pen is pressed against the screen. An optical lens is used to restrict the area of the screen that the pen "sees." Figure 7.58 shows how the aperture and lens arrangement prevents the photo-sensitive device from detecting false traces of the electron beam.

FIGURE 7.58

Light pen focusing.

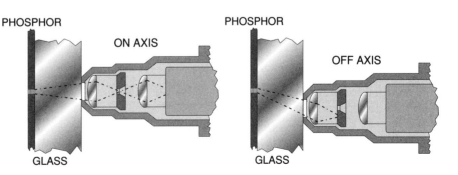

When a phosphor strike occurs within the light pen's field of focus, the photo detector's characteristics change and a digital pulse is created. The pulse is amplified and applied to a level comparator, which compares the amplitude of the pulse to some predetermined threshold level. If the input pulse is large enough, the comparator passes the pulse to the CRT controller as a valid strike.

Light Pen Parameters

A number of factors must be taken into account when setting the threshold level of the pen. Primary factors of concern are the color and type of phosphor used in the monitor, and the **intensity level** at which the screen is set. Phosphor characteristics, such as persistence and peak light emission amplitude, can be problematic in that long-persistence phosphors can cause false strikes to occur. Likewise, low peak amplitude phosphors (especially red) may not produce enough amplitude to register a strike.

Phosphor color and type can be a problem in monochrome monitors as well as color monitors. Monochrome monitors use a single color phosphor, but that color varies among manufacturers. This point should not be overlooked when considering a light pen for use with a particular monitor.

On the other hand, the intensity (brightness) setting of the monitor itself may produce similar problems when set too low or too high. Other factors that affect the response of the light pen are the response characteristics of the photo-detector itself, the type and thickness of the glass face plate, and the distance the photo-detector is actually removed from the screen. All these factors can cause delays that can produce false strikes because the CRT controller counters have advanced by the time the strike is noticed. However, these fixed delays can be overcome by proper software considerations.

Depending on the software used, the location specified by the light pen can be used to address the screen memory so that the computer can examine the contents of that location. The computer can then use this information to identify the character or image of interest on the screen.

The attribute most commonly associated with light pens is that they provide an easy means of choosing commands, options, or programs from an onscreen menu. The light pen also provides the naturalistic method of drawing or creating onscreen graphs and diagrams. Software packages for such light pen applications usually contain routines to draw circles, boxes, or lines; enlarge or reduce the size of graphic images; and shade or change the color of different areas of the screen. More advanced software may enable the user to create truly artistic renderings on the screen.

Troubleshooting Light Pen Problems

> You must consider basically four components when troubleshooting light pen-related problems: the light pen, the monitor, the video adapter card, and the light pen software.

Depress the pen's aperture, and listen carefully to try to hear the mechanical click of the shutter. Examine the light pen's connection to the system and to the video adapter card to see that it is correct and that it makes good contact at each point.

Check the monitor's brightness and intensity settings to see whether the pen functions at different settings of each.

Review the light pen's user's manual and software setup for possible configuration problems and IRQ conflicts. Also, review the monitor's specifications, and compare them to those of the light pen to make sure that they are compatible.

Reinstall the light pen software, carefully reviewing each step. Check for the presence of diagnostic routines in the light pen software. Check the video adapter by substitution. Check the light pen by substitution.

Touch-Sensitive Screens

A+ CORE 1.1

Hewlett-Packard introduced the first **touch-screen monitor** in 1983. Touch-sensitive screens divide the screen into rows and columns that correspond to X and Y coordinates. Two common methods exist for accomplishing this. The first method uses see-through membranes arranged in rows and columns over the screen, as illustrated in Figure 7.59.

FIGURE 7.59

Crossing strips.

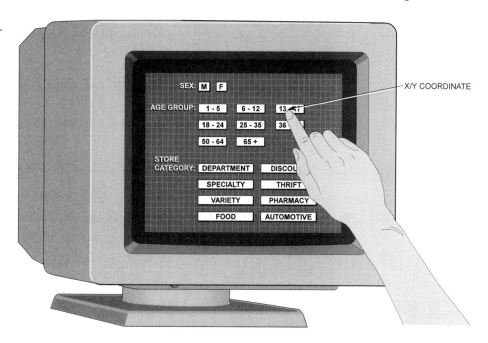

When the user presses the touch-sensitive panel, the Mylar strips are pressed together. When strips from a row and a column make contact with each other, their electrical qualities change. The signal generated between the two strips is decoded to an approximate X/Y position on the screen by the panel's decoding circuitry.

The second type of touch-sensitive screen technology employs infrared techniques to section the screen. Banks of LEDs and sensors arranged around the face of the monitor, as illustrated in Figure 7.60, divide the screen into a grid pattern. When an object interrupts the signal paths between a pair of horizontal and vertical LEDs and sensors, a coded signal is produced that can be related to an X/Y coordinate on the screen.

The main drawback associated with using touch screens involves the excessive arm movements required to operate the system. It is also true that the human fingertip is not a fine enough pointing device to select small points on the screen. Therefore, the location of a small item on the screen may not be exact due to the relative size of the fingertip. The software designer must create screen displays that take this possibility into account and compensate for it where touch screens are used.

FIGURE 7.60

*An LED sensor-detection
arrangement.*

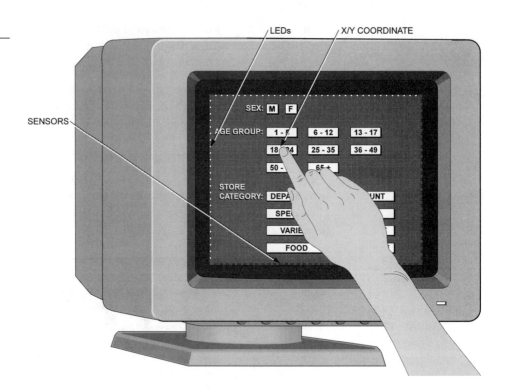

Touch-sensitive panels are available as built-in units in some monitors, but other units are designed as add-ons to existing monitors. These units clip or strap onto the body of the monitor and hang down in front of the screen. In add-on units, the coordinate mismatch problem can be compounded by the addition of **parallax errors**. These errors are caused by the distance between the screen and the sensors, and the angle at which the user views the display. Parallax error causes the image to appear at a different location than it actually is. This concept is illustrated in Figure 7.61.

FIGURE 7.61

Parallax error.

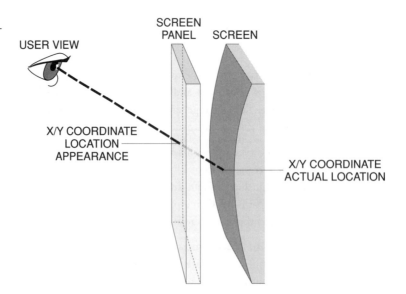

Troubleshooting Touch-Sensitive Screen Problems

A+ CORE 2.1

> You must consider really only three components when troubleshooting problems associated with touch-sensitive screens: the touch-sensitive screen (or the monitor with which it is used), the I/O port to which it is attached, and the screen's driver software.

Review the screen's user manual and software setup for possible configuration problems. Examine the I/O port connection and configuration to make sure it is properly set up to support the touch screen. If the screen is an add-on unit, check the monitor's specifications to make sure that they are compatible with the touch-screen unit.

Reinstall the touch-screen software, carefully reviewing each step. Check for the presence of diagnostic routines in the screen's software. Check the I/O port settings. Check the touch-screen unit by substitution.

Scanners

A+ CORE 1.1

> **Scanners** convert pictures, line art, and photographs into electronic signals that can be processed by software packages such as desktop publishers and graphic design programs.

These programs, in turn, can display the image on the video display or can print it out on a graphics printer.

The scanner borrows technology from the office copy machine. An image is scanned with a light source, and the level of light reflected from the image is applied to a light-sensitive receiver. Unlike the copier, the image is not left on the light-sensitive receiver. Instead, it is converted into an electronic signal stream that can be manipulated by the computer.

Scanners basically come in two types: **handheld scanners** and **flat-bed scanners**. Handheld scanners tend to be less expensive than flat-bed scanners due to less complex mechanics. However, handheld scanners also tend to produce lower quality images than flat-bed scanners. These types normally require two passes to scan an entire page-sized image, but flat-bed scanners can pick up the complete image in one pass. The handheld scanner can be used to scan images from large documents or from irregular surfaces, but they are dependent on the steadiness of the user for their accuracy.

Scanners can also be classified by the type of images they can reproduce. Some scanners can differentiate only between different levels of light and dark. These scanners are called **grayscale scanners**. **Color scanners**, on the other hand, include additional hardware that help them to distinguish among different colors.

Handheld Scanners

The handheld scanner depicted in Figure 7.62 operates by being pulled across an image. The user begins the scanning process by pressing the Scan button and then moving the scanner body across the image. An LED in the scanner projects light on the image as the scanner moves. As the light passes over darker and lighter areas of the page, varying levels of light are reflected back to a focusing lens.

FIGURE 7.62

Inside a handheld scanner.

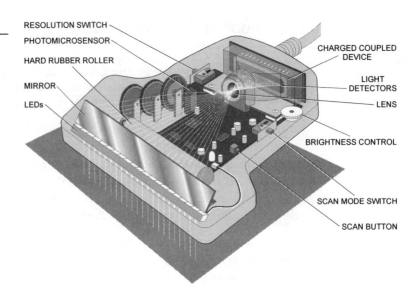

RESOLUTION SWITCH
PHOTOMICROSENSOR
HARD RUBBER ROLLER
MIRROR
LEDs

CHARGED COUPLED DEVICE
LIGHT DETECTORS
LENS
BRIGHTNESS CONTROL
SCAN MODE SWITCH
SCAN BUTTON

The lens focuses the reflected light stream onto a **charge-coupled device** (**CCD**), which converts the intensity of the light into a proportional voltage signal. The CCD is the same type of device used in the lens of a typical handheld video recorder. The voltage level produced corresponds to black, gray, and white light levels.

Internal circuitry processes the voltage signal before passing it to a special adapter card in one of the computer's expansion slots. The scanner's encoding circuitry performs **gamma correction** on the signal to enhance the black levels of the image. This process alters the image to make it more appealing to the human eye. This is necessary because of the eye's tendency to be more sensitive to darker tones than lighter ones.

The color of the light source used in the scanner also affects how the human eye perceives the output. When scans of color material are made, the color of the scanning light used may not produce brightness levels compatible with how the human eye perceives it. This is true in both color and grayscale output. The two most common scanner light source colors are red and green. The green light produces output that looks much closer to the way the eye perceives it than the red light can. For line art and text scans, the color of the light source is not important.

After gamma correction, the voltage signal is applied to an **analog-to-digital converter** (**ADC**). The ADC samples the voltage signal present at its input and generates a corresponding digital value. In low level hand scanners, the digital output is an 8-bit value that can represent up to 256 different shades of gray.

As the scanner moves across the surface, a wide rubber roller turns a series of gears, which in turn rotate a perforated disk. An **opto isolator** shines a light through the slots in the disk as it turns. The light strikes an optical sensor on the other side of the disk and produces pulses as the spokes of the disk interrupt the light stream. The pulses created by the disk are used to coordinate the transmission of the digitized image values with the movement of the scanner. Each time a line of image data is transmitted to the adapter card, the ADC is cleared and begins gathering a new line of image data. Figure 7.63 illustrates how the scanner's mechanical parts are used to coordinate the process of gathering and transmitting images in a hand scanner.

The software included with most scanners provides the user with at least a limited capability to manipulate the image after it has been scanned. Because of the limited width of most hand scanners, the software also provides for integrating two consecutive scans to form a complete picture.

Older hand scanners provided scanning resolutions up to 300 **dots per inch** (**dpi**). Common scanning resolutions are 600 dpi and 1200 dpi. Newer color hand scanners can produce 24-bit, high-resolution (3200 dpi) image editing with 16 million colors.

FIGURE 7.63

The scanner's mechanical structure.

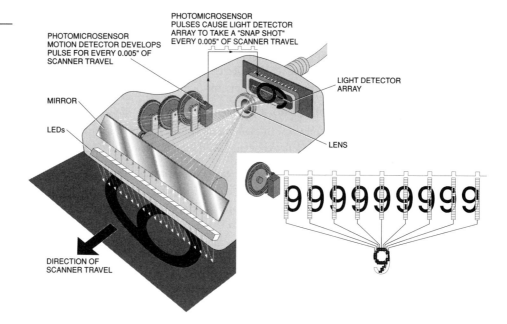

Flat-Bed Scanners

Flat-bed scanners differ from handheld units in a couple of areas. First, the scanner body remains stationary in a flat-bed scanner as a scan head moves past the paper. This process is described in Figure 7.64. The paper is placed facedown on the scanner's glass window. The light source from the scanning mechanism is projected up through the glass and onto the paper. The lighter areas of the page reflect more light than the darker areas do.

FIGURE 7.64

A flat-bed scanner.

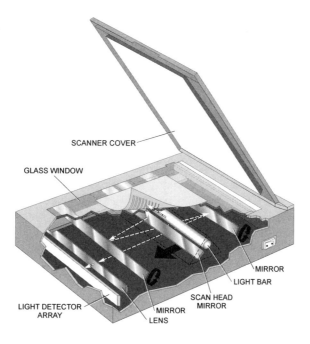

A precision positioning motor moves the scan head below the paper. As the head moves, light reflected from the paper is captured and channeled through a series of mirrors. The mirrors pivot to continually focus the reflected light on a light-sensitive diode. The diode converts the reflected light intensity into corresponding electrical voltages that are applied to an ADC.

The ADC converts the analog voltages into corresponding digital values through the A-to-D process. Each digital value corresponds to a pixel of page information. A normal scanner resolution is 300 dots (or pixels) per inch. Newer flat-bed scanners can achieve resolutions up to 4800 dpi. At these resolutions, each dot corresponds to about 1/90,000 of an inch. The higher the selected scanning resolution, the slower the computer and printer runs, due to the increased amount of data that must be processed.

The digitized information is routed to the scanner adapter card in one of the PC's expansion slots. In main memory, the graphic information is stored in a format that can be manipulated by graphic design software.

Grayscale scanners can differentiate between varying levels of gray on the page. This capability is stated in **shades**. A good quality grayscale scanner can differentiate between 256 levels of gray. Color scanners, on the other hand, use three passes to scan an image. Each scan passes the light through a different color filter to separate them from each other. The red, blue, and green filters create three different electronic images that can be integrated to form a complete picture. For intermediate colors, varying levels of the three colors are blended to create the desired shade. This concept is illustrated in Figure 7.65.

FIGURE 7.65

Color filters.

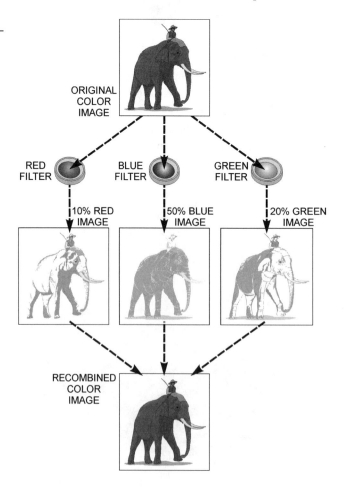

As with the handheld scanners, most flat-bed scanners use a proprietary adapter card and cable to communicate with the system. However, a number of SCSI-interfaced scanners are available. One of the most common problems with installing scanners involves finding a vacant expansion slot for the adapter card. This is particularly true with Pentium boards that use a mixture of ISA and local bus slots. To overcome this problem, scanners are now being produced that operate through the system's parallel printer port. In these units, the printer plugs into the scanner, which, in turn, connects to the port. In older units, such as PCs and XTs, the limited number of available interrupt request lines often became a problem.

Both types of scanners require an adapter card. Although most use proprietary adapters, SCSI adapters are also widely used with scanners.

Optical Character Recognition (OCR)

Scanners are also used to scan written text from a page and convert it into characters that can be manipulated by the computer. In these situations, special **optical character recognition (OCR)** software is used to recognize written characters and convert them into computer characters. In some types of operations, the capability to convert nonelectronic text into an electronic format that is usable by the computer is a great time- and effort-saver.

When the scanner passes over a character, it senses areas of light and dark. The OCR software maps these areas into a character grid pattern similar to the one in Figure 7.66.

FIGURE 7.66

Optical character recognition.

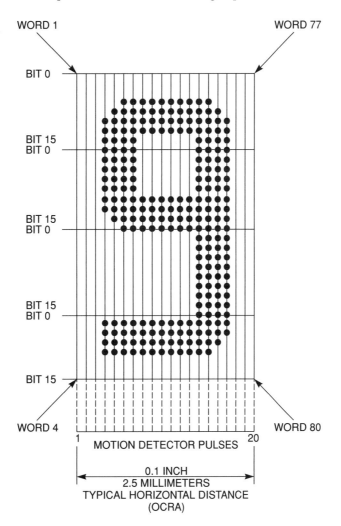

The software then compares the scanned character to character patterns it has stored in its library until a near match is located.

One of the biggest problems with OCR systems lies is their limited capability to recognize different font versions of a character. In addition, the OCR system must be able to overcome spots, stains, colored paper, ink colors, and creases in the paper. Misalignments of the paper being scanned can also cause errors to occur in the character pattern recognition process.

Troubleshooting Scanners

The driver software that comes with the scanner must be configured to match the settings on its adapter card. The adapter card settings are normally established through hardware jumpers. Check the scanner software's setup screen to confirm the settings.

> Most scanners have three important configuration parameters to consider: the I/O address, the IRQ setting, and the DMA channel setting.

Typical I/O address settings for the scanner adapter are 150_h–151_h (default), 170–171, 350–351, or 370–371. Typical IRQ settings are 10 (default) 3, 5, and 11. Likewise, typical DMA channel settings are channel 5 (default), channel 1, channel 3, or channel 7. Figure 7.67 shows the components associated with scanners.

FIGURE 7.67

Scanner-related components.

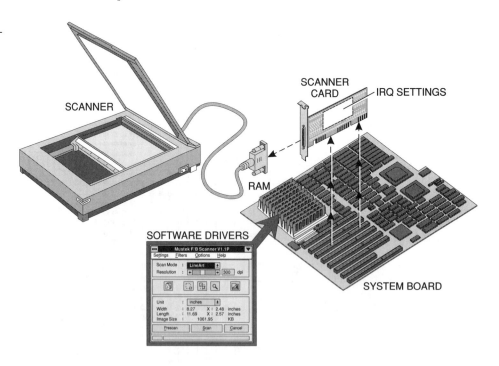

Traditionally, **IRQ conflicts** with network and sound cards tend to be the biggest problem associated with scanners. Typical symptoms associated with IRQ conflicts include the following:

1. The image on the screen appears misaligned.

2. The scanning function appears to be activated and the scanner light comes on, but no image is produced on the screen.

In these cases, a diagnostic package such as MSD can be quite helpful in spotting and correcting the conflicts.

The instance in which the scanning function appears to be activated and the scanner light comes on can also occur if the DMA channel of the interface card conflicts with the DMA setting of another card. Select another DMA channel for the card and software.

If the scanner light does not come on when trying to scan, two possible causes of the problem exist. First, the system may not meet minimum system requirements for the particular scanner being used. If this is the case, the minimum system requirements of the scanner should be researched to make sure that it could be used with the system. If the system requirements are not met, either return the scanner to the supplier, or upgrade the system to meet the minimum specifications for the scanner. The second possible cause of the problem is that the I/O address setting conflicts with another card in the computer. Try other address settings on the adapter card and in the software.

If the problem seems to be a hardware problem, check the quick considerations as described in Chapter 3. Make sure the power to the scanner is plugged in and turned on. Exchange the signal cable for a new one, if available. Refer to the user's guide for troubleshooting hints.

Key Points Review

The first half of this chapter examined standard I/O port assignments in a PC-compatible system. The second half of the chapter dealt with common input devices used with PCs.

- Parallel ports have been a staple of the PC system since the original PCs were introduced. They are most widely used to connect printers to the computer.

- The Centronics standard interface enables the computer to pass information to the printer 8 bits at a time across the eight data lines. The other lines in the connection carry handshaking signals back and forth between the computer and the printer.

- In earlier MI/O cards, all the I/O functions were controlled by discrete circuit devices. On newer MI/O cards, IC manufacturers combined the standard MI/O functions (HDD/FDD/1P/2S/1G ports) into ASIC devices. With Pentium system boards, they have moved to the system board.

- DOS keeps track of the system's installed printer ports by assigning them the logical device names (handles) LPT1, LPT2, and LPT3. Whenever the system is booted up, DOS searches the hardware for parallel ports installed at hex addresses 3BCh, 378h, and 278h consecutively.

- Enhanced parallel port (EPP) and enhanced Centronic parallel (ECP) ports can be converted between unidirectional and bidirectional operation through the CMOS setup screen.

- Two methods are used to provide timing for serial transfers: The data may be sent synchronously (in conjunction with a synchronizing clock pulse) or asynchronously (without an accompanying clock pulse).

- As with parallel ports, DOS assigns COM port designations to the system's serial ports during boot-up. COM port designations are normally COM1 and COM2, but they can be extended to COM3 and COM4 in advanced systems.

- Basically three levels of testing apply to troubleshooting port problems: These are the DOS level, the Windows level, and the hardware level.

- With Pentium systems, it is necessary to check the Advanced CMOS Setup to determine whether a port has been enabled, and if so, whether it has been enabled correctly.

- A new serial interface scheme, called the Universal Serial Bus (USB), has been developed to provide a fast, flexible method of attaching peripheral devices to the computer.

- Input devices convert physical quantities into electronic signals that can be manipulated by interface units. The input devices used with microcomputers convert human physical activity into electronic impulses that can be processed by the computer. The chief devices of this type are keyboards, joysticks, mice, light pens, and touch screens.

- The alphanumeric keyboard is the most widely used input device for microcomputers. It provides a simple finger-operated method of entering numbers, letters, symbols, and special control characters into the computer.

- Inside, a keyboard is basically an X–Y matrix arrangement of switch elements. The keyboard must be capable of detecting and identifying the depressed key, debouncing it, and encoding the key closure into a form usable by the computer.

- On many AT-compatible system boards, a single-chip microcontroller, called an intelligent keyboard controller, performs the keyboard interfacing functions.

- Some keyboard interface circuitry is typically located on the system board. Therefore, the steps required to isolate keyboard problems are usually confined to the keyboard, its connecting cable, and the system board.

- A mouse is a handheld pointing device that produces input data when it is moved across a surface. Basically, the mouse is an X-Y positioning device that enables the user to move a cursor or some other screen image around the display screen.

- Mice can be classified by the method they use to communicate with the host computer. The most common type of mouse sends data to the computer serially. Other mice, called bus mice, use dedicated cards to connect directly to the system's buses and communicate in parallel with the computer.

- The levels of mouse troubleshooting move from configuration problems, to software problems (including DOS, Windows, and applications) to hardware problems.

- As with other input devices, three levels of possible problems exist with a joystick: These are configuration, software, and hardware problems.

- Light pens are handheld light-sensing devices that work in conjunction with the scanning electron beam of a CRT display.

- You must consider four basic components when troubleshooting light pen-related problems: the light pen, the monitor, the video adapter card, and the light pen software.

- You must consider three basic components when troubleshooting problems associated with touch-sensitive screens: the touch-sensitive screen (or the monitor with which it is used), the I/O port to which it is attached, and the screen's driver software.

- Scanners convert pictures, line art, and photographs into electronic signals that can be processed by software packages.

- Most scanners have three important configuration parameters to consider: the I/O address, the IRQ setting, and the DMA channel setting.

At this point, review the objectives listed at the beginning of the chapter to be certain that you understand each point and can perform each task listed there. Afterward, answer the review questions that follow to verify your knowledge of the information.

Multiple Choice Questions

1. What types of integrated circuits are normally found in a PC-compatible keyboard?

   a. The keyboard buffer IC

   b. The keyboard encoder IC

   c. The keyboard output port IC

   d. The keyboard controller IC

2. How are scan codes transmitted from the keyboard to the system?

   a. In parallel

   b. Synchronously

   c. Serially

   d. Isochronously

3. What type of connector is normally found on PC-compatible keyboards?

   a. A 6-pin mini-DIN connector

   b. A 5-pin DIN connector

   c. An RJ-11 connector

   d. An RJ-45 connector

4. What portion of the system board is dedicated to the operation of the keyboard?

   a. The keyboard encoder IC

   b. The keyboard buffer IC

   c. The keyboard controller IC

   d. The keyboard output port IC

5. What is the most common problem encountered when adding a scanner to an 8-bit machine?

   a. Finding an available expansion slot

   b. Configuring a base address

   c. Locating a DMA channel to use

   d. Adding an external power supply unit for the scanner

6. What type of input device detects the electron beam passing by on the CRT screen?

   a. A light pen

   b. A mouse

   c. A scanner

   d. A touch screen

7. What type of device in normally associated with a 15-pin, male D-shell connector?

   a. A mouse

   b. A trackball

   c. A keypad

   d. A joystick

8. What type of device is a mouse?

   a. An I/O device

   b. An output device

   c. A pointing device

   d. A cursor-positioning device

9. Name two types of joysticks.

   a. Analog and trackball

   b. X and Y joysticks

   c. Serial and parallel joysticks

   d. Analog and digital joysticks

10. The input device most widely used with microcomputers is _____.

    a. the alphanumeric keyboard

    b. the mouse

    c. the light pen

    d. the trackball

Review Questions

1. Is a keyboard an input device, an output device, or an I/O device?

2. If a compatible Windows mouse driver is not present, what action should be taken?

3. If swapping the keyboard for a known good one does not clear the problem, what is the second most likely cause of the problem?

4. If the keyboard works properly in DOS but will not work in Windows, where should you check for problems? What type of problem would you be looking for?

5. Why would the troubleshooting routine for a suspected keyboard problem begin with the "Exchange the keyboard for a known good one" instruction?

6. Describe two types of touch screens.

7. How does the color of a grayscale scanner's light source affect its operation?

8. Does the color of the scanner's light source affect line art and text scans?

9. Describe the mechanical operation of an opto-mechanical mouse.

10. If a mouse works under DOS but not in Windows, what area should be checked?

11. Describe the operation of a common light pen.

12. What advantage does a trackball have over a mouse? In what type of application is this useful?

13. Describe how the wiring of a mouse to a COM port is different than that of other common serial devices.

14. List four major types of key switches.

15. Describe how the term *debouncing* applies to keyboards.

Lab Exercises

The lab manual that accompanies this book contains hands-on lab procedures that reinforce and test your knowledge of the theory materials presented in this chapter. Now that you have completed your review of Chapter 7, refer to the lab manual and perform Procedures 20, "Keyboard Problem Isolation," and 21, "Mouse Operations."

MAGNETIC STORAGE

LEARNING OBJECTIVES

Upon completion of this chapter and its related lab procedures, you should be able to perform the following tasks:

1. Describe the format or organization of a typical soft-sectored hard or flexible disk.

2. List the events that occur during a track seek operation.

3. List the events that occur during a typical disk-drive Write operation.

4. List the events that occur during a typical disk-drive Read operation.

5. Describe the responsibilities of the FDD controller.

6. List the signal lines associated with the FDD signal cable.

7. Describe steps to troubleshoot FDD problems.

8. Differentiate between common connecting cables (such as SCSI, IDE, and FDD).

9. Differentiate between different types of hard- and floppy-disk drive types.

10. Install IDE and EIDE devices, including setting Master/Slave/Single designations.

11. Install and configure single and complex SCSI device chains.

12. Establish proper addressing and termination for SCSI devices to avoid conflicts and problems.

13. Describe steps to troubleshoot HDD problems.

14. Discuss the different RAID advisory levels and apply them to given applications.

15. Identify popular tape drive formats.

CHAPTER 8

Introduction

Nearly every microcomputer includes some type of mass information storage system that enables it to store data or programs for an extended period of time. Unlike primary memory devices, which are fast and have a relatively low storage capacity, mass storage systems are usually slower and possess much larger storage potential. These systems represent an acceptable alternative to the IC RAM/ROM devices used on system and video cards. As with the ROM devices, these systems must be capable of holding information even when the computer is turned off. On the other hand, these systems are similar to RAM devices in that their information can be updated and changed often.

The most widely used mass storage systems have typically involved covering some medium with a magnetic coating.

These include flexible Mylar disks (referred to as floppy disks), rigid, aluminum hard disks, and various widths of flexible Mylar tape, as illustrated in Figure 8.1. The information to be stored on the medium is converted into electromagnetic pulses, which, in turn, are used to create tiny positive and negative magnetized spots on the magnetic surface. To retrieve, or read, the information back from the surface, the storage system must detect the spots and decode them. The stored information can be changed at any time by re-magnetizing the surface with the new information.

FIGURE 8.1

Typical magnetic storage systems.

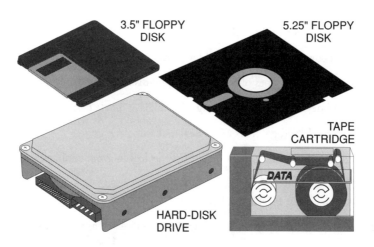

3.5" FLOPPY DISK

5.25" FLOPPY DISK

TAPE CARTRIDGE

DATA

HARD-DISK DRIVE

Magnetic Disks

A+ CORE 1.1

> Magnetic disks resemble phonograph records without grooves, and they fall into two general categories: high-speed hard disks and slower flexible disks. Data bits are recorded serially in concentric circles, called **tracks**, around the disk.

Because the tracks toward the outer edge of the disk are longer than the inner tracks, all tracks are divided into an equal number of equal-size data blocks, called **sectors**. Therefore, each block of data has an address that is the combination of its track number and its sector number. Each sector can be accessed for a read or write operation as quickly as any other sector on the disk, so disk memories are classified as **direct access memory**.

The tracks of the disk are numbered, beginning with 00, from the outer edge of the disk proceeding inward. Each side of the disk can hold 80 or more tracks, depending on the type of disk and the drive used. When disks are stacked, such as in a hard-disk drive, all the tracks with the same number are referred to collectively as a **cylinder**. The number of sectors on each track runs between 8 and 50, also depending on the disk and drive type.

In some floppy-disk systems, the sectors are identified by holes along the outer or inner periphery of the disk. This is referred to as **hard sectoring** because hardware is used to identify the sectors by physically counting the holes as the disk rotates. In other flexible- and hard-disk systems, track and sector address information is contained in a track/sector identification code recorded on the disk. This method of address specification is known as **soft sectoring** because the sector information is written in software. Figure 8.2 depicts a typical soft-sectored track and sector arrangement. PC-compatible systems use soft-sectored disks.

FIGURE 8.2

Disk tracks and sectors.

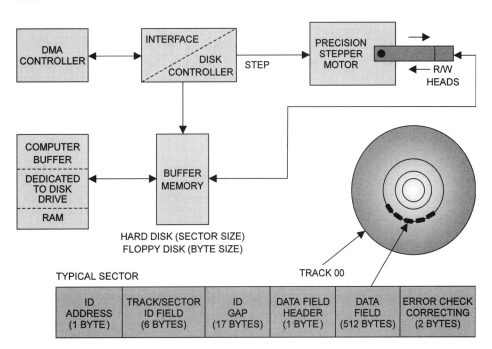

Each sector is separated from the previous and following sectors by a small **gap** of unrecorded space. A typical sector contains 256 (2^8) or 512 (2^9) bytes, but on some systems this value may range as low as 128 (2^7) bytes or as high as 1024 (2^{10}) bytes per sector. The most common sector size in the IBM-compatible/DOS world is 512 bytes. Within these confines, the sector is segmented, beginning with an **ID field header**, which tells the controlling circuitry that an ID area containing the physical address information is approaching. A small **data field header** precedes the actual **data field**. The data field is followed by a **postamble** containing error-checking and correcting codes for the data recorded in the sector.

In their original conditions, hard disks and soft-sectored disks, as well as magnetic tapes, are blank. The system must prepare them to hold data. The system's disk-drive control circuitry accomplishes this by writing track/sector identification and gap locations on the disk, in a process known as **formatting**. This leads to some confusion when disk storage capacity is specified. Capacity may be stated for either formatted or unformatted conditions. Obviously, the capacity of an unformatted disk is greater because no gap or ID information has been added to the disk.

Reading and Writing on Magnetic Surfaces

Data is read from or written to the disk one sector at a time. To perform a read or write operation, the address of the particular track and sector to be accessed is applied to a stepper motor, which moves a **read/write (R/W) head** over the desired track. As the desired sector passes beneath the R/W head, the data transfer occurs.

Information read from or to be written to the disk is usually held in a dedicated part of the computer's RAM memory. The system then accesses the data from this memory location at speeds compatible with the microprocessor.

The R/W head consists of a coil of wire wrapped around a soft iron core, as depicted in Figure 8.3. A small **air gap** in the core rides above the magnetic coating on the disk's surface. Data is written to the disk by pulsing the coil with a surge of current, which produces **magnetic lines of flux** in the soft iron core. At the air gap, the lines of flux dip down into the disk's magnetic coating due to its low reluctance (compared to air). This, in turn, causes the **magnetic domains** in the recording surface to align themselves in a direction dictated by the direction of current flow in the coil. The magnetic domains of the surface can assume one of three possible states, depending on the direction of current flow through the R/W head:

- ▶ Un-magnetized (randomly arranged domains)
- ▶ Domains magnetized in a positive direction
- ▶ Domains magnetized in a negative direction

FIGURE 8.3

A typical R/W head.

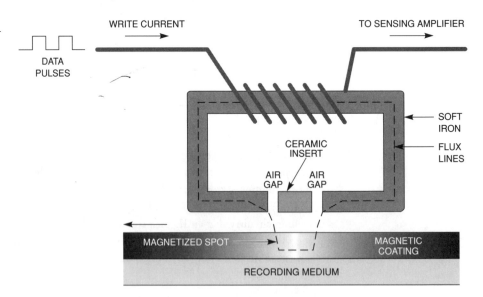

Data is read from the disk in a reversal of this process. As the magnetized spots on the surface pass by the head, changes in magnetic polarity induce lines of flux into the iron core. This, in turn, induces a small voltage in the coil. This voltage is sensed and amplified to the proper digital logic levels by the drive's read circuitry. One significant difference exists between reading and writing on magnetic surfaces, however. **Writing** on the surface records successive zones of positive or negative flux, but **reading** can detect only flux changes (such as the boundaries between zones of differing polarity).

Data Encoding

It may seem logical to simply represent 1s and 0s with positive and negative magnetic spots, but the reality is that this brute force recording method is very ineffective and error prone. To compensate for these drawbacks, several encoding methods have been devised to represent 1s and 0s.

An early example of encoding was the **frequency modulation** (**FM**) method that used two recording frequencies to modulate the data. An advanced FM version called **modified FM** (or **MFM**) cuts out half the pulses and doubles the density of the data on the disk. This method is used to record double-density floppy disks in PC-compatible systems. Additional advancements in data storage are gained by using **group coded recording** (**GCR**) methods. This method uses selective bit patterns to encode blocks of data on the disk. The representative bit patterns are established so that they maximize the magnetic relationship between 0s and 1s to gain the best response from the R/W heads.

Head Construction

R/W heads are constructed in many different ways, depending on their intended application. R/W heads intended for use with disks are usually small and electrically simple compared to R/W heads used with tape drives. These types of heads normally have ferrite cores and a common winding for both reading and writing. Conversely, tape heads may have independent read and write cores, as well as multiple record/playback channels.

Quite often, the R/W head for data recording contains two independent cores, one designed for writing and the other designed for reading. The **Read gap** is placed downstream from the **Write gap** so that data being written to the surface can be read immediately and checked for errors. Some types of R/W heads contain as many as five air gaps, as shown in Figure 8.4. A gap may be only 30 to 100 micro-inches, but this is where all the work of recording and playback occurs.

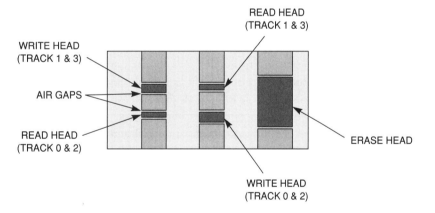

FIGURE 8.4

A multiple-gap R/W head.

Multiple-gap R/W heads are generally used with magnetic tape operations, as opposed to disks, which use single-gap heads. An exception to this trend is the R/W head associated with floppy disks. Floppy-disk heads contain a R/W gap followed by a **trim-erase gap**. The erase gap is used to trim the fringes of the recorded data to improve tracking. This type of head is also referred to as a tunnel or straddle-erase head.

The minimum distance between two successive flux reversals, called the **flux density**, is measured in **flux-changes-per-inch** (**fci**) or **flux-reversals-per-inch** (**frpi**). These terms are a measurement of the number of bits of data that can be stored in a given area of media.

Newer R/W head technologies have been developed to provide very high-density recording capabilities (15,000 fci).

Contact Versus Non-Contact Recording

> Depending on the nature of the magnetic medium being read from or written to, the R/W head may either ride directly on the medium's surface (**contact recording**) or float slightly above it on a thin cushion of air created by the moving surface (**non-contact recording**).

Hard disks, whether fixed or removable, must use flying heads, while flexible media (tapes and disks) generally use contact recording.

Hard disks must unavoidably use non-contact heads that fly over the medium. The extremely high speed of the medium, and the thin and fragile nature of its magnetic oxide coating, makes almost any contact between the R/W head and the disk surface a cause of considerable damage to both the head and the disk. Such contact is known as **head-to-disk interference** (**HDI**), or simply a **crash**. Recent advancements—such as smaller and lighter R/W heads, and ever-harder damage-resistant disk surfaces—have lowered the possibilities of damaging crashes somewhat. Because the medium is dimensionally stable and spins at a high rate of speed, the data density associated with hard disks is relatively high. Complex head architectures are not used with this medium.

Flexible media, such as floppy disks and tape, expand and shrink with temperature and humidity variations. This causes the data tracks on the media to migrate in terms of track-location accuracy of the R/W head. To compensate for such shifting, the R/W heads ride directly on the media's surface, the track density is kept low, and the heads are made more complex to create special zones in the track construction, which compensate for some of the misalignment due to shifting.

Disk-Drive Operations

The basic organization of both hard- and flexible-disk drives is similar in many respects. Both have drive spindles (which are actuated by precision synchronous motors) and one or more movable R/W heads that are positioned by a digital stepper motor, or voice coil. Both systems have intelligent control circuitry to position the R/W head and facilitate the transfer of information between the disk and the computer's memory. Figure 8.5 depicts the major components of the disk drive's electronics systems.

> The heart of the disk drive's circuitry is the **disk-drive controller**. The controller is responsible for providing the necessary interfacing between the disk drive and the computer's I/O channel.

This interfacing consists of decoding the computer's instructions to the disk drive and generating the control signals that the disk drive must have to carry out the instruction. The controller must also move back and forth between the parallel data format of the computer's bus and the serial format of the disk drive.

FIGURE 8.5

Disk drive components.

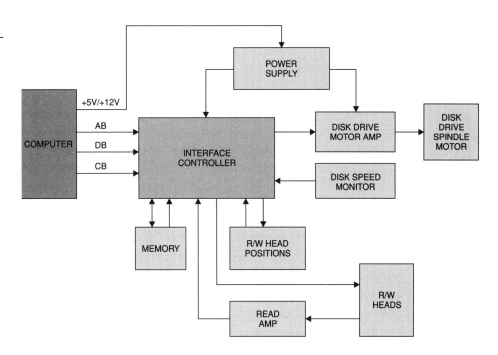

Furthermore, the controller must accurately position the R/W heads, direct the read and write operations, check and correct data received from the processor, generate error-correction codes for outbound data, and mark the location of defective sectors on the disk, closing them to use. After all these responsibilities have been executed, the disk controller must also provide addressing for the tracks and sectors on the disk and control the transfer of information to and from the internal memory.

Due to the high data transfer rates associated with disk systems, a DMA controller is used to permit the disk drive to access the computer's primary memory without the intervention of the CPU. In this manner, the disk drive can exchange data with the computer's main memory while the microprocessor is busy at some chore that doesn't require the use of the address and data bus lines.

The extreme complexity of these responsibilities—and the speed at which they must be performed—usually dictates the presence of a specialized onboard **microcontroller** to control the operation of the drive. In this case, it has been designed expressly to control the operation of a floppy-disk drive. As a matter of fact, the first microprocessors were actually marketed as microcontrollers called **peripheral control units** (**PCUs**) for discrete computers. Only in their second generation were their full processing capabilities realized and brought to use as microprocessors.

In floppy-disk drives, and in hard-disk drives designed around older interface standards, this controller is located on the drive's options adapter card. Drives that use newer interfacing methods have their controllers **embedded** directly on the disk drive unit.

With hard-disk drives, the presence of the onboard microcontroller is usually accompanied by onboard RAM and ROM, as well as any number of other support chips. The drive's RAM capabilities may be as simple as a single 8-bit buffer register or as complex as an array of RAM memory chips that can hold an entire track of information. This memory may be an integral part of the drive's intelligent controller, or it may consist of discrete memory devices.

Hard drives normally have read-only memories that contain an addition to the system BIOS program. This extension historically comes into play after the BIOS startup routine has checked for bootable files in floppy-disk drive A and has not found them. Other support devices in the drive might include clocks (timers), decoders, drive-motor controllers, read and write amplifiers, shift registers, counters, write-protect circuits (on floppy drives), and power supply circuits.

One piece of software is extremely important to the operation of both hard- and floppy-disk drives. This is the DOS **file management system** (**FMS**). Essentially, DOS keeps track of information stored on the disk by creating the **file allocation table** (**FAT**) on the disk. This table specifies where information is stored and what disk space remains available for new data. DOS matches the name assigned to a file with the blocks in the FAT and then refers to a map called a **directory**, which tells the operating system how to get to a specific piece of data.

In addition, the operating system provides disk utility programs to perform functions such as copying and editing files, keeping track of unusable (bad) sectors, and aiding in the formatting of new disks.

Groups of logically related sectors are typically linked into **clusters** (referred to as **allocation units** by DOS) on the disk. For example, if a file on a disk requires several sectors of storage space, DOS looks at the disk's FAT and tries to store the parts of the cluster in sectors that are logically sequential. This strategy takes into consideration the read and repositioning times involved in moving between sectors. This storage method improves the speed at which the total cluster of information can be accessed.

Initialization

Copies of the disk's directory and FAT are written into a dedicated portion of primary memory when the disk is booted to the system. To transfer a file from main memory to the disk (a write operation), the operating system sends the disk-drive controller a write command and initializes its control registers with parameters such as sector length and gap lengths. The system also specifies the track and sector number where writing will begin. It obtains this information by referring to the FAT and finding the address of the next available sector. Refer to Figure 8.6 for an illustration of this process.

The DOS software driver program plugs these parameters into the proper registers within the controller chip. The driver also sets up the DMA controller with information about where the starting address of the data that's to be written from main memory is, how long the block of data is (the number of bytes to be transferred), and in what mode the data transfer is to be performed (block or byte-by-byte). After this has been accomplished, the drivers set up the DMA and disk-drive controllers for interaction and arm them to begin transferring the data.

Track Seek Operations

The controller enables the drive and produces a burst of step pulses to position the R/W head over the proper track. The controller accomplishes this by keeping a record of the current track location of the drive's R/W heads in one of its internal registers. The controller compares the contents of the current location register to the track number specified by the Write command, and decides which direction the head must be moved. The controller then issues a direction signal to the drive on its **Direction** line and begins producing step pulses on its **Step** line. Each pulse on this line causes the drive unit to move the R/W heads one track over, in the direction specified by the direction signal. The value in the current track location register is also increased or decreased (depending on the direction of movement) by a factor of 1 for each step pulse. When the value of the present location register matches the track number specified for the Write operation, the step pulses cease and the R/W heads settle over the desired track. The positioning of the R/W heads is illustrated in Figure 8.7.

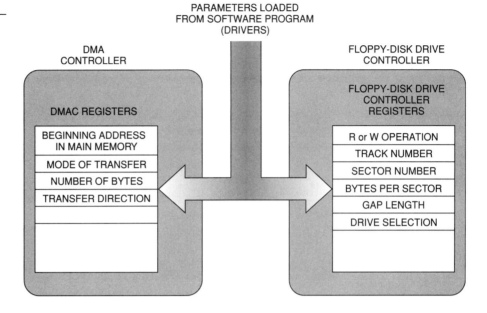

FIGURE 8.6

The initialization process.

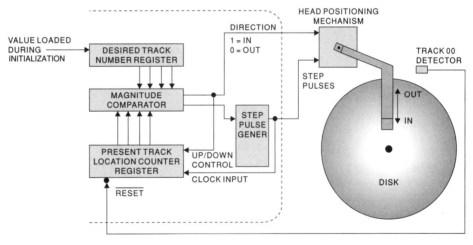

FIGURE 8.7

A Track Seek operation.

Write Operations

When the head is over the track, the controller begins looking for the proper sector by reading the sector headers. The controller is actually waiting for a unique set of flux transitions to occur, which match the starting sector number stored in its registers. When the match is found, **write-splice** occurs (the controller changes from Read to Write operation) during the header gap, and data transfer and serialization begins.

The drive controller requests a byte of data (DREQ) from the DMA controller, which places the byte on the data bus and also sends a DACK signal to the disk controller. The disk controller obtains the byte (assuming byte-by-byte transfer) from the data bus, encodes it into the proper form, serializes it, and applies it to the Write channel of the R/W head, as illustrated in Figure 8.8.

FIGURE 8.8

Data transfers.

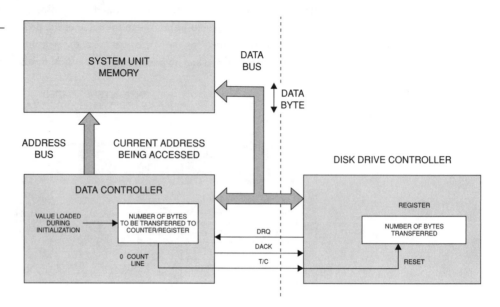

The transfer continues byte-by-byte until the controller requests the last byte from the DMA controller. Counters in both the DMA controller and the disk drive controller count the number of bytes transferred. They do this by decreasing the initialized value of the number of bytes to be transferred by a factor of 1 each time a byte is transferred. When the counter in the DMA controller reaches its terminal count (0), it sends a **terminal count (T/C)** signal to the disk-drive controller. If the counter in the disk drive controller does not equal 0 at this time, an error flag is created in the disk drive controller, and the system must attempt to write the data again.

Data transfers in hard-disk drives must occur at a much quicker pace than those in floppy-disk drives. For this reason, hard-disk drives use onboard RAM buffers to enable transfers to occur in block form rather than byte-by-byte. The buffer is small, usually only large enough to hold one sector of data, although some manufacturers use larger memories. When the controller begins serialization, the data is obtained from the buffer rather than through the DMA channel.

In addition to writing the data, the controller must generate the sector postamble. At the end of the data field, the controller generates the postamble containing the error-detection and correction codes. The sector's **preambles** are written on the disk when it is formatted.

If the data from the computer requires more than one sector to be written, as it usually does, these logically related sectors may not be located sequentially on the disk. When data is transferred a block at a time, some time is required to process each sector of data. To give the drive time to process the information, logically sequential sectors are **interleaved** (separated) by a fixed number of other sectors. This way, the motion of the disk moves the second sector into position to be written (or read) while the drive is processing the previous sector of information. A common **interleaving factor** is 8 sectors between logically related sectors on a floppy drive, a factor of 3 on older hard-disk systems, and a factor of 1 on newer systems.

Read Operations

When a Read operation is performed, the operating system goes to the directory, either in main memory or on the directory track on the disk, to obtain the starting track/sector address of the data to be read. This address is loaded into the disk controller, and a Track Seek operation is performed. The R/W head is stepped to the desired track, and the disk-drive controller selects the proper head. After a few milliseconds delay (to allow the R/W head to settle over the track), the operating system gives the disk controller the command to read the desired sector. The controller begins reading the sector ID headers, looking for the assigned sector.

When the sector is identified, the preamble is read and **bit-sync** is established. As the preamble is read, the controller synchronizes the data separator with the incoming bit stream from the disk drive. At the beginning of the data field, a **data start marker** initiates **byte-sync**, which coordinates the first bit of the first data byte with the controller's internal circuitry. At this point, the controller begins dividing the incoming bit stream into 8-bit words for transmission to the system unit.

After byte-sync has been established, the drive begins reading the data through the controller. The controller decodes the bit stream from its coded form (such as FM, MFM, and GCR) and shifts it into an onboard shift register in 8-bit chunks. Hard-disk drives deliver the bytes to the onboard buffer memory; most floppies set up a DMA request and transfer the data bytes unbuffered into the computer's main memory. The transfer may continue over multiple sectors or tracks until an **end-of-file marker** is encountered, indicating that the entire file has been transferred.

Floppy-Disk Drives

The discussion of general disk drive operations applies to both hard and floppy drives alike. However, the physical construction and operation of the drives are quite different. The FDD is an exposed unit, with an opening in the front to allow the floppy disk to be inserted and removed. In addition, the R/W heads are open to the atmosphere and ride directly on the surface of the disk. Older $5^1/4$-inch units used a locking handle to secure the disk in the drive. A spring-loaded assembly ejected the disk from the drive when the handle was rotated. Newer $3^1/2$-inch units have ejection buttons. Table 8.1 provides a comparison of the two different floppy drive types using the disk formats possible for each.

Table 8.1 *Comparisons of Floppy-Disk Drive Standards*

Diameter	Density	Capacity	Tracks	Sectors
$3^1/2$"	DD	720KB	70	9
	HD	1.44MB	70	18
$5^1/4$"	DD	360KB	40	9
	HD	1.2MB	70	15

Data moves back and forth between the system's RAM memory and the floppy disk surface. Along the way, it passes from the system RAM to the **floppy-disk controller (FDC)** through the floppy drive signal cable and into the floppy drive's **analog control board**. The analog control board converts the data into signals that can be applied to the drive's R/W heads, which, in turn, produce the magnetic spots on the disk surface.

In the original PCs and XTs, the FDC circuitry was located on the FDD controller card. In AT-compatible systems, it migrated onto a multi I/O card along with parallel, serial, game, and HDD control ports. With Pentium-based systems, all this circuitry has been integrated into the system board.

The circuitry on the floppy drive unit is usually distributed between two printed circuit boards: the analog control board and the drive's **spindle motor control board**.

FDD Controller

In older PCs, the FDD control function was performed by a **765 FDC controller** chip and a discrete **digital control port register**. In newer units, the floppy disk control function is provided by the FDC portion of the **integrated I/O ASIC**. This chip can be located on an MI/O card or on the system board. To remain PC-compatible, the FDC registers and signal definitions used must remain identical to those of the 765 FDC and digital control port register. In any case, the FDD controller provides a programmable interface between the system unit and the floppy-disk drive unit. Figure 8.9 depicts a block diagram of the floppy-disk drive control circuitry.

FIGURE 8.9

The floppy-disk drive adapter.

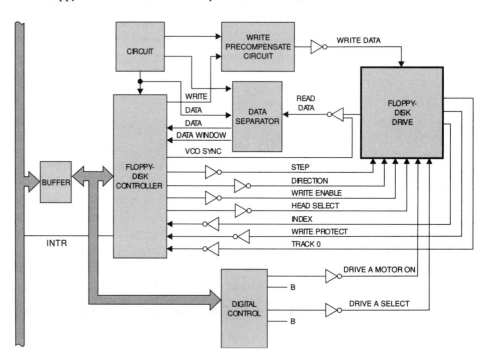

Under direction of the DOS system, the FDC divides the 3½-inch floppy disk into 80 tracks per side, with 9 or 18 512-byte sectors per side. This provides the system with 737,280 (720KB) or 1,474,560 (1.44MB) total bytes of storage on each disk. Table 8.2 lists the operating specifications for a typical 3½-inch floppy-disk drive unit.

Table 8.2   FDD Specifications

Drive Unit Part	DSSD	DSHD
Tracks	80	80
Heads	2	2
Sectors per track	9	18
Bytes per sector	512	512

Drive Unit Part	DSSD	DSHD
Formatted capacity	720KB	1.44MB
Unformatted capacity	1MB	2MB
Rotational speed (RPM)	300	30
Recording density (bits/inch)	8717	17,432
Tracks per inch	135	135
Transfer rate unformatted (Kbps)	250	500

The 765-compatible FDC can carry out at least 15 different commands—such as **Read Sector**, **Write Sector**, **Read Track**, **Seek**, and **Format Track**—under the direction of the disk operating system software. The FDC supports both double-density and high-density (MFM) recording formats and performs all the data-decoding functions for the drive. It has the capability to control two drives (drives A and B) simultaneously, with any mixture of sizes and densities. In addition, the FDC performs all data synchronization and error-checking functions to ensure reliable storage and recall of data.

The ASIC provides the additional circuitry required to complete the entire FDD controller/interface section. The additional circuitry consists of the address recognition circuitry, a clock signal generator to produce master and write clock signals, and a read data separator circuit to remove the data bits from the other information written in a sector. The FDC governs the operation of the data separator.

The ASIC also supplies interface signals that enable it to be connected to microprocessor systems with or without DMA capabilities. However, in most systems, the FDC operates in conjunction with the system's DMA controller and is assigned to the DRQ2 and DACK2 lines. In operation, the FDC presents a DRQ2 request for every byte of data to be transferred. In addition, the disk-drive controller is assigned to the IRQ6 line. The FDC generates an interrupt signal each time it receives a Read, Write, or Format command from the system unit. An interrupt is also generated when the controller receives a Ready signal from one of the disk drive units. Figure 8.10 depicts a block function diagram of the FDC.

Of particular interest is the FDC's internal register set. This register set contains two registers that can be addressed by the system unit's microprocessor: an 8-bit **Main Status register** and a stack of 8-bit registers called the **Data register**. Only one of these data registers can be accessed at a time. Data bytes are written into or read out of the data register to program the controller or obtain results after the completion of an operation. The Main Status register contains status information about the drive and can be accessed by the system at any time.

The operation of the FDC occurs in a three-phase cycle: a **command phase**, an **execution phase**, and a **result phase**.

During the command phase, the system unit initiates an action by writing a multi-byte instruction and all related data into the FDC's data register. At the completion of the command phase, the FDC enters the execution phase, in which the FDC generates the timing and control signals necessary for the drive to carry out the specified command. After the instruction has been carried out, the FDC enters the result phase, in which the disk drive's status information is placed in the Main Status register. Figure 8.11 shows the sequence in which information is moved into the FDC's Data register during Read Sector and Write Sector commands. Although the sequence is identical for these two commands, other instructions occur in different sequences and with other parameters.

FIGURE 8.10

The FDC block diagram.

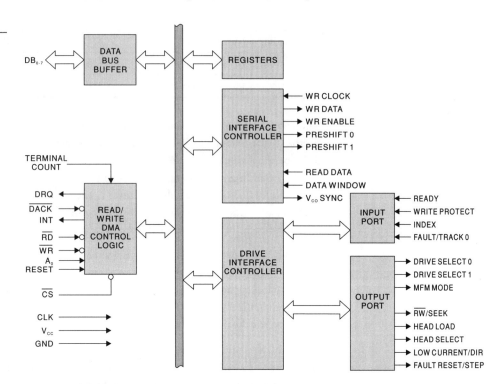

FIGURE 8.11

FDC R/W operations.

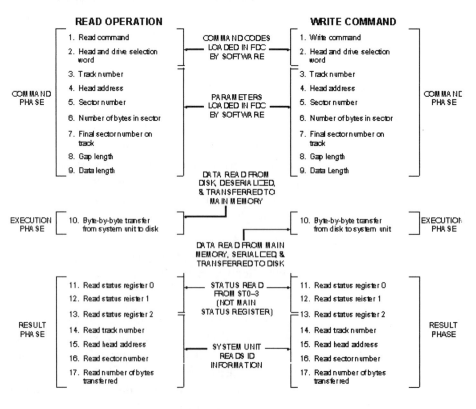

Digital Control Port Register

Operating in parallel with the FDC is the Digital Control Port register. This register is used to control the selection of drive units A and B; the drive motors; and the adapter's FDC Reset, DMA Request (DRQ2), and Interrupt Request (IRQ6) functions. This is a write-only register, selected when the system unit applies an address of 3F2 to the adapter, with the IOW line asserted. The various bits of the Control Port register are used for drive/motor selection, DRQ and IRQ enabling circuitry, and the FDC Reset bit. This register is depicted in Figure 8.12.

FIGURE 8.12

The Digital Control Port register.

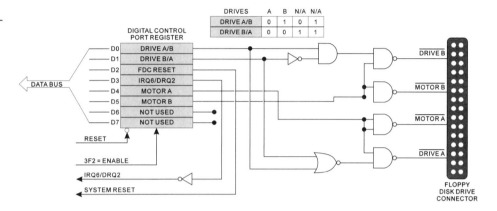

Read Circuitry

Data sent to the FDC from the drive is actually a combination of two signals: the data and the clocking information used to record it. This concept is easier to envision for FM-coded data, where each bit time is marked by the presence of a clock pulse. But MFM-encoded data possesses clocking information embedded in the serial bit stream. To properly read the data, it must be broken into two parts: the clocking information and the data bits. This is the function of the **Data Separator** circuitry.

The Data Separator must synchronize the rate of the serial bit stream coming from the drive unit and the clocking of the FDC's internal circuitry (bit-sync). After synchronization is achieved, the separator creates a **Data Window** timing signal, used by the FDC to differentiate between the clocking information and the data bits in the bit stream. The FDC uses this window to reconstruct the data bits from the bit stream.

In addition to recovering the data bits from the bit stream, the FDC must break the data bits into 8-bit words for transfer to the system unit (byte-sync). This requires that the system unit's DMA controller service the FDC approximately every 15 microseconds for MFM-recorded data. If this servicing does not occur, the FDC detects that a Data Register overrun error has occurred and sets the **Overrun Error flag** in its Main Status register. This action terminates the Data Read command activities.

The disk drive adapter's Read Channel components are shown in Figure 8.13. The MFM-encoded data stream from the disk drive passes through pin 30 of the disk-drive connector. Next, the data stream is applied to the Data Separator, where it is combined with the FDC's clock signal. From the two inputs, the Data Separator produces two outputs: the serial bit stream and the **Read Data Window** (RDW) signal. The RDW signal causes the FDC to sample the **Read Data** (RDD) line. During the window, the FDC loads the data bit on its Read Data input into the internal Data Register.

FIGURE 8.13

FDC Read circuitry.

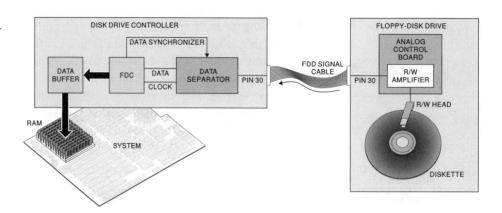

Write Circuitry

The disk drive adapter's Write circuitry is depicted in Figure 8.14. When the system unit places data in the FDC to be written on the disk, the FDC serializes the data, codes the data in the designated form (FM or MFM), and adds error-detection and correction bits (CRCs) to the serial data stream. The data moves in encoded, serial format from the FDC's **Write Data (WD)** output through a Write Precompensate circuit to the adapter's FDD connector at pin 22. The cable carries the WD and **Write Enable (WE)** signals to the disk drive unit.

FIGURE 8.14

FDC Write circuitry.

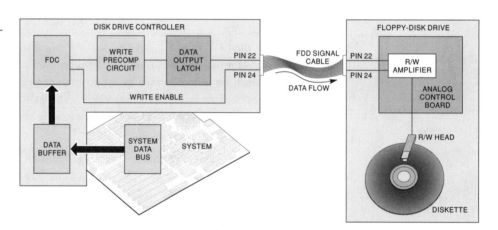

The **Write Precompensate circuit** acts as a time delay to correctly position the data bits for proper read-back. This is necessary because a certain amount of data shift occurs during the read-back process. This shifting is predictable, so the FDC is programmed to precompensate the data stream before it's written.

The precompensation circuitry is required only for MFM-encoded data. MFM-encoded data does not contain a clocking pulse in its bit cell, so it cannot tolerate large amounts of data shifting when the data is read back from the disk.

Floppy-Drive Cables

A single ribbon cable is used to connect the system's floppy drive(s) to the disk-drive controller card. Generally, the cable has two **edge connectors** and two 34-pin, two-row BERG headers along its length.

The edge connectors enable the cable to be connected directly to the printed-circuit board of a 5¼-inch FDD; the BERG connectors are used for 3½-inch drives. The other end of the cable terminates in a 34-pin, two-row BERG header. A small colored stripe normally runs along one edge of the cable, as illustrated in Figure 8.15. This is the **Pin #1 indicator stripe** that marks the side of the cable, which should be aligned with the #1 pin of the FDD adapter's connector and the disk drive's signal connector. The location of this pin is marked on the drive's printed-circuit board.

FIGURE 8.15

The FDD signal cable.

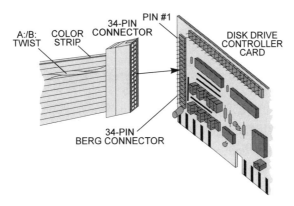

The system assigns the Drive A: designation to the drive attached to the 34-pin header, or edge connector, at the end of the cable. A floppy drive connected to the edge connector in the middle of the cable is designated as Drive B:. A small twist of wires between the A and B connectors reroutes key lines that distinguish between the two drives.

The 34-pin interface connection enables the FDC to control two separate floppy-disk drive units. Figure 8.16 depicts the connections between the disk-drive adapter and the disk drive(s). The direction of signal flow between the drive(s) and adapter is indicated by the arrows.

FIGURE 8.16

FDD cable signal definitions.

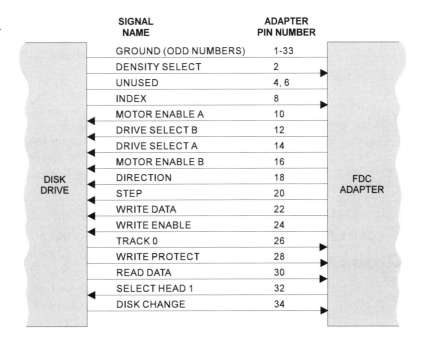

SIGNAL NAME	ADAPTER PIN NUMBER
GROUND (ODD NUMBERS)	1-33
DENSITY SELECT	2
UNUSED	4, 6
INDEX	8
MOTOR ENABLE A	10
DRIVE SELECT B	12
DRIVE SELECT A	14
MOTOR ENABLE B	16
DIRECTION	18
STEP	20
WRITE DATA	22
WRITE ENABLE	24
TRACK 0	26
WRITE PROTECT	28
READ DATA	30
SELECT HEAD 1	32
DISK CHANGE	34

All the adapter's signal lines are TTL-compatible. Furthermore, the functions of the lines are summarized as follows:

WRITE DATA (pin 22): For each high-to-low logic transition on this line, the disk drive stores a flux change on the disk. This action depends on the Write Enable line being activated.

READ DATA (pin 30): The selected disk drive places a pulse on this line for each flux change on the disk that passes under the selected R/W head.

WRITE ENABLE (pin 24): This line disables the drive's Write circuitry unless it is active.

INDEX (pin 8): The selected drive applies a pulse to this line each time the index hole on the disk passes the index sensor (1 pulse/revolution or approximately 300 pulses/min).

TRACK 0 (pin 26): When the R/W heads of the selected drive are positioned over track 0, the drive's track-00 sensor activates this line.

WRITE PROTECT (pin 28): The presence of a write-protected disk in the selected drive activates this line.

DRIVE A (pin 14): This line enables the drive unit attached as drive A when active.

MOTOR A (pin 10): This line starts the drive-A spindle motor when activated and stops it when the line returns to a high logic level.

DRIVE B and MOTOR B (pins 12 and 16): These lines are identical to the drive A and motor A lines, except they control the drive connected as drive B.

STEP (pin 20): During a Seek operation, the FDC issues pulses on this line. The selected drive must move the R/W heads one track per pulse. The direction of movement is in accordance with the condition of the Direction line.

DIRECTION (pin 18): When this line is high, the selected disk drive moves the R/W heads one track away from the center of the disk for each pulse on the Step line. When low, the drive moves the heads one track toward the center for each pulse on the Step line.

SELECT HEAD 1 (pin 32): When this line is high, the upper R/W head (head 0) of the selected drive is activated. When low, the lower head (head 1) is activated.

DENSITY SELECT (pin 2): This line sets the write current level used for double-density or high-density disks. The controller outputs a low when double-density disks are detected, or a high when high-density disks are detected.

FDD Installation

To install a floppy-disk drive, disconnect the system's power cord from the back of the unit. Slide the FDD into one of the system unit's open drive bays, and install two screws on each side to secure the floppy-disk drive to the system unit. If the unit is a 3¹/₂-inch drive, and if it is being installed into a 5¹/₄-inch drive bay, you must fit the drive with a **universal mounting kit**. These kits attach to the drive and extend its form factor so that it fits correctly in the 5¹/₄-inch half-height space. Figure 8.17 illustrates the steps required to install the floppy drive in a tower system.

FIGURE 8.17

Installing a floppy-disk drive.

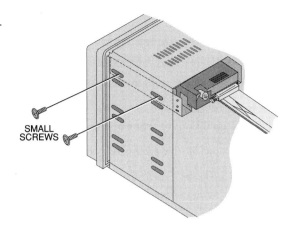

Connect the floppy drive signal cable to the 34-pin, FDD interface header (on an I/O card or system board). Then connect the signal cable to the floppy-disk drive, as illustrated in Figure 8.18. If the drive is the only floppy in the system or is intended to operate as the A drive, connect the drive to the connector at the end of the cable. If it is being installed as a B drive, attach it to the connector toward the center of the cable. On older floppy drives, the cable will connect to an edge connector on the drive's printed-circuit board. With newer units, the connection attaches to a BERG connector. Note the orientation of the color stripe on both ends.

FIGURE 8.18

Connecting the floppy drive.

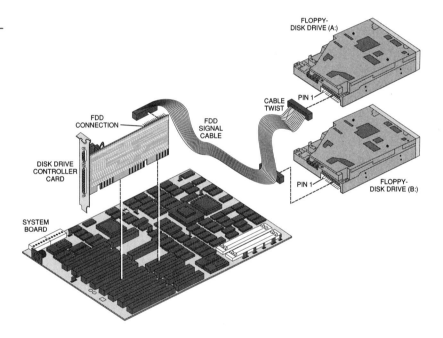

Connect one of the power supply's optional power connectors to the FDD unit. Check for the presence of a **drive select** (**DS**) jumper block on the drive's control board. This jumper is normally set to the DS0 position for drive-A operation. On Pentium and other types of all-in-one system boards, look for an **FDD enabling jumper**, and make certain that it is set correctly for the FDD installed. In newer systems, the FDD enabling function may be set in the Advanced CMOS Setup screen.

Reinstall the system unit's power cord and boot up the computer. As the system boots, move into the CMOS Setup screens and configure the CMOS for the type of FDD just installed.

Troubleshooting FDDs

 A+ CORE 2.1

Typical symptoms associated with floppy-disk drive failures during boot-up include the following:

1. FDD errors encountered during boot-up.

2. Front panel indicator lights are visible, the display is present on the monitor screen, but there is no disk drive action and no boot-up.

3. An IBM-compatible 6xx-error code is displayed.

4. An "FDD Controller Error" message indicates a failure to verify the FDD setup by the System Configuration file.

5. The FDD activity light stays on constantly, indicating that the FDD signal cable is reversed.

Additional FDD error messages commonly encountered during normal system operation include the following:

1. Disk Drive Read Error messages

2. Disk Drive Write Error messages

3. Disk Drive Seek Error messages

4. "No Boot Record Found" message, indicating that the system files in the disk's boot sector are missing or have become corrupt

5. System stops working while reading a disk, indicating that the contents of the disk have become contaminated.

6. The drive displays the same directory listing for every disk inserted in the drive, indicating that the FDD's disk-change detector or signal line is not functional.

> A number of things can cause improper floppy-disk drive operation or disk-drive failure. These items include the use of unformatted disks, incorrectly inserted disks, damaged disks, erased disks, loose cables, drive failure, adapter failure, system board failure, or a bad or loose power connector.

Figure 8.19 depicts the flow of information and control signals associated with the floppy-disk drives throughout the system.

Information is written to and read from the floppy disks by the floppy-disk drive unit. This unit moves information and control signals back and forth between the disk-drive controller and the surface of the disks. The information moves between the controller and the drive through a flat ribbon cable. The small printed-circuit board, located on the drive unit, is called the analog control board. This control board is responsible for turning the digital information received from the adapter card into magnetic information that can be stored on the surface of the disk, and vice versa.

The floppy-disk drive controller is responsible for controlling the flow of information between the system board's circuitry and the disk drive. When the controller is mounted on an options adapter card, information and control signals pass between the card and the system board through the adapter card's edge connector and the system board's expansion-slot connector.

FIGURE 8.19

Flow of FDD data and control signals.

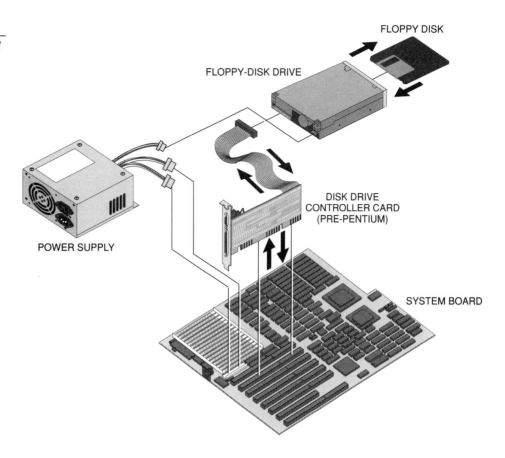

FLOPPY DISK

FLOPPY-DISK DRIVE

DISK DRIVE
CONTROLLER CARD
(PRE-PENTIUM)

POWER SUPPLY

SYSTEM BOARD

Basically three levels of troubleshooting apply to FDD problems: configuration, the DOS level, and the hardware level. No Windows-level troubleshooting applies to floppy drives.

FDD Configuration Checks

Normally, the only time a configuration problem occurs is when the system is being set up for the first time or when a new option is installed. The other condition that cause a configuration problem involves the system board's CMOS backup battery. If the battery fails or has been changed, then the contents of the CMOS setup will be lost. After replacing the battery, it is always necessary to run the CMOS Setup utility to reconfigure the system.

While booting up the system to the DOS prompt, observe the BIOS FDD-type information displayed on the monitor. Note the type(s) of FDD(s) that the BIOS believes are installed in the system. With newer BIOS, you must examine the advanced CMOS setup to check the boot-up order. In these BIOS, the boot order can be set so that the FDD is never examined during startup.

The values stored in this CMOS memory must accurately reflect the type and number of FDDs installed in the system, or an error will occur. These values can be accessed for change during the boot-up procedure.

DOS Checks

If the FDD configuration information is correct and a floppy-disk drive problem is suspected, the first task is to make certain that the system won't boot up from the floppy-disk drive if a disk with a known good boot file is in the drive. Try the boot disk in a different computer to see if it works on that machine. If not, there is a problem with the files on the disk. If the disk boots up the other computer, you must troubleshoot the floppy-drive system.

If possible, run a diagnostic software program from the hard drive or a B floppy drive. Try to use a diagnostic program that conducts a bank of tests on the FDD's components. Run the program's **FDD Tests**, and perform the equivalent of the **ALL tests** function.

From the DOS level, it is also very easy to test the operation of the drive using a simple batch program. At the DOS prompt, type `Copy Con:FDDTEST.BAT`, and press the ENTER key. On the first line, type the DOS `DIR` command. On the second line, type `FDDTEST`. Finally, press the F6 function key to exit, and save the program to the hard-disk drive.

This test program can be executed from the DOS prompt simply by typing its name. When invoked, the program exercises the drive's R/W head-positioning motors and read channel signal-processing circuitry. At the same time, it will test the signal cable and the FDC circuitry.

FDD Hardware Checks

If a floppy-disk drive hardware problem is suspected, begin troubleshooting the hardware by removing all the externally connected devices from the system, except for the monitor and keyboard. Try to boot the system. If the system operates correctly with these options removed, it is safe to assume that one of them is the cause of the problem. To verify which external device is causing the problem, reconnect the devices one at a time until the problem reappears. The last device reinstalled before the problem reappeared is defective. Replace this item and continue reinstalling options, one at a time, until all the options have been reinstalled. If another failure occurs while reinstalling options, replace that option as well. Repair or replace the defective options device(s), and return the system to full service.

If the system will not boot up with the external options removed, turn off the system and remove the system unit's outer cover. Remove all the options adapter cards, except for the video and disk-drive controller cards from the system board's expansion slots. Try to reboot the system.

If the system boots up with the internal options cards removed, it is reasonable to assume that one of them is the cause of the problem. Therefore, you should reinstall the internal options one at a time until the problem reappears. As always, the last option reinstalled before the problem returned is defective. Repair or replace the defective options adapter as indicated, and return the system to full service.

If the system does not boot up with all the options removed, check the components associated with the floppy-disk drives. Begin by exchanging the floppy-disk drive with another one of the same type. If a second floppy-disk drive exists in the system, turn off the computer and exchange its connection to the floppy-disk drive's signal cable so that it becomes the A drive. Try to reboot the system using this drive as A. Also check the floppy-disk drive's signal cable for proper connection at both ends. Check for a drive select jumper on the drive's printed-circuit board, and make certain that it is installed correctly.

Insert the bootable disk in the new drive A, and turn on the system. If the system boots up, reinstall any options removed, and replace the system unit's outer cover. Return the system to full service, and repair the defective floppy drive accordingly.

If the system still refuses to boot up, turn it off and exchange the disk-drive controller card (if present) with a known good one. Disconnect the disk drive's signal cable from the controller card, and swap the controller card with a known good one of the same type. Make certain to mark the cable and its connection point to ensure proper reconnection after the exchange. Reconnect the signal cable to the FDD controller.

Try to reboot the system with the new disk-drive controller card installed. If the controller is built into the system board, it may be easier to test the drive and signal cable in another machine than to remove the system board. If the system boots up, reinstall any options removed, and replace the system unit's outer cover. Return the system to full service and return the defective controller card.

If the system still will not boot up or perform FDD operations correctly, check the disk drive cables for proper connection at both ends. If necessary, exchange the signal cable with a known good one. Finally, exchange the system board with a known good one.

Hard-Disk Drives

Although early PCs did not rely on hard drives, nearly every modern PC has at least one installed. After the original PC, the hard drive became standard equipment. The XT featured a 10MB MFM unit. Modern units feature drives that typically have storage capacities in the gigabyte range. Logically, the hard drive is organized as a stack of disks similar to a floppy disk. Each surface is divided into tracks, which are, in turn, divided into sectors. Each disk possesses a matching set of tracks on the top and bottom of the disk. The disks are stacked on top of each other, and the R/W heads move in and out between them. Because there are corresponding tracks on the top and bottom of each disk in the stack, the HDD controller organizes them into **cylinders**. For example, cylinder 1 of a four-platter HDD would consist of track 1 of each disk surface. The cylinder concept is described in Figure 8.20.

FIGURE 8.20

HDD cylinders.

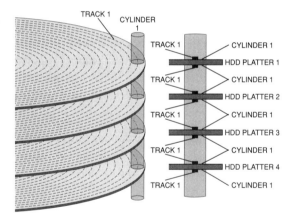

The physical makeup of a hard disk system is depicted in Figure 8.21. This involves a controller (either on an I/O card or built into the system board), one or more signal cables, a power cable, and a disk-drive unit. In some cases, floppy- and hard-disk drive signal cables may look similar. However, some slight differences in their construction prevent them from being compatible. Therefore, great caution must be used when installing these cables. Many skilled technicians have encountered problems by not paying attention to which type of cable they were installing with a particular type of drive.

FIGURE 8.21

Components of the HDD system.

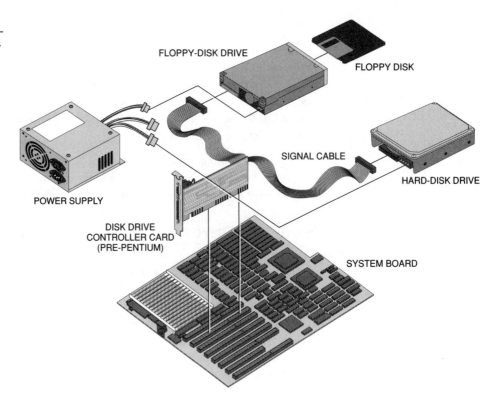

The system's CMOS Setup holds the HDD configuration settings. As with other configuration settings, these must be set correctly for the installed drive. Typical HDD information required for the CMOS setup includes the HDD's capacity, number of cylinders, number of R/W heads, number of sectors/track, amount of precompensation, and the track number to be used as the landing zone for the R/W heads when the drive is shut down. This information must normally be obtained from the drive manufacturer. Figure 8.22 gives typical HDD format information associated with a particular BIOS. Systems using other BIOS may have different values. Most BIOS tables also provide for a user-definable HDD entry, where the values are entered manually into the CMOS settings.

The other important disk-drive specifications are access time, seek time, data transfer rate, and storage capacity. These quantities designate how much data the drive can hold, how fast it can get to a specific part of the data, and how fast it can move data to the system.

Formatting

A+ DOS/WINDOWS 1.5

> Unlike floppy drives, which basically come in four accepted formats, hard-disk drives are created in a wide variety of storage capacities. When the drive is created, its surface is electronically blank. To prepare the disk for use by the system, three levels of preparation, must take place. Their order follows: the **low-level format** (below DOS), the **partition**, and the **high-level format** (or DOS).

A low-level format is very similar to an analogy of a land developer sectioning off a field for a new housing development. The process begins with surveying the property and placing markers for key structures such as roads, water lines, and electrical service. In the same way, the low-level format routine marks off the disk into cylinders and sectors and defines their placement on the disk. In older **device-level drive types** (such as ST-506 and ESDI drives), the user is required to perform the low-level format. This procedure could be accomplished through the DOS Debug program by typing **G=C800:5** at the Debug prompt. In some units, the offset is 6 or 8 instead of 5. Many of the software diagnostic packages come with a low-level formatter program.

Most newer, **system-level drive types** (such as IDE and SCSI drives) come with the low-level format already performed. Attempts to perform low-level formats on IDE and SCSI drives may result in damage to the drive. This is not physical damage, but it involves the loss of pre-recorded bad track and sector information that would occur during a low-level format. The drive also contains alignment information used to control the R/W heads for proper alignment over the tracks. This alignment information would also be lost during a low-level format. If this occurs, it will normally be necessary to send the drive to the manufacturer to restore this information to the disk.

FIGURE 8.22

Typical HDD format values.

Type	Cylin	Heads	W-Pcomp	L-Zone	Capacity
1	306	4	128	305	10MB
2	615	4	300	615	21MB
3	615	6	300	615	31MB
4	940	8	512	940	63MB
5	940	6	512	940	47MB
6	615	4	FFFF	615	21MB
7	462	8	256	511	31MB
8	733	5	FFFF	733	31MB
9	900	15	FFFF	901	112MB
10	820	3	FFFF	820	21MB
11	855	5	FFFF	855	36MB
12	855	7	FFFF	855	50MB
13	306	8	128	319	21MB
14	733	7	FFFF	733	43MB
15	000	0	0000	000	00MB
16	612	4	0000	663	21MB
17	977	5	300	977	41MB
18	977	7	FFFF	977	57MB
19	1024	7	512	1023	60MB
20	733	5	300	732	31MB
21	733	7	300	732	43MB
22	733	5	300	733	31MB
23	306	4	0000	336	10MB
24	925	7	0000	925	54MB
25	925	9	FFFF	925	69MB
26	754	7	754	754	44MB
27	754	11	FFFF	754	69MB
28	699	7	256	699	41MB
29	823	10	FFFF	823	69MB
30	918	7	918	918	54MB
31	1024	11	FFFF	1024	94MB
32	1024	15	FFFF	1024	128MB
33	1024	5	1024	1024	43MB
34	612	2	128	612	10MB
35	1024	9	FFFF	1024	77MB
36	1024	8	512	1024	68MB
37	615	8	128	615	41MB
38	987	3	987	987	25MB
39	987	7	987	987	58MB
40	820	6	820	820	41MB
41	977	5	97	977	41MB
42	981	5	981	981	41MB
43	830	7	512	830	49MB
44	830	10	FFFF	830	69MB
45	917	15	FFFF	918	115MB
46	000	0	0000	000	00MB
47					

Logical and Physical Drives

> Before a high-level format can be performed, the drive must be partitioned. The partition establishes the size and number of **logical drives** on the physical drive.

By partitioning a drive, multiple operating systems can exist on the same drive. The oldest versions of MS-DOS (2.x, 3.x) imposed a limit on the size of a logical drive at 32MB each, identified by different drive letters (such as C, D, E, and so on).

As HDD technology steadily increased, the sizes of the physical drives eventually passed this limit. DOS version 4.0 raised the maximum size of a logical drive to 128MB, and version 5.0 raised it to 528MB. Special disk-management installation packages have extended the size limit of a logical drive up to 2GB. The partitioning program for MS-DOS is named **FDISK**. Likewise, the FDISK utility in Windows 95 provides upgraded support for very large hard drives. The original version of Windows 95 set a size limit for logical drives at 2GB. The FDISK version in the upgraded OSR2 version (b) has extended the maximum disk partition size to 8GB.

Even though newer versions of DOS provide for partitions that are larger than 528MB; another factor limits the size of disk partitions: the BIOS. The standard BIOS has a 504MB capacity limit. To overcome this, newer BIOS include an Enhanced mode that use Logical Block Addressing (LBA) techniques to enable the larger partition sizes available through DOS and Windows to be used. This technique—known as Enhanced Cylinder, Heads, Sectors (ECHS)—effectively increases the number of R/W heads the system can recognize from 16 to 256. The parameters of 1,024 cylinders, 63 sectors/track, and 512 bytes/sector remains unchanged.

Although the connection point along the signal cable (and the Drive Select setting of the drive) is important in determining how the system defines a certain drive, this is not the only determining factor. The system sees hard-disk drives as logical drives assigned by DOS, instead of physical drives. It is not unusual for a single 1GB drive to be partitioned into two 500MB logical drives (C and D).

Figure 8.23 illustrates the concept of creating multiple logical drives on a single hard drive. This is normally done for purposes of organization and increased access speeds. Basically, DOS provides for two partitions on an HDD unit. The first partition, or the **primary partition**, must exist as drive C. The system files must be located in this partition, and the partition must be set to "Active" for the system to boot up from the drive. After the primary partition has been established and properly configured, an additional partition, referred to as an **extended partition**, is also allowed. However, the extended partition may be subdivided into 23 logical drives. The extended partition cannot be deleted if logical drives have been defined in it.

In local area networks (LANs) and wide area networks (WANs), the concept of logical drives is carried a step further. A particular hard-disk drive may be a logical drive in a large system of drives along a peer-to-peer network. On the other hand, a very large centralized drive may be used to create several logical drives for a server/client type of network.

FIGURE 8.23

Partitions on an HDD.

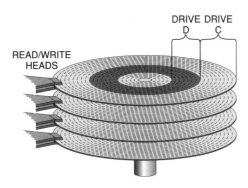

The high-level format procedure is performed by the **Format command** in the MS-DOS program. This format program creates the blank FAT and root directory on the disk.

These elements tell the system what files are on the disk and where they can be found. Never format a disk with an older version of DOS than is currently installed on the disk. The drive can actually be damaged from this action. Before reformatting a drive, use the **DOS VER command** to determine what version of DOS is currently in use.

HDD Interfaces

Four HDD interfaces have been commonly associated with microcomputers. These include two device-level interfaces and two system-level interfaces. The device-level interfaces are the **ST-506/412** and **Enhanced Small Device Interface** (**ESDI**). These types of drives typically use a controller card that contains the system-level interface for the drive. These drive types require the user to perform all three levels of drive preparation.

The system-level interfaces, **Integrated Drive Electronics** (**IDE**) and **Small Computer System Interface** (**SCSI**), place most of the controller circuitry on the drive itself. Therefore, the system sees the entire HDD system as an attachment to its bus systems. As noted in the previous section, these units also come with the low-level format already in place.

The following sections describe the major attributes of the four HDD interface types.

ST-506/412 MFM Interface

Some hard-disk drives, such as those used in 8088-based computers, use a two-cable arrangement to connect the drive to the options adapter card, as depicted in Figure 8.24. This type of drive is referred to as an MFM drive (because they use MFM coding), and the physical connection is specified as an ST-506/412 interface. A similar type, called a **Run-Length Limited** (**RLL**) drive, also uses this interface connection scheme. These drives use the same physical equipment as the MFM drives but employ **group-coded recording** (**GCR**) methods to extend the drive's storage capacity by 50%.

In the ST-506 interface, the smaller, 20-pin **data cable** is easily identified with the MFM or RLL hard drive. However, the larger 34-pin **signal cable** closely resembles the floppy drive's signal cable and can often be confused with it. The two cables are not interchangeable, however. The difference between them is found in the twisted wires located between the two edge connectors. On the floppy cable, the twist begins with the 10th wire in from the indicator stripe and involves seven wires (conductors 10–16). With the hard drive's signal cable, the twist begins with the sixth wire in from the opposite side of the cable and involves five wires (conductors 25–29).

FIGURE 8.24

The ST-506/412 interface cable.

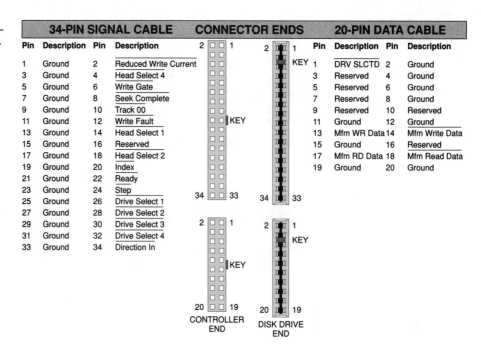

Pin	Description	Pin	Description
1	Ground	2	Reduced Write Current
3	Ground	4	Head Select 4
5	Ground	6	Write Gate
7	Ground	8	Seek Complete
9	Ground	10	Track 00
11	Ground	12	Write Fault
13	Ground	14	Head Select 1
15	Ground	16	Reserved
17	Ground	18	Head Select 2
19	Ground	20	Index
21	Ground	22	Ready
23	Ground	24	Step
25	Ground	26	Drive Select 1
27	Ground	28	Drive Select 2
29	Ground	30	Drive Select 3
31	Ground	32	Drive Select 4
33	Ground	34	Direction In

20-PIN DATA CABLE

Pin	Description	Pin	Description
1	DRV SLCTD	2	Ground
3	Reserved	4	Ground
5	Reserved	6	Ground
7	Reserved	8	Ground
9	Reserved	10	Reserved
11	Ground	12	Ground
13	Mfm WR Data	14	Mfm Write Data
15	Ground	16	Reserved
17	Mfm RD Data	18	Mfm Read Data
19	Ground	20	Ground

The drive unit connected to the edge connector at the end of the cable is normally designated by the system as the C drive. The drive connected to the middle of the cable is usually configured as the D drive. The addition of a second physical MFM drive to the system requires that a second 20-pin data cable be added to the interface to accommodate it. Single-connector versions of the signal cable, called **straight-through cables**, are also available for use in systems that only require one HDD unit.

Enhanced Small Device Interface (ESDI)

The Enhanced Small Device Interface (ESDI) is actually an improved ST-506 standard interface. This interface, described in Figure 8.25, uses the same 20/34-pin, two-cable arrangement as the ST-506. However, the signal definitions and locations have been changed so that the two interfaces are not compatible.

FIGURE 8.25

The ESDI interface cable.

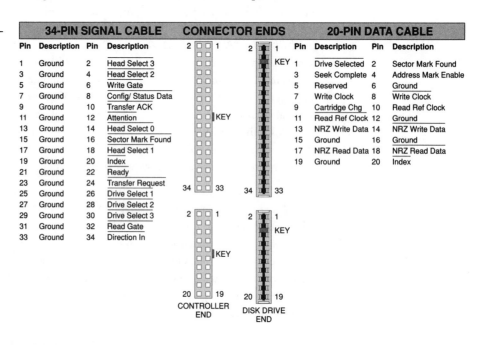

Pin	Description	Pin	Description
1	Ground	2	Head Select 3
3	Ground	4	Head Select 2
5	Ground	6	Write Gate
7	Ground	8	Config/ Status Data
9	Ground	10	Transfer ACK
11	Ground	12	Attention
13	Ground	14	Head Select 0
15	Ground	16	Sector Mark Found
17	Ground	18	Head Select 1
19	Ground	20	Index
21	Ground	22	Ready
23	Ground	24	Transfer Request
25	Ground	26	Drive Select 1
27	Ground	28	Drive Select 2
29	Ground	30	Drive Select 3
31	Ground	32	Read Gate
33	Ground	34	Direction In

20-PIN DATA CABLE

Pin	Description	Pin	Description
1	Drive Selected	2	Sector Mark Found
3	Seek Complete	4	Address Mark Enable
5	Reserved	6	Ground
7	Write Clock	8	Write Clock
9	Cartridge Chg	10	Read Ref Clock
11	Read Ref Clock	12	Ground
13	NRZ Write Data	14	NRZ Write Data
15	Ground	16	Ground
17	NRZ Read Data	18	NRZ Read Data
19	Ground	20	Index

Unlike the ST-506 standard, in which the controller must be configured by the system for the type of drive to which it is being connected, the ESDI interface calls for the drive to provide the controller with its configuration information. This information includes what type of drive it is and how many tracks and sectors it has, as well as bad track and sector information provided about itself. The manufacturer installs the information on the disk at the factory. These drives generally double the capacity and transfer rate of an equivalent MFM drive. Both of these improvements are accomplished primarily by increasing the number of sectors on each track to 34 (as opposed to 17 for most MFM drives).

Integrated Drive Electronics (IDE) Interface

The Integrated Drive Electronics interface is a system-level interface referred to as an **AT Attachment (ATA)** interface. The IDE interface places most of the controller electronics on the drive unit. Therefore, data travels in parallel between the computer and the drive unit. The controller circuitry on the drive handles all the parallel-to-serial and serial-to-parallel conversions. This enables the interface to be independent of the host computer design.

An IDE drive stores formatting information on itself. This information is placed on the drive by its manufacturer and is used by the controller for alignment and sector sizing of the drive. The IDE controller uses a data separator, similar to the FDD data separator, to intercept and isolate the raw data (format and actual information) coming from the R/W heads. This means that the information passed to the drive is comprised of commands and data. The mixed data stream leads to much higher bandwidth requirements between the IDE drive and the host adapter. Although the data-transfer rate varies from model to model, IDE drives have rates several times greater than older ST-506 and ESDI designs.

The IDE interface uses a single 40-pin cable to connect the floppy drives to the adapter card or system board. Its signal cable arrangement is depicted in Figure 8.26. In a system-level interface, the I/O card that plugs into the expansion slot is called a **host adapter** instead of a controller card. It should be apparent from the figure that the IDE host adapter is quite simple because most of the interface signals originate directly from the system's extended bus lines.

FIGURE 8.26

The IDE signal cable.

Pin	Description	Pin	Description
1	Reset	2	Ground
3	Data 7	4	Data 8
5	Data 6	6	Data 9
7	Data 5	8	Data 10
9	Data 4	10	Data 11
11	Data 3	12	Data 12
13	Data 2	14	Data 13
15	Data 1	16	Data 14
17	Data 0	18	Data 15
19	Ground	20	Unused
21	Unused	22	Ground
23	IOW	24	Ground
25	IOR	26	Ground
27	IOCHRDY	28	Bale
29	Unused	30	Ground
31	IRQ14	32	IOCS16
33	A1	34	PDAIG
35	A0	36	A2
37	HDCS0	38	HDCS1
39	SLV ACT	40	Ground

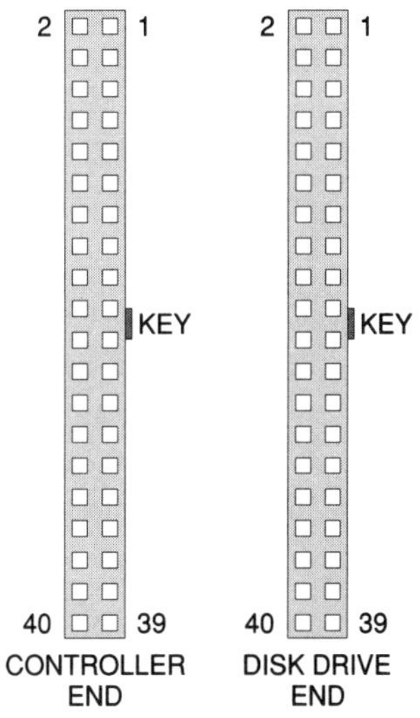

The host adapter basically serves three functions. These include providing the select signals to differentiate between a **single drive** system, or the **master** and **slave** drives. The host adapter also provides the three least-significant address bits (A0–A2) and the interface Reset signal. The HDCS0 signal is used to enable the master drive, and the HDCS1 signal is used to enable the slave drive. The relationship between the host adapter, the system buses, and the IDE interfaces is depicted in Figure 8.27.

FIGURE 8.27

The host adapter, system buses, and IDE interface.

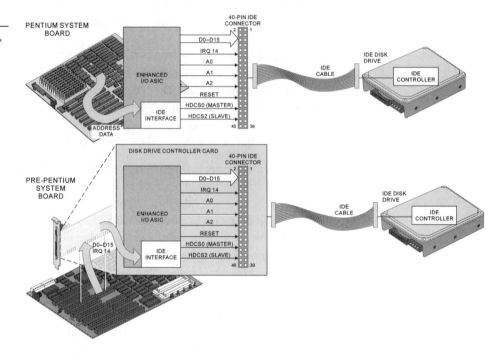

Updated IDE specifications have been developed to provide for more than two drives to exist on the interface. This new specification is called **Enhanced IDE (EIDE)**, or the **ATA-2** interface. Actually, the update covers more than simply increasing the number of drives that can be accommodated; it also provides for improved IDE drivers, known as the **AT Attachment Packet Interface (ATAPI)**, for use with CD-ROM drives as well as new data-transfer methods.

The new standard adds single-word and double-word DMA transfer capability to the interface's standard Programmed I/O mode. The single-word mode provides for one 16-bit word to be transferred during each DMA request cycle. In multiword mode, the data transfer is conducted in a DMA burst mode until the DREQ line is deactivated, or until the DMA controller's terminal count is reached.

Most IDE drives come from the manufacturer configured for operation as a single drive, or as the master drive in a multidrive system. To install the drive as a second, or slave, drive, it is usually necessary to install, remove, or to move a jumper block, as illustrated in Figure 8.28. Some hosts disable the interface's **cable select pin** (pin #28) for slave drives. With these types of hosts, it is necessary to install a jumper for the **Cable Select option** on the drive. Consult the system's user's manual to see whether it supports this function.

In the MS-DOS system, the primary partitions of multiple IDE hard drives are assigned the first logical drive identifiers. If an IDE drive is partitioned into two logical drives, the system identifies them as drives C and D. If a second IDE drive is added as a slave drive with two additional logical drives, it reassigns the partitions on the first drive to be logical drives C and E, with the partitions on the slave drive as D and F.

FIGURE 8.28

IDE master/slave settings.

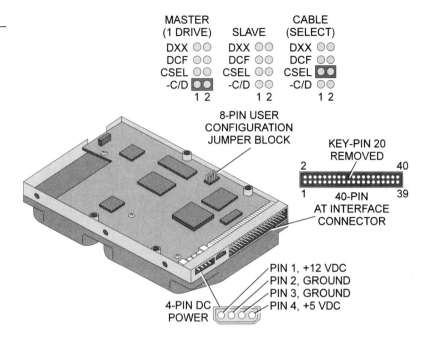

Small Computer System Interface (SCSI)

 A+ CORE 1.6

The Small Computer System Interface (SCSI), often referred to as **scuzzy** standard, provides a true system-level interface for the drive, similar to the IDE concept. Nearly all the drive's controller electronics are located on the peripheral device. As with the IDE host adapter, the duties of the **SCSI host adapter** are reduced to mostly physical connection functions, along with some signal compatibility handling.

Using this arrangement, data arrives at the system interface in a form that is already usable by the host computer. This can be seen through the SCSI interface description in Figure 8.29. Note that the SCSI interface in the figure makes provisions only for 8-bit parallel data transfers.

The SCSI interface can be used to connect up to seven diverse types of peripherals to the system. As an example, a SCSI chain could connect a controller to a hard drive, a CD-ROM drive, a high-speed tape drive, a scanner, and a printer. Additional SCSI devices are added to the system by daisy-chaining them together. The input of the second device is attached to the SCSI output of the first device, and so forth.

In a PC-compatible system, the SCSI interface uses a 50-pin signal cable arrangement, which should not be confused with any other interface cabling arrangements. Although the SCSI interface defined here is the full standard, some manufacturers may not utilize all the functions of the interface. The version of the SCSI interface used in the Apple Macintosh uses a variation of the standard that employs a proprietary miniature 25-pin D-shell connector.

These types of variations create a hardware incompatibility between different SCSI devices. Likewise, some SCSI devices just will not work with each other due to software incompatibilities. In addition, SCSI devices may be classified as internal or external devices. An internal SCSI device has no power supply of its own and, therefore, must be connected to one of the system's options power connectors. On the other hand, external SCSI devices come with built-in or plug-in power supplies that must be connected to a commercial ac outlet. Therefore, when choosing a SCSI device, always inquire about compatibility between it and any other SCSI devices installed in the system.

FIGURE 8.29

The SCSI interface cable.

PIN DESCRIPTION   CONNECTOR ENDS

Pin	Description	Pin	Description
1	Ground	2	Data 0
3	Ground	4	Data 1
5	Ground	6	Data 2
7	Ground	8	Data 3
9	Ground	10	Data 4
11	Ground	12	Data 5
13	Ground	14	Data 6
15	Ground	16	Data 7
17	Ground	18	Data Parity (Odd)
19	Ground	20	Ground
21	Ground	22	Ground
23	Ground	24	Ground
25	No Connection	26	No Connection
27	Ground	28	Ground
29	Ground	30	Ground
31	Ground	32	Attention
33	Ground	34	Ground
35	Ground	36	Busy
37	Ground	38	ACK
39	Ground	40	Reset
41	Ground	42	Message
43	Ground	44	Select
45	Ground	46	C/D
47	Ground	48	Request
49	Ground	50	I/O

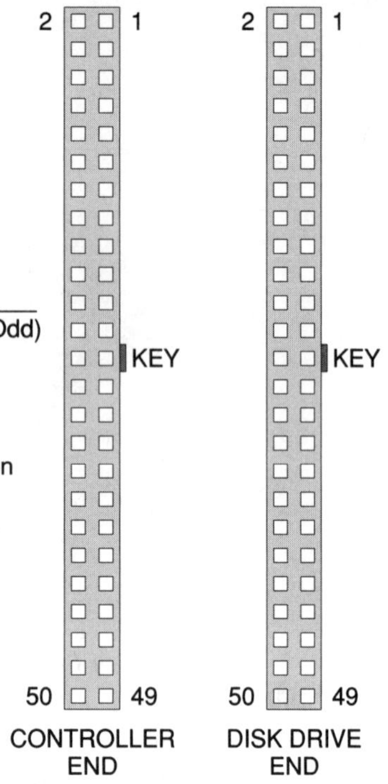

CONTROLLER END

DISK DRIVE END

When installing a SCSI device, addressing is set by jumpers on the host adapter card. In PnP systems, the BIOS configures the address using information obtained directly from the card during boot-up. Unlike other HDD types, SCSI hard drives are not configured as part of the system's CMOS setup function. This is due to the fact that DOS and Windows 3.x never included support for SCSI devices. Therefore, SCSI drivers must be loaded during boot-up, before the system boots, to communicate with the drive when using Windows 3.x. However, Windows 95 does offer SCSI support. SCSI drives also require no low-level formatting. Therefore, the second thing you do when installing a SCSI drive is to partition it.

The SCSI port can be daisy-chained to enable up to six external peripherals to be connected to the system. Even though a total of eight possible **SCSI device numbers** exist, only six are available for external devices. The SCSI specification refers to its SCSI controller as **SCSI-7** (by default) and then classifies the first internal hard drive as **SCSI-0**.

Each SCSI device has either a SCSI number selection switch or configuration jumpers. The SCSI address setting must be unique for every device attached to the host adapter. If two devices are set to the same ID number, one or both will appear invisible to the system.

To connect multiple SCSI devices to a controller, all the devices except the last one must have two SCSI connectors: one for **SCSI-In**, and one for **SCSI-Out**. The order of the connectors does not matter. However, if the device has only one SCSI connector, it must be connected at the end of the chain.

Multiple SCSI adapters can be used in a single system. The first SCSI controller can handle up to seven devices. An additional SCSI controller can boost the system to support up to 14 SCSI devices.

The SCSI daisy chain must be terminated with a terminating-resistor network pack at both of its ends. Single-connector SCSI devices are normally terminated internally. If not, a SCSI terminator cable (containing a built-in resistor pack) must be installed at the end of the chain. SCSI termination is a major cause of SCSI-related problems. Poor terminations cause a variety of different system problems, including the following:

▶ Failed system startups

▶ Hard drive crashes

▶ Random system failures

Maximum recommended length for a complete SCSI chain is 20 feet. However, unless the cables are heavily shielded, they become susceptible to data corruption caused by induced noise. Therefore, a maximum single segment of less than 3 feet is recommended. Don't forget the length of the internal cabling when dealing with SCSI cable distances. You can realistically count on about 3 feet of internal cable, so reduce the maximum total length to about 15 feet. Both a 25-pin and a 50-pin external SCSI connector are depicted in Figure 8.30. Inside the computer, the SCSI specification uses a 50-pin ribbon cable with BERG pin connectors.

FIGURE 8.30

SCSI connectors.

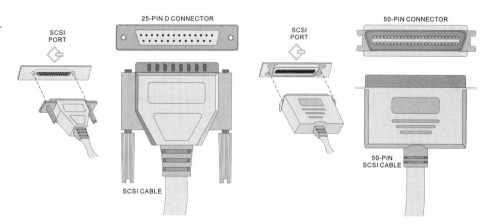

An updated SCSI specification has been developed by the ANSI committee to double the number of data lines in the interface and add balanced, dual-line drivers that provide for much faster data transfer speeds. This implementation is referred to as **Wide SCSI-2**. The specification expands the SCSI specification into a 16/32-bit bus standard and increases the cable and connector specification to 68 pins.

An additional improvement increased the synchronous data transfer option for the interface from 5Mbps to 10Mbps. This implementation became known as **Fast SCSI-2**. Under this system, the system and the I/O device conduct non-data message, command, and status operations in 8-bit asynchronous mode. After agreeing on a larger or faster file transfer format, they conduct transfers using an agreed-upon word size and transmission mode. The increased speed of the Fast SCSI specification reduced the maximum length of the SCSI chain to about 10 feet.

A third version brought together both improvements and became known as **Wide Fast SCSI-2**. An expected update—referred to as **Ultra Wide SCSI**, or **SCSI-3**—makes provisions for a special high-speed serial transfer mode and special communications media, such as fiber optic cabling.

The increased speed capabilities of the SCSI interfaces make them attractive for intensive applications such as large file servers for networks and multimedia video stations. However, the EIDE interface is generally more widely used due to its lower cost and nearly equal performance. The EIDE device also tends to be more compatible with DOS. Most SCSI adapters come with software drivers that must be installed to support them. Table 8.3 contrasts the specifications of the SCSI and IDE interfaces.

Table 8.3 *SCSI/IDE Specifications*

Interface	Bus Size	# Devices	Async. Speed	Synch. Speed
IDE	16 bits	2	4MBps	-
EIDE (ATA-2)	16 bits	4	4MBps	16MBps
SCSI (SCSI-1)	8 bits	7	2MBps	5MBps
Wide SCSI (SCSI-2)	8/16/32 bits	7	2MBps	5MBps
Fast SCSI (SCSI-2)	8/16 bits	7	2MBps	10/20MBps
Wide Fast SCSI(SCSI-2)	8/16/32 bits	7	2MBps	10/20/ 40MBps

HDD Upgrading

One of the key components in keeping the system updated is the hard-disk drive. Software manufacturers continue to produce larger programs. In addition, the types of programs found on the typical PC are expanding. Many newer programs place high demands on the hard drive to feed information—such as large graphics files or digitized voice and video—to the system for processing. Invariably, the system will begin to produce error messages that say that the hard drive is full.

The first line of action is to use software disk utilities to optimize the organization of the drive. These utilities—such as **CHKDSK**, **SCANDISK**, and **DEFRAG**—are covered in detail in Chapter 13, "Preventive Maintenance, Safety, and Customer Service." The second step is to remove unnecessary programs and files from the hard drive. Programs and information that is rarely or never used should be moved to an archival media, such as removable disks or tape.

In any event, there may come a time when it is necessary to determine whether the hard drive needs to be replaced to optimize the performance of the system. One guideline suggests that the drive should be replaced if the percentage of unused disk space drops below 20%.

Another reason to consider upgrading the HDD involves its capability of delivering information to the system. If the system is constantly waiting for information from the hard drive, replacing it should be considered as an option. Not all system slowdowns are connected to the HDD, but many are. Remember that the HDD is the mechanical part of the memory system, and everything else is electronic.

As with the storage space issue, HDD speed can be optimized through software configurations such as a disk cache. However, after it has been optimized in this manner, any further speed increases must be accomplished by upgrading the hardware.

When considering an HDD upgrade, determine what the real system needs are for the hard drive. Also, determine how much performance increase can be gained through other upgrading efforts (check the System Board Upgrading section of Chapter 6, "System Boards") before changing out the hard drive.

If the drive is being upgraded substantially, such as from a 500MB IDE drive to a 1.4GB EIDE drive, check the capabilities of the system's ROM BIOS. If the BIOS does not support Logical Block Addressing (LBA) or Extended Cylinder/Head/Sector (ECHS) enhancements, the drive capacity of even the largest hard drive will be limited to 528MB.

Finally, determine how much longer the unit in question is likely to be used before it must simply be replaced. If the decision to upgrade the HDD stands, the best advice is to get the biggest, fastest hard drive possible. Don't forget that a different I/O bus architecture may add to the performance increase.

HDD Installation

A+ CORE 1.2

A+ CORE 1.7

The installation steps for HDD hardware parallel those of the FDD unit. However, the configuration and preparation of a typical hard-disk drive is much more involved than that of a floppy drive. This procedure is divided into two subsections. The first section deals with installing the hardware of a typical hard-disk drive unit. The second moves through a typical formatting procedure that can be applied to most microcomputer HDD units. If a replacement HDD is being installed for repair or upgrading purposes, the data on the original drive should be backed up to some other media before replacing it, if possible.

Turn off the computer, and remove the outer cover from the system unit. If you are installing a $3^1/_2$-inch drive in a $5^1/_4$-inch bay, attach mounting brackets to both sides of the drive unit.

Obtain and record the drive's type information. In addition, obtain and record any bad track/sector information from the HDD unit. Slide the HDD unit into an empty bay of the disk drive cage, and install the four screws (two on each side) that secure it in the disk drive cage, as illustrated in Figure 8.31.

FIGURE 8.31

Securing the drive unit.

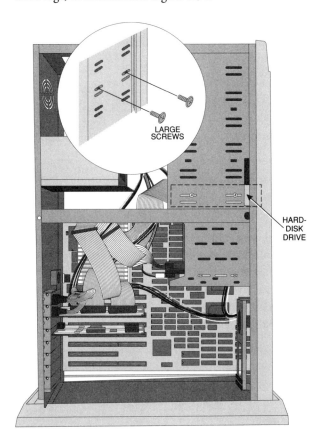

Connect the signal cable(s) to the HDD unit and to the controller. Make certain that the pin #1 indicator stripe on the cable aligns with the pin #1 position of the connectors on both the HDD unit and the controller. Proper connection of a single signal cable interface is depicted in Figure 8.32.

FIGURE 8.32

Connecting the HDD cable.

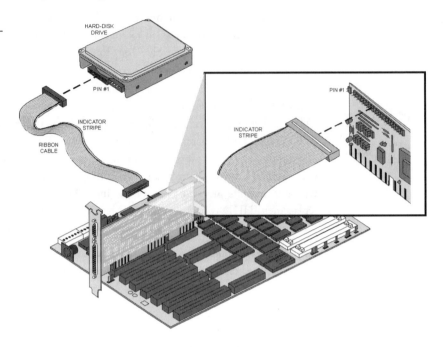

Turn on the computer, and move into the BIOS's CMOS Configuration Setup screen. Move the cursor to the Hard Disk C type position, and scroll through the HDD selections until you find an entry matching the type information of the drive you are installing. Store this parameter in the CMOS configuration file by following the directions given in the screen menu.

The formatting procedure in older drive types is a function of the HDD's BIOS. System-level HDD interfaces, such as IDE and SCSI drives, have automatic low-level formatting routines already installed on them. Therefore, these do not need a low-level format performed before they can be partitioned and high-level formatted.

You must tell the formatting program what type of drive is being formatted and what its parameters are. In newer drives, the information is retrieved from the system's CMOS setup information. In these cases, SCSI drives often require that the CMOS configuration be set to None Installed to operate correctly.

Other information you may be required to supply in older formatting programs includes bad cylinder and sector information. This information can be found on the drive performance sheet that accompanied the program from the factory; it can also typically be found on a sticker attached to the top of the drive. The technician must make certain to enter this information in the format specified by the program and to answer any other questions asked by the program.

A+ DOS/WINDOWS 4.6

Turn off the computer, and place a bootable disk in drive A. Turn on the system and install the operating system on the HDD. If a DOS or DOS/Windows 3.x system is being established, install DOS to the C:\DOS subdirectory. Use the DIR command to ensure that FDISK.COM is present in the DOS directory.

At the DOS prompt, type **FDISK** and press ENTER to reach the DOS FDISK screen.

The following are the options from which you can choose:

1. Create DOS partition or logical DOS drive

2. Set active partition

3. Delete partition or logical DOS drive

4. Display partition information

Press 1 to choose Create a DOS Partition and then press 1 to choose Primary DOS Partition. Finally, press Y to choose Maximum Size for this (Primary) Partition, and then press ENTER to reboot the system and activate the partition.

If the system contains a master and a slave drive, the primary partition of the master drive will logically be drive C. The primary partition of the slave drive will be assigned drive D, with the extended partitions on the master and slave being assigned as drives E and F respectively.

Troubleshooting HDDs

A+ CORE 2.1   Typical symptoms associated with hard-disk drive failures include the following:

1. The computer will not boot up when turned on.

2. The computer will boot up to a system disk in drive A but not to the hard drive, indicating that the system files on the HDD are missing or have become corrupt.

3. No motor sounds are produced by the HDD while the computer is running (in desktop units the HDD should always run when power is applied to the system—this is not true of portables due to their advanced power-saving features).

4. An IBM-compatible 17xx error code is produced on the monitor screen.

5. An "HDD Controller Failure" message indicates failure to verify hard-disk setup by system configuration.

6. A "C: or D: Fixed Disk Drive Error" message indicates a hard-disk CMOS setup failure.

7. An "Invalid Media Type" message indicates that the controller cannot find a recognizable track/sector pattern on the drive.

8. A "No boot record found," "Non-system Disk or Disk Error," or "Invalid System Disk" message indicates that the system boot files are not located in the root directory of the drive.

9. The video display is active, but the HDD's activity light remains on and no boot-up occurs, indicating that the HDD's CMOS configuration information is incorrect.

10. An "Out of Disk Space" message indicates that the amount of space on the disk is insufficient to carry out the desired operation.

11. A "Missing Operating System," "Hard Drive Boot Failure," or "Invalid Drive or Drive Specification" message indicates that the disk's master boot record is missing or has become corrupt.

12. A "No ROM BASIC Interpreter Not Found" message is followed by the system stopping, indicating that no master boot record was found in the system. This message is produced only by PCs, XTs, and some clones.

13. A "Current Drive No Longer Valid" message indicates that the HDD's CMOS configuration information is incorrect or has become corrupt.

Figure 8.33 depicts the relationship between the hard-disk drive and the rest of the system, and also illustrates the control and signal paths through the system.

> Hard-drive systems are very similar to floppy-drive systems in structure. They have a controller, one or more signal cables, a power cable, and a drive unit. The troubleshooting procedure typically moves from setup and configuration to formatting and, finally, into the hardware component isolation process.

The system board is a logical extension of the components that make up the HDD system. However, unless the HDD controller is integrated into it, the system board is typically the least likely cause of HDD problems.

FIGURE 8.33

Hard-disk drive-related components.

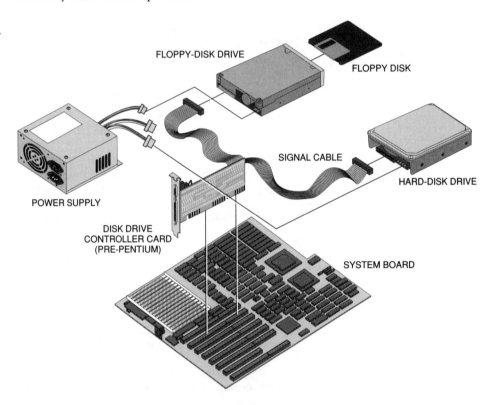

FLOPPY-DISK DRIVE

FLOPPY DISK

SIGNAL CABLE

HARD-DISK DRIVE

POWER SUPPLY

DISK DRIVE
CONTROLLER CARD
(PRE-PENTIUM)

SYSTEM BOARD

Notice that, unlike a floppy drive, there is no Windows component to check with a hard-disk drive. Windows relies on the system's DOS/BIOS structure to handle HDD operations.

HDD Configuration Checks

A+ CORE 4.4 While booting up the system to the DOS prompt, observe the BIOS's HDD-type information displayed on the monitor. Note the type of HDD(s) that the BIOS believes are installed in the system. The values stored in this CMOS memory must accurately reflect the actual format of HDD(s) installed in the system or an error will occur. Possible error messages associated with HDD configuration problems include Drive Mismatch Error, and Invalid Media Type. These values can be accessed for change by pressing the CTRL and DEL keys (or some other key combination) simultaneously during the boot-up procedure.

If the HDD is used with a system board-mounted controller, check for the presence of an **HDD enabling jumper** on the system board. Make certain that it is set to enable the drive, if present. Check the drive to make sure that it is properly terminated. Every drive type requires a terminal block somewhere in the interface. On system-level drives, the master/slave jumper setting should be checked to make sure that it is set properly for the drive's logical position in the system.

Software Checks

If the HDD configuration information is correct and a hard-disk drive problem is suspected, the first task is to determine how extensive the HDD problem is. Place a clean boot disk in drive A, and try to boot the system. Then perform a DOS DIR command to access the C drive. If the system can see the contents of the drive, then the boot files have been lost or corrupted.

Look in the root directory for the system files (denoted by "**..**" and "**...**" entries) and the COMMAND.COM file. It is common to receive a "Disk Boot Failure" message, or one of the other system file-related messages, on the monitor screen, if this type of situation occurs. If the clean boot disk has a copy of the FDISK program on it, attempt to restore the drive's master boot record (including its partition information) by typing `A>FDISK /MBR`.

Providing that the hard disk can be accessed with the DR command, type `SYS C:` at the DOS prompt (with the clean boot disk still in the A drive.

These two lines should copy the DOS system files from the DOS disk to the hard-disk drive. Turn off the system, remove the DOS disk from the A drive, and try to reboot the system from the hard drive.

If the system boots up properly, check to see that the operating system commands are functioning properly. Also check to see that all installed software programs function properly. Recheck the installation instructions of any program that does not function properly. Reinstall the software program, if necessary.

Five conditions will produce a "Bad or Missing COMMAND.COM" error message on the screen. The first condition occurs when the COMMAND.COM file cannot be found on the hard drive and no bootable disk is present in drive A. The COMMAND.COM file is not located in the hard drive's root directory, so this message is likely to occur when installing a new hard drive or a new DOS version. The message will also occur if the user inadvertently erases the COMMAND.COM file from the hard drive.

If the system cannot see the drive after booting to the floppy disk, then the complete HDD system must be examined. Attempt to run a diagnostic software program, if possible. Try to use a diagnostic program that conducts a bank of tests on the HDD's components. Run the program's HDD Tests, and perform the equivalent of the ALL tests function.

HDD Hardware Checks

If the hard-disk drive cannot be accessed and the configuration settings are correct, you must begin troubleshooting the hardware components associated with the hard-disk drive. As with other troubleshooting routines, begin by reducing the components of the system as much as possible. Remove all external options from the system, except the keyboard and video monitor.

Turn on the system. If it boots up properly, reinstall the options in the system one by one until the problem reappears. The last options device reconnected to the system is defective. Repair or replace the defective options device, and return the system to full service.

If no external reason is found for the problems, remove the outer cover from the computer and begin troubleshooting the internal components associated with the hard-disk drive. In a pre-Pentium system, the easiest component to check is the controller card that holds the HDD interface circuitry. Exchange the controller card with a known good one of the same type.

Make certain to mark both the floppy- and hard-drive control/signal cable(s) so as to identify their connection points and direction. This will help to ensure their proper reinstallation. Reconnect the disk-drive signal cables to the new controller card.

Try to reboot the system from the hard drive. If the system boots up properly, check to see that all the DOS commands (DIR, COPY, and so on) are working properly. Also, check the operation of all the hard disk's software programs to make sure they are still functioning correctly. Reinstall any program that does not function properly.

If the system still won't boot up, recheck the System Configuration Setup to see that it matches the actual configuration of the HDD. Record the HDD values from the setup so that they will be available if a replacement drive must be installed.

The next logical step may seem to be to replace the hard drive unit. However, it is quite possible that the hard drive may not have any real damage. It may simply have lost track of where it was and now cannot find its starting point. In this case, the most attractive option is to reformat the hard disk. This action gives the hard drive a new starting point from which to work. Unfortunately, it also destroys anything that you had on the disk before. At the very least, attempting to reformat the drive before you replace it may save the expense of buying a new hard-disk drive. Make certain to use the /s modifier, or repeat the SYS C: operation with the Format command, to restore the system files to the hard drive.

If the system boots up properly after reformatting the drive, reinstall any options removed from the system, replace the system unit's outer cover, and return the system to full service.

If the system does not boot, check the HDD's signal cable for proper connection at both ends. Exchange the signal cable (or cables) for a known good one. Check the HDD's drive select jumper and Master/Slave/Single jumper settings to make sure they set correctly. Exchange the HDD's power connector with another one from the power supply to make certain that it is not a source of problems.

If the reformatting procedure is not successful, or if the system still won't boot from the hard drive, replace the hard-disk drive unit with a working one. Disconnect the signal, control, and power cables from the HDD unit, and exchange them with known good ones of the same type. Reconnect the signal, control, and power cables to the replacement HDD unit.

If a similar computer is being used as a source of test parts, great care should be used in removing the HDD from its original computer and reinstalling it in the defective computer. With some interfaces, such as an MFM drive, it may be advisable to swap both the disk drive and the controller card together.

Try to reboot the system from the new hard drive. If no boot-up occurs, reformat the new drive. Make sure that any information on the replacement drive has been backed up on floppy disks or tape before removing it from its original system.

If the system still won't boot up with a different HDD, swap the hard-disk drive's signal/control cables with known good ones. Make certain to mark the cables for identification purposes so that they will be reinstalled properly. Also, use a different power connector from the power-supply unit to make certain that the current connector is not a source of the problems.

Check the system's configuration setup to see that it matches the actual configuration of the new HDD. Check to see that all installed software programs function properly.

If the system reboots from the replacement drive without reformatting, replace the drive (either with the one you have just installed or with a new one). Also, try reinstalling the original disk-drive controller card to see whether it will work with the new drive.

If the system still boots up and operates properly, reinstall any options removed from the system. Replace the system unit's outer cover, and return the system to full service. Reboot the system and reinstall all software programs to the new hard-disk drive. (See the installation guide from the software manufacturer.) Return the system to full service, and return the defective controller card appropriately.

RAID Systems

As applications push required storage capacities past available drive sizes, it becomes logical to combine several drives together to hold all the data produced. In a desktop unit, this can be as simple as adding an additional physical drive to the system. Wide and local area networks connect computers so that their resources (including disk drives) can be shared. If you extend this idea of sharing disk drives to include several different drive units operating under a single controller, you have a **drive array**. A drive array is depicted in Figure 8.34.

FIGURE 8.34

A drive array stack.

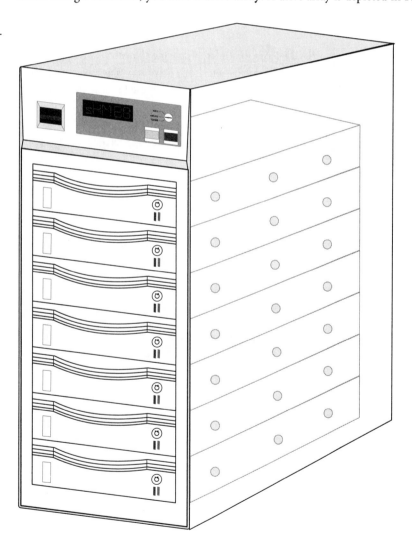

Actually, drive arrays have evolved in response to storage requirements for local area networks. These are particularly useful in client/server networks, where the data for the network tends to be centrally located and shared by all the users around the network.

In the cases of multiple drives within a unit and drives scattered around a network, all the drives assume a different letter designation. In a drive array, the stack of drives can be made to appear as a single, large hard drive. The drives are operated in parallel so that they can deliver data to the controller in a parallel format. If the controller is simultaneously handling 8 bits of data from eight drives, the system will see the speed of the transfer as being eight times faster. This technique of using the drives in a parallel array is referred to as a **striped drive array**.

It is also possible to simply use a small drive array as a data backup system. In this case, which is referred to as a **mirrored drive array**, the drives are each supplied with the same data. If the data from one drive is corrupted, or if one of the drives fails, then the data is still safe. Both types of arrays are created through a blend of connection hardware and control software.

> The most common drive arrays are **Redundant Arrays of Inexpensive Disks** (**RAID**) systems. The RAID Advisory Board gives five levels of RAID technology specifications.

RAID 1 is a redundancy scheme that uses two equal-sized drives, where both drives hold the same information. Each drive serves as a backup for the other. Figure 8.35 illustrates the operation of a mirrored array used in a RAID 1 application.

FIGURE 8.35

Operation of a mirrored array.

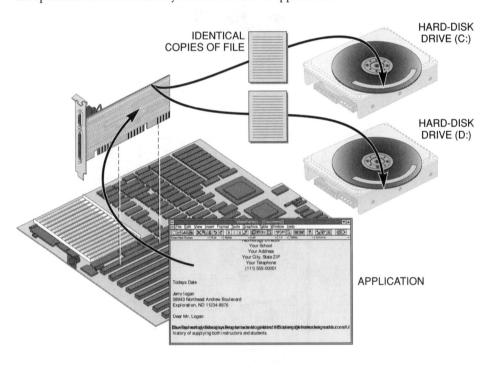

Duplicate information is stored on both drives. When the file is retrieved from the array, the controller reads alternate sectors from each drive. This effectively reduces the data read time by half.

The **RAID 2** strategy interleaves data on parallel drives, as illustrated in Figure 8.36. Bits or blocks of data are interleaved across the disks in the array. The speed afforded by collecting data from the disks in a parallel format is the biggest feature of the system. In large arrays, complete bytes, words, or double words can be written to and read from the array simultaneously.

FIGURE 8.36

Interleaved data on parallel drives.

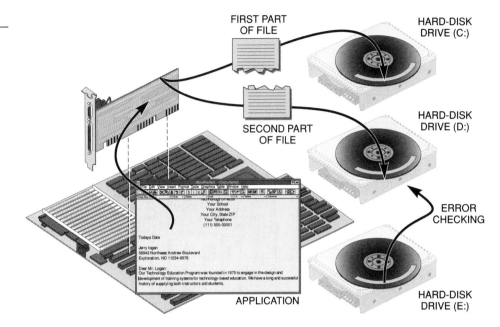

FIRST PART OF FILE

HARD-DISK DRIVE (C:)

SECOND PART OF FILE

HARD-DISK DRIVE (D:)

ERROR CHECKING

APPLICATION

HARD-DISK DRIVE (E:)

The RAID 2 specification uses multiple disks for error-detection and correction functions. Depending on the error-detection and correction algorithms used, large portions of the array are used for non-data storage overhead. Of course, the reliability of the data delivered to the system is excellent, and no need exists for time-consuming corrective read operations when an error is detected. Arrays dealing with large systems may use between three and seven drives for error-correction purposes. Because of the high hardware overhead, RAID 2 systems are not normally used with microcomputer systems.

When the array is used in this manner, a complex **error-detection and correction algorithm** is normally employed. One of the easiest algorithms to understand involves generating a parity bit for each word applied to the array and then grouping the data words into blocks. Each block is then used to generate a parity bit. In this manner, a single error causes a failure in both the word's parity bit and one of the block's parity bit. The intersection of the two failed parity bits marks the location of the erroneous data bit. Because the system is binary, the only action that is required to correct the bit is to change it to the other possible value (0=1 or 1=0). The controller contains circuitry that detects, locates, and corrects the error without retransmitting any data. This is a very quick and efficient method of error-detection and correction. For more critical application, extravagant mathematical formulas may be employed for the error-correction algorithm to ensure the integrity of important data.

In Figure 8.36, the data block being sent to the array is broken apart and distributed to the drives in the array. The data word already has a parity bit added to it. The controller generates parity for the block and stores it on the error-detection drive. When the controller reads the data back from the array, it regenerates the error-check character and compares it to the one written on the error-check drive. By comparing the error-check character to the rewritten one, the controller can detect the error in the data field and determine which bit within the field is incorrect. With this information in hand, the controller can simply correct that bit as it is being processed.

When the data is broken into blocks, as described for RAID 2, the parity bit generated for the whole word is referred to as a **longitudinal parity bit**. The parity bits generated for the block are called **lateral parity bits**. The lateral parity bits are assembled into the **block-check character** (**BCC**) that is stored on the error-detection drive. The block-check character is used in a type of error correction known as **longitudinal redundancy checking**. The more advanced mathematical models for error correction are known as **cyclic redundancy checking** (**CRC**). The concept of lateral and longitudinal parity is depicted in Figure 8.37.

FIGURE 8.37

Lateral and longitudinal parity.

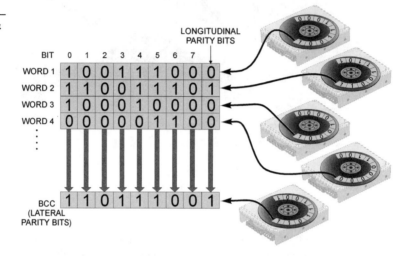

In a **RAID 3** arrangement, the drives of the array operate in parallel as in a RAID 2 system. However, only parity checking is used for error detection and correction, requiring only one additional drive. If an error occurs, the controller reads the array again to verify the error. This is a time-consuming, low-efficiency method of error correction.

A **RAID 4** controller interleaves sectors across the drives in the array. This creates the appearance of one very large drive. The RAID 4 format is generally used for smaller drive arrays but can be used for larger arrays as well. Only one parity-checking drive is allotted for error control. The information on the parity drive is updated after reading the data drives. This creates an extra write activity for each data read operation performed.

The **RAID 5** scheme alters the RAID 4 specification by enabling the parity function to rotate through the different drives. Under this system, error-checking and correction is the function of all the drives. This is usually the most popular RAID system because it can be used on arrays as small as two drives, with a high level of built-in error recovery.

Tape Drives

 A+ CORE 1.1

Tape drive units are another popular type of information storage systems. These systems can store large amounts of data on small **tape cartridges**, similar to the one depicted in Figure 8.38.

Tapes tend to be a more economic choice than other magnetic media for storing large amounts of data. However, access to information stored on tape tends to be very slow. This is caused by the fact that, unlike disks, tape operates in a linear fashion. The tape transport must run all the tape past the drive's R/W heads to access data that is physically stored at the end of the tape.

FIGURE 8.38

Data storage on small tape cartridges.

Tape drives are generally used to store large amounts of information that do not need to be accessed often or quickly. Such applications include making backup copies of programs and data. This type of data security is a necessity with records such as business transactions, payroll, artwork, and so on.

Data backup has easily become the most widely used tape application. With the large amounts of information that can be stored on a hard-disk drive, a disk crash is a very serious problem. If the drive crashes, all the information stored on the disk can be destroyed. This can easily add up to billions of pieces of information. Therefore, an inexpensive method of storing data from the hard drive is desirable.

Early personal computers used audiocassette tapes as storage units for data. The original PCs had an adapter for connecting a cassette recorder. When hard and floppy drives became popular, tape drives began to disappear. However, as the size of hard drives began to make backup on floppies inconvenient, tape systems began to come back into acceptance.

Tape Standards

As more users employed tape as a backup media, standards for tape systems were formed. The most widely used tape standard is the **Quarter Inch Cartridge** (**QIC**) standard. This standard calls for a tape cartridge similar to the one depicted in Figure 8.39. Its physical dimensions are 6 inches by 4 inches by $5/8$ inch. The cartridge has a head access door in the front that swings open when it is inserted in the drive unit.

FIGURE 8.39

A $1/4$-inch tape cartridge.

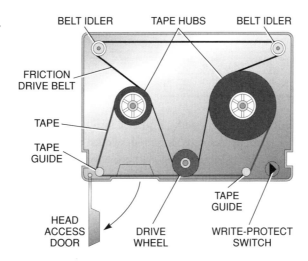

Unlike the audiocassette tape, the cartridge tape is not driven by capstans that extend through the tape spools. Instead, it employs a belt drive system that loops through the cartridge and turns both spools synchronously. The belt is driven by a rubber drive wheel, which, in turn, is driven by the capstan. This design provides smoother, more precise operation than the audiocassette can provide.

The R/W heads magnetize the tape as it passes by, in much the same manner as described for other magnetic storage media. The data is placed on the tape serially as it moves past the head. The tape is organized into sectors of data, separated by intergap blocks. The data can be applied in **parallel tracks** (using multiple R/W heads) in a continuous stream of data (**streaming tape systems**) or in a **serpentine** manner, in which the data is applied to the tape in one direction for **odd tracks** and in the other direction for **even tracks**.

Magnetic tape must be formatted before use, just as with a disk. In the formatting process, the controller marks the tape off into sectors. In addition, it establishes a FAT in its header, similar to that of a floppy or hard disk. The header also contains a bad-sector table to prevent defective areas of the tape from being used. Some of the tape is devoted to the error-detection and correction information that must be used with tape systems. Tape systems use the cyclic redundancy checking and other mathematical algorithm methods described in the discussion of RAID systems.

Cartridge tapes were referred to as **DC-6000**-style tapes. Their model numbers would normally include a reference to their tape capacity as the last digits (for example, DC-6200 would be a 200MB tape). As the cartridge tape industry matured, manufacturers came together to establish standards for tape formats and labeling. In the process, the DC-6000 number has been replaced in discussions about capacity and format.

For the most part, a series of QIC numbers have been used to describe different tape cartridges. Table 8.4 provides a sample list of QIC standard numbers.

Table 8.4   QIC Specifications

Specification	Tracks	Capacity	Cartridge
QIC-02	9	—	DC-3000
QIC-24	9	60MB	DC-6000
QIC-40	20	40MB	DC-2000
QIC-80	32	80MB	DC-2080
QIC-100	12/24	100MB	DC-2000
QIC-150	18	250MB	DC-6000
QIC-1000	30	1.0GB	DC-6000
QIC-1350	30	1.35GB	DC-6000
QIC-2100	30	2.1GB	DC-6000

A **minicartridge** version of the quarter-inch tape cartridge (with dimensions of $3^1/_4$ inches by $2^1/_2$ inches by $^5/_8$ inch) has been developed to provide a more compact form factor to fit in $3^1/_2$-inch drive bays. The internal operation of the cartridge has remained the same, but the amount of tape inside has been reduced. The reduced amount of tape in the cartridge is offset by the use of more advanced data-encoding schemes that store more data on less tape. Minicartridges are referred to as **DC-2000**-style cartridges. As with the DC-6000 tapes, the DC-2000 model numbers normally include a reference to their tape capacity as the last digits.

A number of QIC tape standards have developed over time. The original QIC standard was **QIC-40**. This standard called for a unit that could be connected to a floppy-disk drive interface so that it acted like a large drive B. It specified a 20-track format, with each track consisting of 68 segments, having 29 sectors of 1024 bytes each. This format provided 40MB of data storage. The specification treated the tape's sectors like the sectors of a floppy disk, in that they were organized into files.

An updated **QIC-80** specification was developed to replace the QIC-40 standard. Advanced R/W head structures enable the QIC-80 to place 32 tracks on the tape instead of 20. Coupled with improved data-per-inch storage capabilities, the total capacity of the cartridge was boosted to 80MB. The QIC-80 systems included data-compression software that could effectively double the capacity of the drive from its stated value.

The QIC-80 standard has been superseded by the **QIC-500M** format, which provides for up to 500MB of data to be stored on the cartridge. Newer standards for tape drives continue to emerge. Specifications that depart from the floppy-disk drive interface and use the IDE or SCSI interfaces are producing data storage potentials into the multiple-gigabyte ranges.

Tape Drive Troubleshooting

Because the fundamentals of recording on tape are so similar to those used with magnetic disks, the troubleshooting process is also very similar.

> The basic components associated with the tape drive include: the tape drive, the signal cable, the power connection, the controller, and the tape drive's operating software.

The tape itself can be a source of several problems. Common points to check with the tape include the following:

- ▶ Is the tape formatted correctly for use with the drive in question?
- ▶ Is the tape inserted securely in the drive?
- ▶ Is the tape write-protected?
- ▶ Is the tape broken or off the reel in the cartridge?

As cartridge tapes are pulled back and forth, their Mylar base can become stretched over time. This action can cause the tape's format to fail before the tape actually wears out. To remedy this, the tape should be retentioned periodically using the software's retention utility. Cartridge tapes are typically good for about 150 hours of operation. If the number of tape errors begins to increase dramatically before this time, try reformatting the tape to restore its integrity. After the 150-hour point, the tape should simply be replaced.

If the tape is physically okay and is properly formatted, the next easiest section to check is the tape software. Check the software Setup and Configuration settings to make sure they are correct for any hardware settings. Refer to the tape drive's user's guide for a list of system requirements, and check the system to make sure they are being met.

If any configuration jumpers or switches are present on the controller, verify that they are set correctly for the installation. Also, run a diagnostic program to check for resource conflicts, such as IRQ and base memory addressing that may be preventing the drive from operating.

The software provided with most tape drive units includes some error-messaging capabilities. Observe the system and note any tape-related error messages it produces. Consult the user's manual for error message definitions and corrective suggestions. Check for error logs that the software may keep. These logs can be viewed to determine what errors have been occurring in the system.

Because many tape drives are used in networked and multiuser environments, another problem occurs when you are not properly logged on or are not enabled to work with files being backed up or restored. In these situations, the operating system may not permit the tape drive to access secured files, or any files, because the correct clearances have not been met. The network administrator should be consulted for proper password and security clearances. See Chapter 11, "Data Communications," for more information about the network environment.

Reinstall the drive's software, and reconfigure it. Go through the installation process carefully, paying close attention to any user-selected variables and configuration information requested by the program.

If hardware problems are suspected, begin by cleaning the drive's R/W heads. Consult the user's guide for cleaning instructions, or use the process described in Chapter 13 for the process of manually cleaning floppy-drive R/W heads. The R/W heads should be cleaned after about 20 backups or restores. Also, try using a different tape to see if this works. Make certain that the tape is properly formatted for operation. The tape should also be clean, if possible, to avoid exposing any critical information to possible corruption.

If cleaning does not restore the drive to proper operation, continue by checking the power and signal cables for good connection and proper orientation.

Matching tape drives are not common at a single location, so checking the drive by substitution should be considered as a last step. Check the user's guide for any additional testing information, and call the drive manufacturer's technical service number for assistance before replacing the drive.

Key Points Review

This chapter has explored the use of magnetic media to provide long-term, high-volume data storage for personal computer systems.

▶ Magnetic disks resemble phonograph records without grooves. They fall into two general categories: high-speed hard disks and slower flexible disks. Data bits are recorded on the disk serially in concentric circles, called tracks.

▶ Data is read from or written to the disk one sector at a time. To perform a read or write operation, the address of the selected track and sector is applied to a stepper motor, which moves a read/write (R/W) head over the desired track. As the desired sector passes beneath the R/W head, the data transfer occurs.

▶ Depending on the nature of the magnetic medium being read from or written to, the R/W head may ride directly on the medium's surface (contact recording), or it may "fly" slightly above it on a thin cushion of air created by the moving surface (non-contact recording).

▶ The heart of the disk drive's circuitry is the disk-drive controller. The controller is responsible for providing the necessary interfacing between the disk drive and the computer's I/O channel.

▶ One piece of software is extremely important to the operation of both hard- and floppy-disk drives. This is the DOS File Management System (FMS). Essentially, DOS keeps track of information stored on the disk by creating the FAT on the disk.

- Data moves back and forth between the system's RAM memory and the floppy disk surface. Along the way, it passes from the system RAM to the floppy-disk controller (FDC), through the floppy-drive signal cable, and into the floppy drive's analog control board. This board converts the data into signals that can cause the drive's R/W heads to produce the magnetic spots on the disk surface.

- The operation of the FDC occurs in a three-phase cycle: a command phase, an execution phase, and a result phase.

- A single ribbon cable is used to connect the system's floppy drive(s) to the disk-drive controller card. Generally, the cable has two edge connectors and two 34-pin, two-row BERG headers along its length.

- A number of things can cause improper floppy-disk drive operation or disk drive failure. These items include the use of unformatted disks, incorrectly inserted disks, damaged disks, erased disks, loose cables, drive failure, adapter failure, system board failure, or a bad or loose power connector.

- Three levels of troubleshooting apply to FDD problems: configuration, the DOS level, and the hardware level. There is no Windows-level troubleshooting that applies to floppy drives.

- Hard-disk drives are created in a wide variety of storage capacities. To prepare the hard disk for use by the system, three levels of preparation must take place: the low-level format, the partition, and the high-level format.

- Before a high-level format can be performed, the drive must be partitioned. The partition establishes the size and number of logical drives on the physical drive.

- The high-level format procedure is performed by the FORMAT command in the MS-DOS program. This format program creates the blank FAT and root directory on the disk.

- Hard-drive systems are very similar to floppy-drive systems in structure: They have a controller, one or more signal cables, a power cable, and a drive unit. The troubleshooting procedure typically moves from setup and configuration to formatting and, finally, into the hardware-component isolation process.

- The most common drive arrays are Redundant Arrays of Inexpensive Disks (RAID) systems. The RAID Advisory Board gives five levels of RAID technology specifications.

- Tape drive units are another popular type of information storage systems. These systems can store large amounts of data on small tape cartridges.

- Tape drives are generally used to store large amounts of information that do not need to be accessed often or quickly. Such applications include making backup copies of programs and data.

- The basic components associated with the tape drive include: the tape drive, the signal cable, the power connection, the controller, and the tape drive's operating software.

At this point, review the objectives listed at the beginning of the chapter to be certain that you understand each point and can perform each task listed there. Afterward, answer the review questions that follow to verify your knowledge of the information.

Multiple Choice Questions

1. The maximum size of a disk partition using DOS 3.x is _____.

   a. 500MB

   b. 2GB

   c. 100MB

   d. 2MB

2. What action should always be taken before upgrading a hard-disk drive?

   a. Use the DOS VER command to determine what version of DOS is currently in use.

   b. Use the FDISK command to locate any lost cluster chains on the original drive.

   c. The contents of the installed drive should be backed up to some other media.

   d. The installed drive's CMOS setup values should be recorded for use with the new drive.

3. Head-to-disk Interference (HDI) is also referred to as _____.

    a. a head crash

    b. R/W head bounce

    c. interleaving

    d. data compression

4. If the system will not boot up to the hard drive but can be accessed after booting to a floppy, what type of problem is indicated?

    a. A bad hard-disk drive controller.

    b. A bad hard-disk drive.

    c. Missing allocation units on the HDD

    d. Missing system files on the HDD

5. What precaution should always be taken before reformatting a hard-disk drive?

    a. Use the DOS VER command to determine what version of DOS is currently in use.

    b. Use the FDISK command to locate any lost cluster chains.

    c. Use the Defrag utility to remove any fragmentation from the drive before formatting.

    d. Use an anti-virus utility to remove any viruses from the drive before formatting.

6. In what types of applications should a tape drive backup system be considered?

    a. Applications where high speed is required

    b. Applications where information must be stored in a volatile manner

    c. Applications where information must be stored in a non-volatile manner

    d. Applications where information must be stored for only a very short time

7. A group of logically related disk sectors is called _____.

    a. a FAT entry

    b. a cluster

    c. a byte-sync

    d. a bit-sync

8. What is the main purpose of a RAID 1 drive-array?

    a. To act as an error-checking and correction method

    b. To create the appearance of one very large drive

    c. To act as a redundant data-backup method

    d. To act as a high-speed retrieval system

9. What function does the DOS FDISK program perform?

    a. It removes lost allocation units from the drive.

    b. It creates partitions on the physical disk.

    c. It provides the low-level format for the drive.

    d. It provides the high-level format for the drive.

10. What type of interface does a common tape drive use?

    a. The system's RS-232 serial port

    b. The system's parallel port

    c. An ST-506/412 interface

    d. The system's FDD controller

Review Questions

1. What corrective steps should be taken if the system will not boot up to the C:\> prompt but can be accessed after booting from a floppy boot disk?

2. Which interrupt request channel is normally used with floppy-disk drives in a PC-compatible system?

3. List the types of HDD interfaces that are system-level interfaces. What does this designation imply?

4. How can the A and B floppy drives be differentiated by looking into the system unit?

5. What action should be taken if a "Disk Boot Failure" message is displayed on the monitor screen?

6. List the HDD-related hardware components tested by the chapter's HDD troubleshooting procedure, in the order they were checked.

7. List the non-hardware items checked by the HDD troubleshooting procedure, in the order they were checked.

8. List five conditions that could cause a "Bad or Missing COMMAND.COM" message to be displayed on the screen.

9. Describe how data is stored on a magnetic disk.

10. List the steps involved in installing a hard-disk drive in a desktop system.

11. Describe the differences between the two types of drive array applications.

12. How and why is a cartridge tape different than a standard audio cassette tape?

13. What is formatting, as it applies to a disk?

14. What is the major procedural difference between installing a floppy drive and a hard drive?

15. What is the main function of the DOS high-level format?

Lab Exercises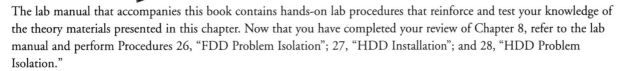

The lab manual that accompanies this book contains hands-on lab procedures that reinforce and test your knowledge of the theory materials presented in this chapter. Now that you have completed your review of Chapter 8, refer to the lab manual and perform Procedures 26, "FDD Problem Isolation"; 27, "HDD Installation"; and 28, "HDD Problem Isolation."

VIDEO DISPLAYS

LEARNING OBJECTIVES

Upon completion of this chapter and its related lab procedures, you should be able to perform the following tasks:

1. Explain how a single dot can be positioned anywhere on the face of the CRT using raster scanning.

2. Describe how a character generator is used to convert ASCII-coded characters into screen images.

3. Describe how color displays are created on the screen.

4. State the characteristics of the MGA, CGA, HGA, EGA, and VGA video standards.

5. Describe the type of physical connector specified for the VGA video standard.

6. Explain how the amount of installed video memory affects the capabilities of a video adapter card.

7. Explain how characters are processed in Text mode.

8. Describe steps to troubleshoot video problems.

9. Discuss safety considerations associated with working around a CRT.

10. List the components commonly found inside a CRT monitor.

11. Describe steps to troubleshoot monitor problems.

12. Identify symptoms associated with common monitor problems.

13. Describe symptoms associated with the monitor's video circuitry.

14. Describe the operation of liquid crystal displays.

15. Describe the operation of gas-plasma displays.

CHAPTER 9

Introduction

The video monitor has long been one of the most popular methods of displaying computer data. At the heart of the monitor is the **cathode ray tube (CRT)**, familiar to us from the television receivers we have in our homes. As a matter of fact, the early personal computers used televisions as video units. The basic difference between the television and a monitor is that no radio-frequency demodulation electronics are used in the video monitor.

As an output device, the monitor can be used to display alphanumeric characters and graphic images. Two possible methods are used to create these displays: the **raster scan** method and the X-Y, or **vector scan**, method. All television sets—and most video displays—are of the raster scan type, so this is the type on which this text focuses. An oscilloscope display is a prime example of vector scanning.

The popularity of portable computers has created a large market for lighter display devices. The main devices used in this market are the LCD and gas-plasma displays. These devices do not use a CRT tube or its supporting circuitry, so the weight associated with the CRT and its high-voltage components is not present. The flat-panel nature of these devices also works well in the portable computer due to its reduced size.

CRT Basics

A+ CORE 1.1

Quite simply, a CRT is an evacuated glass tube with an **electron gun** in its neck and a fluorescent-coated surface opposite the electron gun. A typical CRT is depicted in Figure 9.1. When activated, the electron gun emits a stream of electrons that strike the fluorescent coating on the inside of the screen, producing an illuminated dot.

FIGURE 9.1

A cathode ray tube.

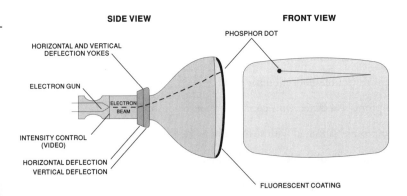

The position of the beam along the face of the screen can be manipulated through horizontal and vertical **deflection coils** attached to the tube. These coils cause the beam to deflect according to electromagnetic attraction and repulsion principles. The deflection coils are usually combined into a single unit, called a **yoke** that slips over the neck of the tube. By applying specific signals to the coils, the beam can be positioned anywhere along the face of the screen. In the raster scan method of creating displays, separate signals are applied to the horizontal and vertical deflection coils to move the electron beam across the screen. As the beam moves, it leaves an illuminated trace, which requires a given amount of time to dissipate. The amount of time depends on the characteristics of the fluorescent coating. This dissipation quality is referred to as **persistence**.

In theory, the electron beam begins at the upper-left corner of the screen and sweeps across its face to the upper-right corner, leaving a line across the screen. This is called a raster line.

Upon reaching the right side of the screen, the trace is blanked-out, and the electron beam is repositioned to the left side of the screen, one line below the first trace (horizontal retrace). At this point, the **horizontal sweep** begins producing the second display line on the screen. The scanning continues until the horizontal sweeps reach the bottom of the screen, as shown in Figure 9.2. At that point, the electron beam is blanked again and returns to the upper-left corner of the screen (**vertical retrace**), completing one **field**.

FIGURE 9.2

Raster scan video.

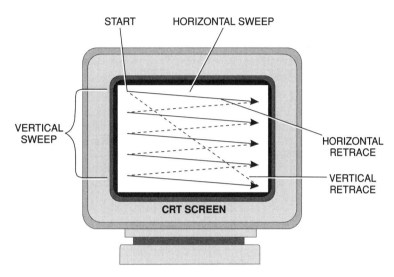

Creating Video Information

Video information is introduced to the picture by varying the voltage applied to the electron gun as it scans the screen.

Typically, a voltage of just above 1V applied to the electron gun's drive circuitry produces no electron emission, and a black (blank) area is created. A signal voltage of approximately 3V causes maximum electron emission, and a white area is created. Voltages between 1V and 3V result in various levels of gray. In this manner, the electron gun paints the desired picture on the fluorescent screen by varying its intensity.

The human eye perceives only the picture, due to the blanking of the retrace lines and the frequency at which the entire process is performed. Typically, a horizontal sweep requires about 63 microseconds to complete, and a complete field requires approximately 1/60 of a second, or 1/30 of a second per frame. The **National Television Standards Committee** (**NTSC**) specifies 525 lines per frame, composed of two fields of 262.5 lines, for television pictures. The two fields—one containing the even-numbered lines, and the other containing the odd-numbered lines—are interlaced to produce smooth images that don't flicker. This method of creating display images is referred to as **interlaced scanning** and is primarily used with television. Most computer monitors use a **noninterlaced scanning** method, as depicted in Figure 9.2. In noninterlaced scanning, the entire image is painted on the screen before a vertical retrace is performed.

CRT Signals

Figure 9.3 depicts a sample voltage signal delivered to the CRT for one raster of a field, containing white and various shades of gray dots on a black background. At the end of each raster scan, a **horizontal synchronization (HSYNC)** signal is applied to the electron gun to cover the retrace. The area, designated as the "back porch," produces a black frame at the right edge. A **vertical synchronization (VSYNC)** signal is introduced at the bottom of the field to cover the movement of the beam back to the top of the screen.

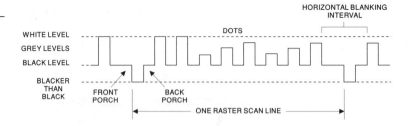

The **cathode-ray tube controller (CRTC)** develops the video signals and the horizontal and vertical synchronization signals for the CRT. The HSYNC and VSYNC signals are applied to free-running horizontal and vertical sweep oscillators so that the video information can be synchronized with the scanning motion of the electron beam.

Other monitors accept a single input signal composed of all three signals, referred to as a **composite video signal**.

Figure 9.4 illustrates the relationship between the HSYNC, VSYNC, and video signals. As the electron beam starts in the upper-left corner of the screen, current through the horizontal and vertical coils is at minimum level. To begin the scanning process, current is applied to the upper-vertical and left-horizontal coils, creating a positive polarity field.

At the same time, the current passing through the lower-vertical and right-horizontal coils sets up a negative field. The polarities of these fields deflect the negatively charged stream of electrons to the right and down the screen, as illustrated in Figure 9.2. The sawtooth waveforms applied to the coils control the positioning of the beam on the screen. As the horizontal waveform becomes more positive, the beam is deflected farther across the screen to the right. Likewise, the more positive the vertical waveform, the farther the beam is pushed down the screen.

In most monitors, the frequency relationships between these signals are fixed. However, some monitors, referred to as multisync monitors, can adapt to various horizontal sweep rates and vertical refresh rates to accommodate a variety of different video standards. Some of these standards are discussed later in this chapter; see Figure 9.20 for an illustration.

A serial line of dot information is applied to the electron gun as the horizontal coil waveform deflects the beam across the viewing area. The data stream is delayed at the beginning and end of each scan line so that the data falls within the boundaries of the screen. The **front** and **back porches** of the video signal create a blank border at the right and left sides of the screen. The horizontal sync pulse produces a **blacker-than-black** situation that covers the horizontal retrace of the electron gun.

FIGURE 9.4

HSYNC, VSYNC, and video signal relationships.

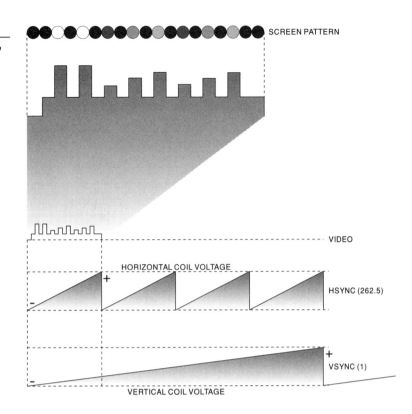

Video Character Generators

So far, we have shown how dots could be displayed on a CRT. The next step is to examine the process of creating meaningful images on the screen. The most widely used monitor application is to display alphanumeric characters on the screen. The dots hold the key to this task. A component of the CRTC, called the **character generator**, converts the ASCII code for each character into a 5-by-7 or 7-by-9 dot-matrix character. A number of other character sizes may also be used.

> The character generator is basically a ROM device containing dot-pattern information for the entire character set. Because only two intensity levels are required (white and black) to display alphanumeric data, simple digital logic levels can be used to produce the two levels.

Figure 9.5 shows one section of a 5-by-7 dot-matrix character generator ROM and some of the circuitry necessary to convert the character code into a pulse train that can be used to drive the electron gun.

Notice that the dot pattern for the letter "C" is stored in seven consecutive addresses. The ASCII-coded "C" is applied to the ROM as part of its address inputs. The other part of the address input is derived from a counter, which counts 0 through 6. The ASCII code accesses the block of memory containing the "C," and the counter selects the first address in the block with its initial count state. The contents of the first address are applied to a parallel-in, serial-out, shift register, which produces the first section of the video pulse train. When the five bits have been shifted out of the register, the line counter is pulsed. With this, the second ROM location is accessed and shifted out. This sequence of events continues until all seven locations have been accessed and serialized. The line counter pulse is synchronized with the HSYNC pulses so that the "C" is reconstructed on the CRT over seven successive horizontal sweeps.

FIGURE 9.5

Character generation.

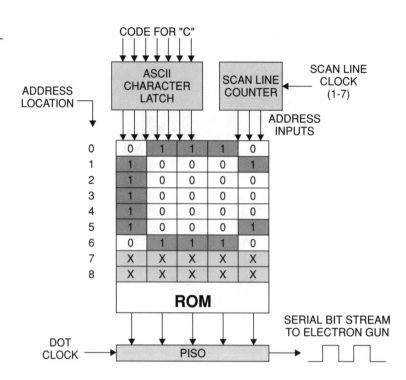

This example contains all the circuitry necessary if only one character is to be displayed on each **character line** of the CRT. Of course, several characters are normally displayed on a character line. A common monitor arrangement calls for 25 lines of text, with 80 characters per line. This requires that the first address of up to 80 character blocks be serialized during the first horizontal trace of the CRT.

By loading the character codes into an 80-character line buffer memory and then sequentially addressing it (while holding the line counter), the characters in the buffer are accessed in order and applied to the character address latch. This produces the first row of each character's dot pattern.

After the first row of 80 characters has been serialized, the line counter is pulsed and the sequential addressing of the line buffer is repeated. This produces the second row of each character during the second horizontal trace of the CRT. Therefore, the line buffer must be accessed through seven cycles to produce the complete line of text on the CRT, as illustrated in Figure 9.6.

FIGURE 9.6

A video text line.

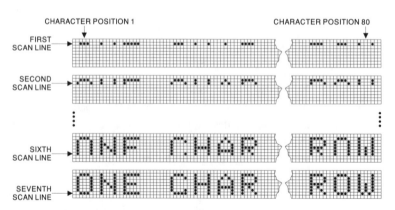

After a line or page of text has been displayed on the screen, it must be rewritten periodically to prevent it from fading away. For the rewrite to be performed fast enough to avoid display flicker, the contents of the display are stored in a special memory, called the **screen memory**. The capacity of the memory is dependent on the characteristics of the display. In our example of 25 lines of text at 80 characters per line, the screen memory must be capable of holding 2,000 bytes of ASCII character information (80 characters x 25 lines = 2,000 characters).

Storing Text Information

The 80-by-25 format listed above is typical for **Alphanumeric Text mode** in most monitor types. When the adapter is in Text mode, it typically requires at least 2 bytes of screen memory for each character position on the screen. As you have seen, the first byte is for the ASCII code of the character itself. The second byte is used to specify the **screen attributes** of the character and its cell. Under this condition, the screen memory in the example must hold at least 4,000 bytes. The **attribute byte** specifies how the character is to be displayed. Common attributes include underlined text, blinking text, and colored text for the color displays. Valid attribute values for monochrome displays are shown in Figure 9.7.

FIGURE 9.7

Monochrome attribute values.

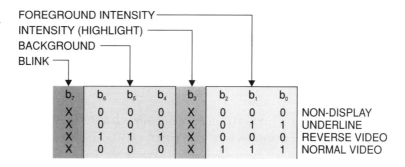

The character box is divided into two parts: the **foreground** and the **background**. The foreground consists of the dots that make up the character itself. The background is made up of the other dots in the character cell. The attribute byte can control the intensity of the foreground and/or background. For monochrome displays, only four combinations of the foreground and background (excluding the highlight and blink) exist.

For color displays, the attribute byte can be used to specify different colors for the foreground and background. The highlight bit is combined with the foreground bits to provide up to 16 different colors for the foreground. Using 3 bits to define the background, it is possible to produce eight different colors for the background.

CRT Controllers

Although a CRT controller can consist of a simple ROM character generator and a few logic devices, the CRT controller arrangement depicted in Figure 9.8 is so common that IC manufacturers produce it in fully integrated packages. In addition to the functions previously stated, the CRTC must perform a number of other tasks. In general, the CRTC is responsible for generating the dot-row, HSYNC, and VSYNC signals to synchronize the timing of the video signals and refresh the display. The CRTC also controls display manipulation functions, such as scrolling, paging, inverse video, character brightness, and cursor positioning (discussed later in this section).

FIGURE 9.8

A CRT controller.

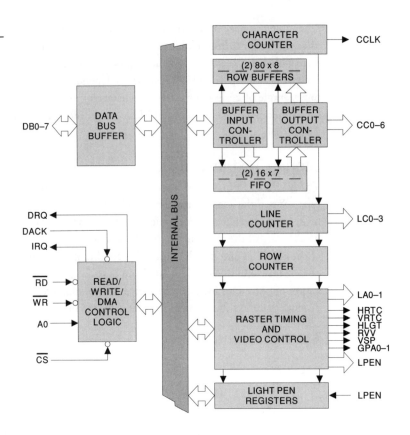

Because the CRTC must continually access the screen memory to refresh the screen, a natural **contention** occurs between the CRTC and the system microprocessor, which must also access the screen memory to enter new data. This contention can be resolved in a number of ways. The microprocessor access times can be limited to certain periods, such as horizontal and vertical retrace, when the CRTC does not need to access the screen memory. In systems that use a two-phase system clock, microprocessors use the system buses only during one phase. Therefore, the CRTC can access the buses during the other phase. An external DMA controller can also be used to multiplex the transfer of information between the microprocessor, or CRTC, and the screen memory. Each of these concepts requires some additional logic circuitry to determine access rights to the screen memory.

Color Monitors and Graphics

The monitor we have been discussing so far is referred to as a **monochrome monitor** because it is capable of displaying only shades of a single **phosphor** color. A **color monitor**, on the other hand, differs from a monochrome monitor. The major variance lies in the construction of color CRTs.

The basic construction of a color CRT is shown in Figure 9.9. The color CRT uses a combination of three-color phosphors—red, blue, and green—arranged in adjacent trios of dots or bars called **picture elements**, **pixels**, or **PELs**. By using a different electron gun for each element of the trio, the individual elements can be made to glow at different levels to produce almost any color desired.

The electron guns scan the front of a screen in unison, in the same fashion described earlier for a monochrome CRT.

Color CRTs add a metal grid called a **shadow mask** in front of the phosphor coating. This ensures that an electron gun assigned to one color doesn't strike a dot of another color.

FIGURE 9.9

Color CRT construction.

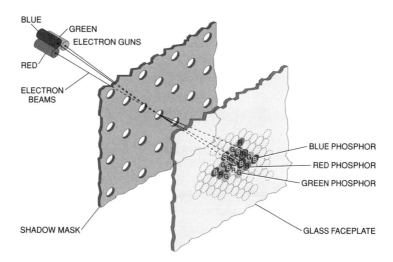

The quality of the image produced on the screen is a function of two factors: the speed at which the image is retraced on the screen, and the number of pixels on the screen. The more pixels on a given screen size, the higher the image quality. This quantity is called **resolution** and is often expressed in an X-by-Y format. The X portion of the specification refers to the number of horizontal dots the monitor can display; the Y function is the number of vertical dots possible. Using this format, the quality of the image is still determined by how big the viewing area is: For example, an 800-by-600 resolution on a 14-inch monitor produces much better quality than the same number of pixels spread across a 27-inch monitor.

Resolution can be expressed as a function of how close pixels can be grouped together on the screen. This form of resolution is expressed in terms of **dot pitch**. A monitor with a .28 dot pitch has pixels that are located .28mm apart. In monochrome monitors, dot pitch is measured from center to center of each pixel. In a color monitor, the pitch is measured from the center of one dot trio to the center of the next trio.

Types of Color Monitors

Color monitors fall into two basic groups, determined by the type of video signal they use. These are **composite color monitors** and **RGB monitors**. Composite monitors combine all the color information, synchronizing information, and brightness into a single signal that must be decoded by the monitor. This type of signal processing is illustrated in Figure 9.10. The RGB (red-green-blue) color monitor uses separate signals for each color and sync signal, thus offering better color control than composite monitors. The RGB method of delivering color signals to the monitor is also depicted in the following figure. Typical composite monitors offer resolutions of about 260-by-300 pixels. High-resolution RGB monitors offer resolutions above 1,024-by-768 pixels.

FIGURE 9.10

Composite and RGB video drives.

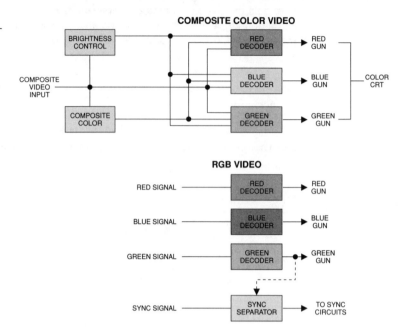

Two subtypes of RGB monitors exist. The first is a **TTL-compatible monitor**, capable of generating a limited number of colors (8). Information presented to the three electron guns is digital in nature, so each gun can be "on" or "off" for only a given phosphor trio. This limits the number of colors the monitor can generate. The other RGB monitor type accepts **analog** input levels that can independently vary the intensity of each gun to produce a nearly endless range of colors.

For displaying alphanumeric text material (letters and numbers), the color monitor presents no significant advantage over the monochrome monitor. However, the monochrome monitor typically offers high resolution at a much lower cost than color monitors do. This is due to the extra complexity of the color monitor, which requires expanded memory capacity, an extra decoder, and amplifier circuitry to process the color signals.

Color monitors have an edge over monochrome monitors when color is added to the display. These applications generally involve **graphics display** (pictorial representations). The average composite monitor possesses sufficient color control and resolution to handle simple color graphics associated with home video games and elementary graphics, such as bar and pie charts. However, advanced high-resolution color graphics require the high resolution and color control offered by analog RGB monitors.

CRT Graphics

Perhaps the simplest form of graphics is contained in the CRTC's character generator. In addition to the ASCII character set, character generators hold a set of special graphic shapes called **block-graphics**. These shapes, depicted in Figure 9.11, can be joined together to generate lines, curves, and other graphic representations, including basic line diagrams.

FIGURE 9.11

Special graphics shapes.

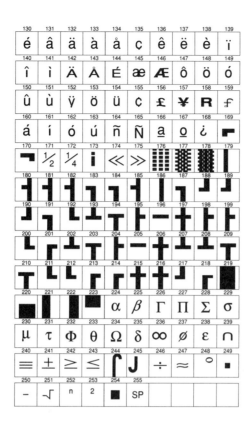

Another simple approach to graphics involves turning all the dots in a character block on or off. In this manner, solid blocks of dark and light spaces are created to form rough geometric shapes. Apply this concept to a 25-line-by-80-character display. In this case, 2,000 pixels are created that can be turned on or off independently. A pixel is defined as the smallest block in a graphic display that may be turned on or off independently.

To improve the quality and resolution of the graphics, character blocks may be subdivided into smaller on-off addressable blocks. By creating more and smaller pixels, the rough edges of the display are smoothed, and the resolution of the display increases in proportion to the number of subdivisions. If the display's character blocks are divided into six sub-blocks, the number of pixels increases to 12,000, and the picture resolution is six times greater.

The ultimate end to subdividing the display occurs when each dot on the screen is mapped to a specific memory data bit. This approach to creating graphics is referred to as **bitmapped graphics**.

Of course, increasing the number of pixels in the display means more data must be stored in memory. Instead of storing 80 character addresses per character line and then repeating them to generate the line (as we did with alphanumeric characters), the system must store 1 bit for each pixel. If color or analog data is also used, the display system must be supported by an extensive RAM memory. For this reason, many systems may offer more than one bitmapped graphic format, using different resolution levels and/or color/shade combinations.

Screen Data Manipulation

The CRTC generates a special symbol so that the operator can determine and control the location on the screen where data is to be entered. This symbol called a **cursor** can be any symbol and can be used to indicate position on the screen. The most common cursor symbols are underscores, squares, and triangles. These symbols can be placed under, over, or on top of a character position on the screen. The cursor can be moved around the screen under the control of special keys on the keyboard or some other input device. The cursor can also be made to blink on and off or can be turned into an **inverse video display** to draw attention to some specific screen location. These actions are programmed through the cursor's attributes. The current position of the cursor is held in a special cursor register in the CRTC. Figure 9.12 depicts the dot pattern representations of the three most common cursor shapes.

FIGURE 9.12

Cursor dot patterns.

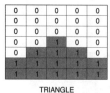

TRIANGLE

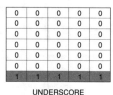

UNDERSCORE

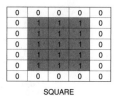

SQUARE

Inverse video displays are achieved by inverting the dot-pattern logic levels so that dark characters are displayed on a bright screen. This provides a means of highlighting text or graphics on the screen. The CRTC may also provide the following functions:

- Produce dark characters on a gray background by substituting a gray-level voltage for the white level

- Cause the display to flash on and off by alternately applying 1V and 3V levels to the light areas of the screen

- Cause the display to pulse by alternately applying 1V and an intermediate gray-level voltage to the light areas of the screen

All these functions are provided to enable the user to accentuate desired areas of the display.

To accommodate text editing, the screen memory may be large enough to hold several pages of text. A page of text is expressed as the capacity of the screen. This means that the display can be scrolled up or down. When the screen is full of text, the CRTC moves the top line of text upward (off the screen) to create a vacant line at the bottom of the screen for new data, or to display lines of data that were written in the memory below the current bottom line address.

The key to **scrolling** operations is the **Top Line Register**, which holds the address of the first line of data displayed on the screen. Figure 9.13 illustrates the concept behind paging and scrolling. When the data on the screen is to be scrolled up, the register is simply incremented to change the address of the first line to be displayed to that of the second display line. In this manner, it appears that each display line is shifted up one line. The display can also be scrolled down by decrementing the Top Line Register.

Scrolling generally involves one line of text at a time. However, an entire page of text can be scrolled at once. This operation is referred to as **paging**. The display may be paged-up or paged-down simply by incrementing or decrementing the Top Line Register by the proper number of addresses. This is a particularly convenient method of changing display data because the data is never actually shifted in the memory; only the address of the first display line of the screen is changed. Thus, the screen memory addressing logic remains fairly simple.

FIGURE 9.13

Paging and scrolling.

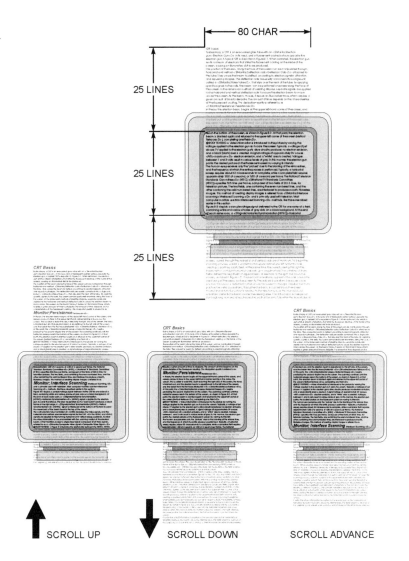

SCROLL UP   SCROLL DOWN   SCROLL ADVANCE

Figure 9.14 depicts the functional relationship of a commercially available CRT controller, screen memory, and control logic unit.

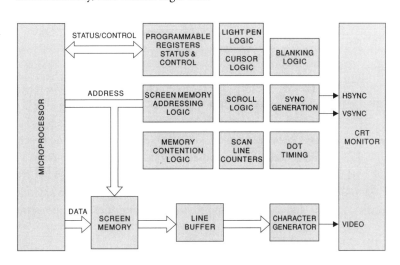

Video Standards

Many different video display standards have been developed for the IBM PC series and their clones. Each standard uses a different connector and/or pin arrangement to transfer video display and control information between the video adapter card and the monitor.

Of course, the monitor and the adapter card must be compatible with each other.

Monochrome/Display/Printer Adapter (MDA)

The **Monochrome/Display/Printer Adapter** (**MDA**) enables PC-compatible monochrome monitors to be attached to the system unit through a nine-pin D-type connector. These monitors differ from other composite monitors in that the HSYNC and VSYNC signals are not sent to the monitor along with the video information. A typical MDA adapter is depicted in Figure 9.15.

FIGURE 9.15

The monochrome card.

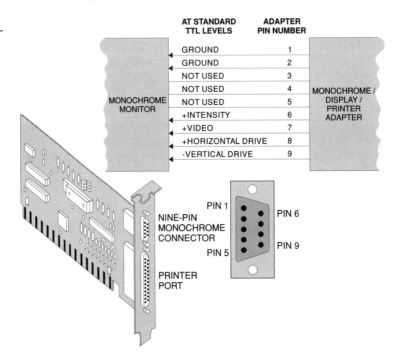

The MDA card supports an 80-character-by-25-row screen display in **Alphanumeric** (**A/N**) **mode**. In this mode, characters are defined as being 7-by-9 dot patterns contained within 9-by-14 character cells. The character cell is made larger than the character itself to create a border between consecutive characters and to provide for characters with **descenders** (portions of the character that hang below the character line). The adapter's ROM character generator is capable of producing 256 different character codes, including the complete standard ASCII character set. It can also produce an extended ASCII character set, which includes special support characters for games, word processing/editing, foreign language, and block-graphics applications. In addition, the adapter supports character attributes of blinking, reverse video, boldface, blanking, and underlining on a character-by-character basis.

In the Graphics mode, the adapter's operation is bitmapped, with each bit of the two pages in the screen memory corresponding to a screen dot. These two pages can be displayed alternately. While one page is being displayed, alterations to the buffer for that page are displayed immediately. Changes to the page not being displayed are shown only when that page is selected.

Under these conditions, each page has a resolution of 720 horizontal dots by 348 vertical dots (720-by-348 pixels). All the adapter's outputs are TTL-compatible, with the HSYNC signal being a positive-level signal and the VSYNC signal being an inverted, or negative-level, signal. The video output signal is semi-composite (the HSYNC and VSYNC signals are separate) and operates in noninterlaced mode with a refresh rate of 50/60Hz. The MDA adapter has a nine-pin female D-shell connector for video output and a 25-pin D-shell for the LPT1 printer output.

Color Graphic/Printer Adapter (CGA)

The first color display offered for the IBM line of computers was the IBM Color Graphics display. This display was introduced to make the IBM PC competitive with the home entertainment computers of the day that used color television sets for video display purposes. As a matter of fact, the original IBM **Color Graphics Adapter** (**CGA**) card included an RF-modulated output port and a composite color output port that enabled it to be connected to a television set.

The CGA standard sets the monitor's horizontal sweep frequency at 15KHz and its vertical refresh rate at 60Hz. Within these confines, the standard produces 7-by-7 dot characters in an 8-by-8 character box. The CGA screen format for text accommodates 80 characters across the screen, with 25 character lines down the screen. The standard also provides for a 40-column operation. Although this resolution (640 by 200) is considerably lower than that found in MDA and MGA cards, the main reason for the introduction of the standard was to provide color. The CGA standard can produce 16 different user-definable colors. The programmer can generate up to 16 different character colors and eight different background colors. These functions are controlled by software through one of the registers in the adapter's **6845 Video Controller IC**.

In addition to its Text mode, the CGA standard provides the capability of producing graphics on the screen. This feature was not available with the original MDA standard. Under that standard, only text characters could be displayed on the screen. However, the CGA standard accommodates two color **graphics modes: low-resolution** and **medium-resolution**. A **high-resolution** graphics mode is possible, but only in monochrome.

In low-resolution mode, the screen is divided into 100 rows of 160 pixels. Each pixel is two dots high by two dots wide and can be assigned one of 16 colors. Medium graphics mode supports 200 rows of 320 pixels each. In this mode, the PELs are one dot high by one dot wide and can be assigned one of four colors. High-resolution mode produces 640 pixels by 200 rows, with each pixel mapped directly to a bit of memory. Because each bit is tied to a bit in memory, only monochrome operation is possible in this mode.

A CGA card, displayed in Figure 9.16, provides two output ports at the rear of the unit. These are the RGB color video output and the parallel printer output (the RF-modulated and composite color outputs of the original CGA card have been discontinued in most later versions of this card). The smaller nine-pin female D-shell connector is used to transfer video signals to a color monitor, and the 25-pin female D-shell connector provides a parallel printer interface connection. This card also includes a light pen interface from a four-pin BERG strip located on the side of the board. As in the MDA card, the CGA's printer port acts as the primary printer port (LPT1) in the system, if it is not disabled.

FIGURE 9.16

The CGA card.

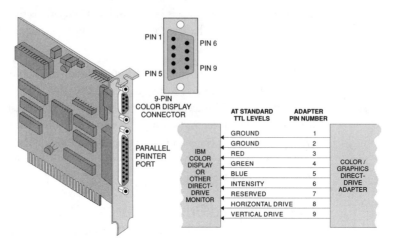

Hercules Graphic/Printer Adapter (HGA)

The **Hercules Monochrome Graphics Adapter (HGA)** card, illustrated in Figure 9.17, was developed to incorporate the best aspects of the IBM MDA and CGA cards. The HGA card combines the bitmapped graphics capabilities of the CGA card with the high-resolution character-mapped text capabilities of the MDA card. It not only matches the MDA's 80-by-25 character format, but it increases the resolution in graphics mode to 720 by 348. To accommodate these levels of resolution, the HGA's horizontal sync frequency is increased to 18.1KHz, with a 50Hz vertical retrace rate.

FIGURE 9.17

The HGA card.

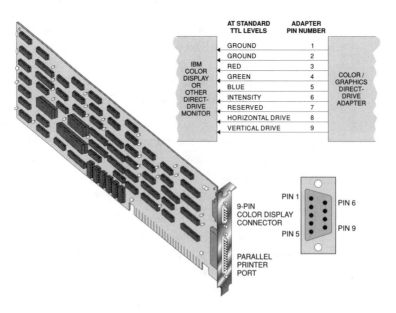

The adapter supports three modes of operation: a high-resolution Alphanumeric Text mode and two **All Points Addressable (APA)** graphics modes. When the unit is first powered up, the adapter is in the Text mode, and its graphics capabilities are masked so that no graphics software can be run. In the graphics modes, the adapter supports 64KB of video information in an onboard video memory. This 64KB buffer is divided into two 32KB buffers for each of the two graphics pages.

In the first of the graphics modes, called the HALF Configuration, the first graphics page (located at addresses between B0000h and B7FFFh) is accessible to graphics software. The second graphics page, located at addresses between B8000h and BFFFFh, is suppressed. This enables other video cards, such as a color/graphics adapter, to be used in the PC as long as their screen buffers do not occupy any part of the first graphics page addresses.

In the second graphics mode, called the FULL configuration, both pages of the adapter's screen buffer are available to graphics software, and other video adapters may not be used in the system.

Enhanced Graphics Adapter (EGA)

The resolution of the CGA card proved too low for the tastes of many users. By 1984, IBM had developed a replacement video standard called the **Enhanced Graphics Adapter (EGA)** standard. The EGA standard defines text characters as a 7-by-9 matrix in an 8-by-14 dot box (640 by 350 dots). The resolution factor remained constant when the display was shifted into Graphics mode. The EGA adapter/monitor interface connection incorporated new signals that provided for up to 64 colors.

To accommodate the high-resolution and expanded color possibilities, the EGA card (depicted in Figure 9.18) incorporated a bank-switching video memory scheme. Its memory was divided into four banks (16KB or 64KB each) that could be switched (redirected) into the system's video address range. To achieve compatibility with software written for the MDA and CGA standards, the EGA's memory could be switched to the base video memory address of these standards (B0000h for MDA and B8000h for CGA). The base address for EGA video memory begins at hex address A0000h.

FIGURE 9.18

An EGA card.

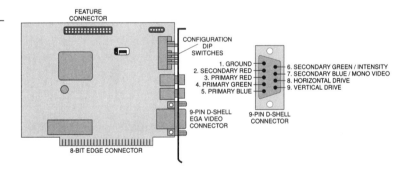

The high-resolution requirements of the EGA standard also called for an increase in the horizontal scan rate. The horizontal scanning frequency in the EGA standard was elevated to 22.1KHz, with a vertical refresh rate of 60Hz. However, the EGA card also had to be capable of producing horizontal and vertical refresh rates that were compatible with previous standards.

Unlike its predecessors, the EGA card was not dependent on the system software for operation. Instead, the EGA standard made use of an onboard **EGA Video BIOS** routine to manage the board's configuration, mode-control, and EGA compatibility functions.

The EGA card was compatible with a number of different video display monitors. In general, EGA cards supported the MGA standard (and could therefore be used to drive monochrome monitors) as well as the CGA standard (so that it could be used with RGB color monitors). To avoid damaging the monitor and the adapter, the EGA card had to be configured to work with the type of monitor being used with the system. This was done by setting DIP switches to reflect the type of monitor in use.

The EGA video signal was passed to the monitor through the nine-pin female D-shell connector on the back plate of the card. This enabled compatibility with the previous MGA and CGA connections. Upon closer examination, some additional signals had been added to the interface. In particular, secondary intensity signals were added to each of the three color signals. The two color lines worked together in a digitally coded manner to furnish four levels of brightness for each color.

Video Graphics Array (VGA) Adapters

The next video standard improvement appeared when IBM announced its Personal System 2 line. This video standard acted as one of the centerpieces of this system and was called the **Video Graphics Array (VGA)** standard. In the PS/2 line, this function was built directly into the system board in the form of a VLSI **logical gate-array IC**. This sometimes led to the VGA acronym being incorrectly expressed as Video Gate Array. In a short time, many PCB manufacturers were producing options adapter card versions of the VGA controller. As with other options adapter cards, these units were designed to fit into the expansion slot of a typical PC-compatible computer and enabled VGA-compatible monitors to be connected to the system through a 15-pin D-shell connector. A VGA card is depicted in Figure 9.19.

FIGURE 9.19

A VGA adapter.

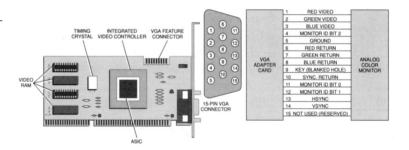

VGA Specifications

> In designing the VGA standard, IBM departed from the signal formats found in its previous display standards. To accommodate a wide range of onscreen color possibilities, the VGA standard resorted to the use of analog video signals.

Because of these analog video signals, the intensity of the image could be varied infinitely over the entire voltage range of the signal (unlike digital signals that can be only on or off). This meant that the VGA standard could support up to 262,144 (256KB) colors.

The digital signals used by the rest of the computer system were converted into analog signals on the video adapter card by circuits called **digital-to-analog Converters (DACs)**. Nearly all VGA cards employed a three-DAC circuit in their VLSI chip to perform this task (one DAC for each of the three video color signals). In addition, the DAC chip contained the adapter's 256KB color palette and circuitry for assigning up to 256 of those colors to be available for use on the screen at any given time.

In addition to offering vastly improved color production capabilities, VGA provided superior resolution capabilities. Standard VGA resolution is defined as 720-by-400 pixels using 16 colors in Text mode, and 640-by-480 pixels using 16 onscreen colors in Graphics mode. However, improved resolution VGA systems—referred to as Super VGAs—are now commonly available in formats of 1,024 by 768 with 256 colors, 1,024 by 768 with 16 colors, and 800 by 600 with 256 colors. The SVGA definition continues to expand, with video controller capabilities ranging up to 1,280 by 1,024 (with reduced color capabilities) currently available in the market.

IBM produced its own **Extended Graphics Array** standard, called the **XGA**. This standard was capable of both 800-by-600 and 1,024-by-768 resolutions, but it added a 132-column, 400-scan line resolution. Unfortunately, IBM based the original XGA on interlaced monitors and, therefore, the standard never gained a large following.

The maximum resolution/color capabilities of a particular VGA adapter were ultimately dependent on the amount of onboard memory the adapter had installed. The standard 640-by-480 display format, using 16 colors, requires nearly 256KB of video memory to operate (640 x 480 x 4 / 8 = 153,600 bytes). With 512KB of video memory installed, the resolution can be improved to 1,024 by 768, but only 16 colors are possible (1,024 x 768 x 4 / 8 = 393,216 bytes). To achieve full 1,024 by 768 resolution with 256 colors, the video memory has to be expanded to a full 1MB (1,024 x 768 x 8 / 8 = 786,432 bytes). Access to this memory is very flexible.

The VGA card's memory-mapping capabilities enable the memory to be accessed from hex base addresses B0000 and B8000 to achieve MDA and CGA compatibility or at base address A0000 for EGA and VGA standards. As with the EGA standard, the full range of the VGA's installed video memory is divided into banks to accommodate bank-switched memory techniques. Under the VGA standard, Plug-and-Play (PnP) VGA cards can automatically adapt to the type of monitor to which they are connected. This function is made possible by the addition of four ID lines (Monitor ID bits 0–3) to the VGA interface port.

Standard VGA monitors employ a 31.5KHz horizontal scanning rate, and SVGA monitors use frequencies between 35KHz and 48KHz for their horizontal sync, depending on the **vertical refresh rate** of the adapter card. Standard VGA monitors repaint the screen (vertical refresh) at a frequency of 60Hz or 70Hz, and SVGA vertical scanning occurred at frequencies of 56Hz, 60Hz, and 72Hz. A summary of the different video standards is presented in Figure 9.20.

VGA Cards

Early non-IBM VGA adapter cards included a special **auxiliary video/feature connector** to remain compatible with the IBM function. Because the Microchannel architecture was patented, the third-party manufacturers resorted to placing the connector elsewhere on their cards. Some cards used a notched-edge connector along the top of the card, and others employed a BERG connector for this function. Although the physical connector was different, the function was the same as the PS/2 versions of the card. These other versions supported add-on units—such as a secondary monitor or a video capture card—to share the VGA signals.

Nearly all VGA adapters were based on an ASIC device called the **Integrated Video Controller (IVC)**.

FIGURE 9.20

Video standards.

Standard	Year Introduced	Mode	Resolution (two pixels)	A/N Display	A/N Character	Refresh Rate	Horizontal Sweep Rate	Buffer Address
MDA (Monochrome Display Adapter)	1981	Alpha Numeric (A/N)	720 x 348 720 x 348	80 x 25	7 x 9 in 9 x 14	50/60	(Non-interlaced)	B0000–B7FFF B0000–B7FFF B0000–BFFFF
CGA (Color Graphics Adapter)	1982	(A/N) Low-resolution Medium-resolution High-resolution (APA) All Points Addressable graphics	640 x 200 160 x 100 320 x 200 640 x 200	80 x 25	7 x 7 in 8 x 8	60	15 kHz	B8000–BBFFF
HGA (Hercules Graphics Adapter)	1982	A/N Diag/Half/Full Graphics	720 x 348	80 x 25	7 x 9 in 9 x 14	50	18.1 kHz	B0000–BFFFF
EGA (Extended Graphics Adapter)	1984	A/N Graphics	640 x 350 640 x 350	80 x 25 80 x 43	7 x 9 in 8 x 14	60 Hz	22.1 kHz	0A0000
VGA (Video Graphics Array Adapter)	1989	Text Graphics	720 x 400 640 x 480	80 x 25 80 x 43	9 x 16	60 or 70 Hz	31.5 kHz	0A0000–0BFFFF
Super VGA (SVGA)	1990	Text Graphics	1280 x 1024 1024 x 768 800 x 600	80 x 25 80 x 43	9 x 16	50, 60, or 72	35-48 kHz	0A0000–0BFFFF
XGA	1992	Text Graphics	1024 x 768 800 x 600	132 x 25	9 x 16 8 x 16	44/70	35.5 kHz	0A0000–0BFFFF

A block diagram of an IVC is depicted in Figure 9.21. This is a single-chip, high-performance, low-cost VGA chip that contains all the circuitry required both to generate the video signal going to the monitor connector and to generate the timing signals for the video memory. The IVC combined a Video DAC, an IBM-compatible Video BIOS, a CRT controller, a graphics controller, and an attribute controller into a single IC device. On older VGA cards, portions of these units were constructed using discrete ICs.

FIGURE 9.21

The blocks of the IVC.

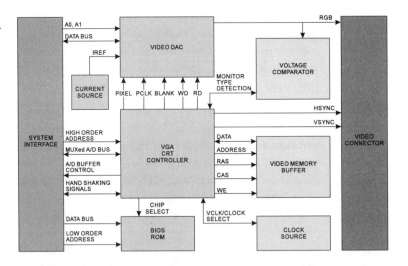

On most newer VGA cards, the only other ICs on the card are the video RAM ICs. These were normally capable of occupying addresses A0000h–BFFFFh, and the ROM BIOS held addresses C0000h–C7FFFh. Video cards came with various levels of video RAM installed. The minimum level had typically been 256KB, but the standard for some time has been 1MB. Advanced video cards may include 2MB or more of video RAM.

> The video RAM is normally implemented through Dynamic RAM devices. However, newer memory types are beginning to offer improved video memory. These memory types include **Extended Data Out DRAM (EDO RAM)**, **Synchronous DRAM (SDRAM)**, and **Video RAM (VRAM)**.

EDO RAM memory operates faster than normal DRAM used in screen memories by not disabling its data output between accesses. Therefore, the turn-on/turn-off times for the outputs are negated. SDRAM uses an external pixel clock to perform high-speed synchronous data accesses.

VRAM employs a special **dual-port access** system to speed up video operations tremendously. In other memory devices, access to the data in the RAM locations is shared between the system's microprocessor and the adapter's video controller. The microprocessor accesses the RAM to update the data in it and also to keep it refreshed. Meanwhile, the video controller must access the same locations to move pixel information to the screen. Both control devices must use the same data bus to get to the data.

Unlike the single data port operation found in the other DRAM devices, VRAM devices provide two access buses to the data. The first is a standard set of parallel data bus pins. The second is a special serial port that enables the data to be accessed for refreshing purposes. VRAM tends to be more expensive than simple DRAM chips, but it delivers much faster data access.

Memory speed is important during complex screen operations, such as scrolling or word wrapping. In Graphics mode, memory speed is particularly important because the entire screen may have to be rewritten bit by bit. If these operations occur too slowly, annoying blinks and flashes are produced on the screen. The access time of the DRAM chips used with the VGA adapter should be no longer than 100 nanoseconds.

Integrated Video Controllers

The Integrated Video Controller (IVC) receives address and data directly from the expansion bus connector. The system applies addresses to the IVC on the system address (SA0–SA19) lines. Likewise, data moves between the chip and the system on data bus lines (SD0–SD7).

The video controller uses a separate address and data bus for each set of DRAM chips. Most IVCs can address video memory using several different formats. For VGA or EGA operation, video RAM is divided into four sections called **maps**. The four maps represent the three colors—red, green, and blue—and intensity. Figure 9.22 illustrates how the controller addresses these maps.

FIGURE 9.22

VGA video RAM addressing.

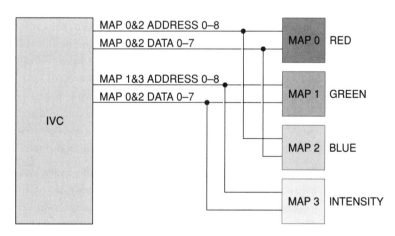

Most VGA adapters come from their manufacturer with a disk full of enhanced software display drivers. These drivers modify the parameters in the registers to optimize the adapter for different software applications such as AutoCAD, Microsoft Windows, and so on. Windows and Windows 95 come with a variety of video drivers already built into them.

RAMDAC Section

The RAMDAC section contains 576 bytes of RAM arranged in a 256-by-18 format. This RAM look-up table, called the color palette, is used to translate a digital value into a corresponding color using a mixture of red, green, and blue. Recall that varying the intensity of the red, green, and blue dots on the screen produces all colors in a CRT. This section also contains three 6-bit DACs. The 6-bit values from the color palette are applied to the inputs of the DACs and converted into corresponding analog output levels.

Because each color is a 6-bit value, 64 levels ($2^6=64$) are present for each basic color. When the red, green, and blue signals are combined, each color produced on the screen relates to an 18-bit value. This produces a maximum of 262,144 ($2^{18}=262,144$) or 256KB colors.

When the RAMDAC section receives the color palette information from the video controller, it stores it in the RAM locations. These values are applied to a DAC to produce the analog video signal for each color. The outputs of the DACs connect directly to the monitor via the adapter's VGA connector. Figure 9.23 shows the RAMDAC section of the video controller.

FIGURE 9.23

RAMDAC block diagram.

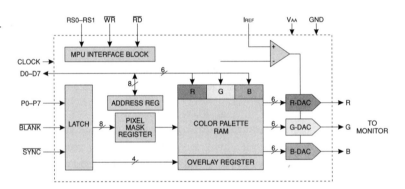

Video BIOS Section

The operation of the VGA adapter is controlled by the card's MASK ROM that provides the video BIOS function calls. This BIOS acts as an extension of the system BIOS and is located between address C0000h and C7FFFh. All the video function calls are accessed through software interrupt INT10. The video BIOS supports 27 distinct modes of operation, as depicted in Figure 9.24. These modes include various character-box sizes and resolution selections and include two different methods of storing screen data in the video memory. The first method is the A/N alphanumeric mode, which is used for text operations. The second method is an APA mode, which is normally used for graphics applications.

The BIOS contains the default font styles for the display's character sets. In alphanumeric modes, characters are passed to the screen memory in ASCII-coded format. However, in graphics modes, the adapter's operation is bitmapped, with information concerning each pixel of the screen stored in the memory. Three possible starting addresses exist for the screen memory: A0000$_h$, B0000$_h$, and B8000$_h$. These addresses correspond to the pixel at the top left corner of the screen for a given mode of operation. When simulating MDA operations, the screen begins at B0000$_h$. CGA simulation begins at B8000$_h$, and EGA/VGA modes begin at A0000$_h$.

FIGURE 9.24

Video BIOS mode table.

Mode (HEX)	T/G	Color	Box Size	Alpha Size	Screen Size	Buffer Start	Pg	Hsync (kHz)	Vsync (Hz)	Crystal (MHz)	RAM (kB)
0,1	A/N	16	8x8	40x25	320x200	B8000	8	31.5	70	25.175	256
2,3	A/N	16	8x8	80x25	640x200	B8000	8	31.5	70	25.175	256
0^,1^	A/N	16	8x14	40x25	320x350	B8000	8	31.5	70	25.175	256
2^,3^	A/N	16	8x14	80x25	640x350	B8000	8	31.5	70	25.175	256
0+,1+	A/N	16	9x16	40x25	360x400	B8000	8	31.5	70	28.322	256
2+,3+	A/N	16	9x16	80x25	720x400	B8000	8	31.5	70	38.322	256
4,5	APA	4	8x8	40x25	320x200	B8000	1	31.5	70	25.175	256
6	APA	2	8x8	80x25	640x200	B8000	1	31.5	70	25.175	256
7	A/N	-	9x14	80x25	720x350	B0000	8	31.5	70	28.322	256
7+	A/N	-	9x16	80x25	720x400	B0000	8	31.5	70	28.322	256
D	APA	16	8x8	40x25	320x200	A0000	8	31.5	70	25.175	256
E	APA	16	8x8	80x25	640x200	A0000	4	31.5	70	25.175	256
F	APA	-	8x14	80x25	640x350	A0000	2	31.5	70	25.175	256
10	APA	16	8x14	80x25	640x350	A0000	2	31.5	70	25.175	256
11	APA	2	8x16	80x30	640x480	A0000	1	31.5	60	25.175	256
12	APA	16	8x16	80x30	640x480	A0000	1	31.5	60	25.175	256
13	APA	256	8x8	40x25	320x200	A0000	1	31.5	70	25.175	256
18	A/N	16	9x16	80x30	720x480	B8000	1	31.5	60	28.322	256
19	A/N	16	9x8	80x43	720x473	B8000	1	31.5	70	28.322	256
1A	A/N	16	9x8	80x60	720x480	B8000	1	31.5	60	28.322	256
1B	A/N	16	9x16	132x25	1188x350	B8000	1	31.2	70	40.0	256
1C	A/N	16	9x16	132x30	1188x480	B8000	1	31.2	60	40.0	256
1D	A/N	16	9x8	132x43	1188x473	B8000	1	31.2	70	40.0	256
1E	A/N	16	9x8	132x60	1188x480	B8000	1	31.2	60	40.0	256
1F	APA	16	8x8	100x75	800x600	A0000	1	31.5	57	36	256
1F V	APA	16	8x8	100x75	800x600	A0000	1	48.0	70	50.35	256
20	APA	16	8x16	120x45	960x720	A0000	1	31.5	43/43	44.9	512
21	APA	16	8x16	128x48	1024x768	A0000	1	31.5	43/43	44.9	512
21 NI	APA	16	8x16	128x48	1024x768	A0000	1	48.5	60	65	512
21 V	APA	16	8x16	128x48	1024x768	A0000	1	56.5	70	75	512
22	APA	16	8x16	96x64	768x1024	A0000	1	38	35/35	44.9	512
23	APA	4	8x16	128x48	1024x768	A0000	1	35.5	43/43	44.9	512
24	APA	256	8x16	64x32	512x512	A0000	1	35.5	62	50.35	512
25	APA	256	8x14	80x25	640x400	A0000	1	31.5	70	50.35	512
26	APA	256	8x16	80x30	640x480	A0000	1	31.5	60	50.35	512
27	APA	256	8x8	100x75	800x600	A0000	1	35.5	57	36	512
27 V	APA	256	8x8	100x75	800x600	A0000	1	48.0	70	50.35	512

Note: NI non-interlaced mode. V VESA mode

Video Controller Section

The block diagram of the **video controller** section is depicted in Figure 9.25. This section consists of the sequencer (SEQR), a cathode ray tube controller (CRTC), a graphic controller, and an attribute controller.

FIGURE 9.25

The video controller.

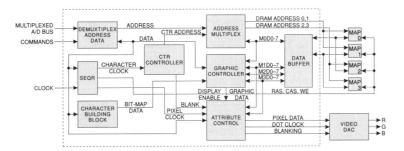

The Sequencer

The **sequencer** generates basic DRAM timing and the character clock for video memory timing control. The VGA adapter's screen memory is known as **dual-ported RAM memory** because both the system microprocessor and the video controller can access it. However, both devices cannot access the memory at the same time. A small problem arises when the system accesses the screen memory for an update. The system access requires more time to complete than the interval between sending character codes to the screen.

The sequencer uses latches and timing circuitry to help the system microprocessor access the screen memory during the active retrace interval of the electron beams. This is accomplished by inserting the system's read and write cycles of the screen memory between the video controller access cycles.

The CRTC

The **cathode ray tube controller (CRTC)** generates the vertical and horizontal synchronization signals (VSYNC and HSYNC) for controlling the electron-gun movement. It also inserts the cursor and underlining for the text modes, and it generates the address for the graphic controller to retrieve pixel data from the DRAM display memory for both the Text and Graphics modes. This section of the chip also performs the video RAM refresh controller function.

The Graphics Controller

The **graphics controller** section performs two functions. First, it provides the interface between the DRAM memory and the system's microprocessor when the display memory is accessed by the microprocessor. Secondly, in graphic modes it formats the pixel data for the attribute controller during the active retrace intervals. When the display is used in Text mode, the data bypasses the graphics controller and is applied directly to the attribute controller.

The Attribute Controller

The last major section of the video controller is the **attribute controller**. This section receives data from the display memory (with the aid of the graphics controller) and formats it for the display. The attribute controller also implements the cursor, underlining, and blinking attributes in Text mode.

Initialization

It should be apparent that the VGA adapter requires a large number of registers to operate. Most of these registers are used to produce a certain mode of operation. Fortunately, the majority of this information is supplied to the adapter through a software interrupt: INT10. During the system startup, the video BIOS intercepts the system's software INT10 function and takes over by substituting its own enhanced INT10 function. When this has been accomplished, the BIOS initializes the VGA adapter's other functions. Three of the more notable setup functions performed by the BIOS are the establishment of the video memory's video maps, the production of the adapter's RAM character generators, and the initialization of the RAMDAC's color palette.

The VGA adapter uses two RAM character generators. By using RAM character generators instead of the ROM generator illustrated in Figure 9.5, user-defined characters can be employed. When the system is started, default character fonts are downloaded from the video BIOS into the RAM character generators. Both character generators are located in memory map 2, and each consists of seven possible 8KB-character sets. These character sets can be easily rewritten by software at any time.

The system loads the default color values into the RAMDAC's color palette at startup. Three 6-bit color values are written into each palette location, one each for the red, green, and blue value. A write operation into a specific palette position begins by writing the address of the palette position; this is followed by three sequential write operations into the DAC Data Register: Red, Green, and Blue. These write operations must be performed in order, and they must be completed. If the sequence is interrupted before it is completed, the entire operation must be performed again. An auto-increment function causes the value of the Write Address Register to be increased by 1 after a complete write sequence has been performed. This provides for consecutive updates of the color palette locations, which enable the system to supply continuous red, green, and blue data until the entire palette has been written.

Text Mode

In Text mode, the adapter accepts screen character information from the system's data bus and stores it in the video screen memory. In this mode, the system sends 2 bytes of information to the adapter for each character to be displayed on the screen. These bytes are stored in sequential order, one after the other. The first byte is the ASCII-coded character and is stored as even-address information in memory map 0.

The second byte is the **attribute byte**, which contains information about how the character is to be displayed. This byte is stored as odd-address information in memory map 1. Bits 0–2 of the attribute byte determine the **foreground** (text) **color**. Bits 4–6 determine the **background** (character box) **color**. Bit 3 indicates a highlighted (bold) character, and bit 7 indicates a blinking character. Bit 3 can also be defined to switch between the character sets stored in map 2. In a similar manner, bit 7 can be redefined to carry background intensity information.

All the VGA adapter's text modes support 16 colors: eight background colors and eight foreground colors, as determined by the character's attribute byte. The serialized character dots are multiplexed with the attribute byte. If the value of the dot is a logic 1, indicating a foreground color, the foreground color bits of the attribute byte (0–3) are read and applied to the color plane enable logic. If the character dot is a logic 0, the background color bits (4–7) are used to drive this circuitry. In the case of nine-dot character cells, the ninth bit is automatically set to the same value as the background color. Table 9.1 lists the default color values loaded into the palette registers by the video BIOS.

Table 9.1 *The Video BIOS Color Set*

Intensity	Red	Green	Blue	Color
0	0	0	0	Black
0	0	0	1	Blue
0	0	1	0	Green
0	0	1	1	Cyan
0	1	0	0	Red
0	1	0	1	Magenta
0	1	1	0	Brown
0	1	1	1	White
1	0	0	0	Gray
1	0	0	1	Light blue
1	0	1	0	Light green
1	0	1	1	Light cyan
1	1	0	0	Light red
1	1	0	1	Light magenta
1	1	1	0	Yellow
1	1	1	1	White (high intensity)

The 8-bit pixel address information from the attribute controller (P0–P7) is latched into the **Pixel Mask Register** of the RAMDAC section. The output of the mask register is used to access one of the 256 color addresses in the color palette. The selected color palette address causes the three 6-bit pieces of color information in that location to be applied to the three DACs.

A value of $3F_h$ drives the DAC to a current output value of 17.62mA. This corresponds to a level of white. Conversely, a value of 00_h produces a 0.0mA output current that corresponds to a **black level**. Other hex values applied to the DAC input produce an output current that is equal to the numerical value of the input plus 9.05mA. The presence of an active BLANK signal overrides the code value applied to the DAC and produces a 0.0mA black level.

Along with the pixel information, the adapter must furnish accurate horizontal and vertical synchronization signals to the monitor. The CRTC section controls this function. Both signals originate with the CRTC and operate at TTL logic levels. A typical range of the HSYNC and VSYNC signals possible with a VGA adapter was illustrated in Figure 9.24. Figure 9.26 depicts the VGA adapter's Text mode operation.

FIGURE 9.26

Text mode circuitry.

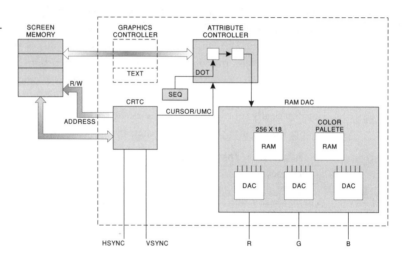

In alphanumeric mode, the adapter supports both 40- and 80-column operations. In 40-column mode, it supports 25 rows of 40 characters. Storing 1 character byte and 1 attribute byte per character requires 2KB of video memory per page. Likewise, a page in 80-column mode requires 4KB of memory.

If the starting address for a particular 80-column text mode is $B0000_h$ and 2 bytes of memory are required for each character, then an 80-character-by-25-line display will use memory addresses up to B0F9Fh for the first screen of memory. The space between B0F9Fh and B0FFFh is reserved so that the next page begins at B1000h. If this Text mode is designated as having a 9-by-14-character cell, then each scan row will be composed of 720 pixels. The total number of scan rows will be 350. Therefore, the resolution of the screen will be 720 by 350 in this mode.

Graphics Mode

In Graphics modes, each pixel on the screen is related to a memory location in each of the adapter's maps. Therefore, the adapter does not use the character generator scheme described in Text mode operation. Instead, the CRTC loads the screen memory locations' contents into the graphics controller section of the IC. Each pixel's color is determined by combining a bit from each of the adapter's four maps in 16-color mode, or eight maps in 256-color mode.

The system writes the screen data into the screen memory through the graphics controller, starting at location A0000$_h$ in default VGA mode. Each of the maps corresponds to the same sets of addresses.

In 320-by-200 graphics modes, the display memory is organized into two banks of 8KB each. Each byte is used to encode four pixels that have four possible colors. The beginning address is B8000$_h$, and image maps 0 and 1 are used to hold the image data. This requires 16KB of video memory. The display is double-scanned to display as 400 rows.

The 640-by-200 graphics mode uses a single-bit plane (C0) that begins at B8000. This mode uses the same addressing and line-scanning techniques as the 320-by-200 mode. Each bit of the data byte is used to distinguish between two colors for a corresponding pixel.

In the 640-by-350 mode, the operation of the adapter is expanded greatly. Blank, video, blinking video, and intensified video attributes are added to the operation, increasing the total memory requirement to 56KB. This mode uses maps 0 and 2, both of which begin at A0000$_h$. The first eight pixels are defined by the byte at A0000, the next eight by the byte at A0001, and so forth.

The 640-by-480 mode provides two-color operations using the same memory format described for the 640-by-200 mode. Instead of starting at B8000, this mode begins at A0000, and no double-scanning is used.

In 16-color modes, the adapter uses all four-bit planes, each of which begins at A0000$_h$. Bit plane C0 holds the blue data, C1 holds the green data, C2 holds the red data, and C3 holds the intensified data. These values are combined to access the palette register in the attribute controller. In 256-color mode, the video memory starts at A0000$_h$ and uses four maps, each of which is 64KB long. Each byte contains the color information for one pixel. Each map is sampled twice to produce eight bit-plane values to address the video DAC.

The color data read from the maps is latched and multiplexed in the graphics controller section. The output from the multiplexer is applied to the graphics controller's four **graphics serializers** (C0–C3). As with the alpha serializer, these shift registers accept the data bytes from the screen memory and convert them into serial bit streams. This data is supplied to the attribute controller's alpha serializer. The attribute controller's foreground and background inputs are deselected so that the serial pixel information is clocked directly through the serializer. The operation of the attribute controller and RAMDAC sections is identical to that described for alphanumeric mode. Figure 9.27 describes the operation of the VGA circuitry in graphics modes.

FIGURE 9.27

Graphics mode circuitry.

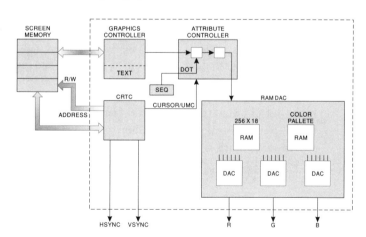

Video Troubleshooting

A+ CORE 1.2 The movement of video information is depicted in Figure 9.28. It may be most practical to think of the video information as starting out on the system board. In reality, the keyboard, one of the disk drives, or some other input/output device may be the actual originating point for the information. In any case, information intended for the video-display monitor moves from the system board to the video adapter card by way of the system board's expansion slots. The adapter card also obtains power for its operation from these expansion slots. Finally, the information is applied to the monitor through the video signal cable.

FIGURE 9.28

Video information movement.

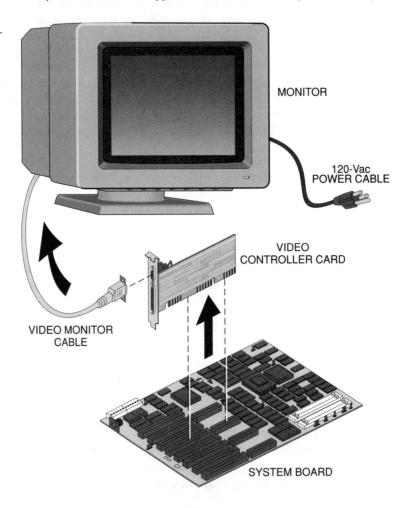

MONITOR

120-Vac
POWER CABLE

VIDEO
CONTROLLER CARD

VIDEO MONITOR
CABLE

SYSTEM BOARD

Three basic levels of troubleshooting apply to video problems. These are the DOS level, the Windows level, and the hardware level. At the DOS level, you have two considerations: configuration problems and hardware problems.

In the case of hardware problems, the components associated with video problems include the video adapter card and the monitor. To a lesser degree, the system board and optional adapter cards—such as sound and scanner cards—can be the cause of video problems.

A+ CORE 2.1 Figure 9.29 illustrates some of the typical symptoms produced by video display failures.

FIGURE 9.29

Video failures.

Other common symptoms associated with display problems include the following:

1. No display

2. Wrong characters displayed on the screen

3. Diagonal lines on the screen (no horizontal control)

4. Display scrolls (no vertical control)

5. An error code of one long and six short beeps produced by the system

6. A "Display Switch Setting Not Proper—Failure to verify display type" error displayed onscreen

7. A "CMOS Display Mismatch—Failure to verify display type" error displayed onscreen

8. An error code of one long and two short beeps, indicating a display adapter problem

The following troubleshooting sections cover the digital portion of the video system. A later section discusses the hardware portion of the monitor. Only experienced technicians should participate in troubleshooting interior monitor problems, due to the very high voltages present there.

Configuration Checks

While booting up the system to the DOS prompt, observe the BIOS video-type information displayed on the monitor. The values stored in this CMOS memory must accurately reflect the type of monitor installed in the system, or an error will occur. These values can be accessed for change by pressing the CTRL and DEL keys (or some other key combination) simultaneously during the boot-up procedure.

DOS Checks

Reboot the system, and run a diagnostic software program. If possible, try to use a diagnostic program that conducts a bank of tests on the video components. Run the program's Video Tests function, and perform the equivalent of the ALL tests function.

Note all the errors indicated by the tests. If a single type of error is indicated, it may be possible to take some corrective actions. However, if more complex system board problems are indicated, exit the diagnostic program and use the troubleshooting information in the Hardware Checks section of this chapter to locate and repair the video problem.

Windows 3.x Checks

If the display operates correctly in DOS but develops problems when Windows is running, then you must troubleshoot the Windows structure as it applies to the system's video. Observe the symptoms created. Is an error message produced when Windows is started? If so, troubleshoot the particular error mentioned in the code. Refer to the Windows user's guide for error code solution information.

Start the Windows video checks by examining the Windows video driver settings. Incorrect settings can cause symptoms that include blank screens, black borders around the screen, and unreadable displays. At the DOS prompt, type **WIN** to start the Windows program. Double-click the MAIN icon, and then double-click the Setup icon. Note the video driver listed in the Setup window.

If the video driver from the list is not correct, reload the correct driver. To change the driver setting, click the Options entry from the tool bar, and click the Change System Settings option from the menu. Use the scroll arrow at the right of the window to move through the available driver options. If the problem persists, reinstall Windows.

If the Windows video problem prevents you from being able to see the driver list, move to the DOS prompt and change directories, so that the current directory is Windows. Type and run **SETUP** from the DOS prompt. Install the generic VGA video driver from the list. This driver will set up a standard 640-by-480 VGA output that will work with most available monitors. If the problem goes away, contact the card maker for a new, compatible video driver. If the problem remains, reinstall Windows. If the video is distorted or rolling, try an alternative video driver from the list. If a blank screen appears after Windows starts up, boot the system from a **Clean Windows Boot Disk**.

To perform deeper Windows video checks, return to the DOS prompt and move to the Windows directory. This is accomplished by typing **CD\WINDOWS** at the DOS prompt. Then type **Edit SYSTEM.INI**, and press the ENTER key to examine the SYSTEM.INI file.

Locate the [boot] section heading, near the top of the file, and check the section's video-related parameters. In particular, note the Grabber (.xgr) and Display (.drv) settings. Figure 9.30 shows a sample of a typical Windows 3.x [boot] section. Also, locate the [386enh] section heading, near the top of the file, and check the section's Display parameters.

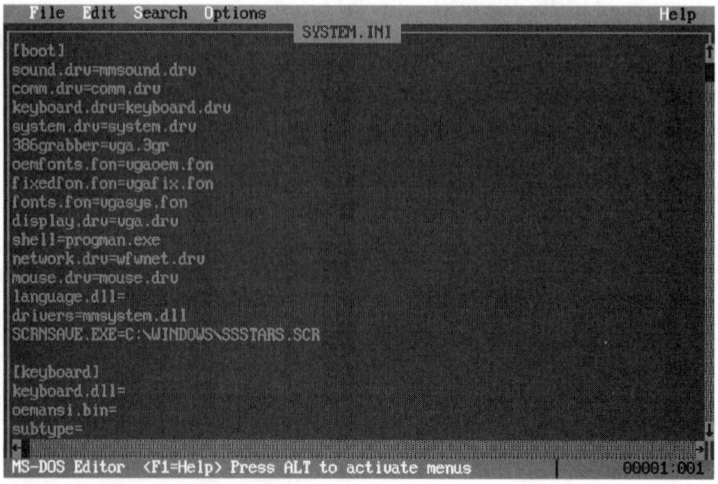

FIGURE 9.30

Typical Windows 3.x [boot] section.

Win 95 Checks

Access to the Win 95 video information can be found by double-clicking the Control Panel's Display icon. From the Display page you can access a series of file folder tabs at the top of the screen. Of particular interest is the Settings tab. Under this tab, the Change Display Type button provides access to both the adapter-type and monitor-type settings.

In the adapter-type window, information about the adapter's manufacturer, version number, and current driver files is given. Pressing the Change button beside this window brings a listing of available drivers from which you can select. You can also use the Have Disk button with an OEM disk to install video drivers not included in the list. Choosing the Show Compatible Devices or Show All Devices options can also alter the manner in which the list is displayed.

In the monitor-type window is an option list for both manufacturers and models. This function can also be used with the Have Disk button to establish OEM settings for the monitor.

Additional Windows 95 video information can be accessed under the Control Panel's System icon. Inside the System Properties page, click the Device Manager tab and select the Display adapters option from the list. Double-click the monitor icon that appears as a branch.

The adapter's Properties page pops up on the screen. From this page, the Driver tab reveals the driver file in use. Selecting the Resources tab displays the video adapter's register address ranges and the video memory address range, as illustrated in Figure 9.31. These settings can be manipulated manually by clicking the Change Setting button. Information about the monitor can also be obtained through the System icon.

FIGURE 9.31

Video adapters resources.

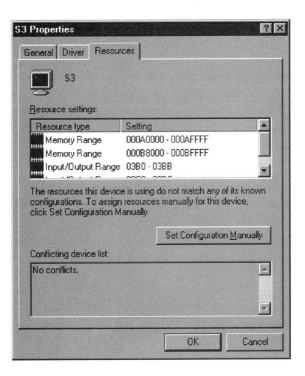

If a blank screen appears after Windows starts up, boot the system from a clean Windows boot disk.

As with the 3.x version of Windows, the first step for isolating Windows 95 video problems involves checking the video drivers. Check for the drivers in the locations specified in the previous paragraphs. If the video driver from the list is not correct, then reload the correct driver. If the problem persists, reinstall Windows 95. If a blank screen appears after Windows starts up, boot the system from a clean Windows boot disk.

If the Windows video problem prevents you from being able to see the driver, restart the system, press the F8 function key when the "Starting Windows 95" message appears, and select Safe mode. This should load Windows with the standard 640-by-480-by-16-colors VGA driver. This is the most fundamental driver available for VGA monitors, and it should furnish a starting point for installing the correct driver for the monitor being used.

If the problem reappears when a higher-resolution driver is selected, refer to the Color Palette box under the Control Panel's Display option/Settings tab, and try minimum color settings. If the problem goes away, contact the Microsoft Download Service (MSDL) or the adapter card maker for a new, compatible video driver. If the problem remains, reinstall the driver from the Windows 95 distribution disk or CD. If the video is distorted or rolling, try an alternative video driver from the list.

Hardware Checks

If a video-display hardware problem is suspected, the first task is to check the monitor's On/Off switch to see that it is in the On position. Also, check the monitor's power cord to see that it is either plugged into the power supply's monitor outlet or into an active 120-Vac commercial outlet. Also check the monitor's Intensity and Contrast controls to make certain that they are not turned down.

If the monitor is using a nine-pin D-shell connector, you should check the type of monitor and video adapter being used. The MGA, CGA, HGA, and EGA monitors all use this connector, so it is possible that they could be interchanged with the incorrect monitor or adapter. This situation can result in damage to both the monitor and the adapter.

The next step is to determine which of the video-related components is involved. On most monitors, this can be done by simply removing the video signal cable from the adapter card. If a raster appears on the screen with the signal cable removed, the problem is probably a system problem, and the monitor is good. If the monitor is an EPA-Certified Energy Star Compliant monitor, this test may not work. Monitors that possess this power-saving feature revert to a low-power mode when they do not receive a signal change for a period of time.

With the system off, remove all the externally connected devices from the system, except for the monitor and the keyboard. Remove any unnecessary options cards from the expansion slots. In particular, remove multimedia-related cards such as sound and video capture cards. Try to reboot the system.

If the system boots up and the display is correct with all the options removed, it is safe to assume that one of them is the cause of the problem. To verify which external device is causing the problem, reconnect the devices one at a time until the problem reappears. The last device reinstalled before the problem reappeared is defective.

Replace this item, and continue reinstalling options one at a time until all the options have been reinstalled. If another failure occurs while reinstalling the options, replace that option as well. When all the options have been reinstalled, return the system to full service and either service or replace the defective options as indicated.

If the display is still wrong or missing, check the components associated with the video-display monitor. Start by disconnecting the monitor's signal cable from the video-controller card at the rear of the system unit, and also disconnect its power cable from the power supply connector or the 120-Vac outlet. Then exchange the monitor for a known good one of the same type (for example, exchange a VGA for another VGA). If the system boots up and the video display is correct, return the system to full service and then service the defective monitor as indicated.

If the display is still not correct, exchange the video controller card with a known good one of the same type. Remove the system unit's outer cover. Disconnect the monitor's signal cable from the video controller card. Swap the video controller card with a known good one of the same type. Reconnect the monitor's signal cable to the new video controller card, and reboot the system.

Other symptoms that point to the video adapter card include a shaky video display and a high-pitched squeal from the monitor or system unit.

If the system boots up and the video display is correct, replace the system unit's outer cover, return the system to full service, and service the defective video controller appropriately. If the system still does not perform properly, the source of the problem may be in the system board.

The Monitor

All the circuitry discussed so far is part of the computer or its video adapter unit.

> The circuitry inside the monitor is responsible for accepting, amplifying, and routing the video and synchronizing information to the CRT's electron gun(s) and the deflection coils.

Figure 9.32 shows the functional circuitry of a typical RGB color monitor.

The RGB monitor accepts and processes separate red, green, and blue signals, which improves the quality of the display by eliminating errors due to signal crossovers. The synchronizing signals may be separate, as shown, or they may be carried with one of the color signals (usually green).

> Great caution must be used when opening or working inside the monitor. The voltage levels present during operation are lethal. Electrical potentials as high as 25,000V are present inside the unit when it is operating.

Operation of a monitor with the cover removed poses a shock hazard from the power supply. Therefore, servicing should not be attempted by anyone unfamiliar with the safety precautions associated with high-voltage equipment.

The high-voltage levels do not necessarily disappear because the power to the monitor is turned off. As with television sets, monitors have circuitry capable of storing high-voltage potentials long after power has been removed. Always discharge the **anode** of the picture tube to the receiver chassis before handling the CRT tube. Due to the high-voltage levels, anti-static grounding straps should never be worn when working inside the monitor.

FIGURE 9.32

The blocks of the RGB monitor designs.

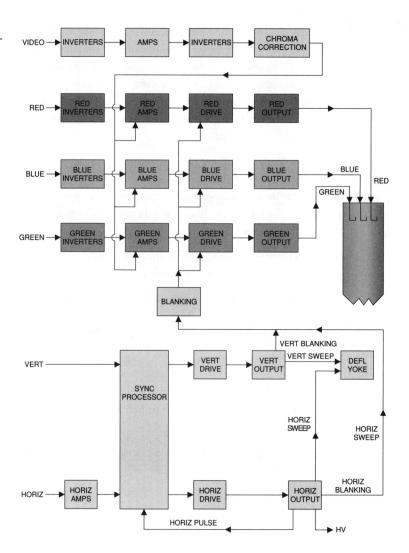

An additional hazard associated with handling CRTs is that the tube is fragile. Extra care should be taken to prevent the neck of the tube from striking any surface. The tube should never be lifted by the neck. This is particularly true when removing or replacing a CRT tube in the chassis. If the picture tube's envelope is cracked or ruptured, the inrush of air will cause a high velocity implosion, and the glass will fly in all directions. Therefore, protective goggles should always be worn when handling picture tubes.

Color monitors produce a relatively high level of **X-radiation**. The CRT tube is designed to limit X-radiation at its specified operating voltage. If a replacement CRT tube is being installed, make certain to replace it with one of the same type, with suffix numbers the same. This information can be obtained from the chassis schematic diagram inside the monitor's housing.

Assembly/Disassembly

Access to the insides of most monitors is gained by removing the back half of the cabinet from the body. The monitor should be placed face-down on a soft material to prevent scratching or other damage to the face of the tube. Begin the disassembly by removing the screws that secure the back half of the cabinet to the front. The number of screws involved varies from model to model. Be aware that some screws may be hidden under removable caps. With the screws removed, the back half of the cabinet should lift away, exposing the inside of the unit.

After the monitor's housing has been removed, the internal components can be accessed. The inside of a typical monitor is depicted in Figure 9.33. The primary components are: the CRT tube, the deflection yoke assembly, the high-voltage anode, the power supply, the CRT socket board, and the signal-processing circuitry (main board).

FIGURE 9.33

Inside the monitor cabinet.

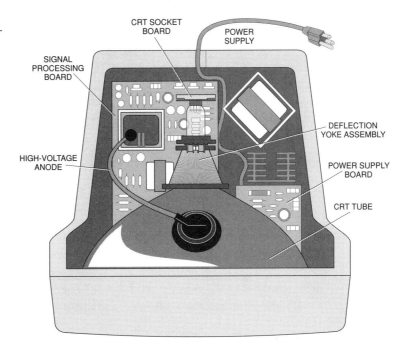

The power supply in a monitor is normally a power supply board with no external cabinet. The function of the board is the same as that of a computer power supply: It receives commercial power and converts it into the various voltage levels required by the different parts of the monitor. Be particularly careful in dealing with the power supply and the high-voltage anode that plugs into the top of the tube. The voltage levels associated with this connection range between 20,000V and 30,000V.

Color monitors also require voltage levels of 4,000V–6,000V for acceleration of the electron beam(s). The current changes involved in going from dark to light images on the screen that require high-voltage regulation to prevent unwanted changes in picture size, linearity, and defocusing. A typical monitor's power supply board is depicted in Figure 9.34.

FIGURE 9.34

A monitor power supply board.

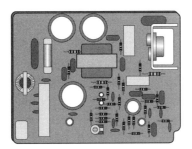

The **monitor's main board** is responsible for accepting video and sync input signals from the video adapter card and then converting them into the signals necessary to control the operation of the picture tube. A main board from a typical color monitor is shown in Figure 9.35. Most of the monitor's service adjustments are located on this board. The monitor's **service/normal switch** is also located here. This switch is used to place the monitor's circuitry in Test mode. The actual connection of the high-voltage anode and deflection yoke harness is made on the main board.

FIGURE 9.35

A typical monitor main board.

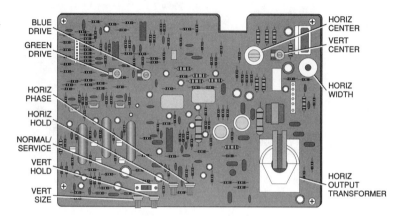

The **CRT socket board**, depicted in Figure 9.36, plugs into the rear of the CRT tube and delivers the video and sync signals. It also supplies control voltage to the CRT grids to accelerate the electron beam(s) toward the screen and sweep them across its face. On some models, this board contains a portion of the service adjustments.

FIGURE 9.36

A CRT socket board.

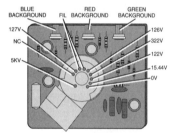

The **yoke assembly** fine-tunes the focus of the electron beams on the face of the screen. In color monitors, the deflection yoke assembly contains several parts. Two sets of coils in the yoke orient the picture on the screen, both horizontally and vertically. Sets of **convergence magnets** fine-tune the alignment of the three electron beams so that they converge into a single dot. In some monitors, the coils and magnets are adjustable, as described in the Adjustments section of this chapter.

This coating resides on the inside face of the picture tube and normally provides a return path to ground for electrons shot from the gun(s).

Handling Picture Tubes

If it becomes necessary to replace a picture tube, extreme care should be taken not to damage the tube. To remove the tube, you must discharge the high-voltage anode and remove it from the tube. The capacitance of the **aquadag coating** stores a high-voltage charge that must be discharged before handling the tube and high-voltage anode.

With the power turned off, unplug the monitor's power cable, and disconnect the signal cable from the system unit. Next, clip one end of an **insulated jumper** wire to the chassis ground, and clip the other end to a screw driver with a well-insulated handle. While touching only the insulated handle of the screwdriver, slide its blade under the cup of the anode and touch its metal contact. Continue the contact for several seconds to ensure that the voltage has been bled off.

Remove the socket board from the rear of the tube, and disconnect the ground leads. Disconnect the deflection yoke circuitry from the monitor's circuit boards. In many monitors, the yoke assemblies are bonded to the neck of the tube and cannot be removed.

Loosen all mounting hardware that holds the tube to the chassis. Position your hands around the sides of the tube, and lift it out of the chassis. Lay the tube face down on a soft, protective surface. As soon as possible, place the tube in protective housing or a shipping box to reduce the implosion hazard.

Tools

For initial monitor checks, only simple tools are required. However, serious monitor diagnostic and repair work calls for a group of specialized CRT testing tools. Among the specialized tools required are a high-voltage probe, a CRT tester, and an RGB video-pattern generator. The simple tools include a medium Phillips screwdriver and a 1/4-inch nut driver. Other tools associated with monitor repair include a TV color-bar generator and a degaussing coil.

Adjustments

In addition to the normal external adjustments, monitors typically possess internal coarse adjustments that are not accessible to the general public. These adjustments usually include the **focus** and **centering adjustments**, found on the monitor's main circuit board. To set the horizontal and vertical centering adjustments, you must connect an RGB video pattern generator to the monitor. With the generator set to a color-bar pattern, adjust the horizontal and vertical centering settings to obtain the best centering of the raster.

Other common internal adjustments include the vertical hold, vertical size, vertical linearity, horizontal hold, and sub-brightness controls. Additional adjustments are present in color monitors to set the color values and mixtures. Color-related adjustments include red, blue, and green background color settings, as well as red, green, and blue drive adjustments. Over time, the monitor's colors tend to fade as the screen's phosphor coating wears away from use. When this happens, it will become more and more difficult to produce good color output. These controls are also normally located on the monitor's main circuit board.

A+ CORE 2.1 Figure 9.37 illustrates how incorrect adjustments of the operating and maintenance controls can create trouble symptoms. The misalignment can be caused by an untrained person attempting to service the unit, or by deterioration in the value of a component. These symptoms are correlated to the likely cause in Table 9.2. In each case, the corresponding control should be adjusted to correct the condition. In addition to the symptoms listed in the table, misalignment of the monitor's **automatic gain control** (**AGC**) adjustment can cause a weak picture, no picture, or a severely distorted contrast in the picture.

FIGURE 9.37

Incorrect adjustment symptoms.

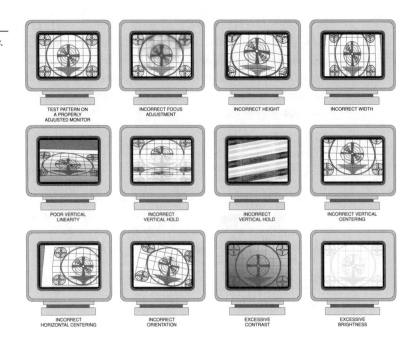

TEST PATTERN ON A PROPERLY ADJUSTED MONITOR	INCORRECT FOCUS ADJUSTMENT	INCORRECT HEIGHT	INCORRECT WIDTH
POOR VERTICAL LINEARITY	INCORRECT VERTICAL HOLD	INCORRECT VERTICAL HOLD	INCORRECT VERTICAL CENTERING
INCORRECT HORIZONTAL CENTERING	INCORRECT ORIENTATION	EXCESSIVE CONTRAST	EXCESSIVE BRIGHTNESS

Table 9.2 *Symptoms/Causes*

Incorrect Condition	Adjust
Out of focus	Focus
Too tall	Vertical size
Too narrow	Width
Stretched at bottom	Vertical linearity
Picture rolls	Vertical hold
Diagonal lines	Horizontal hold
Blank screen above picture	Vertical centering
Blank screen beside picture	Horizontal centering
Slanted picture	Yoke
Picture elements too dark	Contrast
Picture too bright	Brightness

Besides the internal and external operating and maintenance adjustments, the operation of the monitor is affected by a set of magnets in the deflection yoke. A set of **purity magnets** around the neck of the tube provides a color purity adjustment function to produce clean colors. With the blue and green background adjustments turned to minimum and the red background adjustment set so that a red raster is produced on the screen, the deflection yoke is positioned against the purity convergence assembly, as depicted in Figure 9.38. The purity magnets are adjusted until a vertical red stripe is produced at the center of the screen. Then the deflection yoke is moved forward until a uniform red raster is produced. A similar check for both a pure blue and a pure green screen should be performed by adjusting the background colors one at a time.

FIGURE 9.38

The deflection yoke.

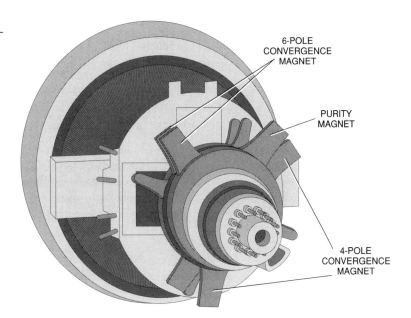

The convergence magnets in the yoke assembly are used to focus the red, green, and blue dot-trios for proper alignment. Adjusting these magnets requires the use of an RGB video-pattern generator. With the generator attached to the monitor's input jack and tuned to produce a dot pattern, the four-pole magnets (also illustrated in Figure 9.35) are adjusted so that the red and blue dots converge at the screen's center. After this, the six-pole magnets are adjusted so that the red and blue dots converge over the green dots.

After converging the dots, tune the generator to a crosshatch pattern and remove the rubber wedges from between the yoke and the neck of the CRT. Tilt the deflection yoke up or down until the vertical lines at the top and bottom of the screen converge with the horizontal lines at the left and right sides of the screen. Then tilt the yoke left or right until the horizontal lines at the top and bottom converge with the vertical lines at the right and left sides of the screen converge. Adjust the yoke for the best convergence possible, and reinstall the rubber wedges.

Some monitors include a **color temperature adjustment** that produces a white color when all three colors are properly balanced. With the red, blue, and green drive settings adjusted to mid-range and the red, blue, and green background adjustments set to minimum, set the unit's service switch to the Service position. Advance the screen control setting from minimum until a dim line of the predominant color appears. Then adjust the other two background colors until a dim white line is produced. Set the service switch back to Normal, and adjust the blue and green drive controls for monochrome operation with the best picture quality and high brightness.

Monitor Troubleshooting

The first step in isolating the monitor as the cause of the problem is to exchange it for a known good one. If the replacement works, then the problem must be located in the monitor.

As with the keyboard, the monitor is easy to swap because it is external and involves only two cables. If the problem produces a blank display, disconnect the monitor's signal cable from its video adapter card. If a raster appears, a video card problem is indicated.

Obvious items should be checked first. Examine the power cable to see that it is plugged in. Check to see that the monitor's power switch is in the On position. Check the external settings to see that the brightness and contrast settings are not turned off.

> Most monitor defects can be associated with the appearance of the output on the screen. These symptoms can generally be grouped into four general categories: power-supply problems, vertical deflection problems, horizontal deflection problems, and video problems.

If these types of problems occur and cannot be corrected through the monitor's operation and maintenance adjustments, then you must exchange sections of the monitor's hardware.

Power Supply Problems

A+ CORE 2.1

As with the power supply unit in the computer, the monitor's power supply can affect all the other subunits in the monitor. The power-supply unit supplies **B+ voltages** for the horizontal and vertical circuits to produce the monitor's raster. The main board derives lower voltage power from the power supply to process the RGB and sync signals. The power supply unit produces the very high voltages for the HV anode.

Check the monitor's internal fuse to ensure that it is good. Make sure that the monitor is unplugged and has been discharged before connecting any test equipment to the unit.

The **blooming effect**, depicted in Part A of Figure 9.39, is an abnormal enlargement of the picture and may involve either the monitor's power supply or its main board circuitry.

FIGURE 9.39

Power supply-related problems.

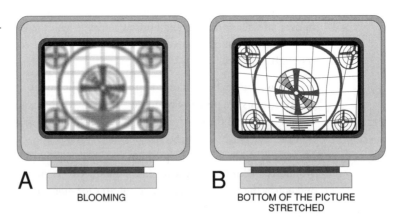

A BLOOMING

B BOTTOM OF THE PICTURE STRETCHED

The stretched appearance of the image in Part B is a result of a change in the value of the vertical height, or linearity value, and can also be attributed to a defective or misadjusted power supply voltage.

Vertical Deflection Problems

A+ CORE 2.1

Faulty operation of the monitor's sync section creates symptoms similar to those depicted in Figure 9.40. Identical symptoms may be created by the vertical or horizontal deflection systems. The horizontal white-line pattern in Part A indicates a loss of vertical deflection. The excessive height in Part B, and the picture that is too short in Part C, are also vertical height and linearity problems. All these problems relate to the vertical circuitry normally found on the main board. Likewise, the **center fold-over**, depicted in Part D and Part E, is caused by circuitry on the main board. The **double-image condition** depicted in Part F is another vertical circuitry problem.

FIGURE 9.40

Vertical deflection problems.

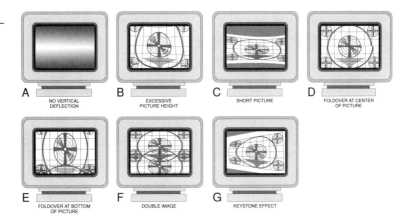

A   NO VERTICAL DEFLECTION
B   EXCESSIVE PICTURE HEIGHT
C   SHORT PICTURE
D   FOLDOVER AT CENTER OF PICTURE
E   FOLDOVER AT BOTTOM OF PICTURE
F   DOUBLE IMAGE
G   KEYSTONE EFFECT

The monitor's power supply should be checked if this condition exists. The **keystone effect**, shown in Part G, is caused by problems with one of the vertical deflection coils in the yoke assembly. The yoke would need to be replaced to correct this problem.

Horizontal Deflection Problems

A+ CORE 2.1

When a monitor loses its horizontal sync signal, a symptom such as the one displayed in Part A of Figure 9.41 is produced. This defect is normally associated with the horizontal sync circuitry located on the main board. Other horizontal sync problems related to the main board include the **piecrust effect**, shown in Part B and the right/left half-reversal symptom in Part C.

FIGURE 9.41

Horizontal sync problems.

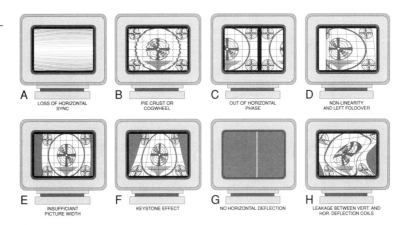

A   LOSS OF HORIZONTAL SYNC
B   PIE CRUST OR COGWHEEL
C   OUT OF HORIZONTAL PHASE
D   NON-LINEARITY AND LEFT FOLDOVER
E   INSUFFICIANT PICTURE WIDTH
F   KEYSTONE EFFECT
G   NO HORIZONTAL DEFLECTION
H   LEAKAGE BETWEEN VERT. AND HOR. DEFLECTION COILS

The horizontal fold-over and insufficient picture-width symptoms illustrated in Part D and Part E, can involve the main board or the deflection yoke assembly. Likewise, the keystone effect caused by a defective horizontal deflection coil, illustrated in Part F, also requires that the yoke assembly be replaced. The vertical white line in Part G and the symptom described in Part H require that the yoke assembly be replaced.

Video Problems

The symptoms depicted in Figure 9.42 represent problems related to the video signal. The blank screen depicted in Part A indicates a complete loss of the video signal; the pale, washed-out picture in Part B indicates a very weak video signal. The other symptoms described (Parts C–H) are also video signal processing problems and can usually be corrected by replacing the main board if operating and maintenance adjustments do not clear up the problem.

FIGURE 9.42

Video signal-related problems.

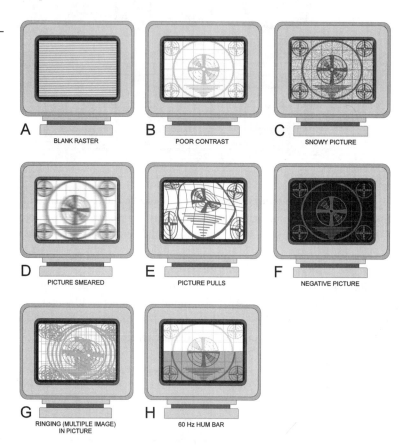

Problems in the video signal circuitry can also produce symptoms associated with loss of vertical and horizontal sync signals.

Other Display Types

Laptop or notebook computers continue to gain popularity because they can travel with the user. This has been made possible by the development of different flat-panel display technologies. Early attempts at developing portable microcomputers used small CRTs that minimized the size of the unit. However, these units quickly gained the label of **luggables** due to their weight. The high-voltage circuitry required to operate a CRT device is heavy by nature and could be reduced only slightly.

The most common of the flat-panel displays used for the smaller PCs are **liquid crystal displays** (**LCD**s). These are flat, lightweight, and require very little power to operate. In addition to reduced weight and improved portability, these displays offer better reliability and longer life than CRT units.

Liquid Crystal Displays

A+ CORE 2.1

The LCD, illustrated in Figure 9.43, is constructed by placing **thermotropic** liquid crystal material between two sheets of glass. A set of electrodes is attached to each sheet of glass. Horizontal (row) electrodes are attached to one glass plate, and vertical (column) electrodes are fitted to the other plate. These electrodes are transparent so that light can pass through them. A pixel is created in the liquid crystal material at each spot where a row and a column electrode intersect. A special plate called a **polarizer** is added to the outside of each glass plate. One polarizer is on the front, and one is on the back of the display.

FIGURE 9.43

LCD construction.

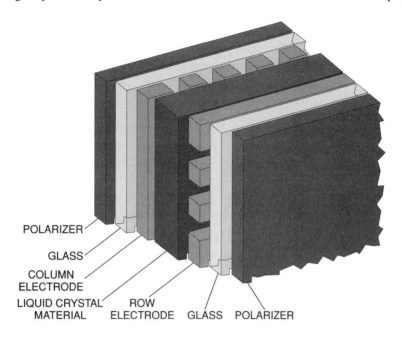

The display is designed so that when the pixel is in the off, or unenergized, condition; the molecules of the liquid crystal twist from one edge of the material to the other, as depicted in Figure 9.44. The spiral effect created by the twist polarizes light and prevents it from passing through the display. When an electric field is created between a row and column electrode, the molecules move, lining up perpendicular to the front of the display. This enables light to pass through the display, producing a single dot on the screen.

FIGURE 9.44

LCD operation.

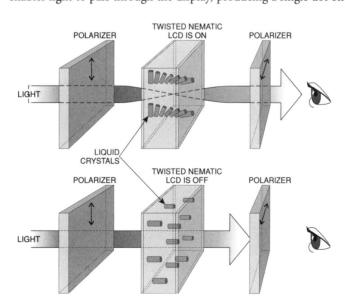

Depending on the orientation of the polarizers, the energized pixels can be made to look like a dark spot on a light screen or a light dot on a dark screen. In most notebook computers, the display is lit from behind the panel. This is referred to as **back-lighting**. Some units are constructed so that the display can be removed from the body of the computer and used with an overhead projector to display computer output on a wall or a large screen.

Because no current passes through the display to light the pixels, the power consumption of LCD displays is very low. The screen is scanned using IC multiplexers and drivers to activate the panel's row and column electrodes. The row-and-column scanning scheme simulates the operation of the sweeping electron beam in the CRT. The scanning circuitry addresses each row sequentially, column by column. Although the column electrode is activated for a short portion of each horizontal scan, the pixels appear to be continuously lit because the scanning rate is very high. The electrodes can be controlled (turned on and off) using standard TTL levels. This translates into less control circuitry required to operate the panel.

LCD displays are available in two types: **passive matrix**, as in the example explained previously, and **active matrix**. The active matrix display is similar in construction to the passive matrix type. However, the active matrix type adds a transistor at each row-column junction (pixel) to improve switching times. With an active matrix display, a small current is sent to the transistor through the row-column lines. The energized transistor conducts a larger current, which is used to turn on the pixel seen on the display.

Color LCD displays are created by adding a three-color filter to the panel. Each pixel in the display corresponds to a red, blue, or green dot on the filter. Activating a pixel behind a blue dot on the filter produces a blue dot on the screen. As with color CRT displays, the dot color on the screen of the color LCD panel is established by controlling the relative intensities of a three-dot (RGB) pixel cluster.

Gas Plasma Displays

The **gas plasma display** is similar to the LCD panel in operation. This display is a gas-filled, sealed glass enclosure. The type of gas used is most typically neon, or a mixture of neon and argon. The enclosure has small wire electrodes arranged in a row-column matrix, as in the LCD panel. Where the electrodes intersect, a pixel is created. When one row and one column are energized, the gas around that intersection discharges, giving off light and producing one dot on the screen. The voltage that is required for this discharge is usually less than 200v. The rows and columns are multiplexed and scanned to produce one full screen of information.

Key Points Review

This chapter has investigated typical video output systems used with personal computer systems.

- ▶ A CRT is an evacuated glass tube with one or more electron guns in its neck and a fluorescent-coated surface opposite the electron gun. When activated, the electron gun emits a stream of electrons that strike the fluorescent coating on the inside of the screen, producing an illuminated dot.

- ▶ Video information is introduced to the picture by varying the voltage applied to the electron gun as it scans the screen.

- ▶ The cathode-ray tube controller (CRTC) develops the video signals and the horizontal and vertical synchronization signals for the CRT.

- ▶ The character generator is basically a ROM (or RAM) device containing dot-pattern information for the entire character set.

- The color CRT uses a combination of three-color phosphors—red, blue, and green—arranged in adjacent trios of dots or bars called picture elements, pixels, or PELS. By using a different electron gun for each element of the trio, the individual elements can be made to glow at different levels to produce almost any color desired.

- The ultimate end to subdividing the display occurs when each dot on the screen is mapped to a specific memory data bit. This approach to creating graphics is referred to as bitmapped graphics.

- Many different video display standards have been developed for the IBM PC series and their clones. Each standard uses a different connector and/or pin arrangement to transfer video display and control information between the video adapter card and the monitor.

- In designing the VGA standard, IBM departed from the signal formats found in its previous display standards. To accommodate a wide range of onscreen color possibilities, the VGA standard resorted to the use of analog video signals.

- Nearly all VGA adapters were based on an ASIC device called the Integrated Video Controller IC.

- The video RAM is normally implemented through Dynamic RAM devices. However, newer memory types are beginning to offer improved video memory. These memory types include Extended Data Out DRAM (EDO RAM), Synchronous DRAM (SDRAM), and Video RAM (VRAM).

- Three basic levels of troubleshooting apply to video problems. These are the DOS level, the Windows level, and the hardware level. At the DOS level, you have two considerations: configuration problems and hardware problems.

- Normally, a configuration problem occurs when the system is being set up for the first time or when a new option is installed. The other condition that causes a configuration problem involves the system board's CMOS backup battery.

- The circuitry inside the monitor is responsible for accepting, amplifying, and routing the video and synchronizing information to the CRT's electron guns and deflection coils.

- Great caution must be used when opening or working inside the monitor. The voltage levels present during operation are lethal. Electrical potentials as high as 25,000V are present inside the unit when it is operating.

- If it becomes necessary to replace a picture tube, extreme care should be taken not to damage the tube. To remove the tube, you must discharge the high-voltage anode and remove it from the tube. The capacitance of the aquadag coating stores a high-voltage charge that must be discharged before handling the tube and high-voltage anode.

- The first step in isolating the monitor as the cause of the problem is to exchange it for a known good one. If the replacement works, then the problem must be located in the monitor.

- Most monitor defects can be associated with the appearance of the output on the screen. These symptoms can generally be grouped into four general categories: power-supply problems, vertical deflection problems, horizontal deflection problems, and video problems.

- The most common of the flat-panel displays used for the smaller PCs are liquid crystal displays (LCDs). These are flat, lightweight, and require very little power to operate.

At this point, review the objectives listed at the beginning of the chapter to be certain that you understand each point and can perform each task listed there. Afterward, answer the review questions that follow to verify your knowledge of the information.

Multiple Choice Questions

1. What portion of the system's address space is allocated to the video display adapter in an EGA system?

    a. 000000h–0FFFFFh

    b. 000000h–0AFFFFh

    c. 0B0000h–0BFFFFh

    d. 0A0000h–0BFFFFh

2. The resolution of a standard VGA card is ____by____.

    a. 1024 by 768, with 265 colors

    b. 640 by 350, with 16 colors

    c. 640 by 480, with 16 colors

    d. 25 by 80, with 16 colors

3. The resolution of an XGA card is _____by_____.

    a. 640 by 480, with 16 colors

    b. 720 by 400, with 16 colors

    c. 1024 by 768, with 265 colors

    d. 25 by 80, with 16 colors

4. A typical Text mode video operation produces a(n)____ character row by ____ column display on the monitor.

    a. 25, 40

    b. 720, 400

    c. 640, 480

    d. 25, 80

5. What video-related component should be checked first if a shaky display is observed?

    a. The monitor

    b. The video controller card

    c. The video signal cable

    d. The power supply unit

6. What is the maximum resolution of a VGA card that has 256KB of video memory installed?

    a. 640 by 480, with 16 colors

    b. 720 by 400, with 16 colors

    c. 1024 by 768, with 265 colors

    d. 25 by 80, with 16 colors

7. If a video problem occurs when Windows 3.x is loaded, where is the most likely place you should look for the problem?

    a. In the Accessories window

    b. In the Setup window

    c. In the Main window

    d. In the Startup window

8. What assumption can be made if the monitor's signal cable is removed from the adapter card and a raster is present on the screen?

    a. The monitor is functioning properly.

    b. The video adapter card is functioning properly.

    c. The video signal cable is defective.

    d. The monitor is not functioning properly.

9. Name the two types of adjustments associated with a typical computer monitor.

    a. Horizontal and vertical position controls

    b. The service switch and RGB controls

    c. Brightness and contrast controls

    d. Horizontal and vertical size controls

10. What type of problem creates a negative image on the screen?

    a. Horizontal synchronization problems

    b. Vertical synchronization problems

    c. Monitor power supply failure

    d. Video processing circuitry

Review Questions

1. How does the operation of an interlaced and noninterlaced monitor differ?

2. What does the term pixel stand for?

3. The resolution of an SVGA card is ____by____.

4. Why should special care be taken when checking an unfamiliar video card with a nine-pin D-shell connector?

5. List the signals associated with the output of a VGA adapter card.

6. If the video controller is operating in Text mode using a character line format of 132 characters by 25 lines, what is the minimum amount of screen memory that must be present on the video card?

7. How is a VGA video signal different than an MGA, CGA, or EGA signal?

8. What is the function of the shadow mask in a color CRT monitor?

9. Where should the troubleshooting sequence for any suspected video problem begin?

10. What are the three primary components that are likely to be involved when a video problem occurs?

11. What type of display paints the complete picture on the screen before a vertical retrace is performed?

12. Describe what is meant by the monitor specification .28 dot pitch. How is this measured?

13. Why should work inside the monitor's cabinet be performed very carefully by trained personnel?

14. In an 800 x 600 display, what is the minimum amount of video memory required to hold two complete screens of information, if 256 colors are possible for each pixel? (8 bits = 256)

15. List the typical components found inside the monitor's cabinet.

Lab Exercises

The lab manual that accompanies this book contains hands-on lab procedures that reinforce and test your knowledge of the theory materials presented in this chapter. Now that you have completed your review of Chapter 9, refer to the lab manual and perform Procedures 22, "Video Problem Isolation"; 23, "VGA Color Tests"; 24, "Screen Attributes"; and 25, "Windows 3.x Video Problems."

THE EXTENDED SYSTEM

PART IV

PRINTERS

LEARNING OBJECTIVES

Upon completion of this chapter and its related lab procedures, you should be able to perform the following tasks:

1. Discuss the types of paper handling common to different printer technologies.

2. List special considerations that must be observed when installing or repairing serial printers.

3. Identify a given type of cable connection between the printer and the computer.

4. Discuss data flow-control methods as they apply to serial printers.

5. Describe troubleshooting techniques associated with dot-matrix printers.

6. Relate symptoms to associated components in a dot-matrix printer.

7. Describe general alignment procedures for printhead mechanisms.

8. Describe the operation of a typical ink-jet printer.

9. Identify the major components of an ink-jet printer.

10. Describe troubleshooting techniques associated with ink-jet printers.

11. Relate symptoms to associated components in an ink-jet printer.

12. Describe the process for applying print to a page in a laser printer.

13. Identify the major components of a laser printer.

14. Describe troubleshooting techniques associated with laser printers.

15. Relate symptoms to associated components in a laser printer.

CHAPTER 10

Introduction

In many instances, you may desire a permanent copy of a computer's output. The leading hard copy output device is the character (letters, numbers, and graphic images) printer. This definition distinguishes the **character printer** (generally referred to simply as the *printer*) from the other hard copy output device referred to as an **X-Y plotter**. Plotters are typically used to create complex graphics and drawings.

Modern character printers, such as the one depicted in Figure 10.1, evolved from earlier typewriter technology. Many different mechanisms have been employed to imprint characters on a page. The earliest methods used with computer printers were simply adaptations of other print mechanisms used with typewriters and teletypewriters. These included print hammers (with characters carved on their faces) like those found in typical electric typewriters. In early computer systems, typewriters were often interfaced to the computer, to provide paper copies of the output. Another adaptation from typewriter technology was the use of IBM's golf-ball printhead, borrowed from the company's very popular Selectric typewriters.

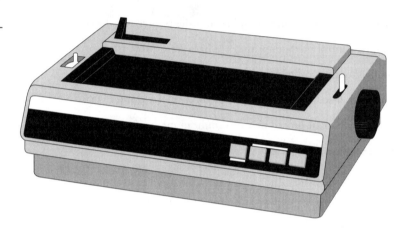

FIGURE 10.1

A typical character printer.

Printer Characteristics

As computer systems and their applications diversified, a wide variety of printer systems were developed expressly to meet the expanding needs dictated by modern computers. Newer printing methods—such as those used in dot-matrix, ink-jet, and laser printers, have yielded much faster and higher-quality printing capabilities than ever before.

Along with the diversity of printer systems came various methods of classifying printers. Character printers can be classified by their method of placing characters on a page (**impact** or **non-impact**), their speed of printing (**low** and **high speeds**), and the quality of the characters they produce (**fully formed**, **letter quality**, **near-letter quality**, or **dot-matrix**).

Printing Methods

The first method of differentiating among printers involves classifying them by how they deliver ink to the page. Basically, the printer can produce the character by causing the print mechanism, or its ink ribbon, to make a physical impact upon the page. Printers that operate in this manner are referred to as **impact printers**.

The other printing methodology delivers ink to the page without the print mechanism making contact with the page. Printers that produce characters in this manner are known as **non-impact printers**.

Impact Printers

Impact printers place characters on the page by causing a hammer device to strike an inked ribbon. The ribbon, in turn, strikes the printing surface (paper).

The print mechanism may have the image of the character carved on its face, or it may be made up of a group of small print wires, arranged in a matrix pattern. In this case, the print mechanism is used to create the character on the page by printing a pattern of dots resembling it.

Generally, the quality—and therefore, the readability—of a fully formed character is better than that of a dot-matrix character. However, dot-matrix printers tend to be less expensive than their fully formed character counterparts. In either case, the majority of the printers in use today are of the impact variety. Figure 10.2 depicts both fully formed and dot-matrix type characters.

FIGURE 10.2

Fully formed and dot-matrix characters.

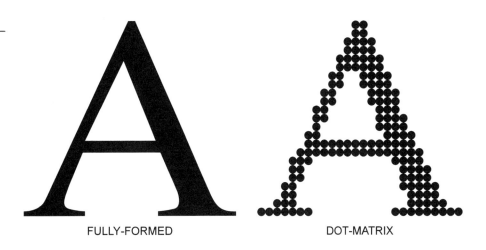

FULLY-FORMED   DOT-MATRIX

Non-Impact Printers

Several non-impact methods of printing are used in computer printers.

Older non-impact printers relied on special heat-sensitive or chemically reactive paper to form characters on the page. Newer methods of non-impact printing use ink droplets, squirted from a jet-nozzle device or a combination of laser/xerographic print technologies, to place characters on a page.

In general, non-impact printers are less mechanical than impact counterparts. Therefore, these types of printers tend to be more dependable. Non-impact printers also tend to be very quiet and faster than comparable impact printers. The major disadvantage of non-impact printers, however, is their inability to produce **carbon copies**.

Non-impact printers tend to occupy the extreme ends of the printer price range. Most of the less expensive printers are non-impact, as are most of the very expensive high-speed printers.

Character Types

Basically, two methods exist for creating characters on a page. One method produces a character that is fully shaped and fully filled-in. This type of character is called a fully formed character. The other method involves placing dots on the page in strategic patterns to fool the eye into seeing a character. This type of character is referred to as a dot-matrix character.

The quality of fully formed characters is excellent. However, creative choices in print fonts and sizes tend to be somewhat limited. To change the size or shape of a character, you must change the print mechanism. Conversely, the flexibility of using dots to create characters means that the shape of the characters can be altered as the document is being created. The quality of dot-matrix characters runs from extremely poor to extremely good, depending on the print mechanism.

Fully Formed Characters

The first, fully formed impact print mechanism devised for computer printers was the **daisy wheel**, depicted in Figure 10.3. Introduced by Diablo, the daisy wheel contained an embossed character on each petal. The center hub rotated until the correct character faced the print area. Then a single hammer struck the petal, which struck the ribbon, which, in turn, struck the paper. The daisy wheel could easily be interchanged with other daisy wheels containing different fonts. The original daisy wheels were metal, but newer models are plastic and correspondingly lighter, faster, and more energy-efficient.

FIGURE 10.3

The daisy wheel.

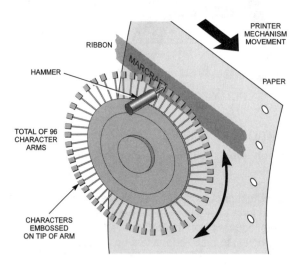

All the fully formed impact printing mechanisms discussed so far print one character at a time. Of the methods discussed, the daisy wheel is by far the fastest. However, for higher-speed letter-quality printing, characters must be printed a line at a time. This requires a line printer.

Dot-Matrix Characters

Dot-matrix characters are not fully formed characters. Instead, dot-matrix characters are produced by printing a dot pattern representing the character, as illustrated in Figure 10.4. The reader's eye fills in the gaps between the dots. Today's dot-matrix printers offer good speed, high-quality characters that approach those created by good typewriters, and nearly limitless printing flexibility.

FIGURE 10.4

Dot-matrix characters.

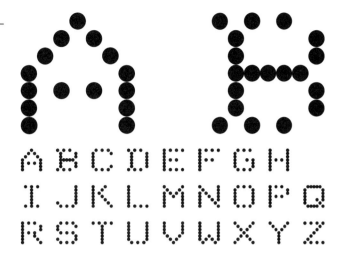

Basically, the printhead in a dot-matrix printer is a vertical column of print wires that are controlled by electromagnets, as depicted in Figure 10.5. Dots are created on the paper by energizing selected electromagnets, which extend the desired print wires from the printhead. The print wires impact an ink ribbon, which impacts the paper. It's important to note that the entire character is not printed in a single instant of time. A typical printhead may contain 9, 18, or 24 print wires. The number of print wires used in the printhead is a major determining factor when discussing a printer's character quality.

FIGURE 10.5

Dot-matrix printer pinheads.

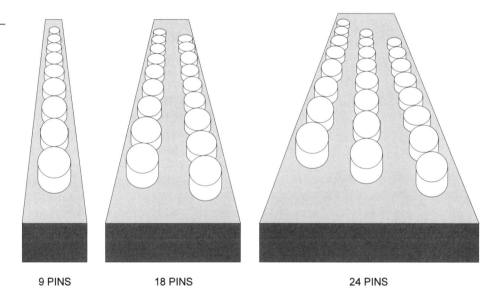

9 PINS   18 PINS   24 PINS

The *matrix* portion of this printer's name is derived from the manner in which the page is subdivided for printing. The page is divided into a number of horizontal rows, or text lines. Each row is divided into groups of columns, called **character cells**. Character cells define the area in which a single character is printed. The size of the character cell is expressed in terms of **pitch**, or the number of characters printed per inch. Within the print cell, the matrix dimensions of the character are defined.

The density of the dots within the character cell determines the quality of the character printed. Common matrix sizes are 5-by-7, 24-by-9, and 36-by-18, to mention only a few of those available. The more dots the printhead produces within the character cell, the better the character looks. This is because the dots are closer together, making the character appear more fully formed and easier to read.

Fonts

The term **font** refers to variations in the size and style of characters. With true fully formed characters, typically only one font is available unless you change the physical printing element. However, all other printing methods typically offer a wide variety of font types and sizes.

Three common classifications of character fonts exist: **bitmapped** (or **raster-scanned**) **fonts**, **vector-based fonts**, and **TrueType outline fonts**.

Bitmapped fonts store dot patterns for all the possible size and style variations of the characters in the set. Font styles refer to the characteristics of the font, such as normal, bold, and italic styles. Font size refers to the physical measurement of the character. Type is measured in increments of $1/72$ of an inch. Each increment is referred to as a point. Common text sizes are 10- and 12-point type.

Vector-based fonts store the outlines of the character styles and sizes as sets of mathematical formulas. Each character is comprised of a set of reference points and connecting lines. These types of fonts can be scaled up and down to achieve various sizes.

The vector-based approach requires much less storage space to store a character set and all its variations than would be necessary for an equivalent bitmapped character set. In addition, vector-based fonts can be scaled and rotated, but bitmapped fonts typically cannot. Conversely, bitmapped characters can be printed directly and quickly, but vector-based characters must be generated when called for.

TrueType fonts are a newer type of outline fonts commonly used with Microsoft Windows. These fonts are stored as a set of points and outlines that are used to generate a set of bitmaps. Special algorithms adjust the bitmaps so that they look best at the specified resolution. After the bitmaps have been created, Windows stores them in a RAM cache that it creates. In this manner, the font is generated only once when it is first selected. Afterward, the fonts are simply called out of memory, thus speeding up the process of delivering them to the printer.

Each TrueType character set requires an .FOT and a .TTF file to create all its sizes and resolutions. Figure 10.6 depicts the TrueType enabling window under the Windows Control Panel.

FIGURE 10.6

TrueType enabling window.

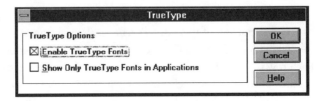

The Control Panel's **Character Map** icon can be used to access the Windows Printer fonts. The Character Map is depicted in Figure 10.7. This listing can also be used to insert special characters into a document.

FIGURE 10.7

Windows Character Map.

Printer Speeds

The second method of classifying printers is by their speed. Low-speed printers print 300 lines per minute (10–300 characters per second), and typical high-speed printers produce in excess of 20,000 lines of print per minute.

Most low-speed printers operate by printing one character at a time across the page, in serial fashion. Therefore, these printers are commonly referred to as **serial printers**. Serial printers are usually associated with personal computers and may use impact or non-impact printing methods. High-speed printers generally achieve their speed by printing characters a line at a time instead of a character at a time. Therefore, they are referred to as line-at-a-time, or simply, **line printers**. Due to their cost, these printers are normally used with larger computer systems. Most line printers use impact printing methods.

Two types of impact line printers exist:

▶ Rotating drum printers

▶ Chain (or band) printers

These printers are depicted in Figure 10.8. **Rotating drum printers** use a spinning, horizontal cylinder that has a complete set of characters embossed around its circumference for each character position across the page. While the drum is rotated at a constant speed, a bank of hammers strike the desired character at each print position. Actually, the hammers strike the page, which strikes the ink ribbon, which strikes the drum characters.

Band printers have characters embossed on a flexible metal band, and chain printers place character sets on a revolving chain. In both cases, the type sets are rotated horizontally behind the paper at a high rate of speed. When the desired character is in the proper print position, a hammer corresponding to that position is fired, imprinting the character on the paper. Both methods use one hammer for each print position along the page. Actually, the entire line is not printed at the same instant, but the characters are produced quickly enough to be classified as line printers. The timing logic for these printers is highly involved because the units must wait for proper character placement before printing.

Laser printers deserve the title of extremely high-speed printers. These printers place lines on the page so rapidly that they virtually print a page at a time. Hence, they are called **page printers**. Laser printers in the past were very expensive and were used only with high-speed, high-volume printing operations. However, recent developments in this technology have produced models in a price range that makes them very attractive for use with personal computers.

FIGURE 10.8

Rotating drum and chain printers.

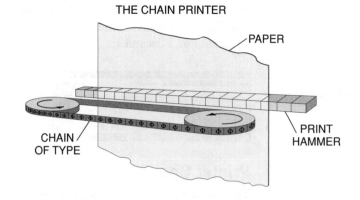

THE CHAIN PRINTER

PAPER

CHAIN OF TYPE

PRINT HAMMER

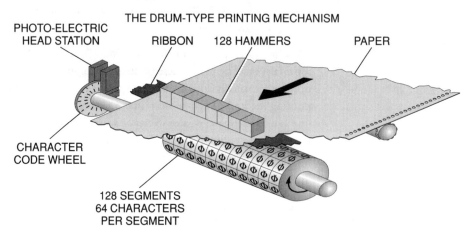

THE DRUM-TYPE PRINTING MECHANISM

PHOTO-ELECTRIC HEAD STATION

RIBBON   128 HAMMERS

PAPER

CHARACTER CODE WHEEL

128 SEGMENTS
64 CHARACTERS
PER SEGMENT

Print Quality

The last criteria for comparing printers is the quality of the characters they produce. This is largely a function of how the characters are produced on the page. Printers using techniques that produce fully formed characters are described as **letter quality** (**LQ**) printers; all elements of the character appear to be fully connected when printed. On the other hand, those using techniques that produce characters by forming a dot pattern are simply referred to as matrix printers; upon close inspection of a character, one can see the dot patterns. The characters produced on some matrix printers are difficult to distinguish from those of fully formed characters. These printers have been labeled **correspondence quality** (**CQ**), or **near-letter quality** (**NLQ**), printers. Often, dot-matrix printers have two printing modes: one in standard dot-matrix (sometimes called **utility mode**), and the other in near-letter quality mode.

Printer Mechanics

> By the very nature of their operation, printers tend to be extremely mechanical peripherals. During the printing operation, the print mechanism must be properly positioned over each character cell in sequence.

Loss of synchronization in contact printers can lead to paper jams, tearing, smudged characters, and/or printhead damage. Non-contact printers may produce totally illegible characters if synchronization is lost. The positioning action may be produced by moving the paper under a stationary printhead assembly, or by holding the paper stationary, and stepping the printhead carriage across the page. In the latter operation, the **printhead carriage** rides on rods extending across the front of the page, as shown in Figure 10.9.

FIGURE 10.9

The printhead carriage.

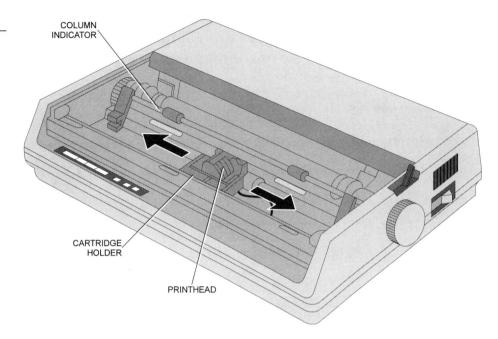

COLUMN INDICATOR

CARTRIDGE HOLDER

PRINTHEAD

Depending upon the type of print mechanism used, the carriage may be stepped across the page at a rate of one character cell at a time (fully formed characters) or in subcharacter cell steps (dot-matrix characters). Printing may occur in only one direction (unidirectional) or in both directions (bi-directional). In bi-directional printers, the second line of characters is stored in the printer's buffer memory and is printed in the opposite direction, saving the time that would normally be used to return the carriage to the start of the second line.

The printhead carriage assembly is stepped across the page by a **carriage motor/timing belt** arrangement. With many printer models, the user can select the number of character columns across the page, producing variable character spacing (expressed in **characters per inch**, or **cpi**), which must be controlled by the carriage position motor. Dot-matrix printers may also incorporate variable dot-densities (expressed as **dot-pitches**). Dot-pitch is also a function of the carriage motor control circuitry. Obviously, this discussion excludes continuous-stream ink-jet printers, in which printing is done by electromagnetic deflection of the ink drops, and laser printers, in which the beam is reflected by a revolving mirror.

Paper Handling

 A+ CORE 5.1

> In addition to positioning the print mechanism for printing, all printer types must feed paper through the print area. The type of **paper-handling mechanism** in a printer is somewhat dependent upon two factors: its speed and the type of form intended to be used with the printer.

Paper forms fall into two general categories: **continuous forms**, which come in folded stacks and have holes along their edges, and **single-sheet forms**, such as common typing paper.

Two common methods exist for moving paper through the printer:

▶ **Friction feed**. Uses friction to hold the paper against the printer's **platen**. The paper advances through the printer as the platen turns.

▶ **Pin feed**. Pulls the paper through the printer by a set of pins that fit into the holes along the edge of the form, as shown in Figure 10.10. The pins may be an integral part of the platen or may be mounted on a separate, motor-driven **tractor**.

FIGURE 10.10

A pin-feed tractor mechanism.

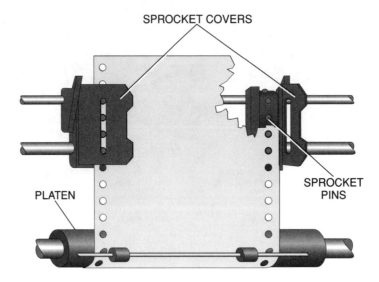

Friction feed is normally associated with single-sheet printers. The sheet-feeding system can be manual or automatic. Platen pin-feed and pin tractors are usually employed with continuous and multilayer forms. These mechanisms can control paper slippage and misalignment created by the extra weight imposed by continuous forms. Platen pin-feed units can handle only one width of paper, but tractors can be adjusted to handle various paper widths. Tractor feeds are used with very heavy forms—such as multiple-part, continuous forms— and are most commonly found on dot-matrix printers. Most ink-jet and laser printers use single-sheet feeder systems.

The gear trains involved in the paper-handling function can be treated as an FRU item in some printers. Although it is possible to replace the gears, or gear packs, in dot-matrix and ink-jet printers (if they can be obtained from the manufacturer as separate items), it is not usually economical to do so. Laser printers, on the other hand, are normally expensive enough to warrant replacing the gear trains and clutch assemblies that handle the paper movement through the printer.

Printer Controls

Although printers vary considerably from type to type and model to model, some elements are common to all printers. These elements are depicted in Figure 10.11.

As with most other peripherals, the heart of a character printer is its **interface/ controller** circuitry. The interface circuitry accepts data and instructions from the computer's bus systems and provides the necessary interfacing (serial or parallel) between the computer and the printer's control circuitry.

FIGURE 10.11

Common printer components.

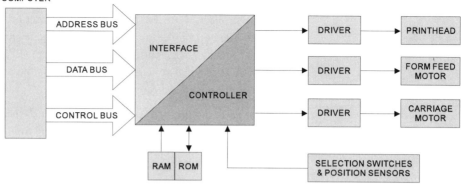

Functions of the interface circuitry include decoding the computer's instructions to the printer, converting signal logic levels between the two, and passing data to the printer's controller.

Parallel port connections are most efficient when the printer is located in proximity to the computer. If the printer must be located remotely, the serial interface becomes more appropriate. Many manufacturers offer both connections as standard equipment. Others offer the serial connection as an option. These two interfaces are covered in greater depth later in this section. A third, less common method of connecting printers to computers uses the SCSI interface as the connection port. As with other SCSI devices, the printer must be set up as a unique SCSI device and must observe proper connection and termination procedures.

The controller section receives the data and control signals from the interface section and produces all the signals necessary to select, or generate, the proper character to be printed. The controller also advances the print mechanism to the next print position and feeds the paper at the proper times. In addition, this mechanism generates status and control signals that tell the computer what is happening in the printer.

Due to the complexity of most character printers, a dedicated **microcontroller** is commonly used to oversee the operation of the printer. The presence of the onboard microprocessor provides greater flexibility and additional options for the printer.

Along with the dedicated processor, the printer normally contains onboard memory in the form of RAM, ROM, or both. A speed mismatch exists between the computer and the printer, however, because the computer is capable of generating characters at a much higher rate than the rate at which the printer can print them. To minimize this speed differential, printers typically carry **onboard RAM** memory buffers to hold characters coming from the computer. In this way, the transfer of data between the computer and the printer occurs at a rate that is compatible to the computer's operating speed. The printer obtains its character information from the onboard buffer.

In addition to character print information, the host computer can also store printer instructions in the buffer for use by the dedicated processor. The printer may also contain **onboard ROM** in the form of **character generators**, or **printer initialization programs**, for startup. Some printers contain EPROM, instead of ROM, to provide a greater variety of options for the printer, such as downloadable type fonts and variable print modes.

In some printers, the microcontroller, RAM chips or modules, and ROM/EPROM devices may be treated as FRU components.

Many laser printers come with a preset amount of RAM on board but enable you to upgrade the memory, if needed. Many high-speed laser printers require that additional RAM be installed to handle printing of complex documents, such as desktop-published documents containing large **encapsulated post script (EPS)** graphics files. Similarly, ROM and EPROM devices that contain BIOS or character sets are often socketed so that they can be replaced or upgraded easily.

As with the gears and gear trains discussed earlier in the chapter, the feasibility of replacing these units depends on whether you can obtain them from a supplier. In most cases, the question is not "Can the device be exchanged?" but "Does this make economical sense to exchange the device?" For a given printer type and model, the manufacturer's service center can provide information about the availability of replacement parts.

Basically, the controller must produce signals to drive the print mechanism, the paper feed motor, the carriage motor, and possibly such optional devices as single-sheet feeders and add-on tractors. Most of these functions are actually performed by precision stepper motors. Hardware driver circuits usually exist between the motors and the controller to provide current levels high enough to activate the motors.

The controller also gathers information from the printer through a variety of sensing devices. These include position-sensing switches and user-operated, front-panel-mounted mode-control switches. Some of the more common sensing switches include the **home-position sensor**, the **end-of-paper sensor**, and the **carriage position sensor**. The controller also responds to manual input command switches, such as **On/Off Line**, **Form Feed (FF)**, and **Line Feed (LF)**.

The sensors and switches can be treated as FRUs in many printers. This is particularly true with more expensive laser printers. In most printers, the entire **operator Control Panel** can be exchanged for another unit. This effectively changes all the user-operated input switches at one time.

Printer Installation

 A+ CORE 5.3

> Generally speaking, one of the least difficult I/O devices to add to a microcomputer system is a parallel printer. This is largely due to the fact that, from the beginning of the PC era, a parallel printer has been one of the most standard pieces of equipment to add.

This standardization has led to fairly direct installation procedures for most printers. Obtain an IBM Centronics printer cable, plug it into the appropriate LPT port on the back of the computer, connect the Centronic-compatible end to the printer, plug the power cord into the printer, load a device driver to configure the software for the correct printer, and print.

> Serial printers are slightly more difficult to set up because the communication definition must be configured between the computer and the printer. The serial port must be configured for speed, parity type, character frame, and protocol.

Regardless of the type of printer being installed, the steps for adding a printer to a system are basically the same. Connect the printer to the correct I/O port at the computer system. Make sure the port is enabled. Set up the appropriate printer drivers. Configure the port's communication parameters, if a serial printer is being installed. Install the paper. Run the printer's self-test, and then print a document. These steps are illustrated in Figure 10.12.

FIGURE 10.12

Printer installation steps.

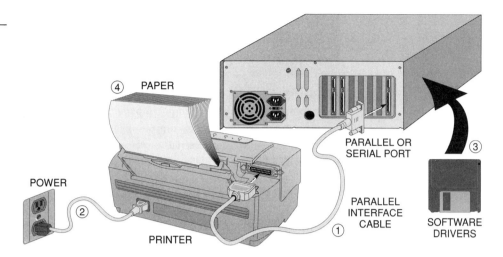

Printer Drivers

As with mice, printers require device driver programs to oversee their operation.

Device driver programs are necessary because, for example, a software developer who is writing a word-processing program will not have any way of knowing what type of printers will be used.

Although most printers use the same codes for alphanumeric data, they may use widely different control codes and special feature codes to produce special text and govern the printer's operation. Therefore, software producers often develop the core of a program and then offer a disk full of **printer drivers** to translate between the software package and different standard printers.

The user normally selects the driver program needed to operate the system through a configuration program that comes with the software. This function is usually performed the first time the software is loaded into the system. Figure 10.13 illustrates the functional position of a printer driver in the system.

FIGURE 10.13

Printer driver position.

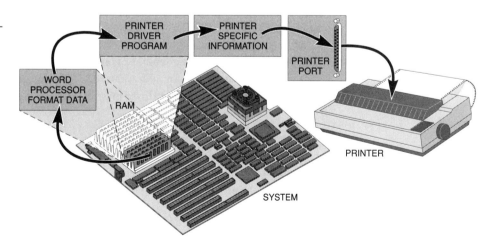

Driver programs may be supplied by the software developer, as part of the package, or by the hardware developer. It is often in the best interests of a hardware developer to offer drivers that make the hardware compatible with popular pieces of application software. Conversely, if a software developer is introducing a new piece of software, that software company often offers drivers that make the software compatible with as many hardware variants as possible.

Serial Printer Considerations

In some applications, it is simply impossible to locate the printer close enough to the host computer to use the parallel connection. In these cases, serially interfaced printers come into play. Printers using a serial interface connection add an extra level of complexity to the system. Unlike the parallel printer interface, which basically works in a plug-and-play manner on most systems, serial interface connections require additional hardware and software configuration steps. Serial printer problems basically fall into three categories:

▶ Cabling problems

▶ Configuration problems

▶ Printer problems

Cabling Problems

A+ CORE 1.4

Not all serial cables are created equal. In the PC world, RS-232 serial cables can take on several configurations. First of all, they may use either 9-pin or 25-pin D-shell connectors. The cable for a particular serial connection must have the correct type of connector at each end. Likewise, the connection scheme inside the cable can vary from printer to printer. Normally, the Transmit Data line (TXD, pin 2) from the computer is connected to the Receive Data line (RXD, pin 3) of the printer. In addition, the Data Set Ready (DSR, pin 6) is typically connected to the printer's Data Terminal Ready (DTR, pin 20) pin. These connections are used as one method to control the flow of information between the system and the printer. If the printer's character buffer becomes full, it signals the computer to hold up sending characters by deactivating this line.

Different or additional pin interconnections can be required for other printer models. The actual implementation of the RS-232 connection is solely up to the printer manufacturer. Figure 10.14 depicts typical connection schemes for both 9-pin and 25-pin connections to a typical printer. The connection scheme for a given serial printer model is normally provided in its user's manual.

Configuration Problems

After the correct connector and cabling scheme have been implemented, the printer configuration must be established at both the computer and the printer. The information in both locations must match for communications to go on. On the system side of the serial port connection, the software printer driver must be set up to match the setting of the printer's receiving section.

First, the driver must be directed toward the correct serial port. In a Windows-based system, this is typically COM2. Secondly, the selected serial port must be configured for the proper character framing. The number of start, stop, data, and parity bits must be set to match what the printer is expecting to receive. These values are often established through hardware configuration switches located on the printer.

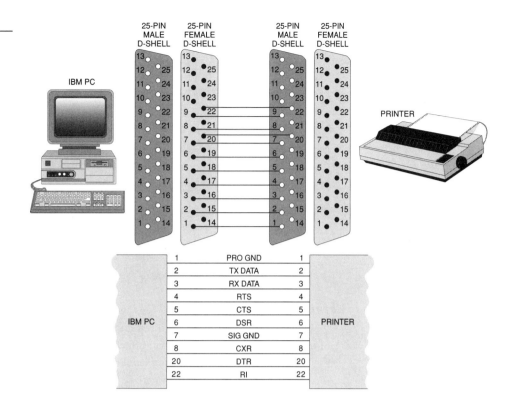

FIGURE 10.14

Serial printer connection schemes.

The printer driver must also be set up to correctly handle the flow of data between the system and the printer. Incorrect flow-control settings can result in slow response, lost characters, or continuous errors and retries. Flow control can be established through **software** or **hardware handshaking**. In a hardware handshaking mode, the printer tells the port that it is not prepared to receive data by deactivating a control line, such as the DTR line. Conversely, in a software handshaking environment, control codes are sent back and forth between the printer and the computer to enable and disable data flow.

> Two popular methods of implementing software flow control are **Xon/Xoff** and **ETX/ACK**. In the Xon/Xoff method, special ASCII control characters are exchanged between the printer and the computer to turn the data flow on and off. In an ETX/ACK protocol, ASCII characters for **End-of-Text** (**ETX**) and **ACKnowledge** (**ACK**) are used to control the movement of data from the port to the printer.

Basically, the computer attaches the ETX character to the end of a data transmission. When the printer receives the ETX character, it checks the incoming data and, when ready, returns an ACK character to the port. This notifies the system that the printer is capable of receiving additional characters. This concept is illustrated in Figure 10.15. In any event, both ends of the interface connection must be set to use the same flow-control method.

Serial communications standards and procedures are covered in greater detail in Chapter 11, "Data Communications." Consult this information for more information about character framing, error-detection and correction methods, and serial transmission protocols.

FIGURE 10.15

Software flow control.

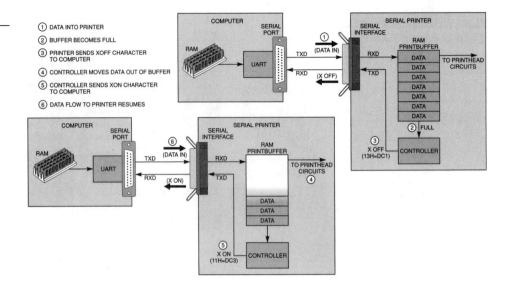

① DATA INTO PRINTER
② BUFFER BECOMES FULL
③ PRINTER SENDS XOFF CHARACTER TO COMPUTER
④ CONTROLLER MOVES DATA OUT OF BUFFER
⑤ CONTROLLER SENDS XON CHARACTER TO COMPUTER
⑥ DATA FLOW TO PRINTER RESUMES

Printer Problems

Problems associated with serial printers differ from those of parallel printer only in the area of the serial interface configuration. As mentioned in the preceding section on configuration, the protocol, character framing, and baud rate of the printer must match that of the system's interface. After ensuring that the interface settings match and that the interface is working, the steps of troubleshooting a serial printer are identical to those given for parallel interfaced printers. Therefore, the only steps that need to be added to the troubleshooting sections later in this chapter are those needed to validate the operation of the serial interface.

Installing Printers in Windows 3.x

To install printers through Windows 3.x, double-click the Printers icon in the Control Panel. This activates the Printers dialog box. The dialog box is divided into three separate sections labeled Default Printer, Installed Printers, and List of Printers. When Windows is first installed, no printers are listed in the Default Printer or Installed Printers sections. To install a printer, select the Add option, which causes the List of Printers to appear. Select the printer to be installed from this list. The specific brand and model of the printer can be obtained from the printer itself. When a match is found and selected, click the mouse on the Install option.

Windows searches drive A: for an appropriate printer driver for the selected printer. None of the drivers are included at the time Windows is installed because most of them are not needed, and because they consume hard-disk drive space. After Windows loads the driver, the printer appears in the Installed Printers section. Figure 10.16 depicts the Windows 3.x Printer Installation window.

Another common solution is to contact the manufacturer of the printer for an appropriate driver. Most of the time, the driver is included when the printer is purchased. When installing a printer that is not listed, select Unlisted Printer from the List of Printers section, and select the Install option. Windows then searches drive A: for the OEM driver software.

After all the drivers have been installed, select the desired printer from the Installed Printers section, using the Set as Default Printer option. The printer appears in the Default Printer section.

520   PART IV   THE EXTENDED SYSTEM

FIGURE 10.16

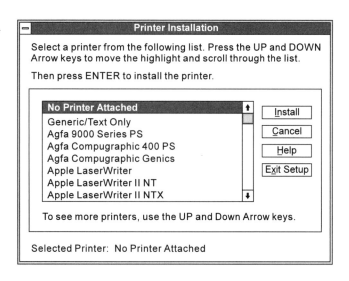

Printers in Windows 95

Printing is significantly improved in Windows 95. The Print Manager function and its support components have been integrated into a single print-processing architecture referred to as the **print spooler**. This integration provides smooth printing in a background mode and quick return-to-application time. The key to this operation lies in how the print spooler sends data to the printer. Data is moved to the printer only when it is ready. Therefore, the system is never waiting for the printer to digest data that has been sent to it.

Windows 95 automatically adopts any printers that have been established prior to its installation. If no printers are already installed, the Setup program runs the new Add Printer Wizard so that a printer can be installed. Each printer in the system has its own print window and icon from which to work. The wizard can be accessed at any time through the Windows 95 desktop and Start menu. In the Start menu, move to Setting and click Printers. Likewise, through the My Computer icon or the Control Panel window, double-click the Printers folder or icon.

To install a printer, open the Printers folder and double-click the Add Printers icon. From this point, the Printer Wizard guides the installation process. Windows 95 has built-in networking support, so the printer can be a local unit (connected to the computer) or a remote unit located somewhere on the network.

If the printer is connected to a remote computer (print server), the remote unit must supply the printer drivers and settings to control the printer. Likewise, the print server must be set up to share the printer with the other users on the network. To install the network printer, simply access the Network Neighborhood icon on the desktop, select the remote computer's network name and the remote printer's name, and right-click the Install option. After the remote printer has been installed, the local computer can access it through the Network Neighborhood icon.

If the printer is not recognized as a model supported by the Windows 95 driver list, OEM drivers can be installed from a disk containing the OEMSETUP.INF file.

To print an open file in Windows 95, simply move to the File menu and click the Print option. If the file is not open, it is still possible to print it by dragging its icon onto the desired printer's icon.

To view documents waiting to be printed from the print spooler, double-click the desired printer's icon. This displays the existing print queue. Unlike the Windows 3.x Print Manager, closing the Print window does not interrupt the print queue in Windows 95. The print jobs in the queue are completed unless the jobs are deleted.

Dot-Matrix Printers

A+ CORE 5.1   The stalwarts of microcomputer printing have been the dot-matrix impact printers.

> The components of a typical dot-matrix printer are depicted in Figure 10.17. They consist of a power supply board, a main control board, a printhead assembly, a ribbon cartridge, a paper feed motor (along with its mechanical drive gears), and a printhead positioning motor and mechanisms.

FIGURE 10.17

Parts of a dot-matrix printer.

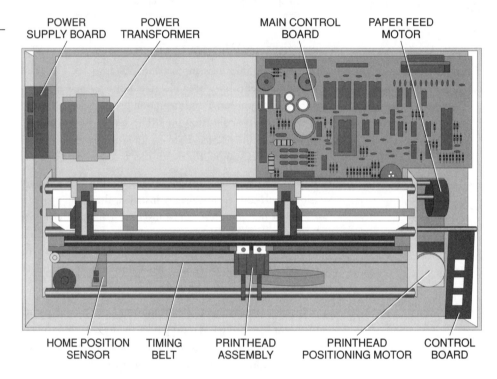

POWER SUPPLY BOARD   POWER TRANSFORMER   MAIN CONTROL BOARD   PAPER FEED MOTOR

HOME POSITION SENSOR   TIMING BELT   PRINTHEAD ASSEMBLY   PRINTHEAD POSITIONING MOTOR   CONTROL BOARD

The Power Supply

The power supply board provides various voltages to power the electronics on the control board. This unit also drives the printhead positioning and paper feed motors and energizes the wires of the printhead so that they strike the ribbon as directed by the control board.

The Main Control Board

The control board is typically divided into four functional sections, as described in Figure 10.18. These functional blocks include the following:

- ▶ The interface circuitry
- ▶ The character generation circuitry
- ▶ The printer controller circuitry
- ▶ Its motor control circuitry

FIGURE 10.18

*Logical parts of the control
board.*

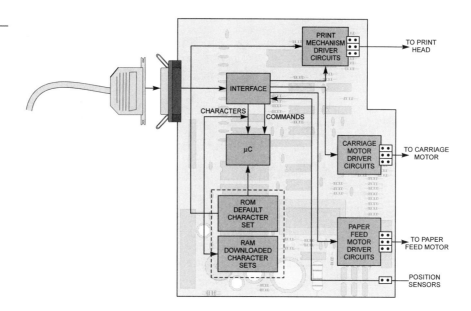

The control board contains the logic circuitry required to convert the signals received from the computer's adapter card into character patterns, as well as to generate the proper control signals to position the printhead properly on the page, fire the correct combination of printhead wires to create the character, and advance the paper properly. The onboard microcontroller, character generators, RAM, and ROM are found on the control board.

The status of the printer's operation is monitored by the control board through a number of sensors. These sensors typically include the following:

▶ Paper Out

▶ Printhead Position

▶ Home Position (for the printhead carriage)

Input from the printer's operator panel is also routed to the control board. Operator panel information includes the following:

▶ Online

▶ Form feed

▶ Line feed

▶ Power/paper out

The control panel may contain a number of other buttons and indicator lights whose functions are specific to that particular printer. Always consult the printer's user's manual for information about the control panel buttons and indicators.

The printer's interface may contain circuitry to handle serial data, parallel data, or a combination of the two interface types. At the printer end of a Centronics parallel port is a 36-pin connector, similar to the one depicted in Figure 10.19.

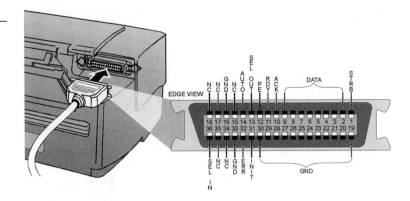

FIGURE 10.19

A parallel connection at the printer.

Dot-matrix printers process bit patterns in much the same way that CRT controllers do. The dot patterns are accessed from a character generator ROM. In addition to the standard ASCII character set, many printers feature preprogrammed sets of block-graphics characters that can be used to create nontext images on a page. Most manufacturers use EPROM (erasable-programmable ROM) character generators instead of the older ROM type. This enables their units to accept **downloadable fonts** from software.

Used with a high-quality printhead, a variety of typefaces—such as Roman gothic, Italic, and foreign language characters—can be loaded into the programmable character generator from software. In addition, it is possible for the user to create his own character sets, typefaces, and graphic symbols. Some manufacturers even offer standard bar-code graphics software sets for their machines.

Printhead Mechanisms

> The **printhead** is a collection of print wires set in an electromagnetic head unit. The printhead assembly is made up of a permanent magnet, a group of electromagnets, and a housing. In the printhead, the permanent magnet keeps the wires pulled in until electromagnets are energized, causing them to move forward.

The printhead is mounted in the **printhead carriage assembly**. The carriage assembly rides on a bar that passes along the front of the platen. The printhead carriage assembly is attached to the printhead positioning motor by a **timing belt**.

Figure 10.20 illustrates a typical dot-matrix printhead control circuit. Although the character generator may appear very similar to the one used with CRT controllers, the data must be processed differently due to the vertical nature of the printhead mechanism (as opposed to the horizontal nature of the CRT's scan lines). In this case, the portion of the character generator containing the dot pattern for an uppercase H is shown. The ASCII dot-column code required to access it is also presented. Each time the dot-column counter is pulsed, the address is incremented, the print wires are activated, and the printhead carriage is stepped over one place in the character cell.

The printhead positioning motor is responsible for moving the printhead mechanism across the page and stopping it in just the right places to print. The printhead rides back and forth across the printer on a pair of carriage rods. A timing belt runs between the printhead assembly and the printhead positioning motor and converts the rotation of the motor into linear movement of the printhead assembly. The printhead must stop each time the print wires strike the paper. If this timing is off, the characters will be smeared on the page and the paper may be damaged. The motor steps a predetermined number of steps to create a character within a character cell. Figure 10.21 illustrates a dot-matrix printhead delivering print to a page.

FIGURE 10.20

A typical dot-matrix printhead control circuit.

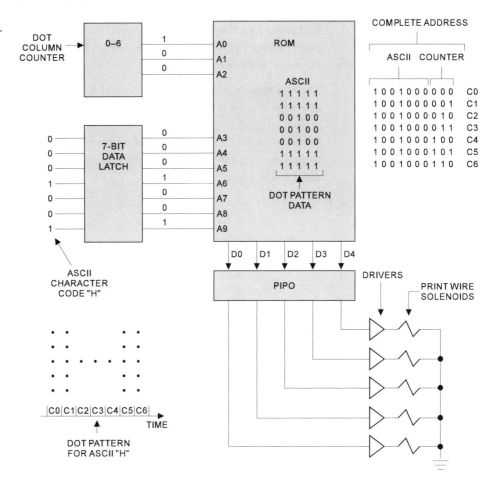

FIGURE 10.21

Dot-matrix printhead.

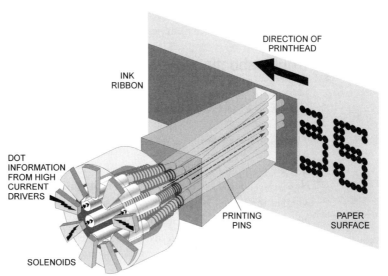

Paper Handling

The paper feed motor and gear train move the paper through the printer. This can be accomplished by driving the platen assembly. The platen can be used in two different ways to move the paper through the printer. After the paper has been wrapped halfway around the platen, a set of rollers is used to pin the paper to the platen as it turns. This is **friction-feed paper handling**. As described earlier, the platen may have small pins that can drag the paper through the printer as the platen turns. In either case, the paper feed motor drives the platen to move the paper.

The feed motor's gear train can also be used to drive the extended gear train of a **tractor assembly**, when it is installed. The gears of the feed motor mesh with those of the tractor, causing it to pull or push the paper through the printer. To use a tractor, the friction-feed feature of the platen must be released. Otherwise, the tractor and the platen may not turn at the same rate, and the paper will rip or jam. The installation of a tractor assembly is illustrated in Figure 10.22.

FIGURE 10.22

Installing a tractor assembly.

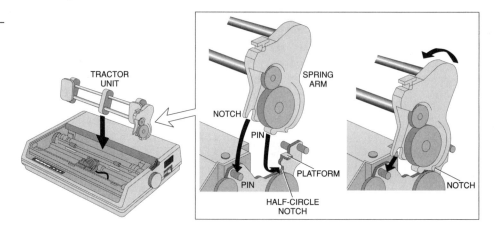

Color Printing

Another interesting innovation available with dot-matrix printers is **color printing**. Color printing capability can be divided into two parts: **dumb colors**, obtained by shifting a multicolor ribbon to the correct level, or **smart colors**, which are created by using multiple print passes to interlace dumb colors from the ribbon (double-strike mode).

Troubleshooting Dot-Matrix Printers

> The classical first step in determining the cause of any printer problem is to determine which part of the printer-related system is at fault: the host computer, the signal cable, or the printer.

Nearly every printer is equipped with a **built-in self-test**. The easiest way to determine whether the printer is at fault is to run its self-test. Consult the printer's user's manual for instructions in running its self-test. Some printers are capable of producing audible tones to indicate the nature of an internal problem. Refer to the printer's user's manual for the definitions of the coded beep tones, if they are available.

If the printer runs the self-test and prints clean pages, then most of the printer has been eliminated as a possible cause of problems. The problem could be in the computer, the cabling, or the interface portion of the printer. However, if the printer fails the self-test, you must diagnose the printer's problem. The following section presents typical problems encountered in dot-matrix printers.

The following are symptoms for dot-matrix printer problems:

- No lights or noise from printer
- Light or uneven print produced
- Printhead moving but not printing
- Dots missing from characters
- Printhead printing, but does not move
- Paper will not advance

Dot-Matrix Printer Configuration Checks

The presence of onboard microcontrollers means that modern printers are very flexible. As with other peripheral devices, printers can be configured to operate in different modes. Operating configuration information can be stored in CMOS RAM on the control board. Some configuration settings can be adjusted through DIP switches mounted inside the printer. These switches are read by the printer's microcontroller at startup.

In the case of dot-matrix printers, the configuration settings are normally entered into the printer through the buttons of its control panel. Typical dot-matrix configuration information includes the following:

- Printer mode
- Perforation skip (for continuous forms)
- Automatic line geed at the bottom of the page
- Paper-handling type
- ASCII character codes (7-bit or 8-bit)
- Basic character sets

Other quantities that can be set up include the following:

- Print font
- Character pitch
- Form length

Most dot-matrix printers contain two or three onboard fonts (character styles) that can be selected through the printer's configuration routines. Typical fonts included in dot-matrix printers are listed here:

- Draft
- Courier
- Prestige
- Bold Prestige

However, in many dot-matrix printer models it is also possible to download other fonts from the computer. The character pitch refers to the number of characters printed per inch. Common pitch settings include 10, 11, 12, and 14 dots per inch. Consult the printer's user's guide to find the definitions of such settings.

Dot-Matrix Printer Hardware Checks

To perform work inside the printer, you must disassemble its case. Begin by removing any add-on pieces, such as dust covers and paper feeders. Next, remove the paper advancement knob located on the right side of most dot-matrix printers. Turn the printer over, and remove the screws that hold the two halves of the case together. These screws are sometimes hidden beneath rubber feet and compliance stickers. Finally, it may be necessary to disconnect the printer's front panel connections from the main board to complete the separation of the two case halves. This procedure is illustrated in Figure 10.23.

FIGURE 10.23

Disassembling the printer.

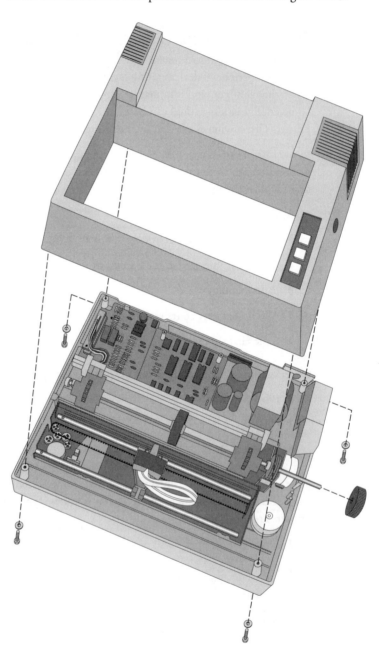

Dot-Matrix Printer Power Supply Problems

If the printer does not function and displays no lights, no sounds, and no actions, the power supply is generally involved. Troubleshoot printer power supply problems in the same manner as a computer power supply. As a matter of fact, the power supply troubleshooting routine is the same.

Check the online light. If the printer is offline, no print action will occur. A missing or improperly installed ribbon cartridge will also prevent the unit from printing. Install the ribbon correctly. Check the power outlet to make certain that it is live. Plug a lamp or other device into the outlet to verify that it is operative. Check to see that the power cord is plugged in securely to the printer and the socket. Make sure the power switch is on.

If everything is plugged in and is in the on position but still is not working, turn off the power and unplug the printer from the outlet. Remove the top of the printer's case, and find the power supply board. Check the power supply's fuse to make sure that it is good. If the fuse is blown, replace it with a fuse of the same type and rating. Do not replace a blown fuse with a conductor or a slow-blow fuse. Doing so could lead to more extensive damage to the printer—and possible unsafe conditions.

Also check the power supply and control boards, as well as the paper feed and printhead positioning motors for burnt components or signs of defect. Fuses do not usually blow unless another component fails. The other possible cause of excessive current occurs when a motor (or its gear train) binds and cannot move. Check the drive mechanisms and motors for signs of binding. If the gear train or positioning mechanisms will not move, they may need to be adjusted before replacing the fuse.

If none of the printer sections work when everything is connected and power is applied, you must exchange the power supply board for a new unit. Unlike the computer's power supply, the typical printer power supply is not enclosed in a protective housing and, therefore, presents a shock hazard anytime it is exposed.

To exchange the power supply board, disconnect the power cable from the printer. Disconnect (and mark) the cabling from the control board and any other components directly connected to the power supply. Remove any screws or clips that secure the power supply board to the case. Lift the board out of the cabinet. Install the new board, and reconnect the various wire bundles to it.

Ribbon Cartridges

The single item in a dot-matrix printer that requires the most attention is the **ribbon cartridge**. The ink ribbon is stored in a controlled wad inside the cartridge and moves across the face of the platen, as depicted in Figure 10.24. A take-up wheel draws new ribbon out of the wad as it is used. As the ribbon wears out, the printing becomes faint and uneven. When the print becomes noticeably faint, the cartridge should be replaced. Most dot-matrix printers use a snap-in ribbon cartridge.

To replace a typical ribbon cartridge, move the printhead carriage assembly to the center of the printer. Remove the old cartridge by freeing it from its clips or holders and then lifting it out of the printer.

Tighten the ribbon tension by advancing the tension knob on the cartridge, in a counter-clockwise direction, until the ribbon is taunt. Snap the cartridge into place, making certain that the ribbon slides between the printhead and the ribbon mask. Slide the printhead assembly back and forth on the rod to check for proper ribbon movement.

FIGURE 10.24

The printer cartridge.

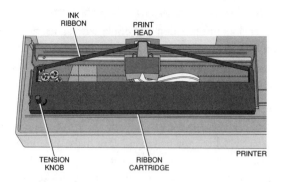

Paper Specifications

Another reason for faint printing is that the paper thickness lever is set to the wrong position for the weight of paper being used.

> Paper is specified in terms of its **weight** per 500 sheets at 22 inches by 17 inches (that is, 500 sheets of 22-by-17-inch 21-pound bond paper weigh 21 pounds).

The thickness setting can also cause smudged characters when the paper is too thick for the actual setting. In this case, adjust the thickness lever one or two notches away from the paper.

Printhead Not Printing

If the printhead is moving but not printing, begin by checking the printer's **head gap lever** to make sure that the printhead is not too far back from the paper. If the printhead does not operate, components involved can include the following:

- The printhead
- The flexible signal cable between the control board and the printhead
- The control board
- Possibly the power supply board

Run the printer's self-test to see whether the printhead will print from the onboard test. Check the flexible signal cable to make sure it is firmly plugged into the control board and that it is not damaged or worn through. If none of the print wires are being energized, then the first step should be to exchange the control board for a known good one of the same type. If the new control board does not correct the problem, replace the printhead. A power supply problem could also be the culprit if the printhead does not print.

A related problem occurs when one or more of the print wires does not fire. If this is the case, check the printhead for physical damage. Also check the flexible signal cable for a broken conductor. If the control board is delivering any of the other print wire signals, the problem is most likely associated with the printhead mechanism. Replace the printhead as a first step. However, if the problem continues after replacing the printhead, exchange the control board for a new one.

To exchange the printhead assembly, make sure that the printhead assembly is cool enough to be handled. These units can get hot enough to cause a serious burn. Unplug the printhead assembly from the control board. Slide the printhead assembly to the center of the printer, and rotate the **head locking lever** to release the printhead from the assembly.

Remove the printhead by lifting it straight up. Install the new printhead by following the disassembly procedure in reverse. Adjust the new printhead for proper printing. If the tops of characters are missing, the printhead is misaligned with the platen; it may need to be reseated in the printhead carriage, or the carriage assembly may need to be adjusted to the proper height and angle.

You may have to adjust the printhead mechanism to obtain proper printing. This procedure is illustrated in Figure 10.25. To print correctly, the printhead should be approximately 0.6mm from the platen when the head position lever is in the center position. Move the printhead to the center of the printer. Adjusting this setting requires loosening the nut at the left end of the rear carriage shaft. Using a feeler gauge, set the distance between the platen and printhead (not the ribbon mask). Tighten the nut, and check the spacing between the printhead and the platen at both ends of the printhead travel.

FIGURE 10.25

Adjusting the printhead spacing.

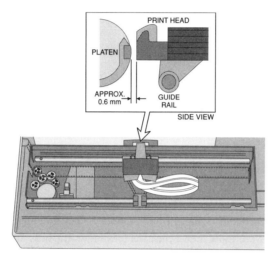

Finally, check the distance between the platen and the ribbon mask. This spacing should be 0.3 mm. If not, loosen the screws that hold the ribbon mask to the printhead assembly, and adjust the gap with feeler gauges. There should also be a 0.1 mm spacing between the printhead and the ribbon mask. After setting the various gaps, run the printer's self-test to check for print quality.

Printhead Not Moving

If the printhead is printing but not moving across the page, a single block of print will be generated on the page. When this type of problem occurs, the related components include the printhead positioning motor, the timing belt, the home position and timing sensors, the control board, and possibly the power supply board.

With the power off, manually move the printhead to the center of the printer. Turn on the printer to see whether the printhead seeks the home position at the far end of the printer. If the printhead moves to the end of the printer and either does not shut off or does not return to the center of the printer, then the home position sensor is malfunctioning and should be replaced. If the printhead moves on startup and will not move during normal printing, the control board should be replaced. If the printhead assembly will not move at any time, check to see whether the printer is in Maintenance mode. In this mode, the printer typically keeps the printhead assembly in the home position. If no mode problems are present, the printhead positioning motor should be replaced. If the print is skewed from left to right as it moves down the page, the printer's bi-directional mode settings may be faulty, or the home-position/end-of-line sensors may be defective.

Testing the timing sensor would require test equipment, in the form of a logic probe or an oscilloscope, to look for pulses produced as the printhead is manually moved across the printer.

Figure 10.26 depicts the components associated with the printhead's timing belt. To replace the timing belt, you must remove the belt from the printhead assembly. In many cases, the belt is secured to the printhead assembly with adhesive cement. This means that the adhesive seal must be cut with a single-edged razor blade or a hobby knife.

After the seal has been broken, it should be possible to move the belt out of the clips that secure it to the printhead assembly. Next, remove the belt from the drive pulley assembly at the positioning motor. You may need to remove the positioning motor from the case to gain access to the pulley.

FIGURE 10.26

Printhead timing.

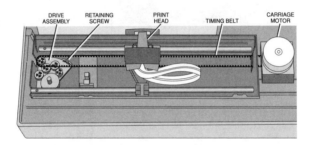

To reinstall the timing belt, apply a small drop of adhesive to the belt and reattach it to the printhead assembly. Wrap the belt around the positioning motor's drive pulley, and reinstall the motor. You must then adjust the tension on the belt. To do so, loosen the adjustment screw on the belt-tension adjustment plate. Tighten the timing belt until it does not move more than $1/4$ inch when the printhead is at either end of the carriage shaft and the belt is pressed inward. Tighten the retaining screw to lock the tension plate in place. Run the printer's self-test, and check the distance between the characters. If the spacing between characters is not uniform, replace the belt and perform the check again.

Paper Not Advancing

When the paper does not advance, the output will normally be one line of dark blocks across the page. Examine the printer's paper feed selector lever to make sure that it is set properly for the type of paper feed selected (whether friction feed, pin feed, or tractor feed). If the paper feed is set correctly, the printer is online, and the paper will not move, you must troubleshoot the paper-handling motor and gear train. Check the motor and gear train by setting the printer to the offline mode and holding down the Form Feed (FF) button.

If the feed motor and gear train work from this point, the problem must exist on the control board, with the interface cable, the printer's configuration, or the computer system. If the motor and/or gear train do not respond, unplug the paper feed motor cable and check the resistance of the motor windings. If the windings are open, replace the paper feed motor.

To replace the paper feed motor and/or gear train, remove the screws that hold the paper feed motor to the frame of the printer. Create a wiring diagram that describes the routing of the feed motor's wiring harness. Disconnect the wiring harness from the control board.

Prepare a drawing that outlines the arrangement of the gear train (if multiple gears are used). Remove the gears from the shafts, taking care not to lose any washers or springs that may be located behind the gears. After reinstalling the gears and new motor, adjust the motor and gear relationships to minimize the gear lash so that they do not bind or lock up. Use the printer's self-test to check the operation of the motor and gears. Never lubricate the gear train or platen assembly of a dot-matrix printer.

Ink-Jet Printers

A+ CORE 5.1

Ink-jet printers produce characters by squirting a precisely controlled stream of ink drops onto the paper, as illustrated in Figure 10.27. The drops must be controlled very precisely in terms of their aerodynamics, size, and shape, or the drop placement on the page becomes inexact and the print quality falters.

FIGURE 10.27

Ink-jet printers.

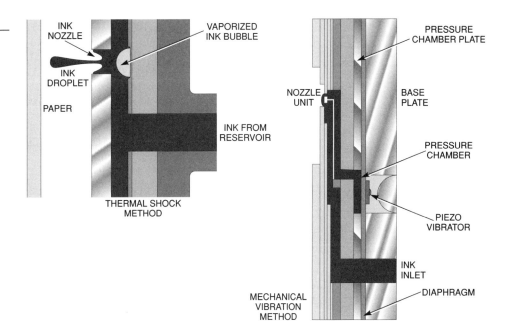

The drops are formed by one of two methods:

▶ Thermal shock heats the ink in a capillary tube, just behind the nozzle. This increases the pressure of the ink in the tube and causes it to explode through the opening.

▶ Vibrations from a piezo-electric crystal force ink through a nozzle.

Ink-jet printers use two methods to deliver the drops to the page: the **interrupted-stream** (drop-on-demand) method and the **continuous-stream** method. The drop-on-demand system forms characters on the page in much the same manner as a dot-matrix printer does. As the printhead mechanism moves across the character cells of the page, the controller causes a drop to be sprayed only where necessary to form the dot pattern of a character. Drop-on-demand printing is illustrated in Figure 10.28.

FIGURE 10.28

Drop-on-demand printing.

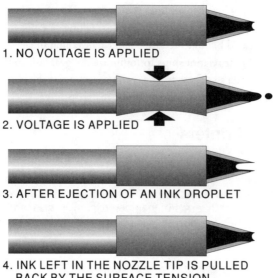

1. NO VOLTAGE IS APPLIED

2. VOLTAGE IS APPLIED

3. AFTER EJECTION OF AN INK DROPLET

4. INK LEFT IN THE NOZZLE TIP IS PULLED
BACK BY THE SURFACE TENSION

Continuous-stream systems, such as the one depicted in Figure 10.29, produce characters that more closely resemble fully formed characters. In these systems, the printhead does not travel across the page. Instead, the drops are given a negative charge in an ion chamber and are passed through a set of deflection plates, similar to the electron beam in a CRT tube. The plates deflect the drops to their proper placement on the page, and unused drops are deflected off the page into an ink-recirculation system.

FIGURE 10.29

Continuous-stream printing.

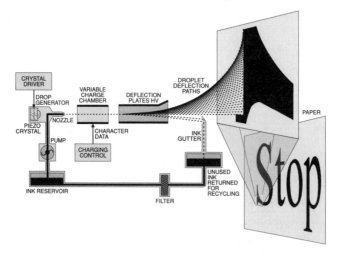

Although capable of delivering very high-quality characters at high speeds, continuous-stream systems tend to be expensive and, therefore, are not normally found in printers for the consumer market. Instead, they are reserved for high-volume commercial applications. The ink-jet printers in this market use drop-on-demand techniques to deliver ink to the page.

Some ink-jet printers incorporate multiple jets to permit color printing. Four basic colors may be mixed to create a veritable palate of colors by firing the ink jets in different combinations.

Ink Jet Printer Components

Aside from the printing mechanism, the components of a typical ink-jet printer are very similar to those of a dot-matrix printer. Its primary components are listed here:

- The printhead assembly
- The power board
- The control board
- The printhead positioning motor and timing belt
- The paper feed motor and gear train
- The printer's sensors

These components are illustrated in Figure 10.30.

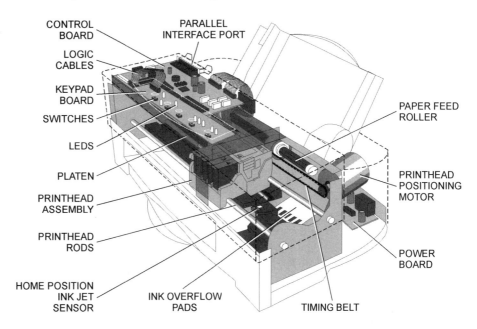

The Printhead Assembly

The ink cartridge snaps into the printhead assembly that rides in front of the platen on a rail or rod. The printhead assembly is positioned by a timing belt that runs between it and the positioning motor. A flexible cable carries ink-jet firing information between the control board and the printhead. This cable folds out of the way as the printhead assembly moves across the printer.

Paper Handling

The paper-feed motor turns a gear train that ultimately drives the platen, as depicted in Figure 10.31. The paper is friction-fed through the printer between the platen and the pressure rollers. Almost all ink-jet printers used with microcomputer systems are single-sheet, friction-feed systems. The control board, power supply board, and sensors perform the same functions in an ink-jet printer that they do in the dot-matrix printer.

Troubleshooting Ink-Jet Printers

As with the dot-matrix printer, the first step in determining the cause of an ink-jet printer problem is to determine which part of the printer system is at fault: the host computer, the signal cable, or the printer.

FIGURE 10.31

Ink-jet paper handling.

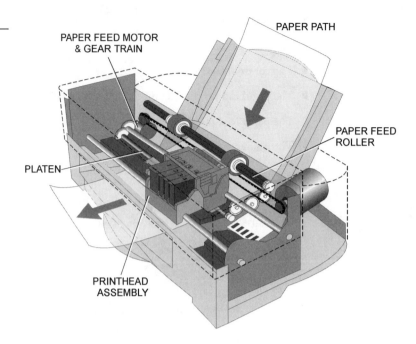

Ink-jet printers are equipped with built-in self-tests. The easiest way to determine whether the printer is at fault is to run its self-tests. Consult the printer's user's manual for instructions on running its self-tests.

If the printer runs the self-tests and prints clean pages, then most of the printer has been eliminated as a possible cause of problems. The problem could be in the computer, the cabling, or the interface portion of the printer. However, if the printer fails the self-tests, you must diagnose the printer problem. The following section presents typical problems encountered in ink-jet printers.

These are symptoms of ink-jet printer problems:

- No lights or noise from printer
- Light or uneven print produced
- Printhead moving but not printing, or printing erratically
- Lines on the page
- Printhead printing, but not moving
- Paper will not advance

Ink-Jet Printer Configuration Checks

The presence of the printer's onboard microcontroller means that modern printers are very flexible. As with other peripheral devices, printers can be configured to operate in different modes. Operating configuration information can be stored in RAM on the control board.

In the case of ink-jet printers, the configuration settings are normally entered into the printer through software. Typical configuration information includes the following:

- Page orientation (landscape or portrait)
- Paper size

- Collation

- Print quality

Landscape printing is specified when the width of the page is greater than the length of the page. **Portrait printing** is specified when the length of the page is greater than the width. In an ink-jet printer, the quality of the print is specified in the number of dots per inch produced. Typical ink-jet resolutions run from 180-by-180 dpi to 720-by-720 dpi. Ink-jet printers have the capability to download additional fonts from the computer.

> You can also configure the basic appearance of color and grayscale images produced by the ink-jet printer. A color ink-jet printer uses four ink colors to produce color images: cyan, magenta, yellow, and black (referred to as **CMYK color**). To create other colors, the printer prints a predetermined percentage of the basic colors in proximity to each other.

The different percentages of color combined determine what the new color will be. The eye does not differentiate the space between them; it perceives only the combined color. This is referred to as **halftone color**. Typical color configurations include setting up the Brightness, the Contrast, and the Saturation settings of images.

Ink-Jet Printer Hardware Checks

To perform work on the printer's hardware, you must disassemble the printer's case. Begin by removing all the add-on pieces, such as dust covers and paper feeders. Remove the screws that hold the outer panels of the case to the printer frame. The process of removing the access panels of a typical ink-jet printer is illustrated in Figure 10.32. The retaining screws are sometimes hidden beneath rubber feet and compliance stickers. Finally, it may be necessary to disconnect the printer's front panel connections from the control board to complete the disassembly of the case.

FIGURE 10.32

Printer case.

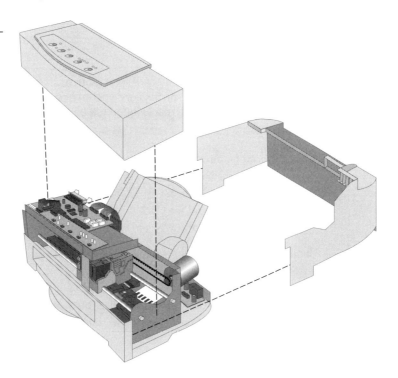

Power Supply Problems

If the printer does not function and displays no lights, no sounds, and no actions, the power supply is generally involved. Check the online light. If the printer is offline, no print action will occur. A missing or improperly installed ink cartridge can prevent the unit from printing. Install the ink cartridge correctly. Check the power outlet to make certain that it is live. Plug a lamp or other device into the outlet to verify that it is operative. Check to see that the power cord is plugged in securely to the printer and the socket. Make sure the power switch is on.

If the unit is plugged in and turned on but still doesn't work, turn it off and unplug it. Remove the top of the printer's case, and locate the power supply board. Check the power supply's fuse to make sure that it is good. If the fuse is blown, replace it with a fuse of the same type and rating. Do not replace a blown fuse with a conductor or a slow-blow fuse. To do so could lead to more extensive damage to the printer—and possible unsafe conditions.

Also check the power supply and control boards, as well as the paper feed and printhead positioning motors, for burnt components or signs of defect. Fuses do not usually blow unless another component fails. The other possible cause of overcurrent occurs when a motor (or its gear train) binds and cannot move. Check the drive mechanisms and motors for signs of binding. If the gear train or positioning mechanisms will not move, you may need to adjust or replace that unit before replacing the fuse.

If none of the printer sections work, everything is connected, and power is applied, exchange the power supply board for a new unit. Unlike the computer's power supply, the typical power supply in a printer is not enclosed in a protective housing and, therefore, presents a shock hazard any time it is exposed.

To exchange the power supply board, disconnect the power cable from the printer. Disconnect (and mark) the cabling from the control board and any other components directly connected to the power supply. Remove any screws or clips that secure the power supply board to the case. Lift the board out of the cabinet. Install the new board, and reconnect the various wire bundles to it.

Ink Cartridges

 A+ CORE 5.2

> The single item in an ink-jet printer that requires the most attention is the ink cartridge (or cartridges). As the ink cartridge empties, the printing eventually becomes faint and uneven, and the resolution of the print on the page diminishes.

When the print becomes noticeably faint, or when the resolution becomes unacceptable, you must replace the cartridge. Most ink-jet printers use a self-contained snap-in ink cartridge, such as the one in Figure 10.33. Some models have combined ink cartridges that replace all three colors and the black ink at the same time. Other models use individual cartridges for each color. In this way, only the colors that are running low are replaced.

The ink cartridges can be popped out of the printhead assembly to inspect its ink jets. If any or all of the jets are clogged, it is normally possible to clear them by gently wiping the face of the cartridge with a swab. A gentle squeeze of the ink reservoir can also help to unblock a clogged jet. Using solvents to clear blockages in the jets can dilute the ink, however, and cause it to flow uncontrollably through the jet.

FIGURE 10.33

Self-contained snap-in ink cartridge.

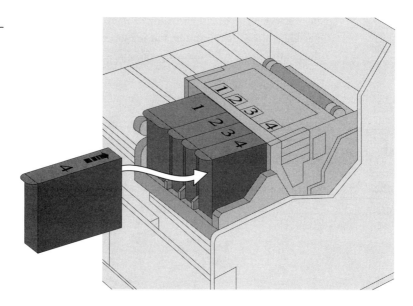

To replace a typical ink cartridge, move the printhead carriage assembly to the center of the printer. Remove the old cartridge by freeing it from its clips or holders and then lifting it out of the printer.

Printhead Not Printing

If the printhead is moving but not printing, begin by checking the ink supply in the print cartridge. The reservoir does not have to be completely empty to fail. Replace the cartridge(s) that appear(s) to be low. Some or all of the jets may be clogged. This is particularly common if the printer has not been used for a while. If the user's manual lists cleaning instructions, clean the jets and attempt to print from the self-test.

If the printer does not print during the self-tests, the components involved include the following:

> The printhead

> The flexible signal cable (between the control board and the printhead)

> The control board

> Possibly the power supply board

Check the flexible signal cable to make sure it is firmly plugged into the control board and that it is not damaged or worn through. If none of the ink jets are firing, the first step should be to exchange the ink cartridges for new ones. If a single ink jet is not firing, replace the cartridge that is not working.

Next, use the ohmmeter function of a multimeter to check the continuity of the conductors in the flexible wiring harness that supplies the printhead assembly. If one of the conductors is broken, a single jet probably is disabled. However, if the broken conductor is a ground or a common connection, all the jets should be disabled. Exchange the control board for a known good one of the same type. If the new control board does not correct the problem, replace the printhead. A power supply problem could also cause the printhead to not print.

If a single jet is not functioning, the output will appear as a white line on the page. If one of the jets is activated constantly, black or colored lines will be produced on the page. Use the steps above to isolate the cause of these problems: Replace the print cartridge, check the flexible cabling for continuity and for short circuits between adjacent conductors, exchange the control board for a known good one, and check the power supply.

Printhead Not Moving

If the printhead is printing but not moving across the page, a single block of print will normally be generated on the page. When this type of problem occurs, the related components include the printhead positioning motor, the timing belt, the home position sensor, the control board, and possibly the power supply. These components are depicted in Figure 10.34.

FIGURE 10.34

Printhead positioning components.

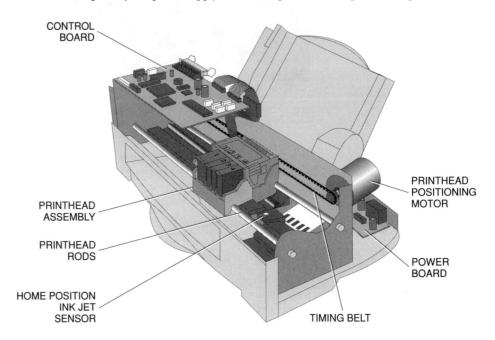

With the power off, manually move the printhead to the center of the printer. Turn on the printer to see whether the printhead seeks the home position at the far left side of the printer. If the printhead moves to the left side of the printer and either does not shut off or does not return to the center of the printer, then the home position sensor is malfunctioning and should be replaced. If the printhead moves on startup and does not move during normal printing, the control board should be replaced. If the printhead assembly does not move at any time, the printhead positioning motor should be replaced.

If characters are unevenly spaced across the page, the timing sensor may be failing. Testing the timing sensor requires test equipment, in the form of a logic probe or an oscilloscope, to look for pulses produced as the printhead is manually moved across the printer.

To replace the timing belt, you must remove the belt from the printhead assembly. In many cases, the belt is secured to the printhead assembly with adhesive cement; cut the adhesive seal with a single-edged razor blade or a hobby knife. After the seal has been broken, it should be possible to move the belt out of the clips that secure it to the printhead assembly. Next, remove the belt from the drive pulley assembly at the positioning motor. You may have to remove the positioning motor from the case to gain access to the pulley.

Paper Not Advancing

A+ CORE 5.2   When the paper does not advance, the output will normally be a thick, dark line across the page. Check the control panel to see that the printer is online. If the printer is online and the paper does not move, you must troubleshoot the paper-handling motor and gear train. Check the motor and gear train by setting the printer to the offline mode and holding down the Form Feed button.

If the feed motor and gear train work from this point, the problem must exist on the control board, the interface cable, the printer configuration, or the computer system. If the motor and/or gear train do not respond, unplug the paper feed motor cable and check the resistance of the motor windings. If the windings are open, replace the paper feed motor.

To replace the paper feed motor and/or gear train, remove the screws that hold the paper feed motor to the frame of the printer. Create a wiring diagram that describes the routing of the feed motor's wiring harness. Disconnect the wiring harness from the control board.

Draw an outline of the gear train arrangement (if multiple gears are used). Remove the gears from their shafts, taking care not to lose any washers or springs that may be located behind the gears. After reinstalling the gears and new motor, adjust the motor and gear relationships to minimize the gear lash so that they do not bind or lock up. Use the printer's self-tests to check the operation of the motor and gears.

Laser Printers

A+ CORE 5.1

The **laser printer** modulates a highly focused laser beam to produce CRT-like raster-scan images on a rotating drum, as depicted in Figure 10.35.

The rotating drum in a laser printer is coated with a photosensitive plastic, which is given a negative electrical charge over its surface. The modulated laser beam creates spots on the rotating drum. The spots written by the laser take on a positive electrical charge. A negatively charged toner material is attracted to the positively charged written areas of the drum. The paper is fed past the rotating drum and the toner is transferred to the paper. A pair of compression rollers and a high-temperature lamp fuse the toner to the paper. Thus, the image written on the drum by the laser is transferred to the paper.

FIGURE 10.35

A typical laser printer.

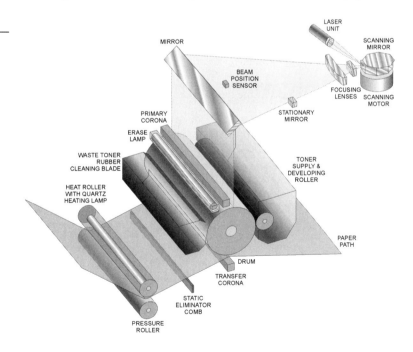

The laser beam scans the drum so rapidly that it is not practical to do the scanning mechanically. Instead, the beam is bounced off a rotating polygonal (many-sided) mirror. The faces of the mirror cause the reflected beam to scan across the face of the drum as the mirror revolves. Using the highest dot densities available, these printers produce characters that rival typeset text. Larger laser printers produce characters at a rate of 20,000 lines per minute. Laser printers intended for the personal computer market generate 6–45 pages per minute.

Laser Printer Components

The exact arrangement and combinations of components may vary among manufacturers and models in laser printers. However, the order of operations is always the same. The six stages of operation in a laser printer include the following:

▶ Cleaning

▶ Conditioning

▶ Writing

▶ Developing

▶ Transferring

▶ Fusing

To accomplish these objectives, all laser printers possess the following logical blocks:

▶ Power supply

▶ Control board

▶ Laser-writing unit

▶ Drum unit

▶ Fusing assembly

▶ Paper feed motor and gear train

▶ System's sensors

▶ Control panel board

The blocks of the typical laser printer are illustrated in Figure 10.36.

FIGURE 10.36

Block diagram of a laser printer.

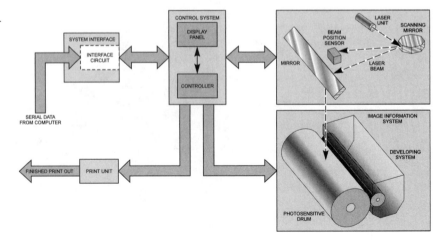

The laser printer power supply unit is the most complex found in any type of printer because it must deliver ac power to the fuser unit. This unit requires power for its fusing heaters and image erase lamps. The power supply also delivers a high-voltage dc supply (+1000 Vdc) to the toner transfer mechanisms in the drum area. The high voltages are used to create the static charges required to move toner from one component to another (for example, from the drum to the paper). Finally, the power supply unit must deliver dc operating voltages to the scanning and paper-handling motors, as well as to the digital electronic circuitry on the control board.

The control board contains all the circuitry required to operate the printer and control its many parts. The control board receives control signals from the computer and formats the data to be printed. This device also monitors the conditions within the printer and responds to input from its various sensors.

When data is received from the host computer, the control board generates all the enabling signals to place the information on the page as directed. The character information is converted into a serial bit stream, which can be applied to the scanning laser. The photosensitive drum rotates as the laser beam is scanned across it. The laser creates a copy of the image on the photosensitive drum, in the form of a relatively positive-charged drawing. This operation is referred to as **registration**.

Laser Printing Operations

Before the laser writes on the drum, a set of erase lamps shines on the drum to remove any residual traces of the previous image. This leaves the complete drum with a neutral electrical charge. A high voltage applied to the **primary corona wire** creates a highly charged negative field that conditions the drum to be written on by applying a uniform negative charge (–600v) to it.

> As the laser writes on the drum, that drum turns through the **toner powder**, which is attracted to the charged image on the drum.

Toner is a very fine powder bonded to iron particles that are attracted to the charges written on the drum. The **developer roller** in the toner cartridge turns as the drum turns and expels a measured amount of toner past a restricting blade, as illustrated in Figure 10.37. A regulating ac voltage assists the toner in leaving the cartridge but also pulls some excess toner from the drum. Excess toner is recycled within the toner cartridge so that it can be used again.

FIGURE 10.37

The developer roller.

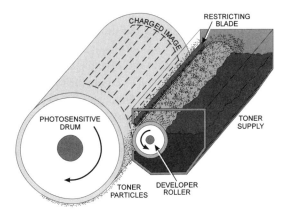

Great care should be taken when installing a new drum unit. Exposing the drum to light for more than a few minutes may damage it. The drum should never be touched, as this, too, can ruin its surface. Keep the unit away from dust and dirt, as well as away from humidity and high-temperature areas.

The **transfer corona wire** (transfer roller) is responsible for transferring the toner from the drum to the paper. The toner is transferred to the paper because of the highly positive charge the transfer corona wire applies to the paper. The positive charge attracts the negative toner particles away from the drum and onto the page. A special static-eliminator comb acts to prevent the positively charged paper from sticking to the negatively charged drum.

After the image has been transferred to the paper, a pair of **compression rollers** in the fusing unit act to press the toner particles into the paper as they melt them to it. The top compression roller, known as the **fusing roller**, is heated by a quartz lamp. This roller melts the toner to the paper as it exits the unit, and the lower roller applies pressure to the paper. A cleaning pad removes excess particles and applies a silicon lubricant to the roller to prevent toner from sticking to the Teflon-coated fusing roller. A demonstration of the complete transfer process is illustrated in Figure 10.38.

FIGURE 10.38

The transfer process.

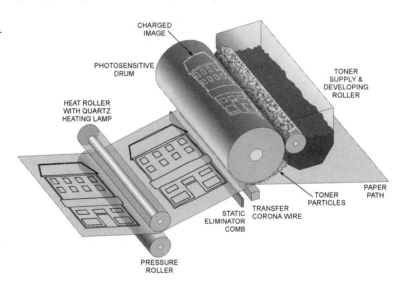

Component Variations

In Hewlett-Packard printers, the main portion of the printing system is contained in the electrophotographic cartridge. This cartridge contains the toner supply, the corona wire, the drum assembly, and the developing roller. The H-P configuration is depicted in Figure 10.39.

In other laser printers, such as the one depicted in Figure 10.40, the basic components are combined so that the printer consists of a developer unit, a toner cartridge, a drum unit, a fuser unit, and a cleaning pad. In this case, the developer unit and toner cartridge are separate units. With this configuration, changing the toner does not involve changing some of the other wear-prone components. Although it is less expensive to change toner, pay attention to how much the other units are wearing. Notice that the photosensitive drum is also a separate component.

FIGURE 10.39

The HP cartridge configuration.

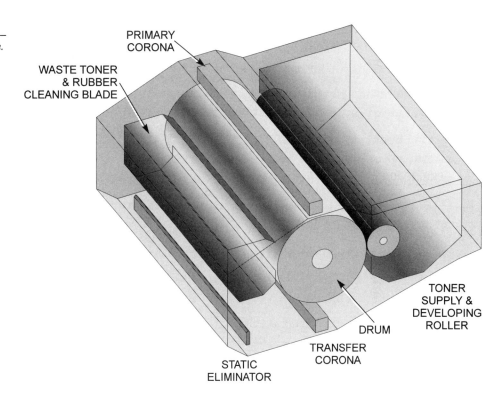

PRIMARY
CORONA

WASTE TONER
& RUBBER
CLEANING BLADE

TONER
SUPPLY &
DEVELOPING
ROLLER

DRUM

TRANSFER
CORONA

STATIC
ELIMINATOR

FIGURE 10.40

*Basic components of a laser
printer.*

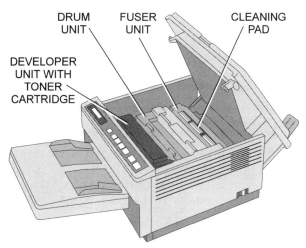

DRUM
UNIT

FUSER
UNIT

CLEANING
PAD

DEVELOPER
UNIT WITH
TONER
CARTRIDGE

Paper Handling

Laser printers are very mechanical in nature. The paper-handling motor and the gear train
assembly perform a tremendous number of operations to process a single sheet of paper.
The paper transport mechanics must pick up a page from the paper tray and move it into
the printer's registration area. After the drum has been written with the image, the paper-
handling mechanism moves the paper into registration. A roller system moves the page past
the drum and into the fusing unit. When the page exits through the fusing rollers, the
printer senses that the page has exited and resets itself to wait for another page to print.

In addition to the motor and gear train, the printer uses a number of sensors and solenoid-
actuated clutches to control the paper movement. Solenoids are used to engage and disen-
gage different gear scts and clutches at appropriate times during the printing process.

A typical laser printer has sensors to determine what paper trays are installed, what size paper is in them, and whether the tray is empty. Sensors also track the movement of the paper through each stage of the printer. This means that the controller knows where the page is at all times and can sequence the activities of the solenoids and clutches properly.

Figure 10.41 summarizes the sensors found in a typical laser printer.

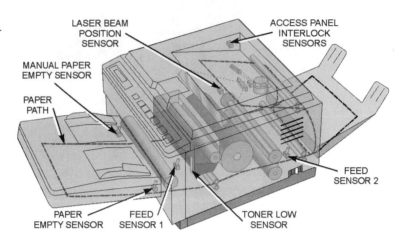

If the page does not show up at the next sensor at the appropriate time, the printer knows that a paper jam has occurred and creates an error message that indicates the area of the printer where the jam occurred. When this happens, you must remove the paper from the inside of the printer and reset the print operation. Gaining access to the area of the printer where the jam is usually requires direction from the printer's user's manual. Always allow the printer to cool and turn off the machine before you reach inside it.

Another set of sensor switches monitors the printer's access doors to protect personnel from potentially dangerous conditions inside the printer. The **interlock switch** blocks the laser beam as a vision-protection measure. Likewise, the high-voltage supplies to various printer components are also shut down. To observe the operation of the printer, you must locate and bypass these interlocks. However, you should always be aware that these interlocks are present for protection, and great care should be taken when they are active.

Still other sensors are used to monitor the temperatures within different sections of the printer. A **thermal sensor** in the fusing unit monitors the temperature of the unit. This information is applied to the control circuitry so that it can control the fuser temperature between 140°C and 230°C. If the temperature of the fuser is not controlled correctly, it may cause severe damage to the printer and present a potential fire hazard. A thermal fuse protects the fuser assembly from overheating and damaging the printer. The thermal fuse should normally snap back after the temperature condition is cleared. If the switch is open under cool conditions, it must be replaced. This is normally an indication that the thermal sensor has failed or that the fuser assembly has been installed improperly.

When the laser beam is turned on, a **beam detector sensor** in the writing unit alerts the control circuitry that the writing process has begun. This signal synchronizes the beginning of the laser-modulating data, with the beginning of the scan line.

Troubleshooting Laser Printers

Many of the problems encountered in laser printers are similar to those found in other printer types. For example, notice that most of the symptoms listed in the following section relate to the printer not printing, not printing correctly, and not moving paper through the printer.

Due to the extreme complexity of the laser printer's paper-handling system, paper jams are a common problem. This problem tends to increase in frequency as the printer's components wear from use. Basically, paper jams occur in all three main sections of the printer:

- The **pickup area**
- The **registration area**
- The fusing area

If the rubber separation pad in the pickup area is worn excessively, more than one sheet of paper may be drawn into the printer, causing it to jam. Furthermore, if additional paper-handling features, such as duplexers (for double-sided copying) and collators (for sorting) are added, they can contribute to the possibility of jams as they wear. Paper problems can also cause jams to occur. Using paper that is too heavy or too thick can result in jams, as can overloading paper trays. Similarly, using the wrong type of paper can defeat the separation pad and allow multiple pages to be drawn into the paper, resulting in a jam. Using coated paper stock can be hazardous as well, because the coating may melt or catch fire.

Unlike other printer types, the laser printer tends to have several high-voltage and high-temperature hazards inside it. To get the laser printer into a position where you can observe its operation, you must defeat some interlock sensors. This action places you in potential contact with the high-voltage, high-temperature areas mentioned above. Take great care when working inside the laser printer.

The following are symptoms of laser printer problems:

- The printer is dead, power is on, but no printing occurs.
- The print on the page is light or washed out.
- A blank page is produced.
- Stains or black dust appear on the paper.
- Vertical lines appear on the paper.
- The printer will not load paper.
- The paper jams in the printer.
- A paper jam has been cleared, and the unit still indicates a jam is present.

Laser Printer Configuration Checks

As with other complex peripheral equipment, laser printers must be configured for the desired operational characteristics. The printer is an extension of the computer system and, therefore, must be part of the overall configuration. To make the system function as a unit, configure the computer, configure the printer, and configure the software. Review and record the computer's configuration information for use in setting up the printer and software. Configure the printer with the parameters that you want it to use, record these settings, and then set up the software to match. Consult the printer's user's manual for configuration information specific to that particular printer.

Laser Printer Hardware Checks

Variations in the hardware organization of different laser printers make it impossible to write a general troubleshooting routine that can be applied to all without being specific to one model. The following troubleshooting discussions are general and require some user interpretation to apply them to a specific laser printer.

Fortunately, laser printer hardware has become highly modularized, as described in Figures 10.39 and 10.40. This means that you can check entire sections of hardware by changing a single module. Unfortunately, the mechanical gear train and sensor systems are not usually parts included in the modules. Therefore, their operation must be checked individually.

Printer Is Dead or Partially Disabled

As usual, when the printer appears to be dead, suspect the power supply: The power supply can affect the operation of basically every section of the printer. In the laser printer, this is particularly complicated because three types of power are being delivered to the various printer components.

If the printer does not start up, check all the normal check points related to power supply (such as the power cord, the power outlet, internal fuses, and so on). If the printer's fans and lights are working, other components that are associated with a defective power supply include the following:

- Main motor and gear train
- High-voltage corona wires
- Drum assembly
- Fusing rollers

Four basic reasons can explain why the main motor may not run when the printer is supposed to print:

- The portion of the power supply that supplies the motor is defective.
- The control circuitry is not sending the enabling signals to turn on the motor.
- The motor is dead.
- The gear train is bound up and will not let the motor turn.

In the latter case, you should hear sounds from the fan running and should see lights on the control panel. Isolate the failure, and troubleshoot the components involved in that section.

If the high-voltage portion of the power supply that serves the corona wires and drum sections is defective, the image delivered to the page will be affected. If the high-voltage section of the power supply fails, then the transfers of toner to the drum and then to the paper cannot occur. The contrast control will not be operational, either.

In cases of partial failure, the image produced will have a washed-out appearance. Replace the high-voltage section of the power supply and/or the drum unit. If a separate corona wire is used, let the printer cool off sufficiently, and replace the wire. Never reach into the high-voltage, high-temperature corona area while power is applied to the printer. Also avoid placing conductive instruments in this area.

If the dc portion of the power supply fails, the laser beam will not be produced, and a "Missing Beam" error message will occur. The components involved in this error are the laser/scanning module, the control board, and the dc portion of the power supply. Replace the L/S module, the dc portion of the power supply, and the main control board.

When the heating element or lamp in the fusing area does not receive adequate ac power from the power supply, the toner will not affix to the page as it should. This condition results in smudged output.

If the printer remains in a constant state of startup, this is equivalent to the computer not passing the POST tests portion of the boot-up process. If the printer starts up to an offline condition, a problem likely exists between the printer and the host computer's interface. Disconnect the interface cable, and check to see whether the printer starts up to a ready state. If so, then the problem is in the host computer, its interface, its configuration, or its signal cable. Troubleshoot the system in this direction.

If the printer still does not start up, note the error message produced, and check the sections of the printer related to that section. Check to see whether the printer is connected to the system through a print-sharing device. If so, connect the printer directly to the system, and try it. It is not a good practice to use laser printers with these types of devices.

A better arrangement is to install or simply use an LPT2 port to attach an additional printer to the system. Beyond two printers, it would be better to network the printers to the system.

Print on Page Is Missing or Bad

A+ CORE 5.2 Many of the problems encountered in laser printers are associated with missing or defective print on the page. Normal print-delivery problems fall into eight categories:

- Black pages
- White (blank) pages
- Faint print
- Random specks on the page
- Faulty print at regular intervals on the page
- White lines along the page
- Print missing from some portion of the page
- Smudged print

A black page indicates that toner has been attracted to the entire page. This condition could be caused by a failure of the primary corona, the laser-scanning module, or the main control board. If the laser is in a continuous on condition, the entire drum will attract toner. Likewise, if the primary corona is defective, then the uniform negative charge will not be developed on the drum to repel toner. Replace the primary corona and/or drum assembly. If the problem continues, replace the laser-scanning module and the main control board.

On the other end of the spectrum, a white page indicates that no information is being written on the drum. This condition basically involves the laser-scanning module, the control board, and the power supply. Another white page fault occurs when the corona wire becomes broken, contaminated, or corroded so that the attracting charge between the drum and paper is severely reduced.

Specks and stains on the page may be caused by a worn-out cleaning pad or a defective corona wire. If the cleaning pad is worn, it will not remove excess toner from the page during the fusing process. If the corona wire's grid does not regulate the charge level on the drum, dark spots will appear in the print. To correct these situations, replace the corona assembly by exchanging the toner cartridge or drum unit. Also replace the cleaning pad in the fusing unit. If the page still contains specks after changing the cartridge, run several pages through the printer to clear excess toner that may have collected in the printer.

White lines along the length of the page are generally caused by poorly distributed toner. Try removing the toner cartridge and gently shaking it to redistribute the toner in the cartridge. Other causes of white lines include damaged or weakened corona wires. Check and clean the corona wires, if accessible, or replace the module containing the corona wires.

Faint print in a laser printer can be caused by a number of different things. If the contrast control is set too low, or if the toner level in the cartridge is low, empty, or poorly distributed, print quality can appear washed-out. Correcting these symptoms is fairly easy: Adjust the contrast control, remove the toner cartridge, inspect it, shake it gently (if it is a sealed unit), and retry it. If the print does not improve, try replacing the toner cartridge. Other causes of faint print include a weakened corona wire or a weakened high-voltage power supply that drives it. Replace the unit that contains the corona wire. Replace the high-voltage power supply. Make sure that latent voltages have been drained off the high-voltage power supply before working with it.

Faults in the print that occur at regular intervals along the page are normally caused by mechanical problems. When roller and transport mechanisms begin to wear in the printer, bad registration and print appear in cyclic form. This can be attributed to the dimensions of cyclic components such as the drum, developing roller in the toner cartridge, or fusing rollers. Examine the various mechanical components for wear or defects.

Missing print is normally attributed to a bad or misaligned laser-scanning module. If this module is not correctly installed, then it will not be capable of delivering lines of print to the correct areas of the page. Likewise, if the scanning mirror has a defect or is dirty, portions of the print will not be scanned on the drum. Another cause of missing print involves the toner cartridge and low, or poorly distributed, toner. If the toner does not come out of the cartridge uniformly, areas of missing print can be created. A damaged or worn drum can also be a cause of repeated missing print. If areas of the drum will not hold the charge properly, toner will not transfer to it or the page correctly.

Smudged print is normally a sign of a failure in the fusing section. If the fusing roller's temperature or pressure is not sufficient to bond the toner to the page, the print will smudge when touched. Examine the fuser unit, the power supply and the fusing roller's heating unit.

Paper Will Not Feed or Is Jammed

A+ CORE 5.2   If the paper will not feed at all, then the place to begin checking is the paper tray area. The paper trays have a complex set of sensors and pickup mechanisms that must all be functioning properly to begin the paper handling. Due to the complexity of the paper pickup operation, jams are most likely to occur in this area. Check the paper tray to make sure that it contains the correct size of paper. Each tray in a laser printer has a set of tabs that contact sensor switches to tell the control circuitry that the tray is installed and what size paper is in it. A mechanical arm and photo detector are used to sense the presence of paper in the tray. The various paper tray sensors are illustrated in Figure 10.42.

FIGURE 10.42

Paper tray sensors.

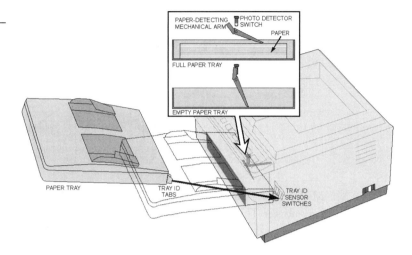

If the printer's display panel indicates a "Paper Out" error message, locate and actuate the paper detector by hand (lift it up). While holding the paper sensor, check the sensor switches by pressing each one individually. If the "Paper Out" message does not disappear when any of the individual switches is pressed, replace that switch. If none of the switches show good, replace the paper sensor and arm. Also check the spring-loaded plate in the bottom of the tray to make sure that it is forcing paper up to the pickup roller when the tray is installed in the printer.

The paper pickup roller must pull the top sheet of paper off the paper stack in the tray. The controller actuates a solenoid that engages the pickup roller's gear train. The pickup roller moves the paper into position against the registration rollers. If the printer's display panel shows a jam in the pickup area, check to make sure that the paper tray is functional, and then begin troubleshooting the pickup roller and main gear train. If none of the gear train is moving, then the main motor and controller board must be checked. The power supply board may also be a cause of the problem.

If the paper feeds into the printer but jams after the process has begun, troubleshoot the particular section of the printer where the jam is occurring: pickup, registration, fusing area, and output devices (collators and duplexers). This information is generally presented by the laser printer's display panel. Figure 10.43 describes the paper's path through a typical laser printer.

In each stage, you must check the action of the gear train in the area. Also inspect the various rollers in that stage for wear or damage. If the motor and gear train operate but no action occurs in the pickup roller or registration rollers, check the solenoid and clutches for these units.

Another cause for jams is the presence of some obstruction in the paper path. Check for pieces of paper that have torn loose and lodged in the printer's paper path. In most laser printers, mechanical components (such as the drum unit, the developing unit, or the fusing unit) are part of a replaceable module. If the motor and all the exposed gears are working, replace these units one at a time.

FIGURE 10.43

The paper's path.

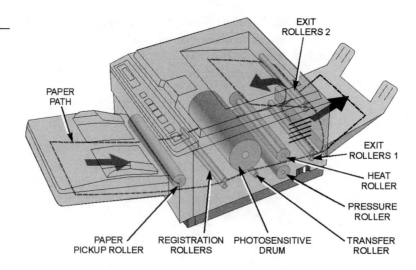

Many times, a paper-jam error will remain even after the paper has been removed from the laser printer. This is typically caused by an interlock error. Simply opening the printer's main access door should clear the error.

Windows-Related Printing Problems

A+ CORE 4.4

In a Windows-based system, the Windows environment controls the printing function through its drivers. When an application presents a particular font type for printing, Windows must locate or create the font codes. If the code is a TrueType code, Windows simply creates the bitmaps required and sends them to the printer. However, if the printer code is some other font style, then Windows must attempt to locate that font in the system.

If the requested font is not available or is not supported by the selected printer, then Windows must substitute a font for it. In these cases, the Windows Font Map is used to decide the most appropriate font to use. Windows bases this choice on several factors, including the character set, family, typeface, height, and width of the possible substitute font.

When Windows is forced to substitute fonts other than the one called for by the application, printing problems can occur. The printer can lock up or simply produce print that is either not correct or out of place.

If you suspect font-related printing problems, check to see that TrueType fonts are selected. Some font converters do not work properly with Windows. Therefore, their output is corrupted and will not drive the printer correctly. This should produce a GP fault message.

The presence of a corrupted font can be determined with the Windows Write text editor. Open the Write program, create a page-long document of MS Sans Serif text, and save the document to disk.

While holding the left mouse button, drag the mouse across the complete page to select the whole body of text. Click the Character entry on the toolbar, and select the Fonts entry from the drop-down list. Select a font from the list, and print the document. Continue this process using each font in the list until you locate the defective font.

Other factors that can cause font problems include low system RAM and third-party video or printer drivers. A minimum of 1MB of RAM is required to print from Windows 3.x, although 2MB is recommended. Use the memory optimization schemes described in Chapter 5, "Microsoft Windows," to free up as much memory as possible. Check the video driver setting in the Windows Setup window to determine which video driver is being used. Substitute the standard VGA driver, and try to print a document. Check the printer driver using the Control Panel's Print icon to make certain that the correct driver is installed.

Some types of drivers are known to conflict with the Windows TrueType fonts. These include the Adobe Type Manager, Bitstream FaceLift, and Hewlett Packard's Intellifont. If any of these font managers are present, they should be disabled and/or removed from the system for troubleshooting purposes.

Use the Notepad utility to examine the font substitution table (fontSubstitutes) in the WIN.INI file. This table determines what Windows substitutes for certain fonts. You can change the values of these entries through the DOS editor. The substitution table can also be accessed through the Substitution window under the Edit Substitution button of the Printer Setup's Advanced Options dialog box.

The TrueType section of the WIN.INI file should also be checked while the file is opened. Normally the system should be set up so that the following are true:

- TTEnable = 1
- TTifCollisions = 0
- TTOnly = 0

The 1 enables the system's TrueType fonts, and the 0s select TrueType as the first choice but also accommodate other fonts in the system.

If printer problems continue, try printing a sample file from a non-Windows environment. The best example of this is to copy the AUTOEXEC.BAT or CONFIG.SYS files to the LPT1 port. If this does not work from the DOS level, a hardware or configuration problem is indicated.

If this is the case, type **EDIT AUTOEXEC.BAT**. Check the file for a SET TEMP = command. If the command is not present, add a SET TEMP statement to the AUTOEXEC.BAT file. At the C:\>> DOS prompt, type **EDIT AUTOEXEC.BAT**. Create a blank line in the file, and type **SET TEMP=C:\WINDOWS\TEMP** into it. Save the updated file to disk, and reboot the system. Make sure to check the SET TEMP= line for blank spaces at the end of the line.

Is there a printer switch box between the computer and the printer? If so, remove the print-sharing equipment, connect the computer directly to the printer, and try to print from the DOS level, as previously described.

If the system prints from DOS but not from Windows, determine whether the Print option from the application's File menu is unavailable (gray). If so, check the Windows Control Panel/Printers window for correct parallel port settings. Make certain that the correct printer driver is selected for the printer being used.

If no printer or the wrong printer type is selected, simply set the desired printer as the default printer. To add the desired printer as the default printer, enter the Main window, double-click the Control Panel icon, double-click the Printer icon, and set the desired printer as the default printer.

Click the Setup button to examine the selected printer's settings. If these settings are correct, click the Connect button to ensure that the printer information is being routed to the correct port. This sequence is depicted in Figure 10.44.

FIGURE 10.44

*The Windows Printers setup
window.*

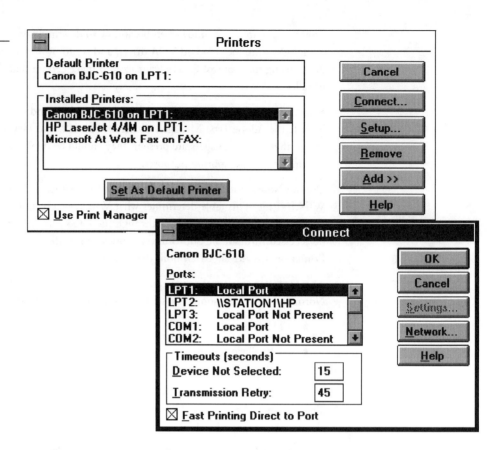

If nothing is being produced by the printer even though print jobs have been sent to it, check the Print Spooler to see whether a particular type of error has occurred. To view documents waiting to be printed, double-click the desired printer's icon. Return to the Printer folder, right-click the printer's icon, click Properties, and then select Details. From this point, select Spool Settings and select the Print Directly to the Printer option. If the print job goes through, you have a spooler problem. If not, the hardware and printer driver are suspect.

To check spooler problems, examine the system for adequate hard-disk space and memory. If the Enhanced Metafile (EMF) Spooling option is selected, disable it, clear the spooler, and try to print. To check the printer driver, right-click the printer's icon, select Properties, and click Details. Reload or upgrade the driver, if necessary.

If a Windows 95 printer operation stalls or crashes during the printing process, some critical condition must have been reached to stop the printing process. The system was running but stopped. Restart the system in Safe mode, and try to print again. If the system still does not print, check the print driver, the video driver, and the amount of space on the hard-disk drive. Delete backed-up spool files (.SPL and .TMP) in the SYSTEM/SPOOL/ PRINTERS directory.

DOS-based applications should have no trouble printing in Windows 95. Windows 95 has enhanced DOS printing capabilities in that they can take part in the new spooling function that usually results in quicker printing of DOS documents. If a particular DOS application has trouble printing, check other DOS applications to see whether they share the problem. If so, use the normal Windows 95 troubleshooting steps outlined previously to locate and correct the problem. If the second DOS application prints correctly, check the print settings of the original malfunctioning application.

In Windows 95, the Help function performs many of the diagnostic steps outlined here in a guided format. In addition, network printing problems and solutions are discussed in Chapter 11.

Key Points Review

The focus of this chapter has been printers.

- Impact printers place characters on the page by causing a hammer device to strike an inked ribbon. The ribbon, in turn, strikes the paper.

- Older non-impact printers relied on special heat-sensitive or chemically reactive Paper to form characters on the page. Newer methods use ink droplets, squirted from a jet-nozzle device, or a combination of laser/xerographic print technologies to place characters on a page.

- Two basic methods exist for creating characters on a page. One method places a character that is fully shaped and fully filled-in on the page. This type of character is called a fully formed character. The other method involves placing dots on the page in strategic patterns to fool the eye into seeing a character. This type of character is referred to as a dot-matrix character.

- The term *font* refers to variations in the size and style of characters. With true fully formed characters, typically only one font is available unless you change the physical printing element. Three common categories of character fonts exist: bitmapped (or raster-scanned) fonts, vector-based fonts, and TrueType outline fonts.

- By the very nature of their operation, printers tend to be extremely mechanical peripherals. During the printing operation, the print mechanism must be properly positioned over each character cell in sequence.

- In addition to positioning the print mechanism for printing, all printer types must feed paper through the print area. The type of paper-handling mechanism in a printer is somewhat dependent upon two considerations: its speed and the type of form intended to be used with the printer.

- As with most other peripherals, the heart of a character printer is the interface/controller that accepts data and instructions from the computer's bus systems and provides the necessary interfacing between the computer and the printer's control circuitry.

- In some printers, the microcontroller, RAM chips or modules, and the ROM/EPROM devices may be treated as FRU components.

- One of the least difficult I/O devices to add to a microcomputer system is a parallel printer. From the beginning of the PC era, the parallel printer has been one of the most standard pieces of equipment to add.

- Serial printers are slightly more difficult to set up because the communication definition must be configured between the computer and the printer. The serial port must be configured for speed, parity type, character frame, and protocol.

- As with mice, printers require device driver programs to oversee their operation.

- Two popular methods of implementing software flow control are Xon/Xoff and ETX/ACK. In the Xon/Xoff method, special ASCII control characters are exchanged between the printer and the computer to turn the data flow on and off.

- The components of a typical dot-matrix printer include a power supply board, a main control board, a printhead assembly, a ribbon cartridge, a paper feed motor (along with its mechanical drive gears), and a printhead positioning motor and mechanisms.

- The printhead is a collection of print wires set in an electromagnetic head unit. The printhead assembly is made up of a permanent magnet, a group of electro-magnets, and a housing.

- The first step in determining the cause of any printer problem is to isolate the part of the printer-related system at fault: the host computer, the signal cable, or the printer.

- Paper is specified in terms of its weight per 500 sheets at 22 inches by 17 inches (that is, 500 sheets of 22-by-17-inch 21-pound bond paper weigh 21 pounds).

- Ink-jet printers produce characters by squirting a precisely controlled stream of ink drops onto the paper. The drops must be controlled very precisely in terms of their aerodynamics, size, and shape, or the drop placement on the page becomes inexact.

- A color ink-jet printer uses four ink colors to produce color images: cyan, magenta, yellow, and black (referred to as CMYK color). To create other colors, the printer prints a predetermined percentage of the basic colors in proximity to each other.

- The single item in an ink-jet printer that requires the most attention is the ink cartridge(s).

- The laser printer modulates a highly focused laser beam to produce CRT-like raster-scan images on a rotating drum.

- As the laser writes on the drum, the drum turns through the toner powder, which is attracted to the charged image on the drum.

- A typical laser printer has sensors to determine what paper trays are installed, what size paper is in them, and whether the tray is empty. The printer also uses sensors to track the movement of the paper through each stage of the printer.

- Many of the problems encountered in laser printers include the printer not printing, not printing correctly, and not moving paper.

- The laser printer tends to have several high-voltage and high-temperature hazards inside it. You may have to defeat some interlock sensors. This action places you in potential contact with the printer's high-voltage, high-temperature areas. Take great care when working inside the laser printer.

At this point, review the objectives listed at the beginning of the chapter to be certain that you understand each point and can perform each task listed there. Afterward, answer the review questions that follow to verify your knowledge of the information.

Multiple Choice Questions

1. List three common pin configurations for dot-matrix printers.

    a. 10, 20, and 30 pins

    b. 5, 10, and 15 pins

    c. 9, 18, and 24 pins

    d. 3, 6, and 9 pins

2. Name the four basic components of a laser printer cartridge.

    a. Laser, toner supply, drum, and fuser

    b. Toner supply, corona wire, drum assembly, and developing roller

    c. Laser, toner supply, corona wire, and drum

    d. Toner supply, corona wire, drum assembly, and fuser

3. What is the purpose of the primary corona wire in a laser printer?

    a. It cleans the paper as it enters the printer.

    b. It conditions the drum for printing.

    c. It transfers toner from the drum to the paper.

    d. It fuses the toner to the paper.

4. What is the first action that should be taken, if the print generated by a dot-matrix printer becomes faded or uneven?

    a. Change the ribbon cartridge.

    b. Add ink.

    c. Adjust the print carriage.

    d. Add toner.

5. What is the first action that should be taken if the print generated by a laser printer becomes faded or uneven?

    a. Adjust the contrast control.

    b. Change the ink cartridge.

    c. Check the toner cartridge.

    d. Adjust the print mechanism.

6. What type of electrical charge must be placed on the corona wire to transfer toner from the drum to the paper?

    a. Negative

    b. None

    c. Neutral

    d. Positive

7. List the six stages of a typical laser printer.

    a. Pick up, registration, transfer, printing, fusing, and finishing

    b. Pick up, conditioning, transfer, developing, fusing, and finishing

    c. Cleaning, conditioning, writing, developing, transferring, and fusing

    d. Cleaning, registration, writing, transferring, fusing, finishing

8. List the fundamental parts of a dot-matrix printer.

    a. Power supply, microprocessor, tractor feed motor, printhead mechanism, and printhead positioning motor

    b. Power supply, interface board, paper feed motor, printhead mechanism, printhead positioning motor, and sensors

    c. Interface board, ink cartridge, printhead mechanism, printhead positioning motor, and sensors

    d. Controller, paper feed motor, ribbon cartridge, and printhead positioning motor

9. What type of ink delivery system is normally found in ink-jet printers built for the personal computers?

    a. Drop-on-demand ink delivery

    b. Continuous-stream ink delivery

    c. Impact ink delivery

    d. Compact-spray ink delivery

10. Describe what the specification for 60-pound bond paper means.

    a. 100 22-by-17-inch sheets weigh 60 pounds

    b. 500 8.5-by-11-inch sheets weigh 60 pounds

    c. 100 11-by-17-inch sheets weigh 60 pounds

    d. 500 22-by-17-inch sheets weigh 60 pounds

Review Questions

1. Referring to the Hardware Checks sections of the troubleshooting procedures for all three printer types, describe three general types of problems common to all printers. Describe the additional type of problem that dot-matrix and ink-jet printers have.

2. What are the common transmission parameters that must be set up for a serial printer interface?

3. Describe the purpose for using pin-feed mechanisms to move paper through the printer.

4. Describe the reason for using tractor-feed paper handling.

5. If the resolution of an ink-jet printer becomes unacceptable, what action should be taken?

6. Describe the function of the fuser assembly in a laser printer.

7. Describe the function of the primary corona (conditioning roller) in a laser printer.

8. If a laser printer continues to show a paper jam problem after the paper has been cleared, what type of problem is indicated, and what action should be taken?

9. List the three primary areas where paper jams occur in a laser printer, as well as any other areas where jams are likely to occur.

10. Describe two methods used by ink-jet printers to put ink on the page.

11. Does a successful self-test indicate that the printer is not the cause of the problem? List the parts of the system that can still cause problems if the self-test runs successfully.

12. How does a dot-matrix printer actually deliver ink to a page?

13. What functions do the printer's controller typically perform?

14. List four things that can be damaging to the photosensitive surface of the laser printer's drum.

15. List the basic components of an ink-jet printer.

Lab Exercises

The lab manual that accompanies this book contains hands-on lab procedures that reinforce and test your knowledge of the theory materials presented in this chapter. Now that you have completed your review of Chapter 10, refer to the lab manual and perform Procedure 30, "Printer Installation and Setup."

DATA COMMUNICATIONS

LEARNING OBJECTIVES

Upon completion of this chapter and its related lab procedures, you should be able to perform the following tasks:

1. Describe the three types of modulation commonly used in data communications.

2. Compare hardware- and software-oriented (code control) protocols.

3. Describe steps to troubleshoot modem problems.

4. Differentiate among typical LAN topologies.

5. Differentiate among different types of network media (10base2, 10base5, and so on).

6. Describe steps to troubleshoot LAN networking problems.

7. Define the term *wide area network (WAN)*.

8. Discuss basic concepts relating to Internet access (such as dial-up ISP connections).

9. Describe the function of routers, hubs, and bridges in network systems.

10. Discuss ISDN connections.

11. Describe FTP operations.

12. Discuss common Internet concepts and terminology (such as email).

13. Identify the purpose of the World Wide Web.

14. Discuss the purpose and use of an Internet browser.

15. Describe steps to troubleshoot WAN networking problems.

CHAPTER 11

Introduction

The most explosive area of personal computer use is in the realm of data communications. Increasingly, personal computers are being connected, and data communications can be as simple as connecting two units so they can *talk* to each other. This can be accomplished by wiring their serial or parallel ports together when the computers are in physical proximity to each other (up to a few feet). Communicating over longer distances requires additional hardware in the form of a modem or a network card and software in the form of drivers and protocols.

When more than two computers are linked so that they can share information, a network is formed. Networks in a relatively confined geographical area are called **local area networks** (**LANs**), and networks distributed over wider geographical areas are referred to as **wide area networks** (**WANs**).

Modems

⌒A+ CORE 1.1

Generally, the most difficult aspect of connecting peripheral equipment to a computer is obtaining the proper interfacing and cabling.

If the peripheral is located at some distance from the computer (greater than 100 feet), it cannot be connected by simply using a longer cable. As the connecting cable gets longer, its resistance combines with distributive capacitance along the wires to form a natural electrical signal integrator, which tends to distort digital signals until they are no longer digital.

To overcome this signal deterioration, a device called a **modem** (short for **modulator/demodulator**) is used to convert the parallel digital signals of the computer into serial, analog signals that are better suited for transmission over wire. A modem enables a computer to communicate with other computers through the telephone lines, as depicted in Figure 11.1.

FIGURE 11.1

Modem communications.

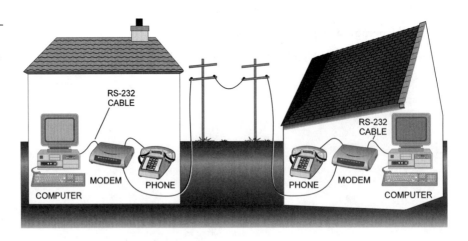

Some of the services available through the modem include **bulletin board services** (**BBSs**), user groups, and a variety of national and worldwide communication services, such as the Internet, Prodigy, and America Online. Many modems incorporate send/receive **facsimile** (**fax**) capabilities that enable the computer to correspond directly with fax machines around the world. Some newer modems incorporate digitized voice-transmission capabilities so that users can employ them as inexpensive telephones.

In its simplest form, a modem consists of two major blocks: a **modulator** and a **demodulator**. The modulator is a transmitter that converts the parallel computer data into a serial format for transmission. The demodulator is the receiver that accepts the serial transmission format and converts it into a parallel format usable by the computer or peripheral.

A modem, which sends signals in only one direction, is referred to as a **simplex-mode** modem. In the case of connecting two computers (or a computer and a remote terminal), it's desirable to transmit data in both directions. This can be accomplished by placing a separate modulator and demodulator at each end of the transmission line. In this configuration, a complete modem unit is present at each end of the line. Modems capable of both transmitting and receiving data are divided into two groups, based on their mode of operation. **Half-duplex mode** modems can exchange data with another modem, but only in one direction at a time, as illustrated in Figure 11.2. Because both modems contain a modulator and a demodulator, adding an extra conductor enables both modems to send and receive data simultaneously. This mode of operation is known as **full-duplex mode**.

FIGURE 11.2

Half- and full-duplex communications.

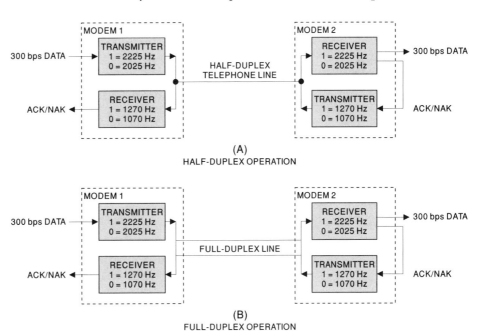

As the distance between terminals increases, it soon becomes impractical to use dedicated wiring to carry data. Fortunately, a very extensive communications network already exists: the public telephone network. Unfortunately, the phone lines were designed to carry analog voice signals instead of digital data. The design of the public phone system limits the frequency at which data can be transmitted over these lines. Again, the modem can be used to enable computers to use public telephone lines to exchange information.

A+ CORE 1.2

A modem can be either an internal or an external device, as illustrated in Figure 11.3. An **internal modem** is installed in one of the computer's expansion slots and has its own UART and interfacing circuitry. The **external modem** is usually a box installed outside the system unit and connected to one of the computer's serial ports by an RS-232 cable. External units also require the use of an internal serial port for its UART. Most computers contain two serial port connections.

In both cases, the modem typically connects to the telephone line using a standard four-pin RJ-11 telephone jack. A second RJ-11 jack in the modem enables an additional telephone to be connected to the line for voice usage. A still smaller four-pin RJ-12 connector is used to connect the telephone handset to the telephone base. Be aware that an RJ-14 jack looks exactly like the RJ-11, but it defines two lines to provide for advanced telephone features such as caller ID and call waiting.

FIGURE 11.3

Internal and external modems.

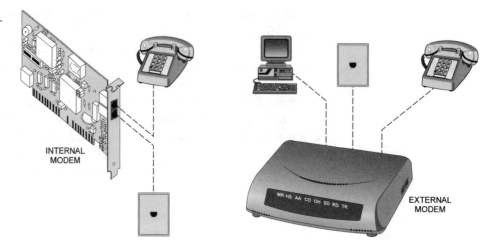

Understanding How Modems Work

The standard telephone system accommodates a range of frequencies between 300Hz and 3300Hz, or a **bandwidth** of 3000Hz. This is quite adequate for transmitting voice, but it severely distorts digital data. To use the audio characteristics of the phone lines to their best advantage, the modem encodes the digital 1s and 0s into analog signals within this bandwidth.

Modems are generally classified by their **baud rate**. Baud rate is used to describe the number of signal changes that occur per second during the transfer of data. Because signal changes are actually being limited by the telephone lines, the baud rate is the determining factor. Most modems begin encoding data into different transmission formats so that a number of data bits can be represented by a single signal change. In this way, the bit rate can be high even though the baud rate is still low. Common bit rates for telecommunications include 2400, 9600, 14400, 28800, and 33600 bits per second (bps). To complete a successful connection at maximum speed, the other party involved must have a compatible modem capable of the same baud rate.

FSK Modulation

The most common method of encoding data is a specialized form of **frequency modulation (FM)** called **frequency-shift keying (FSK)**. Using this method, a specific frequency (such as 1070Hz) is used to represent a "0" (or **space**), and a second frequency (such as 1270Hz) is used to represent a "1" (or **mark**). By using a second pair of frequency tones, the modem can both send and receive a message simultaneously. The sending (or originating) modem uses the frequencies shown in the first row in Figure 11.4, and the receiving (or answering) modem uses the frequency scheme shown in the second row.

FIGURE 11.4

FSK transmission.

		1MARK (Hz)	0SPACE (Hz)
Originate S16=0	Transmitter Receiver	1270 2225	1070 2025
Answer S16=0	Transmitter Receiver	2225 1270	2025 1070
Originate Self-Test S16=1	Transmitter Receiver	2225 2225	2025 2025
Answer Self-Test S16=1	Transmitter Receiver	1270 1270	1070 1070

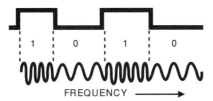

FREQUENCY ⟶

FSK is used in most low-speed, inexpensive modems to transmit data at a rate of 300bps. The terms *baud* and *bps* are sometimes used interchangeably. However, this is true only if a signal change is used to represent each bit. Using FSK modulation, each bit is represented by a signal change, so it's proper to refer to the transfer rate as either 300bps or 300 baud.

PSK Modulation

At the higher transmission rates used by medium- and high-speed modems, FSK becomes increasingly ineffective because of signal losses and noise produced by exceeding the bandwidth of the phone line. To enable higher transmission rates, higher-speed modems use a different form of modulation, referred to as **phase modulation** or **phase-shift keying** (**PSK**). PSK modulation encodes data on a sine wave by shifting the phase of the wave to represent the 1s and 0s. In this manner, a single carrier frequency can be used to carry data, with the relative phase of the waveform indicating the bit-value of data. As an example, a logic "0" can be represented as a 0-degrees phase shift, and a logic "1" by a 180-degrees phase shift.

Phase shift is an analog quantity, so more than two values of phase shift can be used to represent data, as indicated in Table 11.1. When using more than two phase relations to encode data, the method is referred to as **differential phase-shift keying** (**DPSK**). By grouping consecutive data bits in groups of two or three, more than one bit of data can be represented by a single quantity of phase shift. Therefore, the baud rate can be held within the bandwidth of the transmission line, and the number of bits transmitted can be increased. When two bits (**dibits**) are grouped together, four possible bit-pattern combinations result. These combinations can be represented by four increments of phase shift, as depicted in Figure 11.5. Three-bit groups (**tribits**) produce eight possible bit combinations and require eight distinct phase shifts to encode the data. The most common transmission rate for this type of modem is 1800bps, at 600 baud.

FIGURE 11.5

Phase shift keying.

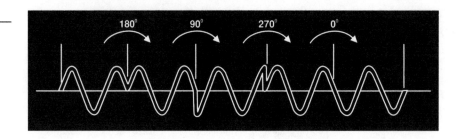

Table 11.1 *DPSK Encoding*

Dibit Pair	Phase Shift	Tribits	Phase Shift
00	0	000	0
01	90	001	45
10	180	010	90
11	270	011	135
		100	180
		101	225
		110	270
		111	315

QAM Modulation

Even higher transmission rates are achieved by combining DPSK techniques with **amplitude modulation** (**AM**), in a method known as **quadrature-amplitude modulation** (**QAM**). The combination of the two methods produces two amplitude states and four distinct phase shifts to represent any of the eight possible combinations of a four-bit group with a single signal change. Therefore, twice as many data bits can be transmitted using quadrature modulation as with PSK alone. In other words, this type of modem commonly transmits data at 2400bps and 600 baud. Using tribits extends the transmission rate to 4800bps, at 600 baud.

Data Compression

In addition to modulation techniques, advanced modems use **data compression techniques** to reduce the volume of data that must be transmitted. These data compression schemes are similar in operation to the techniques used with hard-disk drive recordings, tape backup systems, and the audio/video digitizers described earlier in this text.

Group coding techniques provide for redundant patterns of 1s and 0s to be represented by shorter encoded words. Several group coding techniques have been developed, but they all work on the same basic premise: remove redundant information from the data flow so that it takes less time to transmit. Each method involves a mathematical algorithm that reads the data and converts it into encoded words. The modem at the receiving end must use the same algorithm to decode the words and restore them to their original form.

Some modem compression standards reach ratios as high as 4:1. The major standards for modem data compression have come from a company named Microcom and the **Comité Consultatif International Téléphonique et Télégraphique** (**CCITT**) worldwide standards organization. The **Microcom Networking Protocol** level 7 (MNP 7) standard can produce 3:1 compression ratios, and the CCITT V.42bis standard reaches 4:1.

Transmission Synchronization

Data transmissions between computers, or between computers and peripherals, occur in data blocks consisting of strings of characters.

> Two techniques exist for synchronizing the timing of data transmission between devices. The first method, known as **synchronous transmission**, places timing synchronization signals at the beginning of each data block to synchronize the transmitter and the receiver.

Because the entire block of data is synchronized at the beginning, blocks of data can be transmitted, one block after another, at a maximum rate set by the transmission line and the connecting modems. Because the entire block of data, the timing signals, and the error-checking information must be assembled before transmission, this technique requires the direction of a microcontroller and is usually reserved for high-speed, intelligent modem systems.

> The other technique, called **asynchronous transmission**, places a synchronizing bit at the beginning and end of each 8-bit character.

The bits used in asynchronous transmission are referred to as **start** and **stop bits**. These bits enable characters to be transmitted at irregular intervals. This mode of transmission is usually associated with lower-speed modems (those in the range used with microcomputers and PCs).

Modem Sophistication

The simplest modem operation is provided by manually dialed modems. With this type of modem, an operator at one terminal dials a telephone number to contact an operator at another terminal. After the connection has been made, the operators initiate data transfers between their respective computers. At the end of the transmission, the operators must terminate the connection.

Typically a number of sophisticated functions are available with more intelligent modems. Among these features is **auto-dialing**. Auto-dial modems store lists of telephone numbers, under the control of software. The system can dial these numbers at a particular time you specify (such as at night, when telephone rates are cheaper), and the feature may include automatic redialing of busy numbers. Besides auto-dial, modems may also provide **auto-answer**, **auto logon**, and **auto disconnect** functions to accommodate completely unattended transfers of data. These are commonly referred to as **originate/answer modems** because of their capability of both initiating and answering calls under program control.

Several features have been added to the basic modem that go far beyond simple auto-dial/auto-answer capabilities. The first major feature addition is the capability to communicate with facsimile machines (faxes). Many newer **fax/modems** come with the capability to send information to a remote fax machine, or to receive data from a fax machine, and store it on the hard drive until it can be printed.

Another interesting feature added to modems is the capability to also carry digitized voice.

A **voice modem** communicates with other modems, but it can also digitize voice and communicate this information to another voice modem. Such modems are becoming particularly interesting when used over the Internet. Because of the Internet's organizational structure, voice modems can carry out telephone-like communications between any points in the world, often at the same cost as a local telephone call.

Computer-Modem Transfers

To facilitate the transfer of data from the parallel bus of the computer to the serial bit stream used by the modem (and vice versa), a UART or USART is used. Most modems use a UART. When the computer sends a character to the UART, it is loaded into a character buffer register. The UART shifts a start bit into the buffer, along with the proper error-checking bit and a specified number of stop bits. The character data block is now ready for transmission.

At the receiver, the start bit of the incoming character block is detected. This causes the bits that follow to be shifted into the serial shift register. The error-checking bit is compared to an error bit generated by the receiver as the character block was shifted into the register. The start and stop bits are stripped from the character block, leaving only the data in the character buffer. The system processor can now access the incoming character in parallel form.

The UART and a number of other asynchronous support chips make up the computer/modem interface. The physical location of the interface and its complexity depend on the particular computer system and the type of modem being used.

Standalone modems do not require an onboard UART because one is present in the computer's asynchronous adapter card or serial interface. On the other hand, **dedicated modems** require an onboard UART to facilitate direct communications between the computer and the modem.

Protocols

> To maintain an orderly flow of information between the computer and the modem (and between the modem and another modem) a **protocol**, or set of rules governing the transfer of information, must be in place.

As far as standalone modems are concerned, the most basic hardware standard is the RS-232C serial interface standard. But within the realm of the RS-232 standard, a proliferation of communication methods exist.

RS-232C

The RS-232C standard identifies communication equipment using two categories:

> **Data terminal equipment (DTE)**, usually a computer

> **Data communication equipment (DCE)**, usually a modem

Data terminal equipment is any equipment whose main purpose is to process data. On the other hand, any communication equipment that changes data during transmission is referred to as DCE. Figure 11.6 illustrates a typical DTE/DCE relationship.

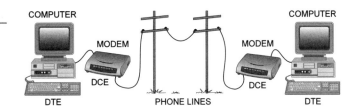

FIGURE 11.6

The DTE/DCE relationship.

The RS-232C serial interface connection is usually made with a 25-pin D-type connector. You should be aware that not all RS-232C connections use the 25-pin DB connector, however, and not all 25-pin DB connectors are RS-232C connections. Table 11.2 describes the pin designations and functions associated with the RS-232C interface, as they apply to modem/computer connections.

Table 11.2 *RS-232C Signal/Pin Definitions*

Pin Number Name	Common Name	RS-232C	Description
1		AA	Protective ground
2	TXD	BA	Transmitted data
3	RxD	BB	Received data
4	RTS	CA	Request to send
5	CTS	CB	Clear to send
6	DSR	CC	Data set ready
7	GND	AB	Signal ground (common return)
8	CD	CF	Received line signal detector (RLSD)
9			Reserved for data set testing
10			Reserved for data set testing
11			Unassigned
12	SI	SCF	Secondary rec'd line sig. detector
13		SCB	Secondary clear to send
14		SBA	Secondary transmitted data
15		DB	Transmission signal element timing
16		SBB	Secondary received data
17		DD	Receiver signal element timing
18			Unassigned
19		SCA	Secondary request to send
20	DTR	CD	Data terminal ready
21		CG	Signal quality detector
22	RI	CE	Ring indicator
23		CH/CI	Data signal rate selector
24		DA	Transmit signal element timing
25			Unassigned

In its most basic form, the RS-232C interface makes provision for full-duplex operating mode through pin 2 (TXD) and pin 3 (RXD). Normally, data passes from the DTE to the

DCE on the **TXD** (**Transmitted Data**) line, and from the DCE to the DTE on the **RXD** (**Received Data**) line, although these two pins may sometimes be reversed.

Of the variations of protocol schemes in use with the asynchronous RS-232C standard, five types are in widespread use today. These five types of protocols can be broken down into two distinct classes:

▶ Hardware-oriented protocols

▶ Control code-oriented protocols

Hardware-Oriented Protocols

The hardware-oriented protocols are tied to the use of a particular pin of the RS-232C connector to control data flow. The two most common forms of hardware protocols are DTR and RTS, named after the **data terminal ready** and **request to send** pins. These lines are toggled between high and low logic levels to control when to send—and not send—data. The DTE uses the RTS (pin 4) to inform the DCE that it is ready to send data. The DTE may also use the DTR (pin 20) to inform the DCE that it is online and functioning.

The DCE uses a trio of reciprocal lines—**CTS** (**Clear to Send**), **DSR** (**Data Set Ready**), and CD (**Data Carrier Detect**)—to signal the data terminal equipment. The DCE uses the CTS to inform the DTE that it is ready to accept data. The data set (or modem) uses the DSR to notify the DTE that it is connected to the phone line.

The RS-232C standard also designates a number of other lines that can be used for specialized functions. The **Speed Indicator** (**SI**) line, connected to pin 12, is used by the DCE to indicate whether the modem is in low- or high-speed mode. The DCE may also use the **Ring Indicator** (**RI**) line to indicate that ring-in voltage is being received. Pin 1 of the DB-25 connector is reserved for the **protective frame ground**, and pin 7 is used for the **signal ground**, to which all other voltages in the interface are referenced.

Control Code-Oriented Protocols

Most data flow control is performed using the control code, or software, class of protocols. Of this class of protocols, three types are in widespread use:

▶ X-OFF/X-ON

▶ ACK/NAK

▶ ETX/ACK

In these protocols, control codes are sent across the data lines to control data flow instead of using separate control lines. A listing of accepted ASCII control codes is presented in Table 11.3.

Table 11.3 *Control Codes*

Hex	EBCDIC	ASCII	Binary	Description
00	NUL	NUL	0000 0000	Null Character (used for padding)
01	SOH	SOH	0000 0001	Start of header (begin session)
02	STX	STX	0000 0010	Start of text (begin data block)
03	ETX	ETX	0000 0011	End of text (end data block)
04	PF	EOT	0000 0100	End of transmission

Hex	EBCDIC	ASCII	Binary	Description
05	HT	ENQ	0000 0101	Inquire (bid for acknowledgment)
06	LC	ACK	0000 0110	Acknowledge (positive response)
07	DEL	BEL	0000 0111	Bell (ring the bell)
08	GE	BS	0000 1000	Backspace
09	RLF	HT	0000 1001	Horizontal tab
0A	SMM	LF	0000 1010	Line feed
0B	VT	VT	0000 1011	Vertical tab
0C	FF	FF	0000 1100	Form feed
0D	CR	CR	0000 1101	Carriage return
0E	SO	SO	0000 1110	Shift out (subscripting)
0F	SI	SI	0000 1111	Shift in (superscripting)
10	DLE	DLE	0001 0000	Data link escape (binary xmission)
11	DC1	DC1	0001 0001	Device control #1 (X-ON)
12	DC2	DC2	0001 0010	Device control #2
13	TM	DC3	0001 0011	Device control #3 (X-OFF)
14	RES	DC4	0001 0100	Device control #4
15	NL	NAK	0001 0101	Not acknowledge
16	BS	SYN	0001 0110	Synchronous idle (sync character)
17	IL	ETB	0001 0111	End of transmission block
18	CAN	CAN	0001 1000	Cancel
19	EM	EM	0001 1001	End of medium
1A	CC	SUB	0001 1010	Substitute character
1B	CU1	ESC	0001 1011	Escape
1C	IFS	FS	0001 1100	Field separator
1D	IGS	GS	0001 1101	Group separator
1E	IRS	RS	0001 1110	Record separator
1F	IUS	US	0001 1111	Unit separator
20	DS	SP	0010 0000	Space (blank character)

The X-ON/X-OFF protocol, where X represents two special control characters, is a relatively simple concept used to regulate data flow. This control is necessary to prevent buffer memories from overfilling. When data overflows the buffer, the result is usually an error code. The X-ON/X-OFF protocol uses special control characters to start and stop data flow.

The ACK/NAK and ETX/ACK protocols are considered high-level protocols because they require special interface programs called **drivers**, or **driver emulators**. In both cases, these protocols use special control characters and escape code sequences to provide functions such as data transmission integrity, flow control, requests for retransmission, and so forth.

The ACK/NAK protocol derives its title from the ASCII control characters for ACKnowledge and Not ACKnowledge. This protocol uses these characters to provide a means of error correction for transmitted data. Basically, the ACK/NAK protocol expects a block of data to be preceded by a **start-of-text** (**STX**) character, and to be followed by both an **end-of-text** (**ETX**) character and an error-checking code, as depicted in Figure 11.7. At the receiving end, the **block check character** (**BCC**) is checked for errors. Depending on the outcome of the check, either an ACK signal is returned to indicate a successful transmission, or a NAK signal is returned to indicate that an error has occurred. If a NAK signal is returned, the transmitting device responds by retransmitting the entire block.

FIGURE 11.7

ACK/NAK transmission.

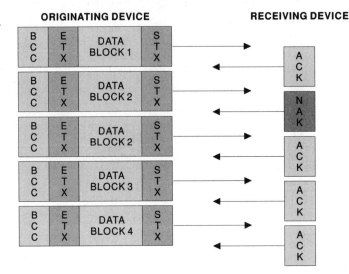

The ETX/ACK protocol is somewhat simpler than ACK/NAK in that no character check is performed. If the receiving device does not return an ACK signal within a predetermined length of time, the sending device assumes that an error or malfunction has occurred and retransmits the character block.

The CCITT and MNP protocols for data compression were mentioned earlier in this chapter. Actually, many protocol standards are in use with data communications equipment.

The CCITT standards are identified by a v.xx nomenclature. The original CCITT standard was the v.22 protocol that established transfers at 1200bps using 600 baud. The v.22bis standard followed, providing 2400bps transfers at 600 baud using QAM methods. The v.32 protocol increased the rate to 4800bps and 9600bps. The 4800bps rate uses QAM modulation at 2400 baud, and the 9600bps rate operates at 2400 baud with additional QAM bit values. A v.32bis modification improves the transmission rate to 14,400bps by providing 128 possible QAM values.

The CCITT standards also include an error-correction and a data-compression protocol. The v.42 standard is the error-correction protocol, and v.42bis protocol is the CCITT equivalent of the MNP5 and MNP7 protocols. Both protocols run as modules along with the v.32 and v.32bis protocols to provide additional transmission speed.

The MNP Microcom standards began with protocols MNP2–MNP4. These standards dealt with error-correction protocols. The MNP5 and MNP 7 standards followed as the first data-compression protocols. The MNP10 standard introduced the first Adverse Channel Enhancement protocol. This type of protocol is designed to provide maximum performance for modems used in typically poor connection applications, such as cellular phones. This protocol features multiple connection attempts and automatically adjusted transmission rates. As with the advanced CCITT protocols, the MNP10 protocol module runs along with a V.42 protocol to maximize the data transmission rate.

Newer CCITT and MNP protocols are under development to provide modems with 56Kbps transmission capabilities. These protocols use a two-step mapping algorithm to map 256 binary values into a data encoder. The encoder produces digital symbols that are applied to a D/A circuit, which converts the data into 256 possible analog signals. The **symbol rate** for 56KB modems is 8Khz. The two-step mapping algorithm provides the best possible trade-off between data table size, error rates, and elevated complexity.

During a special **training period** conducted at lower speeds, the modem tests the integrity of the transmission medium. The modem uses the training information to determine the ultimate group of points in the map to be used for the existing line conditions. The modem then negotiates with the remote modem to determine the maximum transfer rate.

Several error-correcting file transfer protocols have been developed for modem communications packages. Some of the more common protocols include the following:

- Xmodem
- Ymodem
- Zmodem
- Kermit

These protocols use extensive error-detection schemes to maintain the validity of the data as it is being transmitted. The concept of parity checking has already been discussed as a method of detecting data errors. However, parity checking alone is somewhat ineffective when used to check large blocks of data. and it offers no convenient means of error correction.

Error-detecting and correcting protocols generate more exotic error-detection algorithms—such as **checksum** and **cyclic redundancy checks** (**CRC**s)—to identify, locate, and possibly correct data errors.

In Xmodem transfers, the transmitter sends a data block similar to the ones depicted in Figure 11.7. The data section of the block is 128 bytes long. A checksum character is used to detect transmission errors, and the ACK/NAK method of flow control is employed. An improved version of the protocol, called Xmodem CRC, replaces the checksum character with a CRC block check character.

The Ymodem protocol improves on the Xmodem CRC version by increasing the size of the data block to 1024 bytes, although Ymodem can still support the 128 byte xmodem format, if necessary. The 1024-byte version begins with an STX ASCII character, and the 128-byte transmission starts with an SOH character. An improved version, called Ymodem batch, includes filenames and sizes in the transfer so that multiple files can be sent in a single transmission. A further improvement is used in Ymodem G. In this format, the sending unit uses the Ymodem batch method but does not wait for an ACK signal back from the receiver before sending the next data block. This latter format is used only with the MNP protocol functions that supply their own error checking and correcting.

The Zmodem protocol provides a wealth of high-level management features. In addition to using CRC16 and CRC32 error-detection schemes to verify data integrity, the Zmodem protocol offers Autofile Restart crash-recovery techniques and selective file transfers. The files are selected by including their filenames in a batch transfer operation. Zmodem can be used for transferring both text and binary files (such as .exe files).

All the protocols mentioned in this category are used to transmit files over dial-up telephone lines. However, they are not capable of being used with Internet communications.

These are only classes of protocols, and within these classes are many methods of actually implementing a particular protocol. Within a particular protocol, a number of parameters must be agreed upon before an efficient exchange of information can occur. Chief among these parameters are **character type** and **character framing**. Basically, character type refers to the character set (or alphabet) understood by the devices. Depending on the systems, the character set may be an 8-bit ASCII line code, a 7-bit ASCII code (with a parity bit), or an EBCDIC code.

Character-framing, on the other hand, refers to the total number of the bits used to transmit a character. This includes the length of the coded character and the number and type of overhead bits required to send the character. A common character-framing scheme calls for a start bit, seven data bits, an odd-parity bit, and a stop bit, as depicted in Figure 11.8.

FIGURE 11.8

Asynchronous character format.

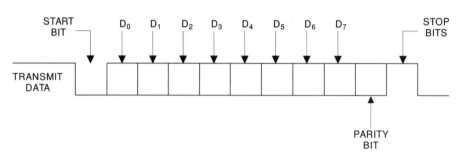

Although this is a typical character-framing technique, it is not universal throughout the industry. The problem here is one of device comprehension. The local unit may be using a 10-bit character frame consisting of a start bit, seven data bits, an odd-parity bit, and a stop bit. However, if the remote system is using something besides 7-bit, odd-parity ASCII with one stop bit, the response from it will be unintelligible.

The Call

To understand the operation of the modem, it is important to understand that it must function in two different modes. The first mode is the **local command state**. In this condition, the modem is offline and communicates with the host system to receive and process commands.

The second mode is the **online state**. In this condition, the modem facilitates the transfer of data between the host computer and a remote computer or device. Two events can cause the modem to shift from the offline state to the online condition. The system can prompt the modem to go online and dial out to another unit. To accomplish this, the host computer places the modem in Originate mode. The second event involves the modem receiving a **ring signal** from a remote device. In this situation, the host system shifts the modem into Answer mode.

The modem automatically shifts from the online state to the local command state whenever the carrier signal from the incoming line is not detected in a given amount of time, or whenever the carrier signal is lost after the connection has been made. An embedded code in the transmitted data can also be used to shift the modem into the local command state.

There are three basic operations that the modem can perform:

▶ Dialing

- Data exchange (the call)

- Answering

Dialing

To place a call using the modem, the same series of events must occur as when you are placing a voice telephone call. When the handset is removed from its cradle, a switch inside the telephone closes, connecting the phone to the line. At this point, the phone is in a state known as **off-hook**, but it is not yet online. When the modem's relay closes and the dial tone is detected, the modem notifies the host computer that it is connected to the line.

To originate a call using an auto-dial modem, you must first place your modem in Originate mode. This requires that the modem be operating in the local command state. Basically, the modem is always in either the local command state or the online state. In the local command state, you can issue commands from the computer to the modem. In the online state, communications between modems occur.

Using an auto-dial modem, the modem automatically places the call by issuing the digital tones equivalent of the desired phone number. The number may come from the keyboard, or it may be one that has previously been entered into memory. Some auto-dial modems are capable of producing both pulse- and touch-tone dialing equivalents.

A number of things can occur to prevent the modem from going into the online state. An intelligent modem waits a specified length of time after pick-up before it starts dialing so that the phone system has time to apply a dial tone to the line. After the number has been dialed, the modem waits for the ring back from the telephone company (this is what you hear when you are making a call). When the ringing stops, indicating that the call has gone through, the modem waits a specified length of time for an answer tone (carrier) from the receiving modem. If the carrier is not detected within the allotted time, the originating modem begins automatic disconnect procedures (hangs up), as depicted in Figure 11.9. If a busy signal is detected, the originating modem hangs up or refers to a second number.

FIGURE 11.9

Auto-dial/Auto-answer modem cycle.

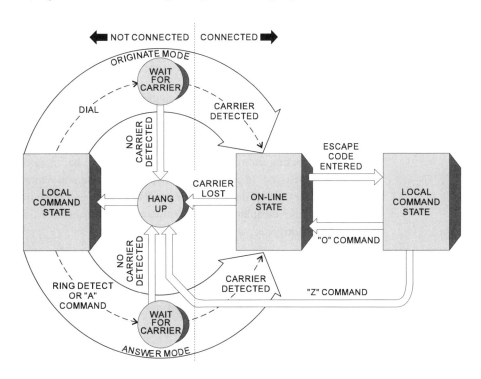

The Conversation

After the phone line connection has been established, a **handshaking sequence** occurs. The originating modem's Carrier Received pin (CD) signals its computer that the receiving modem is online. This is followed by a signal on the Clear To Send (CTS) pin, indicating that its computer is ready to transmit and receive data. The originating modem responds by issuing its own carrier tone frequency, which the answering modem must detect to notify its computer (through its CD and CTS pins) that it is online and ready for data. If both tones have been received successfully, the greetings and handshakes are completed, and the transfer of information begins.

> During the data transfer, both modems monitor the signal level of the carrier to prevent the transfer of false data due to signal deterioration. If the carrier signal strength drops below some predetermined threshold level or is lost for a given length of time, one or both modems will initiate automatic disconnect procedures.

While the modem is in the online state, no commands can be given to it from the keyboard. However, the local command state can be re-entered while still maintaining the connection, by using an escape-code sequence.

Answering

For an auto-answer modem to receive calls, it must be configured to answer the incoming call. When a call comes in, the ring voltage is detected by the modem, which activates its Ring Indicator (RI) pin to notify the computer that a call is coming in. Depending on the configuration of the modem, it may answer the incoming call on the first ring or after some preset number of rings. If the called computer is ready, meaning the data terminal ready (DTR) signal is active, the modem goes off-hook and begins the handshaking routine.

The Serial Interface

In the case of external modems, the serial interface, including the UART, is normally provided by the host system. In pre-Pentium units, the system's multi I/O card provided a pair of fully programmable, asynchronous communication channels through two serial port connections. On earlier I/O cards, a pair of 8250 UARTs were used as the basic port circuitry. In newer MI/O cards, a single VLSI device, called an integrated I/O controller, provided the interfacing and UART functions. In most Pentium systems, the serial port adapter function is incorporated into the system board's integrated I/O controller IC.

The original serial adapters featured programmable baud rates from 50 to 9600 baud, a fully programmable interrupt system, and variable character lengths (5-, 6-, 7-, or 8-bit characters). In addition, the adapter added and removed start, stop, and parity bits; had false start-bit detection, line-break detection, and generation; and possessed built-in diagnostics capabilities. As modems became faster and faster, upgraded UARTs were included or integrated to keep up.

> Notable advanced UART versions include the 16450 and 16550. The 16450 was the 16-bit improvement of the 8250, and the 16550 was a high-performance UART with an onboard 16-byte buffer.

The buffer enables the UART to store or transmit a string of data without interrupting the system's microprocessor to handle them. This provides the 16550 with an impressive speed advantage over previous UARTs. These advanced UARTs enable serial ports to reach data transmission rates of up to 115Kbps. Although some features have changed between these UARTs, and although they are sometimes integrated directly into an integrated I/O chip, they must still adhere to the basic 8250 structure to remain PC-compatible.

In most PC-compatible serial ports, very little circuitry besides the UART is needed to implement the interface. Normally, only an oscillator/clock circuit and some RS-232 line driver/receiver chips are required. Figure 11.10 shows these required sections in block form.

FIGURE 11.10

RS-232C serial interface.

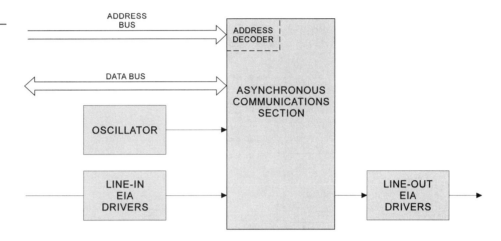

A+ CORE 1.2 Although the basic lines of the serial ports originate on a multi I/O card or system board, they must be connected to RS-232-compatible D-shell connectors to complete the interface. This usually involves connecting a ribbon cable between the board that contains the interface circuitry and the connectors, located on a special expansion slot cover. The connectors on the slot cover are usually a 9-pin DB-9M and a 25-pin DB-25M. The ribbon cables pass the TXD, RXD, DSR, DTR, RTS, CTS, CD, RI, and ground signals to the connectors.

As mentioned earlier, two serial ports are normally provided in a PC-compatible system:

- ▶ RS-232-1
- ▶ RS-232-2

These are hardware settings for the physical ports. The system recognizes the serial ports by their COM port settings. COM port settings are simply port addresses (COM1, COM2, COM3, and COM4) assigned to the serial interfaces by the operating system. These settings enable the hardware and software to work together. The communication protocol is a function of the system software and must be loaded before the interface can be operational.

Software uses the COM setting to address instructions and data to the correct UART. Therefore, both the hardware and software COM settings must agree for the interface to function properly. Either RS-232 port may be designated as COM1, COM2, COM3, or COM4, as long as both ports are not assigned to the same COM port number. In most PCs, COM1 is assigned as port address hex 3F8h, and COM2 is assigned port address hex 2F8h. Normally, IRQ4 is selected for COM1 and COM3, and IRQ3 is selected for COM2 and COM4. Because these COM ports share IRQ settings, it should be apparent that all four ports cannot be in use at the same time. For example, if an external modem is connected to COM2, then no other device should be set up on COM4.

The UART

Whether the UART is located on a multi I/O board, in an integrated I/O controller chip, or is part of an internal modem, it must supply most of the logic and control circuitry for the RS-232C interface. In addition to the classic functions described earlier for a UART, the I/O controller provides all the control and handshake lines required for asynchronous communications to take place (such as RI, DSR, DTR, RTS, CTS, and RLSD). Note that the **Receive Line Signal Detect (RLSD)** line is described as the Carrier Detect (CD) line in the RS-232C standard. Of course, these lines are used by the interface adapter to control the flow of information between the PC and the serial communications equipment. Figure 11.11 shows a block function diagram of an 8250-compatible UART.

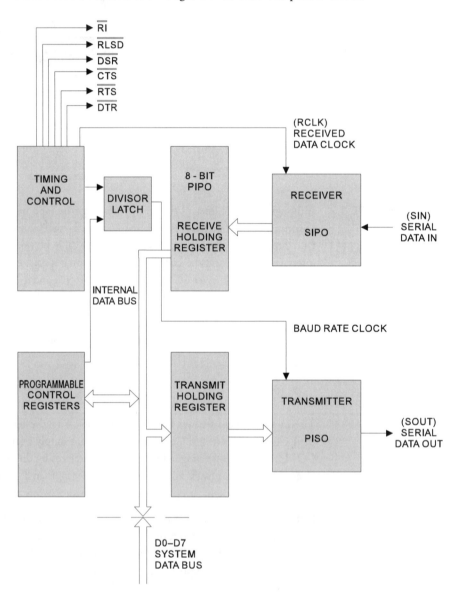

FIGURE 11.11

Inside the UART.

The UART in a PC-compatible system has a number of addressable registers, which help the system unit's software to control its operation. Different modes of operation are selected by programming its registers at port addresses 3F8h–3FFh for the primary RS-232-1 interface, and 2F8h–2FFh for the secondary RS-232-2 interface.

The operation of these registers can be summarized as follows:

TX-RD buffer (3F8/2F8h): This address selects the received data register, which holds the received character if the UART is in read configuration. Conversely, the transmitter holding register is accessed by the same address when the UART is in write configuration and bit 7 is low. If bit 7 is high, this address accesses the least significant byte (LSB) of the programmable baud-rate generator for initialization.

Interrupt enable register (3F9/2F9h): The bits of this register enable four different UART interrupts, which, in turn, activate the chip's INTRPT output. This address also depends on bit 7 of the line-control register. The interrupt enable register is selected by bit 7 being low. If bit 7 is high, this address selects the most significant byte (MSB) of the programmable baud-rate generator for initialization.

Interrupt identification register (3FA/2FAh): The contents of this register are used to prioritize four interrupt levels in the UART. The bits of the register are used by software to identify the highest priority interrupt that may be pending and lock out all other interrupts until that particular interrupt has been serviced.

Line-control register (3FB/2FBh): The contents of this register are used to define the format of the port's data exchange. The logic levels of the various bits of this register define parameters such as word length, number of stop bits, and the type of parity used.

Modem-control register (3FC/2FCh): The bits of this register control the DTE/DCE interface (in particular, the DTR and RTS lines). One bit of this register is used by software to provide loopback diagnostic testing.

Line status register (3FD/2FDh): This register provides the system unit with status information concerning data transfers. This information includes data ready in the receiver register, receiver register overrun errors, parity errors, framing errors, transmitter holding register empty, and transmitter shift register empty.

Modem status register (3FE/2FEh): The contents of this register indicate the status of the DTE/DCE control lines. These lines include the CTS, DSR, RI, and RLSD lines.

Serial Cables

Even though the information in Table 11.2 shows a designation for nearly every pin in the RS-232 connection (except 11, 18, and 25), many of the pins are not actually used in most serial cables. Figure 11.12 illustrates the basic 25-pin-to-25-pin variation of the RS-232 serial cable. In this example, the connection depicted is a straight-through cabling scheme associated with PCs and PC XTs.

Since the advent of the PC AT, the system's first serial port has typically been implemented in a nine-pin D-shell male connector on the DTE. Figure 11.13 depicts a typical 9-pin-to-25-pin connection scheme. Notice the crossover wiring technique employed for the TXD/RXD lines displayed in this example. This type of connection became popular with the nine-pin PC AT serial port.

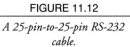

FIGURE 11.12

A 25-pin-to-25-pin RS-232 cable.

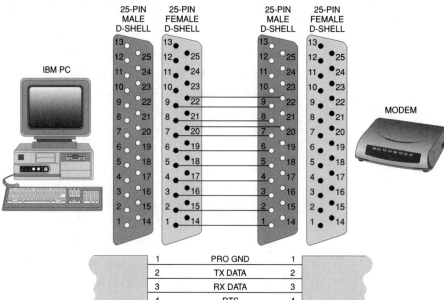

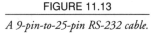

FIGURE 11.13

A 9-pin-to-25-pin RS-232 cable.

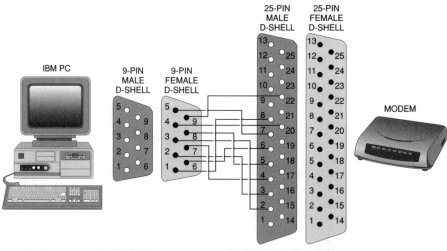

In cases where the serial ports are located close enough to each other, a **null modem** connection can be implemented. A null modem connection enables the two serial ports to communicate directly without using modems. A typical null modem connection scheme is illustrated in Figure 11.14.

FIGURE 11.14

A null modem cable.

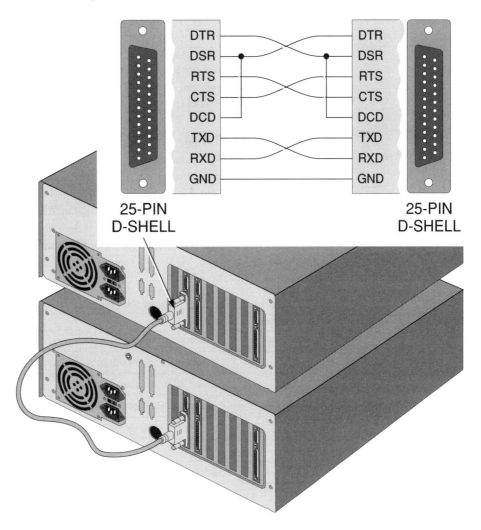

In any event, it should be apparent from the previous trio of figures that all serial cables are not created equal. Incorrect serial cabling can be a major problem when attaching third-party communication equipment to the computer. Read the DCE user's manual carefully to make certain the correct pins are being connected.

Communication Software

All modems require software to control the communication session. This software is typically included with the purchase of the modem. At the fundamental instruction level, most modems use a set of commands known as the **Hayes-compatible command set**.

This set of commands is named after the Hayes Microcomputer Products company that first defined them. The command set is based on a group of instructions that begin with a pair of attention characters, followed by commands words. Because the attention characters are an integral part of every Hayes command, the command set is often referred to as the **AT command set**.

In the Hayes command structure, the operation of the modem shifts back and forth between a command mode (local mode) and a communications mode (remote mode). In the command mode, the modem exchanges commands and status information with the host system's microprocessor. In communications mode, the modem facilitates sending and receiving data between the local system and a remote system. A short guard period between communications mode and command mode enables the system to switch smoothly without interrupting a data transmission.

AT Command Set

Hayes-compatible AT commands are entered at the command line using an ATXn format. The Xn nomenclature identifies the type of command being given (X) and the particular function to be used (n). Except for ATA, ATDn, and ATZn commands, the AT sequence can be followed by any number of commands. The ATA command forces the modem to immediately pick up the phone line (even if it does not ring). The Dn commands are dialing instructions, and the Zn commands reset the modem by loading new default initialization information into it. Table 11.4 provides a summary of the Hayes-compatible AT command set.

Table 11.4 *The AT Command Set Summary*

Command	Function
A/	Re-execute command
A	Go off-hook and attempt to answer a call
B0	Select V.22 connection at 1200bps
B1	* Select Bell 212A connection at 1200bps
C1	* Return OK message
Dn	Dial modifier (see Dial Modifier)
E0	Turn off command echo
E1	* Turn on command echo
F0	Select auto-detect mode (equivalent to N1)
F1	* Select V.21 of Bell 103
F2	Reserved
F3	Select V.23 line modulation
F4	Select V.22 or Bell 212A 1200bps line speed
F5	Select V.22bis 7200 modulation
F6	Select V.32bis or V.32 4800 line modulation
F7	Select V.32bis 7200 line modulation
F8	Select V.32bis or V.32 9600 line modulation
F9	Select V.32bis 12000 line modulation
F10	Select V.32bis 14400 line modulation
H0	Initiate a hang-up sequence
H1	If on-hook, go off-hook and enter command mode

Command	Function
I0	Report product code
I1	Report computed checksum
I2	Report OK
I3	Report firmware revision, model, and interface type
I4	Report response
I5	Report the country code parameter
I6	Report modem data pump model and code revision
L0	Set low speaker volume
L1	Set low speaker volume
L2	* Set medium speaker volume
L3	Set high speaker volume
M0	Turn off speaker
M1	* Turn speaker on during handshaking, and turn speaker off while receiving carrier
M2	Turn speaker on during handshaking and while receiving carrier
M3	Turn speaker off during dialing and receiving carrier, and turn speaker on during answering
N0	Turn off Automode detection
N1	* Turn on Automode detection
O0	Go online
O1	Go online and initiate a retrain sequence
P	Force pulse dialing
Q0	* Allow result codes to PC
Q1	Inhibit result codes to PC
Sn	Select S-Register as default
Sn?	Return the value of S-Register n
=v	Set default S-Register to value v
?	Return the value of default S-Register.
T	Force DTMF dialing
V0	Report short form (terse) result codes
V1	* Report long form (verbose) result codes
W0	* Report PC speed in EC mode
W1	Report line speed, EC protocol, and PC speed
W2	Report modem speed in EC mode
X0	Report basic progress result codes, OK, CONNECT, RING, NO CARRIER (also for busy, if enabled, and dial tone not detected), NO ANSWER, and ERROR.
Xl	Report basic call progress result codes and connections speeds such as OK, CONNECT, RING, NO CARRIER (also for busy, if enabled, and dial tone not detected), NO ANSWER, CONNECT XXXX, and ERROR.

continued

Table 11.4 *continued*

Command	Function
X2	Report basic call progress result codes and connections speeds such as OK, CONNECT, RING, NO CARRIER (also for busy, if enabled, and dial tone not detected), NO ANSWER, CONNECT XXXX, and ERROR.
X3	Report basic call progress result codes and connection rate, such as OK, CONNECT, RING, NO CARRIER, NO ANSWER, CONNECT XXXX, BUSY, and ERROR.

* Default

After a command has been entered at the command line, the modem attempts to execute the command and them returns a result code to the screen. Table 11.5 describes the command result codes.

Table 11.5 *AT Command Result Codes*

Result	Code	Description
0	OK	The OK code is returned by the modem to acknowledge execution of a command line.
1	CONNECT	The modem sends this result code when line speed is 300bps.
2	RING	The modem sends this result code when incoming ringing is detected on the line.
3	NO CARRIER	The carrier is not detected within the time limit, or carrier is lost.
4	ERROR	The modem could not process the command line (entry error).
5	CONNECT 1200	The modem detected a carrier at 1200bps.
6	NO DIAL TONE	The modem could not detect a dial tone when dialing.
7	BUSY	The modem detected a busy signal.
8	NO ANSWER	The modem never detected silence (@ command only).
9	CONNECT 0600	The modem sends this result code when line speed is 600bps.
10	CONNECT 2400	The modem detected a carrier at 2400bps.
11	CONNECT 4800	Connection is established at 4800bps.
12	CONNECT 9600	Connection is established at 9600bps.
13	CONNECT 7200	The modem sends this result code when line speed is 7200bps.
14	CONNECT 12000	Connection is established at 12000bps.
15	CONNECT 14400	Connection is established at 14400bps.
17	CONNECT 38400	Connection is established at 38400bps.
18	CONNECT 57600	Connection is established at 57600bps.
22	CONNECT	The modem sends this result code when establishing a V.23 0riginate. 75TX/1200RX

Result	Code	Description
23	CONNECT	The modem sends this result code upon establishing a V.23 answer. 1200TX/175RX
24	DELAYED	The modem returns this code when a call fails to connect and is considered delayed.
92	BLACKLISTED	The modem returns this result code when an f\call fails to connect and is considered blacklisted.
40	CARRIER 300	The carrier is detected at 300bps.
44	CARRIER 1200/75	The modem sends this result code when V.23 backward channel carrier is detected.
45	CARRIER 75/1200	The modem sends this result code when V.23 forward channel carrier is detected.
46	CARRIER 1200	The carrier is detected at 1200bps.
47	CARRIER 2400	The carrier is detected at 2400bps.
48	CARRIER 4800	The modem sends this result code when either the high or low channel carrier in V.22bis modem has been detected.
49	CARRIER 7200	The carrier is detected at 7200bps.
50	CARRIER 9600	The carrier is detected at 9600bps.
51	CARRIER 12000	The carrier is detected at 12000bps.
52	CARRIER 14400	The carrier is detected at 14400bps.
66	COMPRESSION:	MNP Class 5 is active CLASS 5. CLASS 5
67	COMPRESSION:	V.42bis is active V.42bis. V.42bis
69	COMPRESSION:	No data compression signals NONE.
70	PROTOCOL: NONE	No error correction is enabled.
77	PROTOCOL: LAPM	V.42 LAP-M error correction is enabled.
80	PROTOCOL: ALT	MNP Class 4 error correction is enabled.

Specialized fax and voice software programs are also included, if the modem has these capabilities. Most communication software packages include an electronic **phone book** to hold frequently dialed numbers. Other features include the use of a variety of different software protocols. Common protocols included at this level include XMODEM, YMODEM, and ZMODEM. Both the originating and answering modems must agree on the same protocol, baud rate, and data length for the session to be successful.

To communicate with other computers, some information about how the communication will proceed is needed. In particular, it is necessary to match the protocol of the remote unit, as well as its parity, character framing, and baud rate settings. With older modems, this may involve a telephone call to the other computer user. In the case of online services, the information is provided in the introductory package the user receives when the service is joined.

The Windows 3.x program contains an application called **Terminal** that controls the operation of the system's modem. Terminal is capable of operating with several different modem configurations. This flexibility enables it to conduct transfers with a wide variety of other computer systems. The Communications dialog box under the Settings option, shown in Figure 11.15, provides the options for configuring the communications settings.

FIGURE 11.15

The Communications setting box.

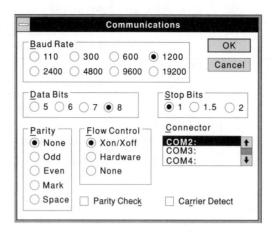

Troubleshooting Modems

A+ CORE 1.7

A+ CORE 1.2

You should mentally divide this section on troubleshooting modems into two segments:

▶ External modems

▶ Internal modems

An internal modem must be checked out in the same basic sequence as any other I/O card. First, check the modem's hardware and software configuration, check the system for conflicts, and check for correct drivers. Improper software setup is the most common cause of modems not working when they are first installed. Inspect any cabling connections to see that they are made correctly and are functioning properly, and test the modem's hardware by substitution. If you are checking an external modem, you must treat it as an external peripheral, with the serial port being treated as a separate I/O port. Figure 11.16 shows the components associated with internal and external modems.

FIGURE 11.16

Internal and external modem components.

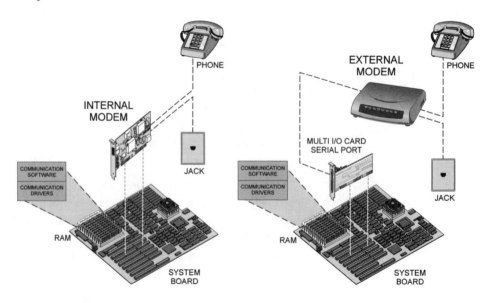

Modem Problem Symptoms

A+ CORE 2.1 Typical symptoms associated with modem failures include the following:

- No response occurs from the modem.

- The modem does not dial out.

- The modem does not connect after the number has been dialed.

- The modem does not transmit after making connection with remote unit.

- The modem cannot be installed properly for operation.

- Garbled messages are transmitted.

- A communication session cannot be terminated.

- Files cannot be transferred.

COM Port Conflicts

A+ CORE 1.3

As stated earlier, every COM port on a PC requires an IRQ line to signal the processor for attention. In most PC systems, two COM ports share the same IRQ line. The IRQ4 line works for COM1 and COM3, and the IRQ3 line works for COM2 and COM4. This is common in PC-compatibles. The technician must make sure that two devices are not set up to use the same IRQ channel.

If more than one device is connected to the same IRQ line, a conflict will occur because it is not likely that the interrupt handler software will be capable of servicing both devices.

For example, if a mouse is set for COM1 and a modem is set for COM3, neither device will be capable of communicating effectively with the system because COM1 and COM3 both use IRQ4. Both the mouse and the modem may interrupt the microprocessor at the same time. The same is true if two devices are connected to IRQ3: COM2 and COM4 use this IRQ. Therefore, the first step to take when installing a modem is to check the system to see how its interrupts and COM ports are allocated. This particular interrupt conflict may be alleviated by using a bus mouse rather than a serial mouse, thereby, freeing up a COM port.

Use a software diagnostic package to obtain information about the serial port's base I/O port address. A typical value for this setting is 02E8. Also obtain the modem's IRQ setting. This setting is typically IRQ=3. Other common modem settings are listed here:

COM1 with IRQ=4, 5, or 7

COM2 with IRQ=3, 5, or 7

COM3 with IRQ=4, 5, or 7

COM4 with IRQ=3, 5, or 7

Care must be taken when using IRQ5 or IRQ7 with the modem. These interrupt channels are typically reserved for LPT1 (IRQ7) and LPT2 (IRQ5). The arrangements in the table assume that IRQ3 and IRQ4 are already taken. The table also assumes that at least one of the LPT interrupts is not being used by a printer.

Modem Software Checks

Many of the software diagnostic packages available include a utility for testing modems. If such a program is available, run the equivalent of its Run All Tests entry to test the modem. If all the configuration settings are correct, attempt to run the modem's DOS-based communications package to test the modem's operation. At the command line, type **ATZ** to reset the modem and enter the Command mode using the Hayes-compatible command set. You should receive a 0 or OK response if the command was processed.

If no result code is returned to the screen, check the modem's configuration and setup again for conflicts. Also check the speed setting of the communication software to make sure it is compatible with that of the modem. On the other hand, a returned OK code indicates that the modem and the computer are communicating properly.

Other AT-compatible commands can be used to check the modem at the DOS level. The ATL2 command sets the modem's output volume to medium to make sure that it is not set too low to be heard. If the modem dials but cannot connect to a remote station, check the modem's speed and DTR settings. Change the DTR setting by entering **AT&Dn**. The following holds true for this equation:

n = 0   The modem ignores the DTR line.

n = 1   Modem goes to asynch command state when DTR goes off.

n = 2   DTR off switches modem to off-hook and back to command mode.

n = 3   DTR switching off initializes modem.

If the modem connects but cannot communicate, check the character framing parameter of the receiving modem, and set the local modem to match. Also, match the terminal emulation of the local unit to that of the remote unit. ANSI terminal emulation is the most common. Finally, match the file transfer protocol to the other modem.

Use the ATDT*70 command to disable call waiting if the transmission is frequently garbled. The **+++** command should interrupt any activity in which the modem is engaged and bring it to the command mode.

In Windows 3.x, the modem-related drivers are located in the Ports section of the Control Panel. The configuration information is found under the Settings and Advanced Settings buttons, as depicted in Figure 11.17.

FIGURE 11.17

Configuration information.

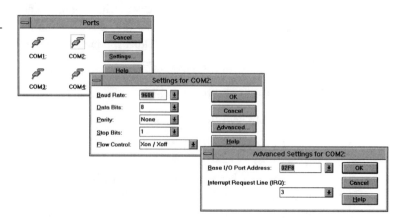

In Windows 95, the modem configuration information is found in the Control Panel under the Modems icon. Under the icon are two tabs: the General tab and the Diagnostics tab. The Properties button in the General window provides port and maximum-speed settings. The Connection tab provides character-framing information, as illustrated in Figure 11.18. The Connection tab's Advanced button provides error- and flow-control settings, as well as modulation type.

FIGURE 11.18

The Connection tab dialog box.

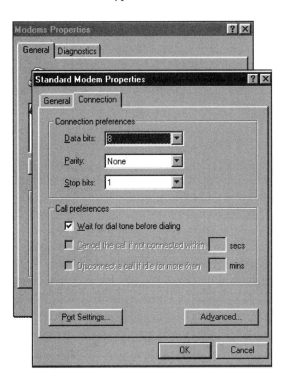

The Diagnostics tab's dialog box, depicted in Figure 11.19, provides access to the modem's driver and additional information. The plug-and-play feature reads the modem card and returns its information to the screen, as demonstrated here.

Windows 95 provides fundamental troubleshooting information for wide area networking through its system of Help screens. Simply select Help from the Control Panel's toolbar and click on the topic you are troubleshooting.

Modem Hardware Checks

From the earlier section concerning UART registers, it should be apparent that modems contain the capability of performing self tests on sections of their circuitry.

> Modems actually have the capability to perform three different kinds of self-diagnostic tests.

The first type of self-diagnostic test a modem can perform is a **local digital loopback test**, in which data is looped through the UART's internal registers. When testing the RS-232 port itself, a device called a **loopback plug,** or **wrap plug**, channels the output data directly back into the received data input, and only the port is tested.

FIGURE 11.19

The Diagnostics tab dialog box.

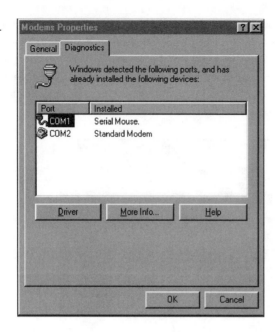

Many modems have the capability to extend this test by looping the data through the local modem and back to the computer (**local analog loopback test**). Some modems even possess the capability to loop back data to a remote computer through its modem (**remote digital loopback test**). In this manner, the entire transmit and receive path can be validated, including the communication line (such as the telephone line). One of the most overlooked causes of transmission problems is the telephone line itself. A noisy line can easily cause garbled data to be output from the modem. Figure 11.20 illustrates adapter, analog, and digital loopback tests.

If transmission errors occur frequently, the various loopback tests should be employed to locate the source of the problem. Begin by running the remote digital loopback test. If the test runs successfully, the problem is likely to be located in the remote computer.

If the test fails, run the local digital loopback test with self tests. If the test results are positive, the problem may be located in the local computer. On the other hand, the local analog loopback test should be run if the local digital test fails.

If the local analog test fails, the problem is located in the local modem. If the local analog test is successful and problems are occurring, the local analog test should be run on the remote computer. The outcome of this test should localize the problem to the remote computer or the remote modem.

If the modem is an internal unit, its hardware can be tested by exchanging it with a known good unit. If the telephone line operates correctly with a normal handset, then only the modem card, its configuration, or the communications software can be causes for problems. If the software and configuration settings appear correct, you must exchange the modem card.

With an external modem, the front panel lights can be used as diagnostic tools to monitor its operation. The progress of a call and its handling can be monitored along with any errors that may occur.

Figure 11.21 depicts the front panel lights of a typical external modem.

FIGURE 11.20

Loopback tests.

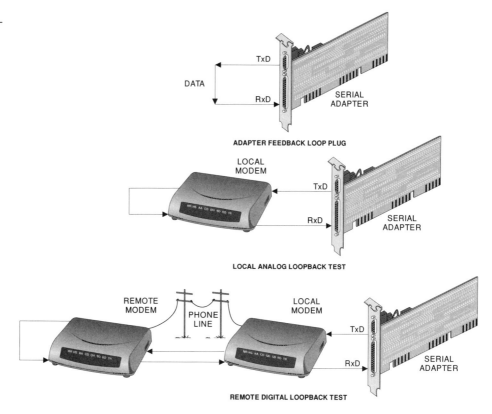

FIGURE 11.21

Modem front panel.

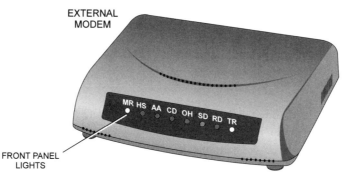

The modem ready (MR), terminal ready (TR), and auto answer (AA) lights are preparatory lights that indicate that the modem is plugged in, powered on, ready to run, and prepared to answer an incoming call. The MR light becomes active when power is applied to the modem and the unit is ready to operate. The TR light becomes active when the host computer's communication software and the modem make contact. The AA light simply indicates that the auto answer function has been turned on.

The off-hook (OH), ring indicator (RI), and carrier detect (CD) lights indicate the modem's online condition. The off-hook light indicates that the modem has connected to the phone line. This action can occur when the modem is receiving a call, or when it is commanded to place a call. The RI light becomes active when the modem detects an incoming ring signal. The CD light becomes active when the modem detects a carrier signal from a remote modem. As long as this light is on, the modem is capable of sending and receiving data from the remote unit. If the CD light will not become active with a known good modem, then a problem with the data communication equipment exists.

The final trio of lights indicates the status of a call in progress. The send data (SD) light flickers when the modem transmits data to the remote unit, and the received data light flickers when the modem receives data from the remote unit. The high speed (HS) light becomes active when the modem is conducting transfers at its highest possible rate. If an external modem will not operate at its highest rated potential, the specification for the UART on the adapter card should be checked to make certain that it is capable of operating at that speed.

Local Area Networks

> **Local area networks (LANs)** are systems designed to connect computers in relative proximity. These connections enable users attached to the network to share resources such as printers and modems. LAN connections also enable users to communicate with each other and share data between their computers.

When discussing LANs, you must consider two basic topics: the LAN's **topology** (hardware connection method) and its **protocol** (communication control method). In concept, a minimum of three stations must be connected to have a true LAN. If only two units are connected, then point-to-point communications software and a simple null modem can be used.

LAN Topologies

Network topologies are connection/configuration strategies. LAN topologies fall into three types of configurations:

- Bus
- Ring
- Star

All three topologies are illustrated in Figure 11.22. In the bus topology, the **stations**, or **nodes**, of the network connect to a central communication link. Each node has a unique address along the bus that differentiates it from the other users on the network. Information can be placed on the bus by any node. The information must contain network address information about the node(s) for which the information is intended. Other nodes along the bus ignore the information.

In a ring network configuration, the communication bus is formed into a closed loop. Each node inspects the information on the LAN as it passes. A **repeater**, built into the ring LAN card, regenerates every message not directed to it and sends it to the next node. The originating node eventually receives the message and removes it from the ring.

In a star topology, the logical layout of the network resembles the branches of a tree. All the nodes are connected in **branches** that eventually lead back to a central unit. Nodes communicate with each other through the central unit. The central station coordinates the network's activity by polling the nodes one by one to see whether they have any information to transfer. If so, the central station gives that node a predetermined slice of time to transmit. If the message is longer than the time allotted, the transmissions is chopped into small segments that are transmitted over several polling cycles.

FIGURE 11.22

*Star, bus, and ring
configurations.*

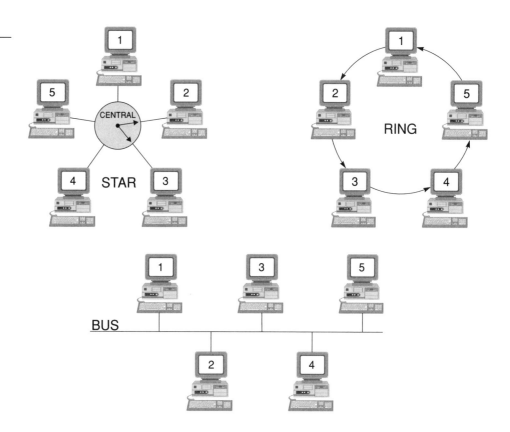

Control of the network can be implemented in two ways: as **peer-to-peer networks**, in which each computer is attached to the network in a ring or bus fashion, and in **client/server networks**, in which workstations (referred to as **clients**) operate in conjunction with a dedicated master (**file server**) computer.

Figure 11.23 illustrates a typical peer-to-peer network arrangement. In this arrangement, the users connected to the network share access to different network resources, such as each other's hard drives and printers. However, control of the local unit is fairly autonomous. The nodes in this type of network configuration usually contain local hard drives and printers that the local computer controls. These items can be shared at the discretion of the individual user.

A typical client/server LAN configuration is depicted in Figure 11.24. In this type of LAN, control tends to be very centralized. The server(s) typically hold(s) the programs and data for all the LAN's users. In some cases, the client units do not even include a local hard or floppy drive unit. Boot-up is performed through an onboard BIOS, and no data is ever stored in the client machine. This type of client is referred to as a **workstation**.

Network Protocols

A+ CORE 7.1

In a network, some method must be used to determine which node has use of the network's communications paths, and for how long the node can have it. The network's protocol handles these functions to prevent more than one user from accessing the bus at any given time.

FIGURE 11.23

A peer-to-peer network.

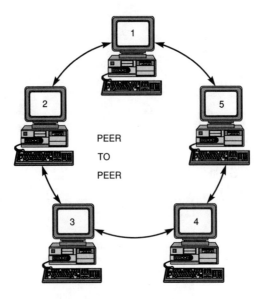

FIGURE 11.24

A client/server network.

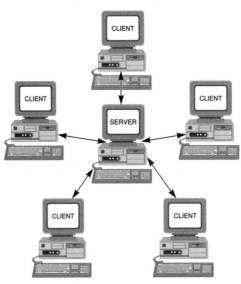

If two sets of data are placed on the network at the same time, a **data collision** occurs and data is lost. Three de facto networking protocols come into play here: **Ethernet**, **ArcNet**, and **Token Ring**.

Ethernet

Ethernet was developed by Xerox in 1976. Its methodology for control is referred to as **Carrier Sense Multiple Access with Collision Detection (CSMA/CD)**. Using this protocol, a node that wishes to transfer data over the network first listens to the LAN to see whether it is in use. If not, the node begins transmitting its data. If the network is busy, the node waits for the LAN to clear for a predetermined time and then takes control of the LAN.

If two nodes are waiting to use the LAN, they periodically attempt to access the LAN at the same time. When this happens, a data collision occurs and the data from both nodes is rendered useless. The receiver portion of the Ethernet controller monitors the transmission to detect collisions. When it senses the data bits overlapping, it halts the transmission, as does the other node. The transmitting controller generates an **abort pattern code** that is transmitted to all the nodes on the LAN to tell them that a collision has occurred. This alerts any nodes that might be waiting to access the LAN that there is a problem.

The receiving node (or nodes) dump(s) any data that it might have received before the collision occurred. Other nodes waiting to send data generate a random timing number and go into a holding pattern. The timing number is a **waiting time** that the node sits out before it tries to transmit. Because the number is randomly generated, the odds against two of the nodes trying to transmit again at the same time is very low. The first node to time out listens to the LAN to see whether any activity is still occurring. Because it almost always finds a clear LAN, the first node begins transmitting. If two of the nodes do time out at the same time, another collision happens and the abort pattern/number generation/time-out sequence begins again. Eventually, one of the nodes will gain clear access to the network and successfully transmit its data.

> The Ethernet strategy provides for up to 1,024 users to share the LAN. However, from the description of its collision-recovery technique, it should be clear that with more users on an Ethernet LAN, more collisions are likely to occur, and the average time to complete an actual data transfer will be longer.

The Ethernet Frame

Under the Ethernet standard, information is collected into a package called a **frame**. A typical Ethernet frame is depicted in Figure 11.25. The frame carries six sections of information:

- A preamble
- A destination address
- An originating address
- A type field
- The data field
- The frame check error-detection and correction information

FIGURE 11.25

A typical Ethernet frame.

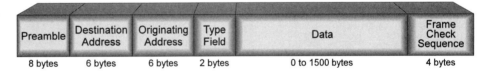

Preamble	Destination Address	Originating Address	Type Field	Data	Frame Check Sequence
8 bytes	6 bytes	6 bytes	2 bytes	0 to 1500 bytes	4 bytes

This organizational structure is very similar to that of a sector on a hard disk. The preamble synchronizes the receiver's operation to that of the transmitter. This action also tells the other nodes that a transmission is under way. The Ethernet preamble is a 64-bit string, made up of alternating 1s and 0s, that ends in two consecutive 1s.

The destination address field is 6 bytes long and is used to define one of three address locations. This number can represent the individual node address of the intended receiver or the address of a grouping of nodes around the LAN, or it can be a broadcast code that enables the node to send a message to everyone on the LAN.

The originating address field contains the identification address for the transmitting node. The type field is a 2-byte field that identifies the user protocol of the frame.

The data field is a variable-length field that contains the actual information. Because it is sent in a synchronous mode, the data field can be as long as necessary. However, the Ethernet standard does not accommodate data fields less than 46 bytes or longer than 1,500 bytes.

The frame check block contains an error-detection and correction word. As with parity and other error-detection schemes, the receiver regenerates the error code from the received data (actually the data, the address bytes, and the type field) and compares it to the received code. If a mismatch occurs, an error signal is generated from the LAN card to the system.

Ethernet Specifications

A+ CORE 7.1

> Ethernet is classified as a bus topology. The original Ethernet scheme was classified as a 10MHz transmission protocol. The maximum length specified for Ethernet is 1.55 miles (2.5km), with a maximum segment length between nodes of 500 meters. This type of LAN is referred to as a **10base5** LAN by the IEEE organization. However, newer implementations—called **Fast Ethernet**—are producing LAN speeds of up to 100Mbps.

Ethernet connections can be made through 50-ohm coaxial cable (10base5), Thin Net coaxial cable (10base2), or unshielded twisted pair (UTP) cabling (1base5). The Fast Ethernet specifications that use UTP are referred to as 10BaseT (10Mbps) and 100BaseT (100Mbps). Ethernet cards capable of supporting these transmission rates are classified as 10/100 cards.

Coaxial cable is familiar to most people as the conductor that carries cable TV into their homes. Coax has a single copper conductor in its center and a protective braided copper shield around it. UTP cable is common telephone cabling with four pairs of twisted wires inside.

The 10base2 Ethernet LAN uses thinner industry-standard RG-58 coaxial cable and has a maximum segment length of 185 meters. The UTP specification is based on telephone cable and is normally used to connect a small number of PCs together. The twisted pairing of the cables uses magnetic-field principles to minimize induced noise in the lines. UTP has a transmission rate that is stated as 1Mbps. Using UTP cable, a LAN containing up to 64 nodes can be constructed with the maximum distance between nodes set at 250 meters. Typical coaxial and UTP connections are depicted in Figure 11.26.

FIGURE 11.26

Typical coaxial and UTP connections.

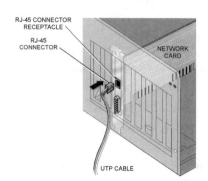
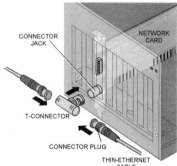

The original 10base5 connection scheme required that special **transceiver units** be clamped to the cable. A pin in the transceiver pierced the cable to establish electrical contact with its conductor. An additional length of cabling, called the **drop cable**, was then connected between the LAN adapter card and the transceiver.

In a 10base2 LAN, the node's LAN adapter card is usually connected directly to the LAN cabling using a **T-connector** (for peer-to-peer networks) or by a **BNC** connector (in a client/server LAN). The 1base5 system uses **RJ-45** jacks and plugs to connect the LAN. RJ-45 connectors are very similar in appearance to the RJ-11 connectors used with telephones and modems. However, the RJ-45 connectors are considerably larger than the RJ-11 connectors. Some Ethernet adapters include 15-pin sockets that enable special systems, such as fiber-optic cable, to be interfaced to them. Other cards provide specialized ST connectors for fiber-optic connectors.

1base5 systems normally use **concentrators**, similar to the one in Figure 11.27, for connection purposes. Both coaxial connection methods require that a terminating resistor be installed at each end of the transmission line. Ethernet systems use 52-ohm terminators.

FIGURE 11.27

UTP between a computer and a concentrator.

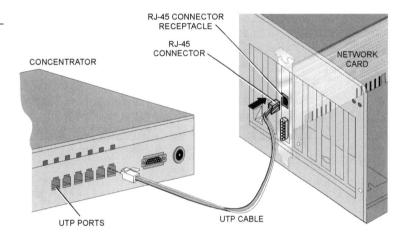

Fiber-optic cable offers the prospects of very high performance links for LAN implementation. It can handle much higher data-transfer rates than copper conductors and can use longer distances between stations before signal deterioration becomes a problem. In addition, fiber-optic cable offers a high degree of security for data communications because it does not radiate EMI signal information that can be detected outside the conductor, it does not tap easily, and it shows a decided signal loss when it is tapped.

Although fiber-optic cable is now widely used in telephone systems, and although some standards are in place for implementing LANs on fiber optic cabling, few LAN hardware manufacturers have switched over to fiber-optic networking at this time.

Table 11.6 summarizes the different Ethernet specifications. Other CSMA/CD-based protocols exist in the market; some are actually Ethernet-compatible. However, these systems may or may not achieve the performance levels of a true Ethernet system. Some may actually perform better.

Table 11.6 *Ethernet Specifications*

Classification	Conductor Max.	Segment Length	Nodes	Max. Length	Trans. Rate
1Base5	UTP	250m	64	500m	1Mbps
10Base2	RG-58	185m	30	250m	10Mbps
10Base5	RG-50	500m	10	2.5km	10Mbps

ArcNet

The **ArcNet** (**Attached Resource Computer NETwork**) protocol was developed by Datapoint and is based on a modified **token-passing** scheme. In a token-passing system, contention for use of the LAN among different nodes is handled by passing an electronic enabling code, called a **token**, from node to node. Only the node possessing the token can have control of the LAN to transmit information. This concept is illustrated in Figure 11.28.

FIGURE 11.28

A token-passing scheme.

The token is passed from node to node along the LAN. Each node is allowed to hold the token a prescribed amount of time. After sending its message, or after its time runs out, the node must transfer the token to the next node. If the next node has no message, it simply passes the token along to the next designated node. Nodes do not have to be in numerical sequence; their sequences are programmed in the network management software. All nodes listen to the LAN during the token-passing time.

In a token-passing network, new or removed nodes must be added to or deleted from the rotational list in the network management software. If not, the LAN will never grant access to the new nodes. Most ArcNet management software and cards are built so that each device attached to the LAN is interrogated when the LAN is started up. In this way, the rotational file is verified each time the network is started.

New nodes that start up after the LAN has been initialized transmit a **reconfiguration burst** that can be heard by all the nodes. This burst grabs the attention of all the installed nodes and erases their token destination addresses. Each node goes into a wait state that is determined by its station number. The node with the highest station number times out first and tries to access the LAN.

The highest-numbered node is responsible for starting the token-passing action after a new unit is added to the LAN. This is accomplished by broadcasting a signal to all nodes telling them what it believes is the lowest numbered node in the LAN and asking if it will accept the token. If no response is given, the node moves to the next known address in the LAN management software's roster and repeats the request. This action continues until an enabled node responds. At this point, the token is passed to the new node, and the forwarding address is stored in the LAN manager's list. Each successive node goes through the same process until all the nodes have been accessed.

The node passing the token must always monitor the LAN, under the ArcNet scenario. This is done to prevent the loss of the token during its passage. If the node remains inactive for a predetermined amount of time, the transmitting node must reclaim the token and search for the next active node to which it must pass the token. In this case, the transmitting node simply increments its next-node address by one and attempts to make contact with a node at that address. If not, it increments the count by one again and retries until it reaches an enabled node. This new node number is stored in the transmitting node and will be the pass-to number for that node until the system is shut down or reconfigured.

ArcNet Specifications

In the ArcNet specification, no particular transmission medium is defined. ArcNet can be used with coaxial cable, twisted-pair cable, or fiber-optic cable. ArcNet coaxial cabling is defined as RG-59 cable, with 75-ohm terminators required for any open nodes. The ArcNet protocol transfers data at a nominal rate of 2.5MHz.

As with the Ethernet rating, this is a maximum rate. Obviously, neither network can push through data at this rate if it is being transmitted to a 1200bps modem, or a serial printer. Other system items, such as hard drives and video adapters, can also limit the true speed of the network.

Although the ArcNet topology is defined as a ring, its actual construction resembles more of a star or tree structure, as illustrated in Figure 11.29. Each station connects to a signal repeater, called a **hub**. Hubs may be active or passive. **Active hubs** actually receive the signal, regenerate it, and resend it. The maximum distance a node can be located from an active hub is 600 meters, while the maximum distance from a **passive hub** is 30 meters. Hubs can be linked to increase the actual distance between nodes.

FIGURE 11.29

The ArcNet tree structure.

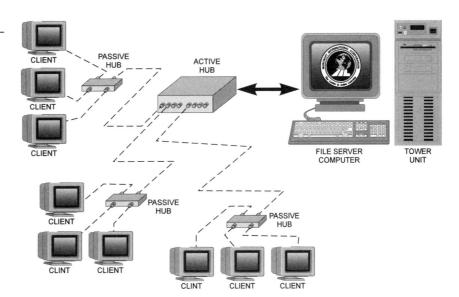

ArcNet Frames

The packet construction for an ArcNet frame is depicted in Figure 11.30. This configuration uses a 1-byte Start field, a 1-byte Access Control field, a 1-byte Frame Control field, 6 bytes of destination address, 6 bytes of source address, a 512-byte (maximum) data field, a 4-byte frame check character, a 1-byte end delimiter mark, and a 1-byte Frame Status field.

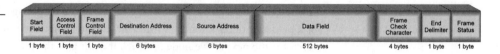

Start Field	Access Control Field	Frame Control Field	Destination Address	Source Address	Data Field	Frame Check Character	End Delimiter	Frame Status
1 byte	1 byte	1 byte	6 bytes	6 bytes	512 bytes	4 bytes	1 byte	1 byte

The Start field contains bits that the nodes can detect as markers for the start of a transmission. The Access Control field establishes the token priority system. One bit is a **monitor bit** that is used by the transmitting node to identify a frame that it should remove from the LAN. The frame control byte declares what type of frame is being transmitted (such as a ring management frame or a data frame). The source and destination frames should be self-explanatory, as should the data frame.

The Frame Check field is a 32-bit **checksum character** that detects single-bit transmission errors. The end delimiter is an encoded bit pattern that tells the receiving node that the frame is ending. One of its bits is used in multipacket transmissions to indicate whether the current frame is an intermediate or final frame. Finally, the Frame Status field is used to determine whether the receiving node is present on the LAN, and if it has received the frame. Because the receiver actually copies the frame and places it back on the LAN, it has an opportunity to set the received bit in this field if it has been received. If not, the bit remains unchanged and will be recognized as an unreceived frame when it gets back to the original node.

Token Ring

In 1985, IBM developed a token-passing LAN protocol it called the **Token Ring**. As its name implies, Token Ring is a token-passing protocol operating on a ring topology. The token is a small frame that all nodes can recognize instantly.

When the ring is idle, the token simply passes counter-clockwise from station to station. A station can transmit information on the ring any time it receives the token. This is accomplished by turning the token packet into the start of a data packet and adding its data to it.

At the intended receiver, the packet is copied into a buffer memory serially where it is stored. The receiver also places the packet back on the ring so that the transmitter can get it back. Upon doing so, the transmitter reconstructs the token and places it back on the ring. This concept is described in Figure 11.31.

IBM uses **trunk coupling units** (**TCUs**) to connect to the cable, as illustrated in Figure 11.32. The cabling is a two-pair, shielded, twisted-pair cable. The main cable is called the **trunk cable**, and the individual drops are referred to as the **interface cable**. The TCUs are grouped in units called **concentrators**. Internally, the concentrator's ports are connected into a ring configuration. In this manner, the concentrator can be placed in a convenient area and enable nodes to be positioned where they are needed. Some Token Ring adapters provide nine-pin connectors for shielded twisted-pair (STP) cables as well.

FIGURE 11.31

Token Ring concept.

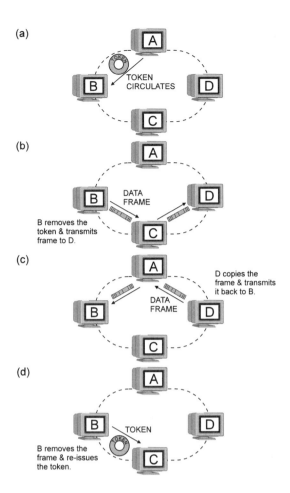

(a)

(b)

(c)

(d)

FIGURE 11.32

TCU connections.

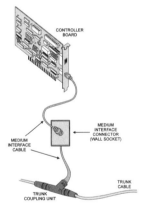

The frame packaging for a Token Ring transmission is very similar to that of an ArcNet frame. The data transfer rate stated for Token Ring systems is 4–16Mbps. Token-passing is less efficient than other protocols when the load on the network is light. However, it evenly divides the net's usage between nodes when traffic is heavy. Token-passing can also be extremely vulnerable to node crashes when that node has the token. LAN adapter cards are typically designed to monitor the LAN for such occurrences so that they can be corrected without shutting down the entire network.

Table 11.7 lists the specifications of the Arcnet and Token Ring topologies.

Table 11.7 *Summary of ArcNet and Token Ring Specs*

Classification	Conductor Max.	Segment Length	Nodes	Trans. Rate
ArcNet	RG-59(75Ω)	600m	9/17	2.5Mbps
Token Ring	STP(150Ω)	185m	30	4Mbps

LAN Adapter Cards

In a LAN, each computer on the net requires a **network adapter card** (also referred to as a **NIC**), and every unit is connected to the network by some type of cabling. These cables are typically twisted-pair wires, thick or thin coaxial cable, or fiber-optic cable.

When dealing with a LAN adapter card, it must have connectors that are compatible with the type of LAN cabling being used. Many Ethernet LAN cards come with both an RJ-45 and a BNC connector so that the card can be used in any type of Ethernet configuration.

A typical LAN card is depicted in Figure 11.33. In addition to its LAN connectors, the LAN card may have a number of configuration jumpers that must be set up. Some cards may have jumper instructions printed directly on the I/O card, but the card's user's manual is normally a must for configuring the card for operation. Great care should be taken with the user's manual, as its loss might render the card useless. At the very least, you would have to contact the manufacturer to get a replacement.

FIGURE 11.33

A typical LAN card.

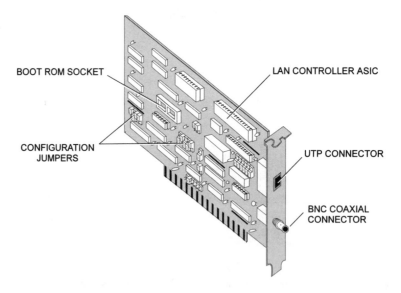

Another item of note on LAN cards includes the presence of a vacant ROM socket. This socket can be used to install a boot-up ROM to enable the unit to be used as a diskless workstation. One or more activity lights may also be included on the card's back plate. These lights can play a very important part in diagnosing problems with the LAN connection. Check the card's user's manual for definitions of its activity lights.

Each adapter must have an **adapter driver** program loaded in its host computer to handle communications between the system and the adapter. These are the Ethernet, ArcNet, and Token Ring drivers that are loaded to control specific types of LAN adapter cards.

In addition to the adapter drivers, the network computer must have a **network protocol driver** loaded. This program may be referred to as the **Transport protocol**, or simply as *the protocol*. It operates between the adapter and the initial layer of network software to package and unpackage data for the LAN. In many cases, the computer may have several different protocol drivers loaded so that the unit can communicate with computers that use other types of protocols.

Typical protocol drivers include the **Internetworking Packet Exchange/Sequential Packet Exchange (IPX/SPX)** model produced by Novell, and the standard **Transmission Control Protocol/Internet Protocol (TCP/IP)** developed by the U.S. military for its ARPA network. Figure 11.34 illustrates the various LAN drivers necessary to transmit or receive data on a network. More specific protocol information is provided throughout the remainder of this chapter.

FIGURE 11.34

Various LAN drivers.

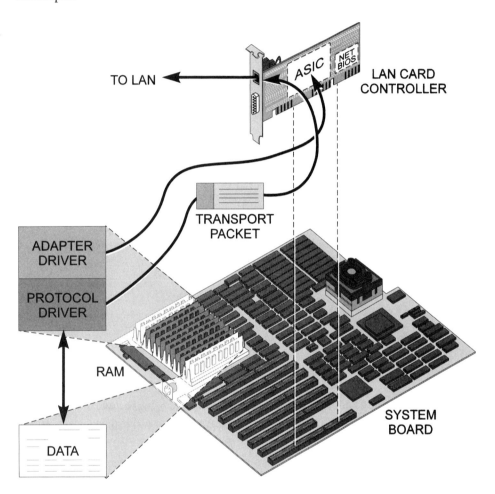

Installing LANs

A+ CORE 1.3

Installing a LAN card in a PC follows the basic steps of installing most peripheral cards. Check the system for currently installed drivers and system settings. Consult the LAN card's installation guide for default settings information, and compare them to those of devices already installed in the system. If no apparent conflicts exist between the default settings and those already in use by the system, place the adapter card in a vacant expansion slot and secure it to the system unit's back plate.

Connect the LAN card to the network as directed by the manufacturer's installation guide, and load the proper software drivers for the installed adapter (see Table 11.8). Figure 11.35 illustrates the process of connecting the computer to the LAN using UTP or coaxial cable. If UTP is being used, the line drop to the computer would come from a concentrator similar to the one depicted.

FIGURE 11.35

Connecting the computer to the LAN.

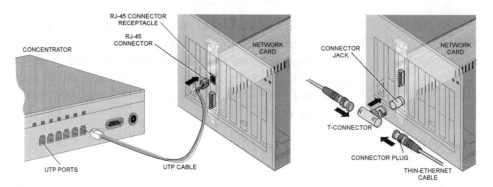

Three pieces of important information are required to configure the LAN adapter card for use:

▶ The interrupt request (IRQ) setting the adapter uses to communicate with the system

▶ The base I/O port address the adapter uses to exchange information with the system

▶ The base memory address that the adapter uses as a starting point in memory for DMA transfers

Some adapters may require that a DMA channel be defined.

Typical configuration settings for the network card's IRQ, I/O port address, and base memory are listed here:

IRQ = 5

Port address = 300h

Base memory = D8000h

If a configuration conflict appears, reset the conflicting settings so that they do not share the same value. Determining which component's configuration gets changed depends on examining the options for changing the cards involved in the conflict. A sound card may have many more IRQ options available than a given network card. In this case, it would be easier to change sound card settings than network card settings.

Table 11.8   LAN Card Configuration Settings

I/O Address Options	Interrupt Request Channels	Extended Memory Addressing
240h	IRQ2	C000h
280h	IRQ3	C400h
2C0h	IRQ4	C800h
320h	IRQ10	CC00h
340h	IRQ11	D000h
360h	IRQ12	D400h
	IRQ15	DC00h

Troubleshooting LANs

Check to see whether any new hardware or new software has been added. Has any of the cabling been changed? Have any new protocols been added? Has any network adapter been replaced or moved? If any of these events has occurred, begin by checking each specifically.

If the system has not been changed and has operated correctly in the past, the next step is to make certain that it functions properly as a standalone unit. Begin by disconnecting the unit from the network and testing its operation. Run diagnostics on the system to see if any problems show up. If a hardware problem is encountered at the standalone level, troubleshoot the indicated portion of the system using the procedures already discussed.

If the problem does not appear in or is not related to the standalone operation of the unit, check the portions of the system that are specific to the network. These elements include the network adapter card, the network-specific portions of the operating system, and the **network drop cabling**. Figure 11.36 depicts the network-specific portions of a computer system.

FIGURE 11.36

Network-related components.

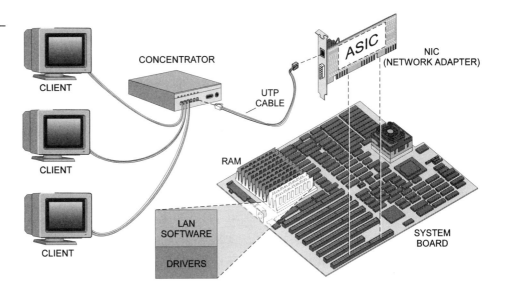

For example, disconnecting a unit from a network that uses coaxial cable creates an unterminated condition in the network. This condition can cause several different types of problems:

▶ Data moving through the network can be lost.

- A general slowing of data movement across the network can occur due to reduced bandwidth.

- Nodes may not be able to see or connect to each other.

If a unit must be removed from the network, it is a good practice to place a terminator in the empty connector where the unit was attached. This should enable the other units to function without the problems associated with an open connection. Care must be taken to ensure that the proper value of terminating resistor is used. Substituting a terminator from an ArcNet system into an Ethernet system may create as many problems as the open connection would have. However, these may be harder to track down. Systems that use concentrators have fewer connection problems when a unit must be removed for servicing.

Even if the unit does not need to be removed from the network, diagnostic efforts and tests run across the network can use up a lot of the network's bandwidth. This reduced bandwidth causes the operation of all the units on the network to slow down. This is due simply to the added usage of the network.

A+ CORE 7.3

Because performing work on the network can affect so many users, it is good practice to involve the network administrator in any such work being performed. This person can run interference for any work that must be performed that could disable the network or cause users to lose data.

LAN Configuration Checks

A+ CORE 1.3

As with any peripheral device, its configuration must be correct for the software that is driving the peripheral, and for the adapter card through which it is communicating. An improperly configured network adapter card can prevent the system from gaining access to the network. Many newer network cards possess plug-and-play capabilities; with other network cards, such as ISA cards, it is necessary to configure the card through hardware jumpers or through EPROM configuration switches.

Check the adapter card's hardware settings to see whether they are set according to the manufacturer's default settings or whether they have been changed to some new setting. If they have been changed, refer to the system information from the software diagnostic tool to see whether there is some good explanation for the change. If not, record the settings as they are and reset them to their default values. Also check the software's configuration settings and change them to match as necessary. If a defective card is being replaced with an identical unit, simply transfer the configuration settings to the new card.

Use a software diagnostic package, such as MSD, to check the system's interrupt request allocations. Try to use a package that has the capabilities of checking the system's I/O port addresses and shadow RAM and ROM allocations. Finally, check the physical IRQ settings of any other adapter cards in the system.

LAN Software Checks

At the LAN system software level, troubleshooting activities diverge. The differences between Novell's Netware, Microsoft's Windows NT, Windows for Workgroups (Windows 3.11), and Windows 95 are significant enough that there are nationally recognized certifications just for Netware and Windows NT. Novell Netware and Windows NT are client/server types of network management software, and Windows 3.11 and Windows 95 are peer-to-peer networking environments.

One of the major concerns in most network environments is data security. Because all the data around the network is potentially available to anyone else attached to the network, all LAN administration software employs different levels of security. Passwords are typically used at all software levels to lock people out of hardware systems as well as programs and data files.

Logon passwords and scripts are designed to keep personnel from accessing the system or its contents. Additional passwording may be used to provide access to some parts of the system and not others. (For example, lower-level accounting personnel may be allowed access to accounts receivable and payable sections of the business management software package, but not allowed into the payroll section.) A series of passwords may be used to deny access to this area.

In other LAN management packages, access and privileges to programs and data can be established by the network administrator through the software's security system. These settings can be established to completely deny access to certain information or to grant limited access rights to it. An example of limited rights would be the capability of reading data from a file but not manipulating it (write, delete, print, or move) in any way.

The reason for discussing security at this point is because established security settings can prevent the technician from using any or all of the system's resources. In addition, having limited access to programs can give them the appearance of being defective. Because of this, the service technician must work with the network administrator when checking a networked machine. The administrator can provide the access and the security relief needed to repair the system. The administrator can also keep you away from data that may not be any of your business.

Windows 3.11

In Windows 3.11, several network-related files and file segments are added to the Windows operating environment to give it peer-to-peer networking capabilities. If a problem exists in the networking operation of 3.11, exit to the DOS level and check the CONFIG.SYS file for a line that states DEVICE=IFSHLP.SYS. Also check the AUTOEXEC.BAT file for a line that states C:\WINDOWS\NET_START.

In Windows 3.11, use the Windows Write program to check the SYSTEM.INI file for a new section titled [network] and to check for the presence of the new NETWORK.INI file.

Check the network selection in Windows Setup for the proper driver. The Change Network Settings option provides access to three important buttons:

▶ The Networks button

▶ The Sharing button

▶ The Drivers button

The Networks button enables network support to be turned on and off. It also enables additional networks to be added to unit. The Sharing button is used to provide sharing of local files and printers with other nodes on the network. The Drivers button is used to install and remove LAN adapters and protocols. Windows 3.11 offers a long list of adapter drivers from which to select and has some capabilities to auto-detect the type of adapter card installed in the unit. Several protocol programs are included to enable Windows 3.11 stations to exchange information with other types of Microsoft networks.

If a compatible driver does not exist in Windows, you must place a manufacturer-supplied driver disk in the floppy drive and click on the Have Disk entry to upload the OEM drivers and protocols needed to operate the card.

Windows 95

In Windows 95, the computer's networking information can be checked through the Network icon, under the Start/Settings/Control Panel path. The network drivers are located under the Configuration tab. Double-click the installed adapter card's driver to obtain its configuration information. The Resource section of a network card's configuration in Windows 95 is depicted in Figure 11.37.

FIGURE 11.37

NE-2000-compatible resources screen.

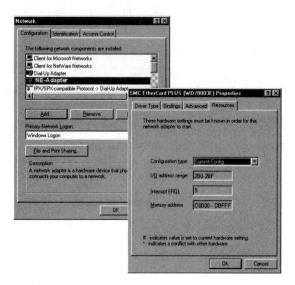

Windows 95 includes a network diagnostic tool, called Net Diag, that can be used to troubleshoot connectivity problems from a second (functional Windows 95) node on the network. To use the Net Diag program, start it from the command line of a second computer on the network. This establishes the second unit as a diagnostic server on the net. Move to the original node and enter the Net Diag command at the command-line level.

Windows 95 provides fundamental troubleshooting information for wide area networking through its system of Help screens. Simply select Help from the Control Panel's toolbar, and click on the topics related to the problem. Also use a word-processing package to read the Windows 95 SETUPLOG.TXT and BOOTLOG.TXT files. These files record where setup and booting errors occur. Use the F8 function key during boot-up to examine each driver being loaded.

Novell NetWare and Windows NT

> In a client/server system such as a Novell NetWare or Windows NT system, the technician's main responsibility is to get the local station to boot up to the network's logon prompt. At this point, the network administrator or network engineer becomes responsible for directing the troubleshooting process.

In a Novell system, check the root directory of the workstation for the NETBIOS and IPX.COM files. Check the AUTOEXEC.BAT file on the local drive for command lines to run the NETBIOS, load the IPX file, and load the ODI (or NETx) files.

The NETBIOS file is an emulation of IBM's **NETwork Basic Input/Output system** and represents the basic interface between the operating system and the LAN. This function is implemented through ROM BIOS ICs, located on the network card. The **Internetworking Packet Exchange (IPX)** file passes commands across the network to the file server. The **Open Datalink Interface (ODI)** file is the network shell that communicates between the adapter and the system's applications. Older versions of NetWare used a shell program called NETx. These files should be referenced in the AUTOEXEC.BAT or NET.BAT files.

In a Windows NT workstation, there are only a few options to get the unit to the logon prompt. If the original installer set up the Windows NT client in FAT mode, you can boot the system to a DOS prompt. Use a DOS 5.0 or higher boot disk to boot the system. Check for the following files in the root directory:

- Windows NT Loader (LDR)

- MSDOS.SYS

- COMMAND.COM

- IO.SYS

If the installer used NTFS format to set up the client site, there is no option to boot the system to a DOS prompt. If an emergency repair disk was created during setup, it can be used to gain access to the system. However, if no such repair disk is available, the Windows NT client software must be reinstalled.

When a Windows NT workstation boots up, the Windows NT LOADER program checks the installed hardware and examines the Windows NT kernel program. If both checks are correct, a blue screen comes up on the monitor. At this point, you are in the Windows NT operating system. As Windows NT takes over, it loads the interface that includes the registry and the SERVICES.LPD file. Next, Windows NT brings in the GUI and the logon prompt. If the indicated files are not present, it may be necessary to reinstall Windows NT.

LAN Hardware Checks

A+ CORE 7.2   Some LAN adapters come with software diagnostic programs that can be used to isolate problems with the adapter. If this type of software is included, use it to test the card. The diagnostic software can also be used to change the adapter's configuration, if necessary.

If the card fails any of the diagnostic tests, check it by exchanging it with a known good one of the same type. Set the replacement card's station address so that it is unique (usually the same as the card being removed). Depending on the type of system being tested, the file server may need to be cycled off and then back on to detect the presence of the new LAN card.

Check the activity light on the back plate of the LAN card (if available) to see whether it is being recognized by the network. If the lights are active, the connection is alive. If not, check the adapter in another node. Check the cabling to make sure that it is the correct type and that the connector is properly attached. A LAN cable tester is an excellent device to have in this situation.

If the operation of the local computer unit appears normal, you must troubleshoot the network from the node out. As mentioned earlier, always consult the network administrator before performing any work on a network beyond a standalone unit. In a network, no node is an island, and every unit has an impact on the operation of the network when it is online. Changes made in one part of a network can cause problems and data loss in other parts of the network. You should be aware that changing hardware and software configuration settings for the adapter can have adverse effects when the system is returned to the network. In addition, changing hard drives in a network node can have a negative impact on the network when the unit is brought back online.

Check the system for concentrators, routers, and bridges that may not be functioning properly. Check the frame settings being used to make sure that they are compatible from device to device, or that they are represented on the file server. The operation of these devices will have to be verified as separate units.

Network Printing Problems

> The reason for including the Network Printing Problems section under the LAN heading of this chapter is that the technician must understand the problems that networking brings to the operation of the system before troubleshooting can be effective.

As described in Chapter 10, "Printers," transferring data from the system to the printer over a parallel port and cable is largely a matter of connecting the cable and installing the proper printer driver for the selected printer. The protocol for sending data consists largely of a simple hardware handshake routine. Even in a serial printer, the protocol is only slightly more complex. However, when a network is involved, the complexity becomes that much greater again, due to the addition of the network drivers.

The first step in troubleshooting network printer problems is to verify that the local unit and the remote printer are set up for remote printing. In Windows for Workgroups and Windows 95, this involves sharing the printer with the network users. The station to which the printer is connected should appear in the Windows 95 Network Neighborhood window. If the remote computer cannot see files and printers at the print server station, file and print sharing may not be enabled there.

In Windows 95, file and printer sharing can be accomplished at the print server in a number of different ways. In the first method, double-click the printer's icon in the My Computer or Windows Explorer. Follow this by selecting Printer/Properties/Sharing and then choosing the configuration. The second method calls for an alternate-click (right-click for right handers) on the Printers icon, followed by selecting Share in the Context Menu and choosing the configuration. The final method is similar except that the path is as follows: alternate-click/Properties/Sharing/choose the configuration.

The next step is to verify the operation of the printer. As described in the "Troubleshooting" section of Chapter 10, run a self-test on the printer to make certain that it is working correctly. Turn the printer off and allow a few seconds for its buffer memory to clear. Try to run a test page to verify the operation of the printer's hardware.

If the test page does not print, a problem obviously exists with the printer. Troubleshoot the printer using the information from Chapter 10 until the self-test works correctly. With the printer working, attempt to print across the network again.

The second step is to determine whether the print server (the computer actually connected to the network printer) can print to the printer. Try to open a document on the print server and print it. If the local printing operation is unsuccessful, move to the MS-DOS prompt, create a small batch file, and copy it to the local LPT port, as described in Chapter 10.

If the file prints, a few possible causes of printing problems exist. The first possibility is that a problem exists with the printer configuration at the print server. Check the print server's drivers.

Another common problem is that not enough memory or hard drive space might be available in the print server. In Windows 3.x, check the available space on the hard drive and clear the contents of the TEMP directory. In Windows 95, check the Spool Settings under the Details entry of the Control Panel/Printers/Properties path. If the spooler is set to EMF, set it to RAW spooling. If the print spool is set to RAW, turn off the spool and click the Print Directly to Printer button. If the unit prints the test page, use the SCANDISK utility to check the disk space. Clear the TEMP directory.

If the file does not print, a hardware problem exists in the local hardware. Refer to the "Hardware Checks" section of the troubleshooting procedure in Chapter 10.

The third step is to verify the operation of the network. This can be accomplished by trying other network functions, such as transferring a file from the remote unit to the print server. If the other network functions work, examine the printer driver configuration of the remote unit. In Windows 3.x, check under Connect/Network in the Control Panel. In Windows 95, open the Control Panel's Printer folder and select the Properties entry in the drop-down File menu. Check the information under the Details and Sharing tabs.

If the print drivers appear to be correct, install a generic or text-only printer driver and try to print to the print server. Also, move to the DOS prompt in the remote unit and create a batch text file. Attempt to copy this file to the network printer. If the generic driver or the DOS file works, reinstall the printer driver, or install new drivers for the designated printer.

If other network functions are operational, the final step is to verify the printer operation of the local computer. If possible, connect a printer directly to the local unit and set up its print driver to print to the local printer port. If the file prints to the local printer, a network/printer driver problem still exists. Reload the printer driver and check the network print path. The correct format for the network path name is \\COMPUTER_name\ SHARED DEVICE_name. Check the network cabling for good connections.

In Windows 95, the Help function performs many of the diagnostic steps outlined here in a guided format.

If the printer operation stalls or crashes during the printing process, a different type of problem is indicated. In this case, the remote printer was functioning, the print server was operational, and the network was transferring data. Some critical condition must have been reached to stop the printing process. Check the print spooler (or print manager) in the print server to see whether an error has occurred. Also check the hard disk space and memory usage in the print server.

Wide Area Networks

The fastest-growing segment of the personal computer world is in the area of **wide area networks (WANs)**.

A wide area network is very similar in concept to a widely distributed client/server LAN. In a WAN, computers are typically separated by distances that must be serviced via modems instead of network cards.

A typical WAN would be a local city- or county-wide network, such as the one in Figure 11.38. This network links members together through a **bulletin board service (BBS)**. Users can access the BBS server with a simple telephone call.

FIGURE 11.38

County-wide network.

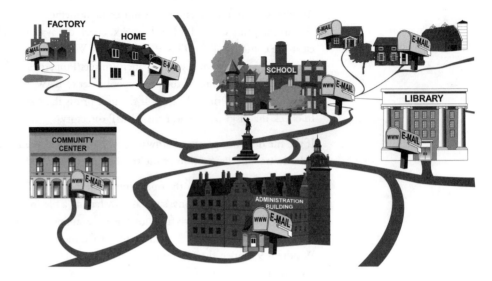

WANs are connected by several different types of communication systems. These communication paths are referred to as **links**. Most users connect to the network via standard telephone lines using dial-up modems, such as those described earlier in this chapter. Dial-up connections are generally the slowest method of connecting to a network, but they are inexpensive to establish and use.

Other users who require quicker data transfers contract with the telephone company to use special, high-speed **Integrated Service Digital Network (ISDN)** lines. These types of links require a digital modem to conduct data transfers. Because the modem is digital, no analog conversion is required.

Users who require very high volumes will lease dedicated **T1 and T3 lines** from the telephone company. These applications generally serve businesses that put several of their computers or networks online. After the information is transmitted, it may be carried over many types of communications links on its way to its destination. These interconnecting links can include fiber-optic cables, satellite up and down links, UHF, and microwave transmission systems. Figure 11.39 illustrates different methods of accessing the Internet.

In some areas, high-speed intermediate-sized networks, referred to as **metropolitan area networks** (MANs), are popping up. These networks typically cover areas up to 50km in diameter and are operated to provide access to regional resources. MANs are like LANs in speed and operation, but they use special high-speed connections and protocols to increase the geographical span of the network in much the same way a WAN does.

The Internet

The most famous wide area network is the **Internet**. The Internet is actually a network of networks working together. The main communication path for the Internet is a series of networks, established by the U.S. government, to link supercomputers at key research sites.

FIGURE 11.39

Methods of accessing the Internet.

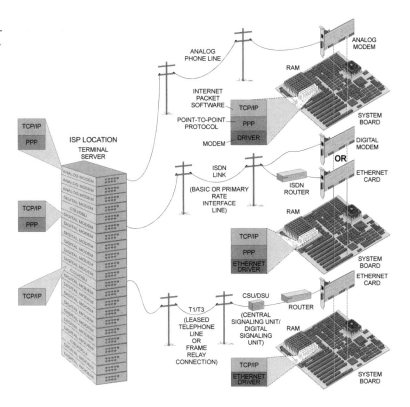

This pathway of the Internet is referred to as the **backbone** and is affiliated with the National Science Foundation (NSF). Since the original backbone was established, the Internet has expanded around the world and offers access to computer users in every part of the globe.

TCP/IP

The language of the Internet is **Transport Control Protocol/Internet Protocol**, or **TCP/IP** for short. No matter what type of computer platform or software is being used, the information must move across the Internet in this format. This protocol calls for data to be grouped together in bundles, called **network packets**.

The TCP/IP packet is designed primarily to provide for message fragmentation and reassembly. It exists through two header fields—the IP header and the TCP header—followed by the data field, as illustrated in Figure 11.40.

Internet Service Providers (ISPs)

A+ DOS/WINDOWS 5.2

> Connecting all the users and individual networks are **Internet service providers (ISPs)**. ISPs are companies that provide the technical gateway to the Internet. These companies own blocks of access addresses that they assign to their customers to give them an identity on the network.

These addresses used to access the Internet are called the **Internet protocol addresses**, or **IP addresses**. The IP address makes each site a valid member of the Internet. This is how individual users are identified to receive file transfers, email, and file requests.

FIGURE 11.40

TCP/IP packet.

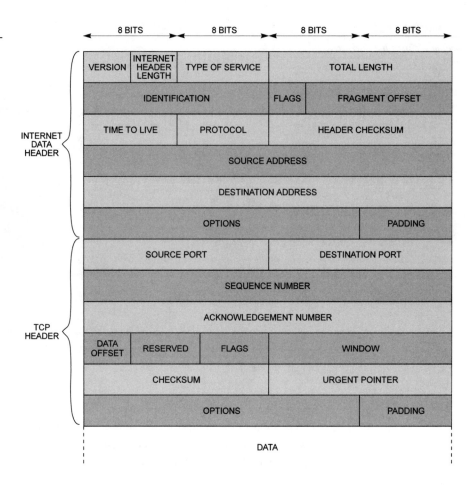

IP addresses exist in the numeric format of XXX.YYY.ZZZ.AAA. Each address consists of four 8-bit fields separated by dots. This format of specifying addresses is referred to as **dotted decimal notation**. The decimal numbers are derived from the binary address that the hardware understands. For example, a binary network address of this format:

10000111.10001011.01001001.00110110 (binary)

corresponds to this format:

135.139.073.054 (decimal)

Internet Domains

A+ DOS/WINDOWS 5.2

The IP addresses of all the computers attached to the Internet are tracked using a listing system called the **domain name system** (**DNS**). This system evolved as a method of organizing the members of the Internet into a hierarchical management structure.

The DNS structure consists of various levels of computer groups called **domains**. Each computer on the Internet is assigned a **domain name**, such as marcraft@oneworld.owt.com. Each domain name corresponds to an additional domain level.

In the example, the .com notation at the end of the address is a major domain code that identifies the user as a commercial site. The following identifies the Internet's major domain codes:

* .com = Commercial businesses

* .edu = Educational institutions

* .gov = Government agencies

* .int = International organizations

* .mil = Military establishments

* .net = Networking organizations

* .org = Nonprofit organizations

The .owt in the example identifies the organization that is a domain listed under the major domain heading. Likewise, the .oneworld entry is a subdomain of the .owt domain; it is very likely one of multiple networks supported by .owt. The Marcraft entry is the address location of the end user. If the end user location is an email address, it is usually denoted by an at symbol (@) between its name and the name of its host domain (as in mcraft@oneworld.owt.com).

In each domain level, the members of the domain are responsible for tracking the addresses of the domains on the next lower level. The lower domain is then responsible for tracking the addresses of domains or end users on the next level below them.

In addition to its domain name tracking function, the DNS system links the individual domain names to their current IP address listings.

The Internet software communicates with the service provider by embedding the TCP/IP information in a **Point-to-Point Protocol** (**PPP**) shell for transmission through the modem in analog format. The communications equipment at the service provider's site converts the signal back to the digital TCP/IP format. Older units running UNIX used a connection protocol called **Serial Line Internet Protocol** (**SLIP**) for dial-up services.

Some service providers, such as America Online (AOL) and CompuServe, have become very well known. However, thousands of lesser-known dedicated Internet access provider companies offer services around the world. Figure 11.41 illustrates the service provider's position in the Internet scheme and shows the various connection methods used to access the net.

When you connect to a service provider, you are connecting to that company's computer system, which, in turn, is connected to the Internet through devices called **routers**. A router is a device that intercepts network transmissions and determines the part of the Internet for which they are intended. The router then determines the best routing scheme for delivering the message to its intended address. The routing schedule is devised on the known, available links through the network and the amount of traffic detected on various segments. The router then transfers the message to a **network access point** (**NAP**).

FIGURE 11.41

Service provider's position.

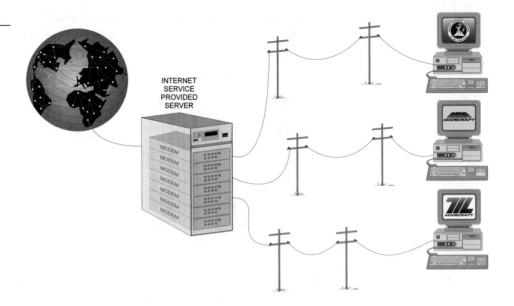

Internet Transmissions

> The TCP/IP protocol divides the transmission into packets of information suitable for retransmission across the Internet. Along the way, the information passes through different networks that are organized at different levels. Depending on the routing scheme, the packets may move through the Internet using different routes to get to the intended address. However, at the destination, the packets are reassembled into the original transmission.

This concept of packet transmission and reassembly is illustrated in Figure 11.42.

FIGURE 11.42

Packets moving through the Internet.

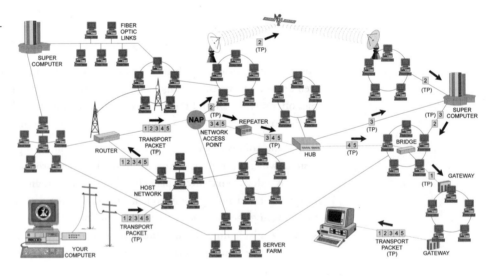

As the message moves from the originating address to its destination, it may pass through LANs, midlevel networks, routers, repeaters, hubs, bridges, and gateways. A **midlevel** network is simply another network that does not require an Internet connection to carry out communications. A router receives messages, amplifies them, and retransmits them to keep the messages from deteriorating as they travel. **Hubs** are used to link networks so that nodes within them can communicate with each other. **Bridges** connect networks so that data can pass through them as it moves from one network to the next. A special type of bridge, called a **gateway**, translates the message as it passes through so that it can be used by different types of networks (Apple networks and PC networks).

ISDN

As discussed earlier in this chapter, ISDN service offers high-speed access to the public telephone system. However, ISDN service requires digital modems (also referred to as **terminal adapters** (**TA**s). Not only does the end user require a digital modem, but the telephone company's switch gear equipment must be updated to handle digital switching.

This discrepancy between the user's equipment and the telephone company's equipment has slowed implementation of ISDN services until recently.

Three levels of ISDN service are available: **basic rate interface** (**BRI**) service, **primary rate interface** (**PRI**) services, and **broadband ISDN** (**BISDN**) services.

BRI services are designed to provide residential users with basic digital service through the existing telephone system. The cost of this service is relatively low, although it is more expensive than regular analog service. BRI service is not available in all areas of the country, but it is expanding rapidly.

Typical residential telephone wiring consists of a four-wire cable. Up to seven devices can be connected to these wires. Under the BRI specification, the telephone company delivers three information channels to the residence over a two-wire cable. The two-wire system is expanded into the four-wire system at the residence through a **network terminator**. The ISDN organization structure is depicted in Figure 11.43.

FIGURE 11.43

ISDN organizational structure.

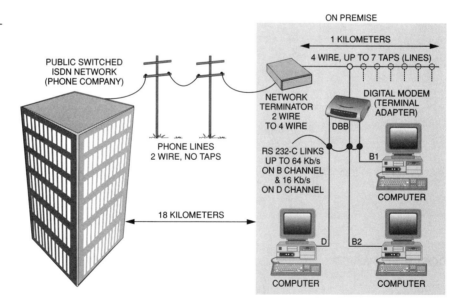

The BRI information channels exist as a pair of 64KBps channels and a 16KBps control channel. The two 64KBps channels—called **bearer**, or **B channels**—can be used to transmit and receive voice and data information. The 16KBps **D channel** is used to implement advanced control features such as call waiting, call forwarding, caller ID, and others. The D channel can also be used to conduct packet-transfer operations.

PRI services are more elaborate ISDN services that support very high data rates needed for live video transmissions. This is accomplished using the telephone company's existing wiring and advanced ISDN devices. The operating cost of PRI service is considerably more expensive than BRI services. The higher costs of PRI tend to limit its usage to larger businesses.

The fastest, most-expensive ISDN service is broadband ISDN. This level of service provides extremely high speed (up to 622Mbps) over coaxial or fiber-optic cabling. Advanced transmission protocols are also used to implement BISDN.

Digital modems are available in both internal and external formats. In the case of external devices, the analog link between the computer and the modem requires D-to-A and A-to-D conversion processes at the computer's serial port and then again at the modem. Of course, with an internal digital modem, these conversion processes are not required.

File Transfer Protocol

A+ DOS/WINDOWS 5.2

A special application, called the **File Transfer Protocol** (**FTP**), is used to upload and download information to and from the net.

FTP is a client/server type of software application. The server version runs on the host computer, and the client version runs on the user's station. To access an FTP site, the user must move into an FTP application and enter the address of the site to be accessed. After the physical connection has been made, the user must log on to the FTP site by supplying an account number and password. When the host receives a valid password, a communication path opens between the host and the user site, and an FTP session begins.

Around the world, thousands of FTP host sites contain millions of pages of information that can be downloaded free of charge. Special servers, called **Archie servers** (archival servers), contain listings to assist users in locating specific topics stored at FTP sites around the world. Another network information-gathering/file-management utility is **Gopher**. Gopher is an Internet tool developed at the University of Michigan that enables users to search (find computers that have informational topics of interest) and browse (look through information at various sites).

In the Windows 3.x environment, a driver that follows the Windows Sockets 1.1 specification is used to interface the Windows operating environment to the TCP/IP protocol. Likewise, a Windows gopher, such as Hgopher, can be loaded so that Windows applications can communicate directly with the network protocol.

Email

A+ DOS/WINDOWS 5.2

One of the most widely used functions of WANS is the **electronic mail** (**email**) feature. This feature enables network users to send and receive electronic messages to each other over the network.

As with the regular postal service, email is sent to an address from an address. However, with email, you can send the same message to several addresses at the same time using a mailing list.

Several email programs are available to provide this function. Normally, email is written as ASCII text files. These files can be created using an ordinary word processing package. An email mailer program is then used to drop the text file into an electronic mailbox. Graphics, audio, and files from other applications can also be attached to email. However, the intended user must have the same application packages that were originally used to create the files to run them.

On the Internet, the message is distributed into packets, as with any other TCP/IP file. At the receiving end, the email message is reassembled and stored in the recipient's mail box. When the designated user boots up on the system, the email program delivers the message and notifies the user that it has arrived. The user can activate the email reader portion of the program to view the information.

The World Wide Web

A+ DOS/WINDOWS 5.2

> The **World Wide Web** (**WWW**) is a menu system that ties together Internet resources from around the world. These resources are scattered across computer systems everywhere. **Web servers** inventory the Web's resources and store address pointers (links) to them.

These links are used to create **hypermedia** documents that can contain information from computer sites around the world. Inside a hypermedia document, the links enable the user to move around the document in a nonlinear manner. For example, in an online encyclopedia, the user can move around the encyclopedia to review all the entries concerning a single topic, without reading through every entry looking for them. The contents of the document can be mixed as well. A hypermedia document can contain text, graphics and animation, and audio and video sequences.

Each Web site has a unique address called its **universal resource locator** (**URL**). URLs have a format that is similar to a DOS command line. To access a Web site, the user must place the desired URL on the network. Each URL begins with the letters http://. These letters stand for **Hypertext Transfer Protocol**, and they identify the address as a Web site. The rest of the address is the name of the site being accessed. (For example, http://www. mic-inc.com is the home page of Marcraft, located on a server at One World Telecommunications.) Each Web site begins with a home page, which is the menu to the available contents of the site.

Web Browsers

> As the Internet network has grown, service providers have continued to provide more user-friendly software for exploring the World Wide Web. These software packages are called **browsers** and are based on **hypertext links**.

Browsers use hypertext links to interconnect the various computing sites in a way that resembles a spider's web, hence the name **Web**.

Browsers are to the Internet what Windows is to operating environments. Graphical browsers such as Mosaic, Netscape Navigator, and Microsoft Internet Explorer enable users to move around the Internet and make selections from graphically designed pages and menus instead of operating from a command line. The original Internet operating environment was a command-line program called UNIX. Fortunately, the UNIX structure—and many of its commands—were the basis used to create MS-DOS. Therefore, users who are DOS-literate do not require extensive training to begin using UNIX. However, with the advent of a variety of browsers, it is unlikely that most users will become involved with UNIX.

The National Center for Supercomputing Applications introduced the first graphical browser in 1993. This program was known as Mosaic. As its name implies, Mosaic enabled the user to create graphical pages using a mixture of text, graphics, audio, and video files. This program translated the **hypertext markup language** (**HTML**) files that were used to create the Web and that ultimately link the various types of files together.

Mosaic was soon followed by Netscape Navigator and the Microsoft Internet Explorer. Figure 11.44 depicts the home page (presentation screen) for the Netscape Navigator from Netscape Communications Corporation.

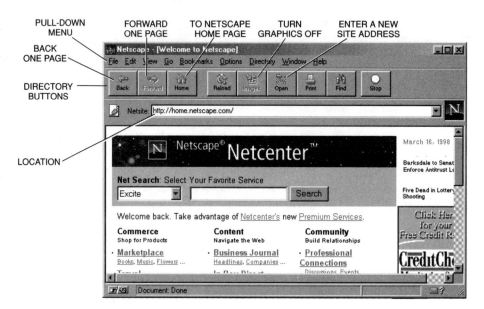

Figure 11.45 illustrates the Microsoft Internet Explorer; its features are similar to those of the Netscape Navigator. Both provide a graphical interface for viewing Web pages. Links to search engines are useful for finding information on the Internet. Both have links to built-in email facilities and to their respective creator's home pages. In the Netscape navigator, searches look at Netscape-recommended sites, and the Explorer checks out Microsoft sites. Operating either browser in Windows versions before Windows 95 requires an external windows socket program to be loaded before running the browser. With Windows 95, the socket was designed into the operating environment.

Several software packages enable users to generate their own Web pages. Programs such as word processors and desktop publishers have included provisions for creating and saving HTML files, called **applets**, that can be used as home pages. Internet browsers, such as Netscape and Internet Explorer, include facilities for generating home page documents. Scripting languages, such as Java, are also used to create HTML applets.

FIGURE 11.45

Internet Explorer home page.

Screen shot reprinted by permission from
Microsoft Corporation.

Troubleshooting WANs

Unless you work for an Internet service provider, most of the work at an Internet site involves the components and software of the local computer. Most of the troubleshooting from the local computer level is identical to the steps given earlier for the modem. Run the loopback tests and try to get online with a local dial-up service using a simple communications software package (such as Terminal). Check the spelling of IP addresses to make sure they are spelled exactly as they should be. If the spelling is wrong, no communications will take place. The major difference in checking WAN problems occurs in checking the Internet-specific software, such as the browser.

> Checking the modem or network card is the major hardware-related activity normally involved with Internet sites. However, you may be called on to work with the customer's local Internet service provider to solve some problems.

Each user should have received a packet of information from his service provider when the service was purchased. These documents normally contain all the ISP-specific configuration information needed to set up the user's site. This information should be consulted when installing and configuring any Internet-related software.

Windows 95 provides fundamental troubleshooting information for WAN networking through its system of Help screens. Simply select Help from the Control Panel's toolbar, and click on the topic that you are troubleshooting.

Key Points Review

This chapter has investigated the two major areas of data communications associated with personal computer systems: LANs and WANs.

▶ Generally, the most difficult aspect of connecting peripheral equipment to a computer is obtaining the proper interfacing and cabling.

▶ In its simplest form, a modem consists of a modulator and a demodulator. The modulator is a transmitter that converts the parallel computer data into a serial format for transmission. The demodulator is the receiver that accepts the serial transmission format and converts it into a parallel format usable by the computer or peripheral.

- The standard telephone system accommodates a range of frequencies between 300Hz and 3300Hz, or a bandwidth of 3000Hz. This is quite adequate for transmitting voice, but it severely distorts digital data. Modems encode digital 1s and 0s into analog signals within this bandwidth.

- In addition to modulation techniques, advanced modems use data-compression techniques to reduce the volume of data that must be transmitted.

- Two techniques exist for synchronizing the timing of data transmission between devices. The first method, known as synchronous transmission, places timing synchronization signals at the beginning of each data block to synchronize the transmitter and the receiver.

- The other technique, called asynchronous transmission, places a synchronizing bit at the beginning and end of each 8-bit character.

- To maintain an orderly flow of information between the computer and the modem (and between the modem and another modem), a protocol, or set of rules governing the transfer of information, must be in place.

- During the data transfer, both modems monitor the signal level of the carrier to prevent the transfer of false data due to signal deterioration. If the carrier signal strength drops below some predetermined threshold level, one or both modems will initiate automatic disconnect procedures.

- Notable advanced UART versions include the 16450 and 16550. The 16450 was the 16-bit improvement of the 8250, and the 16550 was a high-performance UART with an onboard 16-byte buffer.

- All modems require software to control the communication session. At the fundamental instruction level, most modems use a set of commands known as the Hayes-compatible command set.

- As stated earlier, every COM port on a PC requires an IRQ line to signal the processor for attention. In most PC systems, two COM ports share the same IRQ line. The IRQ4 line works for COM1 and COM3, and the IRQ3 line works for COM2 and COM4.

- Modems actually have the capability to perform three different kinds of self-diagnostic possessive tests.

- With an external modem, the front panel lights can be used as diagnostic tools to monitor its operation. The progress of a call and its handling can be monitored along with any errors that may occur.

- LANs are systems designed to connect computers in relative proximity. These connections enable users attached to the network to share resources. LAN connections also enable users to communicate with each other and to share data among their computers.

- Control of the network can be implemented in two ways: as peer-to-peer networks, in which each computer is attached to the network in a ring or bus fashion, and in client/server networks, in which client workstations operate in conjunction with a dedicated file server.

- In a network, some method must be used to determine which node has use of the network's communications paths, and for how long it can have it. The network's protocol handles these functions and is necessary to prevent more than one user from accessing the bus at any given time.

- The Ethernet strategy provides for up to 1,024 users to share the LAN. However, from the description of its collision-recovery technique, it should be clear that with more users on an Ethernet LAN, more collisions are likely to occur and the average time to complete an actual data transfer will be longer.

- Ethernet is classified as a bus topology. The original Ethernet scheme was classified as a 10MHz transmission protocol. The maximum length specified for Ethernet is 1.55 miles (2.5km), with a maximum segment length between nodes of 500 meters. This type of LAN is referred to as a 10base5 LAN by the IEEE organization.

- The ArcNet protocol was developed by Datapoint and is based on a modified token-passing scheme. In a token-passing system, contention for use of the LAN between different nodes is handled by passing an electronic enabling code, called a token, from node to node. Only the node possessing the token can have control of the LAN to transmit information.

- In the ArcNet specification, no particular transmission medium is defined. ArcNet can be used with coaxial cable, twisted-pair cable, or fiber-optic cable. ArcNet coaxial cabling is defined as RG-59 cable, with 75-ohm terminators required for any open nodes. The ArcNet protocol transfers data at a nominal rate of 2.5MHz.

- In 1985, IBM developed a token-passing LAN protocol it called the Token Ring. As its name implies, Token Ring is a token-passing protocol operating on a ring topology.

- In a LAN, each computer on the net requires a **network adapter card,** and every unit is connected to the network by some type of cabling.

- Begin troubleshooting a general network problem by determining what has changed since it was running last. If the installation is new, it must be inspected as a setup problem.

- Be aware that in a network environment no unit really functions alone. Unlike working on a standalone unit, the steps performed on a network computer may affect the operation of other units on the network.

- One of the major concerns in most network environments is data security. Passwords are typically used at all software levels to lock people out of hardware systems, programs, and data files.

- In a client/server system, the technician's main responsibility is to get the local station to boot up to the network's logon prompt.

- In a WAN, computers are typically separated by distances that must be serviced via modems instead of through network cards.

- The most famous WAN is the Internet, which is actually a network of networks working together.

- Connecting all the users and individual networks are Internet service providers. ISPs are companies that provide the technical gateway to the Internet.

- The IP addresses of all the computers attached to the Internet are tracked using a listing system called the domain name system (DNS).

- The TCP/IP protocol divides the transmission into packets of information suitable for retransmission across the Internet. Along the way, the information passes through different networks that are organized at different levels.

- ISDN service offers high-speed access to the public telephone system. However, ISDN service requires digital modems.

- A special application, called FTP, is used to upload and download information to and from the network.

- One of the most widely used functions of WANs is email. This feature enables net users to send and receive electronic messages to each other over the network.

- The World Wide Web is a menu system that ties together Internet resources from around the world. These resources are scattered across computer systems everywhere.

- As the Internet network has grown, service providers have continued to provide more user-friendly software for exploring the World Wide Web. These software packages are called browsers and are based on hypertext links.

- Checking the modem or network card is the major hardware-related activity normally involved with Internet sites. However, you may be called on to work with the customer's local Internet service provider to solve some problems.

At this point, review the objectives listed at the beginning of the chapter to be certain that you understand each point and can perform each task listed there. Afterward, answer the review questions that follow to verify your knowledge of the information.

Multiple Choice Questions

1. What is the minimum number of PCs that must be connected before a true network is formed?

   a. 3

   b. 2

   c. 1

   d. 5

2. What type of topology is Ethernet?

   a. A token-passing topology

   b. A star topology

   c. A ring topology

   d. A bus topology

3. To which topology does ArcNet belong?

   a. A token-passing topology

   b. A star topology

   c. A ring topology

   d. A bus topology

4. State the maximum segment length of a 10base2 Ethernet network.

   a. 100 feet

   b. 185 meters

   c. 185 feet

   d. 100 meters

5. Describe the type of conductor used in a 1base5 network.

   a. Coaxial cable

   b. UTP cable

   c. STP cable

   d. Ribbon cable

6. Define the word *protocol*.

   a. A hardware handshaking method

   b. An error-correction code

   c. An agreed-upon method of doing things

   d. A software handshaking method

7. What is the bandwidth of the telephone system?

   a. 3000Hz

   b. 20,000Hz

   c. 300Hz

   d. 100Hz

8. To which type of communications products do Hayes-compatible commands pertain?

   a. Hubs

   b. Network adapter cards

   c. Routers

   d. Modems

9. Under what conditions is a modem required to transmit data?

   a. For serial transmissions greater than 10 feet

   b. For serial transmissions greater than 1000 feet

   c. For serial transmissions greater than 100 feet

   d. For serial transmissions out of the physical room

10. What language is used to create documents for the World Wide Web?

    a. Hypertext markup language

    b. QBASIC language

    c. FTP language

    d. Mosaic language

Review Questions

1. Describe the function of the World Wide Web.

2. Describe synchronous transmission versus asynchronous transmission.

3. What is the primary difference between a client/server type of network and a peer-to-peer network?

4. Describe the three important configuration settings associated with a network adapter card.

5. What element determines the active unit in a Token Ring network?

6. List three possible places the UART circuitry can be located in a PC-compatible system.

7. What is the purpose of a router in a network?

8. What is TCP/IP, and what do the letters stand for?

9. What function does a browser perform?

10. How does a Token Ring network keep a single unit from dominating the network after it receives the token? What is this called?

11. What is the first step in checking a networked computer?

12. Describe the tests that a typical modem can perform on itself.

13. How are baud and bit rate different?

14. Define the acronym URL and describe its use.

15. Describe the function of an Internet service provider.

Lab Exercises

The lab manual that accompanies this book contains hands-on lab procedures that reinforce and test your knowledge of the theory materials presented in this chapter. Now that you have completed your review of Chapter 11, refer to the lab manual and perform Procedures 31, "Windows 3.x Terminal"; 32, "Modem Installation and Setup"; 33, "Network Installation and Setup"; and 34, "Windows Internet Explorer."

MULTIMEDIA

LEARNING OBJECTIVES

Upon completion of this chapter and its related lab procedures, you should be able to perform the following tasks:

1. Define the term *multimedia*.

2. Discuss Windows multimedia support tools.

3. Describe the function of multimedia authoring programs.

4. Describe the operation of a writable CD-ROM drive.

5. Install and configure a CD-ROM drive for operation.

6. Describe steps to troubleshoot CD-ROM problems.

7. Describe how audio signals are digitized.

8. Install and configure a sound card for operation.

9. Describe the MIDI standard and discuss where it is used.

10. Describe steps to troubleshoot sound card problems.

11. State the characteristics of MPEG and JPEG compression formats.

12. Install and configure a video capture card for operation.

13. Describe steps to troubleshoot video capture card problems.

14. Install and configure a VGA-TV adapter for operation.

15. Describe steps to troubleshoot VGA-TV card problems.

CHAPTER 12

Introduction

The fastest-growing application of microcomputers is in the area of multimedia creation and presentation. **Multimedia** is a term applied to a range of applications that bring together text, graphics, video, audio, and animation to provide interactivity between the computer and its human operator.

The concept of multimedia is illustrated in Figure 12.1. Typical applications for multimedia include interactive presentations, computer-based and computer-assisted instruction materials, and interactive customer service centers, called kiosks.

Computer-based instruction (**CBI**) applies to instructional materials in which the computer is the main source of instructional content. **Computer-assisted instruction** (**CAI**) is a term that is used when the computer is employed as a presentation assistant and class-management tool. A **kiosk** is a computer system set up to advise users about some topic. Large grocery and hardware stores use kiosks to direct customers to the locations of various types of merchandise available in the store.

FIGURE 12.1

Multimedia interactivity.

Multimedia Applications

Several different types of software packages are involved in creating all the pieces that go together to make a **multimedia title**. Graphic design programs are generally used to create the artwork and other graphic elements to be included in the title. Types of artwork employed in a multimedia project run from designing backdrops and scenery to creating individual picture elements. Special-effects graphics packages, or graphics design packages with special-effect features, are used to produce special effects such as animation and morphing.

Video capture software is used to capture frames of television video and convert them into digital formats that can be processed by the system. Graphics packages can be used to manipulate the contents of the video after it has been converted into digital formats that the computer can handle. One of the most popular file formats for video is the Microsoft **Audio Visual Interface** (**AVI**) format.

Audio-digitizing software converts music, voice, and sound effects into formats that can be included in the presentation. These packages typically include utilities that enable the producer to edit and modify the sound files created. The most popular sound formats in use are the **Musical Instrument Digital Interface** (**MIDI**) and the **Wave** (**WAV**) audio file formats. The MIDI format was developed so that electronic musical instruments and controllers can communicate with each other.

A word processor program may be used to prepare text materials for the screens in the production. The text used in multimedia production is normally created as ASCII files. These files can be used simply as text files or can be converted into a graphic format. Typical graphics formats used in multimedia systems include bitmapped graphics as well as two- and three-dimensional renderings.

The elements of the multimedia title are brought together, organized, and finished by a type of software package known as an **authoring system**. This concept is illustrated in Figure 12.2. In addition to combining the elements into a cohesive presentation, the authoring system provides the tools with which to create **interactivity**. Interactivity is the capability of the user to participate with the program while it is running and alter its action. In many cases, the programmer creates scenarios that enable the intended user of the program to select pathways through the software or sections of the software to be used, or to answer questions included in the software.

FIGURE 12.2

Authoring system elements.

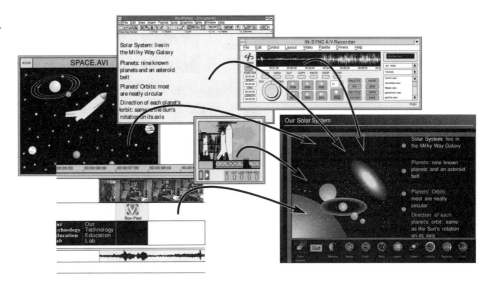

Windows Multimedia Support

Microsoft Windows provides a fundamental set of multimedia tools for the personal computer. These tools are accessed through the **Sound Recorder** and **Media Player** icons in the Accessories window. These utilities, depicted in Figure 12.3, operate in conjunction with the settings in the Driver section of the Windows Control Panel. In addition to the tools mentioned, Windows adds a number of file extension specifications to deal with multimedia applications. The primary multimedia extensions are the RIFF and MIDI file formats. The **RIFF** (**Resource Interchange File Format**) format supplies a standard file format for graphics, animation, and audio. The MIDI format is the standard for recording and playback of digital musical instruments.

Media Control Interface (MCI)

Windows also supports a software interface specification that grants the Windows-based computer control over external multimedia devices, such as VCRs and laser disc systems. This interface is referred to as the **Media Control Interface** (**MCI**). In addition to controlling external devices, the MCI provides a method for Windows-based machines to save or play audio files with its Sound Recorder; to play audio, video, or MIDI files from its Media Player; and to select various musical instrument sounds using the **MIDI Mapper**. The functional position of these utilities is illustrated in Figure 12.4.

FIGURE 12.3

Windows multimedia utilities.

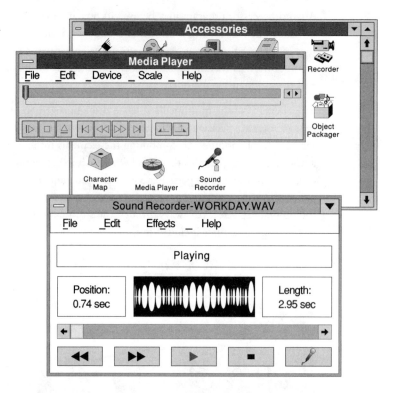

FIGURE 12.4

Windows multimedia utilities in operation.

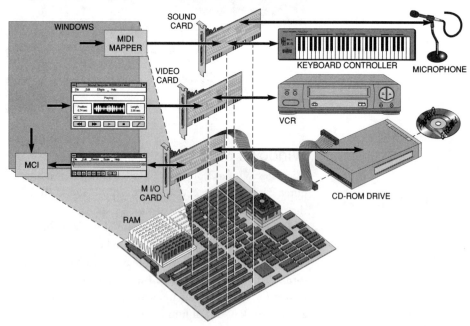

Audio Tools

The Sound Recorder utility enables Windows to communicate with sound adapter cards to record and play audio in the form of WAV files. The sound recorder interface uses start, stop, reverse, fast-forward, fast-reverse, and play icons such as those found on a commercially available audio tape recorder.

The Media Player uses a button scheme that corresponds to the transport control buttons on a VCR machine. This is the main channel to the MCI.

The MIDI interface specification was designed so that electronic music devices can communicate with each other and with a computer. The MIDI mapper directs MIDI files to the MIDI instruments with which they are associated. A MIDI system can contain several electronic instruments that play in conjunction with the computer system.

Video Tools

Windows does not provide any direct support for handling or playing digitized video files. However, certain add-on programs for Windows, such as Microsoft's **Video for Windows**, can be implemented to play **Audio Visual Interface** (**AVI**) files from Windows. This add-on brings several important multimedia-related utilities to the Windows structure. These utilities include the following functions:

> ▶ **VidCap** works with video and sound capture cards to digitize audio and video clips for Windows. In addition, VidCap enables the user to run the video clip in different sizes and speeds. The other utilities are programs that can be used to edit the video and audio clips.

> ▶ **VidEdit** is used to cut and paste video segments.

> ▶ **WavEdit** provides the tools to edit the audio portion of the AVI file.

> ▶ **PalEdit** and **BitEdit** are utilities used to enhance the video by manipulating the color palette and correcting images within the frames of the video clip.

Windows 95 Multimedia Support

In Windows 95, the multimedia tools are located under the Control Panel's Multimedia icon, as illustrated in Figure 12.5. The multimedia tools contained in the icon include Audio, Video, MIDI, CD Music, and Advanced Properties. The Audio tab provides the interface through which the playback driver and volume value can be set. This tab also handles the audio recording driver setting, internal volume control, and quality settings.

FIGURE 12.5

Windows 95 Multimedia Properties window.

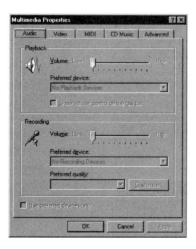

The window size for playing video files on the screen can be adjusted through the Video tab. Typical settings include original size, fractional portions of the screen, and full screen presentation. The onscreen preview window shows the type of video reproduction that can be expected using the selected window size setting.

The MIDI tab enables you to configure the system's MIDI drivers and create custom MIDI configurations. Behind the CD Music tab, you can control the CD-ROM drive's settings. The relative volume level for the CD-ROM output is defined here.

The different drivers available for the various multimedia tools in the system can be viewed under the Advanced tab. Figure 12.6 illustrates the Advanced Multimedia Properties dialog box for a given system.

FIGURE 12.6

Windows 95 multimedia tools.

Authoring Systems

At the heart of the multimedia movement are the authoring systems through which various media types can be pulled together into a complete package.

Figure 12.7 illustrates the relationship between various media sources and the computer hardware.

Designing Multimedia Titles

Unlike word processing and desktop publishing applications, which are used to produce a static page, multimedia authoring programs are used to prepare time-sequenced and interactive presentations. These programs bring together production techniques associated with radio and video production.

To use them to their full potential, the multimedia programmer must think like TV and radio producers. Indeed, multimedia programmers borrow presentation techniques used by people in these fields.

It is very common for a multimedia programmer to begin work on a multimedia title by producing a **story board**, as depicted in Figure 12.8. A story board is a paper description of the various screens that will be developed and a narrative of how the events in the screens will play out. In addition, the programmer may develop a **play list** of audio background or voice clips that will be used in the work.

FIGURE 12.7

Elements of a multimedia title.

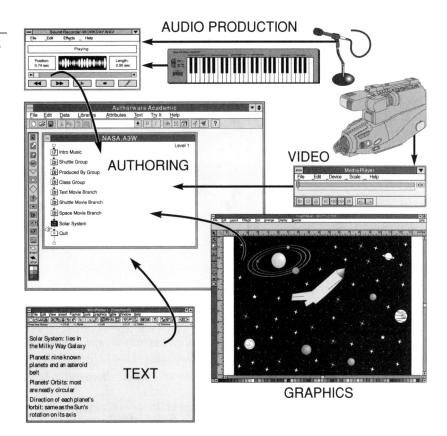

FIGURE 12.8

Story board sheets.

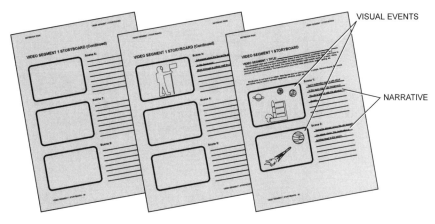

Multimedia Authoring Tools

It might be easiest to visualize a multimedia production as a stack of screens that you can flip through. Each page of the stack uses graphic design composition techniques to maximize its effectiveness. Figure 12.9 illustrates such an authoring system. The program provides a toolbar containing a set of tools with various definitions. The tools are used one at a time to create objects on the screen, such as geometric shapes, text, and colors.

Other tools enable the programmer to create time and event delays between activities. Still other tools enable the programmer to load bitmapped graphics into the page, move different objects around the screen, and cut and paste objects on the screen. Each time a tool is used, an activity and its parameters are logged in the page's object list. When the program is run, the author's **runtime module** simply calls up the activities from the object list one at a time and carries them out as they were defined.

FIGURE 12.9

Object and event list multimedia programming.

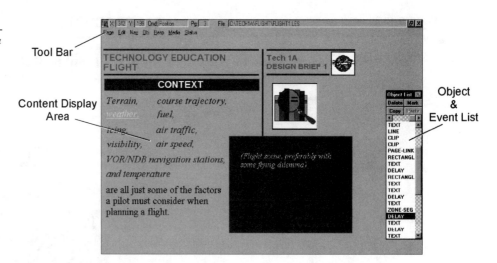

Tool Bar

Content Display Area

Object & Event List

Other authoring programs are more graphical in nature. The programming interface depicted in Figure 12.10 illustrates a flow chart-based method of arranging objects and events in a title. The programmer plots the logical flow of the presentation by linking multimedia pieces in a flow chart. In this manner, the programmer can have multiple activities occurring on the screen simultaneously by placing them in parallel with each other. Objects connected in series with each other happen in sequence, from top to bottom of the flow chart.

FIGURE 12.10

Flow chart-based multimedia programming.

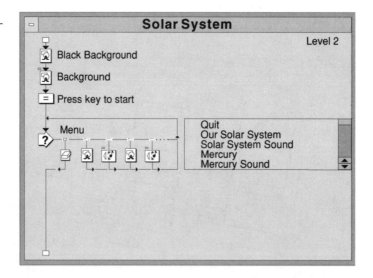

After the concept, design, and layout work have been completed, the next step in producing a multimedia title is to collect the different file types so that they are convenient. This could mean importing all the files into a single drive or having all the files available within a single local network.

Next the multimedia programmer uses the authoring program's tools to bring the files together in the correct sequence. The activities within the title are dynamic. The programmer must be aware of how the screen will look at each instant of time. Figure 12.11 demonstrates how the multimedia programmer brings together the parts and pieces of the title on the screen.

The programmer uses **time delays**, **animated sequences**, and **video clips** to move the user through the presentation. The programmer also injects interactivity by placing menus on the screen with buttons that the user can press to answer questions, get specific information, or alter how the program advances.

The programmer may also include voice clips to narrate the presentation, as well as use music to accompany or highlight the material on the screen. The authoring program is responsible for generating the code necessary to present all the multimedia pieces in the title at the correct time during the presentation.

After the title has been completed, it can be placed on a number of different standard media for distribution. These media include CD-ROMs, interactive laser discs, video CDs, and networks. A section of the authoring program, called the **runtime module**, is included with the title to make it run on other computers. Most multimedia authoring tools are relatively expensive. To include the entire program, along with a multimedia title, would be costly and wasteful. Therefore, only the runtime module required to play back the presentation is normally included with the title.

FIGURE 12.11

Arranging objects and events in a title.

Multimedia Hardware

A typical multimedia system is depicted in Figure 12.12. Some vendors promote a sound card, a pair of speakers, and a CD-ROM drive as a full multimedia package. This is barely enough capability for a system to be called a multimedia system.

> PCs intended for multimedia use normally possess very fast microprocessors; large amounts of installed RAM; big, fast hard-disk drives; a fast CD-ROM drive; a sound card; and a high-resolution video card. They may also include items such as still-frame or full-motion video capture cards, VGA-to-TV converter cards, and digital sound cards.

These items are necessary to efficiently bring together text, graphics, sound, animation, and video into a usable package. The large and fast peripheral equipment associated with multimedia stems from the fact that graphic and animation files tend to be large and require a tremendous amount of time to be manipulated. Digitized sound files also tend to be large. Several seconds of simple speech can take up several kilobytes of memory to process and disk space to store. Full-motion video requires an enormous amount of RAM and disk space to manipulate and store. A few seconds of uncompressed full-motion video can fill a small hard-disk drive.

FIGURE 12.12

A typical multimedia system.

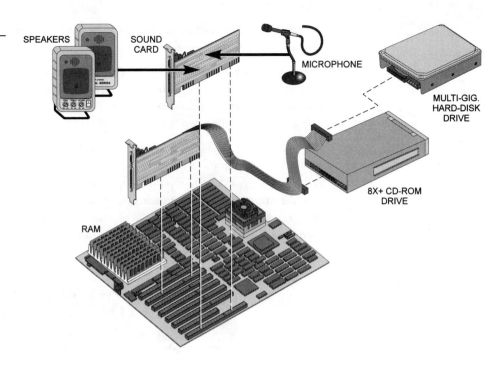

SPEAKERS
SOUND CARD
MICROPHONE
MULTI-GIG. HARD-DISK DRIVE
8X+ CD-ROM DRIVE
RAM

The high-speed peripheral equipment is required for multimedia applications due to the sheer volume of data processing that is required to move sound and video files around the system (for example, to and from the hard drive, to the video memory, and onto the screen). In addition to large hard-disk drives, drive arrays are often included in multimedia systems to hold and help process all the data used to create a serious multimedia title.

A standard has been established to define exactly what makes up a minimal-level multimedia computer. This standard is referred to as the **Multimedia Personal Computer** (**MPC**) standard. The first MPC level (**MPC Level 1**) never gained widespread support due to its lack of true multimedia support components. The **MPC Level 2** specification calls for a minimum 80486SX-25 or better microprocessor, with at least 4MB of RAM, a 150MB or larger hard drive, a 2X or better CD-ROM drive, a 16-bit sound card, and a 640x480 VGA monitor with 64KB color capabilities.

A high-end MPC system, such as the one in Figure 12.13, is normally built around a Pentium MMX microprocessor, with 64MB or more of RAM. The system board should have a large cache and multiple 32-bit PCI expansion slots. The hard drive should be in the multiple-gigabyte range, and an 8X CD-ROM drive should be included. Additional data storage should be available in the form of a tape back-up system, a drive array, or one of several removable storage systems.

Audio/video add-ons include a video capture card, a 16-bit sound card, and a 24-bit graphic accelerator video card. A 17-inch SVGA monitor for viewing the work is a desirable addition, and a speaker and microphone round out the audio/video options. A flat-bed scanner can be a valuable tool for converting existing pictures and artwork into electronic files that can be used by the MPC system. Finally, a modem enables the author to gather and distribute multimedia material without leaving the digital world. The Internet is certainly a valuable asset to the multimedia programmer.

With all the hardware options that can be combined into a multimedia unit, it is necessary to consider the number of system resources that may be required. In particular, the number of IRQ and DMA channels available should be taken into account when considering upgrade options. The number and type of expansions slot available is another point for consideration. For example, it may be necessary to find a scanner that will work off the existing parallel port rather than a unit that has a proprietary adapter card. There may not be enough slots to handle the additional peripheral.

FIGURE 12.13

A high-end multimedia system.

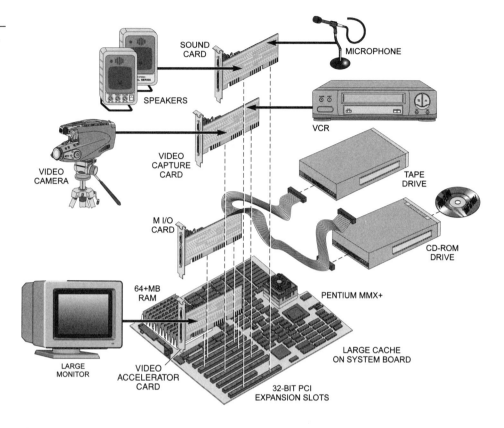

CD-ROM

Soon after the **compact disc** (**CD**) became popular for storing audio signals on optical material, the benefits of storing computer information in this manner became apparent. With a CD, data is written digitally on a light-sensitive material by a powerful, highly focused laser beam.

The writing laser is pulsed with the modulated data to be stored on the disc. When the laser is pulsed, a microscopic blister is burned into the optical material, causing it to reflect light differently from the material around it. The blistered areas are referred to as **pits**, and the areas between them are called **lands**. Figure 12.14 illustrates the process of writing data on the optical disc.

The recorded data is read from the disc by scanning it with a lower-power continuous laser beam. The laser diode emits the highly focused narrow beam that is reflected back from the disc. The reflected beam passes through a prism and is bent 90 degrees, where it is picked up by the diode detector and converted into an electrical signal. Only the light reflected from a land on the disc is picked up by the detector. Light that strikes a pit is scattered and is not detected. The lower power level used for reading the disc ensures that the optical material is not affected during the read operation.

FIGURE 12.14

Writing on a CD-ROM drive.

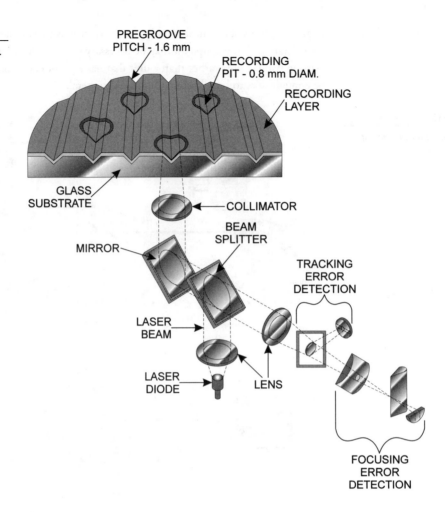

PREGROOVE
PITCH - 1.6 mm

RECORDING
PIT - 0.8 mm DIAM.

RECORDING
LAYER

GLASS
SUBSTRATE

COLLIMATOR

BEAM
SPLITTER

MIRROR

TRACKING
ERROR
DETECTION

LASER
BEAM

LASER
DIODE

LENS

FOCUSING
ERROR
DETECTION

With an audio CD, the digital data retrieved from the disc is passed through a digital-to-analog converter (DAC) to reproduce the audio sound wave. However, this is not required for digital computer systems because the information is already in a form acceptable to the computer. Therefore, CD players designed for use in computer systems are referred to as **CD-ROM drives**, to differentiate them from audio CD players. Otherwise, the mechanics of operation are very similar between the two devices. The ROM designation refers to the fact that most of the drives available are read-only.

CD-ROM Discs

A typical CD-ROM is 4.7 inches in diameter and consists of three major parts:

- ▶ Acrylic substrate
- ▶ Aluminized, mirror-finished data surface
- ▶ Lacquer coating

The scanning laser beam comes up through the disc, strikes the aluminized data surface, and is reflected back. Because no physical contact occurs between the reading mechanism and the disc, the disc never wears out. This is one of the main advantages of the CD system. The blisters on the data surface are typically just under 1 micrometer in length, and the tracks are 1.6 micrometers apart. The data is encoded by the length and spacing of the blisters and the lands between them. This concept is illustrated in Figure 12.15.

The information on a compact disc is stored in one continuous **spiral track**, unlike floppy disks, where the data is stored in multiple concentric tracks. The compact disc storage format still divides the data into separate sectors. However, the sectors of a CD-ROM are physically the same size. The CD spins counter-clockwise and slows down as the laser diode emitter/detector unit approaches the outer perimeter.

FIGURE 12.15

Encoding data on a CD-ROM.

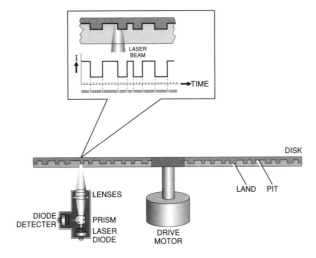

The CD begins spinning at approximately 500RPM at the inner edge of the disc and slows down to about 200RPM at the outer edge of the disc. The spindle motor controls the speed of the disc so that the track is always passing the laser at between 3.95 and 4.6 feet per second. Therefore, CD-ROM drives must have a variable-speed spindle motor and cannot just be turned on and off as with a floppy drive's spindle motor. The variable speed of the drive enables the disc to contain more sectors, thereby giving it a much larger storage capacity. In fact, the average storage capacity of a CD-ROM disc is about 680MB.

CD-ROM Drives

CD-ROM drives that operate at the speed of a conventional audio CD player are called **single-speed drives**. Advanced drives that spin twice and three times as fast as the typical CD player are referred to as **double-speed drives**, **triple-speed drives**, and so forth. Single-speed drives transfer data at a rate of 150KBps. Double-speed drive transfers occur at 300KBps, and so on.

CD-ROM drives are capable of playing audio CDs. However, a CD player cannot produce any output from the CD. CDs are classified by a color-coding system that corresponds to their intended use. CDs that contain digital data intended for use in a computer are referred to as **Yellow Book** CDs. **Red Book** CDs refer to those formatted to contain digital music. **Orange Book** refers to the standard for CDs that are used in WORM drives. **Green Book** CDs are used with interactive CD systems, and **Blue Book** CDs are those associated with laser disc systems.

Common applications for CD-ROM drives include reference material such as these:

▶ Dictionaries

▶ Encyclopedias

▶ Maps

▶ Graphics for desktop publishing

▶ Multimedia

▶ Audio/video clips

▶ Games for entertainment

Older hard drive types, such as MFM, ESDI, and the original IDE drives, were a bit slow for the demands of multimedia, but as technology improved, performance soared. The original CD-ROM drives had a transfer-rate of 150KBps. Some time after, double-spin (2X) drives began to appear with a 300KBps transfer rate. CD-ROM drive makers have continued to increase the transfer rates of their devices so that 3X, 4X, 6X, 8X, 12X, and 24X drives have been produced. Even faster rates seem inevitable for future CD-ROM drives.

Two common methods exist for inserting CDs in the drive. The first method involves inserting the CD into a protective **caddie**, which, in turn, is inserted into the drive. The CD turns inside the caddie, which acts to properly align the disc in the drive.

With the second method, the CD is placed in a shelf that pops out of the drive. Pressing a small button on the front of the drive makes the shelf pop out so that the CD can be placed in it. Pressing the button again causes the shelf to retract into the drive so that it can play the CD. This type of drive is referred to as a **caddie-less drive**. Both caddie and caddie-less drives are depicted in Figure 12.16.

FIGURE 12.16

Caddie and caddie-less CD-ROM drive units.

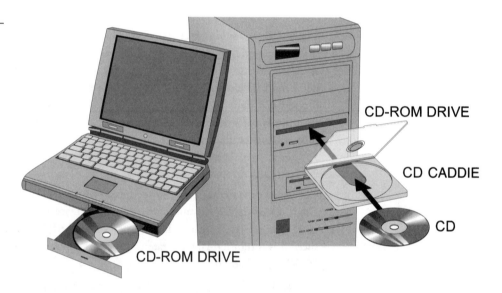

CD-ROM Interfaces

Ⓐ+ **CORE 1.5**

Ⓐ+ **CORE 1.6**

With the many speed choices that exist, there are also three choices of architectures for CD-ROM drives:

▶ SCSI interfaces

▶ IDE interfaces

▶ Proprietary interfaces

The SCSI and IDE drives are capable of using a controller already installed in the computer. However, there are many versions of the SCSI standard, which has not necessarily been standardized. Two versions of the IDE interface also exist: the original IDE and a newer, enhanced IDE, called EIDE. The EIDE interface has been redefined to accommodate faster transfer rates as well as the handling of more storage capacity. EIDE can also be used to control drive units such as a tape or CD-ROM. The EIDE interface is often described as an **ATAPI** (**AT Attachment Packet Interface**) or a **Fast ATA** (**Fast AT Attachment**) interface.

The controllers for proprietary interfaces are often included with the drive or with a sound card. To gain full advantage of a CD-ROM, it is becoming essential to also have a sound card. Many sound cards include a CD-ROM drive interface or controller. However, these controllers may not be IDE- or SCSI-compatible. They often contain proprietary interfaces that work with only a few CD-ROM models.

Software drivers are required to operate a CD-ROM drive from DOS or Windows. Normally, the drivers come packaged with the drive if an IDE interface is being used. Conversely, the drivers are included with the interface card when a SCSI interface is employed.

CD Writers

Another type of CD drive is classified as **Write Once, Read Many (WORM) drive**. As the acronym implies, these drives enable users to write information to the disk once and then retrieve this information as you would with a CD-ROM drive. With WORM drives, the data cannot be changed or deleted after the information is stored on the disc.

Typically, CD-ROMs conform to the International Standards Organization's ISO-9660 specification. This standard is an advancement of an earlier pseudo CD standard called the **High Sierra format**. The presence of established formats have helped CD writing technologies to evolve into a form suitable for use in personal computers.

CD writer technology has developed to the point at which it is inexpensive enough to be added to a typical PC system. CD writers record data on blank **CD-recordable** (**CD-R**). A CD-R is a write once, read many medium that is generally available in 120mm and 80mm sizes. The drives are constructed using a typical 5.25-inch half-height drive form factor. This means that it conveniently fits into a typical PC drive bay.

Even though CD-Rs resemble CD-ROMs, they are not exactly the same. The construction of the CD-R is considerably different than the CD-ROM. The writable disc is constructed as illustrated in Figure 12.17. The CD-R is created by coating a transparent polycarbonate substrate with an opaque dye. The dye is then covered with a thin layer of gold and topped with a protective lacquer layer and a label. The WORM writing mechanism is not as strong as that of a commercial CD-ROM duplicator. Instead of burning pits into the substrate of the disc, the CD-writer drive uses a lower-powered laser to discolor the dye material. Therefore, the WORM disc is difficult to copy.

In other respects, the WORM format is identical to that of a CD-ROM, and information written on it can be read by a typical CD-ROM drive. The spiral track formation and sectoring are the same as that used with CD-ROMs. In addition, the CD writer can produce recordings in the standard CD book formats (such as Red, Yellow, Orange, and Green).

During the write operation, the CD-writer encodes the data into the designated CD storage format. In this process, the writer adds error-correction code information and provides data interleaving. The writer then uses a high-intensity laser to write the data on the thermally sensitive media. The laser light is applied to the bottom side of the disc. It passes through the substrate to the reflective layer and is reflected back through the substrate. The light continues through the drive's optics system until it reaches the laser detector.

FIGURE 12.17

Writable CD-R.

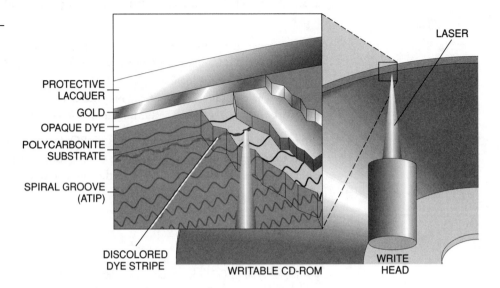

Unlike the pits and lands arrangement of the CD-ROM, the CD-R uses a **polymer dye**, such as Cyanine or Pthalocyanine, as the recording medium. The polymer held in a shallow **pregroove** is molded into the substrate material. This groove is used by the drive's positioning circuitry to maintain track alignment. The drive also uses a built-in **wobble** in the groove for rotational speed control of the disc. The wobble is created so that it delivers a 22.05KHz signal when rotated at the correct velocity. This signal is also encoded with **Absolute Time In Pre-groove** (**ATIP**) information that the system uses to keep track of information stored on the disc.

When the polymer is exposed to the light of the high-intensity writing laser, it heats up and becomes transparent. This exposes the reflective gold layer beneath the polymer. During the read-back process, the reflective layer reflects more light than the polymer material does. The transitions between lighter and darker areas of the disc are used to encode the data.

The data can be written to the CD-R using one of three methods:

▶ As a Disc-at-once

▶ As a Session-at-once

▶ As a Track-at-once

A **session** is the CD equivalent of an HDD partition. The ISO 9660 standard requires that each session contain a **lead-in section**, a **program area**, and a lead-out section. The lead-in section contains the **table of contents** for the session (no FAT exists on a CD-ROM or WORM disc). The **lead-out section** holds information that marks the end of the program area.

Most CD writers are packaged with a SCSI interface and host adapter. This interface must supply the stream of data to the disc at an acceptable rate for encoding and recording on the CD-R. CD writers are typically capable of writing to the CD-R at either one or two times that of CD speeds. These settings have nothing to do with playback speeds.

Installing a CD-ROM Drive

 A+ CORE 1.7 The installation process for a CD-ROM drive is almost identical to that of a hard or floppy drive. For an internal drive, confirm the drive's Master/Slave/Single or SCSI ID configuration setting, install the CD-ROM unit in one of the drive bays, connect the power and signal cables, and load the driver software. External CD-ROM drives are even easier to install. Simply connect the power, run the signal cable between the drive unit and the system, confirm the Master/Slave/Single or SCSI ID setting, and install the driver software.

Internal Units

Figure 12.18 illustrates the installation of an internal CD-ROM drive. If the interface type is different than that of the HDD, you must install a controller card in an expansion slot. To accomplish this, remove the cover from the system unit. To install a controller, locate a compatible empty expansion slot in the system unit. Remove the expansion slot cover and install the internal controller into the expansion slot. Replace the screw to secure the controller card to the system unit's back panel. Finally, refer to the owner's manual regarding any necessary jumper or switch settings.

FIGURE 12.18

Installing an internal CD-ROM drive.

Install the drive in the system by sliding the drive into its bay (near the HDD unit, if possible) and securing it with two screws on each side.

To connect the drive to the system, connect the CD-ROM drive to the HDD signal cable, observing proper orientation (unless a sound card with a built-in controller is being used). Verify that the other end of the cable is connected to the CD-ROM drive. Connect one of the power supply's options connectors to the CD-ROM drive. Connect the audio cable to the drive and to the sound card's **CD INPUT** connection (if a sound card is installed). Finish the job by replacing the system unit's cover and booting up the system.

External Units

Due to the popularity of notebook computers, some manufacturers have produced external CD-ROM drives. These drives typically connect to the SCSI host adapter or to a parallel port. This requires a fully functional, bi-directional parallel port and a special software device driver. Some internal drives include driver software, but beginning with DOS version 6.2, a driver called **MSCDEX** is included to identify and assign a drive letter to the CD-ROM.

Figure 12.19 illustrates the installation of an external SCSI CD-ROM drive. Because the drive is external, connecting the CD-ROM unit to the system usually involves only connecting a couple of cables. First, connect the CD-ROM's power supply to the external drive unit. Before making this connection, verify that the power switch or power supply is turned off. Connect the signal cable to the computer. Finally, connect the opposite end of the cable to the external CD-ROM unit. Complete the installation by installing the CD-ROM driver software on the system's hard-disk drive.

FIGURE 12.19

*Installing an external
CD-ROM drive.*

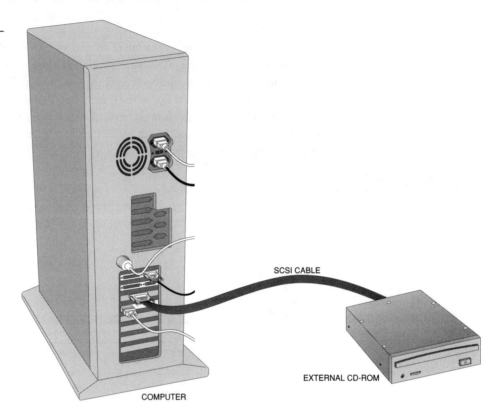

SCSI CABLE

EXTERNAL CD-ROM

COMPUTER

Configuring a CD-ROM Drive

As previously indicated, the CD-ROM drive unit must be properly configured for the system on which it is being installed. In an IDE system, the Master/Slave setting must be confirmed. In a SCSI system, the ID setting must be correct. In a SCSI system the only requirement is that a valid ID setting is configured. However, in an IDE system, some thought may be required as to how to configure the drive.

In a single HDD system, the CD-ROM drive is normally set up as the slave drive on the primary interface. However, in a two HDD system, the CD-ROM drive would most likely be configured as the master or single drive on the secondary interface. If the system also contains a sound card with a built-in IDE interface, it should be disabled to prevent it from interfering with the primary or secondary interfaces.

After the CD-ROM's hardware has been installed, you must install its software drivers. Consult the owner's manual for instructions on software installation. Typically, all that is required is to insert the OEM driver disk in the floppy drive and follow the manufacturer's directions for installing the drivers. If the drive fails to operate at this point, reboot the system using single-step verification, and check the information on the various boot screens for error messages associated with the CD-ROM drive.

If the installation is in a Windows-based system, use the Windows Write program to check the AUTOEXEC.BAT and CONFIG.SYS FILES for updated information. **Microsoft CD Extension (MSCDEX)** driver is used to provide access to the system's CD-ROM drives. This driver must be loaded from the CONFIG.SYS file using a DEVICE= or DEVICEHIGH command. The driver assigns the logical drive letters to all CD-ROM drives in the system along with a unique **driver signature** (name). The signature is used to differentiate one CD-ROM drive from another in the system.

Driver signatures are generally written in the form of MSCD000. To do this, open the Write program from the Windows Accessories window, check the AUTOEXEC.BAT file for a line that says C:\XXX\MSCDEX, and then check the CONFIG.SYS file for a line that says Device=C:\XXX\XXX /D:MSCDXXX. The XXXs will be replaced by the manufacturer's parameters. You can also examine the SYSTEM.INI file for the CD-ROM device statement.

> In Windows 95, an advanced CD-ROM driver called **CDFS (CD-ROM File System)** has been implemented to provide protected mode operation of the drive. Windows 95 retains the MSCDEX files for Real mode operation.

If Windows 95 detects that the CDFS has taken control of the CD-ROM on its initial boot-up, it will REM the MSCDEX lines in the AUTOEXEC.BAT file.

Troubleshooting a CD-ROM Drive

A+ CORE 2.1 The troubleshooting steps for a CD-ROM drive are almost identical to those of an HDD system. The connections and data paths are very similar.

> Four basic levels of troubleshooting apply to CD-ROM problems. These are the configuration level, the DOS level, the Windows level, and the hardware level. Figure 12.20 shows the parts and drivers associated with CD-ROMs.

FIGURE 12.20

Components and drivers associated with CD-ROMs.

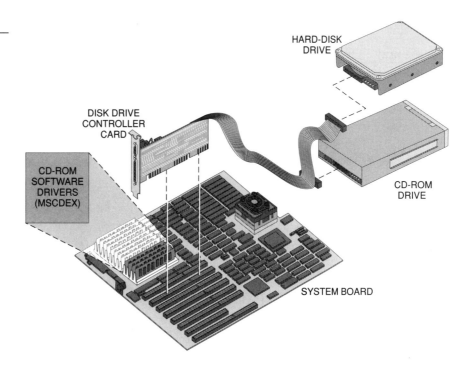

CD-ROM Software Checks

Many of the software diagnostic packages available include test functions for CD-ROM drives. Try to choose a diagnostic package that includes a good variety of CD-ROM test functions. Run the program's CD-ROM function from the Multimedia selection menu. Select the equivalent of the program's Run All Tests option.

Use a diagnostic program, such as MSD, to check the IRQ and I/O address settings for possible conflicts with other devices. If the settings are different than those established by the hardware jumpers on the controller, change the settings so that they match and so that they do not conflict with other devices.

Windows 3.x Checks

Begin by examining the SYSTEM.INI file for the CD-ROM device statement. This is accomplished by typing **Edit SYSTEM.INI** at the DOS prompt and pressing the Enter key. Inside the file, locate the CD-ROM driver by paging down to locate the DEVICE= MSCDEX line. If the line is present, check the CD-ROM documentation for troubleshooting hints. If the line is missing, reinstall the driver software. Check for the MSCDEX statement in the AUTOEXEC.BAT file.

Add a **LANMAN10.DOS** line to the SYSTEM.INI file. At the DOS prompt, type **Edit SYSTEM.INI**. Inside the file, locate the [386enh] section heading, and add the line **DEVICE=LANMAN10.DOS** to the list of device statements. Check the Windows System sub-directory for the LANMAN10.DOS file.

If the correct driver is not installed, load the correct driver, or contact the CD-ROM manufacturer for the correct Windows driver.

Windows 95 Checks

In Windows 95, the CD-ROM can be accessed through the CD icon in the Desktop's My Computer icon. The CD-ROM drive's information is contained in the Control Panel's System icon. The properties of the installed drive are located under the Settings tab. Figure 12.21 shows a typical set of CD-ROM specifications in Windows 95.

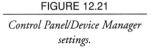

FIGURE 12.21

Control Panel/Device Manager settings.

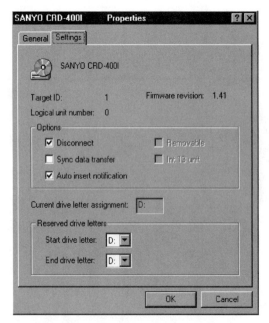

Check the system's AUTOEXEC.BAT and CONFIG.SYS FILES for updated information. To do this, open the WordPad program from the Windows 95 Accessories listing, check the AUTOEXEC.BAT file for a line that says REM C:\XXX\MSCDEX, and then check the CONFIG.SYS file for a line that says REM Device=C:\XXX\XXX /D:MSCDXXX. If the correct drivers are not installed, load the correct driver, or contact the CD-ROM manufacturer for the correct Windows driver.

CD-ROM Hardware Checks

If the configuration and software checks do not remedy the CD-ROM problem, you must troubleshoot the CD-ROM–related hardware. Basically, the hardware consists of the CD-ROM drive, the signal cable, the power cable, and the controller. The controller can be mounted on an MI/O card (host adapter card) or, in a Pentium system, on the system board. For external drives, the plug-in power adapter must be checked as well.

In most systems, the CD-ROM drive shares a controller with the hard-disk drive. Therefore, if the hard drive is working and the CD-ROM drive is not, the likelihood is very high that the problem is in the CD-ROM drive.

Before entering the system unit, check for simple user problems. Is there a CD-ROM in the drive? Is the label side of the disc facing upward? Is the disc a CD-ROM or some other type of CD?

If no simple reasons for the problem are apparent, begin by exchanging the CD-ROM drive with a known good one of the same type. For external units, simply disconnect the drive from the power and signal cables, and substitute the new drive for it. With internal units, remove the system unit's outer cover, and disconnect the signal and power cables from the drive. Remove the screws that secure the drive in the drive bay. Install the replacement unit, and attempt to access it.

If the new drive works, reinstall any options removed, and replace the system unit's outer cover. Return the system to full service, and service the defective CD-ROM drive accordingly.

If the drive does not work, check the CD-ROM drive's signal cable for proper connection at both ends. Exchange the signal cable for a known good one.

If the drive still refuses to operate, turn off the system and exchange the controller card (if present) with a known good one. In Pentium systems, the controller is mounted on the system board. In other systems, the controller is normally mounted on an MI/O card. Disconnect the disk drive's signal cable from the controller card, and swap the card with a known good one of the same type. If the controller is built into the system board, it may be easier to test the drive and signal cable in another machine than to remove the system board. Make certain to mark the cable and its connection points to ensure proper reconnection after the exchange.

Reconnect the signal cable to the controller and try to reboot the system with the new controller card installed. If the system boots up, reinstall any options removed and replace the system unit's outer cover. Return the system to full service, and service the defective controller card as appropriate.

If the drive still refuses to work, check to see whether the CD-ROM drive has been properly terminated. Exchange the CD-ROM's power connector with another one to make sure that it is not a cause of problems. Finally, exchange the system board with a known good one.

Sound Cards

The sound-producing capabilities of early PCs were practically non-existent. These included a single, small speaker that was used to produce beep-coded error messages. Even though programs could be written to produce a wide array of sounds from this speaker, the quality of the sound was never any better than the limitations imposed by its small size.

Audio is an important part of the multimedia world. People typically think of audio in computer systems as voice communication. This is normal, as most of the early work in computer audio applications was performed in the areas of speech synthesis and recognition. This work was fueled by the desire to produce human/computer interfaces that would appeal to the public. If people could communicate with the computer, and if it could talk to them, there would be no need for complicated programming, and the computer would be a handy tool for the masses.

However, the more recent advancements made in the area of multimedia have redirected this research into more computer/TV/radio applications. Voice and music are an integral part of every movie and advertising presentation you hear. People make their living just by creating short musical presentations (called jingles) that catch the interest of the target audience.

A typical **audio digitizer** system is depicted in Figure 12.22. A microphone converts sound waves from the air into an encoded, analog electrical signal. The analog signal is applied to the audio input of the **sound card**. On the card, the signal is applied to an A/D converter circuit, which changes the signal into corresponding digital values, as illustrated in Figure 12.23.

> The sound card takes samples of the analog waveform at predetermined intervals and converts them into corresponding digital values. Therefore, the digital values approximate the instantaneous values of the sound wave.

FIGURE 12.22

A typical audio digitizer system.

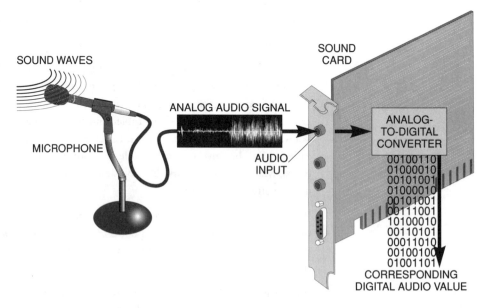

The **fidelity** (the measure of how closely the original sound can be reproduced) of the digital samples is dependent on two factors: the accuracy of the samples taken, and the rate at which the samples are taken. The accuracy of the sample is determined by the **resolution**

capabilities of the A/D converter. Resolution is the capability to differentiate between values. If the value of the analog waveform is 15.55 microvolts at a given point, how close can that value be approximated with a digital value?

Resolution of an A/D converter is determined by the number of digital output bits it can produce. For example, an 8-bit A/D converter can represent up to 256 (2^8) different values. On the other hand, a 16-bit A/D converter can represent up to 65,536 (2^{16}) different sound levels. The more often the samples are taken, the more accurately the original waveform can be reproduced.

FIGURE 12.23

Converting signal changes to digital values.

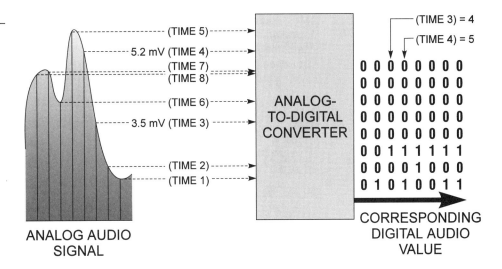

ANALOG AUDIO SIGNAL

ANALOG-TO-DIGITAL CONVERTER

CORRESPONDING DIGITAL AUDIO VALUE

Playback of the digitized audio signal is accomplished by applying the digital signals to a D/A converter at the same rate at which the samples were taken. When the audio files are called for by the application software, the runtime module of the authoring software sends commands to the audio output controller on the sound card. The digitized samples are applied to the audio output IC and are converted back into the analog signal.

The analog signal is applied to an audio preamplifier that boosts the power of the signal and sends it to an **RCA**, or **mini jack**. This signal is still too weak to drive conventional speakers, but it can be applied to an additional amplifier or to a set of speakers that have an additional amplifier built into them.

A **CD quality audio signal** requires a minimum of 16-bit samples, taken at approximately 44KHz. If you calculate the disk space required to store all the 16-bit samples collected in one minute of audio at this rate, the major consideration factor associated with using digitized audio becomes clear (16 x 44,000 x 60 x 8 = 5.28MB). If you want stereo sound, this doubles to a whopping 10.56MB. Therefore, CD-quality audio is not commonly used in multimedia productions. The audio sampling rate used in multimedia titles is generally determined by the producer. Another alternative is to limit the digitized audio used in a product to short clips.

Installation

A+ CORE 1.2   Installing a sound card is similar to installing any other adapter card. Refer to the card's user's guide to determine what hardware configuration settings should be made before inserting the card into the system. It may also be beneficial to run a diagnostic software package to check the system's available resources before configuring the card.

After the hardware configuration is complete, simply install the card in one of the system's vacant expansion slots and secure it to the back panel of the system unit. Plug the microphone and speakers into the proper jacks on the card's backplate. With the card installed the system, load its software drivers according to the directions in the user's guide.

Figure 12.24 depicts the connection scheme of a typical sound card.

> Most sound cards support microphones through stereo RCA jacks. A very similar speaker jack is also normally present on the back of the card. Depending on the card, the jack may be designed for mono or stereo output. An onboard volume control wheel may also protrude through the card's back plate.

FIGURE 12.24

Back-panel connections of a sound card.

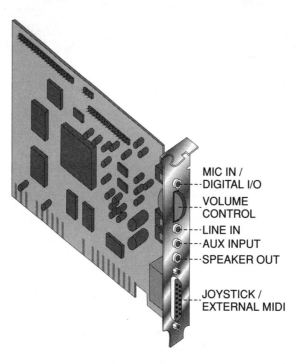

MIC IN /
DIGITAL I/O

VOLUME
CONTROL

LINE IN

AUX INPUT

SPEAKER OUT

JOYSTICK /
EXTERNAL MIDI

A typical sound blaster-compatible I/O address range used by sound cards is 220_h–$22F_h$. Alternative address ranges include 230_h–$23F_h$, 240_h–$24F_h$, and 250_h–$25F_h$. Typically, the sound card uses interrupt request channel 7 as the default. DMA channel 1 is typically used as well.

Some sound cards contain game port adapter circuitry for attaching joy sticks to the sound card. The game port circuitry must conform to the (201_h) I/O addressing specifications, described in Chapter 5, "Microsoft Windows," to remain compatible with the IBM standard. Advanced sound cards may also include a MIDI port connection.

Audio Software

When the run module of a multimedia title encounters a request for an audio file, it locates the file requested and applies it to the sound card's audio driver software. The driver software sets up the sound card to produce the sound file. The sound card has two ways to produce the requested sound file: It can retrieve a pre-recorded file from memory or hard disk and replay it, or it can synthesize the sound file.

A synthesized sound file is one that is created or generated at the time at which it is needed. Two popular synthesis techniques are in use: **FM synthesis** and **wave table synthesis**. FM, or frequency-modulated synthesis, creates sounds by generating programmed combinations of various sine wave frequencies to imitate the desired sound. Most of the sound synthesizers used with PCs are FM synthesizers. Although the actual synthesizer is an IC component, the creation of the sound is controlled by the audio software.

Wave table synthesis is a high-quality sound-generating method used to imitate the sounds made by real musical instruments. The table contains small sound clips of each of the natural instruments to be synthesized. The **synthesizer** processes the small clips to produce all the sounds called for by the software. The small clips for the instruments are generally stored in a compressed format in a ROM chip on the adapter card.

The sound card's audio software may also include a user software interface, such as the one depicted in Figure 12.25. This particular interface is designed so that it resembles the control panels associated with a CD-player, a MIDI player, a tape player, and a graphic equalizer.

FIGURE 12.25

A user interface.

GRAPHIC EQUALIZER

MIDI PLAYER

TAPE PLAYER

CD PLAYER

The software buttons in the interface enable the user to control the system's audio capabilities. The unit can play audio CDs, WAV files, and MIDI files.

MIDI

Most sound cards possess only the capability of capturing audio signals, digitizing them, and playing them back as they were recorded. Some sound cards have the capability of generating synthetic sounds that are not a function of a digitizing process.

> The MIDI standard was created by musical instrument makers to enable music synthesizers and other electronic music devices to communicate with computers and with each other.

The MIDI specification began as a hardware connectivity format. It included a protocol for exchanging data and a cabling scheme for hooking devices together. The agreement was so widely accepted by the music industry that virtually every electronic instrument manufactured today conforms to the MIDI standard.

The MIDI interface protocol lists 16 instrument channels that can be used. Commands can be sent on all channels to control a number of voices. The standard defines 128 MIDI program codes called the **General MIDI Standard**. These codes ensure that the sound produced by different MIDI instruments will be consistent.

Figure 12.26 shows a typical MIDI system. The system contains a MIDI-equipped computer, a keyboard controller/synthesizer, an audio mixer/recorder, and related sound modules. The computer contains a MIDI interface card. Although a mixer has been shown in this figure, advances in MIDI software have led to systems in which the mixer has been eliminated in favor of software mixing. Newer MIDI software contains programming called **MIDI Machine Control** (MMC). Under MMC, the software actually controls the intelligent MIDI devices, such as mixers, stage lights, and so on.

FIGURE 12.26

A typical MIDI system.

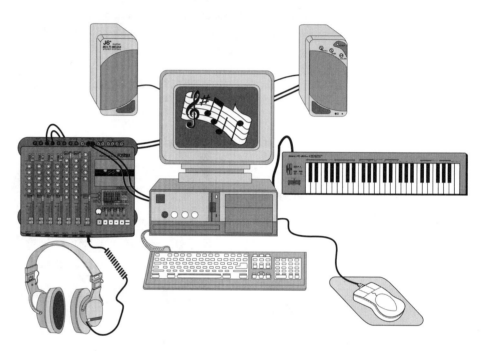

Sophisticated MIDI systems with a large number of instruments still opt for a hardware-mixing console. A sound module is actually a hardware component containing ROM devices that hold the sampled sounds of the real instruments being produced.

All MIDI devices communicate serially through round 5-pin DIN connectors, as described in Figure 12.27. Three types of connections are possible in a MIDI system: **MIDI-In**, **MIDI-Out**, and **MIDI-Thru** connections. A single connection cable can be used for all three connection types. The synthesizer/controller requires two connections to the MIDI interface in the computer. The first deals with the controller portion of the keyboard. A MIDI cable runs from MIDI-Out of the controller to MIDI-In of the interface. On the synthesizer side of the keyboard, a MIDI-In from the keyboard must be connected to MIDI-Out of the interface card.

To continue the MIDI connection scheme, the interface would require an additional MIDI-Out connection. Alternately, MIDI-Thru connections can be used to serially connect all the other MIDI devices to the system, as illustrated in Figure 12.27. The various devices are connected to the mixer/recorder through audio out/in **patch cords**.

FIGURE 12.27

MIDI cable connections.

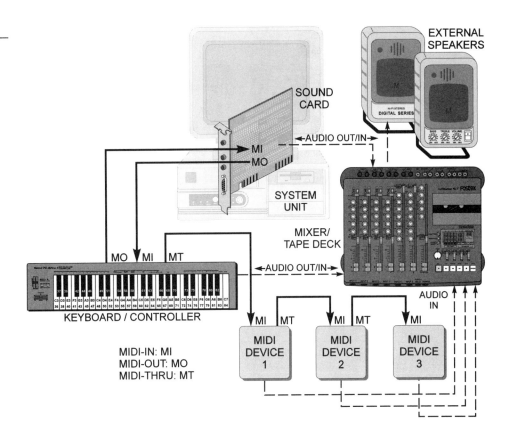

MIDI data transfers are conducted serially. Each MIDI device contains a MIDI controller, as does the MIDI adapter card in the computer system. In the MIDI device, the data produced by the equipment is applied to the MIDI controller, which converts the data into the MIDI data format. The signal passes serially to the MIDI adapter card in the computer. After processing, the computer sends it back to the MIDI device.

The MIDI data stream can contain a large amount of information about the instrument. The information in general MIDI data includes the **patch** (instrument), the **MIDI channel** (1 of 16), the note played, and the **velocity setting** (0–127). The patch code is also referred to as the program change, or PC.

The MIDI note being played is actually controlled by two separate transmissions. The **note-on code** starts the note to be played, and a separate **note-off code** is used to end the note being played. Velocity is a setting for the loudness of the note being played. The data stream can also contain instrument-specific information. This type of transfer is referred to as **system exclusive (SYSX) data**. In this format, all other instruments ignore the data not directed at them.

Speakers

Typically, the output of the sound card requires additional amplification if external speakers are used. The amplification circuitry is normally included in the external speaker units. Power for these speakers is derived from batteries housed in the speaker cabinets or from a small ac power converter. Most sound cards do have the capability of directly driving low-power headphones. Audio output can also be produced by the system's internal speaker, or it can be amplified through external audio amplifier systems for applications such as Surround Sound. Figure 12.28 depicts various speaker arrangements used with multimedia systems.

FIGURE 12.28

Typical speaker arrangements.

Troubleshooting Sound Cards

A+ CORE 2.1

> The components involved in the audio output of most computer systems are very simple. These include a sound card adapter, some speakers, the audio-related software, and the host computer system. Several software diagnostic packages also have the capability of testing sound card operation.

Most sound cards perform two separate functions. The first is to play sound files, and the second is to record them. It may be necessary to troubleshoot problems for either function.

Sound Card Configuration Checks

If sound problems are occurring in the multimedia system, two of the first things to check are the hardware and audio software configuration settings. Refer to the sound card manufacturer's documentation for proper hardware settings. These items usually include checking the card's jumper settings for IRQ and I/O address settings. However, with more plug-and-play cards in the market, software configuration of IRQ and I/O addressing is becoming more common.

In the past, sound cards have been notorious for interrupt conflict problems with other devices. Use a diagnostic program, such as MSD, to check the system for interrupt conflicts.

Sound Card Software Checks

Many diagnostic packages offer testing features for sound cards and other multimedia-related components. Sound card problems should not prevent the system from loading a software diagnostic, so run the All Tests equivalent in the Multimedia section of the diagnostic package. Also run checks to see whether addressing (IRQ or DMA) conflicts are causing a problem. If so, reconfigure the system's components so that the conflicts are removed.

Is the software application running a DOS version? If so, the application may not be capable of outputting audio under Windows. In Enhanced mode, Windows will not hand over control to the DOS application. In such cases, a message saying "This application will not be able to use audio" should appear. Run the application from DOS to see whether it works, or start Windows in Standard mode by typing **WIN** **/S** at the DOS prompt before pressing the Enter key.

The Windows Sound Recorder can be used to check the operation of WAV files under Windows. If the audio file does not play from the sound recorder, make sure the sound recorder is working by attempting to play audio files that have played on the system before. If the files play from the sound recorder, then you must examine the other application being used to try to play the file for proper installation and setup.

If the sound recorder will not play audio files through the sound card, check to see that the multimedia icons are installed in the Control Panel and in Accessories windows. Also check the Control Panel's Drivers icon to see that the correct audio driver is installed and that its settings match those called for by the sound card manufacturer. If the icons are missing, add the icons through the Setup function in the Main window.

If the driver is not installed or is incorrect, add the correct driver from the available drivers list. If the correct driver is not available, reinstall it from the card's OEM disk, or obtain it from the card's manufacturer.

If the Windows Media Player won't play MIDI files, look in the Drivers section of the Control Panel to see that the MIDI driver is set up properly. Set the Media Player to play MIDI files, and make certain that the MIDI mapping is correct. Check to see whether more than one MIDI device is connected. If so, disconnect the other MIDI devices. Also set the MIDI device to Mode 1 for testing purposes. Mode 1 is the most flexible and plays even distorted sounds.

If audio files will not play through the Media Player, check to see that the file is a WAV file. Check in the Device menu to see that the Media player is set up to play audio files. Check the audio driver installation to see that the proper audio driver is installed.

Sound Card Hardware Checks

If the sound card's configuration is properly set, and if the software configuration matches it, you must check the sound card and speakers. The system's sound card-related components are depicted in Figure 12.29. Most of these checks are very simple; they include checking to see that the speakers are plugged into the speaker port. It is not uncommon for the speakers to be mistakenly plugged into the card's MIC (microphone) port. Likewise, if the sound card will not record sound, make certain that the microphone is installed in the proper jack (not the speaker jack) and that it is turned on. Check the amount of disc space on the drive to ensure that there is enough to hold the file being produced.

If the system will not produce sound, troubleshoot the audio output portion of the system. Do the speakers require an external power supply? If so, is it connected, and are the speakers turned on? If the speakers use batteries for their power source, check them to see that they are installed and good. Check the speakers' volume setting to make certain they are not turned down.

Video Capture Cards

Video capture cards are responsible for converting video signals from different sources into digital signals that can be manipulated by the computer. As in the audio conversion process, the video card samples the incoming video signal by feeding it through an A-to-D converter, as depicted in Figure 12.30.

FIGURE 12.29

Sound card-related components.

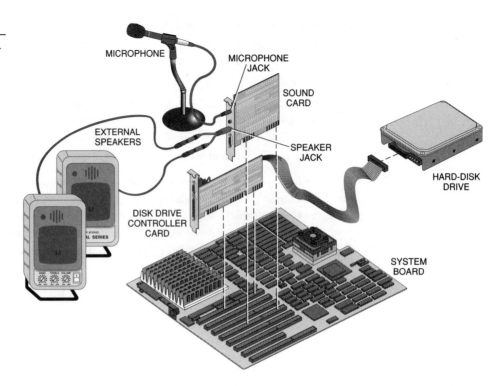

FIGURE 12.30

Converting an incoming video signal.

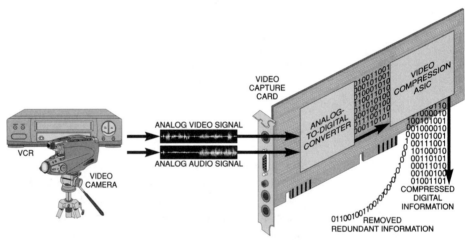

The digitized output from the A-to-D converter is applied to a **video compression ASIC**. The compression chip reduces the size of the file by removing redundant information from consecutive frames. This reduction is necessary due to the extreme size of typical digitized video files. Video-compression schemes can reduce the size of a video file by a ratio of up to 200:1.

As the sections of video are compressed, the reduced files may be applied to the system's RAM memory or may be routed directly to the hard-disk drive. The audio signal is not compressed, but it is synchronized to the video signal so that it will play in the right places when the video is rerun.

When the digitized video is recalled for output purposes, the file is reapplied to the compression chip, which restores the redundant information to the frames. The output from the compression chip is applied to the digital-to-analog portion of the video-processing circuitry. The analog signals are converted back into the proper VGA format and are applied to the video-out connector at the back plate of the card.

Depending on the compression methods used, the video clip can be played back from the Windows AVI structure or through the capture card. This is a major consideration when creating a title that includes a video component. Will the user's computer have a compatible **video digitizer card** installed, or should it be expected that the video clip will play through the Windows multimedia extensions?

Capture Card Signals and Connections

The connection points for a typical video capture card are displayed in Figure 12.31. Sources for video capture normally include VCRs and camcorders. Some capture cards, such as the one shown, include an **RF demodulator** and a **TV tuner** so that video can be captured from a television broadcast signal or a cable TV input.

FIGURE 12.31

Connections of a typical video capture card.

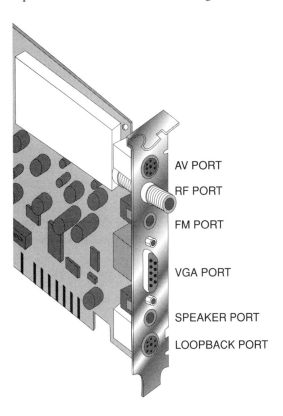

The output from these video-producing devices tends to be **composite TV** or analog **S-video** signals. A video decoder circuit is used to convert the analog signal into a stream of digital signals. However, these are not the RGB digital signals useful to the VGA card. The characteristics of the decoded TV signal are defined in television industry terms as **YUV**. The Y portion of the term refers to the luminance of the signal color, and the UV portion describes the color component of the signal.

One of the jobs of the video capture card is to convert the YUV format into an RGB VGA-compatible signal. An encoding circuit samples the incoming analog signal and then performs an operation known as **color space conversion** on it. Color space conversion is the process of converting the YUV signal into the RGB format acceptable to the VGA card's screen memory. The resolution of a studio-quality TV signal is defined as 512x512 pixels, delivered in two interlaced screens at a rate of 60 pixels per second. The encoder converts this signal scheme into a 640x480 (in VGA mode) image delivered to the screen in a single, non-interlaced screen at a rate of 30 pixels per second.

In addition to changing the format, the capture card also scales the image to fit in the defined video window on the monitor's screen. The capture card's video signal processor adjusts the image to the correct size by **interpolating** (adding or removing) adjacent pixels as necessary.

The encoder samples the analog signal at a rate of 27MBps. This value becomes very important when you realize that, at this rate, a 500MB hard drive would be full in 18.5 seconds. To make the digitized video manageable and useful to the digital computer system, the signal must be compressed into smaller files.

Compression Standards

To date, two common data-compression standards are employed with digitized video. These are the **Joint Photographic Experts Group (JPEG)** and the **Moving Picture Experts Group** (MPEG) compression standards.

JPEG

> For still images, the JPEG compression standard is used. JPEG compression also removes redundant picture information from still video frames. JPEG compresses still frames in 1/30 of a second. Its playback capabilities allow it to also reproduce frames at a rate of 30 per second.

JPEG can play back digitized movies at full-screen sizes. Used in this manner, the format is called **M-JPEG**. However, the M-JPEG format has not been standardized, so it is vendor-specific at this point.

Most compression algorithms use complex mathematical formulas to remove redundant bits, such as successive 0s or 1s, from the data stream. When the modified stream is played back through the decompression circuitry, the formula reinserts the missing bits to return the data to its original state. This concept is depicted in Figure 12.32.

FIGURE 12.32

Examining successive bytes in a frame.

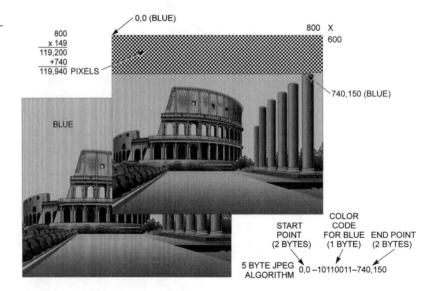

Ideally, you might assume that a compressed/decompressed image would be returned to 100% of its original state. However, in practice, some information from the original image will not be completely restored. In a JPEG system, the fidelity of the image depends on the compression ratio used. JPEG can obtain compression ratios of 100:1, but the quality of the reproduced image may be quite poor. As a matter of fact, when the compression ratio exceeds 20:1, the decompressed image deteriorates noticeably.

The fidelity of the JPEG system depends on the complexity of its compression algorithm. Some expensive compression systems are **lossless JPEG systems**. Their returned image quality is very good, but the compression ratio is typically very low. Other JPEG systems provide better compression, but at the cost of image loss. For this reason, most JPEG capture is performed at less than full-screen size, or with less than every frame. Reduced movie sizes are shown in 1/4-screen windows. **Reduced frame rates** are 1/2 (15 frames per second), or 1/3 (10 frames per second).

MPEG

Although JPEG provides enough compression to allow single-frame digitized images to fit on disk drives, it soon became apparent that **full-motion** pictures were going to need much greater compression to be useful on current technology. Therefore, the MPEG format delivered a compression algorithm that provides compression ratios up to 200:1, with high-quality video and audio.

> As with JPEG, MPEG removes redundant picture information from individual scenes. However, instead of simply removing redundant information from within a single frame, the MPEG compression scheme removes redundant information from consecutive scenes. In addition, the MPEG methodology compresses only key objects within a frame every 15th frame. Between these key frames, only the information that changes from frame to frame is recorded.

In this manner, MPEG compression systems can attain the compression ratios and good image fidelity required by full-motion video.

MPEG files are difficult to edit due to the fact that the content of each frame is heavily related to the contents of the frames around it. The MPEG recording scheme is illustrated in Figure 12.33.

FIGURE 12.33

The MPEG recording scheme.

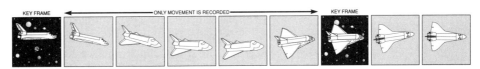

The MPEG standard includes specifications for audio compression and decompression in both MPEG 1 and 2. **MPEG 1** supports a very near CD-quality stereo output, at data rates between 128Kbps and 256Kbps. The **MPEG 2** specification supports CD-quality surround-sound (four-channel) output.

Other Compression Standards

Another data-compression method used with PCs is the **Indeo** compression standard, developed by Intel. Indeo is similar to the MPEG standard, in that it was actually designed to be a distribution format. It was primarily intended to play back compressed video files from the smallest file size possible. Later versions of this standard include the MPEG compression methods.

Another compression/decompression standard supported by Video for Windows is **Cinepak**. This standard uses an AVI file format to produce 40:1 compression ratios and 30 frames per second capture, at 320x200 resolution.

Windows 95 naturally supports several different compression techniques. These include Cinepak, two versions of Indeo, an **RLE** format, and the **Video 1** format.

Video Capture Software

The video capture software normally provides the user with an interface to configure and conduct a video capture operation. A typical video capture software interface is presented in Figure 12.34. As with most other capture software, this interface enables the user to view audio waveforms and video images, perform file creation and control functions, capture video (single-frame or full-motion), and edit video clips or still frames for content and effects.

FIGURE 12.34

A typical video capture software interface.

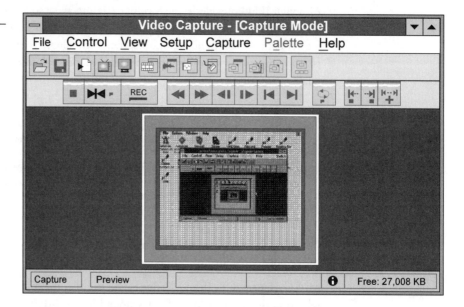

The capture interface screen shown offers a control panel for file-handling and editing functions, as well as a monitor window in which incoming video can be previewed. An audio wave display window, above the control panel, displays the audio waveforms being recorded or played back. This feature is very useful for editing audio files because it is possible to remove sections of the audio and relocate them. The shuttle dial provides quick movement through the file. A set of tape counters at the left side of the panel provides start, length, position, and end values for the video in digital display format.

Normal file-handling features include Open and Save functions. In this example, these features are present in a pair of buttons toward the right side of the screen. Drive and filename listings are available in the windows at the extreme right side of the control panel.

Some file-editing functions typically found in video capture software include the following:

▶ Zoom

▶ Undo

▶ Cut

- Paste
- Crop
- Clear

These functions can be used to edit both audio and video files. Typical **video effects** include Preview and Freeze. The Freeze function captures a still video frame, and the Preview function enables the user to examine the video source without capturing frames.

A full set of audio and VCR control buttons are located on the Control Panel to manipulate the record and playback functions for audio or video. The type of file being examined is determined by the audio/video button that changes from audio to video to AVI.

The **compression controls** enable the user to select the type of compression format to be used. Other compression control settings are used to set a balance between the size and quality of the AVI file produced. The user can select the target (RAM or HDD) for the captured video stream, determine the number of key frames per second, and set the length of the capture buffer that holds the incoming video information.

Typical **capture rates** for full-motion video cards are stated at 30 frames per second. However, many systems are not capable of reaching the full potential of this rate. A number of frames may be dropped from the sequence of frames shot. To record at frame rates above 15 frames per second, the system must have a full arsenal of multimedia-capable components because successful video capture is normally a function of the system's hardware capabilities. If the system's RAM is being used to buffer the incoming video information, the size of the extended memory section must be very large.

Many MPC systems include very large, very fast hard drives for data buffering. The hard drive space accommodates much more captured video, provided that the HDD is fast enough to keep up with the incoming data stream. **Video buffering** is one application in which even the slightly superior performance of SCSI-2 systems becomes more desirable than less-expensive EIDE systems.

Installing Video Capture Cards

 A+ CORE 1.7

Refer to the capture card's documentation and prepare its hardware configuration jumpers (or switches) for operation. The card's factory default settings usually work well, but you should examine the system's installed devices for address and IRQ conflicts.

Install the video capture card in one of the unit's adapter slots. As with any other adapter card, this requires that the outer cover of the system unit be removed. Inside the unit, remove the expansion slot cover of a compatible expansion slot. Many capture cards are full-length cards, so make sure the slot can handle the physical dimension of the card. Make sure the expansion slot type is compatible with the capture card's edge connector.

Connect the capture card to the VGA card as directed by the manufacturer's installation guide. Figure 12.35 depicts a BERG connection between the capture card and the VGA feature connector on the VGA card. Some VGA cards use an edge connector built into the top of the card for the feature connection function.

Install any antennas that must be connected to the card for the intended application. These could include a TV antenna, a coaxial cable from the television, and/or an FM radio antenna.

FIGURE 12.35

Capture card-to-VGA
connection.

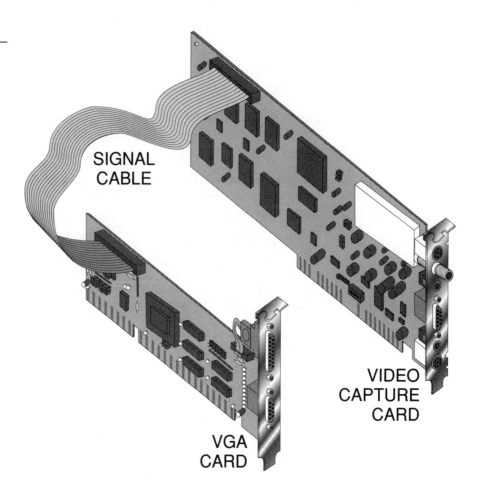

Connect the video-in cables to the audio and video source(s) being used for input. In this case, there is a stereo audio-in (left/right) provision, and two possible sources for video-in. The audio and video connections are typically made with standard RCA cables and connectors.

Connect the VGA monitor's signal cable to the capture card's VGA-out connector, as illustrated in Figure 12.36. The video signal passes through the capture card and is looped to the VGA card. This means that the screen image can be present on the monitor and the video screen simultaneously. A VGA loopback cable is connected between the capture card's loopback input and the VGA card's RGB-out connector.

If external speakers and microphones are being used, connect the microphone to the MIC input, and connect the speaker to the speaker port. This port can also be used as an audio source to the line-in connection of a sound card. This connection is illustrated in Figure 12.37. These types of inputs typically use RCA stereo jacks and plugs.

Troubleshooting Video Capture Cards

A+ CORE 2.1

Troubleshooting problems with a video capture card can involve many parts of the system. Because the capture card can get its input from so many sources, all TV-signal input devices must be considered a possible cause of capture problems.

FIGURE 12.36

*Connecting the monitor's
signal cable.*

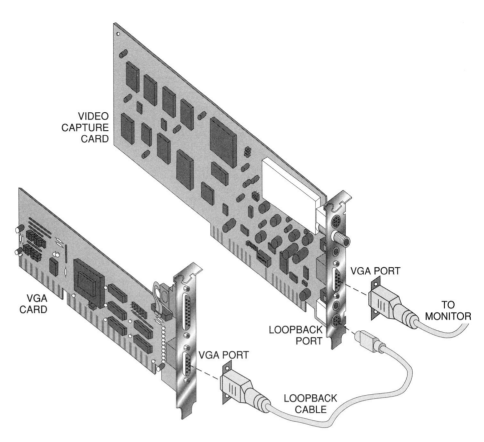

FIGURE 12.37

Connecting the sound card.

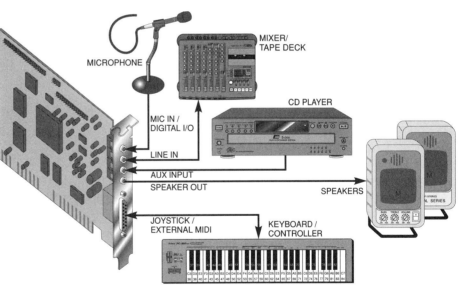

The capture card is directly involved with the video card, so it must always be considered as a source of video capture problems. Due to the complexity of the possible TV/video/sound components, cabling is always a potential source of problems.

Video Capture Card Configuration Checks

A typical capture card's video address range is between 700_h and $70F_h$. Alternate video address settings usually include 400_h–$40F_h$, 500_h–$50F_h$, and 600_h–$60F_h$. These settings may be made through BERG jumpers or through a multiple-switch set mounted in a dual in-line package, as illustrated in Figure 12.38. Address settings for a particular brand of capture card would be found in its installation guide. If the hardware jumper setting is changed on the card, make certain to reset the video capture software configuration to match it. This should be done through the Setup utility of the card's user software.

FIGURE 12.38

Configuring addresses with DIP switches.

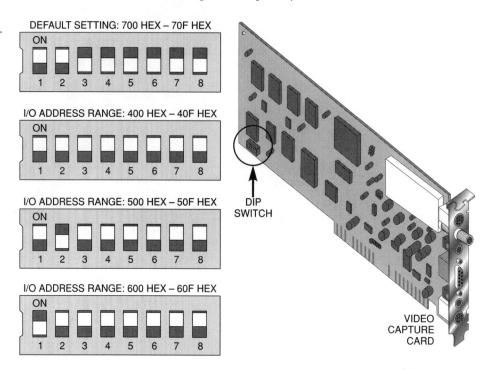

DEFAULT SETTING: 700 HEX – 70F HEX

I/O ADDRESS RANGE: 400 HEX – 40F HEX

I/O ADDRESS RANGE: 500 HEX – 50F HEX

DIP SWITCH

I/O ADDRESS RANGE: 600 HEX – 60F HEX

VIDEO CAPTURE CARD

As with most other adapter cards, the capture card must have an Interrupt Request channel set up for it. IRQ10 is a typical default setting. However, IRQ6, IRQ11, and IRQ12 are possible alternatives. As with the base address value, the IRQ value must be updated in the software if the card's hardware setting is changed.

The capture card's general purpose I/O address must also be configured for correct operation. Capture cards typically use I/O addresses $30C_h$–$30F_h$ or 20Ch–20Fh for I/O purposes. This is the address space at which the capture card's onboard controller communicates with the system, and it is typically used when the system initializes the card for use, or when the system changes the card's operating parameters. Likewise, the system can obtain status information from the card through these addresses.

Capture cards can contain a number of other, more proprietary hardware settings. The manufacturer's installation guide must be consulted to find out what they are and how they should be set up for a particular application. If the hardware settings are changed from the factory defaults, and if power is lost to the system, the software settings may need to be reset to match the true hardware settings.

Video Capture Card Software Checks

No diagnostic utilities are available to test the function of video capture cards. However, a diagnostic package can be run to check for addressing, IRQ, and DMA conflicts. As always, reconfigure the system's components to remove any conflicts detected.

If the capture card's driver software is not installed, or if it is not installed in the correct directory, the card will not be capable of capturing video. Check the installation manual to verify that the drivers are installed correctly. If problems persist, reinstall the video capture software by running the manufacturer's installation disk. Contact the capture card manufacturer for updated drivers or driver corrections (referred to as **patches**).

Check the AVI functions in Windows. Try to play AVI files that have previously worked through the Video for Windows utility. If the display disappears from the screen as soon as the Windows Program Manager appears, check the Startup window for capture card-related .EXE files. You can REM these files for testing purposes.

Check the Drivers window in the Control Panel to see that the card's AVI drivers are properly installed. Consult the manufacturer's user's manual for the names of the card's AVI drivers.

If the Media Player will not run animations, check in the Device section to make certain that it is set to play animation files. Check to see that the animation driver is installed in the Control Panel's driver settings area. Make sure the Microsoft MCI driver for MMP is properly set up.

Under Windows 95, the video capture information is located under the System section in the Control Panel. Check the Device Manager for the capture card's information. Also check under the Advanced tab of the Control Panel's Multimedia section for driver information concerning the sound card. Check the installed driver and its properties to see that it is set up correctly for the installed capture card.

Video Capture Card Hardware Checks

If all the hardware and software configuration settings are correct but capture problems continue, you must troubleshoot the video capture-related hardware. In most systems, this involves a TV signal source (such as a VCR or camcorder), the cabling, the capture card, and the video card. Other parts of the computer system may become involved, but the components presented in Figure 12.39 are those hardware components typically associated with video capture operations.

FIGURE 12.39

Hardware components of a video capture system.

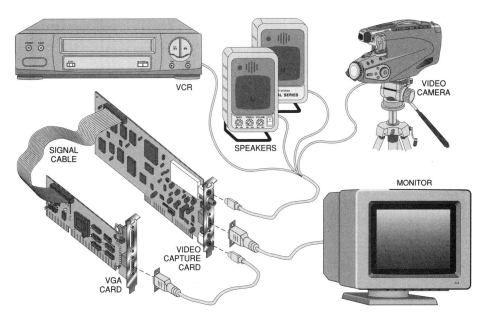

Most capture card software provides a preview window that enables the user to view the video coming from the video source. If the source is visible in this window, then the video source and the video-in cabling can be eliminated as a source of problems. However, simply being able to see the video in the window does not mean that the card will capture video.

If the video is present in the window, and if the video source and cabling check out, then the hardware and software configurations should be checked closely. Check the capture software's setup for video buffer settings. Usual video buffer settings are $D0000_h$, $D800_h$, $E000_h$, or $E800_h$. Change the setting to one of the other possible values. Add a DEVICE= statement to the CONFIG.SYS file that corresponds to the new setting for the video buffer (for example, DEVICE=path\EMM386.EXE X=D000h-D700h). Finally, reinstall and reconfigure the capture software if problems continue.

If the signal from the video source is not present in the preview window, make certain that the video source is turned on. Check the video-in cable to make certain that it is properly connected to the video-out jack of the video source and into the correct video-source input on the capture card. Check the capture card's I/O address setup closely, as well as its setting in the capture software. Check in the video capture software to make sure that the correct video source setting is selected. While in the software settings, check the video type selected, and make sure that it is set for the NTSC standard.

VGA-to-TV Converters

Several companies have developed adapter cards and external adapters to convert VGA signals into NTSC and European PAL-compatible television signals. This enables the computer to use a television as an output device.

This type of converter is particularly useful for presentations conducted in medium-sized rooms. A large-screen or rear-projection television can produce readable output in such a room without dimming the lights. A very large-screen VGA monitor would be expensive by comparison. An overhead projector/LCD panel combination can be difficult to read without lowering the room lights; even with very powerful projectors, the output can be washed out due to normal room lighting.

Figure 12.40 depicts a typical VGA-TV converter card. These converters also come packaged as external units that attach to the output connector of the VGA card. The output signal of the VGA card is routed onto the converter, and it re-emerges to be connected to the VGA monitor. The TV connection is usually made through RCA cables that connect to the TV's video-in jacks. Some converters work in parallel with the VGA card through the IBM PS/2-compatible auxiliary video extension.

The internal operation of the converter is illustrated in Figure 12.41. The converter's operation is straightforward in that its signal-processing circuitry converts the raster scan video and sync signals of a VGA or SVGA card into an NTSC-compatible raster scan signal. For example, the converter might be required to convert an 800-dot-by-600-raster-line signal into a 525.5 raster-line-compatible TV signal.

In the converter, the VGA signal is sampled into an onboard memory, called the **frame buffer**. An onboard clock signal outputs the contents of the buffer at TV-compatible rates. The output RGB signals are fed into a composite signal encoder that performs the final signal conversion into composite-TV, or analog S-Video format.

FIGURE 12.40

*Connecting a VGA-to-TV card
to the system.*

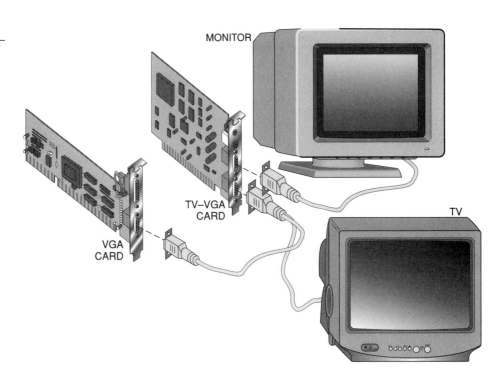

FIGURE 12.41

*Internal operations of
a converter.*

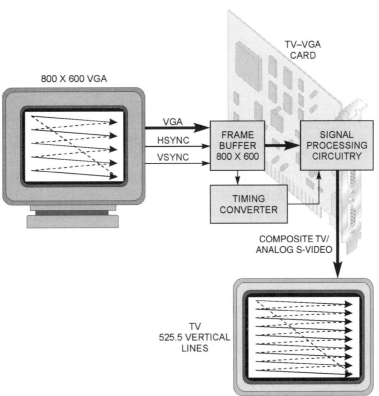

Troubleshooting VGA-to-TV Converters

A+ CORE 2.1   The VGA-TV card becomes part of the computer's video output system. Therefore, troubleshooting problems with a VGA-TV card typically involves the other parts of the display system. Figure 12.42 illustrates the parts of the video output system when a VGA-TV card is involved.

FIGURE 12.42

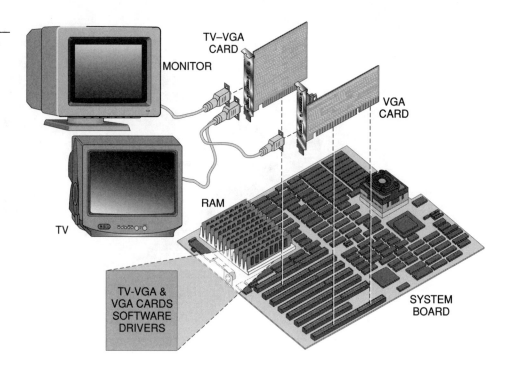

In addition to the hardware components of the system, the VGA-TV card's driver software must also be considered as a potential source of problems.

VGA-to-TV Converters Configuration Checks

Refer to the converter's installation and/or user's guides for configuration information. Check for proper jumper settings if the converter uses hardware jumpers. Check the setup of the converter's driver software. Most VGA-TV converters are software-configurable.

VGA-to-TV Converters Software Checks

Make certain that the VGA-TV driver is loaded. The driver should be a TSR type of driver. Run the TSR function of a diagnostic, such as MSD, to see whether the system sees the VGA-TV driver. The TSR driver may conflict with other system drivers. This will result in operating problems in other applications after the converter has been installed. Refer to the user's guide for alternative installation guidelines for the driver.

Check in the AUTOEXEC.BAT and CONFIG.SYS files for the conflicting TSRs. Create a clean boot disk with no AUTOEXEC.BAT or CONFIG.SYS files, and then load the converter's driver software from the DOS prompt. If a TSR conflict problem exists, it should disappear when the driver is run in this manner.

If you are operating the converter in Windows, check the Windows video setup for the proper display mode. Some converters will not operate in SVGA mode. If the Windows video is set for SVGA mode, select a 640x480 driver, and retry the system. In some cases, the SVGA mode selection will cause the television display to be jumpy even though the VGA output is steady.

VGA-to-TV Converters Hardware Checks

The equipment associated with a VGA-TV converter include the following:

▶ The converter

▶ The VGA card

- The TV

- The cabling

- The computer system

These components are depicted in Figure 12.41. If the video signal does not appear on the TV screen, check the cabling and connectors to make sure they are installed properly, as directed by the manufacturer's installation guide.

Check the TV's channel setting and on/off switch to make sure that the TV is on and set to the correct channel. Also check the TV's video input setting to make sure that it is set to match the actual hardware connection between the TV and the VGA converter.

If a VCR is connected between the TV and the converter, check the TV/VCR channel settings. If the converter is an external unit, make sure that its external power supply is plugged in and that power is available.

If the computer is a notebook with an auxiliary VGA output (the LCD panel is the primary VGA output), then check to make sure that the external VGA switch is set properly. The notebook may also have a software hot key that switches the output from the LCD panel to the external VGA output. Consult the notebook's user's manual for this possibility.

General Multimedia Problems

Typical symptoms associated with multimedia failures include the following:

- The sound does not work.

- The system will not capture video.

- The user cannot access the CD-ROM.

- The system will not play video.

Various multimedia support systems include a sound card, a CD-ROM drive, external speakers, and a video capture card. Most or all of these devices will be included in any particular multimedia system. These types of equipment typically push the performance of the system and, therefore, require the most services from technicians. This is very true during setup and configuration.

One of the major points to be aware of when building or upgrading a multimedia PC is the interrupt channel usage of the system. It is important that all the devices have access to unique, acceptable interrupt request lines. To ensure this, the technician should map out the system's IRQ capabilities with the number and level of interrupts needed by the different devices being installed. In some instances, it will also be necessary to map the DMA capabilities of the system to the number of available DMA channels.

The wide variety of I/O systems that come together to create a true multimedia machine can quickly use up all the available I/O slots on most system boards. This is particularly prevalent in Pentium systems, where the expansions slots are often a mix of ISA and PCI buses. This sometimes leads to problems getting I/O cards with the right mix of bus connectors. IRQ and DMA availability and utilization is covered in detail in Chapter 6, "System Boards."

Key Points Review

The focus of this chapter has been on multimedia components, methods, and applications.

▶ *Multimedia* is a term applied to a range of applications that bring together text, graphics, video, audio, and animation to provide interactivity between the computer and its human operator.

▶ At the heart of the multimedia movement are the authoring systems that bring various media types together into a complete package.

▶ Unlike word processing and desktop publishing applications, which are used to produce a static page, multimedia authoring programs are used to prepare time-sequenced and interactive presentations.

▶ PCs intended for multimedia use normally possess very fast microprocessors; large amounts of installed RAM; big, fast hard-disk drives; a fast CD-ROM drive; a sound card; and a high-resolution video card.

▶ Soon after the compact disc became popular for storing audio signals on optical material, the benefits of storing computer information in this manner became apparent.

▶ The information on a compact disc is stored in one continuous spiral track, unlike floppy disks, where the data is stored in multiple concentric tracks.

▶ Another type of CD drive is classified as Write Once, Read Many (WORM) drive. These drives enable users to write information to the disc once and then retrieve this information as with a normal CD-ROM drive.

▶ In Windows 95, an advanced CD-ROM driver called CDFS (CD-ROM File System) has been implemented to provide Protected mode operation of the drive.

▶ Four basic levels of troubleshooting apply to CD-ROM problems. These are the configuration level, the DOS level, the Windows level, and the hardware level.

▶ The sound card takes samples of the analog waveform at predetermined intervals and converts them into corresponding digital values. Therefore, the digital values approximate the instantaneous values of the sound wave.

▶ Playback of digitized audio is accomplished by applying the digital signals to a D/A converter at the same rate at which the samples were taken. When the audio files are called for by the application software, the runtime module of the authoring software sends commands to the audio output controller on the sound card. The digitized samples are applied to the audio output IC and are converted back into the analog signal.

▶ Most sound cards support microphones through stereo RCA jacks. A similar speaker jack is also normally present on the back of the card. Depending on the card, the jack may be designed for mono or stereo output.

▶ The MIDI standard was created by musical instrument makers to enable music synthesizers and other electronic music devices to communicate with computers and each other.

▶ The components involved in the audio output of most computer systems are very simple: There is a sound card adapter, some speakers, the audio-related software, and the host computer system.

▶ Video capture cards are responsible for converting video signals from different sources into digital signals that can be manipulated by the computer.

▶ For still images, the JPEG compression standard is used. JPEG compression also removes redundant picture information from still video frames. JPEG compresses still frames in 1/30 of a second. Its playback capabilities enable it to also reproduce frames at a rate of 30 per second.

▶ As with JPEG, MPEG removes redundant picture information from individual scenes. However, the MPEG compression scheme removes redundant information from consecutive scenes. In addition, MPEG compresses only key objects within every 15th frame. Between these key frames, only the information that changes from frame to frame is recorded.

▶ Because the video capture card can obtain its input from so many sources, all TV-signal input devices must be considered a possible cause of capture problems.

- Several companies have developed adapter cards and external adapters to convert VGA signals into National Television Standards Committee and European video signals. This means that the computer can use a television as an output device.

At this point, review the objectives listed at the beginning of the chapter to be certain that you understand each point and can perform each task listed there. Afterward, answer the review questions that follow to verify your knowledge of the information.

Multiple Choice Questions

1. How is data stored on a CD?

   a. As 1s and 0s

   b. As colored spots on a light-sensitive material

   c. As opaque spots on a light-sensitive material

   d. As blisters written on a light-sensitive material

2. What type of file is a .WAV file?

   a. A standard video file

   b. A standard audio file

   c. A standard musical file

   d. A standard authoring file

3. Describe the two types of video capture cards.

   a. Video only and audio/video

   b. VGA-to-TV capture and VGA-to-VGA capture

   c. Still-frame capture and full-motion capture

   d. Monochrome and RGB color capture

4. What hardware component is associated with the MSCDEX file?

   a. The video capture card

   b. The sound card

   c. The CD-ROM drive

   d. The VGA-TV card

5. What type of signal conversion is performed by a VGA-TV card?

   a. RGB video to composite TV

   b. RGB video to composite video

   c. Composite video to composite TV

   d. Composite TV to composite RGB video

6. List the hardware items that should be checked if sound card problems are encountered.

   a. The speakers, the sound card, and the CD-ROM

   b. The speakers, the sound card, and the system board

   c. The sound card, the CD-ROM, and the system board

   d. The speakers, the sound card, and the amount of free space on the HDD

7. In what type of multimedia application are you most likely to find MIDI equipment and software?

   a. Video editing

   b. Electronic music production

   c. Multimedia composition

   d. Audio/video mixing

8. What type of standard is YUV?

   a. A multimedia industry color signal standard

   b. An audio industry sound standard

   c. A television industry color signal standard

   d. A television industry transmission standard

9. What is the major limiting factor in using full-motion video in a multimedia title?

   a. RAM and HDD capacity

   b. Microprocessor speed

   c. Bus speed

   d. Codex processing speed

10. Which Windows utility is the primary channel used with the MCI interface?

    a. The Round Recorder

    b. The Media Player

    c. The MIDI Player

    d. The VidCap utility

Review Questions

1. How do CD players differ from CD-ROM drives?

2. List six hardware components typically found in a multimedia system.

3. What is the purpose of an authoring system?

4. Why are fast peripherals desirable with multimedia systems?

5. Describe interactivity as it applies to multimedia applications.

6. Name the two types of video compression standards and describe the type of application in which each can be found.

7. List at least four types of software packages generally associated with the production of a multimedia title.

8. Describe three hardware configuration settings normally associated with setting up a video capture card.

9. How is a multimedia authoring system different than a word processing or desktop publishing program?

10. How is MIDI data exchanged between system components?

11. Describe the process that takes place in creating digitized audio.

12. What is the purpose of including a video capture card in a multimedia PC?

13. How is digitized video different from digitized audio?

14. Why is cabling such a cause of problems in video capture cards?

15. Describe the three compression techniques involved in MPEG compression.

Lab Exercises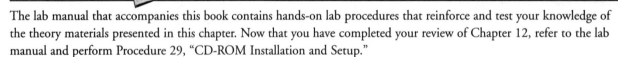

The lab manual that accompanies this book contains hands-on lab procedures that reinforce and test your knowledge of the theory materials presented in this chapter. Now that you have completed your review of Chapter 12, refer to the lab manual and perform Procedure 29, "CD-ROM Installation and Setup."

SKILL ENHANCEMENT

PART V

Chapter 13 Preventive Maintenance, Safety, and Customer Service

PREVENTIVE MAINTENANCE, SAFETY, AND CUSTOMER SERVICE

LEARNING OBJECTIVES

Upon completion of this chapter and its related lab procedures, you should be able to perform the following functions:

1. Demonstrate proper cleaning procedures for various system components.

2. Describe ESD hazards and methods of preventing ESD.

3. Define the term *ground*.

4. Describe the two types of uninterruptable power supplies (UPSs) and state their qualities.

5. State typical precautions that should be observed when working on computer equipment.

6. Perform generic preventive maintenance routines as required (for example, remove excess toner, replace printer ribbons, defragment hard drives, and create back-up copies).

7. Detail routine preventive maintenance procedures as they apply to hard and floppy disks.

8. Perform basic disk-management functions on a hard drive, including using SCANDISK, CHKDSK, and Defrag utilities.

9. Use software utilities to identify and remove viruses from computer systems.

10. List precautionary steps that should be taken when handling floppy disks.

11. List steps to clean a dot-matrix, ink-jet, or laser printer.

12. Establish and maintain preventive maintenance schedules for users.

13. Differentiate between various UPS specifications and state how they apply to a given situation.

14. State potential hazards that are present when working with laser printers, monitors, and other equipment.

15. Describe various customer service skills that will lead to improved customer satisfaction.

Introduction

It has long been known that one of the best ways to fix problems in complex systems is to prevent them before they happen. This is the concept behind preventive maintenance procedures. Breakdowns never occur at convenient times. By planning for a few minutes of nonproductive activities, hours of repair and recovery work can be avoided. This chapter covers common preventive maintenance activities and scheduling.

Most of the text in this chapter centers on safety-related issues. The personal computer is a relatively safe piece of equipment to own or repair, but it is still an electronic device that carries potentially hazardous conditions with it. This section should make you aware of these potential hazard areas.

Cleaning

A+ CORE 3.1

> Cleaning is a major part of keeping a computer system healthy. Therefore, the technician's tool kit should also contain a collection of cleaning supplies. Along with hand tools, this kit should include a lint-free, soft cloth (**chamois**) for cleaning the outer surfaces of the system.

Outer-surface cleaning can be accomplished with a simple soap-and-water solution, followed by a clear-water rinse. Care should be taken to make sure that none of the liquid splashes or drips into the inner parts of the system. A damp cloth is easily the best general-purpose cleaning tool for use with computer equipment.

The cleaning should be followed by the application of an antistatic spray or antistatic solution to prevent the build-up of static charges on the components of the system. A solution composed of 10 parts water and 1 part common household fabric softener makes an effective and economical antistatic solution. To remove dust from the inside of cabinets, a small paint brush is handy. These items are summarized in Figure 13.1.

FIGURE 13.1

Computer cleaning supplies.

CORE 3.1 Another common problem is the build-up of oxidation or corrosion at electrical contact points. These build-ups occur on electrical connectors and contacts, and can reduce the flow of electricity through the connection. Some simple steps can be used to keep corrosion from becoming a problem. The easiest step in preventing corrosion is observing the correct handling procedures for printed circuit boards and cables, as shown in Figure 13.2. Never touch the electrical contact points with your skin; the moisture on your body can start corrosive action.

FIGURE 13.2

How to handle a PC board.

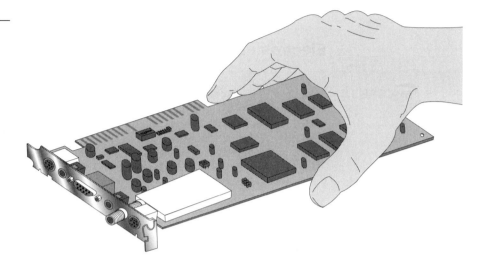

Even with proper handling, some corrosion may occur over time. This oxidation can be removed in a number of ways. The oxide build-up can be sanded off with emery cloth, rubbed off with a common pencil eraser or special solvent-wipe, or dissolved with an electrical-contact cleaner spray. Socketed devices should be reseated as a part of an anti-corrosion cleaning. However, they should be handled according to the MOS handling guidelines in this chapter to make certain that no static discharge damage occurs.

If you use the emery cloth or rubber eraser to clean your contacts, always rub toward the outer edge of the board or connector to prevent damage to the contacts. Rubbing the edge may lift the foil from the PC board. Printed-circuit board connectors are typically very thin. Therefore, rub only hard enough to remove the oxide layer. Also, take time to clean up any dust or rubber contamination generated by the cleaning effort.

Cleaning other internal components, such as disk drive Read/Write heads, can be performed using lint-free foam swabs and isopropyl alcohol or methanol. It's most important that the cleaning solution be one that dries without leaving a residue. The following list details the tools and equipment recommended for a well-prepared computer repair toolbox:

▶ Assorted flat-blade screwdrivers

▶ Assorted Phillips screwdrivers

▶ Assorted small nut drivers

▶ Assorted small torx bit drivers

▶ Needle-nose pliers

▶ Diagonal pliers

▶ Contact cleaner

- Foam swabs
- Tweezers
- Cleaning supplies
- Magnifying glass
- Clip leads
- IC extractors

Electrostatic Discharge

 A+ CORE 3.5

Electrostatic discharges (ESDs) are the most severe form of **electromagnetic interference (EMI)**. The human body can build up static charges that range up to 25,000 volts. These build-ups can discharge very rapidly into an electrically grounded body or device. Placing a 25,000v surge through any electronic device is potentially damaging to it.

Static can easily discharge through digital computer equipment. The electronic devices that are used to construct digital equipment are particularly susceptible to damage from ESD. As a matter of fact, ESD is the most damaging form of electrical interference associated with digital equipment.

The most common causes of ESD are listed here:

- Moving people
- Low humidity (hot and dry conditions)
- Improper grounding
- Unshielded cables
- Poor connections

Elementary school teachers demonstrate the principles of static to their students by rubbing different materials together. When people move, the clothes they are wearing rub together and can produce large amounts of electrostatic charge on their bodies. Walking across carpeting can create charges in excess of 1,000v. ESD is most likely to occur during periods of low humidity. If the relative humidity is less than 50%, static charges can accumulate easily. ESD generally does not occur when the humidity is more than 50%. Anytime the charge reaches around 10,000v, it is likely to discharge to grounded metal parts.

ESD won't hurt humans, but it will destroy certain electronic devices. The high-voltage pulse can burn out the inputs of many IC devices. This damage may not appear instantly; it can build up over time and cause the device to fail. Electronic logic devices constructed from **metal oxide semiconductor (MOS)** materials are particularly susceptible to ESD. The following section describes the special handling techniques that should be observed when working with equipment containing MOS devices.

MOS Handling Techniques

In general, MOS devices are sensitive to voltage spikes and static electricity discharges. This can cause a great deal of problems when you have to replace MOS devices, especially **complementary-symmetry metal oxide semiconductor** (**CMOS**) devices. The level of static electricity present on your body is high enough to destroy the inputs of a CMOS device if you touch its pins with your fingers.

To minimize the chances of damaging MOS devices during handling, special procedures have been developed to protect them from static shock. ICs are generally shipped and stored in special conductive plastic tubes or trays. You may want to store MOS devices in these tubes, or you may simply ensure their safety by inserting the IC's leads into aluminum foil or antistatic (conductive) foam, not Styrofoam. PC boards containing static-sensitive devices are normally shipped in special antistatic bags. These bags are good for storing ICs and other computer components that may be damaged by ESD. The bags are also the best method of transporting PC boards with static-sensitive components.

Professional service technicians employ a number of precautionary steps when they are working on systems that may contain MOS devices. These technicians normally use a **grounding strap**, similar to the one depicted in Figure 13.3. These antistatic devices may be placed around the wrists or ankle to ground the technician to the system on which he is working. These straps release any static present on the technician's body and pass it harmlessly to ground potential.

Antistatic straps should never be worn while working on higher-voltage components, such as monitors and power supply units. Some technicians wrap a copper wire around their wrist or ankle and connect it to the ground side of an outlet. This is not a safe practice because the resistive feature of a true wrist strap is missing. As an alternative, most technicians' work areas include antistatic mats made out of rubber or other antistatic materials on which the technicians stand while working on the equipment. This is particularly helpful in carpeted work areas because carpeting can be a major source of ESD build-up. Some antistatic mats have ground connections that should be connected to the safety ground of an ac power outlet.

FIGURE 13.3

Typical antistatic devices.

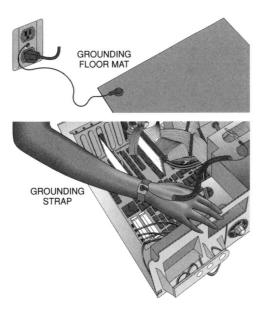

GROUNDING
FLOOR MAT

GROUNDING
STRAP

To avoid damaging static-sensitive devices, follow these procedures to help minimize the chances of destructive static discharges:

1. Computers and peripheral systems may contain a number of static-sensitive devices, so before touching any components inside the system, you should touch an exposed part of the chassis or the power supply housing with your finger, as illustrated in Figure 13.4. Grounding yourself in this manner ensures that any static charge present on your body is removed. This technique should be used before handling a circuit board or component. Of course, you should be aware that this technique works safely only if the power cord is attached to a grounded power outlet. The ground plug on a standard power cable is the best tool for overcoming ESD problems.

FIGURE 13.4

Discharging through the power supply unit.

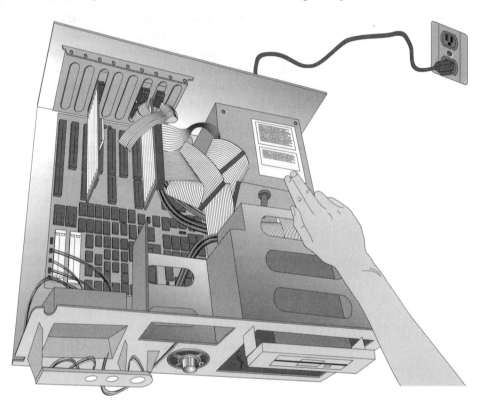

2. Do not remove ICs from their protective tubes (or foam packages) until you are ready to use them. If you remove a circuit board or component containing static-sensitive devices from the system, place it on a conductive surface, such as a sheet of aluminum foil.

3. If you must replace a defective IC, use a soldering iron with a grounded tip to extract the defective IC when soldering the new IC in place. Some of the ICs in computers and peripherals are not soldered to the printed circuit board. Instead, an IC socket is soldered to the board, and the IC is simply inserted into the socket. This makes for easy replacement of these ICs.

   If you must replace a hard-soldered IC, you may want to install an IC socket along with the chip. Be aware that normal operating vibrations and temperature cycling can degrade the electrical connections between ICs and sockets over time. It is a good practice to reseat any socketed devices when handling a printed circuit board. Before removing the IC from its protective container, touch the container to the power supply of the unit in which it is to be inserted.

4. Some devices used to remove solder from circuit boards and chips can cause high static discharges that may damage the good devices on the board. The device in question is referred to as a **solder-sucker** and is available in antistatic versions for use with MOS devices.

5. Use antistatic sprays or solutions on floors, carpets, desks, and computer equipment. An antistatic spray or solution applied with a soft cloth is an effective deterrent to static.

6. Install static-free carpeting in the work area; you can install an antistatic floor mat as well. Install a conductive table top to carry away static from the work area. Use antistatic table mats.

7. Use a room humidifier to keep the humidity level greater than 50% in the work area. Figure 13.5 summarizes proper IC handling precautions.

Grounds

The term **ground** is often a source of confusion for the novice because it actually encompasses a collection of terms. Generically, *ground* is simply any point from which electrical measurements are referenced. However, the original definition of *ground* actually referred to the physical ground. This ground is called **earth ground**.

The movement of the electrical current along a conductor requires a path for the current to return to its source. In early telegraph systems and even modern power transmission systems, the earth provides a return path and, hypothetically, produces an electrical reference point of absolute zero. This type of ground is illustrated in Figure 13.6.

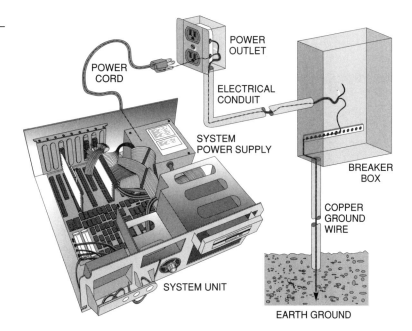

Many electronic circuits use an actual conductor as a return path. This type of ground is referred to as a **signal ground**. Electronic devices may also contain a third form of ground called **chassis**, or **protective ground**. In any event, ground still remains the reference point from which most electrical signals are measured. In the case of troubleshooting computer components, measurements referenced to ground may be made from the system unit's chassis.

The other measurement reference is the signal ground point, on the printed circuit board where the test is being performed. This point isn't too difficult to find in a circuit board full of ICs because most DIP-style chips use the highest-numbered pin for the positive supply voltage, and the last pin on the pin-1 side of the chip as the ground pin. This type of ground is illustrated in Figure 13.7. Some caution should be used with this assumption because not all ICs use this pin for ground. However, if you examine a number of ICs and connectors on the board, you should be able to trace the ground foil and use it as a reference.

As mentioned in Chapter 1, "Microcomputer Fundamentals," grounding is an important aspect of limiting EMI in computer systems. Left unchecked, EMI can distort images on the video display, interfere with commercial communication equipment (such as radios and televisions), and corrupt data on floppy disks. In addition, EMI can cause signal deterioration and loss caused by improper cable routing. If a signal cable is bundled with a power cable, radiation from the power cable may be induced into the signal cable, affecting the signals that pass through it. Unlike ESD, which is destructive, the effects of EMI can be corrected without damage.

FIGURE 13.7

Grounds on IC chips.

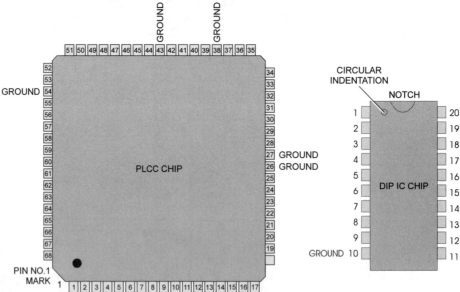

Because the computer system is connected to an actual earth ground, it should always be turned off and disconnected from the wall outlet during electrical storms. This applies to the computer and all its peripherals. The electrical pathway through the computer equipment can be very inviting to lightning on its way to earth ground. The extremely high electrical potential of a lightning strike is more than any computer can withstand.

Power Line Protection

A+ CORE 3.2

Digital systems tend to be sensitive to power variations and power losses. Even a very short loss of electrical power can shut down a digital computer, resulting in a loss of any current information that has not been saved to a mass storage device.

Typical power supply variations fall into two categories:

▶ **Transients**—An over-voltage condition. Such conditions can be classified as **spikes** (measured in nanoseconds) or as **surges** (measured in milliseconds).

▶ **Sags**—An under-voltage condition. Sags can include **voltage sags** and **brownouts**. A voltage sag typically lasts only a few milliseconds, but a brownout can last for a protracted period of time.

Inexpensive **power line filters**, also called **surge suppressors**, are good for cleaning up "dirty" commercial power. These units passively filter the incoming power signal to smooth out variations. You should consider two factors when choosing a surge suppressor:

▶ Clamping speed

▶ Clamping voltage

These units will protect the system from damage, up to a specified point. However, large variations such as surges created when power is restored after an outage can still cause considerable data loss and damage. In the case of startup surges, make sure that the system is turned off, or even disconnected from the power source, until after the power is restored. In the case of a complete shutdown or a significant sag, the best protection for saving programs and data is an **uninterruptible power supply** (**UPS**).

Uninterruptible Power Supplies

Uninterruptible power supplies are battery-based systems that monitor the incoming power and kick in when unacceptable variations occur in the power source. The term **UPS** is frequently used to describe two different types of power backup systems.

The first type of UPS is a **standby power system**; the second is a truly **uninterruptible power system**. A typical UPS system is depicted in Figure 13.8.

The standby system monitors the power input line and waits for a significant variation to occur. The batteries in this unit are held out of the power loop and draw only enough current from the ac source to stay recharged. When an interruption occurs, the UPS senses it and switches the output of the batteries into an inverter circuit that converts the dc output of the batteries into an ac current and voltage that resembles the commercial power supply. This power signal is typically applied to the computer within 10 milliseconds.

The uninterruptible systems do not keep the batteries offline. Instead, the batteries and converters are always actively attached to the output of UPS. When an interruption in the supply occurs, no switching of the output is required. The battery/inverter section simply continues under its own power. Figure 13.9 shows how a UPS connects into a system.

FIGURE 13.8

UPS systems.

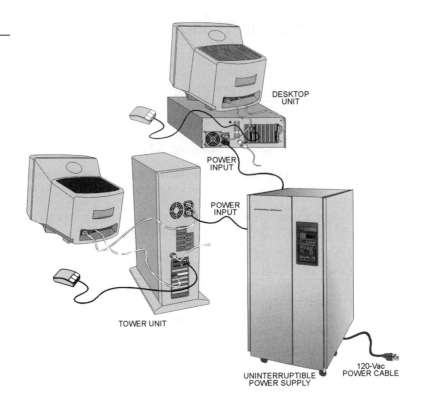

DESKTOP UNIT

POWER INPUT

POWER INPUT

TOWER UNIT

120-Vac POWER CABLE

UNINTERRUPTIBLE POWER SUPPLY

FIGURE 13.9

Connecting the UPS in the system.

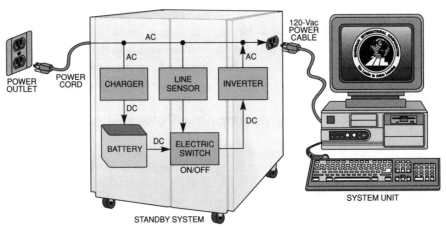

POWER OUTLET

POWER CORD

AC

AC

CHARGER

DC

BATTERY

DC

LINE SENSOR

ELECTRIC SWITCH
ON/OFF

INVERTER

AC

DC

120-Vac POWER CABLE

SYSTEM UNIT

STANDBY SYSTEM

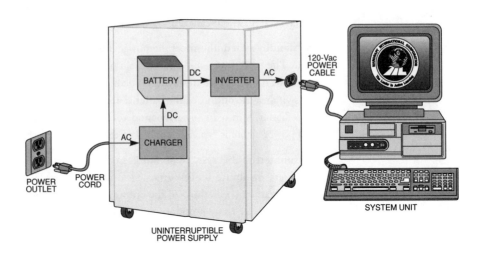

POWER OUTLET

POWER CORD

AC

CHARGER

DC

BATTERY

DC

INVERTER

AC

120-Vac POWER CABLE

SYSTEM UNIT

UNINTERRUPTIBLE POWER SUPPLY

Standby systems don't generally provide a high level of protection from sags and spikes. However, they do include additional circuitry to minimize such variations. Conversely, an uninterruptible system is an extremely good power-conditioning system. Because this type of system always sits between the commercial power and the computer, it can supply a constant power supply to the system.

When dealing with either type of UPS system, the most important rating to be aware of is its **volt-ampere (VA) rating**. The VA rating indicates the capability of the UPS system to deliver both voltage (V) and current (A) to the computer, simultaneously. This rating is different than the device's **wattage** power rating, and the two should not be used interchangeably. The **wattage rating** is a factor of multiplying the voltage and current use, at any particular time, to arrive at a power consumption value. The VA rating is used in ac systems because peak voltage and current elements do not occur at the same instant. This condition is referred to as being **out-of-phase** with each other and makes it slightly more difficult to calculate power requirements. In general, always make sure that the UPS system has a higher wattage capability than the computer requires and, likewise, that the VA rating of the UPS is higher than that required by the computer. High power-consumption peripheral devices, such as laser printers, should not be connected directly to the UPS. These devices can overload the UPS and cause data loss.

The other significant specification for UPS systems is the length of time they can supply power. Because the UPS is a battery-powered device, it uses an **ampere-hour rating**. This is the same time-notation system used for automobile batteries and other battery-powered systems. The rating is obtained by multiplying a given current drain from the battery for a given amount of time (for example, a battery capable of sustaining 1.5 amps of output current for an hour would be rated at 1.5 amp-hours).

Preventive Maintenance

The environment around a computer system, and the manner in which the computer is used, determines greatly how many problems it will have. Occasionally dedicating a few moments of care to the computer can extend its **mean time between failures (MTBF)** period considerably. This activity involving maintenance not normally associated with a breakdown is called **preventive maintenance (PM)**.

The following sections of this chapter describe PM measures for the various areas of the system.

As with any electronic device, computers are susceptible to failures caused by dust build-up, rough handling, and extremes in temperature. Dust build-up can be taken care of by the cleaning and inspection procedures stated earlier. Likewise, conquering rough handling is a simple matter of adjusting practices. However, identifying and controlling heat build-up problems can require some effort and planning. Microcomputers are designed to run at normal room temperatures. If the ambient temperature rises above about 85 degrees F, heat build-up can become a problem. High humidity can also lead to heat-related problems.

To combat heat problems, make sure that the area around the system is uncluttered so that free air flow around the system can be maintained. Make sure the power supply's fan is operational. If not, replace the power supply unit. Likewise, be sure that the microprocessor fan is plugged in and operational. It is very easy for a high-speed microprocessor to fry if its fan fails. A good rule of thumb is to install a fan on any microprocessor running above 33MHz.

If heat build-up still exists, check to make sure that the outer cover is secured firmly to the machine and that all the expansion slot covers are in place. These items can disrupt the designed air-flow characteristics of the case. Finally, add an additional case fan to draw more air through the system unit.

Monitors

The PM associated with video-display monitors basically consists of periodic cleaning, dusting, and common-sense practices around the monitor. The monitor's screen and cabinet should be dusted frequently and cleaned periodically. Dust and smoke particles can build up very quickly around the monitor's screen, due to the presence of static charges on its face. When cleaning the screen, some caution should be used to avoid scratching its surface and, in the case of antiglare screens, preserve its glare-reduction features.

Aerosol sprays, solvents, and commercial cleaners should be avoided because they can damage the screen and cabinet. The simple cleaning solution described earlier is also fine for cleaning the monitor. Make sure that the monitor's power cord is disconnected from any power source before washing. The monitor's screen should be dried with a soft cloth after rinsing.

The monitor should not be left on for extended periods with the same image displayed on the screen. Over a period of time, the image will become permanently "burnt" into the screen. If it is necessary to display the same information on the screen for a long period of time, turn down the intensity level of the monitor, or install a **screen saver** program to alter the screen image periodically.

Inside the monitor's housing are very dangerous voltage levels. Therefore, you should remove the monitor's outer cabinet only if you are fully qualified to work on CRT-based units. Even if the monitor has been turned off and unplugged for a year, it may still hold enough electrical potential to be deadly. Figure 13.10 shows the areas of the monitor that should be avoided if you must work inside its housing.

FIGURE 13.10

Caution areas inside the monitor.

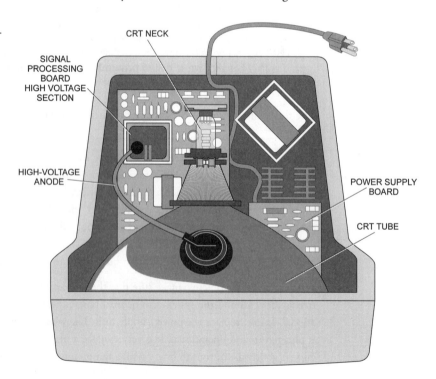

CRT NECK

SIGNAL
PROCESSING
BOARD
HIGH VOLTAGE
SECTION

HIGH-VOLTAGE
ANODE

POWER SUPPLY
BOARD

CRT TUBE

Hard-Disk Drives

Hard-disk drives don't require much preventive maintenance because the R/W heads and disks are enclosed in sealed, dust-tight compartments. However, some things can be done to optimize the performance and lifespan of hard-disk systems. Rough handling is responsible for more hard-disk drive damage than any other factor. The drive should never be moved while you can still hear its disks spinning. The disk is most vulnerable during start-up and shutdown, when the heads are not fully flying. Even a small jolt during these times can cause a great deal of damage to both the platters and the R/W heads. If the drive must be moved wait for 1 full minute after turning off the system.

If the drive is to be transported or shipped, make sure to pack it properly. The forces exerted on the drive during shipment may be great enough to cause the R/W heads to slap against the disks, causing damage to both. Pack the drive unit in an oversized box, with antistatic foam all around the drive. You may also pack the drive in a box-within-a-box configuration, again using foam as a cushion. This concept is illustrated in Figure 13.11.

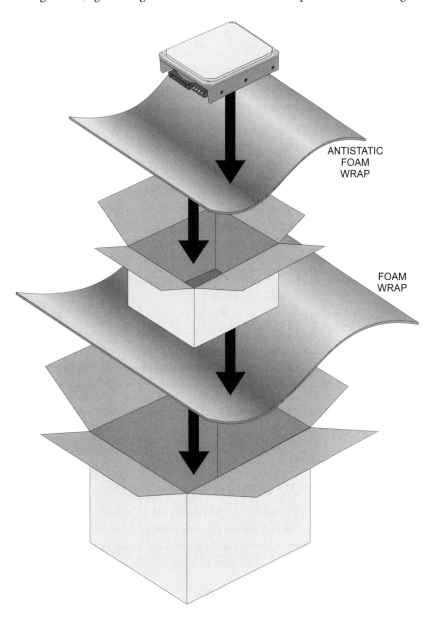

FIGURE 13.11

Proper packing of a hard drive for shipment.

ANTISTATIC FOAM WRAP

FOAM WRAP

The mechanisms of the drive should never be positioned by hand. The weighted drive spindle and the track-zero sensor may be accessible with the drive's outer cover removed. Moving these mechanisms by hand can cause the R/W heads to drag across the disk, damaging the heads and disk surfaces. At no time should the internal housing, which protects the platters, be removed in open air. The contaminants in normal air will virtually ruin the drive. If the drive malfunctions, the electronic circuitry and connections may be tested, but when it comes to repairs within the disk chamber, the factory service or a professional service facility with a proper clean room is a must!

To recover quickly from hardware failures, operator mistakes, and acts of nature, some form of software backup is essential with a hard-disk system. The most common backup for larger systems is high-speed, streaming-tape cartridges, which can automatically back up the entire contents of the disk drive on magnetic tape. In the event of data loss on the disk, a full reinstall from the tape is possible in a matter of a few minutes.

Backup may also be kept on disks. However, the volume of data stored on modern hard disks requires a tremendous number of floppies to back up. The floppies must also be stored. Other high-volume disk-based devices, such as **optical drives** and **removable hard drives**, have become attractive methods for backing up the contents of large hard drives. Various backup methods are depicted in Figure 13.12. In any case, failure to maintain backups will eventually result in a great deal of grief when the system goes down due to a hardware or software failure.

FIGURE 13.12

Data backup systems.

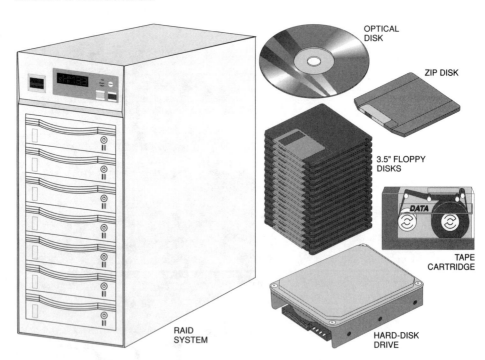

HDD Utilities

The operation of hard drives can slow with general use. Files stored on the drive may be erased and moved, causing parts of them to be scattered around the drive. This causes the drive to reposition the R/W heads more often during read and write operations, thereby requiring more time to complete the process.

Five important utilities can be used to optimize and maintain the operation of the hard-disk drive. These are the CHKDSK, SCANDISK, DEFRAG, BACKUP, and Anti-Virus utilities. With the exception of SCANDISK, which is a Windows utility, all these utilities have been available since early MS-DOS versions.

In Windows 3.x, these functions were typically located in the Applications window. In Windows 95, they are located in several areas of the system. The icons for SCANDISK and DEFRAG are located in the Program\Accessories\System tools path. The executable file for SCANDISK can be found in C:\Windows\Command; the Defrag icon is simply under C:\Windows. The Backup icon is in the Program\Accessories path, and the file is located in C:\Programfiles\accessories. The built-in anti-virus function is missing from Windows 95, so an add-on program from a second party should be used. The MSAV and MWAV programs from DOS and Windows 3.x can be found in the C:\DOS directory if Windows 95 was installed as an upgrade.

CHKDSK

DOS systems offer a number of commands that can be used to maintain and optimize the performance of the hard drive. The DOS **CHKDSK (Check Disk)** command is used to recover **lost allocation units** from the hard drive. These lost units occur when an application terminates unexpectedly.

Over a period of time, lost units can pile up and occupy large amounts of disk space. To remove these lost units from the drive, a **/f Modifier** is added to the command so that the lost units can be converted into files that can be investigated and removed. In some cases, the contents of the converted file is a usable data file that can be rebuilt for use with an application. The **CHKDSK /f** command is often used before running a drive-defragmentation program.

SCANDISK

A+ DOS/WINDOWS 4.3
A similar program, called **SCANDISK**, is available in DOS 6.x and Windows 95. SCAN-DISK searches the disk drive for disconnected file clusters and converts them into a form that can be checked and manipulated. This enables the user to determine whether any information in the lost clusters can be restored. SCANDISK also detects and deletes **cross-linked files**, which occur when information from two or more files is mistakenly stored in the same sector of a disk.

The standard SCANDISK operation examines the system's directory and file structure. However, a thorough SCANDISK option can be selected to examine the physical disk surface, as well as its files and directories. If potential defects exist on the surface, SCANDISK can be used to recover data stored in these areas.

DOS and Windows offer a number of utility programs that enable the user to periodically clean up the drive and ensure its top performance. Among these programs are the **Defrag**, **Backup**, and **Anti-Virus** utilities.

The Backup Utility

A+ DOS/WINDOWS 1.4
Backup utilities enable the user to quickly create extended copies of files, groups of files, or an entire disk drive. This operation is normally performed to create backup copies of important information in case the drive crashes or the disk becomes corrupt.

The **DOS Backup** and **Restore** commands can be used to back up and retrieve one or more files to another disk.

Because a backup of related files may be much larger than a single floppy disk, serious backup programs ensure that information can be backed up to a series of disks; these programs also provide file-compression techniques to reduce the size of the files stored on the disk. Of course, it is impossible to read or use the compressed backup files in this format. To be usable, the files must be decompressed (expanded) and restored to the DOS file format.

Backup Types

Most backup utilities provide for backups to be performed in a number of ways. Typically, backups fall into three categories:

- Total

- Selective

- Differential (or modified-only)

In a **full** or **total backup**, the entire contents of the designated disk are backed up. This includes directory and subdirectory listings and their contents. In a **selective backup** operation, the operator moves through the tree structure of the disk, marking or tagging directories and files to be backed up. After all the desired directories/files have been marked, they are backed up in a single operation. Specifying a **differential backup** causes the backup utility to examine each file to determine whether it has changed since the last backup was performed. If not, the file is bypassed. However, if the file has been altered, it will be backed up. This option is a valuable time-saving feature in a periodic backup strategy.

In DOS, the basic backup command can be modified through command switches. A /s switch causes all files and subdirectories to be backed up. The /m switch modifies the command so that only those files that have changed are backed up. The /d and /t switches examine the date and time stamps of each file and back up only those files modified after a specified data or time. Other switches can be used to format the backup media and to maintain a backup log on the disk.

Data Backup

From the C:\>> prompt, use the CHKDSK/f command to clean up lost file clusters. Instruct the program to convert any lost chains into files that can be checked later. Windows 3.x and Windows 95 use a program called MWBACKUP for data conservation on floppy disks.

The operation of the Microsoft Windows 3.x Backup utility is described in the following paragraphs.

Start the backup program. Select the MWBACKUP icon to start the backup program. The MWBACKUP main screen should appear, similar to the one described in Figure 13.13.

Set the backup parameters. Move through the Backup Type drop-down selection box, and select the Full entry to highlight it. Then click the C: entry in the Backup From: list box. Finally, click the desired drive and disk size entries in the Backup To: list box.

Select the backup options by clicking the OPTIONS button. This provides access to the Backup Options screen depicted in Figure 13.14. Select the desired backup options from the window by clicking on the box next to each option. An X will appear beside each item when it is selected.

FIGURE 13.13

*The Windows Backup
main screen.*

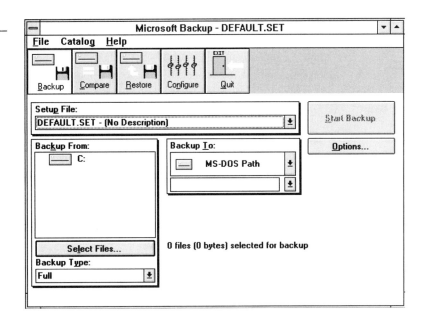

FIGURE 13.14

The Backup Options screen.

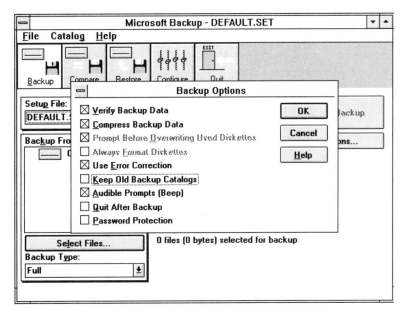

Select directories and files to back up. This is accomplished by double-clicking the SELECT FILES button. To choose files to be included in the backup, click the C:\ folder at the top of the files tree. Click the INCLUDE button, click the ADD button, and click the Include circle.

Choose special files to be marked by clicking the SPECIAL button and then clicking various parameters in the Special Selections dialog box.

Back up the desired portions of the HDD to a series of backup disks. Click the Backup box to highlight it. Then click the SELECT FILES button, click File from the drop-down menu bar, and click Select All. Finally, click the Start Backup box, answer the FDD prompt, and insert a blank disk in drive A. The program will conduct the backup operation with no further action from the user, except for exchanging floppy disks when prompted.

Restoring Data

To restore data in Windows, start the MWBACKUP program. The program's main screen should appear, as previously depicted in Figure 13.11.

Set the restore parameters by clicking on the Restore box. Next, verify the floppy disk type in the Restore From: window, and verify the C: entry in the Restore Files window. Click the Restore To: window to select it, and then select the location for the restore position.

Select the restore options. Click the OPTIONS button to access the Restore Options screen depicted in Figure 13.15. Select the restore options from the window by clicking on the box next to each option. An X will appear beside each item when it is selected.

FIGURE 13.15

The Restore Options screen.

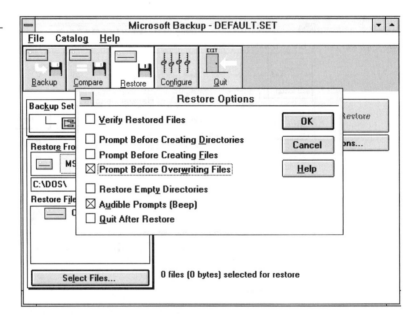

Restore the specified directories and files to the HDD from the backup disks. Click the SELECT FILES button. Click the C:\ file folder to select it. Click File from the drop-down menu bar, and click Select All. Click the OK button to return to the Main screen, and then click the Start Restore box to begin the restore process.

Other Backup Methods

The backup utilities included in DOS and Windows are not the only—or necessarily the best—backup options available. Using DOS or Windows backup utilities can create a huge pile of floppy disks if a large HDD unit is being backed up. Several backup systems using different media have been developed for use with personal computer systems. The most noteworthy are **RAID systems**, **magnetic tape**, **optical disks**, and **digital audio tape (DAT)** backup systems. Many of these systems have already been discussed in earlier chapters.

In most larger backup operations it is common to use a **tape drive** for storage due to its relatively low cost-per-bit of storage.

Figure 13.16 depicts the opening screen of a typical tape backup GUI package. As you can see, this screen incorporates many of the Windows compatibility functions. The toolbar at the top of the screen provides the usual assortment of Windows menu utilities. On the left side of the main screen is a graphical listing of the system's disk drives. The window in the middle of the screen displays the contents of the tape currently in the tape drive. The icon structure provides for the contents of drives and tape to be moved and copied using the normal Windows drag-and-drop techniques.

FIGURE 13.16

A tape drive's main screen.

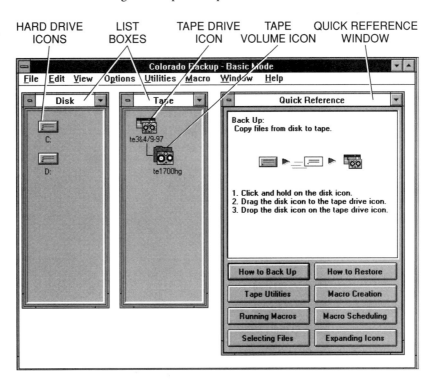

The software's Utility screen, depicted in Figure 13.17, enables users to specify parameters for the backup and restore operations such as Copy or Move; Total, Selective, or Modified; and Immediate or Scheduled Start of the operation. An additional screen area enables the user to provide a volume title for the stored information and set up data compression to reduce the amount of tape required to store the data.

If a selective backup is selected, a file manager screen such as the one in Figure 13.18 appears on the display. This screen is used to **tag** (mark) all the files and directories desired for inclusion in the backup operation.

Most effective tape-storage routines involve rotating multiple tapes to record important data from different days of the week. In a three-tape operation, a relatively small number of tapes can be used to ensure the availability of relatively recent backup data. If only one tape is used, the backup data would be destroyed if the system crashed during the backup. A two-disk rotation creates too much wear on the tapes, causing them to fail prematurely.

FIGURE 13.17

The tape drive's Utility screen.

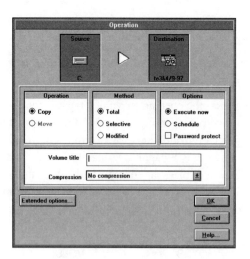

FIGURE 13.18

Tagging selected files for backup.

ROOT DIRECTORY

FILES ON CURRENT DIRECTORY LEVEL

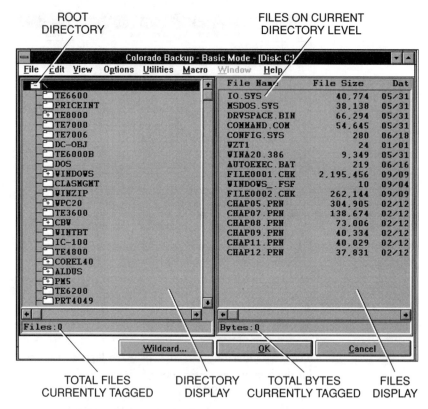

TOTAL FILES CURRENTLY TAGGED DIRECTORY DISPLAY TOTAL BYTES CURRENTLY TAGGED FILES DISPLAY

HDD Defragmentation

A+ DOS/WINDOWS 1.4

In the normal use of the HDD, files become **fragmented** on the drive, as illustrated in Figure 13.19. This file fragmentation creates conditions that cause the drive to operate slower. Fragmentation occurs when files are stored in noncontinuous locations on the drive. This happens when files are stored, retrieved, modified, and rewritten due to differences in the sizes of the before and after files.

Because the fragmented files do not enable efficient reading by the drive, it takes longer to complete multisector read operations. The **defragmentation** program realigns the positioning of related file clusters to speed up the operation of the drive.

FIGURE 13.19

Data sectors.

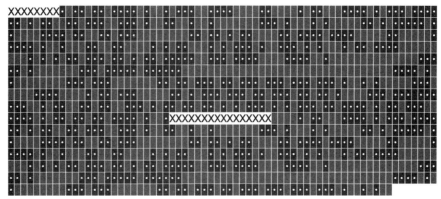

■ – USED   FRAGMENTED HARD DISK DRIVE
▓ – UNUSED
X – UNMOVABLE
1 BLOCK = 53 CLUSTERS

Some portions of files may become lost on the drive when a program is unexpectedly interrupted, such as after a software crash or a power failure. These **lost allocation units** (chains) also cause the drive to operate slowly. Therefore, it is customary to use the DOS **Check Disk** command to find and remove these chains before performing a Defrag operation.

It may also be necessary to remove some data from the drive to defragment it. If the system is producing "Out of Disk Space" error messages, the Defrag utility will not have enough room on the drive to realign clusters. When this happens, some of the contents of the drive must be transferred to a backup media (or must be discarded) to free up some disk space for the realignment process to occur.

The operation of the MS-DOS Defrag utility is described as follows:

1. Start the Defrag program by typing **DEFRAG** at the C:\>> prompt. The DEFRAG main screen should appear similar to that described in Figure 13.20.

2. Select the drive to optimize by highlighting drive C: and pressing the ENTER key.

3. Specify the type of optimization. Highlight Configure, and press ENTER. Select the optimization method, and select the Unfragment Files Only entry.

4. To specify the type of optimization, press F10 and access the drop-down menu. Use the DOWN ARROW key to select the optimization method. Use the SPACEBAR to select full optimization. Start the defragmentation procedure by selecting the Begin Optimization entry.

Viruses

A+ DOS/WINDOWS 4.4

Computer viruses are destructive software programs designed to replicate and spread on their own. Viruses are created to sneak into personal computers. Sometimes these programs take control of a machine to leave a humorous message, and sometimes they destroy data. When they infiltrate one machine, they can spread into other computers through infected disks that friends and co-workers pass around, or through local and wide area network connections.

FIGURE 13.20

The DEFRAG main screen.

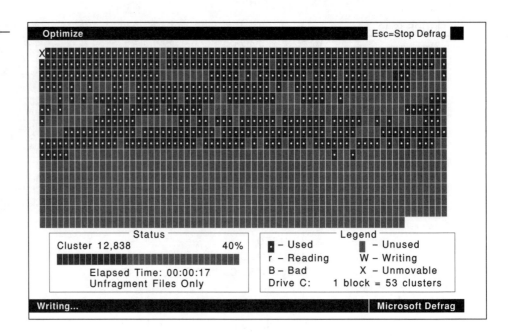

Researchers at the **National Computer Security Association** estimate that between 200 and 300 new viruses are being introduced into the computer community every month. However, the top 10 viruses in the United States account for about 80 percent of virus infections.

Most viruses are written for DOS. Therefore, as more users switch to Windows, it is expected that the number of viruses being written will decrease. Three basic types of viruses exist, based on how they infect a computer system. One type of virus is known as a **boot sector virus**. This type of virus copies itself onto the boot sector of floppy and hard disks. The virus replaces the disk's original boot sector code with its own code. This enables it to be loaded into memory before anything else is loaded.

After it is in memory, the virus can spread onto other disks. Another type of virus is known as a file infector. **File infectors** are viruses that add their virus code to executable files. When the file with the virus is executed, it spreads to other executable files. A similar type of virus, called a **macro virus**, hides in the macro programs of word processing document files. These files can be designed to load when the document is opened or when a certain key combination is entered. In addition, these types of viruses can be designed to stay resident in memory after the host program has been exited (similar to a TSR program), or they may simply stop working when the infected file is terminated.

The third type of virus is known as a **Trojan horse.** This type of virus appears to be a legitimate program that may be found on any system. Trojan-horse viruses are more likely to do damage by destroying files, and they can cause physical damage to disks.

A number of different viruses have been created from these three virus types. They have several different names, but they all perform basically the same. After the virus file has become active in the computer, it may perform a number of different types of operations. These operations can be as complex and damaging as the author designs them to be.

As an example, a strain of boot sector virus known as **CMOS virus** infects the hard drive's master boot record and becomes memory resident. When activated, the virus writes over the system's configuration information in the CMOS area. Part of what is overwritten is the HDD and FDD information. Therefore, the system cannot boot up properly. The initial infection comes from booting from an infected floppy disk. The virus overwrites the CMOS once in every 60 boot-ups.

A similar boot sector virus, referred to as the **FAT virus**, becomes memory resident in the area of system memory where the IO.SYS and MSDOS.SYS files are located. This enables it to spread to any non-write-protected disks inserted into the computer. In addition, the virus moves the system pointers for the disk's executable files to an unused cluster and rewrites the pointers in the FAT to point to the sector where the virus is located. The result is improper disk copies, an inability to backup files, large numbers of lost clusters, and all executable files cross-linked with each other.

In another example, a file infector virus strain, called the **FAT table virus**, infects .EXE files but does not become memory resident. When the infected file is executed, the virus rewrites another .EXE file.

Virus Symptoms

Because virus programs tend to operate in the background, it is sometimes difficult to realize that the computer has been infected. Typical virus symptoms include the following:

- Hard-disk control failures occur.

- Disks continue to be full even when files have been deleted.

- The system cannot read write-protected disks.

- The hard disk stops booting; files are corrupted.

- A system boots to a floppy but will not access the HDD. An "Invalid drive specification" message is usually displayed when attempting to access drive C:.

- CMOS settings continually revert to default even though the system board battery is good.

- Files change size for no apparent reason.

- System operation slows down noticeably.

- A blank screen occurs when booting (flashing cursor).

- Windows crashes.

- The hard drive is set to DOS compatibility, and 32-bit file access suddenly stops working.

- Network data transfers and print jobs slow dramatically.

A few practices increase the odds of a machine being infected by a virus. These include use of shareware software, software of unknown origin, or bulletin board software. One of the most effective ways to reduce these avenues of infection is to buy shrink-wrapped products from a reputable source.

Another method of dealing with virus protection involves installing a virus-scanning program that checks disks and files before using them in the computer. MS-DOS provides a minimal anti-virus scanner called VSAFE that can be installed as a TSR to continuously monitor the system for viruses. DOS also includes an MSAV command that can be run from the DOS prompt to scan for and remove viruses.

Several other companies offer third-party virus-protection software that can be configured to operate in various ways. If the computer is a standalone unit, it may be anti-productive to have the anti-virus software run each time the system is booted up. It would be much more practical to have the program check floppy disks only because this is the only possible entry way into the computer. However, a networked or online computer has more opportunity to contract a virus because viruses can also enter the unit over the network or through the modem. In these cases, setting the software to run at each boot-up is more desirable.

Anti-virus Programs

To run the MS-DOS anti-virus program, type **msav.exe** at the DOS command line. This should produce the anti-virus program's main screen, as depicted in Figure 13.21.

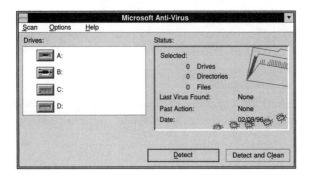

Complete the following steps:

1. Select the Virus List from the Scan menu to produce the virus list window. In this window, you can read the information about the viruses recognized by the current version of the program. The list of viruses is long, so you can search for virus names by typing the first few letters of the virus in the Search For: dialog box.

2. Configure the Anti-Virus program. Select Options to see the menu. Verify that an X appears in the boxes for Verify Integrity, Create New Checksums, Prompt While Detect, and Check All Files, as depicted in Figure 13.22.

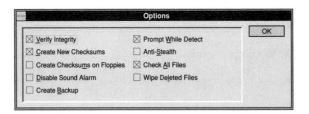

3. Select the Anti-Stealth and Wipe Deleted Files entries to activate them. An X should appear in the boxes beside them. Click C: in the Drives: box. A small window will show that the program is reading the directories for drive C:. The Status: window shows the number of drives, directories, and files found on the system.

4. Run the Anti-Virus program. Activate the DETECT button to search for viruses. The program first scans RAM memory for any viruses. If any are found in memory, they are cleaned from the system memory. The program then searches the files on the hard drive. Select the Update option if the program tells you that a file has been changed.

5. When the program is finished scanning the drive, a Statistics window appears. Exit the Statistics window, and select the Scan option to see the menu.

6. Alter the AUTOEXEC.BAT file to automatically start the anti-virus program when the computer is booted up. Type **C:\DOS\VSAFE.COM** into the AUTOEXEC.BAT file so that the program checks for viruses when you start a program, copy a file, or save a file to disk. VSafe will notify you if any viruses infect your computer.

Floppy-Disk Drives

Unlike hard-disk drives, floppy drives are at least partially open to the atmosphere, and the disks may be handled on a regular basis. This opens the floppy-disk drive to a number of maintenance concerns not found in hard-disk drives. In addition, the removable disks are subject to extremes in temperature, exposure to magnetic and electromagnetic fields, bending, and airborne particles that can lead to information loss.

Protecting Disks

The disk stores information in the form of magnetized spots on its surface, so it is only natural that external magnetic fields will have an adverse effect on the stored data. Never bring disks near devices that produce magnetic fields, such as CRT monitors, television sets, or power supplies. Disks should also never be placed on or near appliances such as refrigerators, freezers, vacuum cleaners, and other equipment containing motors. Any of these can alter the information stored on the disk.

Proper positioning of the drive and proper connection of peripheral interface cables helps to minimize noise and **radio frequency interference** (**RFI**). RFI can cause the drive to operate improperly. Magnetic fields generated by power supplies and monitors can interfere with the magnetic recording on the disk. The drive and signal cables should be positioned away from these magnetic-field sources. Magnets should never be brought near the drive unit.

Another major cause of floppy disk failures is surface contamination. Several preventive measures can minimize disk contamination and lengthen the life expectancy of your disks. Even though the disk is enclosed in a protective case or envelope whose liner sweeps contaminants from its surface, enough dust particles may collect to overpower the liner over time. Care should be taken to never touch the exposed surfaces of the disk. Store disks in their protective envelopes, and keep your computer area as clean and free from dust as possible.

There should be no smoking around the computer. Residues from tobacco smoke are a problem for floppy-disk drives because they tend to build up on the exposed surfaces of both the disks, and the drive. These deposits are detrimental to both the drive and the disk because they gum up the close-tolerance mechanics of the drive and can scratch the disk surface and the faces of the R/W heads. This makes the heads less effective in reading and writing information to and from the disk, and it eventually leads to failure of the disk and the drive.

The fact that the R/W heads ride directly on the disk surface produces a certain amount of contamination and wear on the disk and the heads. During read and write operations, the abrasion between the heads and disk cause some of the oxide coating on the disk to be transferred to the head. This makes the head less effective in reading and writing operations, and it eventually leads to the failure of the disk.

Additional measures to protect your disks include storing them in a cool, dry, clean environment out of direct sunlight. Excessive temperature can warp the disk and its jacket. Take care when inserting the disk into the drive so as not to damage its jacket or the drive's internal mechanisms.

Maintaining the Floppy Drive

So far, each preventive action has involved the disk. However, two procedures are available for the user to perform on the disk drive to ward off bigger maintenance problems. These are routine cleaning of the R/W heads (to remove oxide build-ups) and periodic disk-drive speed tests and adjustments, when necessary.

A+ CORE 3.1

Cleaning R/W heads removes residue and oxide build-ups from the face of the head to ensure accurate transfer of data from the head to the disk. Two accepted methods can be used to clean the heads: special head-cleaning disks and manual cleaning of the heads. Head-cleaning disks are convenient to use, but some precautions must be taken when using them. Two basic types of cleaning disks exist: **dry disks** (abrasive) and **wet disks** (chemical). Abrasive head-cleaning disks remove build-ups as the disk spins in the drive. This is similar to using sandpaper to remove paint from a surface. These disks can be damaging to the head if used for too long at a time.

The dry disk must be left in the drive just long enough to remove the build-up on the head, but not long enough to scratch the head surface. Due to the difficulties of timing this operation, manufacturers have developed nonabrasive, cloth-covered disks that are used with a solvent solution. Depending on the type of kit you purchase, the disk may be premoistened or may come with a separate solvent solution that must be applied to the disk before cleaning, as illustrated in Figure 13.23. The chance that abrasion of the head might occur still exists with this type of cleaning disk, but it is not as great as with the dry disks. The instructions that come with the cleaning kit should be consulted for proper usage and cleaning-time duration.

FIGURE 13.23

FDD cleaning disks.

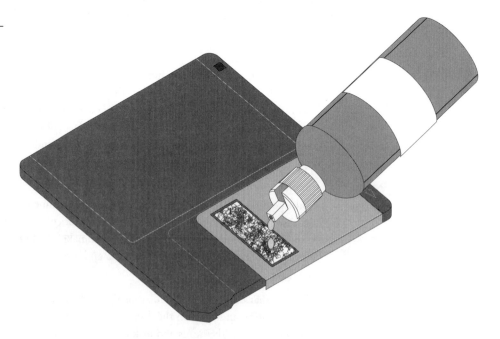

A somewhat more complicated method of cleaning R/W heads is to clean them manually, as depicted in Figure 13.24. This operation involves removing the cover of the drive, gaining access to the R/W heads, and cleaning the heads manually with a swab that has been dipped in alcohol. This may appear to be a lot of work compared to the cleaning disk, but manual cleaning is much safer for the drive. This is particularly true when combined with other cleaning, oiling, and inspection work. Together, these steps provide an excellent preventive maintenance program that should ensure effective long-term operation of the drive.

FIGURE 13.24

Manually cleaning the R/W heads.

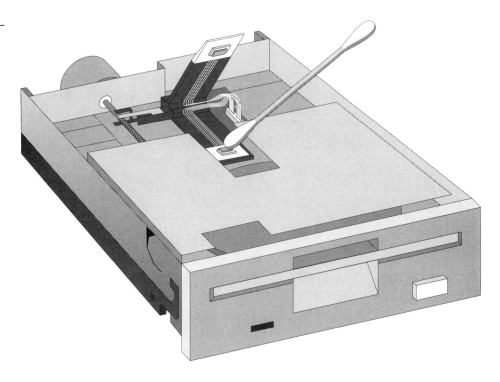

The cleaning solution can be isopropyl alcohol, methanol, or some other solvent that does not leave a residue when it dries. Common cotton swabs are not recommended for use in manual cleaning because they tend to shed fibers. These fibers can contaminate the drive and, in certain circumstances, damage the R/W heads. Instead, cellular foam swabs or lint-free cloths are recommended for manual head cleaning. Using either cleaning method, the interval of time between head cleanings depends on several factors, such as the relative cleanliness of your computer area and how often you use your disk drive. A good practice is to clean the heads after 40 hours of disk-drive operation. If read/write errors begin to appear before this time elapses, you may need more frequent cleaning or higher-quality disks.

Input Devices

A+ CORE 3.1

Input peripherals generally require very little in the way of preventive maintenance. An occasional dusting and cleaning should be all that's really required.

Keep in mind a few common-sense items when using input devices so as to prevent damage to the device and ensure its longevity.

The keyboard should be vacuumed, as described in Figure 13.25, when you are cleaning around your computer area. To remove dirt and dust particles from inside the keyboard, disassemble the keyboard and carefully brush particles away from the board with a soft brush. A lint-free swab can be used to clean between the keys. Take care not to snag any exposed parts with the brush or swab. To minimize dust collection in the keyboard, cover your keyboard when not in use.

FIGURE 13.25

Cleaning the keyboard.

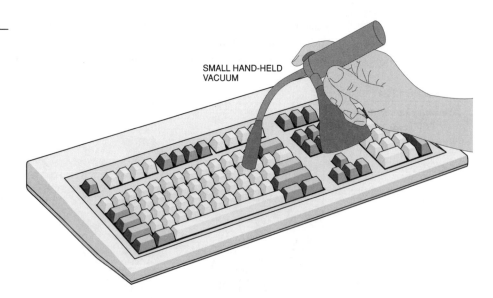

SMALL HAND-HELD
VACUUM

Never set keyboards or pointing devices on top of the monitor or near the edge of the desk, where they may fall. To prevent excessive wear on special keys, avoid applications and game programs that use keys in a repetitive manner. For these applications, use an appropriate pointing device, such as a mouse or joystick, for input.

When using a mouse, keep its work space clear, dry, and free from dust. The trackball should be removed and cleaned periodically. Use a lint-free swab to clean the X and Y trackball rollers inside the mouse, as depicted in Figure 13.26.

Never touch the lens of a light pen with your finger, as the sensitivity of the pen will be diminished by the resulting smudge. As with detachable keyboards, keep the connecting cables of all pointing devices out of harm's way.

FIGURE 13.26

Cleaning the rollers in a trackball mouse.

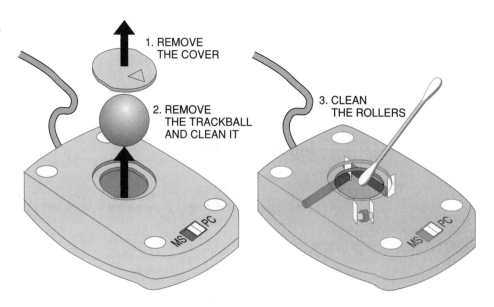

1. REMOVE
   THE COVER

2. REMOVE
   THE TRACKBALL
   AND CLEAN IT

3. CLEAN
   THE ROLLERS

Printers

Because printers tend to be much more mechanical than other types of computer peripherals, they require more effort to maintain. Printers generate pollutants, such as paper dust and ink droplets, in everyday operation. These pollutants can build up on mechanical parts and cause them to wear. As the parts wear, the performance of the printer diminishes. Therefore, printers require periodic cleaning and adjustments to maintain good performance.

Dot-Matrix Printers

Adjust the printhead spacing, as illustrated in Chapter 10, "Printers." If the printhead is too far away from the platen, the print should appear washed out. The tension on the printhead positioning belt should be checked periodically. If the belt is loose, the printer's dot-positioning will become erratic; the belt should be reset for proper tension.

Cleaning the printer and its mechanisms periodically adds to its productivity by removing contaminates that cause wear. Vacuum the inside of the unit after applying antistatic solution to the vacuum's hose tip. Wipe the outside with a damp cloth, also using antistatic solution. Brush any contaminate build-up from the printer's mechanical components, using a soft-bristled brush. Never lubricate the platen assembly of the printer.

Clean the printer's roller surfaces. Use a damp, soft cloth to clean the surface of the platen. Rotate the platen through several revolutions. Do not use detergents or solvents on the rollers.

Use a non-fibrous swab dipped in alcohol to clean the face of the dot-matrix printhead. This should loosen paper fibers and ink that may cause the print wires to stick. Apply a small amount of oil to the face of the printhead.

Clean the paper-handling motor's gear train. Use a swab to remove build-up from the teeth of the gear train. If the gear train has been lubricated before, apply a light oil to the gears using a swab. Turn the platen to make sure the oil is distributed throughout the gear train. Apply a light coating of oil to the rails on which the head-positioning carriage rides. Move the carriage assembly across the rails several times to spread the lubricant evenly.

The following are the steps to cleaning a dot-matrix printer:

1. Adjust the printhead spacing.

2. Check the tension on the printhead positioning belt.

3. Clean the printer and its mechanisms.

4. Clean the printer's roller surfaces.

5. Clean the surface of the platen.

6. Clean the surface of the dot-matrix printhead.

7. Clean the paper-handling motor's gear train.

8. Apply light oil to the gears using a swab.

9. Turn the platen to distribute the oil.

10. Apply light coating of oil to the rails.

11. Move the carriage assembly to distribute the oil.

Ink-Jet Printers

The spacing of the printheads in some ink-jet printers means that these devices require cleaning adjustments similar to those described for dot-matrix printers.

Clean the paper-handling motor's gear train. Use a swab to remove build-up from the teeth of the gear train. If the gear train has been lubricated before, apply a light oil to the gears using a swab. Turn the platen to make sure the oil is distributed throughout the gear train. Apply a light coating of oil to the rails on which the printhead-positioning carriage rides. Move the carriage assembly across the rails several times to spread the lubricant evenly.

The following are steps to cleaning an ink-jet printer:

1. Adjust the printhead spacing.

2. Check the tension on the printhead positioning belt.

3. Clean the printer and its mechanisms.

4. Clean the printer's roller surfaces.

5. Clean the surface of the platen.

6. Clean the surface of the ink-jet printhead.

7. Clean the paper-handling motor's gear train.

8. Apply light oil to the gears using a swab.

9. Turn the platen to distribute the oil.

10. Apply a light coating of oil to the rails.

11. Move the carriage assembly to distribute the oil.

Laser Printers

Use a vacuum cleaner to remove dust build-up and excess toner from the interior of the laser printer. Care should be taken to remove all excess toner from the unit. Vacuum the printer's ozone filter. Because water can mix with the toner particles in the printer, using wet sponges or towels to clean up toner inside the laser printer can create a bigger mess than the original one. Remove the toner cartridge before vacuuming.

Clean the laser printer's rollers using a damp cloth or denatured alcohol. Also clean the paper-handling motor's gear train. Use a swab to remove build-up from the teeth of the gear train. If the gear train has been lubricated before, apply a light oil to the gears using a swab. Make sure the oil is distributed throughout the gear train.

Clean the writing mechanism thoroughly. Use compressed air to blow out dust and paper particles that may collect on the lenses and shutters. If possible, wipe the laser lens with lint-free wipes to remove stains and fingerprints.

If accessible, use a swab dipped in alcohol to clean the corona wires. Rub the swab across the entire length of the wires. Take extra care to not break the strands that wrap around the corona. If these wires are broken, the printer will be rendered useless until new monofilament wires can be reinstalled.

The following are steps to cleaning a laser printer:

1. Remove dust build-up and excess toner from the interior.

2. Clean the laser printer's rollers.

3. Clean the paper-handling motor's gear train.

4. Apply light oil to the gears using a swab.

5. Distribute the oil throughout the gear train.

6. Clean the corona wires.

In some laser printer models, the toner cartridges are designed so that they can be refilled. At this time, the third-party refill cartridges are not typically as good as those from the manufacturer. However, they tend to be much cheaper than original equipment cartridges. If the output from the printer does not have to be very high-quality, then refilled toner cartridges might be an interesting topic to examine. To date, no regulations govern the disposal of laser printer cartridges.

Preventive Maintenance Schedule

No perfect **Preventive Maintenance** (**PM**) schedule exists, but the following is a reasonable schedule that can be used to effectively maintain most computer equipment. The schedule is written from the point of view of a personal computer. From an outside maintenance perspective, some of the steps must be shared with the daily user. As a matter of fact, most of the daily and weekly PM activities are carried out by the user.

Daily

Back up important data from the unit. This can be done to a floppy disk, a backup tape, another network drive, or some other backup media. Check computer ventilation to make sure that papers and other desk clutter are not cutting off air flow to the unit. Check for other sources of heat build-up around the computer and its peripherals. These sources include the following:

- Direct sunlight from an outside window

- Locations of portable heaters in the winter

- Papers or books piled up around the equipment

Weekly

Clean the outside of the computer and its peripheral equipment. Wipe the outsides of the equipment with a damp cloth (the cloth can be slightly soapy). Wipe dry with an antistatic cloth. Clean the display screen using a damp cloth with the antistatic solution described earlier in this chapter. An antistatic spray can also be used for static build-up prevention.

Run CHKDSK/f on all hard drives to locate and remove any lost clusters from the drives. Run a current virus-check program to check for hard drive infection. Back up any revised data files on the hard drive. Inspect the peripherals (mice, keyboard, and so on), and clean them if needed.

Monthly

Clean the inside of the system. Use a long-nozzle vacuum cleaner attachment to remove dust from the inside of the unit. Wipe the nozzle with antistatic solution before vacuuming. A soft brush can also be used to remove dust from the system unit.

Clean the inside of the printer using the same equipment and techniques used with the system unit. Check system connections for corrosion, pitting, or discoloration. Wipe the surface of any peripheral card's edge connectors with a lubricating oil to protect it from atmospheric contamination.

Vacuum the keyboard. Clean the X and Y rollers in the trackball mouse using a lint-free swab and a non-coating cleaning solution.

Defragment the system's hard drive using the Defrag utility. Remove unnecessary .TMP files from the hard drive. Check software and hardware manufacturers for product updates that can remove problems and improve system operation. Back up the entire hard-disk drive.

Six Months

Every six months, perform an extensive PM check. Apply an antistatic wash to the entire computer/peripheral work area. Wipe down books, desk top, and other work area surfaces with antistatic solution. Disconnect power and signal cables from the system's devices, and reseat them. Clean the inside of the printer. Run the printer's self-tests.

Use a software diagnostic package to check each section of the system. Run all system tests available, looking for any hint of pending problems.

Annually

Reformat the hard drive by backing up its contents and performing a high-level format. If the drive is an MFM, RLL, or ESDI drive, a low-level format should also be performed annually. Reinstall all the applications software from original media, and reinstall all user files from the backup system. Check all floppy disks in the work area with a current anti-virus program.

Clean the R/W heads in the floppy drive using a lint-free swab. Cotton swabs have fibers that can hang up in the ceramic insert of the head and can damage it. Perform the steps outlined in the monthly and semi-annual headings.

A+ CORE 3.1
A+ CORE 3.2

Although this is a good model PM schedule, it is not the definitive schedule. Before establishing a firm schedule, you should take several other points into consideration. These points include any manufacturer's guidelines for maintaining the equipment. Read the user's guides of the various system components, and work their suggested maintenance steps into the model.

Also take note of the environment in which the equipment is being used and how heavy its usage is. If the system is located in a particularly dirty area or an area given to other environmental extremes, it may need to be cleaned and serviced more frequently than if it were in a clean office environment. This is also true for systems that are subjected to heavy or continuous use. In an industrial environment, check with the management to see whether any office or industry maintenance standards for servicing are applicable.

Finally, use simple observation of the wear and tear on the equipment to gauge the need for additional or spot-maintenance steps. Look for signs of extended use, such as frayed cords, missing slot covers, and keyboards with letters worn off to spot potential problems due to age or usage.

Over time, adjust the steps and frequency of the plan to effectively cope with any environmental or usage variations. After all, the objective isn't to complete the schedule on time; it is to keep the equipment running and profitable.

Safety Considerations

In most IBM compatibles, only two potentially dangerous areas exist. One of these is inside the **display monitor**; the other is inside the **power-supply unit**. Both of these areas contain electrical voltage levels that are lethal. However, both of these areas reside in self-contained units, and you will normally not be required to open either unit.

As a matter of fact, you should never enter the interior of a CRT cabinet unless you have been trained specifically to work with this type of equipment. The tube itself is dangerous if accidentally cracked. In addition, extremely high-voltage levels may be present inside the CRT housing up to a year after electrical power has been removed from the unit.

Never open the power-supply unit, either. Some portions of the circuitry inside the power supply carry extremely high-voltage levels.

Generally, no open shock hazards are present inside the system unit. However, you should not reach inside the computer while power is applied to the unit. Jewelry and other metallic objects do pose an electrical threat, even with the relatively low voltage present in the system unit.

Never have liquids around energized electrical equipment. It's a good idea to keep food and drinks away from the computer equipment at all times. When cleaning around the computer with liquids, make certain to unplug all power connections to the system and its peripherals beforehand. When cleaning external computer cabinets with liquid cleaners, take care to prevent any of the solution from dripping or spilling into the equipment.

A+ CORE 1.4

Do not defeat the safety feature of three-prong power plugs by using two-prong adapters. The equipment ground of a power cable should never be defeated or removed. This action removes a very important level of protection from the equipment and can place service personnel in danger.

Periodically examine the power cords of the computer and peripherals for cracked or damaged insulation. Replace worn or damaged power cords promptly. Never allow anything to rest on a power cord. Run power cords and connecting cables safely out of the way so that they don't become **trip**, or **catch**, hazards. Remove all power cords associated with the computer and its peripherals from the power outlet during thunder or lightning storms.

Don't apply liquid or aerosol cleaners directly to computer equipment. Spray cleaners on a cloth, and then apply the cloth to the equipment. Freon-propelled sprays should not be used on computer equipment because they can produce destructive electrostatic charges.

Check equipment vents to see that they are clear and have ample free-air space to allow heat to escape from the cabinet. Never block these vents, and never insert or drop objects into them.

A+ CORE 3.3

Laser printers contain many hazardous areas. The laser light can be very damaging to the human eye. In addition, you should be aware of multiple high-voltage areas in the typical laser printer and a high-temperature area.

The technician is normally protected from these areas by interlock switches built into the unit. However, it is often necessary to bypass these interlocks to isolate problems. When doing so, proper precautions must be observed, such as avoiding the laser light, being aware of the high temperatures in the fuser area, and taking proper precautions with the high-voltage areas of the unit.

Another potential burn hazard is the printhead mechanism of a dot-matrix printer. During normal operation, the printhead can become hot enough to be a burn hazard if touched.

Because computers do have the potential to produce these kinds of injuries, it is good practice to have a well-stocked first-aid kit in the work area. In addition, a class-C fire extinguisher should be on hand. Class-C extinguishers are the type specified for use around electrical equipment. You can probably imagine the consequences of applying a water-based fire extinguisher to a fire with live electrical equipment around. The class or classes for which the fire extinguisher is rated are typically marked on its side.

You may think that there's not much chance for a fire to occur with computer equipment, but this is not so. Imagine if a capacitor from a system board blew up and a small piece landed in a pile of packing materials in the work area. This would quickly become a fire.

This section has covered the major safety precautions and considerations that you need to be aware of while working on computer equipment. Most of all, use common sense and sound safety practices around all electronic equipment.

Disposal Procedures

 A+ CORE 3.4
As with any mechanical device, a computer eventually becomes obsolete in the application for which it was originally intended. Newer machines with improved features arise to replace earlier models. Slowly, but surely, those components fail and get replaced. Then comes the question: What to do with the old stuff? Can it simply be placed in the garbage bin so that it is hauled to the land fill and buried?

In today's world of environmental consciousness, you might not think so. Computers and peripherals contain some environmentally unfriendly materials.

> Most computer components contain some level of hazardous substances. Printed circuit boards consist of plastics, precious metals, fiberglass, arsenic, silicon, gallium, and lead. CRTs contain glass, metal, plastics, lead, barium, and rare earth metals. Batteries from portable systems can contain lead, cadmium, lithium, alkaline manganese, and mercury.

Although all these materials can be classified as hazardous materials, so far there are no wide-spread regulations when it comes to placing them in the land fill. Conversely, local regulations concerning acceptable disposal methods for computer-related components should always be checked before disposing of any electronic equipment.

As mentioned in an earlier section, laser printer toner cartridges can be refilled and recycled. However, this should be done only in draft mode operations in which very good resolution is not required. Ink cartridges from ink-jet printers can also be refilled and reused. As with laser cartridges, these cartridges can be very messy to refill and often do not function as well as new cartridges. In many cases, the manufacturer of the product will have a policy of accepting spent cartridges.

For both batteries and cartridges, the desired method of disposal is recycling. It should not be too difficult to find a drop site that handles recycling these products. On the other hand, even nonhazardous Subtitle D dump sites can handle the hardware components if needed.

Fortunately, several charitable organizations around the country take in old computer systems and refurbish them for various applications. Contact your local Chamber of Commerce for information about such organizations. The Internet also has several computer disposal organizations that take old units and redistribute them. In addition, a few companies will dispose of your old computer components in an "environmentally friendly" manner—for a fee.

In addition to the computer parts that provide hazardous materials, many of the cleaning substances used on computer equipment can be classified as hazardous materials. When it comes to disposing of the chemical solvents used to clean computers—as well as the containers in which they come—it will normally be necessary to clear these items with the local waste management agencies before disposing of them. Many dump sites will not handle free liquids, so solvents and other liquid cleaning materials must be properly categorized and disposed of at an appropriate type of disposal center.

All hazardous materials are required to have **material safety data sheets** (**MSDS**) that accompany them when they change hands. They are also required to be on hand in areas where hazardous materials are stored and commonly used. The MSDS contains information about the following:

1. What the material is

2. Its hazardous ingredients

3. Its physical properties

4. Fire and explosion data

5. Reactivity data

6. Spill or leak procedures

7. Health hazard information

8. Any special protection information

9. Any special precaution information

This information sheet is required to be provided by the supplier of the hazardous material. If you supply this material to a third party, you must also supply the MSDS for the material. The real reason for the sheets are to inform workers and management about hazards associated with the product and how to handle them safely. The sheets also provide instructions about what to do if an accident occurs involving the material. For this reason, employees should know where the MSDS are stored in their work area.

Customer Service Skills

A+ CORE 8.0
The object of this section is to discuss customer service skills that employers find desirable in their employees. Many companies have formal customer service guidelines that they make all employees aware of. However, these guidelines are not universal.

Everything discussed so far in this text has concerned the development of good technical skills.

For the most part, a high level of technical proficiency alone is not enough to sustain a career in the world of computer service. For most of the service jobs available, good customer skills are just as important as good technical skills. In most cases, these skills are equal partners for a successful career. Good customer service skills are a must for those who work directly with the public.

The field, or bench, technician must possess a good set of interpersonal skills to be able to handle customers. It has been said that we don't fix computers; we fix customers. How we are perceived is as important as how well we perform. In the end, it is customer satisfaction (with the product, the service, and the supplier) that creates a successful business and continued employment.

Customer service skills are generally referred to as **soft skills** because they cannot be tested easily with a written or hands-on test. However, these are skills that can be learned and practiced. The following paragraphs contain key points to consider in the area of providing customer service.

Prepare

Review the customer's history before contacting the company or going to its site to perform work. In particular, see if the problem you are going to work on is a repetitive problem or a new occurrence. Check the urgency of the call and the customer's priority level.

Research the type of equipment the call is concerning. Determine whether any special tools will be needed or whether any parts may be involved in the repair. Make sure your documentation is in order. It may be necessary to check the customer's status with your company. Make sure that you have all the manuals, replacement parts, and tools you will likely need. Do you have the ESD equipment, meters, hand tools, and other items needed? Make sure the tools and parts are in good working order. Set realistic schedules. Make appointments that you can keep. Always notify customers, as soon as possible, about any appointment changes, service delays, complications, or setbacks that may occur. These things happen to everyone, and your best defenses against customer dissatisfaction are promptness and good communication.

Establish Rapport

A+ CORE 8.1

A good practice is to learn your customers by name. Collect business cards, and include copies in customer folders—have them in your pocket during the call. Always deal with them as individuals, not by stereotypes such as order/entry person, receptionist, manager, and so on. Be as open, friendly, and approachable as your personality will allow. This is an area that most of us can always work on. Politeness is a valuable quality to possess, but it should never be forced, contrived, or overdone. Your greatest weapon in this area is your expertise. Avoid politically or racially sensitive topics: These have no place in business settings.

Establish Your Presence

Make eye contact when you speak to customers. Maintain alert body posture and calm facial expressions. Keep a calm voice level when perplexing situations arise. Your presence can be used to set the excitement level of the customer. If you appear calm, collected, and confident, the customer probably won't get too excited, either. Avoid moodiness in the work place. This can undermine your credibility with the customer. You begin each new customer contact with a 100% rating. At the end, you will be left with whatever points you have not given away.

> Doing an efficient, professional, and complete job does more to ingratiate you to customers than almost anything else you can do.

If customers are sure that you will always be able to solve their problems, you have the best rapport that could be achieved in a business setting.

Be Proactive

Provide a customer with a PM plan, and explain how it contributes to the continued productivity of the customer's equipment. Take time to illustrate proper methods of handling consumables and items to be on the watch for. Show them how to install and change printer ribbons, ink cartridges, toner cartridges, and so on. Demonstrate the use of virus-protection products and backup utilities, and advise them of potential environmental hazards, such as disposing of toner cartridges.

Scenario 1

A customer calls with a RAM problem that has been common in a particular model of computer your company sells. What should you tell the customer about the product?

    a. "Oh yeah, we have that happening all over. We'll be getting everyone fixed up real soon."

    b. "We've had a whole batch of bad RAM."

    c. Troubleshoot the problem as you would any other phone support problem.

    d. Offer to send the customer replacement RAM.

Alert customers of potential system problems or productivity-related issues concerning their systems. Identify noisy system components that may need care in the near future. Suggest system changes that could improve performance, and explain how this is possible. Keep customers aware of service bulletins and advisories concerning their equipment.

Research customer requests for recommendations, and advise about future directions and equipment. However, this option should normally be taken only if requested by the customer. Also be sensitive to the level of the person to whom you are making recommendations. Some workers have never met a new piece of hardware or software they didn't like. However, their superiors may be quite happy without the production/down-time/cost trade-offs that changing could bring. Don't incite the customer's employees with the latest and greatest product if their management hasn't signaled the way.

Listen and Communicate

One of the attributes that makes a good customer service or repair person is the ability to actively listen to the customer. Real listening means not just hearing what the customer has to say, but trying to pin down what he means. Mentally (and maybe physically) identify key points as the customer describes the nature of the problem. Don't interrupt customer descriptions before you have all the details. Even if you are sure that you know what is going on after the first sentence, have patience to listen to the complete description. This is not only common courtesy, but it also serves to uncover extra data about the problem.

Scenario 2

You are sent to set up a desktop publishing computer for a publisher, and you discover that the company is using a publishing program that you know does not have all the features of a competing program. You are sure that the company could be much more productive using the other program. How do you convey this to the customer?

   a. You don't because the company is installing a new program and does not need to be told this isn't the best.

   b. Get the supervisor alone, and recommend the other program in private.

   c. Mail an advertisement of the better product to the manager.

   d. Tell the operators about the features of the other product in confidence so that they will know what to look for the next time.

Pay attention to the customer's body language and other nonverbal clues. Pay attention to body posture, hand gestures, facial cues, and voice inflection to gauge anger, anxiety, and other emotions.

A+ CORE 2.2 Listening is also a good way to eliminate the user as a possible cause of the problems occurring. Many cartoons have been created in service newsletters about the strangest user-related calls ever received. Part of your job is to determine whether the user could be the source of the problem—either trying to do things with the system that it cannot do, or not understanding how some part of it is supposed to work. If you find this to be the case, work with the user to clarify the realistic uses of the system. This is a point where it may be appropriate to suggest advanced training options available. However, such suggestions should be made discretely.

Scenario 3

You arrive on a service call, and the office supervisor turns on the malfunctioning machine. She begins to explain what she thinks the problem is, but you can tell from the operation of the machine that it is something else. What course of action should you pursue?

   a. Listen to the explanation until she is finished, and then fix the machine.

   b. Sit down and fix the machine while she is describing the rest of the problem to you.

   c. Begin troubleshooting the problem she is describing until she leaves, and then fix the problem.

   d. Stop the explanation, and tell her that you are pretty sure that you already know what the problem is.

A+ CORE 8.1 The ability to communicate clearly is the other trait most looked for in service people. Allow customers to talk through their problems. Use probing questions for clarification purposes and to make sure you understand what the user is describing at each step. In doing so, the customer may come up with clues he hasn't thought of before. Help him to think through the problem by asking organized questions. With equipment down, the customer may be under some stress and might not be thinking as rationally as possible. Choose words and questions that do not put the customer, or the employees, in a bad light (for example, "What have you done now?" is not likely to set the proper tone with a customer who has more problems than he needs for the moment). Adjust the pace and flow of your conversation to accommodate the customer.

Avoid quick analysis statements. Repeatedly changing your position kills customer confidence. Also, avoid or minimize surprises that pop up (such as unexpected charges or time requirements). Try to manage the customer's expectations by being as up-front as possible about what you can accomplish and the scope of services you can provide. If the customer has a networking problem and you are the computer repair person, the customer shouldn't be allowed to believe that you are going to get everything working before you leave (unless the network falls within the scope of your normal work).

A+ CORE 8.1 If the person you are working with in a company is the MIS person, network administrator, or engineer, take his lead and follow his instructions. Avoid competitive situations of who knows more. Try to quickly recognize the technical abilities of the people with which you are working. Adjust your conversation to accommodate them. For technically challenged customers, avoid jargon; it will be confusing to them and can be a cause of customer dissatisfaction with you, even if you do a great job. Clarify your terminology with such people, and be careful to avoid talking down to them or patronizing them. On the other hand, if the customer is technically literate, be careful not to insult his intelligence by over-explaining things. In this case, use technical terms as appropriate, and use them correctly. Watch for signs of misunderstanding, and explain things in greater detail as necessary.

Scenario 4

While working with a relatively inexperienced customer over the telephone, you become aware that the customer is having great difficulty following your directions. How can you help the customer even though he cannot see you?

a. Send the customer fax drawings of steps to perform.

b. Ask the customer if you can talk to someone else to get a fresh perspective on the problem.

c. Check your conversation, and try to communicate more clearly.

d. Ask the customer to fax you drawings of what he is experiencing.

Follow up on unresolved issues. For incomplete calls, such as those requiring additional parts, assess the customer's need and restore as much functionality to the system as possible or as needed. Clean up and organize parts removed from the system so that they will not be in the way or will be removed before your return to the site. Keep the customer informed about progress of unresolved issues, such as when parts are expected. If problems are intermittent, set up a schedule and procedure to work with the customer to pin down circumstances that cause the problem to reoccur.

Be Responsive

Concentrate on the customer's problem or request. Give consideration to the customer's sense of urgency. Relegate paper work and administrative duties to a secondary level until the customer's problems have been fully aired. Don't undermine the customer's sense of urgency. Work with his priorities. Schedule steps to fulfill any unresolved problems to show commitment to getting the customer's problems solved. In this way, the customer will be assured that he is not being left adrift. Don't multitask while working directly with a customer. Focus on the task at hand, and keep it in the forefront. Avoid distractions in the customer's presence. Act on the customer's complaints.

Be Accountable

Document your promises and dates so that you may demonstrate accountability to your customers. Follow up on return dates for yourself and/or equipment. Take personal responsibility for being the single point for the service call when contacting specialists, dealing with parts vendors, and so on. It's your show; run it.

Scenario 5

An irate customer calls, complaining that a technician from your company has recently performed a software upgrade on their system and now the modem will not connect with other modems. How should you handle the customer?

    a. "I'm sure none of our technicians would have left a condition like that. Let's see what the problem is."

    b. "Give me the technician's name, and I'll have him get back to you as soon as he returns to the office."

    c. "Please describe the symptoms to me, so I can see what might be causing the problem."

    d. "This is really easy. Take the top off of the computer, and check to see that the card is installed securely."

Be Flexible

If a problem runs beyond your capabilities, take the initiative to move it to the next level of authority. Never leave a customer hanging without a path to get the problems settled. Provide alternatives to the customer when possible (such as down time scheduling, loaner equipment availability, and so on).

Be Professional

You should always make certain that your attire is clean, neat, and appropriate. You should establish a good rapport with your customers, but you should always maintain a professional distance from them. You cannot afford to be their support or confidant in dealings with the company for which you work. The apparent opportunity to gain the inside track with the customer, at your company's expense, cannot work out in your favor. Remember, the customer sees you as an extension of that company, so you can only be as good as your company is to the customer. If my computer is broken, I don't need a friend; I need the best repair person I can find.

All the listening and communications skills are equally valuable when performing phone support work. Because you cannot see the customer or interpret body language, it is even more important to assess the state of the customer quickly. It is also important to determine the technical abilities of the user as quickly as possible. Asking a receptionist to remove the cover of a computer is not normally an accepted practice.

When giving instructions over the phone, be precise. Provide detailed instructions for work to be done, and ask lots of questions about what is happening on the other end. Cellular or cordless phones are extremely valuable tools for customers using phone support. At your end of the phone, take good notes of what the user has been instructed to do so that you can review them as needed.

It is much more beneficial to establish the relationship with the customer based on your abilities and integrity. Have something good to say about the customer's facilities, if possible. If not, don't comment on them at all. The same goes for the equipment. The company isn't paying you for consulting services, and disparaging comments about its choices won't win you any points.

From time to time, you may be exposed to customer information that is of a sensitive nature. Respect the confidentiality of this information. Never reveal financial information that you have obtained from a customer's system. This includes friends and especially employees of the customer.

Scenario 6

The technician received a telephone call from a customer who buys thousands of dollars of computer equipment from his company each year. The purchaser cannot get the company's computer to work with a printer that was purchased through another supplier. She wants the technician to get the system running. How should the technician react?

   a. "I'm really sorry, but we can't work on equipment purchased from another vendor."

   b. "Sure, how can I help you?"

   c. "Let me clear this with my supervisor."

   d. "You'll have to tell my supervisor that you want me to do this. I'm sure that it will be all right because you do so much business with us."

Avoid distracting employees while you are working at a customer's site. Work as unobtrusively as possible. Ask permission to use the customer's facilities, such as the telephone, copier, or other equipment. For example, if paper is required to test a printer you are repairing, ask an appropriate person for it; don't just get it for yourself. Straighten up the work area before leaving it (for instance, don't leave the paper from the print tests laying around).

Never break copyright regulations by loading or giving away illegal software. One of the leading causes of computer virus infection is pirated software. Not only do you run this risk in giving away copies, but it's illegal and can get you introduced to various people you never really wanted to meet, such as lawyers and judges. On top of that, it could cost you your job.

Handle Conflicts Appropriately

Inevitably, you will run into a customer who is having a bad day. No matter what you do, you will not be able to keep him from getting angry over the situation. What you can do is realize that this is the case, and attempt to de-escalate the situation. The easiest thing to do is let the customer vent verbal frustrations without reply. Try to avoid taking a defensive stance, as this signals a conflict point. Redirect the conversation to creating solutions to the problems.

Remain calm, talk in a steady voice, and avoid making inflammatory comments. As soon as possible, withdraw from the confrontation and let the situation cool off. Inform your superiors as quickly as possible so that you have inside support and so that a plan of relief can be implemented.

Handle Paper Work—and Follow Up

A number of non-troubleshooting, non-repair activities must be handled to have an efficient organization. As a service person, you are not alone. You are part of a team that must communicate effectively for the system to operate smoothly. Other members of the team won't be able to do their jobs effectively if you don't follow through on yours. Process paper work as soon as possible so that it can be moving through your system.

Scenario 7

A customer who has picked up a repaired computer from your store brings it back within a few hours, complaining that it doesn't work. What should you say?

    a. "What happened to it?"

    b. "Sometimes I can't believe our technicians can find their way home at night. I'll get this thing fixed up for you."

    c. "It was working when it left here. I don't know what could have happened to it. Let's take a look at it."

    d. "Did it ever work when you got it home?"

Follow up with people to which you have delegated tasks to make sure that those tasks are being completed. Use an organizational aid to coordinate jobs, appointments, and activities with co-workers. Prioritize commitments, and resist the urge to overbook appointments. If it takes 30 minutes to get across town, never schedule an appointment there for a half hour after you should be finished at the first site. Maintain time allotments established for completion of different tasks.

Maintain an Orderly Work Area

Handle jobs one at a time so that components from one job do not get mixed up with components from another job. Store equipment not being used so that there is ample room to work and so that these items do not become a safety hazard.

Keep an inventory of parts and equipment in your area of responsibility. Order parts needed for a job promptly, and keep a log of when they should arrive. If the parts do not arrive as scheduled, you should have a reminder that they are still missing. This reminder will enable you to track repair parts so that when a customer calls to check on equipment or a problem you will have the information at hand.

Tag parts brought into the work area so that they do not get lost or mishandled. Store them so that they will not be damaged by environmental factors, such as ESD. Include all pertinent information about the part, including the problem description, repair notes, and customer name and location.

Key Points Review

The focus of this chapter has been to present important points for inclusion in the preventive maintenance programs associated with personal computer systems.

▶ Cleaning is a major part of keeping a computer system healthy. Therefore, the technician's tool kit should also contain a collection of cleaning supplies.

▶ The human body can build up static charges that range up to 25,000v. These build-ups can discharge very rapidly into an electrically grounded body or device. Placing a 25,000v surge through any electronic device is potentially damaging to it.

▶ In general, MOS devices are sensitive to voltage spikes and static electricity discharges. This can cause a great deal of problems when you have to replace MOS devices. The level of static electricity present on your body is high enough to destroy the inputs of a CMOS device.

▶ The term *ground* is often a source of confusion for the novice because it actually encompasses a collection of terms. Generically, ground is simply any point from which electrical measurements are referenced.

- Digital systems tend to be sensitive to power variations and power losses. Even a very short loss of electrical power can shut down a digital computer, resulting in a loss of any information that has not been saved to a mass storage device.

- Uninterruptible power supplies are battery-based systems that monitor the incoming power and kick in when unacceptable variations occur in the power source.

- The environment around a computer system, and the manner in which the computer is used, determines greatly how many problems it will have. Occasionally dedicating a few moments of care to the computer can extend its mean time between failures considerably. This activity, involving maintenance not normally associated with a breakdown, is called preventive maintenance (PM).

- DOS systems offer a number of commands that can be used to maintain and optimize the performance of the hard drive. The DOS CHKDSK command is used to recover lost allocation units from the hard drive.

- Backup utilities enable the user to quickly create extended copies of files, groups of files, or an entire disk drive. This operation is normally performed to back up important information in case the drive crashes or the disk becomes corrupt.

- File fragmentation creates conditions that cause the drive to operate slower. Fragmentation occurs when files are stored, retrieved, modified, and rewritten due to differences in the sizes of the before and after files.

- Computer viruses are destructive software programs designed to replicate and spread on their own. Sometimes these programs take control of a machine to leave a humorous message, and sometimes they destroy data.

- Unlike hard-disk drives, floppy drives are at least partially open to the atmosphere, and the disks may be handled on a regular basis. This opens the floppy-disk drive to a number of maintenance concerns not found in hard-disk drives.

- Input peripherals generally require very little in the way of preventive maintenance. An occasional dusting and cleaning should be all that's really required.

- Because printers tend to be much more mechanical than other types of computer peripherals, they require more effort to maintain. Printers generate pollutants, such as paper dust and ink droplets, in everyday operation. These pollutants can build up on mechanical parts and cause them to wear.

- In most IBM compatibles, only two potentially dangerous areas exist. One of these is inside the display monitor; the other is inside the power-supply unit. Both of these areas contain electrical voltage levels that are lethal.

- Laser printers contain many hazardous areas. The laser light can be very damaging to the human eye. In addition, you should be aware of multiple high-voltage areas and a high-temperature area in the typical laser printer.

- Most computer components contain some level of hazardous substances. Printed circuit boards consist of plastics, precious metals, fiberglass, arsenic, silicon, gallium, and lead. CRTs contain glass, metal, plastics, lead, barium, and rare earth metals. Batteries from portable systems can contain lead, cadmium, lithium, alkaline manganese, and mercury.

- For the most part, a high level of technical proficiency alone is not enough to sustain a career in the world of computer service. For most of the service jobs available, good customer skills are just as important as good technical skills.

- Doing an efficient, professional, and complete job does more to ingratiate you to customers than almost anything else you can do.

At this point, review the objectives listed at the beginning of the chapter to be certain that you understand each point and can perform each task listed there. Afterward, answer the review questions that follow to verify your knowledge of the information.

Multiple Choice Questions

1. What is the most common cause of ESD in micro-computer systems?

   a. Moving people

   b. High humidity

   c. Rubber mats

   d. Grounded power supply cables

2. Do viruses normally attack the system's CMOS settings?

   a. Yes; this is how a virus attacks most computers.

   b. No; viruses do not normally attack CMOS settings.

   c. Yes; this is how viruses attack all computers.

   d. No; viruses never attack CMOS settings.

3. How is excess toner normally removed from a laser printer?

   a. With a vacuum cleaner

   b. With a wet cloth

   c. With a dry cloth

   d. With compressed air

4. How are most computer viruses spread from computer to computer?

   a. By downloading programs from networks

   b. By passing infected disks between individuals

   c. By not formatting disks before use

   d. By transferring files over modems

5. If the DOS defrag option is not available, what other DOS command could be used to eliminate file chaining on a hard-disk drive?

   a. The Restore utility

   b. The MSAV utility

   c. The CHKDSK or SCANDISK utilities

   d. The Backup utility

6. ESD is most likely to occur during periods of _____.

   a. Low humidity

   b. High humidity

   c. Medium humidity

   d. Rain

7. What is the best method of cleaning a keyboard?

   a. Spraying with an anti-static solution

   b. Blowing with compressed air

   c. Vacuuming and cleaning with a damp cloth

   d. Washing with soap and water

8. What type of backup device is typically used to store large banks of information for an extended period of time?

   a. A floppy disk

   b. A tape drive

   c. A hard drive

   d. A CD-ROM drive

9. How often should the platen assembly of a dot-matrix printer be lubricated?

   a. Annually

   b. Monthly

   c. Weekly

   d. Never

10. Define a voltage sag.

    a. An over-voltage condition that lasts for a few milliseconds

    b. An under-voltage condition that lasts for an extended period

    c. An over-voltage condition that lasts for an extended period

    d. An under-voltage condition that lasts for a few milliseconds

Review Questions

1. List the two most dangerous areas of a typical microcomputer system, and describe why they are so dangerous.

2. Name three devices used to minimize ESD in the repair area.

3. The best general-purpose cleaning tool for computer equipment is _____.

4. List three types of backups that can be performed with most backup utilities.

5. Describe common PM procedures for laser printers.

6. Are there any restrictions on disposing of a spent toner cartridge?

7. List three types of computer viruses, and describe how they are different.

8. Why are defragmentation programs run on computers?

9. What is the purpose of running a CHKDSK operation before performing a backup or defrag operation on the hard drive?

10. The best method of protecting computer equipment from a thunderstorm is to _____.

11. The best method for transporting electronic devices is _____.

12. Describe the disadvantage of using the DOS or Windows Backup utility to perform a total backup of a large hard-disk drive.

13. List computer-related PM items that should be performed annually.

14. Name two characteristics that should be checked carefully before purchasing a UPS for a given computer system.

15. Describe the normal duration of a voltage spike.

Lab Exercises

The lab manual that accompanies this book contains hands-on lab procedures that reinforce and test your knowledge of the theory materials presented in this chapter. Now that you have completed your review of Chapter 13, refer to the lab manual and perform Procedures 35, "DOS Anti-Virus"; 36, "HDD Utilities"; and 37, "Logical Versus Physical Drives."

A+ OBJECTIVES MAP

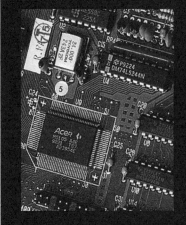

APPENDIX A

Core Examination

The CompTIA organization has established the following objectives for the Core portion of the A+ Certification examination.

1.0 Installation, Configuration, and Upgrading

This section challenges the test taker to identify, install, configure, and upgrade microcomputer modules and peripherals. Established procedures for system assembly and disassembly must be followed. Test elements include the ability to identify and configure IRQs, DMAs, and I/O addresses and to properly set configuration switches and jumpers.

1.1 Identify basic terms, concepts, and functions of system modules, including how each module should work during normal operation. Examples of concepts and modules include

- ▶ System board—Chapters 2 and 6
- ▶ Power supply—Chapter 2
- ▶ CPU/Microprocessor—Chapters 1, 2, and 6
- ▶ Memory—Chapters 1, 2, and 3
- ▶ Storage devices—Chapters 1, 2, and 8
- ▶ Monitor—Chapters 1, 2, and 9
- ▶ Modem—Chapters 1 and 11
- ▶ Firmware—Chapter 4
- ▶ Boot process—Chapter 4
- ▶ BIOS—Chapters 1 and 4
- ▶ CMOS—Chapter 4

1.2 Identify basic procedures for adding and removing field replaceable modules. Examples of modules include

- ▶ System board—Chapter 6, Lab Procedure 1
- ▶ Power supply—Chapter 3, Lab Procedure 1
- ▶ CPU/Microprocessor—Chapters 3 and 6
- ▶ Memory—Chapter 6, Lab Procedure 12
- ▶ Storage devices—Chapter 8, Lab Procedures 1, 27, and 29
- ▶ Input devices—Chapter 7, Lab Procedure 1

1.3 Identify available IRQs, DMAs, and I/O addresses with procedures for configuring them for device installation. Examples include

- ▶ Standard IRQ settings—Chapter 6
- ▶ Modems—Chapter 11

719

- Floppy Drives—Chapters 6 and 8
- Hard drives—Chapters 6 and 8

1.4 Identify common peripheral ports, associated cables, and their connectors. Examples include

- Cable types—Chapter 7
- Cable orientation—Lab Procedures 1, 20, 21, 26, 28, 29, 30, 32, and 33
- Serial versus parallel—Chapter 7
- Pin connections—Chapter 7

Examples of connector types include

- DB-9—Chapters 7 and 10
- DB-25—Chapters 7 and 10
- RJ-11—Chapter 11
- BNC—Chapter 11
- RJ-45—Chapter 11
- PS2/Mini-DIN—Chapter 7

1.5 Identify proper procedures for installing and configuring IDE/EIDE devices. Examples include

- Master/slave—Chapter 8
- Devices per channel—Chapter 8

1.6 Identify proper procedures for installing and configuring SCSI devices. Topics include

- Address/termination conflicts—Chapter 8
- Cabling—Chapter 8
- Types (standard, wide, fast, ultrawide)—Chapter 8
- Internal versus external—Chapter 8
- Switch and jumper settings—Chapter 8

1.7 Identify proper procedures for installing and configuring peripheral devices. Topics include

- Monitor/video card—Chapter 9
- Modem—Chapter 11
- Storage devices—Chapter 8

1.8 Identify procedures for upgrading BIOS

- Methods for upgrading—Chapter 4
- When to upgrade—Chapter 4

1.9 Identify hardware methods of system optimization and when to use them. Examples include

- ▶ Memory—Chapter 6
- ▶ Hard drives—Chapter 8
- ▶ CPU/microprocessors—Chapter 6
- ▶ Cache memory—Chapter 6

2.0 Diagnosing and Troubleshooting

This item requires the test taker to apply knowledge relating to diagnosing and trouble-shooting common module problems and system malfunctions. This includes knowledge of the symptoms relating to common problems.

2.1 Identify common symptoms and problems associated with each module and how to troubleshoot and isolate the problems. Contents may include

- ▶ Processor/memory symptoms—Chapter 6, Lab Procedures 7 and 13
- ▶ Keyboards/mouse/trackball/pen/microphones/touchpad—Chapters 7, 20, and 21
- ▶ Floppy drive failures—Chapter 8, Lab Procedures 7 and 26
- ▶ Parallel ports/scanners/tape drives—Chapter 7
- ▶ Hard drives—Chapter 8, Lab Procedures 7 and 28
- ▶ Sound card/audio—Chapter 12
- ▶ Monitor/video—Chapter 9, Lab Procedures 7, 22, 23, 24, and 25
- ▶ Motherboards—Chapter 6
- ▶ Modems—Chapter 11
- ▶ BIOS—Chapters 4 and 6
- ▶ CMOS—Chapter 4
- ▶ Power supply—Chapter 3, Lab Procedures 7, 17, and 18
- ▶ Slot covers—Chapter 5
- ▶ POST audio/visual error codes—Chapter 4
- ▶ Troubleshooting tools, for example, multimeter—Chapter 3

2.2 Identify basic troubleshooting procedures and good practices for eliciting problem symptoms from customers. Topics include

- ▶ Troubleshooting/isolation/problem determination—Chapters 3 and 13
- ▶ Determine whether hardware or software problem—Chapter 3

Gather information from user regarding:

- ▶ Customer environment—Chapter 13
- ▶ Symptoms/error codes—Chapter 3
- ▶ Situation when the problem occurred—Chapter 13

3.0 Safety and Preventive Maintenance

This section requires that the test taker show knowledge of safety and preventive maintenance. With regard to safety, it includes the potential hazards to personnel and equipment when working with lasers, high-voltage equipment, ESD, and items that require special disposal procedures that comply with EPA guidelines. With regard to preventive maintenance, this includes knowledge of preventive maintenance products, procedures, environmental hazards, and precautions when working on microcomputer systems.

3.1 Identify the purpose of various types of preventive maintenance products and procedures, and when to use/perform them. Examples include

- ▶ Liquid cleaning compounds—Chapter 13

- ▶ Types of materials to clean contacts and connections—Chapter 13

- ▶ Vacuum out systems, power supplies, fans—Chapter 13

3.2 Identify procedures and devices for protecting against environmental hazards.

- ▶ UPS (uninterruptible power supply), suppressers, noise filters, and plug strips—Chapter 13

- ▶ Determining the signs of power issues—Chapter 13

- ▶ Proper methods of component storage for future use—Chapter 13

3.3 Identify the potential hazards and proper safety procedures relating to lasers and high-voltage equipment.

- ▶ Lasers can cause blindness—Chapter 13

- ▶ High-voltage equipment, such as the power supply or CRT, can cause electrocution—Chapter 13

3.4 Identify items that require special disposal procedures that comply with EPA guidelines. Examples include

- ▶ Batteries—Chapter 13

- ▶ Toner kits/cartridges—Chapter 13

- ▶ Chemical solvents and cans—Chapter 13

- ▶ CRTs—Chapter 13

- ▶ MSDS (Material Safety Data Sheet)—Chapter 13

3.5 Identify ESD (Electrostatic Discharge) precautions and procedures, including the use of ESD protection devices.

- ▶ What ESD can do, and how it may be apparent or hidden—Chapter 13

- ▶ Common ESD protection devices—Chapter 13

- ▶ Situations that could present a danger or hazard—Chapter 13

4.0 Motherboard/Processors/Memory

This section requires the test taker to demonstrate knowledge of specific terminology, facts, ways and means of dealing with classifications, categories, and principles of motherboards, processors, and memory in microcomputer systems.

4.1 Distinguish between the popular CPU chips in terms of their basic characteristics.

- ▶ Popular CPU chips—Chapter 6

Characteristics include

- ▶ Physical size—Chapter 6
- ▶ Voltage—Chapter 6
- ▶ Speed—Chapter 6
- ▶ Onboard cache or not?—Chapter 6
- ▶ Sockets—Chapters 2 and 6
- ▶ Number of pins—Chapter 6

4.2 Identify the categories of RAM (random access memory) terminology, their locations, and physical characteristics. Terminology includes

- ▶ EDO RAM (Extended Data Output RAM)—Chapter 6
- ▶ DRAM (Dynamic RAM)—Chapter 6
- ▶ SRAM (Static RAM)—Chapter 6
- ▶ VRAM (Video RAM)—Chapter 6
- ▶ WRAM (Windows Accelerator Card RAM)—Chapter 6

Locations and physical characteristics:

- ▶ Memory bank—Chapters 2 and 6
- ▶ Memory chips (8-bit, 16-bit, and 32-bit)—Chapter 2
- ▶ SIMMS (Single In-line Memory Module)—Chapters 2 and 6
- ▶ DIMMS (Dual In-line Memory Module)—Chapters 2 and 6
- ▶ Parity chips versus non-parity chips—Chapters 2 and 6

4.3 Identify the most popular types of motherboards, their components, and their architecture (bus structures and power supplies, for example).

Types of motherboards:

- ▶ AT (Full and Baby)—Chapter 6
- ▶ ATX—Chapter 6

Motherboard components include

- ▶ Communication ports—Chapter 7
- ▶ SIMM and DIMM—Chapter 2

- ▶ Processor sockets—Chapter 6

- ▶ External cache memory (Level 2)—Chapter 6

Bus Architecture:

- ▶ ISA—Chapters 2 and 6

- ▶ EISA—Chapters 2 and 6

- ▶ PCI—Chapters 2 and 6

- ▶ USB (Universal Serial Bus)—Chapter 6

- ▶ VESA local bus (VL-BUS)—Chapters 2 and 6

- ▶ PC Card (PCMCIA)—Chapters 2 and 6

Basic compatibility guidelines

4.4 Identify the purpose of CMOS (Complementary Metal-Oxide Semiconductor), what it contains, and how to change its basic parameters. Examples include

- ▶ Printer parallel port—Uni, bidirectional, disable/enable, ECP, EPP—Chapters 4 and 7

- ▶ COM/serial port—memory address, interrupt request, disable—Chapters 4 and 7

- ▶ Hard drive—size and drive type—Chapters 4 and 8

- ▶ Floppy drive—enable/disable drive or boot, speed, density—Chapters 4 and 8

- ▶ Boot sequence—Chapter 4

- ▶ Memory—parity, non-parity—Chapters 4 and 6

- ▶ Date/time—Chapter 4

- ▶ Passwords—Chapter 4

5.0 Printers

This domain requires knowledge of basic types of printers, basic concepts, printer components, how they work, how they print onto a page, paper path, care and service techniques, and common problems.

5.1 Identify basic concepts, printer operations, printer components, and field replaceable units in primary printer types.

Types of printers include

- ▶ Laser—Chapter 10

- ▶ Ink jet—Chapter 10

- ▶ Dot matrix—Chapter 10

- ▶ Paper feeder mechanisms—Chapter 10

5.2 Identify care and service techniques and common problems with primary printer types. Examples include

- Feed and output—Chapter 10

- Errors—Chapter 10

- Paper jam—Chapter 10

- Print quality—Chapter 10

- Safety precautions—Chapter 13

- Preventive maintenance—Chapter 13

5.3 Identify the types of printer connections and configurations. Topics include

- Parallel—Chapter 10

- Serial—Chapter 10

- Network—Chapter 10

6.0 Portable Systems

This section requires the test taker to demonstrate knowledge of portable computers and their unique components and problems.

6.1 Identify the unique components of portable systems and their unique problems. Examples include

- Battery—Chapter 2

- LCD—Chapters 1, 2, and 9

- AC adapter—Chapter 2

- Docking stations—Chapter 2

- Hard drive—Chapters 1 and 2

- Types I, II, III cards—Chapters 2 and 6

- Network cards—Chapter 2

- Memory—Chapter 2

7.0 Basic Networking

This section requires the test taker to demonstrate knowledge of basic network concepts and terminology, ability to determine whether a computer is networked, knowledge of procedures for swapping and configuring network interface cards, and knowledge of the ramifications of repairs when a computer is networked.

7.1 Identify basic networking concepts, including how a network works. Examples include

- Network access—Chapter 11, Lab Procedure 33

- Protocol—Chapter 11, Lab Procedure 33

- Network interface cards—Chapter 11, Lab Procedure 33

- Full duplexing—Chapter 11

- Cabling—twisted pair, coaxial, fiber optic—Chapter 11

- Ways to network a PC—Chapter 11

7.2 Identify procedures for swapping and configuring network interface cards.

- ▶ Network interface card—Chapter 11

7.3 Identify ramifications of repairs on the network. Examples include

- ▶ Reduced bandwidth—Chapter 11
- ▶ Loss of data—Chapter 11
- ▶ Network slowdown—Chapter 11

8.0 Customer Satisfaction

This section requires the test taker to show knowledge of—and sensitivity about—those behaviors that contribute to satisfying customers. More specifically, these behaviors include such things as the quality of technician-customer personal interaction; the way a technician conducts himself or herself professionally within the customer's business setting; the credibility and confidence projected by the technician that, in turn, engenders customer confidence; the resilience, friendliness, and efficiency that can unexpectedly delight the customer above and beyond the solving of a technical problem.

8.1 Differentiate effective from ineffective behaviors as these contribute to the maintenance or achievement of customer satisfaction. Some of the customer satisfaction behaviors and factors addressed include

- ▶ Communicating and listening (face to face or over the phone)—Chapter 13
- ▶ Interpreting verbal and nonverbal cues—Chapter 13
- ▶ Responding appropriately to the customer's technical level—Chapter 13
- ▶ Establishing personal rapport with the customer—Chapter 13
- ▶ Professional conduct—Chapter 13
- ▶ Helping and guiding customers with problem descriptions—Chapter 13
- ▶ Responding to and closing a service call—Chapter 13
- ▶ Handling complaints and upset customers, conflict avoidance and resolution—Chapter 13
- ▶ Showing empathy and flexibility—Chapter 13
- ▶ Sharing the customer's sense of urgency—Chapter 13

DOS/Windows Module Examination

In addition to the Core objectives, the following objectives have been established for the DOS/Windows portion of the A+ examination.

1.0 Function, Structure, Operation, and File Management

This section requires the test taker to demonstrate knowledge of DOS, Windows 3.x, and Windows 95 operating systems in terms of their functions and structure, for managing files and directories, and running programs. It also includes navigating through the operating system from DOS command-line prompts and Windows procedures for accessing and retrieving information.

1.1 Identify the operating system's functions, structure, and major system files. Examples include

- ▶ Functions of DOS, Windows 3.x, and Windows 95—Chapters 4 and 5

- ▶ Major components of DOS, Windows 3.x, and Windows 95—Chapters 4 and 5

- ▶ Contrasts between Windows 3.x and Windows 95—Chapter 5

Describe major system files: what they are, where they are located, and how they are used. Examples include

- ▶ System, configuration, and user interface files—Chapters 4 and 5

DOS

- ▶ Autoexec.bat—Chapter 4

- ▶ Config.sys—Chapter 4

- ▶ Io.sys—Chapter 4

- ▶ Ansi.sys—Chapter 4

- ▶ Msdos.sys—Chapter 4

- ▶ EMM386.exe—Chapter 4

- ▶ Himem.sys—Chapter 4

- ▶ Command.com—Chapter 4

Windows 3.x

- ▶ Win.ini—Chapter 5

- ▶ System.ini—Chapter 5

- ▶ User.exe—Chapter 5

- ▶ Gdi.exe—Chapter 5

- ▶ Win.ini—Chapter 5

- ▶ Win.com—Chapter 5

- ▶ Progman.ini—Chapter 5

- ▶ Progman.exe—Chapter 5

- ▶ Krnlxxx.exe—Chapter 5

Windows 95

- ▶ Io.sys—Chapter 5

- ▶ Msdos.sys—Chapter 5

- ▶ Command.com—Chapter 5

- Regedit.exe—Chapter 5

- System.dat—Chapter 5

- User.dat—Chapter 5

1.2 Identify ways to navigate the operating system and how to get to needed technical information.

- Procedures (that is, menu or icon-driven) for navigating through DOS to perform such things as locating, accessing, and retrieving information—Chapter 4

- Procedures for navigating through the Windows 3.x/Windows 95 operating system, accessing and retrieving information—Chapter 5, Lab Procedures 3, 4, 5, and 6

1.3 Identify basic concepts and procedures for creating and managing files and directories in DOS/Windows. Examples include

- File attributes—Chapter 3

- File-naming conventions—Chapter 4, Lab Procedure 2

- File types, file formats—Chapter 4, Lab Procedure 2

- Command syntax—Chapter 4, Lab Procedure 2

- Read-only, hidden, system, and archive attributes—Chapter 4

1.4 Identify the procedures for basic disk management. Examples include

- Using disk-management utilities—Chapter 13, Lab Procedure 36

- Backing up—Chapter 13, Lab Procedure 36

- Formatting—Chapter 8, Lab Procedures 27, 28, and 37

- Partitioning—Chapter 8, Lab Procedures 27, 28, and 37

- Defragmenting—Chapter 13, Lab Procedure 36

- Scandisk—Chapter 13

- FAT 32—Chapter 5

- File Allocation Tables (FAT)—Chapters 4 and 5

- Virtual File Allocation Tables (VFAT)—Chapter 5

2.0 Memory Management

This section requires the test taker to demonstrate knowledge of the types of memory used by DOS and Windows and the potential for memory address conflicts.

2.1 Differentiate between types of memory. Examples include

- Conventional—Chapter 4

- Extended/upper memory—Chapter 4

- High memory—Chapter 4

- Expanded memory—Chapter 4

- Virtual memory—Chapter 4

2.2 Identify typical memory conflict problems and how to optimize memory use. Examples include

- What a memory conflict is—Chapter 5

- How it happens—Chapter 5

- When to employ utilities—Chapter 5

- System Monitor—Chapter 5

- General Protection Fault—Chapter 5

- Illegal operation occurrences—Chapter 5

- MemMaker or other optimization utilities—Chapters 4, 5, and 6, Lab Procedure 12

- Himem.sys—Chapters 4 and 5

- SMARTDRV—Chapter 4

- Use of expanded memory blocks (using Emm386.exe)—Chapter 4

3.0 Installation, Configuration, and Upgrading

This section requires the test taker to demonstrate knowledge of installation, configuration, and upgrading DOS, Windows 3.x, and Windows 95. This includes knowledge of system boot sequences.

3.1 Identify the procedures for installing DOS, Windows 3.x, Windows 95, and bringing the software to a basic operational level. Examples include

- Partition—Chapter 8, Lab Procedures 27, 28, and 37

- Format drive—Chapter 8, Lab Procedures 27, 28, and 37

- Run appropriate setup utility—Chapter 8

- Loading drivers—Chapter 8

3.2 Identify steps to perform an operating system upgrade. Topics include

- Upgrading from DOS to Windows 95—Chapter 5

- Upgrading from Windows 3.x to Windows 95—Chapter 5, Lab Procedure 5

3.3 Identify the basic system-boot sequences and alternative ways to boot the system software, including steps to create an emergency boot disk with utilities installed. Examples include

- Files required to boot—Chapters 4 and 5

- Creating an emergency boot disk—Chapter 5

- Startup disk—Chapter 4

- Safe mode—Chapter 5

- DOS mode—Chapter 5

3.4 Identify procedures for loading/adding device drivers and the necessary software for certain devices.

 ▶ Windows 3.x procedures—Chapter 4

 ▶ Windows 95 Plug and Play—Chapters 4 and 5

3.5 Identify the procedures for changing options and configuring and using the Windows printing subsystem—Chapter 10, Lab Procedure 30

3.6 Identify the procedures for installing and launching typical Windows and non-Windows applications—Chapter 5

4.0 Diagnosing and Troubleshooting

This section requires the test taker to demonstrate the ability to apply knowledge to diagnose and troubleshoot common problems relating to DOS, Windows 3.x, and Windows 95. This includes understanding normal operation and symptoms relating to common problems.

4.1 Recognize and interpret the meaning of common error codes and startup messages from the boot sequence and identify steps to correct the problem:

 ▶ Incorrect DOS version—Chapter 4

 ▶ Error in Config.sys line XX—Chapter 4

 ▶ Bad or missing Command.com—Chapter 4

 ▶ Himem.sys not loaded—Chapter 5

 ▶ Swapfile corrupt—Chapter 5

 ▶ A device referenced in System.ini could not be found—Chapter 5

 ▶ Missing or corrupt Himem.sys—Chapter 5

 ▶ No operating system found—Chapter 5

 ▶ Safe mode—Chapter 5

4.2 Recognize Windows-specific printing problems and identify the procedures for correcting them. Examples include

 ▶ Print spool is stalled—Chapter 10

 ▶ Incorrect/incompatible driver for print—Chapter 10

4.3 Recognize common problems and determine how to resolve them. Topics include

Common problems:

 ▶ General Protection Faults—Chapter 5

 ▶ Illegal operation—Chapter 5

 ▶ Invalid working directory—Chapter 4

 ▶ System locks up—Chapters 4 and 5

 ▶ Option will not function—Chapter 5

- Application will not start or load—Chapter 5

- Cannot log on to network—Chapter 11

DOS and Windows-based utilities:

- MSD.exe—Chapter 3, Lab Procedure 8

- Scandisk—Chapter 13, Lab Procedure 36

- Defrag.exe—Chapter 13, Lab Procedure 36

- Mem.exe—Chapter 4, Lab Procedure 12

- Edit.com—Chapters 4 and 5

- Fdisk.exe—Chapter 8, Lab Procedure 27

- Attrib.exe—Chapter 4

- Device manager—Chapter 5

- Sysedit.exe—Chapter 5, Lab Procedure 6

- Extract.exe—Chapter 5

4.4 Identify concepts relating to viruses and virus types—their danger, symptoms, and sources, and how they infect, how to protect against them, and how to identify and remove them. Topics include

- What they are—Chapter 13

- Sources—Chapter 13

- How to determine their presence—Chapter 13

5.0 Networks

This section requires the test taker to demonstrate knowledge of the network capabilities of DOS and Windows, and how to connect to networks, including what the Internet is about, its capabilities, basic concepts relating to Internet access and generic procedures for system setup.

5.1 Identify the networking capabilities of DOS and Windows including procedures for connecting to the network. Topics include

- Sharing disk drives—Chapter 11, Lab Procedure 33

- Sharing print and file services—Chapter 11, Lab Procedure 33

- Network type and network card—Chapter 11

5.2 Identify concepts and capabilities relating to the Internet and basic procedures for setting up a system for Internet access. Topics include

- TCP/IP—Chapter 11

- Email—Chapter 11

- HTML—Chapter 11

- HTTP://—Chapter 11
- FTP—Chapter 11
- Domain Names (Web sites)—Chapter 11
- ISP—Chapter 11
- Dial-up access—Chapter 11

TEST TAKING TIPS

The A+ exam is an objective-based timed test. It covers the objectives listed in Appendix A in a multiple-choice format. There are two general methods of preparing for the test. If you are an experienced technician using this material to obtain certification, use the testing features at the end of each chapter and on the accompanying CD to test each area of knowledge. Track your weak areas and spend the most time concentrating on them. If you are a newcomer to the subject of serious computer repair, plan a systematic study of the materials, reserving the testing functions until each chapter has been completed.

In either case, after completing the study materials, use the various testing functions available on the CD to practice, practice, practice taking the test. Test yourself by topic—as a mixture of questions from all areas, as a flash card review, and so on—until you are comfortable that you are ready. The CD will allow you to immediately reference the area of the text that covers material that you might miss.

- Answer all the questions you know first. You can always go back and work on harder questions.

- Don't leave any questions unanswered. They will be counted as incorrect.

- There are no trick questions. The most correct answer is there somewhere.

- Be aware of A+ questions that have more than one correct answer. They are identified by a special formatting of the letters for the possible answers. They are enclosed in a square box. When you encounter these, make sure to mark every answer that applies.

- Get plenty of hands-on practice before the test. Practice against the time limit set for the test.

- Make certain to prepare for each test category listed above. The key is not to memorize, but to understand the topics.

- Take your watch. The A+ exam is a timed test. You will need to keep an eye on the time to make sure that you are getting to the items that you are most sure of.

- Get plenty of rest before taking the test.

GLOSSARY

access time (1) When specifying memory access, the amount of time required to transfer a character to/from the MPU to/from RAM. This speed is normally given in nanoseconds. (2) When specifying disk access, the average time required to position the R/W head over a specific track. This speed is normally given in milliseconds.

accumulator A special-purpose register used by the MPU to store the results of ALU operations. It also serves as the source of one of the operands for most ALU operations.

ACK (ACKnowledge) A data communications code used by the receiver to tell the transmitter it is ready to accept data. During a data transfer this signal is continually used to indicate successful receipt of the last data character or block and to request more.

adapter A device that permits one system to work with and connect to another. Many I/O device adapters interface with the microcomputer by plugging into the expansion slots on the system board. These specialized circuit boards are often called adapter cards. See *daughter board.*

ADC (Analog-to-Digital Converter) A device that converts a continuously varying signal (analog) into a binary coded signal (digital) for use by a computer.

address The unique location number of a particular memory storage area, such as a byte of primary memory, a sector of disk memory, or a peripheral device itself.

address bus A unidirectional pathway that carries address data generated by the MPU to the various memory and I/O elements of the computer. The size of this bus determines the amount of memory a particular computer can use and therefore is a direct indication of the computer's power.

A: drive The commonly understood term designating the first floppy-disk drive in Microsoft's DOS microcomputer operating system.

alphanumeric data Data such as names and addresses, and distinguished from numeric data such as monetary or quantity figures.

ALU (Arithmetic Logic Unit) The subsection of the CPU where the actual math and logic operations are performed, two binary numbers at a time.

AM (Amplitude Modulation) A method of data transmission that modulates the data into a carrier by varying the carrier amplitude.

analog monitor A video display that is designed for use with a variety of computer or television standards, including the common NTSC composite video standard. Analog monitors offer a high-resolution picture. Some models are capable of many different sweep frequencies (multisync), and most accept separate red, green, and blue (RGB) signals for sharper contrast than digital monitors.

ASIC (Application Specific Integrated Circuit) An ASIC called the serial communication controller manages the activities of the ports. It is a USART device that allows the port to be used for both asynchronous and synchronous communications. The SCC performs the serial/parallel and parallel/serial conversions between the system's bus and the peripheral device. It also handles the handshaking protocol between the port and the system.

ASCII (American Standard Code for Information Interchange) The 7-bit binary data code used in all personal computers, many minicomputers and also in communications services. Of the 128 possible character combinations, the first 32 are used for printing and transmission control. Because of the 8-bit byte used in digital computers, the extra bit can be used either for parity checking or for the extended ASCII set of characters, which includes foreign language characters and line-draw graphic symbols.

asynchronous transmission A method of serial data transmission where the receiving system is not synchronized, by a common clock signal, with the transmitting system.

AT bus Also referred to as ISA (Industry Standard Architecture) bus. The 16-bit data bus introduced in the AT class personal computer.

attribute byte A data byte specifying the display characteristics of a single character of text such as highlight, underline, reverse video, or blinking.

attribute controller The portion of the VGA video controller that converts data from the video memory and formats it for display on the video display.

auto dial A modem feature that automatically accesses the line and dials the telephone of the answering modem in order to establish a connection.

B

BASIC (Beginners All-purpose Symbolic Instruction Code) A high-level programming language originally developed in the mid 1960s for timesharing mainframe use. It now has become widely used on all types of computers.

BAT file (BATch file) A file extension name used to identify a batch file in Microsoft DOS versions. A batch file, created by a word processor, contains a list of DOS commands that are executed as if each were typed and entered one at a time.

baud rate The number of electrical state changes per second on a data communication line. At lower speeds, the baud rate and the bits-per-second rate are identical. At higher speeds, the baud rate is some fraction of the bits-per-second rate.

BCD (Binary Coded Decimal) A binary coding system in which individual decimal numbers 0-9 (digits) are converted into separate groups of four binary bits, one group for each decimal digit.

B: drive The commonly understood term designating the second floppy-disk drive in the DOS and OS/2 microcomputer operating systems.

binary This means two. In conjunction with digital computers, all data is processed only after being converted into binary numbers consisting of the digits 0 and 1.

BIOS (Basic Input/Output System) See *ROM BIOS*.

bit (binary digit) One digit of a binary number (0 or 1). Groups of bits are manipulated together by a computer into various storage units called nibbles, bytes, words, or characters.

bit map A term used in computer graphics to describe a memory area containing a video image. One bit in the map represents one pixel on a monochrome screen, whereas in color or grayscale monitors, several bits in the map might represent one pixel.

bit stream A continuous flow or transfer of binary signals.

boot To start the computer. It refers to the word bootstrap because the straps help in pulling boots on, just as the bootable disk helps the computer to get its first instructions.

bootable disk Normally refers to a floppy disk containing the computer operating system.

bps (bits per second) A term used to measure the speed of data being transferred in a communications system.

buffer   (1) Also known as bus drivers; a special class of digital amplifying device used to match dissimilar circuit characteristics of various IC devices and to increase the number of device inputs that an output can successfully drive. These devices usually are equipped with tri-state capabilities. See *tri-state*. (2) A class of memory registers and devices used to match data transfer speeds between the computer and a peripheral. Can be as simple as a single register or as complex as a large portion of RAM storage being used to accommodate large data transfers, such as DMA operations.

bulk storage   Refers to any data storage medium (tape or disk) not used for high-speed execution.

bus   A parallel collection of conductors that carry data or control signals from one unit to another.

bus master   Any class of MPU having the capability to take control of the system buses of a computer.

bus mouse   A type of mouse that plugs into an adapter card rather than a serial port.

byte   The most common word size used by digital computers. It is an eight-bit pattern consisting of both a high and a low order nibble. Computers of any size are frequently described in terms of how many bytes of data can be manipulated in one operation or cycle.

C

cache   An area of high-speed memory reserved for improving system performance. Blocks of often-used data are copied into the cache area to permit faster access times. A disk cache memory area is actually located on board the disk controller card.

cache controller   An MPU with the specific task of managing a sophisticated cache memory system.

carriage   The part in a printer or typewriter that handles the feeding of the paper forms.

cartridge   A removable data storage module, containing disks, magnetic tape or memory chips, and inserted into the slots of disk drives, printers, or computers.

CCP (Chip Carrier Package)   A very popular IC package style that, unlike the DIP, has pins around its entire circumference. A CCP takes up to 50 percent less surface area on a printed circuit board than an identical circuit in DIP form. Pins are "gull-wing" shaped and set on solder pads of the PCB. These chips are more difficult to test and replace than DIPs.

C: drive   The commonly understood term designating the system or first hard-disk drive in the DOS and OS/2 microcomputer operating systems.

Centronics interface   The 36-pin standard for interfacing parallel printers and other devices to a computer. The plug, socket, and signals are defined.

CGA (Color Graphics Adapter)   A low-resolution, IBM video standard for text and graphics, requiring the use of a digital RGB color display monitor. It has been superseded by the EGA, VGA, and SuperVGA standards.

character cell   A dot matrix used to produce a single character on a printer or a display screen. The matrix must be designed in such a way to allow enough blank space between characters and lines to produce an acceptable level of legibility.

character printer   Any printer that prints one character at a time, such as a dot matrix printer of a daisy wheel.

check sum   In error-checking systems, a numeric value assigned to a block of data. Check sums are capable of detecting single bit errors and some multiple bit errors.

chip   The common name for an integrated circuit (IC). Preceded by the development of the transistor, ICs can contain from several dozen to several million electronic components (resistors, diodes, transistors, and so on) on a square of silicon approximately 1/16- to 1/2-inch wide and around 1/30 inch in thickness. The IC can be packaged in many different styles, depending on the specific use for which it is intended. The term "chip" is synonymous with *microelectronic device*.

chip set   A group of specifically engineered ICs designed to perform a function interactively.

client/server network   Workstations or clients operate in conjunction with a master file server computer to control the network.

clock   An internal timing device. Several clock varieties are used in computer systems. Among them are the CPU clock, the realtime clock, a timesharing clock, and a communications clock.

CMOS (Complementary Metal Oxide Semiconductor)
A MOS device fabricated by combining both P and N MOS components. It has a lower packing density than NMOS alone, but it operates at higher speed and lower power consumption than NMOS devices. CMOS ICs are very sensitive to voltage spikes and static discharges and must be protected from static shock.

CMOS diagnostics   ROM-based diagnostic routines available on the MC-2000 system board for testing hard-disk drives, floppy-disk drives, keyboards, video displays, and miscellaneous ports.

CMOS setup   A software setup program used to provide the system with information about what options are installed. The configuration information is stored in special CMOS registers that are read each time the system boots up. Battery backup prevents the information from being lost when power to the system is removed.

cold boot   Booting a computer by turning the power on.

color monitor   Also known as RGB monitors, these displays enable the user to run text and color-based applications such as graphics drawing and CAD programs. There are two basic RGB type monitors: digital (TTL) and analog. Analog RGB monitors allow the use of many more colors than digital RGB monitors.

color palette   A set of VGA registers that contain digital red, green, and blue values that can be converted into analog signals to drive a color CRT's electron guns to create colors on the screen.

color printer   Any printer capable of printing in color, using thermal-transfer, dot matrix, electrophotographic, electrostatic, ink jet, or laser printing techniques.

COM1   The label used in Microsoft DOS versions assigned to serial port 1.

compatible   A reference to any piece of computer equipment that works or looks like a more widely known standard or model. A PC compatible, or clone, is a PC that, although somewhat different physically than the IBM-PC, runs software developed for the IBM-PC and accepts its hardware options.

composite video   The video-only portion of the standard NTSC TV signal with all video signals mixed together. Some computers offer this type of signal for use with home TV sets.

computer word   The data format that exists inside the computer. There are three types of computer words. (1) Numeric words that contain only numeric information in binary, octal, hexadecimal, or binary coded decimal (BCD) code. (2) Alphanumeric words that contain codes representing letters, numbers, and special characters. As these codes are identified, the characters are reconstructed from specific bit patterns stored in the output device. (3) Instruction words that are used to tell the computer what type of operation to perform and where to find any data needed to complete the operation.

config.sys file   A Microsoft DOS file that, upon start-up, is used to customize the system's hardware environment. The required peripheral device drivers (with SYS file extensions) are initialized.

configuration   A customized computer system or communications network composed of a particular number and type of interrelated components. The configuration varies from system to system, requiring that some means be established to inform the system software about what options are currently installed. See *configuration switches* and *CMOS setup*.

continuous forms   Paper sheets that are joined together along perforated edges and used in printers that move them through the printing area with motorized sprockets. Sprockets may fit into holes on both sides of the paper.

control bus   A pathway between the MPU and the various memory, programmable and I/O elements of the system. Control bus signals are not necessarily related to each other and can be unidirectional or bi-directional.

control character   A special type of character that causes some event to occur on a printer, display, or communications path, such as a line feed, a carriage return, or an escape.

control unit   The subsection of the CPU that sends the control signals to and receives control signals from all the other parts of the system, such as memory chips, programmable controllers, other bus masters, disk drives, and the various peripherals. It regulates the data traffic between all devices.

coprocessor   A high-speed numeric microprocessor designed to work with a matching MPU and usually installed in an empty IC socket specifically provided for it by the system board manufacturer. It extends the system's arithmetic and instruction set to provide for high-speed mathematical calculation capabilities.

CPU (central processing unit)   The part of the computer that does the thinking. It consists of the control unit and the ALU. On personal computers, the CPU is contained on a single chip, whereas on a minicomputer it occupies one or several printed circuit boards. On mainframes, a CPU is contained on many printed circuit boards. Its power comes from the fact that it can execute millions of instructions in a fraction of a second.

CRC (Cyclic Redundancy Check)   The error-checking technique that ensures communications channel integrity by utilizing division to determine a remainder. If the transmitter and receiver do not agree on what the remainder should be, an error is detected.

CRT (cathode ray tube)   The vacuum tube used as the display screen for both televisions and computer terminals. The term is sometimes used to mean the terminal itself.

CRT controller   The name given to the circuitry or IC responsible for providing the horizontal and vertical synchronization signals, writing screen data into the screen memory, refreshing the screen, and controlling all of the display manipulation functions.

CTS (Clear To Send)   An RS-232 handshaking signal sent from the receiver to the transmitter indicating readiness to accept data.

cursor   The movable display screen symbol that indicates to the user where the action is taking place. The text cursor is usually a blinking underline or rectangle, whereas the graphics cursor can change into any predetermined shape at different parts of the screen.

cursor keys   The keyboard cluster of keys that move the cursor around the display screen. Enhanced keyboards have two clusters of cursor keys in case the numeric keypad is in use.

cycle stealing   A mode of DMA operation whereby the DMA controller senses periods during which the bus system is not being used and performs data transfers during these periods. In this way both processing and peripheral operations can occur simultaneously with some degree of overlap.

cylinder   The combination of all tracks, normally on multiple-platter disk drives, that reside at the same track number location on each surface.

D

DAC (digital-to-analog converter)   A device that converts a binary coded signal (digital) into a continuously varying signal (analog) for use by an analog device.

DACK (DMA ACKnowledge)   A signal issued by the DMA controller to the requesting I/O device indicating that a high-speed data transfer can now commence.

daisy wheel printer   A printer utilizing a print mechanism containing a plastic or metal hub with characters embossed on the ends of spokes. The hammer waits until the correct character is spun under it, and then hits the ribbon onto the paper.

data   Information assembled in small units of raw facts and figures.

data bus   A bi-directional pathway linking the MPU to memory and I/O devices, the size of which usually corresponds to the word size of the computer.

data compression   Most compression algorithms use complex mathematical formulas to remove redundant bits, such as successive 0s or 1s from the data stream. When the modified word is played back through the decompression circuitry, the formula reinserts the missing bits to return the data stream to its original state.

DCE (Data Communications Equipment)   A communications device, usually a modem, that establishes, maintains, and terminates a data transfer session. It also serves as a data converter when interfacing different transmission media.

decoder   A device similar to a demultiplexer. A binary coded input (several input lines) is used to activate a single output. The number of the activated output line corresponds with the number of the binary input code.

default   The normal action taken, or setting used, by the hardware or software when the user does not otherwise specify.

demodulator A device that removes the data from the carrier frequency and converts it to its originally unmodulated form.

diagnostics Software programs specifically designed to test the operational capability of the computer memory, disk drives, and other peripherals. The routines are available on disks or ROM chips. Errors might be indicated by beep codes or visual reports. They can normally point to a board-level problem, but not down to a particular component, unless the routine has been written for a particular board being used in the system under test. A complete system failure would require a ROM-based diagnostic program, as opposed to a disk-based routine.

dibit A term used to describe a combination of two consecutive bits. A dibit can be transmitted as a single entity using phase modulation techniques.

digital A term referring to either a device or a process that can manipulate information pulses. These pulses can take only two distinct voltage states or values: on or off, high or low. In most cases, the term "digital" is synonymous with computer.

DIMMs (Dual In-line Memory Modules) DIMMs are 168-pin plug-in memory modules similar to SIMMs.

DIP (Dual In-line Package) The most common form of IC package, available in 8-pin mini-DIPs, and 14-, 16-, 20-, 24-, 28-, and 40-pin DIPs. Measurements taken at the various pins provide the information used by the technician when troubleshooting electronic equipment containing these digital devices.

direct access Accessing data stored at only a specific location, without having to scan the data that occupies memory space either in front of or behind it.

direct I/Ov An I/O addressing method that uses no address allocations but requires extra control lines.

directory A collection of disk files organized under one heading and simulating a file drawer.

disk controller The printed circuit board, normally plugged into a system board expansion slot, that contains the circuitry responsible for communicating with the disk drive(s).

disk drive The peripheral storage device that reads and writes data to spinning magnetic or optical disks. The drive can either hold removable disks or contain permanent platters.

disk A term usually applied to a removable, floppy-disk memory storage device.

DMA (direct memory access) The capability of certain intelligent, high-speed I/O devices to perform data transfers themselves, with the help of a special IC device called a DMA controller.

DMA controller An intelligent (programmable) IC chip specifically designed to perform high-speed data transfers when asked to do so by an I/O device. The DMA controller has the capability to take over the entire bus system for short lengths of time.

DOS (Disk Operating System) Can be a generic term, but in most cases it refers to the Microsoft family of computer operating systems (PC-DOS for IBM equipment or MS-DOS for compatibles).

DOS prompt A screen symbol that indicates to the user that the system is ready for a command. It usually consists of the current drive letter, followed by a colon and a blinking cursor.

dot matrix printer A type of printer that forms its images out of one or more columns of dot hammers. Higher resolutions require a greater number of dot hammers to be used.

dot pitch A measurement of the resolution of a dot matrix. The width of an individual dot in millimeters describes a display's resolution, with the smaller number representing the higher resolution. The number of dots per linear inch describes a printer's resolution, with the higher number representing the higher resolution.

DPSK (Differential Phase Shift Keying) A common form of phase modulation in modems in which the phase is incrementally altered to reflect multiple bit combinations, yielding multiple bits per baud of bandwidth. See *PSK*.

DRAM (dynamic random access memory) A type of RAM that loses its data, regardless of power considerations, unless it is refreshed at least once every two milliseconds.

DREQ (DMA REQuest)   A peripheral signal sent to the DMA controller requesting a high-speed data transfer without MPU intervention.

DSR (Data Set Ready)   An RS-232 handshaking signal sent from the modem to its own computer, indicating its readiness to accept data.

DTE (Data Terminal Equipment)   A piece of data communications equipment that is serving as either the source or destination of a data transfer. A DTE is normally a computer terminal.

DTR (Data Terminal Ready)   An RS-232 handshaking signal sent to a modem by its own computer, indicating its readiness to accept data.

E

edge connector   The often double-sided row of etched lines on the edge of an adapter card that plugs into one of the computer's expansion slots.

EEPROM (Electrically Erasable Programmable Read Only Memory)   A type of nonvolatile semiconductor memory device that allows erasure and reprogramming from within a computer using special circuitry. These devices allow specific memory cells to be manipulated, rather than requiring a complete reprogramming procedure as in the case with EPROMs.

EGA (Enhanced Graphics Adapter)   The IBM video display standard providing medium-resolution text and graphics and requiring a digital RGB enhanced color display monitor. This standard has been superseded by VGA.

EIA (Electronics Industries Association)   An organization, founded in 1924, made up of electronic parts and systems manufacturers. It sets electrical and electronic interface standards, such as the RS-232C.

EISA (Extended Industry Standard Architecture)   A PC bus standard that extends the AT bus architecture to 32 bits and allows older PC and AT boards to plug into its slot. It was announced in 1988 as an alternative to the IBM Micro Channel.

electron beam   A continuous stream of electrons specifically directed toward a receiving target.

electron gun   The device by which the fine beam of electrons is created that sweeps across the phosphor screen in a CRT.

EMI (electromagnetic interference)   A system-disrupting electronic radiation created by other electronic devices. The FCC sets allowable limits for EMI in Part 5 of its Rules and Regulations. Part A systems are designed for office and plant environments, and Part B systems are designed for home use.

EMM (Expanded Memory Manager)   Any software driver that permits and manages the use of expanded memory in 80386 and higher machines.

EMS (Expanded Memory Specification)   A method of using memory above one megabyte on computers using DOS. Codeveloped by Lotus, Intel, and Microsoft, each upgrade has allowed more memory to be used. EMS is dictated by the specific application using it. In 80286 machines, EMS is installed on an adapter card and managed by an EMS driver. See *EMM*.

EOP (End OPeration)   A control line activated by an I/O device to indicate the termination of a DMA transfer.

EPROM (Erasable Programmable Read-Only Memory)   A type of nonvolatile semiconductor memory device that can be programmed more than once. Selected cells are charged using a comparatively high voltage. EPROM's can be erased by exposure to a source of strong ultraviolet light, at which point they must be completely reprogrammed.

ergonomics   The study of people-to-machine relationships. A device is considered to be ergonomic when it blends smoothly with a person's body actions.

error checking   The act of testing the data transfer in a computer system or network for accuracy.

escape character   Used in conjunction with other codes to perform specific actions. It is a control code with a numeric value of 27 in ASCII.

Esc key (Escape key)   The keyboard key used to cancel an application operation or exit some routine.

ESDI (Enhanced Small Device Interface)   A hardware interface standard for connecting disk and tape drives to computers, allowing these devices to hold up to 1 GB of data with a transfer rate between one to three megabytes per second.

execution cycle   The second part of a two-step process that occurs repeatedly until a program is completely executed by the computer. During an execution cycle, the instruction, which was fetched, decoded, and identified during the instruction cycle, is carried out. Another instruction cycle is entered immediately after an execution cycle, unless the current execution cycle is the last one.

execution time   The time required for a computer to execute a single instruction and making up the last half of an instruction cycle.

expansion slot   The receptacle mounted on the system board into which adapter cards are plugged into in order to achieve system expansion. The receptacle interfaces with the I/O channel and system bus; therefore, the number of slots available determines the expansion potential of the system.

extended memory   The memory above 1 MB in Intel 80286 and higher computers, and used for RAM disks, disk caching routines, and for locating the operating system files in recent versions of Microsoft DOS.

external command   A DOS command that requires the loading of its COM or EXE file prior to its execution.

F

FAT (File Allocation Table)   The part of the DOS file system that keeps track of where specific data is stored on the disk.

FDC (Floppy Disk Controller)   A specialized IC that provides an intelligent interface between the system unit and the disk-drive unit.

FDISK command   The DOS utility program that permits the partitioning of the hard disk into several independent disks.

FDM (Frequency Division Multiplexing)   A widely used data transmission method used to send multiple signals over a single channel. Each signal is modulated onto a separate carrier.

FIFO (First In First Out)   A data storage method that retrieves the data that has been stored for the longest time.

file   Any program, record, table, or document that is stored under its own filename.

filename   A name created by the user or programmer to identify a file. It must adhere to specific operating system rules for naming a file.

firmware   A term used to describe the situation in which programs (software) are stored in ROM ICs (hardware) on a permanent basis.

floppy disk   Sometimes called a diskette, it is a removable secondary storage medium for computers, composed of flexible magnetic material and contained in a square envelope or cartridge. A floppy disk can be recorded and erased hundreds of times.

FM (Frequency Modulation)   (1) A method of data transmission that modulates the data into a carrier by varying the carrier frequency. (2) A method of recording data onto magnetic medium using one clock bit with each bit of data recorded.

font   One set of alphanumeric characters possessing matching design characteristics, such as typeface, orientation, spacing, pitch, point size, style, and stroke weight.

form feed   The moving of the next paper form into the proper print position, accomplished either by pressing the form feed (FF) button on the printer or by sending the printer the ASCII form feed character.

FORMAT command   A Microsoft DOS utility that prepares a disk for use by the system. Track and sector information is placed on the disk while bad areas are marked so that no data will be recorded there.

formatting   The act of preparing a hard or floppy disk by using the FORMAT command.

frame   One screen of computer graphics data or the amount of memory required to store it.

FRU (Field Replaceable Unit)   The portions of the system that can be conveniently replaced in the field.

FSK (Frequency Shift Keying)   A simple, data transmission modulating technique that uses only two frequencies, one for a logic 1, and the other for a logic 0.

full-duplex   A method of data transmission that allows data flow in both directions simultaneously.

function keys   A set of keyboard keys used to give the computer special commands. They are frequently used in combination with other keys and can have different uses depending on the software application being run.

G

gap   (1) The space between the blocks of data on disk or tape. (2) The space in the R/W head over which magnetic flux passes when data transfer occurs.

GHz (GigaHertZ)   One billion hertz, or cycles per second.

graphics   The creation and management of pictures using a computer.

graphics controller   The portion of the VGA video controller that supplies an interface between the video memory and the attribute controller during active display periods. It also acts as an interface between the system and the video memory when the display is being updated. See *attribute controller*.

ground   (1) Any point from which electrical measurements are referenced. (2) Earth ground is considered to be an electrical reference point of absolute zero and is used as the electrical return path for modern power transmission systems. This ground, often incorporated by electronic devices to guard against fatal shock, is called chassis or protective ground. (3) An actual conductor in an electronic circuit being used as a return path, alternately called a signal ground.

GUI (graphical user interface)   A form of operating environment that uses a graphical display to represent procedures and programs that can be executed by the computer.

H

handset   The speaker and microphone portion of the telephone.

handshaking   A system of signal exchanges conducted between the computer system and a peripheral device during the data transfer process. Their purpose is to produce as orderly a flow of data as possible.

hard disk   A metal disk for external storage purposes, coated with ferromagnetic coating and available in both fixed and removable format.

hardware   Any aspect of the computer operation that can be physically touched. This includes IC chips, circuit boards, cables, connectors, and peripherals.

hexadecimal (hex)   Meaning sixteen; a numbering system with a base of sixteen. It provides a quick shorthand method of representing all the possible values of a byte. Each nibble (four bits) represents one hex digit. The hex digits themselves are composed consecutively of Arabic numerals 0 through 9, followed by uppercase letters A through F.

HGC (Hercules graphics card)   This is the monochrome graphics standard developed by Hercules Computer Technology to meet the needs of early PC users for graphics capabilities. Introduced in 1982, it provides a text and graphics resolution of 720x348 pixels.

high-level language   A programming language that is machine-independent, such as BASIC, COBOL, FORTRAN, Pascal, and C. When using a high-level language, the programmer can concentrate on the logic of the problem to be solved without having to be concerned about the specific architecture of the machine.

high resolution   A term used to describe a printer or display screen image of high quality. Actual quality depends of the number of dots used per square inch to create the image.

I

IC (integrated circuit)   The technical name for a chip. See *chip*.

IDE (Integrated Drive Electronics)   A method of disk drive manufacturing that locates all the required controller circuitry on the drive itself, rather than on a separate adapter card. Also known as AT Attachment interface.

impact printer   Any printer that produces a character image by hammering onto a combination of embossed character, ribbon, and paper.

ink-jet printer   A high-resolution printer that produces its image by spraying a specially treated ink onto the paper.

input device   Any computer input generating peripheral device, such as keyboard, mouse, light pen, scanner, or digitizer.

instruction cycle   The first part of a two-step process that occurs repeatedly until a program is completely executed by the computer. During an instruction cycle, an opcode is fetched, decoded, and identified.

instruction word   A class of binary coded data word that tells the computer what operation to perform and where to find any data needed to perform the operation.

intelligent controller   Usually an IC or a series of ICs with built-in microprocessor capabilities dedicated to the controlling of some peripheral unit or process. Single-chip controllers are sometimes referred to as smart chips.

interface   The joining of dissimilar devices so that they function in a compatible and complementary manner.

interlaced   The method of rewriting the monitor screen repeatedly by alternately scanning every other line and then the unscanned every other line.

INT (INTerrupt)   A signal sent to the microprocessor from an I/O device, that is capable of interrupting the microprocessor during program execution. An interrupt is usually generated when an input or output operation is required.

INTA (INTerrupt Acknowledge)   A signal sent on the control bus by the MPU to indicate that it has received an interrupt request.

Internet   The most famous wide area network is actually a network of networks networking together. The main communication path is a series of networks established by the U.S. government and has expanded around the world and offers access to computers in every part of the globe.

interrupt controller   A special programmable IC responsible for coordinating and prioritizing interrupt requests from I/O devices and sending the MPU the starting addresses of the interrupt service routines so that the MPU can service the interrupting device and then continue executing the active program.

interrupt vector   One of a possible 256 four-byte address pointers that reside in the first kilobyte of memory in a PC-based system. Each vector points to the location, in another area of memory, where a specific interrupt service routine is stored. These routines contain instructions for handling a wide variety of peripheral activities and internal system functions.

I/O (input/output)   A type of data transfer occurring between a CPU and a peripheral device. Whenever any data transfer occurs, output from one device becomes an input to another.

I/O channel   The actual high-speed pathway between the peripheral device and the computer.

I/O interface   The connecting channel between the CPU and a I/O device in a large computer. In a small computer, the interface also includes the interface controller and the connecting cable between the computer and the I/O device.

I/O port   The external window or connector on a computer, used to affect an interface with a peripheral device. The I/O port may appear as either parallel data connections or serial data connections.

IRQ (Interrupt ReQuest)   See *INT*.

ISA (Industry Standard Architecture)   A term that refers to the bus structures used in the IBM PC series of personal computers. The PC and XT uses an 8-bit bus; the AT uses a 16-bit bus.

ISPs (Internet service providers)   Companies that provide the technical gateway to the Internet. It connects all of the users and individual networks together.

J

joystick   A computer input device that offers quick, multidirectional movement of the cursor for CAD systems and video games.

jumper   Normally, a two- or four-pin BERG connector, located on the system board or an adapter card, which permits the attachment of a wired, hardware switch or the placement of a shorting bar to affect a particular hardware function or setting.

K

keyboard   The most familiar computer I/O device, incorporating a standard typewriter layout with the addition of other specialized control and function keys.

keyboard controller   Usually a dedicated MPU, located in the keyboard itself, that translates a key closure into the appropriate scan code.

L

laser printer   Any printer that utilizes the electrophotographic method of image transfer. Light dots are transferred to a photosensitive rotating drum, which picks up electrostatically charged toner before transferring it to the paper.

LCD (liquid crystal display)   The type of output display created by placing liquid crystal material between two sheets of glass. A set of electrodes is attached to each sheet of glass. Horizontal (row) electrodes are attached to one glass plate, while vertical (column) electrodes are fitted to the other plate. These electrodes are transparent and let light pass through. A pixel is created in the liquid crystal material at each spot where a row and a column electrode intersect. When the pixel is energized, the liquid crystal material bends and prevents light from passing through the display.

LED (light emitting diode)   A particular type of diode that emits light when conducting and is used in computers and disk drives as active circuit indicators.

letter quality   Refers to a print quality as good or better than that provided by an electric typewriter.

light pen   An I/O device meant to be used in conjunction with a video terminal in the selection of items from a screen menu or the drawing of images directly. The pen, when activated by the user, senses the scanning CRT electron beam during screen refresh, and thereby is able to tell the system its on-screen location.

line feed   This is a character control code (LF) used to kick the printer down to the next line or to move the screen cursor down to the next line. Some printers have a line feed button that accomplishes the same action.

line printer   An expensive and high-speed printer characterized by its capability to print a line of text all at once.

loopback   A modem test procedure that allows a transmitted signal to be returned to its source for comparison with the original data.

low-level format   The procedure that initializes a harddisk drive according to a sector layout plan dictated by its controller.

low resolution   A term used to describe a printer or display screen image of low quality, due to the limited number of dots used per square inch to create the image.

LPT1   The label used in Microsoft DOS versions assigned to parallel port 1, usually reserved for printer operation.

LSB (Least Significant Bit)   The bit occupying the rightmost position in the byte or word.

LSI (Large Scale Integration)   IC devices containing a large number of electronic components (from 3,000 to 100,000, approximately).

luminance   A screen pixel's degree of brightness, measured in lumens.

M

machine instruction   Any instruction that requires no further translation in order for the computer to carry it out. It is composed of an op code and any number of operands.

magnetic disk   The most popular form of secondary data storage for computers. Shaped like a platter and coated with an electromagnetic material, magnetic disks provide direct access to large amounts of stored data and can be erased and rerecorded many times.

magnetic tape   The most popular form of secondary data storage backup for computers. Because access to data is sequential in nature, magnetic tape is primarily used to restore a system that has suffered a catastrophic loss of data from its hard-disk drive.

maskable interrupts   A specific class of interrupts which the computer can ignore under certain conditions. See *interrupt mask*.

MCA (Micro Channel Architecture)   The 32-bit bus introduced by IBM on the high end of its PS/2 line of computers. MCA is totally incompatible with the original PC bus.

MDA (Monochrome Display Adapter)   The original video display standard introduced in the IBM PC line, having only monochrome text capabilities (no graphics).

memory management   Methodology used in handling a computer's memory resources, including bank switching, memory protection, and virtual memory.

memory map   A layout of the memory or I/O device addressing scheme used by a particular computer system.

memory-mapped I/O   An I/O addressing method where I/O devices are granted a portion of the available address allocations, thus requiring no additional control lines to implement.

memory unit   The section of the digital computer where instructions and data to be used by the computer are stored. Volatile memory that interfaces directly with the MPU is called internal memory, while nonvolatile memory stored on peripheral devices is called external memory. See *primary memory* and *secondary memory*.

menu   A screen display of available program options or commands that can be selected through keyboard or mouse action.

MFM (Modified Frequency Modulation)   An improvement over early FM magnetic disk recording techniques that reduces the number of required synchronization bits.

MGA (Monochrome Graphics Adapter)   The Hercules-compatible adapter card containing output connectors for both a monochrome monitor and a parallel printer.

MHz (MegaHertZ)   One million hertz, or cycles per second.

microcomputer   Meaning the same thing as a personal computer or a computer using an MPU as its CPU.

M/IO card (multi-input/output card)   The I/O adapter card that contains a floppy disk controller capable of running two floppy drives, two serial ports, one parallel printer port, one game port, and a clock/calendar circuit.

modem (MOdulator-DEModulator)   Also called a DCE device, it is used to interface a computer or terminal to the telephone system for the purpose of conducting data communications between computers often located at great distances from each other.

monitor   (1) Another name for a computer display. (2) Any hardware device or software program that checks, reports about, or automatically oversees a running program or system.

monochrome   Used to describe a computer display capable of operating with only one foreground and one background color.

MOS (Metal Oxide Semiconductor)   A category of logic and memory chip design that derives its name from the use of metal, oxide, and semiconductor layers. Among the various families of MOS devices are PMOS, NMOS, and CMOS. The first letter of each family denotes the type of construction used to fabricate the chip's circuits. MOS families do not require a highly regulated +5V DC power supply, like TTL devices do.

mouse   A popular computer I/O device used to point or draw on the video monitor by rolling it along a desktop as the cursor moves on the screen in a corresponding manner.

MSB (Most Significant Bit)   The bit occupying the leftmost position in the byte or word.

MSI (Medium Scale Integration)   IC devices containing a small number of electronic components (from 100 to 3,000, approximately). These ICs include the digital logic circuits such as multiplexers, demultiplexers, and decoders.

MTBF (Mean Time Between Failures)   Corresponds to the average working time for a component before failure occurs. It is equal to the total number of hours tested divided by the total number of failures.

multimedia   A term applied to a range of applications that bring together text, graphics, video, audio, and animation to provide interactivity between the computer and its human operator.

multitasking   The capability of a computer system to run two or more programs simultaneously.

MUX (multiplexer)   A device that accepts many different digital logic input signals and passes only one at a time to its single output line. It is also known as a data selector.

N

NAK (Negative ACKnowledge)   A data communications code used by a receiver to tell the transmitter that the last message was not properly received.

nibble   A four-bit binary pattern that can easily be converted to a single hexadecimal digit.

NLQ (Near Letter Quality)   A quality of printing nearly as good as an electric typewriter. The very best dot matrix printers can produce NLQ.

NMI (nonmaskable interrupt)   A type of interrupt that cannot be ignored by the MPU during program execution. Three things can cause a nonmaskable interrupt. (1) A numeric coprocessor installation error. (2) A RAM parity check error. (3) An I/O channel check error.

nonimpact printer   Any printer that does not form its characters by using a hammer device to impact the paper, ribbon, or embossed character.

nonvolatile memory   Memory, such as ROM, that is not lost after the power is turned off.

NOP (No OPeration)   A machine code instruction used to take one byte of memory when contained in a program or to waste some execution time during certain operations such as HALT DMA mode data transfers. Although the MPU is idling, it does get to refresh its memory in order to prevent a system crash during the DMA operation. See *HALT DMA*.

NTSC (National Television Standards Committee)   This organization created the television standards in the United States and is administered by the FCC.

NuBus   A type of expansion slot bus that is a Texas Instruments specification. It uses intelligent cards that communicate with the system during startup to determine what type of card is in the slot.

null modem cable   A cable meeting the RS-232C specification, used to cross-connect two computers through their serial ports by transposing the transmit and receive lines. The computers must be located close together, eliminating the need for a modem.

O

octal   A method of representing binary numbers by grouping them into three-bit patterns. Because this system uses a base of 8, the highest digit that can be represented is a 7, or 111 in binary.

odd parity   The form of parity checking where the parity bit is used in order to make the total number of ones contained in the character an odd number.

off-hook   A condition existing on a telephone line that is now capable of initiating an outgoing call, but unable to receive an incoming call.

offline   Any computer system or peripheral device that is not ready to operate, not connected, not turned on, or not properly configured.

on-hook   A condition that exists on any telephone line that is capable of receiving an incoming call.

online   Any computer system or peripheral device that is not only powered up, but is also ready to operate.

op code (OPeration Code)   The part of an instruction word telling the computer what to do. The operation code is usually a verb, such as input, add, or branch.

operand   The data upon which the given operation is to be carried out. Can also refer to a specific peripheral device for I/O operations.

operand address   The data containing the memory address where the operand is located.

operating system   A special software program, first loaded into a computer at power up and responsible for running it. The operating system also serves as the interface between the machine and other software applications.

optical mouse   A mouse that emits an infrared light stream to detect motion as it is moved around a special x-y matrix pad.

output device   Any peripheral device, such as a monitor, modem or printer, that accepts computer output.

P

page printer   Any printer capable of printing a page at a time, such as a laser printer.

parallel interface   The multiline channel through which the simultaneous transfer of one or more bytes occurs.

parallel mode   The mode of data transfer where an entire word is transferred at once, from one location to another, by a set of parallel conductors.

parallel port   The external connector on a computer that is used to affect an interface between the computer and a parallel peripheral, such as a printer.

parity bit   Used for error checking during the sending and receiving of data within a system and from one system to another. The parity bit's value depends on how many 1 bits are contained in the byte it accompanies. See *even parity* and *odd parity*.

parity checking   A method to check for data transmission errors by using a ninth bit to ensure that each character sent has an even (even parity) or odd (odd parity) number of logic 1s before transfer. The parity bit is checked for each byte sent.

parity error   This error occurs when a data transfer cannot be verified for integrity. At least one data bit or the parity bit has toggled during the transfer process.

PC bus   Refers to the bus architectures used in the first IBM PCs, the original 8-bit bus, and the 16-bit bus extension used with the AT.

PCI (Peripheral Component Interconnect) bus   A low-cost, high-performance 32-/64-bit local bus developed jointly by IBM, Intel, DEC, NCR, and Compaq.

PDS (Processor Direct Slot) bus   The various PDS slots consist of between 90 and 140 pins. The PDS bus goes directly into the microprocessor's address, data, and control buses without any buffering. It is a very fast

expansion slot. It is not standardized between different MAC models.

peer-to-peer network   Each computer is attached to the network in a ring or bus fashion to control the network.

pel (Picture ELement)   See *pixel*.

peripherals   Also called I/O devices, these units include secondary memory devices such as hard-disk drives, floppy-disk drives, magnetic-tape drives, modems, monitors, mice, joysticks, light pens, scanners, and even speakers.

peripheral controller   A dedicated IC or circuit that interprets system commands to its unit and sends it the required control signals.

persistence   The amount of time that a CRT phosphor dot continues to emit light after being struck by an electron beam.

pin feed   A method of moving continuous forms through the print area of a printer by mounting pins on each side of a motorized platen to engage the holes on the right and left side of the paper.

PISO (Parallel In Serial Out)   Refers to a type of shift register that loads a parallel word in a single clock pulse. After the word has been loaded into the register, the bits are shifted out, one clock pulse per bit.

pitch   A unit of measurement for print type, it lists the number of characters per inch.

pixel   Also called a pel, or picture element, it is the smallest unit (one dot for monochrome) into which a display image can be divided.

pointing device   Any input device used for the specific purpose of moving the screen cursor or drawing an image.

polarizer   An optical device that will either block or allow the passage of light through it depending upon the polarity of an electrical charge applied to it.

polling   A system of initiating data transfer between a computer system and a peripheral, where the status of all the peripherals is examined periodically under software program control by having the MPU check the READY line. When it is activated by one of the peripherals, the

MPU will begin the data transfer using the corresponding I/O port.

POST (Power-On Self-Tests)   A group of ROM BIOS diagnostic tests that are performed on the system each time it is powered up.

power supply   The component in the system that converts the alternating current voltage from the wall outlet to the direct current voltages required by the computer circuitry.

preventive maintenance   Any regularly scheduled checking and testing of hardware and software with the goal of avoiding future failure or breakdown.

printer   A peripheral device for the printing of computer text or graphics output.

printer buffer   A special-purpose memory area or device that accepts high-speed transfer of print data from the computer and transfers the data to the printer at printer-compatible speeds, freeing the computer for other tasks during the printing process.

printer font   A prescribed character set properly formatted for use by the printer.

program   Any group of instructions designed to command a computer system through the performance of a specific task. Also called *software*.

programmed I/O   A system of initiating data transfer between a computer system and a peripheral, where the MPU alerts the specific device by using an address call. The I/O device can signal its readiness to accept the data transfer by using its BUSY line. If BUSY is active, the MPU can perform other tasks until the BUSY line is deactivated, such as which time the transfer can begin.

programming language   Any one of a number of languages used to write computer instructions in symbolic form, without regard to a machine's specific hardware makeup.

prompt   A software-supplied message to the user, requiring some specific action or providing some important information. It can also be a very simple symbol, indicating that the program is successfully loaded and waiting for a command from the user.

protected mode   An operational state that allows an 80286 or higher computer to address all of its memory.

protocol   A set of rules that govern the transmitting and receiving of data communications.

PSK (Phase Shift Keying)   A method of modulation in modems through which the phase of the signal is altered to reflect the transmission of 0s and 1s. See *DPSK*.

Q

QAM (Quadrature Amplitude Modulation)   A data communication transmission method, combining both AM and PSK modulation techniques, that provides for much higher bit transfer rates than using either system alone.

queue   A special and temporary storage (RAM or registers) area for data in printing or internal program execution operations.

QWERTY keyboard   A keyboard layout that was originally designed to prevent typists from jamming old-style mechanical typewriters, it is still the standard English language keyboard. The name spells out the first six leftmost letters in the first alphabetic row of keys.

R

RAM (random access memory)   A type of semiconductor memory device that holds data on a temporary or volatile basis. Any address location in the RAM memory section can be accessed as fast as any other location.

RAMDAC   A section of the VGA video controller circuitry that contains the RAM color palette and three DACs. The DACs translate the coded digital values stored in the color palette into corresponding analog output levels. These voltage levels drive the CRT's electron guns to produce a corresponding color using a mixture of red, green, and blue. When the red, green, and blue signals are combined, each color produced on the screen relates to an 18-bit value. This produces a maximum of 262,144 (2^{18}) or 256K colors.

raster graphics   A graphics representation method that uses a dot matrix to compose the image.

raster scan   The display of a video image, line by line, by an electron beam deflection system.

read Any act of inputting prerecorded digital data, whether it be on disk or tape, or in ROM or RAM.

read only (1) A file parameter setting that prevents a file from being altered. (2) Refers to data that is permanently stored on the media or to such media itself.

Ready A control bus signal line, used by an I/O device, to cause the microprocessor to suspend its internal operations, temporarily, until it's prepared to engage in data transfer.

read/write head Usually abbreviated "R/W" head, the device by which a disk or tape drive senses and records digital data on the magnetic medium.

real mode A mode of operation in 80286 and higher machines in which the computer functions under the same command and addresses restrictions as an 8086 or 8088.

reboot To restart the computer or to reload the operating system.

refresh A required method of re-energizing a memory cell or display pixel in order for its data to be held continually.

RESET A control bus signal, activated either by a soft or hard switch, which sets the system MPU and all programmable system devices to their startup, or initialization, values. This allows the computer to begin operation following the application of the RESET input signal.

resolution A measurement of the sharpness of an image or character, either of a printer or a display monitor. For a monitor, resolution consists of the number of dots per scan line times the number of scans per picture. For a printer, resolution consists of the number of dots present per linear inch of print space.

reverse video A method commonly used to highlight specific screen characters by reversing their foreground and background colors.

RGB monitor Any video display, either analog or digital, requiring separate red, green, and blue input signals from the computer.

RLL (Run Length Limited) An improvement over the MFM magnetic disk encoding technique, allowing more data to be packed into the same space.

ROM (read-only memory) A type of semiconductor memory device that holds data on a permanent or non-volatile basis.

ROM BIOS A collection of special programs (native intelligence) permanently stored in one or two ROM ICs installed on the system board. These programs are available to the system as soon as it is powered up, providing for initialization of smart chips, POST tests, and data transfer control.

RS-232C The most widely used serial interface standard, it calls for a 25-pin D-type connector. Specific pins are designated for data transmission and receiving, as well as a number of handshaking and control lines. Logic voltage levels are also established for the data and the control signals on the pins of the connector.

RS-422 An enhancement to the original RS-232C interface standard and adopted by the EIA, it uses twisted-pair transmission lines and differential line voltage signals resulting in higher immunity for the transmitted data.

RS-423 Another enhancement to the original RS-232C interface standard and adopted by the EIA, it uses coaxial cable to provide extended transmission distances and higher data transfer rates.

RTS (Request To Send) The RS-232 handshaking signal sent from the originating modem to the receiving modem requesting permission to begin the data transmission.

S

scan code A code supplied by the keyboard MPU that corresponds to a keypress from the keyboard.

scan rate The total number of times per second that a video raster is horizontally scanned by the CRTs electron beam.

SCSI (Small Computer System Interface) bus Apple was the first personal computer maker to select the SCSI interface as the bus standard for peripheral equipment. The Macintosh's SCSI port can be daisy-chained to allow it to connect up to six external peripherals to the system. Even though there are a total of eight possible SCSI device address numbers, only six are available for external devices.

SCSI (Small Computer System Interface) An interface standard adapter card for PCs that can provide high-speed data transfer control (4MB/sec) for up to seven devices, while occupying only one expansion slot.

sector   One of many individual data-holding areas into which each track of a disk is divided during the format process.

sector interleave   A method by which a disk drive's read and write operations can be optimized. The interleave number indicates the order in which the sectors will contain the data pertaining to the same file.

seek time   The amount of time required for a drive's R/W head to settle over a particular disk track following an I/O command.

sequential access   A data access method in which all data, existing in the media ahead of the desired data, must be sequentially checked and identified.

serial interface   A channel through which serial digital data transfer occurs. Although multiple lines may be used, only one of these will actually carry the data. The most popular serial interface standard is the EIA RS-232C.

serial mode   The mode of data transfer where the word bits are transferred one bit at a time, along a single conductor.

serial mouse   A type of mouse that plugs into a serial port rather than an adapter card.

serial port   The external connector on a computer that is used to effect an interface between the computer and a serial device, such as a modem. A typical serial port uses a DB-25 or a DB-9 connector.

serial transmission   The transmission of data one bit at a time, one bit following the next.

shadow RAM   An area of RAM used for copying the system's BIOS routines from ROM. Making BIOS calls from the RAM area improves the operating speed of the system. Video ROM routines are often stored in shadow RAM also.

SIMM (Single In-line Memory Module)   A memory chip, circuit board module, containing eight (without parity) or nine (with parity) memory chips and designed to plug into special sockets.

simplex   A term used to describe one-way data transmission.

SIPO (Serial In Parallel Out)   Refers to a type of shift register that loads in a serial word, one bit per clock pulse. After the bits have been loaded into the register, they are immediately available to the system and might require tri-state buffering to isolate them from the data bus.

soft sectored   A type of storage disk noted for its programmed method of sector identification.

software   Any aspect of the computer operation that cannot be physically touched. This includes bits, bytes, words, and programs.

software interrupt   Any interrupt caused by a program instruction. See *interrupt*.

speaker   The computer system's audio output device. Measuring 2-1/4 inches in diameter and rated at 8 ohms, 1/2 Watts, the speaker is usually used as a system prompt and as an error indicator. It is also capable of producing arcade sounds, speech, and music.

spindle   The center spinning shaft in a disk drive unit that fits through and grasps the disks during drive operation.

SRAM (static random access memory)   A type of RAM that can store its data indefinitely as long as power to it is not interrupted.

SSI (Small Scale Integration)   IC devices containing a very small number of electronic components (from 2 to 100, approximately). These ICs include the basic digital logic gates, such as AND, OR, NAND, NOR, and INVERTER circuits.

ST506   For hard-disk drives up to 40MB, this hard-disk controller for PCs uses MFM encoding techniques with data transfer rates of 500Kbps.

ST506 RLL (ST506 Run-Length Limited)   An improved version of the ST 506 hard-disk controller for PCs, allowing the use of higher-capacity disks and transfer rates of 750Kbps.

stack   A special memory storage area that is used to keep track of internal program operations during interrupt requests, or when the program being executed contains calls or subroutines that jump to nonsequential memory locations. The address information, needed to return to the proper point in the program after the subroutine, is contained in the stack. The stack operates on a LIFO (Last In First Out) basis; the last address pushed onto the stack is the first address popped off.

stack pointer   A special memory address register used in the operation of the stack memory area to record the location of the next push or pull operation. See *stack*.

start bit   In asynchronous serial data transmission, this bit denotes the beginning of a character and is always a logic low pulse, or space.

static electricity   Can be a serious problem in environments of low-humidity, a stationary charge of electricity normally caused by friction, and potentially very damaging to sensitive electronic components.

stepper motor   A special class of motor used in disk-drive access arms and dot matrix print head mechanisms. Very precise movements are obtained by applying voltage pulses, one pulse per step, to the motor control circuitry.

stop bit   The bit sent after each character in an asynchronous data communications transmission that signals the end of a character.

sync character   A character that is transmitted in synchronous data communications to synchronize the timing between the transmitter and receiver.

synchronous transmission   A method of serial data transmission in which both the transmitter and the receiver are synchronized by a common clock signal.

system board   The large printed circuit board (mother board) into which peripheral adapter boards (daughter boards) may plug into, depending on the number of devices working with the system. The system board is populated with 100 or more IC chips, depending on how much onboard memory is installed. Besides RAM chips, the system board contains the MPU, BIOS ROM, several programmable controllers, system clock circuitry, switches, and various jumpers. Also, most system boards come with an empty socket into which the user may plug a compatible coprocessor chip to give the computer some high-level number crunching capabilities.

system-level interface   An interface that allows the system to directly access the I/O device through an expansion slot without an intermediate interface circuit. The system is isolated from the peripheral device and only sees its logical configuration.

system software   A class of software dedicated to the smooth control and operation of a computer system and its various peripherals.

system unit   The main computer cabinet housing containing the primary components of the system. This includes the main logic board (system or mother board), disk drive(s), switching power supply, and the interconnecting wires and cables.

T

tape drive   The unit that actually reads, writes, and holds the tape being used for backup purposes.

task switching   The changing of one program or application to another, either manually by the user or under the direction of a multitasking operating system environment.

TDM (Time Division Multiplexing)   A method of sending many individual digital data signals over one high-speed data channel by sharing the amount of time allotted to each signal sequentially.

text mode   Refers to a screen display mode that displays only text (no graphics) or to any application mode allowing the entry and editing of text.

thermal printer   A printer requiring the use of specially treated paper and electrically heated print pins, which are selectively pushed against the paper to produce areas of darkness at the contact points. A thermal printer is considered a nonimpact type and is very quiet, producing a print image that is of medium to low resolution.

toner   A form of powdered ink that accepts an electrical charge in laser printers and photocopying machines. It adheres to a rotating drum containing an image that has been oppositely charged. The image is transferred to the paper during the printing process.

track   A single disk or tape data storage channel on which the R/W head places the digital data in a series of flux reversals. On disks, the track is a concentric data circle, whereas on tapes, it is a parallel data line.

track ball (1) A pointing device that enables the user to control the position of the cursor on the video display screen by rotating a sphere (ball). (2) The sphere inside certain types of mice that the mouse rides on. As the mouse moves across a surface, the trackball rolls, creating xy movement data.

tractor feed A paper-feeding mechanism for printers that use continuous forms. The left and right edges of the forms contain holes by which the tractor pins pull the paper through the print area.

transceiver A device capable of both transmitting and receiving analog or digital signals. In computers, an example of a transceiver is the 74LS245 digital octal transceiver IC.

transmit Although this term usually means to send data between a transmitter and receiver over a specific communications line, it can also describe the transfer of data within the internal buses of a computer or between the computer and its peripheral devices.

U

UART (Universal Asynchronous Receiver Transmitter) A serial interface IC used to provide for the parallel-to-serial and serial-to-parallel conversions required for asynchronous serial data transmission. It also handles the parallel interface to the computer's bus, as well as the control functions associated with the transmission.

URL (Universal Resource Locator) A unique address on the World Wide Web used to access a Web site.

USART (Universal Synchronous Asynchronous Receiver Transmitter) A serial interface IC used to provide for the parallel-to-serial and serial-to-parallel conversions required for both asynchronous and synchronous serial data transmission. It also handles the parallel interface to the computer's bus, as well as the control functions associated with the transmission.

USRT (Universal Synchronous Receiver Transmitter) A serial interface IC used to provide for the parallel-to-serial and serial-to-parallel conversions required for synchronous serial data transmission only.

utility program A term used to describe a program designed to help the user in the operation of the computer.

V

vertical refresh A rate or frequency per second during which the entire display screen is rewritten.

VESA (Video Electronics Standards Association) bus A 64-bit local bus standard developed to provide a local bus connection to a video adapter. Its operation has been defined for use by other adapter types, such as drive controllers, network interfaces, and other hardware.

VGA (Video Graphics Array) Another video standard, developed by IBM, providing medium and high text and graphics resolution. It was originally designed for IBM's high-end PS/2 line, but other vendors have created matching boards for PC and AT machines also, making it the preferred standard at this time. Requiring an analog monitor, it originally provided 16 colors at 640x480 resolution. Third-party vendors have boosted that capability to 256 colors, while adding an even greater 800x600 resolution, calling it Super VGA.

video adapter Sometimes referred to as a display adapter, graphics adapter or graphics card, it is a plug-in peripheral unit for computers, fitting in one of the system board option slots and providing the interface between the computer and the display. The adapter usually must match the type of display (digital or analog) it is used with.

video capture Software is used to capture frames of television video and convert it into digital formats that can be processed by the computer.

virtual disk A method of using RAM as if it were a disk.

virtual memory A memory technique that allows several programs to run simultaneously even though the system does not have enough actual memory installed to do this. The extra memory is simulated.

VLSI (Very Large Scale Integration) IC devices containing a very large number of electronic components (from 100,000 to 1,000,000, approximately).

volatile memory Memory (RAM) that loses its contents as soon as power is discontinued.

VOM (Volt Ohm Milliammeter) A basic piece of electronic troubleshooting equipment that provides for circuit measurements of voltage, current, and resistance in logarithmic analog read-out form.

W

wait state   A machine cycle in which the MPU is marking time, usually waiting for an I/O device to ready itself, or for the last instruction to be executed and a new instruction to be loaded.

warm boot   Booting a computer that has already been powered up.

Windows   A graphical user interface from Microsoft Corporation. It uses a graphical display to represent procedures and programs that can be executed by the computer. Multiple programs can run at the same time.

word   Refers to the amount of data that can be held in a computer's registers during a process and is considered to be the computer's basic storage unit.

word length   The major determining factor when considering the power of a given computer, because its internal hardware is chosen to conduct operations on data units composed of a specific number of bits. The larger the word length, the more data a machine can be expected to process per unit of time.

write   Any act of recording digital data, whether it be on disk or tape, or in ROM or RAM.

write gap   A slot in the R/W head across which the flux travels into the disk or tape media, from the head, during write operations.

X

x-axis   (1) In a two-dimensional matrix, the horizontal row/rows such as on an oscilloscope screen. (2) The dimension of width in a graphics representation.

Xmodem   A very early and simple asynchronous data communications protocol developed for personal computers and capable of detecting some transfer errors, but not all.

Xon-Xoff   An asynchronous data communications protocol that provides for synchronization between the receiver and transmitter, requiring the receiver to indicate its capability to accept data by sending either an Xon (transmit on-buffer ready) or Xoff (transmit off-buffer full) signal to the transmitter.

x-y matrix   Any two-dimensional form or image, where x represents width and y represents height.

Y

y-axis   (1) In a two-dimensional matrix, the vertical column/columns such as on an oscilloscope screen. (2) The dimension of height in a graphics representation.

Z

zero wait state   Describes high-speed data transfer memory operations requiring absolutely no cycle delay whatsoever.

answering calls, modems, 574

anti-virus programs, 696

antistatic cleaning, 674

APIs (application programming interfaces), updating processors, 282

Apple systems, 56

applets, 618

applications

    DOS, 153

    multimedia, 626

    video capture, 658

    see also programs

Applications group, Windows 3.x, 187

aquadag coating, monitors, 490

AR register (Address Register), 22

arbitration, bus mastering, 308

Archie servers, 616

ArcNet, 596-598

    cabling specifications, 597

    frames, 597-598

ASCII code (American Standard Code for Information Interchange)

    control codes, 7-9

    converting to dot-matrix characters, 459

ASICs (Application Specific Integrated Circuits), 11, 86, 415

Assembly Language, 49

asterisk wild card, 160

asynchronous

    SRAM, 298

    transmissions

        modems, 565

        serial ports, 344

AT (Advanced Technology), 57

    command set, 579-584

    see also IBM PC-AT

ATA interface, IDE hard drives, 431

ATAPI (AT Attachment Packet Interface), 432, 639

Atari PCs, 56

ATTRIB command, DOS, 159

attribute byte, CRTs, 461

attribute controller, video controllers, 478

attributes, DOS files, 152

ATX system boards, 263

audio, 646

    CD quality audio signal, 647

    digitizing, 629, 646

    drivers, 648

    fidelity, 646

    files, 627

    MIDI, 627, 649-650

    multimedia, 646

    output devices, 91

    resolution, 646

    Sound Recorder, 628

    speakers, 651

    synthesized sound files, 649

    Windows 95, 630

authoring systems for multimedia, 627, 630-631

Auto Feed line, parallel printer ports, 339

Auto-configuration mode, BIOS, 141

auto-dialing modems, 565

AUTOEXEC.BAT file, 161, 172

automatically starting Windows 85 programs, 222

auxiliary clock signals, system boards, 285

auxiliary video extension, MCA bus, 309

AVI files (Audio Visual Interface), 626, 629

Award BIOS, 138

B

B channels (ISDN), 615

BA signal (buses available), processors, 31

Baby ATs, 61, 261

back-lighting, LCDs, 498

backbone of Internet, 611

backplanes, 61

BACKUP utility, 688

backups, 686

    hard drives, 688

    RAID systems, 690

    tape drives, 447, 691

backward compatibility, Windows 95, 221

band printers, 511

bandwidth, modems, 562

bank switching, 166

banks, RAM, 299

BAS extension, 154

Base Architecture registers, 80486 processors, 275

base memory, DOS, 163

Base Pointer register, 8088 processors, 266

Base-2 number system, 4

BASIC, 48

Basic Rate Interface (BRI) service, 615

BAT extension, 153

batch command, DOS test files, 110

Batch mode, single process operating systems, 131

crashes, hard disks, 408
CRC (cyclic redundancy checking), 446, 571
cross-linked files, 151
CRTC (cathode ray tube controller), 458, 478
CRT monitors (Cathode Ray Tube), 39, 93
  Alphanumeric Text mode, 461
  attribute byte, 461
  bitmapped graphics, 465
  block-graphics, 464
  CGA, 469
  character box, 461
  character lines, 460
  composite color monitors, 463
  controllers, 461
  EGA, 471-472
  HGA, 470
  inverse video display, 466
  MDA, 468
  paging, 466
  pixels, 463
  resolution, 463
  RGB color, 463
  screen
    attributes, 461
    data manipulation, 465
    memory, 461-462
  scrolling operations, 466
  shadow mask, 463
  socket board, 490
  Top Line Registers, 466
  troubleshooting, 482
  TTL-compatible monitors, 464
  VGA, 472
  XGA, 473
  see also monitors
CSMA/CD (Carrier Sense Multiple Access with Collision Detection), 593
Ctrl key, 93
CTS (Clear to Send) line, 568
[Current] section, CONTROL.INI file, 202
Current_User key, Registry, 229
cursor
  control keys, 93
  Windows 3.x, 185
[Custom Colors] section, CONTROL.INI file, 202
customer service skills, 707
  accountability, 711
  communication, 709-710
  establishing rapport, 708
  exam objectives, 726
  handling conflicts, 713

handling paperwork, 713
positive presence, 708
preparing for service calls, 708
proactivity, 709
professionalism, 712
responsiveness, 711
customizing
  Windows 3.x, 215
    desktop, 190
  Windows 95 desktop, 226
cycle stealing DMA mode, 31
Cyclic Redundancy Checks (CRCs), 571
cylinders, hard disks, 90, 405, 425
Cyrix
  486 processors, 277
  Pentium clone processors, 284

D

D channels (ISDN), 615-616
DACK signal (DMA acknowledge), 31
DACs (digital-to-analog Converters), VGA monitors, 472
daily maintenance, 703
daisy wheels (printers), 508
daisy-chaining SCSI ports, 434
data available strobe signal, parallel ports, 337
data bit entries, serial ports, 161
data bus, 20
data cable, ST-506/412 hard drives, 429
data collisions, 592
Data Communication Equipment (DCE), 566-567
data communications, *see* networks
data compression
  modems, 564-565
  see also compression
data field headers, magnetic disks, 405
data latch, parallel printer ports, 341
data register, FDC, 415
data restoration, 690
Data Segment register, 8088 processors, 266
Data Separator, FDC, 417
Data Set Ready (DSR) line, serial interfaces, 348
data start markers, magnetic disks, 413
Data Strobe line, parallel printer ports, 339
Data Terminal Equipment (DTE), 566-567
Data Terminal Ready (DTR) line, serial interfaces, 348, 568

Frequency Modulation data encoding, 407

Frequency-Shift Keying, *see* FSK modulation

friction feed (printers), 514, 526

front panel
> connectors, system boards, 77, 327
>
> PC case, 63

frozen system, *see* system lock ups, troubleshooting

FRUs (Field Replaceable Units)
> system boards, 320
>
> troubleshooting, 117

FSDs (file system drivers), Windows 95, 233

FSK modulation (frequency-shift keying), modems, 562-563

FTP (File Transfer Protocol), 616

full backups, 688

full cycle DMA stealing, 31

full-duplex mode modems, 561

full-height drive units, 63

full-screen mode, Windows 3.x, 205

full-size adapter cards, 85

fully formed characters (printers), 507-508

function keys, 93

fuses, troubleshooting, 103

fusing roller (laser printers), 544

G

games, 50
> interface, 350, 385
>
> joysticks, 387
>
> MI/O adapter card connections, 88
>
> ports, 87, 336
>
> paddles, 349, 383-385
>
> software interaction, 386
>
> sound cards, 648

Games group, Windows 3.x, 187

gamma correction, scanners, 394

gas plasma displays, 39, 498

gateways, Internet packet transmissions, 615

GDI files, Windows 95 install, 220, 228

general protection faults, Windows 3.x, 212

gigabytes, 37

gimbal, joysticks, 383-385

Gopher, 616

Grant line PCI local bus, 312

graphical interface managers, 184

graphical operating systems, 56

graphics
> bitmapped, 47, 465
>
> files, 516
>
> multimedia, 627
>
> pixels, 47
>
> programs, 47
>
> serializers, VGA monitors, 481
>
> vector images, 47
>
> video controllers, 478

graphics mode
> MDA monitors, 469
>
> VGA monitors, 480-481

grayscale scanners, 393, 396

Green Book CDs, 637

ground, 679

grounding straps, 677

group coded recording data encoding, 407

group coding techniques, data compression, 564

group files, Windows 3.x, 204

[Groups] section, PROGMAN.INI file, 204

GUI program, CheckIt diagnostic program, 114

GUIs (graphical user interfaces), 184

H

half-duplex mode modems, 561

Half-Height Adapter Cards, 85

half-height drive units, 63

half-size
> adapter cards, 85
>
> system boards, 262

halftone color, 537

hand-held scanners, 393

handles
> joysticks, *see* gimbal
>
> PnP, 313

handshakes
> data transfers, 28
>
> modems, 574

hang ups, Windows 3.x, 211

hard disks, 90
> clusters, 410
>
> crashes, 408
>
> cylinders, 90, 405
>
> data start markers, 413
>
> directories, 410
>
> end-of-file markers, 413
>
> formatting, 405, 426
>
> head-to-disk interference, 408

Hayes-compatible command set, 579-584

hazardous materials disposals, 707

HDCs (Hard Disk Drive Controllers), 87, 425

HDD controller cards, BIOS extensions, 136

HDI (head-to-disk interference), 408

head gap lever, printers, 530

head keys, Registry, 229

head locking lever, printers, 530

head-cleaning floppy disks, 698

heat build-up problems, 683

Help system, Windows 95, 225, 250

hexadecimal number system, 5

HGA monitors (Hercules Monochrome Graphics Adapter), 470

high logic levels, 4

high-level
> formatting, hard disks, 426
> programming languages, 48

high-speed printers, 511

HIMEM.SYS memory manager, 165, 170, 238

historical overview of PCs, 56

hits, cache, 297

HLDA signal (hold acknowledge), processors, 31

HMA (High Memory Area), 165, 215

HOLD input signal, DMA controllers, 30

home-position sensor, printers, 516

horizontal adjustments, monitors, 491

horizontal deflection, monitors, 495

horizontal synchronization, VGA monitors, 480

host adapters, hard drives
> IDE, 431
> SCSI, 433

host bridge, PCI local bus, 311

host controllers, USB, 358

hosts, USB, 358

hot insertion, PCMCIA slots, 318, 361

HTML (HyperText Markup Language), 618

HTTP (HyperText Transfer Protocol), 617

hubs
> ArcNet, 597
> Internet packet transmission, 614
> USB, 358

hyper page mode RAM, 299

hypermedia, 617

HyperText Markup Language, *see* HTML

HyperText Transfer Protocol, *see* HTTP

I

I/O (Input/Output), 25
> adapter cards, 61
> addressing
>> *direct I/O, 301*
>> *memory-mapping, 300*
>> *move instructions, 301*
>> *redundant, 302*
>> *scanners, 398*
>> *system boards, 300-301*
> connectors, ATX system board, 263
> devices, 27
>> *adapter cards, 33*
>> *DMA controllers, 30*
>> *see also peripherals*
> DOS commands, 160
> ports
>> *addresses, 302*
>> *testing, 110*
> transfers
>> *DMA, 293*
>> *processors, 27*

IBM
> 80386SLC processors, 273
> 80486SLC2 processors, 277
> parallel printer ports, 338-342
> PC, 56-57, 260
> PC-AT, 57, 261, 267
> PS/2, 58, 80
> TopView GUI, 184

icons, Windows 3.x, 185

ICs (Integrated Circuits), 11, 678
> cooler fans, 64
> extractors, 101
> replacing, 678

ID field headers, magnetic disks, 405

ID register (Instruction Register), 22

IDE (Integrated Drive Electronics), 429
> CD-ROM drives, 638
> hard drives, 427
>> *cable select pin, 432*
>> *host adapter, 431*
>> *specifications, 436*

Idle mode, DMA controllers, 293

IFS (Installable File System), 228, 233

Illegal Operation error messages, Windows 95, 249

impact printers, 506-507

Indeo data compression, 657

index hole, floppy disks, 34-36

Index register, 23

indicator lights, 63

.INI files

    keynames, 194

    Windows 3.x, 193-194

Initialize Printer line, parallel printer ports, 339

initializing hardware, 41

ink-jet printers, 533-540

    cartridges, 538

    components, 534

    configuration checks, 536-537

    continuous-stream method, 533

    hardware checks, 537-541, 546

    interrupted-stream method, 533

    landscape printing, 537

    maintenance, 702

    portrait printing, 537

    recycling ink cartridges, 706

    troubleshooting, 535-536

        ink cartridges, 538

        paper not advancing, 540

        power supply problems, 538, 546

        printhead, 539-540

input buffer, keyboard, 373

input devices, 59, 91

    alphanumeric keyboard, 362

    maintenance, 699

input/output devices, *see* I/O, devices

inspecting system when troubleshooting, 104

INSTALL command, DOS, 170

installation utilities, 169

[Installed] section, CONTROL.INI file, 203

installing

    CD-ROM drives, 641

    DOS, 175

        exam objectives, 729

    floppy drives, 420-421

    hard drives, 437

    LAN adapter cards, 602-603

    objectives of exam

        DOS, 719-720

        Windows, 729

    printers, 516-522

        drivers, 517

        serial printer problems, 518-520

        software/hardware handshaking, 519

        Windows 3.x, 520

        Windows 95, 521-522

    SCSI hard drives, 434

    sound cards, 647-648

    video capture cards, 659

    Windows 3.x, 186

    Windows 95, 216

        bootstrap process, 219

        Configuration Manager, 220

        DOS drivers/TSRs, 220

        GDI files, 220

        kernel files, 220

        logons, 221

        PnP devices, 220

        Program Manager, 217

        static VxDs, 220

        USER files, 220

instruction cycles, processors, 13, 24

Instruction Decoding Unit, 80286 processors, 268

instruction fetches, memory access, 298

instruction jumps, processors, 14

Instruction Pointer register, 8088 processors, 266

Instruction queue, Pentium Pro processor, 281

instruction sets

    processors, 14

    registers, 23

instruction words, 9

INT (Interrupt) signals, 29

INTA (Interrupt Acknowledge) signals, 29

INTE (Interrupt Enable) lines, peripherals, 30

Integrated Services Digital Network (ISDN), 610

Integrated Video Controller IC, VGA adapter cards, 86, 473

Intel processors

    80286, 57, 74, 267-269

    80386, 75, 269-271

    80386SL, 273

    80386SX, 75, 272

    80486, 75, 274-275

    80486DX2, 276

    80486DX4, 277

    80486SLC2, 277

    80486SX, 276

    8086, 74

    8088, 56, 74, 260-261, 264-266

    OverDrive processors, 284

    Pentium, 75, 277

        ATX system boards, 263

        clones, 284-285

    Pentium II, 282

    Pentium MMX, 279

    Pentium Pro, 280-281

    see also processors

intelligent keyboard controllers, 260, 372

intensity level, light pens, 390

Interactive mode, single process operating systems, 131

IVCs (Integrated Video Controllers), 475
    attribute controller, 478
    CRTCs, 478
    graphics controller, 478
    RAMDAC section, 476
    sequencer, 477
    Video BIOS section, 476

J

joysticks, 383
    analog, 384
    digital, 385
    fire buttons, 350
    game ports, 349
    gimbal, 383
    troubleshooting, 387
JPEG (Joint Photographic Experts Group) compression, 656
jump instructions, PC register, 22
jumpers
    hard drives, troubleshooting, 441
    MI/O adapter cards, 88
    system boards, 76

K

K (kilobytes), 19
kernel
    operating systems, 131
    Windows 3.x, 187
    Windows 95, 220, 228
key bounce, 365
keyboard, 91-92
    A20 Enable pin, 374
    Alt key, 93
    break codes, 371
    buffer, 370
    Caps Lock key, 93
    character-ready signal, 366
    Clock Enable bit, 373
    clock signal, 371
    controllers, 374-376
    Ctrl key, 93
    cursor control keys, 93
    Data Enable bit, 373
    detachable, 369
    DIN connectors, 72
    DVORAK, 363
    echoing strokes, 376

    encoder, 365, 371
    Enter key, 93
    ergonomics, 363
    function keys, 93
    input buffers, 373
    interfaces, 372
    key switches, 367
    keyboard clock signal, 371
    maintenance, 699
    microcontroller, 366
    multiple key closures, 371
    notebook computers, 66
    numeric keypad, 93, 363
    phantom switch closures, 371
    QWERTY, 363
    Real/Protected mode switching, 374
    Reset CPU (RC) line, 375
    Return key, 93
    row-scan oscillator, 366
    row strobe ring counter, 366
    scan codes, 371
        scan code latch, 366
    Scroll Lock key, 93
    Tab key, 93
    testing, 377
    time delay, 365
    troubleshooting, 323, 376-377
    typematic delay/rate, 377
    X-Y matrix encoding, 365
KEYBOARD.SYS file, 171
[Keyboard] section, SYSTEM.INI file, 200
keylock switches, 77, 373
keynames, .INI files, 194
keys, Registry, 229
keystone effect, monitors, 495
kiosks, 626

L

L1 cache, 297
L2 cache, 275, 297
lands, CDs, 635
landscape printing, 537
LANs (local area networks), 560, 590
    adapter cards, 600-601
        installing, 602-603
    protocols, 592
        ArcNet, 596-598
        Ethernet, 593-596
        Token Ring, 598-600
    topologies, 590-592

network access point (NAP), 613
network adapter cards
    BIOS extensions, 136
    see also adapter cards
Network icon, Windows for Workgroups, 209
Network Neighborhood icon, Windows 95, 222
networking
    DOS exam objectives, 731
    exam objectives, 725
    passwords, 206
    security, 206
    shared resources, 207
    Windows exam objectives, 731
    Windows for Workgroups, 206
networks, 560
    client/server, 591-592
    drop cabling, troubleshooting LANs, 603
    Internet
            packets, 611
            see also *Internet*
    ISDN, 615-616
    LANs, *see* LANs
    MANs (Metropolitan Area Networks), 610
    modems, 560-566, 571-579
    peer-to-peer, 591-592
    protocol drivers, 601
    WANs, *see* WANs
NexGen Pentium clone processors, 284
nibbles, 5
NICs (Network Interface Cards), *see* adapter cards
NMIs (non-maskable interrupts), 30, 292
nodes
    ArcNet, 596-597
    bus topology, 590-591
    Ethernet, 593
    USB, 358
non-classified problem troubleshooting, 121
non-contact recording, hard disks, 408
non-impact printers, 506-507
non-volatile memory, 73
non-volatile ROM, 15
[NonWindowsApp] section, SYSTEM.INI file, 202
NOP (No OPeration) instructions, 31
Normal mode, Windows 95, 234
note-off code, MIDI, 651
note-on code, MIDI, 651
notebook PCs, 66
    displays, 496
    exam objectives, 725
    system boards, 264

NotePad, editing INI files, 194
Novell NetWare, troubleshooting LANs, 606-607
null modems, 348, 579
Num-Lock key, 93
numeric data words, 6
numeric keypad, 93, 363

O

observing problems for troubleshooting, 104
obsolete equipment disposal, 706
OCR software (optical character recognition), 397
octal number system, 7
odd parity, 8, 296
ODI (Open Datalink Interface) file, 607
off-hook state, modems, 573
offset address, 8088 processors, 266
OLE (Object Linking and Embedding), 194
on-board I/O, system boards, 300
onboard RAM (printers), 515
onboard ROM (printers), 515
one-byte instructions, 9
online state (modems), 572
op codes, 9
Open Datalink Interface (ODI) files, 607
opening
    DOS programs in Windows, 205
    see also starting
operands, memory accesses, 9, 298
operating environments, 184
operating specifications, floppy drives, 414
operating system loader, boot process, 145
operating systems, 43, 130
    BIOS system initialization, 134
    boot process
            command processor, 145
            interrupt routines, 145
            master boot record, 144
            operating system loader, 145
    bootstrapping, 132
    command-line interpreters, 130
    DMA controllers, system initialization, 134
    interrupt controllers, system initialization, 134
    kernel, 131
    keyboard test, system initialization, 135
    multiple process, 131
    POST tests, 133-135
    RAM testing, system initialization, 134
    ROM BIOS services, 146

power LED connector, 77

power light, 63

power line protection, 681

power supply, 60, 68

    ATX system board connections, 263

    cable bundles, 69

    connectors, 69

    dot-matrix printers, 522

    fans, 64

    monitors, 489

        troubleshooting, 494

    Pentium clone issues, 285

    portable PCs, 70

    troubleshooting, 119, 322

power switch, 63, 69

power-on defaults, BIOS, 141

POWER.EXE program, 172

PPIs (Parallel Peripheral Interfaces), 8088 processors, 260-261

PPP (Point-to-Point Protocol), 613

pre-emptive multitasking, Windows 3.x, 206, 232

pregroove, CD-R discs, 640

presentations, multimedia, 630-632

preventive maintenance

    antistatic solutions, 674

    CMOS devices, 677

    corrosion, 675

    daily tasks, 703

    electrostatic discharge, 676

    exam objectives, 722

    floppy drives, 697

    grounding straps, 677

    hard drives, 685-686

    heat build-up, 683

    ICs, removal, 678

    input devices, 699

    monitors, 684

    monthly tasks, 703

    MOS devices, 677

    mouse, 382

    outer surfaces, 674

    outmoded equipment disposal, 706

    oxidation, 675

    power line protection, 681

    printed circuit boards, 675

    printers, 701-702

    R/W heads, 675

    repair toolbox contents, 675

    safety issues, 705

    six month tasks, 704

    surge suppressors, 681

    UPSes, 681

    viruses, 694-696

    yearly tasks, 704

PRI (Primary Rate Interface) service, 615-616

primary corona wire (laser printers), 543-544

primary memory, 14

primary partitions, 428, 439

Primary Rate Interface (PRI) service, 615-616

Print Manager

    Windows 3.x, 193

    Windows 95, 225

    Windows for Workgroups, 207

Print Troubleshooter, Windows 95, 357

printed circuit boards

    cleaning, 675

    signal ground, 680

    see also system boards

printer ports, 338

    Acknowledge line, 339

    adapter tests, 109

    Auto Feed line, 339

    Busy line, 339

    data latch, 341

    Data Strobe line, 339

    Error line, 339

    Initialize Printer line, 339

    interface, 340

    interrupt enable, 341

    LPT handles, 342

    Paper End line, 339

    reading data, 341

    Select Input line, 339

    spooler, 521

    status buffer, 341

    TTL signal levels, 341

[Printer Ports] section, WIN.INI file, 199

printers, 39, 91, 94

    bi-directional printers, 513

    carriage motor/timing belt, 513

    characters, 507-511

        character generators, 515

        characters per inch (cpi), 513

    controller circuitry, 514-516

    daisy wheel, 508

    drivers, 171, 517

    dot-matrix printers

        color printing, 526

        configuration checks, 527-528

        hardware checks, 528-533

        main control board, 522-524

S

Safe mode, Windows 95, 234

safety
    exam objectives, 722
    laser printer issues, 705
    preventive maintenance, 705

sagging power variations, 681

scan codes, keyboard, 371

scan code latch, keyboard, 366

SCANDISK utility, 687

scanners, 393
    analog-to-digital converter, 394
    charge-coupled device, 394
    flat bed, 395
    gamma correction, 394
    grayscale, 396
    hand-held, 393
    opto isolator, 394
    troubleshooting
        DMA channels, 399
        I/O address settings, 398
        IRQ conflicts, 398

scheduler module, operating systems, 132

screens, monitors
    attributes, 461
    data manipulation, 465
    fonts, 196
    memory, 461-462
    screen savers, 226, 684

Screen tab, DOS Properties window, Windows 95, 228

[Screensaver.*] section, CONTROL.INI file, 203

screwdrivers, 101

Scroll Lock key, 93

scrolling operations, monitors, 466

SCSI (Small Computer System Interface), 429
    CD-ROM drives, 642
    daisy-chaining SCSI devices, 434
    hard drives, 427-429
        device numbers, 434
        host adapter, 433
        installing, 434
        specifications, 436
        terminating chains, 435
    interface, 515

SCSI-3 standard, 435

SDRAM (Synchronous DRAM), 299, 474

second-level cache, *see* **L2 cache**

secondary memory, 14, 33

sectors
    DOS disks, 150
    magnetic disks, 404
    root directory, 152
    tracks, 34

security
    passwords, 206
    troubleshooting LANs, 605

seek operations, hard disks/floppy disks, 410

segments
    80386 processors, 271
    8088 memory addresses, 266

select lines, parallel printer ports, 339

selective backups, 688

self-booting DOS disks, 178

sequencers, video controllers, 477

serial buses, 26

serial cables, 577-579

serial connections, 515

serial interface, 346
    advanced standards, 348
    modems
        COM port settings, 575-576
        serial cables, 577-579
        UARTs, 574-577

Serial Line Internet Protocol (SLIP), 613

serial mode, transferring words, 9

serial mouse, 379-380

Serial Port Loopback Plug, COM port test, 109

serial ports, 87, 161, 342
    character frames, 349
    DOS
        configuring, 160
        names, 349
    marks, 344
    parity, 161, 344
    protocols, 349
    redirecting output, 161
    spaces, 344
    start bits, 344
    stop bits, 161, 344
    transmission modes, 343
    troubleshooting
        DOS, 353-354
        Windows 3.x, 356
        Windows 95, 358
    UARTs, 345

serial printers, 94, 511
    cabling problems, 518
    configuration problems, 518-519

T

volatility
    memory, 73
    RAM, 18
voltage
    sags, 681
    troubleshooting system capacitors, 102
VOMs (Volt-Ohm Milliammeters), 101
VRAM (video RAM), 299, 475
VxDs (Virtual Device Drivers), 219
    initializing, 242
    loading, 241
    static, Windows 95 install, 219-220
    verifying, 242

W

waiting time, Ethernet nodes, 593
wallpaper, Windows 3.x, 190
WANs (Wide Area Networks), 560, 609-611
    BBSs, 610
    email, 616-617
    Internet, 611
        see also Internet
    troubleshooting, 619
warm booting, 41, 133
wattage rating, UPSes, 683
WAV files, 627
wave table audio file synthesis, 649
WavEdit utility, 629
WD output (Write Data), FDC, 418
WE signal (Write Enable), FDC, 418
Web (World Wide Web), 617-619
Web browsers, 617-619
Web servers, 617
WfW (Windows for Workgroups), 184
Wide Area Networks, see WANs
Wide Fast SCSI-2 standard, 435
Wide SCSI-2 standard, 435
wild cards, * and ?, 160
WIN.COM file, 187
WIN.INI file, Windows 3.x
    [Colors] section, 198
    [Desktop] section, 195
    [Embedding] section, 197
    [Extensions] section, 195
    [FontSubstitutes] section, 197
    [Fonts] section, 196
    [International] section, 195
    [MCI Extensions] section, 197

[Ports] section, 196
[Printer Ports] section, 199
[Sound] section, 199
[TrueType] section, 197
[Windows Help] section, 198
[Windows] section, 194
Windows, 184
    Control Panel, Character Map icon, 511
    evolution of system, 184
    exam objectives, 726-728
    installing, 729
    Media Control Interface, 627
    Media Player, 627-629
        troubleshooting MIDI files playback, 653
    memory, 728
    MIDI Mapper, 628
    mouse driver, 381
    multimedia
        Media Control Interface, 627
        Media Player, 629
        RIFF files, 627
        Sound Recorder, 628
    networking, 731
    PalEdit utility, 629
    ports, 355
    printing problems, 552-555
    Sound Recorder, 627-628
        testing WAV files, 653
    troubleshooting, 730
    versions and features, 185
    VidCap utility, 629
    VidEdit utility, 629
    Video for Windows, 629
    WavEdit utility, 629
Windows 3.11, troubleshooting LANs, 605-606
Windows 3.x, 185
    386 Enhanced mode, 205
    Accessories group, 187
    Add/Remove Windows Components option, 193
    Applications group, 187
    boot disks, 210
    Clipboard Viewer, 193
    Control Panel, 190
    CONTROL.INI file, 202-204
    cooperative multitasking, 206
    cursor, 185
    customizing desktop, 190
    desktop, 187
    disk cache, 192
    Dr. Watson, system event monitoring and diagnosis, 212
    Drivers option, 190
    Enhanced mode, 186
    FastDisk driver, 191

X

Y

Z